CAMBRIDGE INTERNATIONAL TRADE AND ECONOMIC LAW

As the processes of regionalisation and globalisation have intensified, there have been accompanying increases in the regulations of international trade and economic law at the levels of international, regional and national laws.

The subject matter of this series is international economic law. Its core is the regulation of international trade, investment and cognate areas such as intellectual property and competition policy. The series publishes books on related regulatory areas, in particular human rights, labour, environment and culture, as well as sustainable development. These areas are vertically linked at the international, regional and national level, and the series extends to the implementation of these rules at these different levels. The series also includes works on governance, dealing with the structure and operation of related international organisations in the field of international economic law, and the way they interact with other subjects of international and national law.

Series editors:

Dr Lorand Bartels, *University of Cambridge*
Professor Thomas Cottier, *University of Berne*
Professor William Davey, *University of Illinois*

Books in the series:

Trade Policy Flexibility and Enforcement in the WTO: A Law and Economics Analysis
Simon A. B. Schropp

The Multilaterization of International Investment Law
Stephan W. Schill

The Law, Economics and Politics of Retaliation in WTO Dispute Settlement
Edited by Chad P. Bown and Joost Pauwelyn

THE LAW, ECONOMICS AND POLITICS OF RETALIATION IN WTO DISPUTE SETTLEMENT

Edited by

CHAD P. BOWN

JOOST PAUWELYN

CAMBRIDGE
UNIVERSITY PRESS

CAMBRIDGE UNIVERSITY PRESS
Cambridge, New York, Melbourne, Madrid, Cape Town,
Singapore, São Paulo, Delhi, Tokyo, Mexico City

Cambridge University Press
The Edinburgh Building, Cambridge CB2 8RU, UK

Published in the United States of America by Cambridge University Press, New York

www.cambridge.org
Information on this title: www.cambridge.org/9780521119979

First published 2010

A catalogue record for this publication is available from the British Library

Library of Congress Cataloguing in Publication data
The law, economics and politics of retaliation in WTO dispute settlement /
[editors] Chad P. Bown, Joost Pauwelyn.
p. cm. – (Cambridge international trade and economic law)
ISBN 978- 0-521-11997-9 (hardback)
1. World Trade Organization–Rules and practice. 2. Dispute resolution (Law)
3. Foreign trade regulation. 4. Dumping (International trade) 5. Tariff – Law and
legislation. 6. Import quotas. I. Bown, Chad P. (Chad Philips), 1972–
II. Pauwelyn, Joost.
K4610.L39 2010
382′.5–dc22 2009035292

ISBN 978-0-521-11997-9 Hardback

CONTENTS

List of tables and figures ix

Contributors xi

Introduction: trade retaliation in WTO dispute settlement: a multi-disciplinary analysis 1

CHAD P. BOWN AND JOOST PAUWELYN

PART I **Background and goal(s) of WTO retaliation** 21

1 The nature of WTO arbitrations on retaliation 23

GIORGIO SACERDOTI

2 The calculation and design of trade retaliation in context: what is the goal of suspending WTO obligations? 34

JOOST PAUWELYN

Comment on chapter 2 66

JOHN H. JACKSON

Comment on chapter 2 70

ALAN O. SYKES

3 Extrapolating purpose from practice: rebalancing or inducing compliance 73

GREGORY SHAFFER AND DANIEL GANIN

PART II **A legal assessment after ten arbitration disputes** 87

4 The law of permissible WTO retaliation 89

THOMAS SEBASTIAN

Comment on chapter 4 128
NICOLAS LOCKHART

5 From *Bananas* to *Byrd*: damage calculation coming of age? 135
YVES RENOUF

PART III **An economic assessment after ten arbitration disputes** 147

6 The economics of permissible WTO retaliation 149
CHAD P. BOWN AND MICHELE RUTA

Comment on chapter 6 194
L. ALAN WINTERS

7 Sticking to the rules: quantifying the market access that is potentially protected by WTO-sanctioned trade retaliation 198
SIMON J. EVENETT

PART IV **The domestic politics and procedures for implementing trade retaliation** 233

8 The United States' experience and practice in suspending WTO obligations 235
SCOTT D. ANDERSEN AND JUSTINE BLANCHET

9 The European Community's experience and practice in suspending WTO obligations 244
LOTHAR EHRING

10 The politics of selecting trade retaliation in the European Community: a view from the floor 267
HÅKAN NORDSTRÖM

11 Canada's experience and practice in suspending WTO obligations 277
VASKEN KHABAYAN

12 Is retaliation useful? Observations and analysis of Mexico's experience 281
JORGE A. HUERTA-GOLDMAN

13 Procedures for the design and implementation of trade retaliation in Brazil 297

LUIZ EDUARDO SALLES

14 Retaliation in the WTO: the experience of Antigua and Barbuda in *US–Gambling* 310

MARK E. MENDEL

PART V **Problems and options for reform** 317

15 Evaluating the criticism that WTO retaliation rules undermine the utility of WTO dispute settlement for developing countries 319

HUNTER NOTTAGE

16 Optimal sanctions in the WTO: the case for decoupling (and the uneasy case for the *status quo*) 339

ALAN O. SYKES

Comment on chapter 16 355

PETROS C. MAVROIDIS

17 Sanctions in the WTO: problems and solutions 360

WILLIAM J. DAVEY

18 WTO retaliatory measures: the case for multilateral regulation of the domestic decision-making process 373

RETO MALACRIDA

19 The WTO Secretariat and the role of economics in panels and arbitrations 391

CHAD P. BOWN

Comment on chapter 19 434

RETO MALACRIDA

20 The equivalence standard under Article 22.4 of the DSU: a 'tariffic' misunderstanding? 446

SIMON SCHROPP

Comment on chapter 20 503

FRITZ BREUSS

PART VI **New frontiers and lessons from other fields 513**

21 Cross-retaliation and suspension under the GATS and TRIPS agreements 515
WERNER ZDOUC

22 Cross-retaliation in TRIPS: issues of law and practice 536
FREDERICK M. ABBOTT

23 Preliminary thoughts on WTO retaliation in the services sector 589
ARTHUR E. APPLETON

24 Compensation assessments: perspectives from investment arbitration 623
GABRIELLE KAUFMANN-KOHLER

25 Reforming WTO retaliation: any lessons from competition law? 641
SIMON J. EVENETT

Index 648

LIST OF TABLES AND FIGURES

Tables

Table 2.1 The possible goals of WTO suspension 38
Table 6.1 WTO DSU, Article 22.6 arbitrations, 1995–2007 151
Table 6.2 Does Bagwell–Staiger describe dispute arbitration? 197
Table 7.1 Calculating the amount of non-actionable exports for each country 208
Table 7.2 Calculating the proportion of exports that are 'actionable' by country 211
Table 7.3 Growth of actionable exports varies greatly across countries: 1990s 214
Table 7.4 Identifying the number of potential 'enforcers' that each nation faces 217
Table 7.5 Can only OECD nations play a credible enforcement role? No 221
Table 7.6 What percentage of each economy's imports come from the potential enforcers? 225
Table 12.1 Level of sensitivity of the products subject to the dispute 292
Table 19.1 The arbitrators in the disputes 406
Table 19.2 WTO members, disputes, and the distribution of Secretariat staff positions within various divisions, 2000–2007 414
Table 23.1 Modes of supply 594

Figures

Figure 6.1 Reciprocity compensation when the respondent implements a WTO-inconsistent tariff 158
Figure 6.2 Reciprocity compensation when the respondent implements a WTO-inconsistent quota and/or implements an inconsistent licensing scheme 162
Figure 6.3 Reciprocity compensation when the respondent imposes a WTO-inconsistent non-tariff measure on a trading partner's exports (for example violating national treatment) 171

Figure 6.4 Reciprocity compensation when the respondent implements a WTO-inconsistent production subsidy to an import-competing industry 174
Figure 6.5 Reciprocity compensation when the respondent imposes a WTO-inconsistent export subsidy (three-country model) 179
Figure 6.6 Reciprocity compensation when the respondent imposes a WTO-inconsistent export subsidy (two-country model) 184
Figure 6.7 Reciprocity compensation when the respondent implements a WTO-inconsistent tariff after a supply shock 189
Figure 7.1 Not all exports are sanctionable and the proportions vary considerably across countries 213
Figure 7.2 Although most nations saw a growth in actionable exports in the 1990s, the variation across countries is substantial 215
Figure 7.3 There is little evidence of convergence in the percentage of actionable exports in the 1990s 215
Figure 7.4 Countries differ in the number of trading partners that can act as 'enforcers' 219
Figure 7.5 Non-actionable exports tend to erode deterrent value of the DSU more than exports to lesser markets 223
Figure 7.6 Imports from nations that are potential enforcers, or the amount of each nation's market access that can be defended through WTO dispute settlement 227
Figure 7.7 Are developing economies exposed to greater potential sanctions than the United States? 228
Figure 7.8 Are developing economies exposed to greater potential sanctions than India? 229
Figure 10.1 Splitting the bill for *US–Steel Safeguards* 269
Figure 10.2 Splitting the bill for *US–Foreign Sales Corporations* 270
Figure 12.1 Time-line for *US–Brooms Safeguards* 285
Figure 19.1 Page length of DSU, Article 22.6 arbitration reports, 1999–2007 421
Figure 20.1 Reliance damages as baseline for the calculation of NoI 458
Figure 20.2 Restitution damages as baseline for the calculation of NoI 460
Figure 20.3 Expectation damages as baseline for the calculation of NoI 462
Figure 20.4 Comparing reliance (*I*), restitution (*II*) and expectation damages (*III*) 462
Figure 20.5 Different standards of measuring the intensity of NoI 470
Figure 20.6 The calculation baseline according to WTO arbitrators' practice 481

CONTRIBUTORS

FREDERICK ABBOTT
Damon House, Room 203
Edward Ball Eminent Scholar
Florida State University College of Law
425 W. Jefferson Street
Tallahassee, FL 32306-1601
USA

SCOTT ANDERSEN
Managing Partner, Geneva Office
Sidley Austin LLP
139 rue de Lausanne
CH-1202 Geneva
Switzerland

ARTHUR E. APPLETON
Appleton Luff International Lawyers
17 rue de Contamines
CH-1206 Geneva
Switzerland

JUSTINE BLANCHET
International Trade Analyst
Sidley Austin LLP
139 rue de Lausanne
CH-1202 Geneva
Switzerland

CHAD P. BOWN
Department of Economics
Brandeis University
MS 021, 415 South Street
Waltham, MA 02454-9110
USA

FRITZ BREUSS
Research Institute for European Affairs
Vienna University of Economics and Business Administration
Europainstitut
WU-Wien
Althanstrasse 39–45
A-1090 Vienna
Austria

WILLIAM J. DAVEY
University of Illinois College of Law
504 E Pennsylvania Avenue
Champaign, IL 61820
USA

LOTHAR EHRING
European Commission
Directorate-General for Trade
Unit for Legal Aspects of Trade Policy
European Commission
CHAR 9/46
BE-1049 Brussels
Belgium

SIMON EVENETT
SIAW-HSG
Universität St. Gallen
Bodanstrasse 8
9000 St. Gallen
Switzerland

DANIEL GANIN
University of Minnesota–Twin Cities
420 Delaware St. SE
Minneapolis, MN 55455
USA

JORGE A. HUERTA-GOLDMAN
Mission of Mexico to the WTO
Mexican Ministry of Trade
c/o Misión de México ante la OMC
Av. de Budé 16
CH-1202 Geneva
Switzerland

JOHN JACKSON
Georgetown University Law Center
McDonough Hall, Room 456
600 New Jersey Avenue, NW
Washington, DC 20001
USA

GABRIELLE KAUFMANN-KOHLER
University of Geneva Faculty of Law
102 Bd Carl-Vogt
CH-1205 Geneva
Switzerland

VASKEN KHABAYAN
Department of Foreign Affairs and International Trade Canada
125 Sussex Drive, C6-189 (JLT)
Ottawa
Ontario K1A 0G2
Canada

NICOLAS LOCKHART
Sidley Austin LLP
139 rue de Lausanne
CH-1202 Geneva
Switzerland

RETO MALACRIDA
Legal Affairs Division
World Trade Organization
154 rue de Lausanne
CH-1211 Geneva 21
Switzerland

PETROS C. MAVROIDIS
Edwin B. Parker Professor of Law at Columbia Law School
Professor of Law at the University of Neuchatel
Research Fellow at CEPR
4 Chemin de la Riaz
CH-1291 Commugny (VD)
Switzerland

MARK E. MENDEL
Mendel Blumenfeld, LLP
21 Cook Street, 2nd Floor
Cork
Co. Cork
Ireland

HÅKAN NORDSTRÖM
National Board of Trade
(Kommerskollegium)
Box 6803
113 86 Stockholm
Sweden

HUNTER NOTTAGE
Counsel, Advisory Centre on WTO Law
Avenue Giuseppe-Motta 31–33
C.P. 132
CH-1211 Geneva 20
Switzerland

JOOST PAUWELYN
Professor of International Law
Co-Director Centre for Trade and Economic Integration (CTEI)
Graduate Institute of International and Development Studies
Rue Richard Wagner 1
CH-1202 Geneva
Switzerland

YVES RENOUF
Legal Affairs Division
World Trade Organization
154 rue de Lausanne
CH-1211 Geneva 21
Switzerland

MICHELE RUTA
Economic Research and Statistics Division
World Trade Organization
154 rue de Lausanne
CH-1211 Geneva 21
Switzerland

GIORGIO SACERDOTI
Bocconi University, Milan
and Appellate Body, World Trade Organization
Via Albricci 10
I-20122 Milan
Italy

LUIZ EDUARDO RIBEIRO SALLES
Graduate Institute of International and Development Studies
Rua Joaquim Floriano, 209, apto 103
Bairro Itaim Bibi
São Paulo–SP
Brazil
CEP 04534-010

SIMON SCHROPP
Sidley Austin LLP
3 rue du 1er Juin
CH-1207 Geneva
Switzerland

THOMAS SEBASTIAN
Allen & Overy LLP
1 Bishop's Square
London E1 6AD
United Kingdom

GREGORY SHAFFER
Melvin C. Steen Professor
University of Minnesota Law School
N230 Mondale Commons
229-19th Avenue South
Minneapolis, MM 55455
USA

ALAN O. SYKES
James and Patricia Kowal Professor of Law
Stanford University
Stanford Law School
559 Nathan Abbott Way
Stanford, CA 94305-8610
USA

L. ALAN WINTERS
Professor of Economics
Department for International
Development (DFID) and
University of Sussex
School of Social Sciences
University of Sussex
Falmer
Brighton BN1 9QN
UK

WERNER ZDOUC
Appellate Body
World Trade Organization
154 rue de Lausanne
CH-1211 Geneva 21
Switzerland

Introduction

Trade retaliation in WTO dispute settlement: a multi-disciplinary analysis

CHAD P. BOWN AND JOOST PAUWELYN*

It is hard to think of a better topic for multi-disciplinary study than trade retaliation in the WTO. When a country violates WTO rules, the remedy of last resort is bilateral, state-to-state trade sanctions. Such trade sanctions are imposed against the violating country by one or more other WTO members who took the initiative to challenge the breach. WTO retaliation must, however, be multilaterally authorized by the WTO following, first, an elaborate procedure establishing (continued) breach in the first place and, second, an arbitration on whether the retaliation is 'equivalent' or 'appropriate' in the light of the harm caused by the original violation. This is where the law comes in: arbitrators must apply legal criteria to assess the harm caused by a WTO violation, select benchmarks and counterfactuals to do so, as well as decide, where requested, on whether the conditions for so-called cross-retaliation are met (that is, retaliation in the form of, for example, suspending intellectual property rights in response to a WTO-inconsistent import restriction). This process obviously involves economics as well, both economic theory (what is the role of *violation-cum-retaliation* in an incomplete contract?; what is the optimal design of remedies for breach of contract?) and applied or quantitative economics (how does one calculate lost trade, lost royalties or other economic harm caused by a WTO violation?; how does one make sure that the retaliation in response is 'equivalent'?). Finally, the design, implementation and effectiveness of WTO retaliation is deeply political, ranging from the decision of whether to retaliate in the first place

* The editors of this volume would like to offer a special thanks to Miguel Burnier, Ph.D. candidate at the Graduate Institute in Geneva, for his excellent help in editing the many contributions to this book.

(especially salient in developing countries) to selecting specific products to retaliate against (for example, with a view to compensate or protect domestic, import-competing industries at home, say, Mexico keeping out US corn syrup to please Mexican cane sugar producers; or, alternatively, to exert maximum political pressure in the violating country, say, the EC restricting Florida orange juice to affect US President Bush's re-election chances in 2004).

Given that GATT-authorized retaliation required consensus (including approval by the violating country itself!), retaliation under GATT (to be distinguished from unilateral retaliation under, for example, US section 301) was authorized only once from 1947 to 1995. Retaliation in the WTO, though subject to multilateral control, once found to be 'equivalent' or 'appropriate' is automatically authorized. This explains why in the 14 years since the establishment of the WTO, trade retaliation has been multilaterally approved no less than seventeen times in eight different trade disputes (one of which involved eight complainants, namely *Byrd Amendment*; in two other disputes, *EC–Bananas* and *EC–Hormones*, two complainants were authorized to retaliate). These disputes combined have spawned eleven arbitration reports (*EC–Bananas (US)*, *EC–Hormones (US)*, *EC–Hormones (Canada)*, *EC–Bananas (Ecuador)*, *Brazil–Aircraft*, *US–FSC*, *Canada–Aircraft II*, *US–1916 Act*, *US–Byrd Amendment*, *US–Gambling* and *US–Cotton Subsidies*).

With this critical mass of experience in the field, and given the multi-disciplinary character of the problem, the newly established multi-disciplinary Centre for Trade and Economic Integration at the Graduate Institute of International and Development Studies in Geneva, Switzerland convened a Workshop on 18–19 July 2008 entitled 'The Calculation and Design of Trade Sanctions in WTO Dispute Settlement'. This book is the outcome of that Workshop. It includes contributions from specialists in both trade law and economics. In addition, it narrates the practical experiences of most WTO members who were authorized to use trade retaliation from the perspective of diplomats or practising lawyers working for those countries.

Part I of the book offers an introductory background to the nature of WTO arbitrations on retaliation (Sacerdoti, Chapter 1) and the contested goal (or goals) that are set out, or can be expected to be achieved by trade retaliation based on both the history, text and context of the GATT/WTO treaty and the arbitration reports and country experiences and practices so far (Pauwelyn with comments by Jackson and Sykes, Chapter 2; Shaffer and Ganin, Chapter 3). Part II of the book summarizes and discusses the state of play after ten arbitration disputes on

WTO retaliation from a legal perspective (Sebastian with comment by Lockhart, Chapter 4; Renouf, Chapter 5). Part III does the same from an economic perspective (Bown and Ruta with comment by Winters, Chapter 6; Evenett, Chapter 7).

Part IV examines the domestic politics and procedures for implementing WTO-authorized trade retaliation in individual countries, more specifically: the United States (Andersen and Blanchet, Chapter 8); the European Community (Ehring (Chapter 9) and Nordström (Chapter 10)); Canada (Khabayan, Chapter 11); Mexico (Huerta Goldman, Chapter 12); Brazil (Salles, Chapter 13); and Antigua and Barbuda (Mendel, Chapter 14). Part V looks at problems that have arisen in the practice so far, be they real or imagined, more specifically: problems faced by developing countries (Nottage, Chapter 15); problems resulting from the absence of compensation to individual economic operators (Sykes with comment by Mavroidis, Chapter 16); and problems and possible solutions related to timing, counterfactuals, causation and changed circumstances (Davey, Chapter 17). Schropp (with comment by Breuss, Chapter 20) offers a broader critique of the current arbitration practice based on a welfare analysis of WTO retaliation. Part V of the book also includes proposals for reform regarding the domestic decision-making process implementing trade retaliation (Malacrida, Chapter 18) and the role of the WTO Secretariat and interaction between lawyers and economists in WTO arbitrations (Bown with comment by Malacrida, Chapter 19).

Finally, Part VI of the book offers analyses of two new frontiers of WTO retaliation, namely retaliation taking the form of suspending intellectual property rights and retaliation in trade in services (Zdouc, Chapter 21; Abbott, Chapter 22; Appleton, Chapter 23). Part VI concludes with similarities and differences between, on the one hand, WTO retaliation and, on the other hand, compensation in investor–state arbitration (Kaufmann-Kohler, Chapter 24) and remedies in antitrust or competition law (Evenett, Chapter 25).

Rather than attempting to summarize the thirty-two contributions in this volume, this Introduction limits itself to pointing out three general lines of argument or critique that recur throughout the book. For ease of reference we refer to them as: (i) 'trade retaliation is shooting yourself in the foot'; (ii) 'trade retaliation simply does not work when developing countries win a case'; and (iii) 'accurately calculating the authorized level of retaliation is a myth and close to impossible'. To avoid all doubt, we are not here agreeing with any of these statements. To the contrary, what we plan to do in this Introduction is to debunk them or, at least, to qualify them.

1 'Trade retaliation is shooting yourself in the foot' (reciprocity versus welfare; definition of nullification; choice of counterfactual)

The WTO remedy of last resort, that is, *restricting* trade, is, indeed, somewhat of a puzzle if one considers that the goal of the WTO is to *liberalize* trade. To authorize in response to a first trade restriction (the original violation) a second trade restriction (WTO retaliation) seems to assume that somehow 'two wrongs' (that is, twice reducing welfare) will make things 'right' again. Yet, as Winters points out, '[t]he exercise highlights an eternal dilemma that the WTO raises ... The institution is mercantilist through and through ... Reciprocity seems misconceived for most countries – I will stop hurting my economy [that is, I will comply with WTO rules] ... if you will stop hurting yours! Yet the GATT/WTO has harnessed reciprocity to preside over a massively welfare-increasing liberalisation of international trade'. Put differently, trade retaliation as a remedy against an illegal trade restriction may not make much economic sense (it is, in many cases, 'shooting yourself in the foot' and harms innocent bystanders). Yet, since the GATT/WTO is inherently based on a mercantilist game of 'reciprocal exchanges of market access', and this model has, in practice, offered us high degrees of trade liberalization, should we not accept this odd remedy of retaliation as part and parcel of the, after all, rather effective mercantilist game?

Brown and Ruta, in their assessment of the economics of permissible WTO retaliation, do follow this reciprocity model (based on the Bagwell and Staiger theory of trade agreements). For them, '[u]nder the reciprocity approach, the complainant is allowed to introduce a retaliatory policy measure ... i.e. a trade restrictive measure ... such that the value of export and import trade volumes between the two countries is stabilized'. In other words, in their view, the goal is that both the original violation and the retaliation have an equal effect on *volumes of trade*. Brown and Ruta subsequently apply this benchmark to original violations taking the form of tariffs, quotas, national treatment discrimination and subsidies, and find that in standard cases arbitrators have, indeed, followed the reciprocity model. Indeed, if retaliation is (i) engaged in by a 'large country' (in the terms-of-trade sense of being able to affect world prices) or even by a small country which can affect the world price of the products retaliated against (a country which thereby becomes 'large' for those specific imports), and (ii) calibrated at the level of a so-called 'optimal tariff' (most likely to be much lower than the standard 100 per cent duties currently imposed!), retaliation should *increase overall welfare* in the retaliating country (and, to that extent, *not* be 'shooting yourself in the foot', see Bown and Ruta as well as Nordström). Breuss's empirical study referred to in this volume shows, for example, that in *US–FSC*, the EC retaliation (even combined with the original US violation) was actually slightly welfare increasing for the EC. What is more, in the WTO context, the traditional argument against 'optimal tariffs', that is, that they are likely to trigger retaliation, even a trade war, which in the end makes everyone worse off, is, at least under the law, no longer pertinent: WTO rules authorize retaliation against a continuing breach of WTO law; retaliation by the violator against such retaliation is *not* permitted.

In contrast, when it comes to WTO case law on retaliation in response to prohibited export subsidies (where retaliation is permitted up to the *entire amount of the subsidy*) Bown and Ruta are more critical, on the ground that the full subsidy amount 'is not necessarily a good proxy for the size of the *trade effects* of the export subsidy – i.e., the volume of lost trade for the complainant'. On this very point, Sebastian, in his contribution on the law of permissible WTO retaliation, thinks along the same lines, arguing that in none of the arbitrations so far has the decision to take the *full amount of the subsidy* as a benchmark been adequately explained (in his words, '[t]he convoluted reasoning in *US–FSC* does not inspire any confidence'). As a result, Sebastian is of the view that 'it is likely that arbitrators will come under some pressure in future cases to adopt uniform approaches across these provisions (notwithstanding differences in the wording used in the DSU and the SCM Agreement)'. Huerta Goldman, however, takes a polar opposite position: if retaliation is limited to only that share of trade represented by the complainant(s), instead of the full amount of subsidy or other violation, the violator is 'better off to face retaliation ... than to comply with the WTO contract; a system which, under Huerta Goldman's 'chocolate cake scenario', 'significantly diminishes the effectiveness of retaliation and provides negative incentives for compliance and compensation'.

Returning to the GATT/WTO dilemma between 'reciprocity' and 'welfare' referred to by Winters, the contributions by Schropp and Breuss take a resolutely different approach as compared with the reciprocity model of Bown and Ruta. For Schropp, in what is essentially a welfare analysis, the goal of WTO retaliation is not reciprocity or rebalancing the scale of trade concessions and trade volumes, but rather 'to compensate the Complainant for its true damage from the violation of the contract'. As a result, in Schropp's view, WTO retaliation ought to be calculated not in order to stabilize the value of export and import trade volumes between the two countries (reciprocity), but 'based on a counterfactual that puts the injured party in as good a position as it had been if the violating party had performed as promised ("expectation damages")'.

Consequently, and this is hugely important, whereas under a reciprocity model (as in standard WTO arbitrations and Bown and Ruta) 'nullification or impairment' defined in Article 22.4 of the *Dispute Settlement Understanding* (DSU) amounts to the *trade effects* of the WTO-inconsistent measure on the complaining country, under a welfare model (Schropp and Breuss) 'nullification or impairment' amounts to the *net economic loss* caused by the WTO-inconsistent measure to the complaining country. It goes without saying that, in most cases, these two different starting points lead to very different dollar amount results. As Breuss puts it, 'equal trade effects will only coincidentally, if ever, proxy for equal welfare effects'.

The above debate among economists (reciprocity versus welfare) is, interestingly enough, also reflected in the contributions to this volume by lawyers. Sykes, for example, construes the goal and calculation of WTO retaliation as being aimed at broadly rebalancing the scales between the parties and essentially putting an *upper limit* on retaliation in order to 'facilitate arguably desirable deviations from the letter of the bargain under politically exigent circumstances'. Lockhart implies a reciprocity model when arguing that in the selection of 'metrics' to calculate the amount of authorized retaliation the 'punishment should fit the crime'. In his view, '[t]he crime scene here comprises the nature of the measure at issue and the nature of the obligation violated. Together, these two factors seem to influence the choice of metric'. In contrast, other lawyers contributing to this volume shift the focus from reciprocity between measures and/or trade effects, to compensation for harm caused (see, for example, Mavroidis and Davey, both arguing in favour of some form of compensation instead of, or in addition to, retaliation) and/or rule compliance (see, for example, Jackson and Shaffer and Ganin, for whom the core aim of WTO retaliation is not restoring reciprocity but 'inducing compliance'). On the assumption that compliance with WTO rules enhances overall welfare, this shift is somewhat analogous to a shift from a reciprocity model to a welfare analysis.

In sum, it is not that economists as a group focus on rebalancing or reciprocity and lawyers as another group favour rule compliance. Instead, in both disciplines the dilemma or tension between reciprocity and welfare can be detected. The practical consequences of these different approaches should not be underestimated. The debate has a direct impact on which benchmarks or counterfactuals ought to be chosen to calculate WTO retaliation. Reciprocity models tend to focus on trade volume effects. Welfare, compensation and rule compliance models tend to focus on net economic loss or the amount of the violation (for example, the full amount of the subsidy).

A similar tension prevails when it comes to the all-important choice of counterfactual (that is, in order to calculate trade effects or economic loss what hypothetical situation should the current situation be compared with?). One group of contributors to this volume (including Sebastian and Davey), as well as prevailing WTO arbitration practice, take as counterfactual the hypothetical, alternative situation where *the defendant would comply with WTO rules.* In *US–Gambling*, for example, this would be a US regime on Internet gambling that complies with the GATS (for example, full market access or, according to some, allowing foreign suppliers to compete in the horse-race gambling sector). Opting for the counterfactual of 'rule compliance' opens the difficult question of what to do in case different, alternative measures, with varying degrees of trade or economic impact, would comply with the WTO treaty? The arbitrators in *US–Gambling* adopted the criterion of a 'plausible or reasonable compliance scenario' without, however, ruling on whether the counterfactual eventually selected was, indeed, WTO-consistent. The arbitrators in *US–Gambling* found that this question of consistency fell outside the mandate of WTO arbitration on retaliation. This finding was strongly contested by a number of contributors to this volume (see, for example, Sebastian, Lockhart and Davey), all finding that a decision on the amount of authorized retaliation based on a counterfactual necessarily requires and allows finding that this counterfactual is, contrary to the original measure, consistent with WTO rules. As Sebastian puts it, '[i]t would appear that a threshold requirement for a counterfactual is that it is indisputably WTO-consistent'. Interestingly, Mendel, who is legal adviser to Antigua and Barbuda in the *US–Gambling* dispute, supports the arbitrators' refusal to examine consistency on the ground that arbitration reports on retaliation cannot be appealed to the Appellate Body and, hence, should not decide on questions of substantive WTO compliance. Ehring, along similar lines, argues that 'the question of legality of a counterfactual is often not suitable for a reliable resolution within a sanctions arbitration'.

Another group of contributors to this volume does not opt for the counterfactual of 'what would be the situation if the defending country were to comply with WTO rules' (that is, what would the situation be '*but for the violation*'). Instead, they advocate the counterfactual of, as

Ehring puts it, 'the hypothetical situation where the illegal market access restriction does not exist' (that is, what would be the situation '*but for the trade restriction*', an approach that was followed in *EC–Hormones*). In *US–Gambling* this counterfactual would have led to a much bigger award as it would have assessed the impact on Antigua of the US ban on online gambling *tout court*, as opposed to only the impact of the discriminatory US ban on online horse-racing bets. This 'but for the trade restriction' counterfactual is not only supported by Ehring and (not surprisingly) Mendel, but also in Schropp's welfare analysis of trade retaliation. Similarly to Ehring, Schropp advocates the counterfactual of a 'hypothetical situation that would exist if the illegality had never been committed and the injurer had always performed according to the contract (*expectation* measure)'. With such expectation damages, 'the victim of a contractual violation is fully compensated for all its efficiency losses due to the Respondent's measure in question'. Whether WTO retaliation must be calculated to offset the effects of WTO *violation* (as in *US–Gambling* and most other arbitrations) or of the *trade restriction as such* (as in *EC–Hormones*) is certain to remain an important element of debate in the future.

In conclusion, there is no doubt that in many cases trade retaliation (especially at the level of 100 per cent duties) has, or would, end up with the country 'shooting itself in the foot' (unless the two conditions set out above for welfare-enhancing retaliation are met, that is, being a 'large country' and setting the tariff at the right or optimal level). However, within the mercantilist reciprocity model of the GATT/WTO this should not come as too much of a surprise. Similarly, WTO retaliation can be criticized for not compensating the actual victims of a trade violation, even for causing additional harm to innocent bystanders. Yet, if one views WTO retaliation as a sanction to induce compliance it is hardly surprising that trade retaliation is also costly to the one imposing it (imprisonment costs money to the state). As Pauwelyn puts it '[w]ithout fixing this goal or benchmark [of WTO retaliation], any debate on effectiveness of the system is meaningless, with some authors saying that WTO remedies are "too weak", others saying that they are "too strong" and yet others concluding that they are "about right"'. In contrast to the WTO regime, the goal of damages in investor–state arbitration is clear. As Kaufmann-Kohler writes, 'there is no doubt that the primary purpose of the remedies provided by investment law is to compensate an investor for the losses caused by an act of a State'. Similarly, in antitrust or competition law, Evenett illustrates that one of the core goals of fines, even imprisonment, is to punish and deter violators. Returning to the WTO regime, Pauwelyn concludes that although full compensation of all victims or outright punishment cannot realistically be met with the current purely prospective 'equivalent retaliation' instrument, WTO retaliation does serve variable, overlapping goals which at times creates confusion. Yet, in Pauwelyn's view, 'different types of legal entitlements should be matched with different types of protection and enforcement goals (referred to as liability rules, property rules and inalienability)'.

2 'Trade retaliation simply does not work when developing countries win a case' (informal remedies; the WTO enforcement club; smart sanctions; cross-retaliation)

Besides the one-liner that 'trade retaliation is shooting yourself in the foot', another idea or critique that is often voiced in discussions on WTO retaliation is that 'trade retaliation simply does not work when developing countries win a case'. What impact can, for example, trade sanctions by Antigua have on the United States? In other words, what to do when faced with what Mendel refers to as '[m]assive inequalities between two economic and political systems'?

Nottage, working as a trade lawyer for the Advisory Centre on WTO Law whose task it is to assist developing countries, critically evaluates whether weaknesses in WTO retaliation rules undermine the utility of WTO dispute settlement for developing countries. His answer is negative and reached by distinguishing between what he calls 'theory' and 'practice'. Nottage agrees with 'the theoretical proposition that WTO retaliation rules are skewed against developing countries as a means of inducing compliance by WTO Members of asymmetrical market size'. At the same time, however, Nottage disagrees with 'the consequential argument that shortcomings in WTO retaliation rules undermine the utility of the WTO dispute settlement system for developing countries'. The core reason for his conclusion is that 'GATT and WTO dispute settlement *practice* demonstrates high rates of compliance with adverse dispute settlement rulings *even when smaller and developing countries are complainants*' (emphasis in the original). As a logical matter, Nottage argues, it must, therefore, be true that 'the capacity to retaliate effectively is often not a significant factor for government compliance with adverse panel and Appellate Body rulings'. Pawley similarly refers to the informal remedies of reputation and 'community' costs as major driving forces behind WTO compliance.

Of the so far seventeen authorizations to retaliate, eight were granted to developing countries and only in one instance did a developing country actually implement the retaliation (Mexico against the United States in *Byrd Amendment*). One explanation, Nottage suggests, is that in the seven other cases 'actual retaliation may no longer have been necessary or of limited incremental purpose' (he refers, for example, to US retaliation in *EC–Bananas* and a pending settlement with the EU as possible reasons for why Ecuador did not implement retaliation in *EC–Bananas*). The *threat* or *authorization* to impose sanctions may, therefore, mean as much as (if not more than) actually imposing sanctions. Or as Khabayan puts it when talking about Canada's retaliation against the United States in *Byrd Amendment:* 'the product targets [live swine, ornamental fish, oysters and cigarettes, selected because the supporters of the offending legislation were from Virginia and Maine] appear to have more to do with sending a political message to the US Congress rather than having a real economic impact. But the political message was underscored by the fact that several of the co-complainants in this case sought retaliation authorization nearly concurrently'.

In sum, Nottage concludes that '[d]eveloping countries should not be overly dissuaded from using WTO dispute settlement to achieve their trade objectives due to a lack of retaliation capacity'. Huerta Goldman, working for the Mexican mission to the WTO in Geneva, puts it somewhat differently: 'Retaliation as a legal remedy is not very effective. But it is much preferable to have a system which offers these mechanisms, as deficient as they may be, than not to have any such system at all.'

Evenett's economic analysis ('Sticking to the rules') confirms Nottage's conclusion from a different perspective. Evenett uses data on international trade flows to estimate the potential impact of trade sanctions (or the threat thereof) in the bilateral relationships of twenty-two countries (twenty major developing countries, Japan and the United States). By gauging the possible impact of trade sanctions Evenett hopes to find a proxy of the varying incentives for countries to stick to WTO rules. Evenett agrees that a country's capacity to enforce WTO rules, that is, to protect market access negotiated under the WTO, does, of course, depend on the size of its market. Yet, he also finds that sanctioning capacity does *not* depend on a country's level of development (market size matters as much for Switzerland as it does for Costa Rica or Antigua). Crucially, Evenett further explains that the impact of trade sanctions not only depends on the market size of the *retaliating country*, but also on the amount and distribution of exports, and the types of products exported, by the *violating country.* Trade sanctions will, for example, work better against a country that exports a lot, and mainly parts and components (or what Evenett refers to as 'actionable exports'): think of countries like Japan, Korea, China and Taiwan. In contrast, trade sanctions will present less of a threat against countries that have few exports, or export mainly homogeneous or fungible goods, such as oil or other raw materials which can be easily diverted or sold to other countries: think of countries like Nigeria, Venezuela or Saudi Arabia. On that basis, Evenett concludes that there exists a 'clear WTO enforcement club' of nations whose bilateral trade flows are sufficiently large that they have some clout over several importing nations.

Interestingly, and here is where Evenett meets Nottage, according to Evenett, this 'WTO enforcement club' increasingly includes developing countries, especially in East Asia. One of Evenett's conclusions is, therefore, that East Asian countries should step up their role in WTO enforcement and play a more active part in WTO dispute settlement.

One way to possibly make trade retaliation more effective for smaller developing countries is to learn from the experience of developed WTO members. The contributions in this volume on the United States, EC, Canadian and Mexican experience all refer to various techniques to impose what one could call 'smart sanctions'. The general guidelines for such 'smart sanctions' should be to (i) *minimize* the harm caused to the sanctioning country, while at the same time (ii) *maximize* the impact of the sanctions in the violating country.

A crucial way to *minimize harm at home* is to conduct internal consultations with stakeholders (especially importers) before actually imposing sanctions. In this way, products sourced from the violating country which cannot be easily replaced by imports from other countries can be identified and avoided. Khabayan refers to Brazilian orange juice that is not easily substituted in the same quantities for importation into Canada. Nordström talks of the vehement objections raised by the importer and dealer of Harley-Davidson motorbikes in the EC when motorbikes were put on a potential retaliation list against the United States. In the EC a notice for comments on a proposed retaliation list against the United States in *US–FSC*, explained that the list had on purpose been limited to 'products for which the average US import share (in value) in the period 1999–2001 represents a maximum of 20% of the average total imports into the EU'.[1] Malacrida goes as far as proposing that explicit rules should be included in the DSU to oblige retaliating countries to set up a domestic

[1] 'Notice relating to the WTO Dispute Settlement proceeding concerning the United States tax treatment of Foreign Sales Corporations (FSC) – Invitation for comments on the list of products that could be subject to countermeasures' (2002/C 217/02), *Official Journal of the European Communities*, 13 September 2002.

notice-and-comment procedure before finalizing retaliation lists. Salles, in turn, criticizes the implementation system currently in place in Brazil for not providing such public consultations. Yet, as Ehring illustrates, even with such consultations, surprises may still occur, as in the upset caused to American football clubs based in the EC when the EC blocked US imports under a relatively broad tariff line which turned out to include cheerleader pom-poms that could be sourced only from the United States!

Nordström is less enthusiastic about internal consultations as a tool with which to strengthen WTO retaliation. In his experience, EC member states and industries do all they can to 'keep the sanctions out of their own backyard ... What was supposed to be a carefully laid out strategy became a free-for-all party ... Everyone agrees with the objective, but no one wants to pay the bill.' To avoid what he calls the 'substitution mess' Nordström makes two (alternative) suggestions. First, innocent victims within the retaliating countries should be compensated by the government ('It is not unreasonable, in my opinion, to compensate individual firms that carry a disproportionate burden of a trade dispute on behalf of the Community. The common burdens should be carried equitably and not distributed at will.'). Second, Nordström proposes what he calls a 'long list' approach which would replace the currently prevailing method of imposing 100 per cent duties on a 'short list' of products with the alternative of imposing a very small additional percentage (he refers to 1 per cent in *US–FSC*) on *all imports* coming from the violating country. This would do away with internal consultations (since all products would be automatically on the 'long list'), equitably share the burden of retaliation (thereby avoiding any government compensations) and even have a positive (tariff) revenue side (in *US–FSC*, with a 1 per cent additional tariff on all US imports amounting to approximately $US2 billion a year). In response to the objection that this may take away the 'bite' of the retaliation as it is felt in the violating country, Nordström argues that 'the power of trade sanctions is overrated ... Economic coercion can certainly add some extra pressure to comply, but the decisive factor is often the legal ruling *per se* and the bad reputation it would earn a government that refuses to stand by its international obligations. Even a "small" punishment would signal the resolve of the Community and the additional tariffs, however small, will be an irritant for the export industry in the targeted country, and hence also a problem for the government concerned.'

Similarly, and although imposed on a 'short list' of imports (instead of all imports as proposed by Nordström), Ehring explains that the EC retaliation in *US–FSC* was not in the form of the traditional 100 per cent duty but in the 'cleverer' form of 'a 5 per cent additional import duty, to be increased by 1 per cent every month for a period of one year, until the level of 17 per cent'. Along similar lines, Huerta Goldman explains how Mexico in *US–Byrd Amendment* imposed varying duties depending on the product (9 per cent for chewing gums, 30 per cent for certain dairy products and 20 per cent for certain wines, champagnes and other sparkling wines). Illustrating yet another method to minimize harm in the sanctioning country (or even to create some benefits), the first guideline for 'smart sanctions' mentioned earlier, Huerta Goldman describes how Mexico in a NAFTA dispute (*US–Brooms*) focused its retaliation on 'defensive interests', namely US imports of high fructose corn syrup, so as to offer protection to Mexican cane sugar producers who were more than happy to substitute for any lost imports. Along the same lines, Andersen and Blanchet point out that 'pursuant to Section 407 of the Trade and Development Act of 2000, [US retaliation lists] must include, where possible, at least some reciprocal goods of the industries affected by the failure of the foreign country or countries to implement the recommendation'.

Turning now to the second guideline for 'smart sanctions', namely, *maximize the impact* of the sanctions *in the violating country*, the impact thus sought could be economic or political, or both. That the EC retaliated against Florida orange juice and other products from 'battle ground' or 'swing' states in US President Bush's 2004 re-election campaign is well known. The political pressure (or at least message) exerted by such targeted sanctions is clear. As Renouf puts it, 'skilful targeting of economic sectors in the losing party may ultimately have more impact than the total amount of countermeasures'. Ehring further explains how relatively low duties, rather than prohibitive tariffs, may actually exert more pressure on the violating country. As 'irritants' rather than 'bans' they may keep the pressure on for much longer: 'a frustrated exporter can have a more powerful voice domestically than an eliminated exporter that has gone out of business entirely or that has lost a certain export market without hope to re-conquer it quickly'. Put differently, it is not enough to take the 'hostage' that 'screams the loudest' (that is, to select a product whose producer has a lot of clout with the government of the violating county). In addition, retaliating countries should keep in mind that, in most cases, a 'screaming hostage' (trade irritants) is worth more than a 'dead hostage' (trade bans).

To further drive up the pressure, Andersen and Blanchet refer to the option in the United States of a so-called carousel (where products on the retaliation list are changed every 6 months). Yet, they note that, even in the United States, such a carousel has so far not been activated. Interestingly, however, after the Workshop and just before sending this book to press, the United States did change its 1999 retaliation package in *EC–Hormones*, a move that is likely to trigger a WTO dispute over 'equivalence'. In what many saw as a 'parting shot' (against France) from outgoing President Bush on 14 January 2009, the United States not only changed the product list but also increased the retaliatory duty from 100 to 300 per cent on one single product, namely, Roquefort cheese.[2] The duty is thereby clearly meant to be punitive rather than compensatory (contrary to the 'screaming' versus 'dead' hostage analogy made above). Yet, the product chosen may be an exceptional case and a near perfect example of a 'screaming hostage'. It exemplifies the political targeting referred to earlier. Although US sales of Roquefort represent only 2 per cent of annual sales, as *Time* reported, '[y]ou can laugh at their accents, mock their leaders, and even ban their fries from the Congressional menu without getting much of a rise from the *French*. But start messing with their beloved cheeses, as the U.S. has now done, and *the famous Gallic shrug* will rapidly give way to outraged shouts of protest'.[3] Indeed, within a week, Roquefort producers, led by media star and former presidential candidate, José Bové (himself a Roquefort farmer), protested in the streets of Paris and hand-delivered 7 kg of Roquefort to the US Ambassador to France.[4]

Cross-retaliation is often referred to as another way for smaller developing countries to use WTO retaliation more effectively as a tool to induce compliance by larger WTO members. Whereas sanctions in the form of trade restrictions may harm one's own economy (especially where sanctions are imposed on inputs), not paying royalties to foreign patent holders or otherwise suspending intellectual property rights of nationals in the violating country may both increase welfare in the sanctioning economy (at least in the short term) and exert greater political pressure in the violating countries. Yet, the economic, legal and political complications raised by WTO retaliation under the TRIPS as well as GATS agreements are manifold, as discussed in Zdouc, Abbott and Appleton.

[2] 'Modified list of EU products subject to additional duties', 14 January 2009, available at: www.ustr.gov/assets/Document_Library/Federal_Register_Notices/2009/January/asset_upload_file64_15289.pdf.

[3] 'France fumes over US Roquefort Tax', *Time*, 16 January 2009, available at: www.time.com/time/world/article/0,8599,1872241,00.html.

[4] 'Roquefort: une délégation d'élus locaux reçue à l'ambassade des US sans Bové', L'Express, 21 January 2009, available at: www.lexpress.fr/actualites/1/roquefort-une-delegation-d-elus-locaux-recue-a-l-ambassade-des-us-sans-bove_734993.html.

Contributors (see, for example, Sebastian, Hunter and Zdouc) agree, however, that arbitrators have liberally interpreted the DSU's pre-conditions for countries to be authorized to cross-retaliate (thus far not a single developing country that so requested has been denied the right to cross-retaliate). Nonetheless, Sebastian expresses the view that 'even this deferential review arguably goes beyond what was envisaged by the negotiators of the DSU'. Along the same lines, Zdouc points to a DSU review proposal by Cuba, India and Malaysia whereby developing countries would be completely free to cross-retaliate against developed countries in any trade sector and under any covered agreement without having to state reasons. Zdouc argues that '[i]f the objective is to induce compliance by using the most effective form of retaliation or to punish the perpetrator for its non-compliance, then [this reform proposal] is the more promising alternative'. In any event, one point on which several authors in this volume agree is that IP conventions concluded under the auspices of WIPO should not stand in the way of WTO members implementing an authorization to suspend parallel IP obligations under the TRIPS Agreement (see Abbott, Ehring and Zdouc). Zdouc, Director of the WTO Appellate Body Secretariat, for example, makes the point that '[c]ross-retaliation under the TRIPS Agreement cannot effectively induce compliance unless structures are developed to avoid a situation where a WTO Member exercising its DSB-authorized right to suspend TRIPS obligations faces conflict with its obligations under other international or national regimes'.

Finally, that developing countries may, therefore, be able to design 'smart' and effective sanctions, or at least credibly threaten with such sanctions especially when viewed in combination with other, 'informal remedies', is underscored by the somewhat enigmatic statement by Mendel (counsel for Antigua) that, for Antigua in *US–Gambling* 'the ultimate application of the sanctions should not be ruled out. Even at the low level approved by the two arbitrators, the application of the authorised sanctions might prove to be effective. Antigua has a strategy for the application of its remedies which could very well have the intended effect.'

3 'Accurately calculating the authorized level of retaliation is a myth and close to impossible'

A third and final recurring theme in discussions on trade retaliation, including in this volume, is that whatever the goal, metric or benchmark selected, the calculation of authorized levels of WTO retaliation is, at present, not 'very scientific'. Cynics point out, for example, that in many arbitrations the final amount awarded was suspiciously close to the average between what the complainant asked for and what the defendant suggested as the 'nullification or impairment'. The disarming, but nonetheless troubling, statement by the arbitrators in *US–Gambling* below was referred to several times during the Workshop as well as in this volume:

> we feel we are on shaky grounds solidly laid by the parties. The data is surrounded by a degree of uncertainty. For most variables, the data consists of proxies … and observations are too few to allow for a proper econometric analysis … we are left with preciously little information and guidance. Nevertheless, we will attempt to stay as closely to the approaches proposed by parties as possible and to make a maximum use of the limited information base we were given.[5]

Based on this and other observations, Schropp concludes that 'Arbitrators have failed to fulfill their mandate of safeguarding the equivalence standard … The calculation of the level of [nullification or impairment] was under-compensatory for the complaining parties, arbitrary in its choice of counterfactuals, and inept to address violations of non-market access WTO entitlements.' Ehring, in no hidden terms, refers to the *US–Gambling* arbitration as a 'judicial disaster'.

If the arbitrators' calculation of 'nullification or impairment' caused by the original violation is controversial, as many contributors to this volume have pointed out, this may only be the first part of a more complex three-step exercise. The instruction to arbitrators in DSU, Article 22.4 requires that (i) the level of 'suspension of concessions or other obligations' (SCOO) is (ii) 'equivalent' to (iii) the level of 'nullification or impairment' (NoI) caused by the violation. Arbitrators have, however, so far limited themselves to only the third element, that is, putting a dollar figure on NoI. With one exception (*EC–Hormones*), they have not checked or determined the level or impact of the SCOO proposed by the retaliating country (point (i) above), nor evaluated whether the two (that is, NoI and SCOO) are 'equivalent' (point (ii) above). Schropp, Sebastian and Davey in contributions to this volume all agree that arbitrators can, and should, examine not just one but all three of these steps. Following this track, Zdouc, Abbott and Appleton explain some of the complications in calculating the impact or effect of suspending obligations under the TRIPS or GATS agreements (including when calculating the level of SCOO in cross-retaliation cases).

[5] *US–Gambling*, Arbitration under Article 22.6, DSU, paras. 3.173–4.

Bown and Ruta, in their economic assessment of the ten arbitration reports so far, are more positive, concluding that '[i]n many of the DSU cases that we examine ... the arbitrators' actual approach appears quite consistent with the Bagwell and Staiger reciprocity formulation theory'. Sebastian ends his legal assessment with a mixed message: 'arbitral panels have been broadly consistent in the basic approaches'; however, '[g]iven the open texture of the standards involved and the limited number of awards so far, there remains considerable room for refinement and development in this area of law'.

If the work of WTO arbitrators on retaliation is tested against the standard of accurately setting the precise amount of 'nullification or impairment' so as to fully compensate (yet not *over*compensate) the complainant or to carefully rebalance the scales, getting it 'exactly right' is crucial. Indeed, if the theory of 'efficient breach', referred to by Sykes, is to have any currency in the WTO, the system must be able to accurately 'value' WTO entitlements so as to avoid the cost related to error and, more importantly, not to *under*compensate (which would lead to 'too many' breaches) nor to *over*compensate (which would lead to 'not enough' breaches). Sykes concedes that his reference to 'expectation damages' and 'efficient breach' in private contract theory is only a 'crude analogy', first, because nothing in the DSU ensures or obliges the actual imposition of retaliation (thereby running the risk that the 'price of breach' is *too low*) and, second, because 'the question of how to measure and operationalize "equivalence" [in WTO retaliation] is much less clear than in the private contract setting'.

Indeed, most contributors to this volume seem to think that the current system is *under*-compensatory. Davey, for example, disagrees with Sykes 'that we need to worry about making breach more costly or too costly ... the consequences of breach are often not very costly at all, compared to the damage done ... because remedies are prospective and available only after a very long legal process is completed ... breach is, if anything, cheap'. Schropp is of the same view: 'Opting for reliance damages as the baseline counterfactual and taking the end of the [reasonable period of time, instead of the time at the which the illegality arose] as starting-point of damage-calculation results in an under-compensatory benchmark ... this prompts excessive breach on the part of injuring parties and inefficiently little *ex ante* trade liberalization by prospective complainants.' Pauwelyn concludes that 'the nature of WTO entitlements is such that putting an accurate value or price on WTO entitlements is difficult, costly and prone to either over- or (especially) undervaluation. The limited practice of WTO suspension arbitrations ... leaves no doubt that the calculation of "equivalent" suspension – that is, the pricing of WTO entitlements – is at best an approximation, at worst an educated guess; it clearly is an art, not a science.'

If, in contrast, the idea of calculating and authorizing WTO retaliation is to put an upper limit on sanctions that can be imposed so as to effectively induce compliance (without really punishing the violator), then getting it 'about right' may be more acceptable (the way countermeasures in public international law, think of an armed counteract, need only to be 'proportional' to the original breach). As Winters puts it with reference to former GATT Director-General Arthur Dunkel: '[r]eciprocity is difficult to pin down precisely ... "[it] cannot be determined exactly, it can only be agreed upon"'. Along those lines, Malacrida's suggestion of optional or even mandatory 'final offer arbitration' is intriguing. Under such systems both parties would simultaneously submit their final best 'estimates' of the level of nullification or impairment to the arbitrator. The arbitrator would then have to select one of the two proposed levels. Since both parties know in advance that the arbitrator has to select the more appropriate estimate, each party has an incentive to submit an estimate that is reasonable.

Apparently supporting the idea that getting it 'about right' is as much as we can hope for, Sacerdoti puts WTO arbitrations on retaliation in the context of 'discretionary' determinations 'similar to an *aequo et bono* decision' and the distinction between legal and non-legal disputes (arguing that the absence of the possibility to appeal retaliation awards 'confirms that the subject matter was viewed as involving predominantly non legal issues'). Mendel goes a step further, arguing that the award in *US–Gambling* 'bears many of the features of an essentially political approach'. On the question of appealing retaliation awards, Ehring, in contrast, suggests that the legal issues in such awards should be made subject to review by the Appellate Body. Making the comparison to investor–state arbitration awards on compensation, Kaufmann-Kohler defends the idea of giving broad discretion to the arbitrators. In her view, this allows them 'to take into consideration the nature of the investment and all the surrounding circumstances, which can vary significantly' as well as possibly 'to factor into their end result some considerations of fairness'.

That said, mere complexity of the facts and economics involved should not lead arbitrators to throw up their hands and simply make an educated guess. The contribution by Bown and Ruta underlines the fact that economic formulas are available to 'get it right'. In addition, two recurring suggestions to facilitate the process are made in this volume. First, arbitrators should increase the input of economics and economists in their calculation process. Bown, and Malacrida in his comment to Bown, agree on that point. A debate remains on whether economists themselves should be on the arbitration panel and what the precise involvement of economists on the WTO Secretariat support staff should be. Malacrida is less enthusiastic than Bown in this respect. He calls for 'a healthy degree of caution ... in view of the limitations of quantitative economics' and stresses that input by economists must be limited to 'non-binding guidance'. Most contributors agree, however, that arbitrators can and should appoint independent economic experts to assist them. Sacerdoti, a current member of the WTO Appellate Body, describes the situation as follows:

> It is clear that competence in trade, economy, statistics, consumer behaviour, price elasticity and products substitution are called for. Although the DSU is silent in this respect, recourse to experts by the arbitrators, as panels are authorized to do under Art. 13 DSU, should be possible. Such a possibility should be welcome, because it might supplement the material that the litigants themselves may supply in disputes generally.

Kaufmann-Kohler draws on her experience as a long-standing arbitrator in investor–state disputes to come to the same conclusion. She refers to the difficulty for arbitrators to assess 'the accuracy of conflicting expert valuations produced by the parties' and suggests, as possible solutions, 'the appointment by the tribunal of its own damage expert to assist it in evaluating the evidence of the party-appointed experts' as well as the 'need for more involvement of economists in investment arbitration'.

A second recurring suggestion to improve the accuracy of WTO retaliation calculations is for arbitrators to find ways to collect more data and evidence from the parties or elsewhere (see Bown, Huerta Goldman, Lockhart, Renouf and Zdouc). As Huerta Goldman points out, having sufficient data available is important not only for WTO arbitrators, but also (if not more so) for the retaliating country itself to enable that country to calibrate an optimal retaliation package ('A policy maker considering the selection of goods to be subject to retaliation is handicapped if he or she does not have a comprehensive set of trade data available.'). Lockhart, pointing to the problem of the strict time frame within which arbitrators must finish their work (in principle, sixty days only), suggests that in order to improve the flow of information to arbitrators the parties should be given 'more time to address ... concerns regarding methodologies and data' and arbitrators should be pushed to 'pose a first set of questions to the parties for written answer *before* the hearing' (instead of holding these questions until the hearing). In Lockhart's view, 'if the arbitrators do not receive satisfactory answers, they should have the courage to draw adverse inferences and apply the burden of proof rigorously'. For Renouf, a WTO official acting regularly as legal adviser to WTO arbitrators, '[t]he cooperation of the parties in providing data is ... essential and all arbitrators have insisted on the need for parties to provide the latest and most accurate data available. Arbitrators sometimes went as far as threatening to use publicly available (and presumably less accurate) data if the parties were not forthcoming' (Renouf here refers to *Canada–Aircraft*).

Kaufmann-Kohler's conclusion on the capacity of arbitrators to calculate damages in the investment context (notwithstanding increasingly high levels of complexity) does send a hopeful message for WTO retaliation calculations. In her view, 'practice shows that with a fair level of discretion in the choice of the methodology and valuation techniques and an increasing measure of expert assistance, investment arbitrators are in a position to assess direct compensation'. The sophisticated modelling and calculation of trade effects in *US–Byrd Amendment*, for example, is generally referred to as a big step forward and an example for future cases. To use Renouf's terms, arbitration an WTO retaliation 'has grown up' and is 'coming of age'. Our hope is that this volume will further nurture this learning process.

PART I

Background and goal(s) of WTO retaliation

1

The nature of WTO arbitrations on retaliation

GIORGIO SACERDOTI

1 Novelties in the WTO dispute settlement system

The dispute settlement system established by the WTO Agreement and set forth in the Dispute Settlement Understanding (DSU) is one of the major achievements of the Marrakesh Agreement of 1994. The establishment of what is in substance a compulsory and exclusive third-party adjudication based on law to settle all disputes arising under the WTO Agreement and its annexes among the WTO members is a key feature of the 'rule-based' WTO, as opposed to the more soft and 'power-based' GATT. At the same time the mechanism did not go as far as full judicialization: it resorts to a combination of diplomatic means (the initial consultations), arbitral and judicial organs (the panels and the Appellate Body) and the bestowing of overall and final responsibility upon the political organs of the WTO, mainly the Dispute Settlement Body (DSB) within a strictly defined mandate ('automatic' adoption of the reports).

There are two other novelties worth underlining. The first is that this system is unique among specific regimes established to govern definite sectors of international relations beyond regional arrangements. The law of the sea regime as governed by the UNCLOS Convention of 1982 includes a court, that is, the Tribunal of the Law of the Sea. Its competence is, however, quite limited and there is no obligation for the parties to the Convention to resort to its jurisdiction except for narrowly defined types of disputes.

The second feature, which is more central to our examination and discussion, concerns the implementation of the decisions of the panels and the Appellate Body, once adopted by the DSB. Implementation of binding international decisions, be they issued by political institutions or by judicial organs, has always been the Achilles' heel of the international order, undermining the operation of international justice. Faced with a recalcitrant obligee, the pendulum swings between resorting to coercive measures – a momentous choice often not practicable – and leaving the responsibility to comply to that very party, with the risk that effectiveness of the legal order becomes a mockery.[1]

The WTO has dealt with these problems through a complex system that relies on various elements:

(1) first, the willingness and cooperation of the party which must comply with a decision, on the assumption that trade obligations (which should not be loaded in principle with political sensitivity) will be carried out spontaneously in good faith;
(2) mutual agreement between this party (the 'losing' party) and the 'winning' party, in order to facilitate compliance or develop alternatives such as compensation;
(3) pressure put upon the losing party by the continuous multilateral surveillance of implementation by the DSB;
(4) flexibility resulting from the fact that implementation entails the removal of the objectionable conduct and withdrawal of domestic measures in conflict with a WTO obligation only for the future (*ex nunc*, not *ex tunc*) without any obligation to pay damages for past breach;
(5) and, finally, recourse to compulsory third-party adjudication if key steps in the implementation phase should be blocked by disagreement.

This last element is also novel and is an integral element of the objective to obtain effective compliance, removing the loss of trade, basically the prejudice caused to the market access guaranteed and expected by the other trading partner(s). As a last remedy, this includes authorizing trade sanctions in the form of countermeasures offsetting the prejudice suffered by the winning party. They are allowed as long as non-compliance persists and in proportion to such prejudice. However, suspension, that is countermeasures, result in a lose–lose game, while trade negotiation and commitments aim at producing a win–win situation in international trade. They are a second-best solution, and it is, therefore, a euphemism to state that they lead to 'rebalancing mutual trade benefits', albeit at a lower level.[2] Their purpose is in any case to induce compliance; the ultimate aim remains the removal of the inconsistent restriction (Article 22.1, DSU).

[1] J. G. Merills, *International Dispute Settlement*, 3rd edn. (Cambridge, 1998), 117.
[2] See WTO, *A Handbook on the WTO Dispute Settlement System* (Cambridge University Press, 2004), 81.

2 Third-party adjudication in the DSU implementation phase

Recourse to third-party adjudication is provided in a number of instances in the implementation phase. First, Article 21.3, DSU provides that if immediate compliance is impracticable and the parties in dispute do not agree a reasonable period of time to comply, such period shall be determined by binding arbitration.

Secondly, where there is disagreement as to the existence or consistency with a WTO agreement of measures taken to comply with the recommendations and rulings of the DSB, Article 21.5, DSU provides for recourse to the original panel, with the possibility of appeal to the Appellate Body.

Thirdly, under Article 22, DSU, if proper compliance is not effected within such reasonable period of time, upon request of the winning party the DSB shall authorize suspension of concessions or other obligations under the WTO Agreement, that 'shall be equivalent to the level of the nullification or impairment' caused to the party that makes the request. The granting of the authorization by the DSB is ensured by the 'reversed consensus' that applies when the DSB is so requested. To ensure the equivalence between sanctions imposed and prejudice caused, since the level of suspension is proposed by the winning party, compulsory arbitration is mandated by Article 22.6 in case of challenge by the other party in order to prevent 'overshooting'. Article 22.7 makes this explicit where it states that the task of the arbitrator(s) is to 'determine whether the level of such suspension is equivalent to the level of nullification or impairment'. This arbitration, to be entrusted to the original panel with no possibility of appeal, was the main object of the Workshop that led to the present volume. I will accordingly focus on some legal features of this mechanism, considering it within the framework of the other third-party adjudication procedures, highlighted above, which are provided within implementation.

I wish to recall that resort to these mechanisms has been rather frequent, a practice that confirms the success of the whole dispute settlement system and its centrality as a key element of the functioning of the multilateral rule-based trade system of the WTO. From 1995 to the end of 2008 there have been twenty-eight arbitrations on the length of the reasonable period of time under Article 21.3, all of which were carried out by individual arbitrators chosen by the Director-General from among the past or current Appellate Body members.[3] There have been twenty-eight panel

[3] For the complete list of arbitrations from 1995 to 2008 see *Appellate Body Annual Report 2008* (WTO, 2009), 89ff.

proceedings to resolve disputes on the correctness of compliance under Article 21.5 (of which fifteen have resulted in appellate proceedings), with a substantial increase in recent years. Finally, there have been seventeen arbitrations on the level of concession to be suspended.[4]

Within the WTO, binding arbitration in order to settle disputes concerning market access has also been resorted to beyond the DSU. Specifically the 'banana waiver', granted to the EC by the Ministerial Conference at Doha in 2001 in favour of the African, Caribbean and Pacific (ACP) countries in accordance with Article IX:3 of the WTO Agreement, provided for two arbitrations in case of dispute concerning the maintenance of the previous 'total market access for MFN banana suppliers' to the EC.[5] In fact, both arbitrations took place in 2005–2006, although they failed to resolve the dispute.[6]

3 WTO arbitrations during the implementation phase: legal versus non-legal disputes; lawyers versus non-lawyers

The legal question which I would like to address concerns the nature of these arbitrations since they present some novel features in the panorama of international arbitration and judicial settlement, especially that provided by Article 22.6.

Since the development of arbitration based on due process and the application to the substance of the dispute of legal rules and principles of international law in the second half of the nineteenth century, this method of interstate dispute settlement has been considered appropriate to deal with 'legal disputes', thereby deciding who is right and who is wrong. Arbitration of this kind, on the other hand, has been considered inappropriate for settling 'political disputes' because of their sensitivity and/or the absence of pre-existing rules on the basis of which they could be resolved. Political disputes have been considered the province of negotiation and agreement, through mediation, diplomacy, equitable

[4] For the complete list of Article 21.5 Panel proceedings and arbitrations from 1995 to 2007 see 'Dispute Settlement Body, Annual Report 2007, Overview of the State of Play of WTO Disputes', WT/DSB/43/Add.1. Available at: www.wto.org.

[5] See Doha Ministerial Conference, The ACP–EC Partnership Agreement Decision of 14 November 2001, Annex I.

[6] See Award of the Arbitrator, *EC–The ACP–EC Partnership Agreement*, Recourse to Arbitration Pursuant to the Decision of 14 November 2001, WT/L/616, 1 August 2005 (DSR 2005:XXIII, 11667); Award of the Arbitrator, *EC–The ACP–EC Partnership Agreement*, Second Recourse to Arbitration Pursuant to the Decision of 14 November 2001, WT/L/625, 27 October 2005 (DSR 2005:XXIII, 11701).

solutions and decisions by competent organs of international organizations. There is a long tradition at the root of this distinction.[7] Let me recall here in Geneva the statement of one of the founding fathers of the doctrine of international law, the Swiss jurist, de Vattel, in the middle of the eighteenth century in his treatise *Le droit des gens*: 'Arbitration is a most reasonable instrument to settle a dispute and most in conformity with natural law, provided that the dispute does not directly affect the preservation of the Nation.'[8]

More recently, when institutional arbitration and judicial proceedings have largely replaced ad hoc arbitration, this principle is set forth in Article 36.3 of the UN Charter dealing with Pacific Settlement of Disputes: 'In making recommendations under this Article the Security Council should also take into consideration that legal disputes should as a general rule be referred by the parties to the International Court of Justice in accordance with the provisions of the Statute of the Court.' This reflects the fact that under Article 36.2 of the latter the court is competent in respect of 'legal disputes'.

The criteria to distinguish a legal dispute from other types of disputes are far from clear and undisputed. Basically, a legal dispute is one where the claimant bases its claim on a right to which it argues it is entitled based on a legal provision binding the other party, which the claimant complains has been breached by such other party.[9] A legal standard must exist against which the alleged breach can be evaluated so that the conduct of the respondent may be labelled as unlawful, if so proved in fact and in law. By contrast, in a political dispute the claimant does not base itself on a legal entitlement but relies on arguments of political expediency, security needs, economic satisfaction, of moral or other nature. In such a dispute, the claimant often relies on principles generically recognized by the legal order though running counter to an existing legal regulation (such as invoking the right of self-determination of peoples to modify a border agreed by treaty). A political pretension may thus aim at changing the legal situation and may be unfounded in strict legal terms.

[7] See G. Morelli, 'La théorie générale du procès international', *RC*, 61 (1937: III), 253–373; A. Cassese, 'The Concept of "Legal Dispute" in the Jurisprudence of the ICJ', *Comunicazioni e Studi*, vol. XIV (Milano, 1975), 173ff; C. Santulli, *Droit du contentieux international* (2005), 4.

[8] Emmerich de Vattel, 'De l'Arbitrage', *Le Droit des Gens*, vol. II, para. 329.

[9] See also Publications of the Permanent Court of International Justice, Series B, No. 3, 1924; PCIJ, Series A, No. 2; *The Mavrommatis Palestine Concessions* case, where the classical definition of legal dispute is found. Accordingly, '[a] dispute is a disagreement on a point of law or fact, a conflict of legal views or of interests between two persons'. *Ibid.*, 6.

But a grey area subsists. Legal disputes can be resolved though diplomatic means by mutual concessions. Decisions *ex aequo et bono* may settle both legal and non-legal disputes. Procedural justice, due process in the proceedings, appointment of jurists as arbitrators are indices of a legal dispute, but are not incompatible with the settlement of other types of controversy. An international tribunal may be empowered to settle any dispute under well-defined terms of reference.[10] The preference expressed recently in some fora for conciliation, rather than resorting to formal adjudication, may be aimed at overcoming the very distinction in the interest of an effective settlement of a dispute that one party may view as legal and the other as political. Alternatively, formal adversarial proceedings based on the application of international law to the dispute may not result in a binding decision, but rather in a recommendation that is subsequently incorporated into an authoritative decision of a political organ of the organization to which the proceedings pertain. This is the case with regard to panels and the appellate mechanism at the WTO, a feature that does not rule out at the outset the judicial nature of those proceedings.[11]

I believe that the distinction between legal and non-legal disputes is still valuable, even beyond an Aristotelian logic. Determining whether a dispute has a legal character may be relevant for jurisdictional purposes, helps in organizing dispute settlement mechanisms that are consistent with the nature of the disputes to be resolved, assists in pinpointing the obligations that are at stake, the content of any decision and what compliance entails. The various WTO mechanisms in the implementation phase show an expansion of the category of legal disputes amenable to third-party adjudication – arbitration and judicial – beyond the traditional realm.

The expansion of international law and dispute settlement mechanisms into new realms has added interest to the issue. Norms refer more and more to non-legal standards that become direct or indirect content of, or parameters relevant to determine the content of, international obligations, just as is current in domestic law and litigation or in commercial arbitration. The judge and the arbitrator are called upon to decide what is

[10] See the competence that may be bestowed upon the European Court of Justice to settle as an arbitrator disputes between member states of the EU under Article 239 of the EC Treaty.

[11] See, in general, our contribution 'The Dispute Settlement System of the WTO in Action: A Perspective of the First Ten Years' in G. Sacerdoti, A. Yanovich and J. Bohanes (eds.), *The WTO at Ten – The Contribution of the Dispute Settlement System* (Cambridge University Press, 2006), 42ff.

the applicable non-legal standard of human conduct and whether such a standard has been complied with or not; the legal consequence may be just a mechanical follow-up.[12] Medical malpractice cases, disputes concerning technical standards to be applied in public works, manufacturing, provision of services are good examples. In domestic legal orders questions of life or death (for the accused) may be entrusted to juries of laymen and women.

The law itself, including international law, refers to standards of conduct which must be applied in the light of circumstances and where precedents fulfil an important role: thus, in the area of protection for foreign investors and ensuing litigation, the fair and equitable, reasonable and other standards of conduct applicable to host governments. Finally, establishing damages caused by the breach of an obligation entails mostly non-legal, but rather technical, accounting, economic determinations and estimates. Nonetheless, this is recognized as an integral part of litigation and arbitration, both domestically and internationally, in private and interstate disputes.

The legal profession has by and large maintained its competence to decide these issues; lawyers are more commonly chosen to perform the task of assessing damages than accountants, engineers or other professionals. Judges and arbitrators, of course, rely heavily on experts in order to discharge their mandate in this respect, but maintain the last word: *judex peritus peritorum*, the judge is the expert among the experts. The set up and practice of WTO panels is consistent with this approach.[13]

In the light of the above framework how should we view the various arbitration proceedings envisaged by the DSU in the implementation phase? As to disputes under Article 21.5 concerning implementation of a previous panel or Appellate Body adopted report, there is no doubt that the dispute shares the same legal nature as the original case. The task of the adjudicators is to decide the conformity of a measure taken to comply with the previous holding and generally with WTO obligations. This is a typical legal operation entailing interpretation of both the domestic measures and WTO law. It is not by chance that the report of an Article 21.5 panel may be appealed to the Appellate Body, which in this respect exercises its usual functions: namely, to review the issues of law covered

[12] *Cf.* Article 36.2(c) of the Statute of the ICJ under which the court may be given competence in respect of 'the existence of any fact which, if established, would constitute a breach of an international obligation'.

[13] See Article 13 DSU, 'Right to seek information': 'Each panel shall have the right to seek information and technical advice by any individual or body which it deems appropriate.'

in the panel report and legal interpretations developed therein that have been appealed and uphold, modify or reverse the panel's legal findings and conclusions.

The characterization of arbitration under Article 21.3 for determining the reasonable period of time for implementation is more complex. No determination of non-compliance is at issue here, nor any determination of fact that may be relevant to ascertain who is right and who is wrong. The task of the arbitrator is to make declarative and prospective determination, applying *in casu* the right accorded to the losing party, spelled out in that provision: that of having a reasonable period of time to comply.[14]

At this point one may wonder whether this a discretionary determination by the arbitrator, similar to an *aequo et bono* decision, although even such a decision is not to be equated to arbitrariness and requires the expression of grounds. 'Reasonable' in the light of what? And in the interest of whom? Article 21 supplies fundamental criteria in this respect: first, 'prompt compliance with recommendations or rulings of the DSB is essential in order to ensure effective resolution of the disputes to the benefit of all Members' (Article 21.1). Secondly, 'a guideline for the arbitrator should be that the reasonable period of time to implement panel or Appellate Body recommendations should not exceed 15 months from the date of adoption of a panel or Appellate Body Report. However, that time may be shorter or longer, depending upon the particular circumstances' (Article 21.3(c)).

In practice the yardstick has been the time needed to adopt the implementing measure by the member that has to comply, considering the length of the domestic proceedings required. More precisely several arbitrators have held that 'the reasonable period of time, as determined under Article 21.3(c), should be the shortest period possible within the legal system of the member to implement the recommendations and rulings

[14] See on Article 21.3, 'arbitration': Alvarez-Jiménez Alberto, 'A Reasonable Period of Time for Dispute Settlement Implementation: An Operative Interpretation for Developing Country Complainants', *World Trade Review*, 6:3 (2007), 451–76; Gambardella Maurizio and Rovetta Davide, 'Reasonable Period of Time to Comply with WTO Rulings: Need to Do More for Developing Countries?', *Global Trade and Customs Journal*, 3:3 (2008); Monnier Pierre, 'The Time to Comply with an Adverse WTO Ruling: Promptness with Reason', *Journal of World Trade*, 35:5 (2001), 825–45; Peng Shin-yi, 'How Much Time is Reasonable? – The Arbitral Decisions under Article 21.3(c) of the DSU', *Berkeley Journal of International Law*, 5 (2008); Zdouc Werner, 'The Reasonable Period of Time for Compliance with Rulings and Recommendations Adopted by the WTO Dispute Settlement Body' in R. H. Yerxa and S. B. Wilson (eds.), *Key Issues in WTO Dispute Settlement: The First Ten Years* (Cambridge University Press, 2005).

of the DSB'.[15] Thus, the deadline has been shorter when administrative action was required, in contrast to instances where legislative measures are indispensable. The period granted has varied between six and fifteen months.[16]

Notwithstanding the accumulated precedents and the parties' input have in the proceedings (including briefs and a hearing), the arbitrator enjoys a substantial degree of discretion. His or her tasks are not typical of an arbitrator in a legal dispute; rather, they are more akin to those of an expert entrusted with the completion of an element of a contract, such as to determine the 'fair market value' of an asset in a sale. The fact that the Director-General has up till now always appointed former or current members of the Appellate Body, supported by members of the Appellate Body's Secretariat, indicates the importance of entrusting with such a sensitive task (the decision is final in all respects, not subject to review or adoption) experienced and prudent senior figures, well acquainted with the system.

4 Specific features of WTO arbitration on the level of retaliation

I come now to the Article 22.6–7 arbitration for determining the equivalence between the level of nullification or impairment of benefits caused by a WTO-inconsistent measure not withdrawn by the non-complying party, on the one hand, and the level of concessions that the winning party proposes to suspend, on the other hand.

It must be recalled that it is the winning party that proposes the suspension of certain concessions, usually in the form of an increase in custom duties on exports from the non-complying party. The task of the panel in arbitration is then to determine whether the negative effect of that increase on those exports will be equivalent to the prejudice caused by the restriction in the opposite direction that has been maintained in breach of its WTO obligations by the other party. Thus, the comparison is between an actual and prospective loss of trade (in respect of the hypothetical situation had the measure been withdrawn), on the one hand, and the prospective trade loss that the retaliation is likely to cause. It is

[15] Award of the Arbitrator, *Canada–Pharmaceuticals Patents*, para. 45, WT/DS114/13, 18 August 2000 (DSR 2002:I, 3).

[16] For details, see *WTO Appellate Body Repertory of Reports and Awards 1995–2006* (Cambridge University Press, 2007), 880ff.

clear that competence in trade, economy, statistics, consumer behaviour, price elasticity and products substitution is called for. Although the DSU is silent in this respect, recourse to experts by the arbitrators, as panels are authorized to do under Article 13 DSU, should be possible. Such a possibility should be welcome, because it might supplement the material that the litigants themselves may supply. Since the original panel members are chosen as arbitrators, if available, it is apparent that they may well lack the competence that would be required. No appeal is envisaged in these proceedings. This confirms that the subject matter was viewed as involving predominantly non-legal issues, considering that the Appellate Body is competent to review the panel decisions in order to correct legal errors.[17]

In my view, the task of panels acting as arbitrators under Article 22 can be assimilated to the determination of future damages, specifically loss of profits (*lucrum cessans*) in commercial disputes as a consequence of breach of contract, or of unlawful state action in foreign investors' disputes against the host state under investment protection treaties. There are established rules, though not undisputed, for valuation of different types of productive assets, as well as for future losses (as discussed in the contribution by Kaufmann-Kohler, see Chapter 24). The use of one or another parameter, such as the discount rate for future cash flows, may bring considerable differences in the results. Valuation experts are usually relied upon by judges and arbitrators, since the latter recognize their lack of competence in this respect, except when valuers or accountants are themselves appointed to decide. A common feature in all such disputes is that the losses are measured and, hence, the damages are liquidated in monetary terms.

At the WTO the losses, mostly prospective, are instead measured in monetary terms, but the damage suffered is somehow liquidated in kind: namely, the creditor may inflict an equivalent loss on the liable party by suspending a trade concession of an equivalent value. This, however, entails the additional difficulty of estimating what loss will be caused in the future by the retaliation: namely, by the authorized increase in certain tariffs on imports from the non-complying party.

[17] Determining damages is in any case a proper object of a legal dispute. See Article 36.2(d) of the Statute of the ICJ, listing among the legal disputes on which the court may be given jurisdiction 'the nature and extent of the reparation to be made for the breach of an international obligation'.

A careful examination of all issues involved, including evaluating past cases and discussing possible improvements, is therefore timely and appropriate, especially in view of the limited attention devoted to these issues up to now, notwithstanding their importance. The launching of this interdisciplinary Workshop and the present volume is, therefore, most welcome.

2

The calculation and design of trade retaliation in context: what is the goal of suspending WTO obligations?

JOOST PAUWELYN

> [I]t is not completely clear what role is to be played by the suspension of obligations in the DSU and a large part of the conceptual debate that took place in these proceedings could have been avoided if a clear 'object and purpose' were identified. (*US–Byrd* arbitration, paragraph 6.4)

1 Introduction

This volume concerns the calculation and design of trade retaliation in response to continued non-compliance with the WTO treaty. In subsequent chapters, detailed questions related to this broad topic are examined. One red line that frequently runs through these assessments of legal or economic detail (be it the application of the 'equivalence' standard, the choice of 'counterfactual',[1] the benchmark to determine 'nullification'[2] or the selection of products to target[3]) regards the purpose or goal(s) of suspending WTO concessions. When the WTO permits, or a WTO member engages in, trade retaliation in response to continued non-compliance, what is it trying, or can it legitimately hope, to achieve? This question, as we examine it here, does not relate to what the *retaliating country's* preferences are in this situation (obviously, as complainant, its first goal is most likely to be compliance by the defendant). The question is rather what the drafters of the Dispute Settlement Understanding (DSU) as a whole (drafting

[1] See Thomas Sebastian, 'The Law of Permissible WTO Retaliation', Chapter 4, section 3(a)(i), below.

[2] See Simon Schropp, 'The Equivalence Standard under Article 22.4, DSU: A "Tariffic" Misunderstanding?', Chapter 20, section A, below.

[3] See Håkan Nordström, 'The Politics of Selecting Trade Retaliation in the EC: A View from the Floor', Chapter 10, below.

as both potential complainants *and* potential defendants) intended with the instrument of WTO retaliation. Although clarification of this purpose or goal surely does not solve all problems, nor is it able to provide exact numbers,[4] it can offer crucial insights as a contextual element.

To thus put the calculation and design of trade retaliation in context, this chapter attempts to clarify the goal(s) of WTO suspension from both an historical, descriptive perspective (what has been and currently is the goal of GATT/WTO suspension?) and a prescriptive, normative point of view (ideally, what should be the goal of WTO suspension?). This will be done mainly for the calculation (or *quantity*) aspects of trade retaliation, but will have repercussions also on questions of design (or *quality*).

First, when it comes to the permitted level or quantity of WTO suspensions (how many US$ per year?), WTO rules impose a multilaterally controlled 'equivalence' standard, that is, suspensions cannot go beyond what is 'equivalent' to the level of nullification or impairment caused by the original violation.[5] Notwithstanding this, at first sight, rather strict and clear standard of 'equivalence', ample 'wiggle room' remains to interpret and apply this standard in the light of its goal or 'object and purpose' as called for in the rules of treaty interpretation of the Vienna Convention on the Law of Treaties (incorporated also in the WTO through Article 3.2 of the DSU).

Second, as regards the design or quality of WTO suspensions (which products should be targeted, at what level of additional duty and for how long?), WTO rules leave most of the decisions (with the exception of some limits on cross-retaliation[6]) to the discretion of the retaliating country. As the arbitrators in *EC–Hormones* put it: '*qualitative* aspects of the proposed suspension touching upon the "nature" of concessions to be withdrawn ... fall outside the arbitrators' jurisdiction'.[7] Yet, when making those decisions, retaliating countries will most likely be guided by what they perceive to be the purpose or goal of the suspension in the particular case at hand. Hence, at this level as well – and possibly more so than at the calculation level where the legal confines are stricter – the question of the goal or purpose of WTO suspension matters.

[4] As pointed out by Thomas Sebastian in his contribution to this volume, 'The Law of Permissible WTO Retaliation', Chapter 4, section 7.

[5] Article 22.4, DSU.

[6] These limits are set out in Article 22.3, DSU.

[7] *EC–Hormones*, Decision by the arbitrators under Article 22.6, DSU, WT/DS26/ARB (DSR 1999:III, 1105), WT/DS48/ARB (DSR 1999:III, 1135), para. 19 (original emphasis).

This chapter concludes that the goal of multilaterally controlled GATT/WTO suspension has historically been, and remains to this day, murky and confused (ranging from simple rebalancing of concessions to punishment). Yet, if anything, there has been a gradual evolution from 'compensation' (or simple rebalancing) to 'sanction' (or rule compliance). Hence, instead of one goal, there seem to be multiple and sometimes overlapping goals. Since retaliation for continued non-compliance is, in practice, the only formal remedy provided for by the system (compensation for past harm is not awarded), all possible cures seem to be expected from it. From a normative perspective, however, the argument will be made that this flexibility in the goals pursued by trade suspension, when carefully calibrated, can be a good thing. Although certain perceived goals (such as full compensation of all victims or outright punishment) cannot possibly be met with the current purely prospective 'equivalent retaliation' instrument, the case will be made that different types of legal entitlements should be matched with different types of protection and enforcement goals (referred to as liability rules, property rules and inalienability). Rather than one fixed goal of WTO suspension, there are (and should be) several possible goals. Put differently, optimal protection of WTO entitlements implies variable protection of WTO entitlements.

2 What could be the goal(s) of WTO suspension?

Let us take the *EC–Hormones* case as an example. The United States wins the substantive dispute. Yet, because the EC does not implement the ruling within the set reasonable period of time and no compensation can be agreed on pursuant to DSU, Article 22.2, the United States obtains the right to suspend concessions 'equivalent' to the nullification or impairment caused to it by the EC hormone beef ban (*in casu*, US$116.8 million per year). When the United States subsequently imposes 100 per cent duties on selected EC imports (ranging from Italian scarves to French Roquefort cheese), what is the United States trying, or can it legitimately expect, to achieve? In other words, what is the goal of WTO suspension? As noted in the Introduction, what interests us here is not what *US* preferences are in this situation (obviously, as complainant, its first goal is most likely to be compliance by the EC). The question is rather what the drafters of the DSU as a whole (drafting as both potential complainants *and* potential defendants) intended with the instrument of WTO retaliation. Shaffer and Ganin (Chapter 3) do focus on the practice of retaliating countries to discern the overall purpose of WTO retaliation (namely, in their view, inducing compliance). Yet, in doing so, they can, obviously, paint only part of the picture and not account for the practice or preferences of the victim of retaliation, that is, the original wrongdoer (who may well prefer mere rebalancing or compensation as much as the retaliator is likely to prefer compliance).

Two broad sets of goals could be pursued by trade retaliation, defined here as compensation versus sanction. First, by restricting EC imports, the United States could be authorized to, or seek to, obtain some form of compensation, broadly defined. By suspending some of its earlier granted trade concessions as against the EC, the United States would then reciprocate, rebalance the scales or return to the situation as it existed before the respective concessions were exchanged (reciprocal non-performance, return to the *status quo ante* or invocation of the so-called *inadimpleti non est adimplendum* exception). The retaliation could also compensate the United States in more precise, monetary terms: keeping out EC agricultural products, for example, may compensate US farmers, that is, alleviate the damage caused to the victims of the EC hormone beef ban. As a large country, US duties may also improve US terms of trade and thereby overall US welfare pursuant to the theory of optimal tariffs.[8]

Second, by restricting EC imports, the United States could be authorized or seek to impose some form of sanction, broadly defined, on the EC. This sanction could aim at inducing compliance or rule conformity by the EC or at least a bilateral settlement agreeable to the United States. Suspension as sanction could also go beyond the goal of rule compliance in the particular case and seek to impose punishment or deterrence as regards possible future violations.

The four possible goals of WTO suspension are depicted in Table 2.1 below. Note that the two types of 'compensation' (reciprocal withdrawal of concessions and compensating the victims of the original violation) focus on what happens in or with the *victim state*, here the United States. The goal of compensation, broadly defined, also seems to be the focus of most economists contributing to this volume.[9] In contrast, the two types of 'sanction' (inducing compliance and punishment) focus on changing

[8] See Fritz Breuss, 'A General Equilibrium Interpretation of some WTO Dispute Settlement Cases – Four EU–US Trade Conflicts', Comment on Chapter 20, below.

[9] See Chad Bown and Michele Ruta, 'The Economics of Permissible WTO Retaliation', Chapter 6, below, whose entire study is predicated on pure reciprocity; Alan Sykes, 'Optimal Sanctions in the WTO: The Case for Decoupling (and the Uneasy Case for the *Status Quo*)', Chapter 16, below, who regards WTO dispute settlement as aimed at efficient breach with retaliation acting as a compensation device. See also Simon Schropp,

Table 2.1. *The possible goals of WTO suspension*

I. Compensation (focus on victim)		II. Sanction (focus on violator)	
1. rebalance	2. damages	3. induce compliance	4. punishment

the situation in the *violating state*, here the EC. WTO suspension as sanction to induce rule compliance is (not surprisingly) the goal most often referred to by the lawyers contributing to this volume.[10] The same is true for WTO arbitrations on the question[11] and retaliating complainants actually imposing WTO suspensions (yet, as noted earlier, what retaliating countries aim for must be distinguished from what the drafters of the DSU intended to be the goal of WTO suspension and what, as a result, WTO suspension can realistically be expected to achieve).[12]

3 Why does the goal of WTO suspension matter?

As pointed out in the Introduction, the goal of WTO suspension matters for both the calculation and the design of trade retaliation. This section, while not being exhaustive in any way, lists a number of areas where the intended goal of WTO suspension may have a material impact.

First, when arbitrators are asked to decide on the permitted *level* of retaliation pursuant to the equivalence standard in DSU, Article 22.4, they may come up with a higher number if they perceive the goal of the retaliation to be 'sanction' than if they are of the view that the goal is mere 'compensation'.[13] Put differently, inducing compliance or punishment

'The Equivalence Standard under Article 22.4, DSU: A "Tariffic" Misunderstanding?' and Fritz Breuss, 'A General Equilibrium Interpretation of some WTO Dispute Settlement Cases – Four EU–US Trade Conflicts'; both focusing on welfare and calibrating WTO remedies, including trade retaliation, so as to achieve Pareto efficiency or expectation damages.

10 See William Davey, 'Sanctions in the WTO: Problems and Solutions', Chapter 17, below and Reto Malacrida, 'WTO Retaliatory Measures: the Case for Multilateral Regulation of the Domestic Decision-making Process', Chapter 18, below, as well as the discussion in Thomas Sebastian, 'The Law of Permissible WTO Retaliation', Chapter 4, below.

11 See section 6, below.

12 As reflected in the contributions to Part IV of this volume on the politics of selecting and implementing trade sanctions.

13 For instance, in *Canada–Export Credits and Guarantees*, the arbitrators adjusted the result of the calculation based on the amount of the subsidy by 20 per cent in order to

may necessitate a *higher* level of retaliation than merely rebalancing the bargain.

Second, the goal of WTO suspension may influence what is taken as the *benchmark* to calculate the amount of *nullification* caused by the original violation as well as the amount of *retaliation* authorized in response. If the goal is to compensate the victims of the violation (for example, US farmers harmed by the EC ban on hormone-treated beef), then the most appropriate benchmark to assess nullification may well be the economic harm or loss of profits suffered by the victims of the violation (as, for example, advocated by Schropp (Chapter 20), who sees the goal of retaliation as 'to compensate the Complainant for its true damage from the violation of the contract'[14]). If, in contrast, the goal of the suspension is to restore the broader balance of trade concessions between the two countries, then a more appropriate benchmark could be the trade effects or value of lost bilateral trade caused by the violation (to be distinguished from the actual economic harm caused by the violation). Similarly, if the goal of retaliation is rebalancing then the retaliation could be set at an equivalent 'level of trade', instead of an equivalent 'monetary level of compensation' (for example, a prohibitive tariff keeping out as much trade as the original violation, as is the case in practice so far, instead of, for example, adding up tariff revenues up to the total amount of harm caused by the original violation).

Third, if the goal of WTO suspension is seen as sanctioning the violator to induce compliance, then the retaliating country would be well-advised to retaliate against those sectors and products where the violating country will be hurt the most (for example, politically-sensitive products or suspension of intellectual property rights). In contrast, if the goal of the suspension is to compensate the victims of the original breach, then the retaliating country would be better advised to retaliate against those sectors or products that compete with its domestic industry, especially the industry harmed by the original violation (for example, EC agricultural products kept out of the United States in *EC–Hormones*). Similarly, Nordström's proposal[15] of retaliation in the form of a 2 per cent additional

cause Canada to reconsider its position, which was then to maintain the subsidy in breach of its obligations. See *Canada–Export Credits and Guarantees*, Decision by the arbitrator under Article 22.6, DSU and Article 4.11, SCM Agreement, WT/DS222/ARB (DSR 2003:III, 1187), paras. 3.119–22.

14 Simon Schropp, 'The Equivalence Standard under Article 22.4, DSU: A "Tariffic" Misunderstanding?', section A.

15 See Håkan Nordström, 'The Politics of Selecting Trade Retaliation in the EC: A View from the Floor'.

tariff on a wide range of products makes more sense if the goal is compensation (including improving one's terms of trade with an optimal tariff), than when the objective is to sanction or induce compliance (a 2 per cent tariff on a wide range of products is likely to have less of a punishment or inducement effect than prohibitive, 100 per cent duties on politically-sensitive products).

Fourth, the goal of WTO suspension may also guide questions of timing. If the goal is compliance, then there would be good reason to start calculating the level of nullification and corresponding retaliation as of the date of enactment of the illegal measure or, at least, as of the date of adoption of the WTO ruling finding the measure to be WTO inconsistent.[16] If, in contrast, the goal is simply to rebalance concessions or compensate during the time of continued non-compliance, a later starting point could be chosen. Similarly, a so-called 'carousel' practice where the list of products against which sanctions are imposed is altered every six months may fit well with the goal of inducing compliance (the chilling effect related to the regular change is likely to keep out more trade); the justification for a 'carousel' practice is less clear when the goal is simply to rebalance or compensate.

Fifth, one of the preconditions to cross-retaliate, that is, to retaliate, for example, under the TRIPS Agreement in response to a violation under GATT, is that it is 'not practicable or *effective* to suspend concessions or other obligations with respect to the same sector' or 'the same agreement',[17] in our example, GATT. In *US–Gambling*, the arbitrators interpreted the question of whether suspension is 'effective' as follows:

> the thrust of the 'effectiveness' criterion empowers the party seeking suspension to ensure that the impact of that suspension is strong and has the desired result, namely to induce compliance by the Member which fails to bring WTO inconsistent measures into compliance with DSB rulings within a reasonable period of time.[18]

In other words, whether or not a WTO member has the right to cross-retaliate depends in part on the goal of WTO suspension: if the goal is simply to rebalance trade concessions then retaliation in the same sector

[16] As proposed by William Davey, 'Sanctions in the WTO: Problems and Solutions', section 3.

[17] Article 22.3(b), (c), DSU.

[18] *US–Gambling*, Decision by the arbitrator under Article 22.6, DSU, WT/DS285/ARB, para. 4.29, referring to *EC–Bananas (Ecuador)*, Decision by the arbitrators under Article 22.6, DSU, WT/DS27/ARB/ECU (DSR 2000:V, 2237), para. 72.

or agreement is more likely to be 'effective' (so that cross-retaliation is *not* allowed), than when the goal is to induce compliance (as the arbitrators in *US–Gambling* found, leading them to allow Antigua to cross-retaliate against the United States).

Finally, any assessment of the effectiveness of the WTO dispute settlement system more generally depends on what one regards as the goal of WTO suspension and WTO dispute settlement more broadly. Without fixing this goal or benchmark, any debate on effectiveness of the system is meaningless, with some authors[19] saying that WTO remedies are 'too weak', others[20] saying that they are 'too strong' and yet others[21] concluding that they are 'about right'. More specifically, if the goal is to rebalance concessions, then continued non-compliance in, for example, *EC–Bananas*, *EC–Hormones* and *US–Gambling* combined with reciprocal suspensions by the winning party, should not be seen as failures of the system. In contrast, if the goal is set at inducing compliance or rule conformity then those cases are examples of where the system has (not yet?) achieved its objective.

4 How can we figure out the intended goal(s) of WTO suspension?

Given the multiple options (section 2, above) and the importance of the question (section 3, above), how then can we answer the descriptive question of what is now the intended goal of WTO suspension?

First, we could engage in reverse engineering and based on the *level* of permitted retaliation deduce the implied *goal* of retaliation and WTO dispute settlement more generally. Sykes, for example, looks at the current rule that WTO suspension must be 'equivalent' to the nullification caused, to conclude that the intended goal of WTO suspension is mere rebalancing and that the underlying objective of WTO dispute settlement more generally is 'efficient breach'.[22] Put differently, if WTO members wanted WTO suspension to genuinely induce compliance, Sykes argues,

[19] See, for example, Petros Mavroidis, 'Remedies in the WTO Legal System: Between a Rock and a Hard Place', 11 *European Journal of International Law* (2000), 763.

[20] See, for example, Steve Charnovitz, 'Rethinking WTO Trade Sanctions', 95 *American Journal of International Law* (2001), 792.

[21] See Alan Sykes, 'Optimal Sanctions in the WTO: The Case for Decoupling (and the Uneasy Case for the *Status Quo*)'.

[22] See Alan Sykes, 'Optimal Sanctions in the WTO: The Case for Decoupling (and the Uneasy Case for the *Status Quo*)'.

they would have allowed retaliation to go beyond mere 'equivalence'. The fact that they put the ceiling at 'equivalence' implies that WTO members wanted simply to rebalance the scales and avoid punitive retaliation[23] (something *smaller* or *developing* countries have always been afraid of), and wanted to keep some flexibility to deviate from the rules where such was politically or otherwise expedient (a door that especially *large* or *developed* countries were glad to leave open). As noted below, however, some caution is warranted when engaging in such reverse engineering. The objective of WTO dispute settlement may be achieved not only by the formal remedy of (equivalent) retaliation but also by informal remedies, such as reputation and community costs. If so, the goal of WTO dispute settlement may go beyond what can be expected from 'equivalent' suspension alone, that is, it may nonetheless be to induce compliance rather than merely rebalancing the scales. The historical background, context and actual implementation of the equivalent retaliation standard all support this proposition (indeed, rule compliance follows in the huge majority of WTO disputes, and not a single WTO member has expressed the view that when it retaliates it merely seeks compensation and no longer expects compliance).

Second, we could figure out the goal of WTO suspension by examining the historical background and evolution of trade retaliation in the GATT/WTO. In this process, we could compare with, and draw lessons from, suspension or countermeasures in general international law. This exercise is conducted in section 5, below.

Third, and perhaps most relevant to practice, we could consider what arbitrators say is the intended goal of WTO suspension. As explained below (in section 6), however, the message is mixed and confused (although there seems to be a majority view that the goal is to 'induce compliance').

Fourth, we could consider what retaliating countries themselves have said is their goal when they retaliate, or look at how they designed their retaliation to learn more about what it is they are trying to achieve (for example, where they impose 100 per cent duties on a select list of politically-sensitive products in the violating state, as the United States normally does, retaliating countries are probably first and foremost seeking

[23] This argument is based on Pieter Jan Kuijper's personal comments to the presentation of a draft of this chapter at the CTEI's Interdisciplinary Conference on the Calculation of Trade Sanctions, Graduate Institute of International and Development Studies, 18–19 July 2008.

to induce compliance; if, in contrast, they were to impose 2 per cent duties on products that heavily compete with their own domestic industries, then the aim is probably also, if not predominantly, to compensate some of their own producers). Yet, as repeatedly pointed out, the question of interest here is not so much what retaliating countries seek with WTO suspension (as complainants most likely seek compliance), but rather what the drafters of the DSU as a whole intended to be the legitimate goal of WTO suspension.

It may come as a surprise that after more than 60 years, the GATT/WTO has still not nailed down the intended goal of its core formal remedy. There is, however, an explanation. During the GATT days, suspension of concessions under GATT, Article XXIII was authorized only once (in 1952, in a case between the Netherlands and the United States). Because of the possibility of defendant countries blocking the establishment of panels and the adoption of panel reports, the situation of continued non-compliance after adoption of a GATT ruling simply did not arise: if compliance was seen as a problem, defendants would have long blocked the panel process and, if anything, complainants would impose unilateral trade sanctions without GATT approval (as happened regularly under section 301 of the US Trade Act). It is only with the abolishment of this veto and the establishment of the automatic WTO dispute settlement system that recalcitrant defendants could be pushed all the way against the wall of non-compliance and into an arbitration proceeding on levels of retaliation. Hence, it is only since 1995 that the question of multilaterally authorized trade retaliation and how to calibrate it arose.

5 The historical evolution of the goal(s) of trade suspension from GATT to WTO

The raw text of what the GATT/WTO allows in terms of trade retaliation has not always been set at 'equivalence' to nullification. GATT, Article XXIII:2, the precursor to DSU, Article 22.4 which sets out the current 'equivalence' standard, provided a more flexible benchmark, namely suspension as 'appropriate in the circumstances'. This 'appropriateness' standard seems to allow for retaliation that goes beyond mere 'equivalence'.[24] Put differently, and following the reverse engineering exercise hinted at earlier, whereas today's 'equivalent retaliation' would seem to imply a goal of mere rebalancing or compensation (*quod non*, as

[24] See the opinion of the GATT Legal Adviser referred to in note 31, below.

discussed below), 'appropriate retaliation' could lend itself to the more ambitious goal of sanction or even punishment. From this purely textual perspective, one could then think that there has been an evolution in the goal of multilaterally controlled GATT/WTO retaliation (to be distinguished from self-help or unilateral sanctions taken, for example, by the United States under Section 301 of the Trade Act) from 'sanction' in the GATT to mere 'compensation' in the WTO.[25]

When looking at the negotiating history of GATT and putting the GATT/DSU texts in context, however, if there is a trend to be discerned, it is one in the opposite direction. Indeed, if anything, and somewhat counterintuitively based on the texts alone, the movement from GATT to WTO has been one from regarding retaliation as aimed at rebalancing or compensation in GATT, to inducing compliance or sanction in the WTO.[26]

Let us first look at the negotiating history of GATT, Article XXIII:2. Some delegations wanted to provide for punitive sanctions so as to ensure compliance with the rules rather than simply rebalance the scales.[27] Yet, a Working Group examining the question in the context of the Havana Charter recommended that, even in the case of legal violation, the remedy should be compensatory suspension of concessions and no more.[28] As a result, in the final Havana Charter, the provision corresponding to GATT, Article XXIII:2 referred to suspensions that are 'appropriate *and compensatory*'. To clear all doubt, an interpretative paragraph stated that 'the nature of the relief to be granted is compensatory and not punitive' and that the word 'appropriate' should not be read to provide relief

[25] Note, moreover, that Article XXIII:2 permitted suspensions only if 'the circumstances are serious enough to justify such action'. In contrast, whenever a WTO member wins a dispute and the other party does not implement in time, the complainant has an automatic right to equivalent retaliation, even if, somehow, the circumstances were *not* 'serious enough'. In sum, retaliation in the WTO is allowed *more often* (no need for 'serious circumstances'), but, at least based on the text alone, at a *lower level* ('equivalent' as opposed to 'appropriate').

[26] In support see Steve Charnovitz, 'Rethinking WTO Trade Sanctions', 792.

[27] See Robert Hudec, *The GATT Legal System and World Trade Diplomacy* (New York: Praeger, 1975), 26–31; John Jackson, *World Trade and the Law of GATT* (Indianapolis, In: Bobbs-Merril, 1969), 169, note 21.

[28] United Nations Conference on Trade and Employment, 'Report of the Working Party 3 of Sub-committee G', E/Conf.2/C.6/W.80, 30 January 1948, available at: http://trade.wtosh.com/gatt_docs/English/SULPDF/90200202.pdf (accessed on 15 January 2009). The proposals were adopted without debate (see United Nations Conference on Trade and Employment, 'Sub-committee on Chapter VIII, Notes of the 17th Meeting', E/Conf.2/C.6/W.102, 16 February 1948, available at: http://trade.wtosh.com/gatt_docs/English/SULPDF/90200228.pdf (accessed on 15 January 2009).

'beyond compensation'.[29] In other words, if anything, the Havana Charter set rebalancing or compensation as the goal of suspensions, not sanction or punishment.[30]

Moving to the context of GATT, Article XXIII, it is interesting to note that Article XXIII was negotiated hand-in-hand with what are now Article XIX on safeguards and Article XXIII on tariff renegotiations. In both Article XIX and Article XXIII retaliation is also permitted in case no mutually acceptable compensation can be agreed. Yet, the reciprocal suspension in those articles must be 'substantially equivalent' to the concessions withdrawn as opposed to 'appropriate in the circumstances' under Article XXIII or 'equivalent' under DSU, Article 22.4. This 'substantially equivalent' standard seems to fall somewhere between the more flexible 'appropriateness' standard (in GATT, Article XXIII) and the stricter 'equivalence' standard (in the DSU).[31] Yet, in the one GATT case where suspensions under Article XXIII were authorized, the level of suspension was determined 'having regard to its *equivalence* to the impairment suffered by the Netherlands as a result of the United States restrictions'.[32]

[29] United Nations Conference on Trade and Employment, 'Reports of Committees and Principal Subcommittees for the International Trade Organization' (Geneva, 1948), 155, available at: www.wto.org/gatt_docs/English/SULPDF/90180096.pdf (accessed on 15 January 2009).

[30] What complicates matters, however, is that these Havana Charter clarifications occurred *after* the GATT itself was concluded and were subsequently not incorporated into the GATT. Article XXIII, GATT was, indeed, taken from the earlier Geneva draft of the failed ITO Charter. The legal value of those later Havana Charter clarifications is, therefore, questionable. On the one hand, one could say that they are an *ex post* confirmation of what the drafters of GATT also perceived as the goal of suspensions (compensation, not sanction). On the other hand, one could argue *a contrario* and focus on the fact that the Havana clarifications were *not* subsequently incorporated into the GATT so that the goal of GATT suspension was set at more than mere rebalancing and could include sanctions or punishment. According to John Jackson, one element which could explain this position is that the Havana Charter dealt with a broader range of obligations than GATT so that it made sense to offer softer remedies (compensation only) in the Havana Charter and harder remedies (sanction or even punishment) in the eventual GATT (see John Jackson, *World Trade and the Law of GATT*, 169).

[31] In support, see this 1988 statement by the GATT Legal Adviser where, after noting that suspension under Article XIX (safeguards) and Article XXVIII (tariff renegotiations) was limited to 'substantially equivalent' concessions, he added: 'In the case of Article XXIII, the wording was wider, referring to measures determined to be appropriate in the circumstances, which meant that there was a wider leeway in calculating the retaliatory measures under Article XXIII than under Articles XIX or XXVIII' (GATT doc. C/M/220, at 36, quoted in WTO, *Analytical Index: Guide to GATT Law and Practice* (Cambridge University Press, 1995), 698; and confirmed by the then Deputy Director-General (GATT doc. C/M/224, at 19), quoted in WTO, *Analytical Index: Guide to GATT Law and Practice*, 699.

[32] *Netherlands Action Under Article XXIII:2 to Suspend Obligations to the United States*, BISD 1S/62 (1/61), para. 2, see also para. 3 (italics added).

Thus, even when applying the 'appropriateness' standard in Article XXIII, an 'equivalence' standard along the lines of DSU, Article 22.4 was adopted. Rather than sanction or punishment, the goal of GATT suspension in the one and only GATT ruling on the issue seemed, therefore, to be rebalancing or compensation; not sanction or punishment. This philosophy was explicitly confirmed in the GATT-era Tokyo Code on Technical Barriers to Trade (1979), which provided for suspension in response to non-compliance 'in order to restore mutual economic advantage and balance of rights and obligations', thereby expressing the goal of rebalancing or compensation; not sanction or compliance.

As noted earlier, however, the biggest change from GATT to WTO in terms of suspension is no doubt that under GATT a consensus of all contracting parties was required to authorize retaliation. Hence, it was for the contracting parties *as a whole* to determine by consensus whether the retaliation is 'appropriate in the circumstances'. This meant that multilaterally approved retaliation (to be distinguished from unilateral sanctions, especially by the United States under section 301 of the Trade Act) only occurred once during the close to 50 years of GATT and, more importantly for our purposes, that any scope for harsh sanctions or punishment under Article XXIII remained purely illusionary: since the victim of the sanctions itself would have to agree to authorizing such sanctions, there was simply no way to impose punishment under GATT, Article XXIII. In the WTO, in contrast, the right to retaliation is automatic (under DSU, Article 22.6 only a consensus of all WTO members, including the complainant, can block retaliation). Yet, in return, the level of retaliation was made subject to multilateral control in the form of an arbitration that decides on whether proposed retaliation is 'equivalent' to nullification. In sum, with the WTO, retaliation became automatic both in the sense that there is no need for 'serious circumstances' (as Article XXIII provided for[33]) and no need for positive consensus to get it authorized. In return, however, the level of retaliation was limited to 'equivalence' and made subject to arbitration. Multilaterally controlled equivalence (requested, especially, by countries that had in the past been victims of unilateral US trade sanctions) was the *quid pro quo* for automatic sanctions (a demand formulated, especially, by the United States which had grown frustrated with the veto blocking of the old GATT dispute process).

[33] See note 25, above.

If the intended goal of GATT, Article XXIII suspension could be said to be focused on rebalancing or compensation (with an original idea or rather fictional option to move toward sanctions based on the flexible term 'appropriate'), the contextual message elucidating the goal of WTO suspension, in contrast, points toward sanction or rule compliance (albeit tempered by the 'equivalence' standard in DSU, Article 22.4). Indeed, whereas GATT, Article XXIII provided for 'appropriate' suspension only in 'serious circumstances', made subject to consensual approval of all GATT parties, and without follow-up or indication as to when such suspension would be ended (thereby implying that suspension could be a permanent rebalancing of concessions), the DSU repeatedly underlines that suspension does *not* end the matter (as in compensation that substitutes for rule compliance) but is rather a temporary instrument to achieve the ultimate goal of compliance or mutually agreed settlement. DSU, Article 22.1 stresses, for example, that 'compensation and suspension ... are *temporary* measures' and that 'neither compensation nor ... suspension ... is preferred to full implementation'.[34] Crucially, by providing when suspension must be ended – that is, when the inconsistent measure is removed or when a mutually satisfactory solution is reached – DSU, Article 22.8 implicitly gives us the goal of WTO suspension: only if the illegality is removed or a settlement is found (not when, for example, the victim state is fully compensated) must suspension be removed. Hence, suspension is not a permanent rebalancing of concessions (as in tariff renegotiations under GATT, Article XXVIII), but a temporary solution that must be ended if, but only if, WTO rulings are implemented or a settlement is reached. The fact that the Dispute Settlement Body (DSB) must keep the matter under surveillance and that violating countries must submit regular status reports[35] underlines that suspension is temporary and not a substitute compensation for compliance.

In sum, the contextual goal of WTO suspension as expressed in the DSU is not rebalancing or compensation as such, but compliance or settlement. As further explained below, this goal is not only backed up by the formal 'equivalent retaliation' remedy, but also by informal remedies such as reputation and community costs linked to continued non-compliance. Indeed, it is the repeated expression in the DSU that the ultimate goal of the system is compliance that nurtured a general perception that compliance *is*, indeed, the goal. And it is precisely this general perception which,

[34] See also Articles 3.7 and 22.8, DSU

[35] See Articles 21.6 and 22.8, DSU.

in turn, is the trigger of, and necessary precondition for, the reputation and community costs linked to continued non-compliance (if, in contrast, the WTO community did not share the goal of compliance, breach combined with compensatory suspension could end the matter and would not create any further reputation or community costs; put differently, community costs do not depend on a sense of legal obligation *held by the violator*, but on the shared expectations of *other* WTO members). These informal costs must be added to the formal costs of equivalent retaliation and are, in combination, what explains, according to Davey (Chapter 7), the 83 per cent compliance rate with WTO dispute rulings,[36] notwithstanding the, at first sight, relatively weak remedy of equivalent suspension. In sum, to deduce from the formal remedy of equivalent retaliation alone that the goal of WTO suspension and dispute settlement more generally is mere rebalancing (or efficient breach) is too simple.

To summarize this brief historical overview, although the treaty texts could lead one to think otherwise ('appropriate' suspension in GATT versus 'equivalent' suspension in the WTO) and nothing was set in stone in either GATT or the DSU, the gradual evolution of what seems to be the commonly shared goal of trade suspension in the multilateral trade system is one from rebalancing/compensation in the GATT to compliance/settlement in the WTO.

To make an analogy with the default remedies in general international law, suspension under GATT, Article XXIII is best compared with treaty suspension in Article 60 of the Vienna Convention on the Law of Treaties where 'material breach' (similar to the 'serious circumstances' condition in GATT, Article XXIII) is a ground for 'suspending' treaty obligations. Like GATT, Article XXIII which refers only to 'appropriate' suspension, Article 60 of the Vienna Convention does not include an equivalence or proportionality standard. In addition, both Article XXIII and Article 60 are silent as to if and when suspension must be ended thereby implying that it could be a permanent state of affairs that settles the matter.

Suspension in the WTO, in contrast, is best compared with countermeasures in Article 49 of the International Law Commission's Articles on State Responsibility. There, any continuation of an 'internationally wrongful act' (as with WTO suspension, there is no need for 'material breach' or 'serious circumstances') gives rise to a right to take 'countermeasures'. Yet, such countermeasures are subject to a proportionality standard, comparable with (but somewhat more flexible than) the equivalence standard

[36] See, William Davey, 'Sanctions in the WTO: Problems and Solutions', section 1.

in the DSU.[37] Similarly to DSU, Article 22.8 stating that 'suspension … shall only be applied until such time as the [inconsistent] measure … has been removed', Article 49.2 explains that countermeasures 'are limited to the non-performance for the time being of international obligations'.[38] In addition, the goal of countermeasures is explicitly stated 'to induce [the violating State] to comply with its obligations'.

That the evolution from GATT to WTO suspension has been one from 'treaty suspension' under the Vienna Convention to 'countermeasures' under the Articles of State Responsibility is confirmed in the gradual change of terminology commonly used to refer to GATT/WTO 'suspension'. Whereas in the GATT days, and even in the early days of the WTO, countries insisted on reference to 'suspension' (and chided the language of sanctions, retaliation or countermeasures), today, it is commonly accepted to use what Steve Charnovitz calls the 'S-word' and even more common to refer to WTO 'retaliation' or 'countermeasures'. WTO arbitrators on suspension when seeking guidance from general international law have also referred to countermeasures in the Articles on State Responsibility, not suspension under the Vienna Convention. Hence, although we are stuck with the old GATT/Vienna Convention term of 'suspension' even in the DSU (but not in the Subsidies and Countervailing Measures (SCM) Agreement which does use the term 'countermeasures', as discussed below), for all intents and purposes, what we now have in the WTO is something more akin to retaliation or countermeasures as they are expressed in the Articles on State Responsibility.

6 Statements in WTO arbitration reports as to the goal(s) of WTO suspension

Another avenue to pursue in order to figure out the intended goal of WTO suspension is to check what WTO arbitrators themselves have said about the issue. As with the historical evolution sketched above, statements in WTO arbitration reports on suspension have often been less than clear

[37] See Article 51, ILC Articles on the Responsibility of States for Internationally Wrongful Acts (ILC Articles), Annex to A/RES/56/83 of 12 December 2001, as corrected by UN doc. A/56/49 (vol. I), Corr. 4, which provides that '[c]ountermeasures must be commensurate with the injury suffered, taking into account the gravity of the internationally wrongful act and the rights in question'.

[38] See also Article 53, ILC Articles: 'Countermeasures shall be terminated as soon as the responsible State has complied with its obligations under Part Two in relation to the internationally wrongful act'.

and made reference to multiple goals. Moreover, as with the evolution from GATT (rebalancing or compensation) to WTO (compliance or settlement), there has been an evolution in WTO case law on the stated goal of WTO suspension. This time, three phases or trends can be detected:

(i) unequivocal statements that 'inducing compliance' is *the* goal of WTO suspension (*EC–Bananas (US)*, *EC–Hormones*, *EC–Bananas (Ecuador)* and *US–Gambling*);
(ii) rulings where close to (and, in one case, genuine) punitive suspension was authorized in response to prohibited subsidies ('appropriate countermeasures' in *Brazil–Aircraft*, *US–FSC*, *Canada–Export Credits and Guarantees*); and
(iii) a sense of crisis or disillusion in regular cases (other than prohibited subsidy cases) with statements that the goal of WTO suspension in the DSU is not clear and might, given its 'equivalence' benchmark, not be compliance (*US–1916 Act*, *US–Byrd*).

Phase 1: induce compliance (albeit with equivalent suspension)

Phase I could be referred to as 'the lion roars but realizes it has no teeth'. The following statement in the very first WTO arbitration on suspension (*EC–Bananas (US)*) – is emblematic:

> the authorization to suspend concessions or other obligations is a temporary measure pending full implementation by the Member concerned. We agree with the United States that this *temporary* nature indicates that it is the purpose of countermeasures to *induce compliance*.[39]

Yet, in the same breath, the roaring lion (announcing that suspension is there to achieve the rather ambitious goal of 'inducing compliance'), faces reality and must add the following:

> But this purpose does not mean that the DSB should grant authorization to suspend concessions beyond what is *equivalent* to the level of nullification or impairment. In our view, there is nothing in [the DSU] that could be read as a justification for counter-measures of a *punitive* nature.[40]

Therefore, from the very beginning the tension between, on the one hand, the *more ambitious goal* of compliance (newly expressed in the DSU) and,

[39] *EC–Bananas (US)*, Decision by the arbitrators under Article 22.6, DSU, WT/DS27/ARB (DSR 1999:II, 725), para. 6.3 (italics in original, underlining added).

[40] *EC–Bananas (US)*, *ibid.*

on the other hand, the *weakened instrument* of equivalent (rather than appropriate) suspension to achieve that goal, was acknowledged.[41]

The goal of 'inducing compliance' was subsequently also confirmed in *EC–Bananas (Ecuador)*, where the arbitrators decided that retaliation by Ecuador against the EC under GATT was not 'effective' to induce compliance and, on that ground, granted Ecuador the right to cross-retaliate under TRIPS (pursuant to DSU, Article 22.3):

> Our interpretation of the 'practicability' and 'effectiveness' criteria is consistent with the object and purpose of Article 22 which is to induce compliance. If a complaining party seeking the DSB's authorization to suspend certain concessions or certain other obligations were required to select the concessions or other obligations to be suspended in sectors or under agreements where such suspension would be either not available in practice or would not be powerful in effect, the objective of inducing compliance could not be accomplished and the enforcement mechanism of the WTO dispute settlement system could not function properly.[42]

Phase 2: inducing compliance requires more than equivalent suspension ('appropriate countermeasures' in response to prohibited subsidies)

As further explained by Sebastian (Chapter 4), WTO suspension in response to prohibited subsidies under the SCM Agreement is not bound by the 'equivalence' standard in DSU, Article 22.4, but by what seems to be a more flexible standard of 'appropriate countermeasures' (SCM, Article 4.10). This, of course, reminds us of the 'appropriateness' standard under GATT, Article XXIII. Note, also, that in this case, the old term 'suspension' (reminiscent of treaty suspension under the Vienna Convention) was dropped in favour of the term 'countermeasures' (as in the Articles on State Responsibility). This confirms the above argument that from GATT to WTO we have witnessed a gradual shift from suspension as 'treaty suspension' under the Vienna Convention, to 'countermeasures' under the Articles on States Responsibility.

[41] See also *EC–Hormones*, Decision by the arbitrators under Article 22.6, (DSR 1999:III, 1135), para. 39: 'The DSU characterizes full and prompt implementation of DSB recommendations as the *first* objective and *preferred* solution. The suspension of concessions, in contrast, is only a temporary measure of last resort to be applied only until such time as full implementation or a mutually agreed solution is obtained. To allow the effect of suspension of concessions to exceed that of bringing the measure into conformity with WTO rules would not be justifiable in view of DSU objectives' (italics in original).

[42] *EC–Bananas (Ecuador)*, Decision by the arbitrators under Article 22.6, DSU, WT/DS27/ABR/ECU, para. 76 (underlining added).

Recall, however, that unlike the 'appropriateness' standard in GATT, Article XXIII, the 'appropriateness' standard under SCM, Article 4.10 is not subject to consensual approval by all GATT/WTO members. Whereas under GATT 'appropriateness' was kept within strict bounds because of the consensus requirement (and in the one GATT case on the issue reduced to 'equivalence'[43]), in the SCM Agreement, the decision on 'appropriateness' was transferred to third-party arbitration. This prompted the drafters of the SCM Agreement to add the cautionary footnote 10 to the Agreement, stating that the expression 'appropriate' is 'not meant to allow countermeasures that are disproportionate in light of the fact that the subsidies dealt with under these provisions are prohibited'. Ironically, however, arbitrators tasked to interpret what seems to be a softening footnote have used it rather to bolster their conclusion that retaliation in response to prohibited subsidies calls for something *more than* 'equivalent' suspension.

The arbitrators in *Brazil–Aircraft*, for example, the first dispute under SCM, Article 4.10, started by confirming that the goal of WTO suspension is to induce compliance: 'We conclude that a countermeasure is 'appropriate' *inter alia* if it *effectively* induces compliance.'[44] It then went on, however, to find that this objective requires more than 'equivalent' suspension, referring, *inter alia*, to footnote 10:

> [R]equiring that countermeasures in the form of suspension of concessions or other obligations be equivalent to the level of nullification or impairment would be contrary to the principle of effectiveness by significantly limiting the efficacy of countermeasures in the case of prohibited subsidies.[45]

On this and other grounds, the arbitrators saw no problem in selecting the *entire amount of the subsidy* as the benchmark for calculating

[43] See note 32, above.

[44] *Brazil–Aircraft*, Decision by the arbitrators under Article 22.6, DSU and Article 4.11, SCM Agreement, WT/DS46/ARB (DSR 2002:I, 19), para. 3.44. The objective of 'inducing compliance' was subsequently confirmed in all prohibited subsidy cases. See, for example, *US–FSC*, Decision by the arbitrators under Article 22.6, DSU and Article 4.11, SCM Agreement, WT/DS108/ARB (DSR 2002:VI, 2517), para. 5.52 ('countermeasures are taken against non-compliance, and thus its authorization by the DSB is aimed at inducing or securing compliance with the DSB's recommendation'), and *Canada–Export Credits and Guarantees*, Decision by the arbitrators under Article 22.6, DSU and Article 4.11, SCM Agreement, WT/DS222/ARB, para. 3.48 ('We agree that the need to induce compliance is a factor that should be considered in evaluating the appropriateness of the level of proposed countermeasures.').

[45] *Brazil–Aircraft*, para. 3.58.

'appropriate countermeasures' in response to prohibited subsidies, even if this benchmark could go beyond the 'equivalent' trade effects caused by the original violation. As the arbitrators in *US–FSC* put it, with reference to Article 51 of the Articles on State Responsibility quoted earlier:[46]

> [A] Member is entitled to act with countermeasures that properly take into account the gravity of the breach and the nature of the upset in the balance of rights and obligations in question. This cannot be reduced to a requirement that constrains countermeasures to trade effects.[47]

At the same time, the Arbitrators did add that: '[t]here is nothing in the text or in its context which suggests an entitlement to manifestly punitive measures'.[48] The tough approach in prohibited subsidy cases (defining 'appropriate countermeasures' as something going beyond equivalence but not 'manifestly punitive') culminated in the *Canada–Export Credits and Guarantees* dispute. In that case, the arbitrators not only opted for the entire amount of the subsidy as the benchmark for 'appropriateness' but, in addition, increased this amount by 20 per cent on the ground that Canada had provoked the arbitrators by saying that it would not comply with the entire ruling:

> we are of the view that Canada's statement that, for the moment, it does not intend to withdraw the subsidy at issue suggests that in order to induce compliance in this case a higher level of countermeasures … would be necessary and appropriate.[49]
>
> … we have decided to adjust the level of countermeasures … by an amount which we deem reasonably meaningful to cause Canada to reconsider its current position … We consequently adjust the level of countermeasures by an amount corresponding to 20 per cent of the amount of the subsidy.[50]

This no doubt means that, at least in response to prohibited subsidies, punitive suspension, beyond equivalence, is a possibility. In other words, whereas in ordinary DSU cases, arbitrators felt reigned in by the equivalence standard when attempting to give effect to what they perceived to be the goal of 'inducing compliance', arbitrators in SCM cases, in contrast, jumped on the flexibility in the appropriateness standard to boost the amount of WTO suspension in the hope of more effectively achieving

[46] See note 37, above. [47] *US–FSC*, para. 5.55. [48] *US–FSC*, para. 5.56.
[49] *Canada–Export Credits and Guarantees*, para. 3.107.
[50] *Canada–Export Credits and Guarantees*, para. 3.121.

the stated goal of compliance. Put differently, whereas in Phase 1 the lion roared but realized it lacked teeth, in Phase 2, the lion roared, found its teeth and eagerly attacked.

Phase 3: identity crisis and doubt as to the goal of WTO suspension in regular DSU cases

After the euphoria of arbitrators authorizing what is effectively punitive suspension in prohibited subsidy cases, arbitrators in ordinary DSU disputes quickly faced reality, as expressed in the equivalence standard, and started to question the very goal of WTO suspension. Indeed, if earlier arbitrators said that inducing compliance cannot be achieved effectively with equivalent suspension (see *Brazil–Aircraft* quoted above), are we sure that under the DSU, where there is the ceiling of equivalent suspension, the goal really is compliance (as early arbitrators quoted under Phase 1 so categorically claimed)? In *US–1916 Act*, the arbitrators clung to 'inducing compliance' as *a key* objective of WTO suspension, but acknowledged that WTO suspension may also have other goals:

> The European Communities stressed that 'the basic purpose of the suspension of concessions or other obligations is to induce compliance of the other Member with its WTO obligations'. The United States suggested other possible purposes, such as 'to restore the balance of benefits under the covered agreements between the parties to the dispute'.[51]
>
> ... in our view, a key objective of the suspension of concessions or obligations – whatever other purposes may exist – is to seek to induce compliance by the other WTO Member with its WTO obligations.[52]

The move away from putting up 'inducing compliance' as the goal of WTO suspension culminated in *US–Byrd*, where the arbitrators turned the statements made during Phase I on their head, concluding essentially that they are far from certain that inducing compliance is even one of several goals of WTO suspension:

> The concept of 'inducing compliance' ... is not expressly referred to in any part of the DSU and we are not persuaded that the object and purpose of the DSU – or of the WTO Agreement – would support an approach where the purpose of suspension ... would be exclusively to induce compliance. [We] cannot exclude that inducing compliance is part of the objectives

[51] *US–1916 Act*, Decision by the arbitrators under Article 22.6, DSU, WT/DS136/ARB (DSR 2004:IX, 4269), para. 5.3.

[52] *US–1916 Act*, para. 5.5. See also para. 5.7: 'We agree that a fundamental objective of the suspension of obligations is to induce compliance'.

> behind suspension ... but at most it can be only one of a number of purposes in authorizing the suspension ... By relying on 'inducing compliance' as the benchmark for the selection of the most appropriate approach we also run the risk of losing sight of the requirement of Article 22.4 that the level of suspension be *equivalent* to the level of nullification or impairment.[53]

The Arbitrators in *US–Byrd* ended their report with a note on the tension, explained earlier, between, on the one hand, the repeated statements in the DSU implying that the goal of suspension is compliance or settlement and, on the other hand, the relatively weak instrument offered in the DSU to achieve this goal, namely, equivalent suspension:

> the DSU does not expressly explain the purpose behind the authorization of the suspension ... On the one hand, the general obligation to comply with DSB recommendations and rulings seems to imply that suspension of concessions or other obligations is intended to induce compliance ...
>
> On the other hand, the requirement that the level of such suspensions remain equivalent to the level of nullification or impairment suffered by the complaining party seems to imply that suspension ... is only a means of obtaining some form of temporary compensation, even when the negotiation of compensations has failed.[54]

These doubts, almost an identity crisis around what WTO arbitrations on suspension are all about, led the *US–Byrd* arbitrators to make the statement quoted on the first page of this chapter, expressing dismay at the fact that the goal of WTO suspension is simply 'not clear' and that 'a large part of the conceptual debate that took place in these proceedings could have been avoided' if only the goal of suspension were identified.[55]

Conclusion on WTO arbitration case law

If the narrative above is convincing, the evolution of WTO case law on the goal of WTO suspension is a cyclical move from muted ambition (Phase 1) to assertive ambition (Phase 2) that turned into frustration (Phase3). That this evolution may, indeed, be cyclical is supported by the most recent arbitration report in *US–Gambling* which seems to wipe away the doubts expressed in *US–1916 Act* and, especially, *US–Byrd*, to

[53] *US–Byrd*, Decision by the arbitrator under Article 22.6, DSU, WT/DS217/ARB/EEC (DSR 2004:IX, 4591), WT/DS234/ARB/CAN (DSR 2004:IX, 4425), para. 3.74 (emphasis original).

[54] *US–Byrd*, paras. 6.2–3 (underlining added).

[55] *US–Byrd*, para. 6.4.

revert to the muted ambition of Phase 1, with a categorical statement that *the* goal of WTO suspension, even in normal DSU cases, is to 'induce compliance':

> the purpose of suspension of concessions or other obligations under the covered agreements ... is to 'induce compliance' ...[56]
>
> ... the thrust of the 'effectiveness' criterion [in DSU, Article 22.3 on cross-retaliation] empowers the party seeking suspension to ensure that the impact of that suspension is strong and has the desired result, namely to induce compliance . . .[57]

7 Proposition A: suspension in the GATT/WTO has variable goals

From the above analysis (sections 2–6), a first proposition to offer is this: the goal of retaliation or suspension in the GATT/WTO has, from the very beginning, been unclear and confused. This lack of clarity and confusion remains today, after more than 60 years of operation, as expressed most recently in the *US–Byrd* arbitration. What can be detected, however, is a gradual change in the intended, or at least perceived, goal of suspension from (i) rebalancing or compensation in the GATT to (ii) compliance, settlement and, in some prohibited subsidy cases, punishment in the WTO and WTO arbitration cases. In general international law terms this evolution can be seen as one from regarding GATT/WTO suspension as 'treaty suspension' under Article 60 of the Vienna Convention, to 'countermeasures' under Article 49 of the Articles on State Responsibility.

Whereas the ultimate intended, or at least perceived, goal of the current suspension system is 'inducing compliance', there is, however, no doubt that, from the perspective of the retaliating country in a specific dispute, WTO suspension may also achieve other (ancillary) objectives along the way. These can range from (temporary) rebalancing of trade concessions and some form of political or (if the retaliator is a large country) economic compensation, to deterrence of possible future violations (as against both the violator in dispute and other WTO members). As indicated earlier, depending on the goal pursued, retaliating WTO members should then calibrate and, as the case may be, change the design of their retaliation package accordingly (in terms of, for example, product coverage, amount

[56] *US–Gambling*, Arbitration under Article 22.6, DSU, WT/DS285/ARB, para. 2.7.
[57] *US–Gambling*, para. 4.84.

of extra duties or carousel). Indeed, while retaliating is, in most cases, costly for the retaliator itself, not to retaliate once given WTO authorization to do so risks eroding the objective of deterrence and the impact of future threats of retaliation. For small or weak countries mere WTO authorization to retaliate (at the highest possible level) may, however, be enough to trigger the reputation and community costs sought to induce compliance by even the biggest WTO players (without actually implementing the retaliation). This, in turn, may explain why small countries like Ecuador and Antigua have gone all the way to request and vigorously arbitrate the highest possible retaliation package only *not* to use it once authorized to do so.

The beauty of the current system is that such case-by-case calibration of suspension is allowed due to the fact that (i) the equivalence standard in the DSU is a maximum ceiling (not a fixed amount that must be imposed) and (ii) most elements of design (other than quantity and the right to cross-retaliate) remain within the discretion of the retaliating country itself.

That said, one must remain realistic and not expect from trade suspension what it cannot possibly offer. Indeed, since (prospective) suspension is, ultimately, the only formal remedy offered by the system (compensation is an alternative, but since it requires mutual agreement it is extremely rare), both WTO members and commentators tend to expect too much from suspension. As a result, they criticize the remedy of suspension (or what it does or does not do) for reasons that are inherent in the very instrument of suspension or retaliation. Most commonly, commentators lament the fact that retaliation is shooting oneself in the foot. This is correct, but it is the case for any type of retaliation or punishment: when the state puts someone in prison for assault, the remedy of imprisonment is costly to the state but that is what it takes to punish or deter the offender. Conversely, critics argue that retaliation does not compensate the victims of breach. Again, this is correct, but it is the case for any type of stick with which to induce compliance or to deter breach: when in primitive societies the rule of 'an eye for an eye' applied, taking someone's eye in response to that person having taken mine does not restore my eyesight.

In sum, with the current remedy of prospective and equivalent suspension on the books, some of the potential goals of suspension described in section 2 above simply cannot be achieved, more specifically (i) full compensation of harm suffered by the victims (unless we have an extreme case of a large country retaliating, improving its terms of trade and subsequently refunding damages to individual victims), and (ii) genuine punishment (with the possible exception of 'appropriate countermeasures' in response to prohibited subsidies, particularly as interpreted in *Canada–Export Credits and Guarantees*).

8 Proposition B: equivalent suspension can (and normally does) induce compliance largely because it can be tailor-made and is combined with reputation and community costs

The above conclusion that the ultimate goal of WTO suspension is 'to induce compliance' faces one serious obstacle, referred to earlier on several occasions and exploited most successfully by Sykes: how can the goal of 'inducing compliance' be taken seriously if the instrument offered to effect compliance is mere 'equivalent' suspension? Put differently, are the DSU texts referring to the goal of compliance or settlement simply overshooting or wishful thinking when matched to the relatively weak instrument of 'equivalent' suspension, so that when looking at the DSU in action, rebalancing and compensation ('efficient breach') are the true goals? Looked at from a different perspective: how is it possible that equivalent suspension can (and in 83 per cent of WTO rulings does) achieve compliance?

First, inclusion of the relatively strict 'equivalence' standard (as opposed to 'appropriateness' in the old GATT) was not meant to undermine the objective of compliance. Instead, as noted earlier, multilaterally controlled equivalence was the *quid pro quo* for automatic authorization of WTO retaliation. When one takes away the veto right for defendants to block retaliation, making retaliation authorizations automatic, is it not normal that WTO members insisted on limiting and controlling the level of such automatic retaliation? Small and/or developing countries especially were afraid of the punitive or uncontrolled retaliations that they had experienced, particularly under Section 301 of the US Trade Act. Thus, imposing the ceiling of 'equivalent' retaliation was meant to avoid punitive sanctions, not to justify continued non-compliance.

Second, equivalent retaliation as such may well be stronger than one might suppose. Take the earlier example of *EC–Hormones*, where the ceiling of WTO retaliation was not set based on the gains made by the EC, but rather based on the losses suffered by the United States. Since, in many violations, the loss suffered by the victim (in this case the United States) is higher than the gains made by the violator (in this case the EC), for the violator, the cost of equivalent retaliation is likely to outweigh the gains made by the original breach. If so, the violator has a clear incentive to comply even when faced only with equivalent retaliation. Add to this the fact that in the WTO, each and every WTO member affected by breach can bring a dispute and, if it wins, retaliate, and the impact of equivalent retaliation only becomes bigger. Moreover, in many cases it is not so much the *amount* of retaliation that matters, but rather the *type* of retaliation (such as suspension of IP rights versus tariffs on imported goods) or the *sectors or products* retaliated against (goods that are politically sensitive in the violating country versus goods that are competing with domestic industries in the retaliating country). To put it bluntly, it is often more important to pick the *right* hostage (or the hostage that screams the loudest) than the highest *number* of hostages.

Third, as stressed earlier, even if equivalent suspension may be the only formal remedy offered by the DSU, to this formal remedy one must add the informal remedy of reputation and community costs, such as loss of reputation or trust when a country engages in long-term non-compliance, which, in turn, can make future complaints by the violator against other WTO members, as well as credible future trade deals, more difficult; activation of internal support within the violating country for that country to comply with WTO rules based, for example, on the reciprocal and long-term benefits to be derived from the system; belief in the value of liberalized trade and the importance of keeping promises, etc. These community costs are not predicated on a firm legal obligation imposed on *the violating country*, or normative beliefs held by *the violating country* that it must comply with the rules. On the contrary, such community costs are conditioned on, and triggered by, the shared beliefs and perceptions of *other members of the WTO community*: if there is a shared belief that the goal of WTO dispute settlement is to induce compliance or settlement, continued non-compliance will trigger community costs. If, in contrast, the shared belief is that WTO suspension simply rebalances the scales and ends the matter, other WTO members will not frown upon the target of WTO suspension, and with such rebalancing suspension most, if not all, community costs created by the original violation will stop. Here resides, for example, the crucial difference between suspension under the DSU or the SCM Agreement in response to an established breach of the rules, as compared with suspension in response to tariff renegotiations under GATT, Article XXIII or safeguards under Article XIX. Temporary suspension in response to a safeguard is the 'price' to be paid for the safeguard, and restores the country imposing the safeguard in good standing.

The clock of community costs stops ticking once the safeguard is offset by the reciprocal suspension. The same happens when tariff renegotiations fail, and the country imposing the higher tariff is subjected to 'substantially equivalent' suspensions of concessions. Such rebalancing of the scale under GATT, Article XXIII is permanent and ends the matter. After that, the community costs linked to imposing the higher tariff end. Suspension in response to continued breach is crucially different. It is not the 'price' to be paid for breach, but a 'sanction' to induce compliance. As a result, even with the suspension in place, community costs keep mounting, and will stop only once compliance or a settlement is reached.

If this reasoning is correct, then the informal remedy of community costs may at times be higher than the formal cost of retaliation, especially when we are talking, for example, of retaliation by small countries such as Ecuador or Antigua against large countries or blocs like the EC or the United States. If the EC or the United States comply in those disputes, it will not be because of the (threat of) retaliation, but rather because of the community costs referred to earlier. I am not saying that these community costs will always be enough to induce compliance, nor will they always be the same or necessarily persist after long periods of non-compliance. What I am saying, however, is that equivalent suspension is not the only element available to meet the stated goal of compliance. To that, one must add the admittedly flexible and unpredictable incentive of community costs. In combination both equivalent suspension and community costs can, and normally do, achieve compliance. That is what, in my view, explains the DSU's 83 per cent success rate. As a result, the intended goal of compliance or settlement is not some form of legal pipe-dream or overly ambitious goal written down by a group of idealistic internationalists. Instead, it is an objective that the system, when carefully utilized and nurtured, is able to deliver on.

9 Proposition C: optimal protection of WTO entitlements is variable protection

The two commentators to this chapter – Professors Jackson and Sykes – have taken rather different views on the goal or ultimate objective of WTO suspension and WTO dispute settlement more generally. Professor Jackson is of the opinion that, in the current system, WTO rulings are legally binding and must be complied with. Hence, in his view, the ultimate goal of WTO suspension is to induce compliance. Jackson not only sees this as an accurate description of what the negotiators intended and agreed to in the DSU, but also as the normatively most desirable or optimal goal with reference, in particular, to the predictability and stability that comes with rule compliance or keeping one's promise. In sum, for Jackson, the objective of WTO dispute settlement is, *and should be*, compliance with the rules (WTO obligations are, and should be, in other words, protected by a so-called 'property rule' or, to some extent, even be considered as 'inalienable').

Professor Sykes, in contrast, is of the opinion that the current system does not impose a legal obligation to comply with WTO rulings and that suffering WTO suspension or paying compensation are equally valid alternatives to compliance. Hence, in his view, the ultimate goal of WTO suspension is not to induce compliance in each and every case, but to rebalance the bargain and, as the case may be, to compensate the victim. Sykes not only regards this as an accurate description of what the negotiators intended and agreed to in the DSU, but also as the normatively most desirable or optimal goal. In sum, for Sykes, the objective of WTO dispute settlement is, *and should be*, compliance where the gains of compliance outweigh its costs; however, where compliance has a net cost, breach combined with compensation or suspension is, and should be, preferred as the most efficient outcome. On this view, the WTO not only tolerates but should promote 'efficient breach' as welfare maximizing (WTO obligations are, and should be, in other words, protected by a so-called 'liability rule').

Rather than taking sides in this debate, this chapter claims that both Professors Jackson and Sykes overlook the historically, and to date, *variable* nature of the goal or ultimate objective of GATT/WTO suspensions and dispute settlement in general. First, the goal of GATT/WTO suspension was ambiguous from the very beginning when GATT, Article XXIII was drafted in 1947, and remains ambiguous today both in the DSU and in subsequent WTO arbitrations on the level of WTO suspensions. Second, the commonly perceived goal of GATT/WTO suspension has, nonetheless, varied over time – essentially from mere tit-for-tat to some form of sanction – and did so as much because of changes in perceptions as changes in the actual treaty language. Third, in the current system, the goal varies depending on the type of WTO obligation that is defected from. For example, tariffs and specific commitments under GATS can be unilaterally withdrawn as long as compensation is paid, pursuant to the 'liability rules' in GATT, Article XXVIII and GATS, Article XXI. For other WTO obligations, however, suspension is, as explained earlier, not the 'price' to be paid for defection, but the 'sanction' for breach, pursuant to the 'property rule' in the DSU and SCM Agreement, Article 4.10. Fourth, WTO members may, and do, have different views on the goal of WTO suspension, depending on the case, the side they are on, and the relative market size and power of the disputing parties.

What is more, this *variable* nature of the goal or ultimate objective of GATT/WTO suspension and dispute settlement in general is not only historically and descriptively more accurate, but also normatively desirable. If carefully calibrated – both in the WTO rule book, and when WTO members design their actual suspensions – such a variable goal allows for optimal protection and enforcement of WTO entitlements depending on the circumstances. Therefore, rather than debating and having to choose between black and white, or compliance versus efficient breach, property rule versus liability rule, a better way forward is to clarify the variable nature of the current system and to think of objective guidelines or criteria as to when compliance (or property protection) is the optimal goal and when efficient breach (or liability protection) is more suitable,[58] depending essentially on the *nature* of the WTO obligations in question (contrasting, for example, purely reciprocal market access concessions to certain GATT, SPS, TBT or TRIPS obligations of a more regulatory type).[59] WTO suspensions can then be calculated, selected and otherwise designed accordingly.

In addition, whereas both Jackson and Sykes provide crucial insights into the WTO system, each, in their own way, overemphasizes just one side of what is in essence a balanced spectrum. Jackson, for example, underestimates the benefits of rule flexibility that underpins liability rules and the theory of efficient breach. Rule flexibility – as opposed to, for example, constitutionalizing the WTO – allows for contractual freedom and the maximization of welfare. Rule flexibility also enables higher

[58] For such exercise, see Joost Pauwelyn, *Optimal Protection of International Law: Navigating between European Absolutism and American Voluntarism* (Cambridge University Press, 2008).

[59] After conducting such objective analysis, it is doubtful, for example, whether the current distinction between 'normal' DSU suspensions and 'appropriate countermeasures' in response to prohibited subsidies (Article 4.10, SCM) (which have been broadly interpreted in case law so as to effectively induce compliance, for example, by awarding suspension rights equivalent to the total sum of the subsidy) should be maintained. There seems to be little reason to be harsher, by definition, against prohibited export subsidies than against, for example, prohibited tariffs or quotas (see A. Green and M. Trebilcock, 'Enforcing WTO Obligations: What Can We Learn from Export Subsidies', *Journal of International Economic Law*, 10 (2007), 653 and R. Lawrence and N. Stankard, 'Should Export Subsidies be Treated Differently?', Mimeo, May 2005, on file with author).

levels of commitment. Without it, a stronger dispute settlement system would probably not have been possible. Moreover, by providing certain safety valves, rule flexibility offers negotiators a way to deal with uncertainties in the future and thereby prevents exit from the system. In sum, rule flexibility enables and fosters a legitimate and stable normative WTO system, rather than undermines it.

Sykes, in contrast, underestimates the potential force of WTO suspension and, more importantly, the informal remedies that drive the system, as explained earlier. In addition, Sykes mischaracterizes the current system as one that promotes genuine 'efficient breach': it is most probably not what the DSU negotiators had in mind, nor what they actually wrote into the DSU; it is not the commonly held belief either when reading post-1994 government statements in and outside the WTO. More importantly, there can be no doubt that non-compliance in combination with reciprocal WTO suspensions is *not* a situation of 'efficient breach' in any *economic* sense of the word: by their very nature WTO suspensions do not compensate the victim (like other sanctions, they are costly to the victim and intended rather to punish the wrongdoer). Even if one could somehow characterize WTO suspensions as a form of compensation, they work only prospectively and cannot, therefore, possibly make the victim whole. Moreover, when shifting focus from the state to the actual beneficiaries of the WTO system, that is, traders, a violation in, for example, the beef sector is not in any way compensated by a tariff concession or reciprocal suspension in, for example, the textile sector. As a result, it is difficult to speak of breach with the victims of breach being fully compensated, a true *conditio sine qua non* for there to be 'efficient breach'.

Finally, even if the system could somehow be adjusted to fully compensate all victims of breach, the nature of WTO entitlements is such that putting an accurate value or price on WTO entitlements is difficult, costly and prone to either over- or (especially) undervaluation. The limited practice of WTO suspension arbitrations underscores this point and leaves no doubt that the calculation of 'equivalent' suspension, that is, the pricing of WTO entitlements, is at best an approximation, at worst an educated guess; it clearly is an art, not a science. As the arbitrators in *US–Gambling* put it disarmingly, and yet somewhat troublingly:

> we feel we are on shaky grounds solidly laid by the parties. The data is surrounded by a degree of uncertainty. For most variables, the data consists of proxies ... and observations are too few to allow for a proper econometric analysis ... we are left with preciously little information and guidance. Nevertheless, we will attempt to stay as closely to the approaches

> proposed by parties as possible and to make a maximum use of the limited information base we were given.[60]

The approximate nature of suspension calculations and admitted difficulty of getting it right, confirm that WTO suspension is not an appropriate tool to offer exact and full compensation or to rebalance the scales with minute precision. These calculation difficulties and inherent inaccuracies underline, and are ultimately justified and made acceptable by, the fact that suspension will always be a somewhat unwieldy stick whose ultimate goal is to induce compliance, not to compensate. In the exercise of controlling the use of this stick (that is, in WTO arbitrations on equivalent suspension), getting equivalence exactly right then may well be secondary to imposing a general limit so as to avoid abusive retaliation.

10 Conclusion

This chapter has argued that the goal of GATT/WTO suspension has historically been, and remains to this day, murky and confused, ranging from simple rebalancing of concessions to punishment. Yet, if anything, there has been a gradual evolution from 'compensation' (or simple rebalancing) in GATT, Article XXIII to 'sanction' (or rule compliance) in the DSU. Hence, instead of one goal, there seem to be multiple and sometimes overlapping goals.

Most importantly, whereas the ultimate intended, or at least perceived, goal of the current suspension system is 'inducing compliance' or 'settlement', there is no doubt that, depending on the countries and products in dispute, WTO suspension or the threat thereof may also achieve other, ancillary objectives, such as temporary rebalancing of trade concessions, triggering of what has been referred to as reputation or community costs, offering some form of political or (if the retaliator is a large country) economic compensation or deterrence of possible future violations. Depending on the goal(s) pursued, retaliating WTO members should then calibrate and, as the case may be, change the design and implementation of their retaliation package accordingly (in terms of, for example, product coverage, amount of extra duties or carousel). The beauty of the current system is that such case-by-case calibration of trade retaliation is allowed due to the fact that: (i) the equivalence standard in the DSU is a maximum ceiling (not a fixed amount that must be imposed); and (ii) most elements

[60] *US–Gambling*, Arbitration under Article 22.6, DSU, paras. 3.173–4.

of design (other than quantity and the right to cross-retaliate) remain within the discretion of the retaliating country itself.

From a normative perspective, this chapter has argued that the flexibility in the goals pursued by WTO suspension, when carefully calibrated, can be a good thing. Although certain perceived goals (such as full compensation of all victims or outright punishment) cannot realistically be met with the current purely prospective 'equivalent retaliation' instrument, different types of legal entitlements should be matched with different types of protection and enforcement goals (referred to as liability rules, property rules and inalienability). Rather than one fixed goal of WTO suspension, there are (and should be) several possible goals. Put differently, optimal protection of WTO entitlements implies variable protection of WTO entitlements.

Comment on chapter 2

JOHN H. JACKSON

Professor Pauwelyn's chapter is an excellent overview of a highly technical but nevertheless serious and important aspect of the remarkable "remedial" provisions of the WTO dispute settlement system.

While I do not completely agree with Professor Pauwelyn's account of some of the history of this remedial system (GATT plus WTO), and I do not agree with some of his characterization of my views (for example, my writings do not support an "overlooking" of the variable nature of the goal or goals of the system), I do agree with his stated conclusion that there has been a gradual evolution in the GATT and the WTO toward a goal of rule compliance, and that there seem to be multiple and sometimes overlapping goals of the system. Indeed, I would go further and suggest that there is noticeable conflict between some of these goals.

The chapter notes and the conference discussion elaborated on the different views of Professor Sykes and myself about goals, which are sometimes reflected in the analysis of whether an adopted WTO DS report (panel or appellate body) engages an international law obligation to comply as I have written,[1] or rather is subject to a theory of 'efficient breach' with contrary results. Professor Pauwelyn notes that his chapter is directed mostly to the question, of what is (or should be) the goal of the DS system? I share his endeavor, but in my own writing looking more generally at multiple goals of international tribunals or "juridical institutions," I can inventory at least twelve goals for such institutions, not all of which apply to each institution including some goals on the list which can be seen to conflict with each other. In an appendix to this comment I give a brief summary of some of my earlier research on the multiple goals of international dispute settlement.

[1] John H. Jackson, "Editorial Comment: International Law Status of WTO DS Reports: Obligation to Comply or Option to 'Buy-Out'?," *American Journal of International Law*, 98 (2004), 109–25.

Such goals include keeping the peace, addressing the asymmetry of power in a system, and many others. We see this in the WTO itself. The WTO lists variously security, predictability, and a rapid and efficient conclusion among its goals. These goals clearly will not always be compatible. The goal to redress harm is, interestingly enough, not included in the WTO. One goal that might be important in the WTO context is to address asymmetry of power, to allow each state to have its day in court in a way that addresses the unevenness of economic power.

In the WTO, a lot of emphasis is placed on the issue of sovereignty. The term sovereignty really refers to the allocation of power between the state and the international body. The choice among different goals at the international tribunal level is underpinned by this constant question of sovereignty, in tension with an international goal of cooperation. This allocation of power is similarly occurring within the WTO, and the goals of the WTO must be understood in the context of this balance.[2]

I think Joost's second proposition regarding community costs is an important one. The remedies and sanctions themselves may not be as important as one would think. I agree with the argument that "community costs" are an important factor. Given the remarkably good rate of compliance in the WTO, the sanctions in place may be less consequential.

The interpretations of the WTO agreements have lead to the dynamic evolution of the WTO jurisprudence. Consider, for example, the decision to interpret the language of GATT, Article XXIII, that a violation of WTO law is a *prima facie* nullification or impairment. This interpretation, which took place without any change in the language of the treaty, was a constitutional evolution in the GATT–WTO. This interpretation drove the jurisprudence for years. This fundamental change in the interpretation of the language moreover was illustrative of a broader change in the international relations environment.

I should note that internationally, in the many countries I that have had contact with in this regard, there is a widespread and high degree of support for the DSU. Furthermore, this system mostly operates without reliance or need for remedies and sanctions. The point is that the nature of remedies and sanctions may not be so critical to the whole WTO system.

I have one important caveat to this conclusion, however. The most important goal of the WTO system is to afford predictability to the international trading system. It is not the governments themselves that are the

[2] John H. Jackson, *Sovereignty, the WTO, and Changing Fundamentals of International Law* (Cambridge University Press, 2006), ch. 3, 62–76.

primary beneficiaries of the WTO, it is the economic actors. These actors need the predictability that comes with a well developed jurisprudence. A recent statement of a diplomat at the WTO confirms the importance of predictability above all to developing countries.

Of all complaints that are filed about half do not make it to a dispute panel, presumably because they are settled. This settlement can take place because there is a body of jurisprudence with which the parties can make predictions on the outcome and make decisions to come to a negotiated solution.

Finally, it is important to mention the important role of some sort of "precedent" in any significant juridical institution. The WTO system clearly has some level of precedent operating (5,800 citations to prior WTO cases in one WTO panel report!). However, by precedent, I mean something different than *stare decisis*. Precedent can have a range of meanings that are not necessarily *stare decisis*. This reliance on precedent in the jurisprudence enhances the predictability of the system, and this in turn lowers the risk premium of trade for all market participants – an important contribution to economic welfare.

Appendix Policy underpinnings of international juridical institutions[3]

- At least twelve goals, as follows:
  (1) Undo harm done by respondent, to redress complainant's injury: seems not to be a goal of WTO DS.
  (2) Settle the differences amicably to restrict international tensions, avoid conflict or even war.
  (3) Settle the differences efficiently ("promptly," for example, DSU, Article 3.3). Efficient breach idea can conflict with rule stability?
  (4) Provide jurisprudence or "precedents" for prediction, stability; DSU, Article 3.2; especially when beneficiaries are not just governments, for example, entrepreneurs.
  (5) Fill gaps and resolve ambiguities in the treaty text; (inevitable when large multinational groups negotiate a treaty); dysfunction of "*in dubio mitius*," that is, to presume in favor of nation-state sovereignty whenever gap or ambiguity.

[3] John H. Jackson, note 2, above, ch. 5.3, 147–51.

(6) Promote compliance with DS outcome: the procedure enhances compliance; brings pressure, etc. (coupled with sanction?). Implies obligation to perform? To comply? International law rule as persuasion.
(7) Redress asymmetries of power; fairness to weaker entities.
(8) Re-establish balance of benefits, "rebalance" (especially GATT? Reciprocity ideas? Outmoded now? Use safeguards for this goal?).
(9) Give the participating parties sense of "day in court," right to fair procedure? But: Question who is the real party? Governments? Or their citizens? Or international businesses? (Market participants?) Note WTO *US–Section 301* case; Need private right of action? Non-government access to DS?
(10) Provide reasoned judgments to enhance broader public acceptance of the application and development of the rules. Useful to governments to persuade their constituents to do "right thing."
(11) Reasoned analysis of important policy implications of the rule application, so as to shed light on complex issues and dilemmas requiring a balancing approach. Thus, assist other governmental processes.
(12) Define and rationalize allocation of governmental powers, that is, to "repair" the constitution and provide for evolution.

- Each of these goals can sometimes clash with other goals so balancing is necessary.
- Most, but not all, of these goals apply in all legal systems, national or international, in varying importance. Constitutionalism? Proportionality?

Comment on chapter 2

ALAN O. SYKES

In his contribution to this volume, Joost Pauwelyn provides a thoughtful overview of the debate regarding the goal associated with the suspension of concessions in the WTO system. In the course of his review, Pauwelyn offers a valuable summary of the academic commentary, the pertinent treaty text, and relevant statements from WTO adjudicators. He also makes clear the reasons why it may be important to identify the goal of the system. Pauwelyn is to be commended for a fine job of synthesizing these diverse strands.

I have been a contributor to this debate through the years, and the essence of my views may be found elsewhere, including in my own contribution to this volume (Chapter 16). As I do not wish to be repetitive here, these remarks will be brief.

My central quarrel with certain others in the debate can perhaps be restated as a conviction that the system does not have "a goal," but rather that it serves multiple purposes simultaneously, much like the rule of expectation damages in contract law. In this respect, I welcome Pauwelyn's conclusion (slightly at odds with his title) that perhaps the system indeed has multiple goals.

Any enforcement system for any body of law has, more or less by definition, a goal of inducing compliance with that body of law. The same may certainly be said of the WTO DSU. The harder question is whether "a goal of compliance" should be interpreted as a desire to induce compliance 100 percent of the time. For complex agreements negotiated under conditions of uncertainty – unquestionably characteristic of the treaty agreements that comprise WTO law – it is inevitable that the drafters will not have anticipated all contingencies in which deviation from the bargain may be jointly optimal. Even if they have included some built-in mechanisms for adjusting the bargain, those mechanisms, too, are likely to be imperfect, suggesting the possible utility of a "fall-back" mechanism to facilitate efficient deviation.

One such mechanism is simply renegotiation in the face of changed circumstances, as the defenders of the "specific performance" remedy in private contract law emphasize. But it is well known that bargaining breakdowns attributable to strategic behavior can undermine that mechanism even in bilateral contracts. In the WTO system, with over 150 members and a most-favored-nation obligation on most matters, the challenges of renegotiation can escalate exponentially.

The alternative mechanism for private contracts is an appropriate damages rule. Expectation damages, in particular, tend to encourage performance when the benefits of performance to the promisee outweigh the costs to the promisor, and tend to encourage breach when the reverse situation arises. Such a rule, therefore, in a no doubt crude and imperfect way given litigation costs, measurements errors, and the like, simultaneously serves to encourage efficient compliance and to facilitate efficient breach. Concurrently, when breach occurs, it serves to compensate aggrieved promisees. The suspension of equivalent concessions can also be understood to "rebalance" the bargain.

The analogy to the suspension of "equivalent concessions" in the WTO suggests itself immediately. The suspension of "equivalent concessions," with an appropriate calibration of equivalence, can pose to WTO members contemplating breach the prospect of a sanction that roughly induces them to internalize the externality to others from the breach. It can, in principle, thereby serve to induce efficient compliance and facilitate efficient breach. Likewise, it affords political officials in aggrieved trading partners an opportunity to take an action that can restore their lost political welfare, and thus affords a crude "compensation" to them as well.

Of course, this mechanism will not function perfectly, because the calibration of equivalence is difficult even as a theoretical matter, and the linkage between calibrated equivalence and lost political welfare may exhibit considerable slippage. Nevertheless, the fact that the drafters of the DSU designed the mechanism that they did, in my view, can be understood by the analogy to expectation damages. Recent theoretical work on the economics of trade agreements, cited in my contribution to this volume, provides support to this proposition.

In short, when commentators or adjudicators ask whether the goal of the system is compliance, efficient breach, compensation, or rebalancing, my answer is "yes" – all of the above. Pauwelyn ultimately seems to accept this possibility in his conclusion, at least in broad brush if not in every detail. But I will briefly note one quibble. At one point in his contribution, he remarks: "if anything, and somewhat counterintuitively based on the texts alone, the movement from GATT to WTO has been one from regarding retaliation as aimed at rebalancing or compensation in GATT, to inducing compliance or sanction in the WTO."

His reading of the texts is plausible, and I will not take the time to quibble here as I have set out my own textual discussion elsewhere. But this remark highlights the folly of searching for answers to the questions he poses in text alone. As I explain in Chapter 16, the transition of the system from GATT, with its late stage "aggressive unilateralism," to the new WTO DSU, had the practical effect of *reducing* the price for deviation from WTO obligations. *Ceteris paribus*, the result will be a lower level of compliance. The WTO innovation responded to the perception that the price of deviation from the bargain had become too high in the waning years of GATT and, by implication, that the "goal" of compliance was if anything being overserved.

The arguable tension between the evolution of the text and the evolution of the dispute system as a practical matter need not surprise us. Often, the drafters of sophisticated agreements create mechanisms that serve useful economic functions without fully articulating them or even understanding them. For that reason, in the analysis of treaty mechanisms just as in the analysis of commercial agreements, it is often more reliable to focus on what actors do rather than on what actors say.

3

Extrapolating purpose from practice: rebalancing or inducing compliance

GREGORY SHAFFER AND DANIEL GANIN*

Scholars continue to debate over the aim of WTO remedies in light of the ambiguity of the legal texts. As Joost Pauwelyn writes, the goal of WTO remedies remains "murky and confused."[1] Some commentators contend that the overarching objective is, and should be, to induce compliance with WTO obligations.[2] Others maintain that the central goal is, and should be, rebalancing – that is, to ensure that the overall balance of concessions is maintained.[3] Rebalancing is to be achieved by permitting the successful complainant to suspend concessions in an equivalent amount.[4] This chapter confronts the question inductively through an assessment of WTO members' practice.

One method of discerning purpose is by examining members' practice, constituting the law-in-action of WTO remedies. State practice implicates, at least in part, how WTO complainants view the primary objective of WTO remedies, and, in particular, whether they focus on rebalancing

* Gregory Shaffer is Melvin C. Steen Professor of Law, University of Minnesota Law School. Daniel Ganin is a third year student at the University of Minnesota Law School.

1 Joost Pauwelyn, "The Calculation and Design of Trade Retaliation in Context: What is the Goal of Suspending WTO Obligations?" Chapter 2, above.

2 Pauwelyn, above, note 2 (citing the work of John Jackson). See, for example, Article 3:7, Dispute Settlement Understanding (DSU) ("the first objective of the dispute settlement mechanism is usually to secure the withdrawal of the measures concerned if these are found to be inconsistent with the visions of any of the covered agreements"). See "Understanding on Rules and Procedures Governing the Settlement of Disputes," Article 3:7, WTO Agreement, Annex 2, 1869 U.N.T.S. 401, 33 I.L.M. 1226 (1994).

3 See Alan O. Sykes, "Optimal Sanctions in the WTO: The Case for Decoupling (and the Uneasy Case for the *Status Quo*)," Chapter 16, below.

4 The remedy provided by the WTO for violations of its rules is retaliation through the withdrawal of concessions in an equivalent amount, as authorized by a WTO panel pursuant to Article 22, DSU when a respondent fails to comply with a WTO ruling by a specified date. Panels, however, have varied in their methodologies as to how to calculate the authorized amount of retaliation.

or compliance. This chapter's conclusions are supported by the five case studies in this volume regarding complainants' use of retaliation, respectively covering the United States, the European Union (EU), Mexico, Canada, Brazil, and other developing country members. Our conclusions are necessarily tentative given the few cases of authorized retaliation under Article 22 of the DSU (nine disputes involving eighteen nations in 13 years), and the even smaller number actually implemented. Nevertheless, our assessment of current practice leads to five interrelated findings: (1) the process for applying an authorized WTO remedy is driven primarily by domestic export interests demanding compliance, not rebalancing; (2) complainant government practice has responded accordingly, focusing on compliance; (3) governments have done so by strategically targeting politically influential foreign export interests, as opposed to politically influential domestic protectionist interests, while attempting to minimize harm to domestic consumers and consuming industries; (4) constituencies within the complainant member who fear that their products may be on a retaliation list (that is, importers and import-consuming industries) have been catalyzed to lobby to exempt goods from the retaliation list, apparently more so than producers who would benefit from rebalancing through the imposition of protective tariffs;[5] and (5) overall, members have not implemented retaliatory countermeasures as frequently as would be predicted were the primary goal rebalancing.

Our findings raise the prospect that WTO member practices could have systemic impacts within the WTO in the course of time. If the ministries representing WTO members perceive that the objective of WTO remedies is compliance, then such beliefs could affect formal law over time, whether through the negotiation of new legal texts or the interpretation of existing ones. In any case, members' practices constitute the WTO law-in-action, that is, how formal WTO remedies are actually applied.

Our hypotheses

Practice should vary with perception of purpose. If compliance is paramount to a complainant, and not rebalancing, one will expect to see certain patterns of behavior and not others. First, if the primary purpose is compliance, as opposed to rebalancing, members should, on average, be

[5] We have been told by US and EU government officials that this has been the case, which is supported by the case studies in this volume, but we are not aware of any quantitative study in this respect.

more reluctant to apply authorized retaliation. They should be reluctant because there is no guarantee that retaliation will induce compliance, and retaliation may injure domestic groups by making the goods that they input and consume more expensive.[6] Thus, members seeking compliance, as opposed to rebalancing, should rely to a greater extent upon retaliatory threats to incentivize compliance, without having to implement sanctions in practice. In contrast, if members seek a rebalancing of trade concessions, then they should impose retaliatory awards more frequently and with less hesitation where a respondent fails to comply with a ruling. Government officials should, in such cases, respond to those domestic constituencies who desire greater protection, and they should receive compensatory political payoffs for doing so.

Second, we contend that members should more likely impose incremental or partial countermeasures, as opposed to immediate retaliation in full, if the primary aim is compliance and the amount of authorized retaliation is significant. Partial countermeasures calculated to increase over time can exert pressure on foreign constituencies to lobby their governments to comply, but they accomplish this end with less injury to domestic importers, retailers, and consumers.[7] In this way, compliance can be achieved through using smaller, less prohibitive countermeasures. In contrast, if members are primarily interested in rebalancing, they should immediately implement retaliation in full, and withdraw it only once a respondent complies fully with a ruling.

Third, if inducing compliance is the primary goal, members should be more likely to strategically target a small number of politically influential exporters in the respondent state rather than a broad array of products.[8]

[6] Donald McRae, "Measuring the Effectiveness of the WTO Dispute Settlement System," *Asian Journal of WTO & International Health Law and Policy* 3 (2008), 5.

[7] See Lothar Ehring, "The European Community's Experience and Practice in Suspending WTO Obligations," Chapter 9, below. In this vein, Ehring argues that non-prohibitive "smart sanctions" offer advantages both in terms of minimizing domestic harm and inducing compliance. Partial measures can still be "irritants" without entirely cutting off foreign imports. Additionally, they can be more useful in facilitating compliance insofar as "a frustrated exporter can have a more powerful voice domestically than an eliminated exporter that has gone out of business entirely or that has lost a certain export market without hope to re-conquer it quickly." *Ibid.*

[8] Joost Pauwelyn and Håkan Nordström both argue that the most efficient strategy for inducing compliance is to selectively target influential sectors that will hurt the non-complying state the most, though the latter believes that broader targeting may be preferable for ethical, logistical, and possibly legal reasons. Pauwelyn, see note 2, above; Håkan Nordström, "The Politics of Selecting Trade Retaliation in the EC: A View from the Floor," Chapter 10, below. See also Jide Nzelibe, "The Credibility Imperative: The

On the one hand, comparatively higher tariffs imposed on a select number of products create greater incentives for foreign exporters to lobby for compliance. On the other hand, targeting a small number of carefully selected products will harm fewer domestic importers and consumers. In contrast, if a complainant government's main concern is rebalancing from an economic or political perspective, then it should determine retaliation targets in a different manner. From an economic perspective, a government should choose targets in the most cost-effective manner so as to reduce deadweight transaction costs while raising revenue, possibly through application of an across-the-board tariff increase. From a political perspective, a government should more frequently target products that provide it with political payoffs from protectionist domestic constituencies.

Finally, where the aim is compliance, decisions should be driven primarily by affected export interests, rather than protectionist, import-competing ones. Unlike domestic protectionist groups, injured exporters have a vital interest in the removal of illegal measures through compliance, rather than in erecting reciprocal trade barriers through a rebalancing which benefits other sectors. In practice, these export interests invest considerable resources in the preparation of WTO cases, so that government representatives must demonstrate that they will exert significant pressure for compliance,[9] otherwise, export groups will be less inclined to provide the government with support in the future.

Complainant practice

Since its inception in 1995, the WTO has authorized the use of retaliatory sanctions in nine disputes involving eighteen members.[10] In addition, the

Political Dynamics of Retaliation in the World Trade Organization's Dispute Resolution Mechanism," *Theoretical Inquiries in Law*, 6 (2005).

9 See Gregory Shaffer, *Defending Interests: Public–Private Partnerships in WTO Litigation* (Washington, DC: Brookings Institution Press, 2003); Gregory Shaffer, Michelle Ratton Sanchez, and Barbara Rosenberg, "Winning at the WTO: What Lies Behind Brazil's Success?" *Cornell International Law Journal*, 41:2 (summer 2008). See also Jide Nzelibe, "The Case Against Reforming the WTO Enforcement Mechanism," *University of Illinois Law Review* (2008).

10 Decision by the arbitrators, *EC–Measures Concerning Meat and Meat Products (Hormones)*, Original Complaint by Canada, Recourse to Arbitration by the European Communities under Article 22.6 of the DSU, WT/DS48/ARB (July 12, 1999) (DSR 1999:III, 1135) [hereinafter *EC–Hormones (Canada)*]; Decision by the arbitrators, *EC–Measures Concerning Meat and Meat Products (Hormones)*, Original Complaint by the United States, Recourse to Arbitration by the European Communities under

EU successfully threatened to impose sanctions under Article 8 of the Agreement on Safeguards in the *US–Steel Safeguards* case, and it informally applied them in order to induce compliance in the *US–Wheat Gluten Safeguards* case.[11] In total, five WTO members have implemented retaliatory measures in four WTO disputes.[12] The United States, the EU, and Canada each have applied countermeasures on two occasions. The United

Article 22.6 of the DSU, WT/DS26/ARB (July 12, 1999) (DSR 1999:III, 1105) [hereinafter *EC–Hormones (US)*]; Decision by the arbitrators, *EC–Regime for the Importation, Sale and Distribution of Bananas*, Recourse to Arbitration by the European Communities under Article 22.6 of the DSU, WT/DS27/ARB (April 9, 1999) (DSR 1999:II, 725) [hereinafter *EC–Bananas (US)*]; Decision by the arbitrators, *EC–Regime for the Importation, Sale and Distribution of Bananas*, Recourse to Arbitration by the European Communities under Article 22.6 of the DSU, WT/DS27/ARB/ECU (March 24, 2000) (DSR 2000:V, 2237) [hereinafter *EC–Bananas (Ecuador)*]; Decision by the arbitrators, *US–Antidumping Act of 1916*, Original Complaint by the European Communities, Recourse to Arbitration by the United States under Article 22.6 of the DSU, WT/DS136/ARB (February 24, 2004) (DSR 2004:IX, 4269) [hereinafter *US–1916 Act*]; Decision by the arbitrators, *US–Continued Dumping and Subsidy Offset Act of 2000*, Original Complaint by the European Communities, Recourse to Arbitration by the United States under Article 22.6 of the DSU, WT/DS217/ARB/EEC (August 31, 2004) (DSR 2004:IX, 4591) [hereinafter *US–Byrd Amendment*] (similar awards were given to Brazil, Chile, India, Japan, South Korea, Canada, and Mexico); Decision by the arbitrators, *Brazil–Export Financing Programme for Aircraft*, Recourse to Arbitration by Brazil under Article 22.6 of the DSU and Article 4.11 of the SCM Agreement, WT/DS46/ARB (August 28, 2000) (DSR 2002:I, 19) [hereinafter *Brazil–Aircraft*]; Decision by the arbitrator, *US–Tax Treatment for "Foreign Sales Corporations"*, Recourse to Arbitration by the United States under Article 22.6 of the DSU and Article 4.11 of the SCM Agreement, WT/DS108/ARB (August 30, 2002) (DSR 2002:VI, 2517) [hereinafter *US–FSC*]; Decision by the arbitrator, *Canada–Export Credits and Loan Guarantees for Regional Aircraft*, Recourse to Arbitration by Canada under Article 22.6 of the DSU and Article 4.11 of the SCM Agreement, WT/DS222/ARB (February 17, 2003) (DSR 2003:III, 1187) [hereinafter *Canada–Aircraft*]; Decision by the arbitrator, *US–Measures Affecting the Cross-Border Supply of Gambling and Betting Services*, Recourse to Arbitration by the United States under Article 22.6 of the DSU, WT/DS285/ARB (December 21, 2007) [hereinafter *US–Gambling*].

11 Article 8 permits WTO members to apply countermeasures against invalid safeguards. See Ehring, above, note 7, citing to Appellate Body Report, *US–Definitive Safeguard Measures on Imports of Certain Steel Products*, WT/DS248/AB/R (November 10, 2003) (DSR 2003:VII, 3117) [hereinafter *US–Steel Safeguards*]; Appellate Body Report, *US–Definitive Safeguard Measures on Imports of Wheat Gluten from the European Communities*, WT/DS166/AB/R (December 22, 2000) (DSR 2001:II, 717) [hereinafter *US–Wheat Gluten Safeguards*]. See also, Delegation of the European Commission to the USA, "EU Welcomes WTO Ruling Confirming US Steel Tariffs Are Illegal," European Union, available at www.eurunion.org/eu/index.php?option=com_content&task=view&id=2068&Itemid=58.

12 Retaliatory measures were implemented in *EC–Hormones* by the United States and Canada, in *EC–Bananas* by the US, in *US–FSC* by the EC, and in *US–Byrd Amendment* by the EC, Canada, Japan, and Mexico.

States did so in each case where it has been authorized, and the EU and Canada have formally pursued authorization to retaliate in seven disputes and received authorization in three of them.[13] The United States imposed 100 percent tariffs on selected products in both cases, while the EU, in the *FSC* case, opted for partial tariffs which would be increased incrementally if the United States did not comply.[14] The only other countries to impose retaliatory measures were Mexico and Japan, which did so in the *US–Byrd Amendment* case, together with the EU and Canada. Brazil, Ecuador, and the island of Antigua and Barbuda have received authorization to adopt countermeasures, but have not implemented them.[15]

Export interests have driven the process. For example, in both cases where the United States implemented retaliatory measures – the *EC–Hormones* and *EC–Bananas* disputes – the decision to secure and implement retaliatory measures was based on pressure from injured exporters.[16] When existing countermeasures proved to be ineffective in inducing EU compliance, the US Congress enacted "carousel" legislation that required the United States Trade Representative (USTR) to rotate the list of targeted products every 180 days.[17] Contemporaneous press reports indicated that the legislation was again the product of political pressure from banana and beef exporters frustrated with the lack of EU compliance.[18] Although carousel retaliation has yet to be implemented, it is still considered.[19]

The process for selecting and implementing retaliatory measures, at least in larger WTO members, has generally proceeded as follows. When

[13] Scott D. Andersen and Justine Blanchet, "The United States' Experience and Practice in Suspending WTO Obligations," Chapter 8, below; Håkan Nordström, see above, note 8; Vasken Khabayan, "Canada's Experience and Practice in Suspending WTO Obligations," Chapter 11, below.

[14] Andersen and Blanchet, see above, note 13, section 2; Ehring, see above, note 7, section 2(b) ("... countermeasures were applied in the form of a 5 per cent additional import duty, to be increased by 1 per cent every month of a period of one year, until the level of 17 per cent").

[15] Hunter Nottage, "Evaluating the Criticism that WTO Retaliation Rules Undermine the Utility of WTO Dispute Settlement for Developing Countries," Chapter 15, below. See also, Daniel Pruzin, "Ecuador Gets WTO Go-Ahead to Retaliate against European Union," *BNA International Trade Daily*, May 19, 2000, d12; Daniel Pruzin, "Group Argues IP Retaliation Feasible in WTO Disputes against U.S. Measures," *International Trade Daily*, May 13, 2008, d10.

[16] Andersen and Blanchet, see above, note 13, section 2.

[17] Nzelibe, see above, note 8, 226.

[18] Andersen and Blanchet, see above, note 13, section 2.

[19] See Gary Yerkey, "USTR Seeks Input on Possible Change to Sanctions in Beef Trade Dispute with EU," *BNA International Trade Reporter*, 25:44 (2008), 1576.

retaliation rights are sought, the complainant government first will compile a broad, non-specific, provisional list of targets.[20] The EU's provisional retaliation list in *US–Tax Treatment for Foreign Sales Corporations* provides a salient example in that the list contained references to ninety-nine product categories rather than to particular goods.[21] The government then solicits public comments in order to narrow the list of targets.[22]

The government receives comments from three categories of domestic constituencies: exporters affected by the challenged trade barrier who demand compliance; domestic importers and users who wish to remove goods of interest to them from the retaliation list; and protectionist groups seeking inclusion of goods with which they compete. Domestic groups seeking to exclude goods from the list appear to provide the greatest number of comments.[23] In both the *EC–Bananas* and *EC–Hormones* disputes, US officials state that they received many more comments from domestic importers than protectionist groups. As Andersen and Blanchet (Chapter 8) write in this volume, the USTR received comments "from hundreds of U.S. businesses and Members of Congress petitioned USTR … to avoid imposition of sanctions on particular industry sectors," wishing to have goods removed from the list.[24]

The practice of issuing broad, provisional retaliation lists appears to serve two primary functions: (1) to create diffuse uncertainty and anxiety among exporters in the respondent member, increasing their incentives to lobby for compliance; and (2) to allow various domestic constituencies to voice their interests in order to mitigate the domestic political and economic costs of retaliation.[25] These dual objectives underlie the US decision

[20] For example, this general practice is followed in the United States, the EC, and Canada. Andersen and Blanchet, see above, note 13, section 2; Ehring, see above, note , section 2; Khabayan, see above, note 13.

[21] Daniel Pruzin and Tim King, "EU Unveils FSC Hit List, Asks WTO to Clear More than $4 billion in Trade Sanctions," *BNA International Trade Daily*, November 20, 2000, d2; Paul Meller, "Europeans Seek $4 billion in Trade Sanctions Against U.S.," *The New York Times*, November 18, 2000, C1.

[22] Ehring, see above, note 7, section 2; Khabayan, see above, note 13.

[23] Andersen and Blanchet, see above, note 13, section 2. In *US–FSC*, for example, the EU removed nearly a thousand products from the initial list of 2,556 based on comments from EU member states, companies, and trade associations. Nordström, see above, note 8.

[24] Andersen and Blanchet, see above, note 13, section 2.

[25] Steve Charnovitz, "Rethinking WTO Trade Sanctions," *American Journal of International Law*, 95 (2001), 814; Rosemary A. Ford, "The Beef Hormone Dispute and Carousel Sanctions: A Roundabout Way of Forcing Compliance with World Trade Organization Decisions," *Brooklyn Journal of International Law*, 27 (2002), 547, 568–9.

to enact carousel legislation in response to continued non-compliance in the *EC–Hormones* and *EC–Bananas* disputes.[26] The United States wished to maximize pressure on the EU by creating widespread anxiety about possible targets, but included a mechanism for the USTR to receive comments from domestic constituents. Once again, most comments requested goods to be excluded from the list.[27]

After gathering input from domestic actors, the complainant member generally issues a final, shortened list of retaliatory targets.[28] Such lists have generally not targeted the sectors in the respondent member that benefited from the WTO-inconsistent measure. Rather, they appear calibrated to spur politically influential foreign exporters to lobby their governments to comply with the WTO ruling, while excluding products on which domestic industries and consumers are dependent.[29] Thus, in the *EC–Bananas* case, the United States threatened and ultimately imposed 100 percent duties on luxury goods from specific EU industries and countries, including Louis Vuitton handbags from France, pecorino cheese and handbags from Italy, and cashmere sweaters from Britain.[30] Similarly, in the *EC–Hormones* dispute, the United States imposed 100 percent duties on select, high-end agricultural products from France, Germany, Italy, and Denmark, including Roquefort cheese, Dijon mustard, and Danish ham.[31] In both cases, the EU member states targeted were perceived to be the strongest supporters, respectively, of the banana regime and of the ban on hormone-treated beef.[32] Although the United States initially targeted European pork products in the hormones dispute, it scaled back

[26] Gary G. Yerkey, "U.S. Meat Industry Expresses Concern about Delay in Publication of 'Carousel' List," *BNA International Trade Daily*, September 12, 2000, d3; Mark L. Movsesian, "Enforcement of WTO Rulings: An Interest Group Analysis," *Hofstra Law Review*, 32 (2003), 11.

[27] Andersen and Blanchet, see above, note 13, section 2; Yerkey, see above, note 26, d3; Movsesian, see above, note 26, 11. Andersen and Blanchet note that the carousel provision expressly directed the USTR to revise the list to increase the chances of compliance or a satisfactory solution.

[28] Andersen and Blanchet, see above, note 13, section 2; Khabayan, see above, note 13.

[29] Kym Anderson, "Peculiarities of Retaliation in WTO Dispute Settlement," *World Trade Review*, 1 (2002), 130.

[30] Helen Cooper, "U.S. Starts its Threatened Banana Fight with Europe," *Wall Street Journal*, March 4, 1999, A2; John Simons, "Handbags, Bed Linens Included in List of Goods Covered by Trade Sanctions," *Wall Street Journal*, April 12, 1999, A24.

[31] Yerkey, see above, note 26, d3; Andersen and Blanchet, see above, note 13, section 3.

[32] Andersen and Blanchet, see above, note 13, section 3.

because Denmark – the EU's largest pork producer – lacked sufficient political influence that could help spur EU compliance.[33] In both cases, the targeted products were luxury items so that most US consumers would not be harmed. Likewise, in the *US–Byrd Amendment* dispute, Canada selectively targeted items which were produced in US states whose representatives supported the offending legislation.[34] Although the chief US beneficiaries of the legislation manufactured ball bearings and steel, Canada targeted non-reciprocal goods, such as swine, ornamental fish, oysters, and cigarettes, for which it had alternative foreign or domestic sources of supply.[35]

The EU's use of retaliatory threats in the *US–Steel Safeguards* dispute was perhaps the most successful in terms of achieving quick compliance. Pursuant to Article 8 of the Agreement on Safeguards, the EU threatened to impose countermeasures on products produced in US states critical to the 2004 presidential election, largely ignoring US steel products that benefited from the safeguards.[36] On the eve of the EU's retaliation deadline, the threat of countermeasures paid off. The United States capitulated, scrapping the challenged steel tariffs.[37] The EU strategy paralleled those of the United States and Canada, while avoiding actual implementation. All three governments selectively targeted politically significant exporters in the non-complying member with little or no regard to reciprocal rebalancing in terms of the affected sectors.

Developing country WTO members have shown even greater reluctance to implement retaliatory measures, although they have threatened to impose them, in particular in the form of a suspension of intellectual property protection. Brazil, Ecuador, and Antigua and Barbuda, for example, have not imposed retaliatory measures where they have been authorized to do so.[38] Ecuador and Antigua and Barbuda obtained rights

[33] Charnovitz, see above, note 25, 815; Ford, see above, note 25, 559.

[34] Khabayan, see above, note 13.

[35] Daniel Pruzin, "WTO Complainants still Hesitant to Levy Sanctions on U.S. Imports in Byrd Dispute," *International Trade Daily*, February 18, 2005, d18; Khabayan, see above, note 13.

[36] Gary G. Yerkey, "EU Draws up List of U.S. Products Targeted for Sanctions in Steel Dispute," *International Trade Daily*, March 27, 2002, d2; Elizabeth Becker, "Visiting Europe Trade Chief Warns of Sanctions Monday," *The New York Times*, February 27, 2004, C5; Nzelibe, see above, note 8, 255.

[37] Nzelibe, see above, note 8, 255.

[38] Nottage, see above, note 15, section 3.

to "cross-retaliate" by suspending intellectual property protection for intellectual property owners in the EU and United States, respectively.[39] While Brazil pursued measures in the form of increased product tariffs in the *Canada–Aircraft* case,[40] it has considered and threatened to suspend intellectual property protection to induce US compliance in the *US–Cotton Subsidies* dispute.[41] In this way, developing countries can maximize their ability to press for compliance because of the political sensitivity of intellectual property issues within the United States and the EU, while tariff measures would exert less pressure, especially for developing countries with small markets.[42] A developing country will also minimize domestic economic harm in this way, and arguably may even benefit economically due to increased access to otherwise protected information, goods, and technology.[43]

In sum, most WTO members have followed a similar strategy of targeting products from politically influential exporters in the respondent member state to maximize pressure on it to comply, while minimizing harm to the complainant's constituencies, including its import-consuming industries.

Conclusion: extrapolating purpose from practice

Members' practice in selecting and implementing countermeasures suggests that complainants' primary purpose is to induce compliance and not to achieve a rebalancing of concessions. To start, complainants infrequently apply authorized countermeasures where a respondent has not complied with a WTO ruling. According to Hunter Nottage (Chapter 15), WTO members have formally requested authorization to retaliate in only seventeen of the sixty disputes in which retaliation was possible, fully litigated and received authorization to implement countermeasures in only nine of these cases, and implemented such measures in only five of them.[44]

[39] Daniel Pruzin, see above, note 15, d12; Daniel Pruzin, see above, note 15, d10. *Cf. Canada–Aircraft* and Daniel Pruzin, "WTO Decision Puts Pressure on Brazil, Canada to Resolve Aircraft Subsidy Dispute," *International Trade Daily*, October 23, 2001.

[40] In the civil aircraft disputes, Brazil and Canada decided to negotiate a settlement after each receiving authorization to retaliate. Khabayan, see above, note 13; and Pruzin, see above, note 39, d6.

[41] See Appellate Body Report, *United States–Subsidies on Upland Cotton*, WT/DS267/AB/R (March 3, 2005) (DSR 1996:I, 3); Pruzin, see above, note 15, 746.

[42] Marco Bronckers and Naboth van den Broek, "Financial Compensation in the WTO," *Journal of International Economic Law*, 8 (2005), 102.

[43] Pruzin, see above, note 15.

[44] Nottage, see above, note 15, section 3(a) (citing Reto Malacrida's figures, from the WTO Secretariat).

That is, members have sought retaliatory measures in only 28 percent of the disputes in which they would have been able to do so, and have implemented authorized retaliation in only 8 percent. Moreover, only one-third of the members whom the WTO has authorized to impose countermeasures have done so. Even the WTO's two most powerful members have infrequently applied retaliation. The United States has sought and implemented retaliation in only two disputes, while the EU has formally sought retaliation rights on seven occasions and implemented them only twice.[45] These practices would not occur if members' primary purpose were rebalancing. If rebalancing were complainants' primary aim, then members should be more aggressive in seeking and implementing retaliation rights so as to restore the balance of trade benefits and concessions where a respondent has violated WTO rules and failed to comply with a WTO ruling.

Even when authorization is obtained, complainant parties often resort to mechanisms aimed at exerting pressure on foreign exporters to comply without having to retaliate in practice. Complainants first commonly promulgate broad, non-specific provisional lists of potential targets in order to foment anxiety among export interests in the respondent member. Through these lists, complainants aim to spur foreign exporters to lobby for compliance. Complainants frequently threaten to impose countermeasures and then postpone their implementation. For example, the EU delayed implementing countermeasures in the *US–FSC* case, instead relying on the threat that it would increase countermeasures over time. Similarly, in the *EC–Agricultural Biotech* dispute, the United States has threatened to seek authorized retaliation in the context of ongoing negotiations with the EU over compliance, but had not done so two years after the adoption of the panel report.[46] We should not expect these delaying tactics were the objective to rebalance trade concessions fully and immediately.

We have posited that incremental and partial countermeasures might be applied where the authorized amount is significant if the primary goal is compliance, and not rebalancing. The EU applied this strategy in the *US–FSC* dispute where the amount of authorized retaliation was to the order of US$4 billion per year. The EU was reluctant to impose retaliation immediately, especially where the US Congress had to change the

[45] Nordström, see above, note 8.

[46] See, for example, "Commission Presses for Continued GMO Dialogue, US Non-Committal," 26:43, *Inside US Trade* 1 (October 31, 2008).

underlying US legislation, and rather hoped to induce compliance through gradually increasing the amount of retaliation. There are also means to increase pressure over time to induce compliance where the authorized amount of retaliation is less significant. For example, although the United States implemented full countermeasures in its two cases, it continued to exercise pressure to induce compliance through the threat of "carousel" retaliation. If rebalancing were the aim, there would have been no need for the United States to enact and threaten the use of "carousel" retaliation in the face of continued EU non-compliance. The United States could have simply maintained existing countermeasures that achieved a rebalancing of concessions. The US threat to use carousel retaliation parallels the EU"s threat to increase retaliation over time in that both decisions aimed to induce compliance.

The strategy of targeting a small number of politically significant producers within the respondent again suggests that compliance, and not rebalancing, is the complainants' primary goal. Complainants have found that concentrating retaliatory measures on politically influential export groups is a more effective way to induce compliance than increasing tariffs by a lower rate across the board or targeting the sector that benefited from the WTO-inconsistent measure. These choices are less understandable if rebalancing were the complainants' primary aim. If rebalancing were the primary objective, then complainants should be driven to placate domestic protectionist interests from a political perspective, and should pay more attention to minimizing transaction costs and raising revenue in selecting targets from an economic one. As Håkan Nordström (chapter 10) writes, the use of longer retaliation lists could reduce the time and expense of consulting domestic constituencies and selecting specific retaliation targets, and could also generate greater revenue by avoiding the imposition of prohibitive product tariffs.[47]

Small developing country complainants' practices likewise suggest that their primary objective is to induce compliance. While large WTO members (that is, large in terms of their exercise of market power) have imposed countermeasures in the form of increased tariffs, small developing country members have sought and secured retaliation rights in the form of suspending intellectual property protection. They claim to have done so because this form of retaliation is most likely to place pressure on influential constituencies within the respective respondent (the United States and the EU) to lobby for compliance. While the imposition of tariffs

[47] Nordström, see above, note 8.

could lead to a rebalancing of trade concessions, these members find that they exercise too little market power for such tariffs to catalyze domestic groups to lobby their government to comply. In addition, smaller developing country members have been even more reluctant actually to impose countermeasures, apparently again because they believe that such countermeasures would exert little pressure in inducing compliance.[48]

In sum, WTO member practice suggests that complainants are driven primarily by the aim of compliance, not rebalancing. This practice reflects, in particular, the impact of domestic export groups within the complainant who have invested significantly in the case. These groups wish to have the trade barrier removed. They are not interested in a rebalancing that would not benefit them. Their governments have responded accordingly.

Over time, WTO member practices can have systemic impacts within the WTO. Members are represented by foreign affairs and trade ministries who develop and pool expertise on WTO law within governments. If these ministries all perceive that the aim of WTO remedies is compliance, then such beliefs could affect formal law over time, whether through the negotiation of new legal texts or the interpretation of existing ones. In any case, members' practices determine the WTO law-in-action, that is, how formal WTO remedies are actually used.

[48] Bronckers and Broek, see above, note 42, 102.

PART II

A legal assessment after ten arbitration disputes

4

The law of permissible WTO retaliation

THOMAS SEBASTIAN*

Introduction

This chapter seeks to provide an account of the manner in which Article 22.6 arbitrators have gone about their task of fitting 'punishment' (retaliation) to 'crime' (the continuing violation of WTO law). The treaty text provides only sparse instructions on how to carry out this task and, as a consequence, arbitrators and WTO members have been left to develop their own solutions in individual cases.

The task of this chapter is essentially descriptive. As a 'state-of-play' account it looks back at the arbitral awards issued to date and isolates the legal approaches used by arbitrators, examines the issues they have confronted, while applying those approaches in individual cases and discusses the justifications offered for particular approaches and choices. The chapter does touch (lightly) on the thorny matter of evaluation of arbitral awards and the related issue of what the proper 'purpose' or 'objective' of WTO remedies is or should be, but, on the whole, its task is to construct an accurate description. The task of providing prescriptions is left for other contributors to this volume.

It is structured as follows: section 1 provides an overview of the basic features of the WTO enforcement mechanism; section 2 describes the procedural aspects; sections 3–6 are the core of the chapter and describe how arbitral panels have controlled the form and magnitude of retaliation in the ten cases decided to date; and section 7 briefly discusses the question of how the arbitral panels have viewed the purpose of retaliation.

* Allen & Overy LLP. The views expressed are the personal views of the author. An earlier version of this chapter was presented at the Workshop on the Calculation and Design of Trade Sanctions in WTO Dispute Settlement at the Graduate Institute in Geneva. I am grateful to Chad Bown, Todd Friedbacher, Nic Lockhart, Joost Pauwelyn and Simon Schropp for their comments. All errors remain mine.

Readers who are familiar with the WTO enforcement mechanism can skip sections 1 and 2.

1 Basic features of the WTO enforcement mechanism

(a) The sole remedy for continuing non-compliance is retaliation

Bilateral and multilateral treaties provide for a wide variety of responses to non-compliance by state parties. These can include fines, judgments for monetary damages enforceable through the domestic courts of state parties or specially tailored packages of financial aid and technical assistance conditional on compliance. The WTO agreements do not envisage these types of responses to non-compliance. The only response to non-compliance envisaged in the WTO agreements is the 'suspension of concessions or other obligations' owed to the violating state under the WTO agreements by complainant states (or 'retaliation' in short). In other words, the only response to violation of the treaty is a further offsetting violation of the treaty, a particular type of 'countermeasure'.

There is some debate as to whether attempts to redress non-compliance by taking other types of measures, including measures that are wholly consistent with the WTO agreements, could contravene the Dispute Settlement Understanding (DSU). The panel in *EC–Commercial Vessels* ruled that the grant of WTO-consistent countersubsidies by the EC constituted an impermissible response to alleged violations of the SCM Agreement by Korea.[1] In that case, the EC resorted to the WTO-consistent countersubsidies without first resorting to the DSU. The panel concluded that Article 23.1 of the DSU proscribes WTO-consistent measures taken by the EC as long as the purpose of those measures was to induce Korea to cease conduct which the EC considered to be inconsistent with the WTO agreements.[2] Thus, there is authority for the view that perfectly legal measures (sometimes referred to as measures of retorsion: suspension of foreign aid is an example) which seek to redress purported violations of the WTO agreements could contravene Article 23.1 of the DSU. The panel's

[1] See Panel Report, *EC–Commercial Vessels* (DSR 2005:XV, 7713), paras. 7.184–7.222, especially para. 7.196 ('As discussed above, the Panel considers that Article 23.1 must be interpreted to mean that Members may not seek to obtain results that can be achieved through remedies of the DSU by means other than recourse to the DSU').

[2] *EC–Commercial Vessels* (DSR 2005:XV, 7713), paras. 7.196, 7.207.

reasoning also implies that measures which involve the suspension of obligations under non-WTO treaties (non-WTO countermeasures, such as an expropriation in violation of a Bilateral Investment Treaty (BIT)), if taken to redress a purported WTO violation, could also contravene Article 23.1 of the DSU.[3]

Doubts can be raised about whether the panel's reasoning is correct.[4] Still, this case implies that the use of measures that are not specifically provided for in the DSU to redress a WTO violation, such as measures of retorsion and non-WTO countermeasures, involves a failure to 'have recourse to, and abide by' the DSU within the meaning of Article 23.1 of the DSU.[5] Whether this jurisprudence will be reversed or limited by the Appellate Body remains to be seen.

(b) *Collective retaliation is not envisaged*

Article 22.2, DSU limits the use of retaliation to 'any party having invoked the dispute settlement procedures'. Retaliation by WTO members which did not bring a complaint is, therefore, explicitly ruled out. Thus, there is no notion of centralised or collective enforcement in the WTO system. Instead, retaliation is left to individual WTO members who have enough of an interest in enforcement to incur the costs of bringing a WTO complaint and taking it through the dispute settlement process. This can be usefully contrasted with the systems under treaties where non-compliance can provoke a response by all parties to the treaty regardless of whether or not they have prevailed in dispute settlement proceedings. For instance, collective measures could, at least in theory, be imposed under Article

[3] Because neither category of measures is contemplated in the DSU, their use cannot be the result of a 'recourse' to the DSU and, arguably, implies a corresponding failure by the imposing member to 'have recourse to' the DSU.

[4] See Pieter-Jan Kuijper, 'Does the WTO Prohibit Retorsions and Reprisals? Legitimate "Contracting Out" or "Clinical Isolation Again"' in Merit E. Janow, Victoria Donaldson and Alan Yanovich (eds.), *The WTO: Governance, Dispute Settlement & Developing Countries* (Huntington, NY: Juris Publishing, 2008), 701–2 ('*It must be considered extremely doubtful that the WTO founding fathers had this in mind ...*' (emphasis added). Nevertheless, the panel's legalistic analysis, referring to the general terms of Article 23.1 is *prima facie* correct: members should not try to obtain results they can obtain through DSU procedures by other means, outside those procedures).

[5] Antonis Antonidas, 'Unilateral Measures and WTO Dispute Settlement: An EC Perspective', 41 *Journal of World Trade Law*, 605 (2007), 625 ('In its proper construction, Article 23 contains a broad prohibition of unilateralism which excludes all measures outside those prescribed in the DSU').

94.2 of the UN Charter in response to non-compliance with judgments of the International Court of Justice.

(c) *Retaliation is subject to multilateral disciplines on form and magnitude*

The WTO agreements impose significant disciplines on the form and magnitude of retaliatory measures.

As far as the magnitude of retaliatory measures is concerned, the WTO agreements provide for different standards depending on the nature of the underlying violation:

(1) Article 22.4 of the DSU provides that the 'level of suspension of concessions or other obligations' must be '*equivalent*' to the nullification and impairment. This equivalence standard is the general rule.
(2) Special rules apply in cases involving actionable and prohibited subsidies:

    (a) Article 7.9 of the SCM Agreement specifies that in cases involving actionable subsidies countermeasures must be '*commensurate*' with the degree and nature of the adverse effects determined to exist.
    (b) Article 4.10 of the SCM Agreement specifies that in cases involving prohibited subsidies the countermeasures must be '*appropriate*' and a further footnote clarifies that countermeasures should not be 'disproportionate in light of the fact that the subsidies dealt with under these provisions are prohibited'.

As far as form of retaliation is concerned, Article 22.3 of the DSU provides that the obligations or concessions suspended should usually be in the same 'sector' and 'agreement' as the 'sector' and 'agreement' in which the underlying violation occurred. The terms 'sector' and 'agreement' have a specific meaning in this context. Article 22.3 imposes certain conditions that must be met before retaliation in a different 'sector' or under a different 'agreement' can be authorised. These disciplines impose a preference for the underlying violation and retaliation to be symmetrical; that is, broadly speaking, a TRIPs violation should be met with a retaliatory measure which also violates TRIPs, a GATS violation should be met with a retaliatory measure which also violates GATS, etc. However, non-symmetrical or 'cross-retaliation' is permitted under certain conditions (see the contributions in this volume by Appleton (Chapter 23) on GATS retaliation and Abbott (Chapter 22) on TRIPS retaliation).

These disciplines on the form and magnitude of retaliation are enforced through a system of binding arbitration. Their content is more fully discussed in sections 3–6 of this chapter.

(d) Retaliation is temporary

The authorisation to retaliate is conditional on continued non-compliance by the violating state.[6] So retaliation is a temporary measure and operates as a substitute for compliance. If compliance is forthcoming the retaliatory measure must be revoked. Accordingly, retaliation involves the *suspension* of WTO obligations but not a permanent alteration or termination of those obligations.

(e) Retaliation does not respond to non-compliance occurring before the expiry of the RPT

Article 19.1 of the DSU prescribes that the end result of a successful complaint under the DSU is a recommendation to the violating state to 'bring the measures into conformity' with the WTO agreements. Under Article 21.3 of the DSU, the violating state is usually given a period of grace within which to accomplish this task. This is referred to as the 'reasonable period of time for implementation' or 'RPT' for short.

Articles 19.1 and 21.3 of the DSU read together are understood to limit the scope of what can be required of a violating state. A violating state is required to cease its illegal conduct by the end of the RPT but cannot be required to make reparation for injury caused on account of illegal conduct which predates the expiry of the RPT. It is in this sense that WTO remedies are understood to be 'prospective'.[7]

The position under general public international law is different. All violations of a treaty, regardless of when they occur, entail obligations to make reparation for consequent injury. Unlike WTO law, in general public international law there is no period of grace within which a violation has no legal consequence. For this reason, retaliation in the WTO system should be viewed as a response to non-compliance occurring during the period following the expiry of the RPT. Acts or omissions outside this period (that is, those acts or omissions occurring *prior* to the expiry of the RPT) would not, ordinarily, generate retaliatory measures.

[6] DSU, Article 22.8.

[7] For a recent statement see Appellate Body Report, *US–Cotton (Recourse to Article 21.5 – US)*, footnote 494.

2. The process

(a) *The initial request for authorisation to retaliate*

The DSU is understood to require a complainant to request authorisation to retaliate no later than thirty days after the expiry of the RPT.[8] This deadline is usually waived by the parties to a dispute under bilateral 'sequencing agreements'. These agreements oblige the complainant to initiate Article 21.5 proceedings in order to obtain a multilateral determination of whether the losing state has brought itself into compliance during the RPT. Only if the Article 21.5 process concludes with a determination that the losing state has failed to bring itself into compliance with its WTO obligations is the complainant allowed to proceed to request authorisation to retaliate from the Dispute Settlement Body (DSB).

The request for authorisation to retaliate must meet fairly minimal requirements of form. It must identify: (i) a specific level of suspension of concessions and other obligations sought; and (ii) the agreement and sector under which concessions or other obligations would be suspended.[9] This basic information is required in order to assess whether the legal requirements regarding the permissible magnitude and form of retaliation have been complied with.

More elaborate information on features of the proposed retaliatory measures, for instance, details of particular obligations that are to be suspended,[10] products that are to be subjected to additional tariffs or the extent of tariff increases, need not be specified in the request.[11] The reasoning typically given to justify these meagre disclosure requirements is that under Article 22.7 of the DSU arbitral panels cannot examine these features of the proposed retaliatory measures and, therefore, information regarding these features is not material and cannot be demanded from the retaliating state.[12] It should be noted that arbitral panels have not

[8] DSU, Article 22.2 read with Article 22.6.

[9] *EC–Bananas III (US)* (Article 22.6) (DSR 1999:II, 725), para. 16; *EC–Bananas III (Ecuador)* (Article 22.6) (DSR 2000:V, 2237), para. 21.

[10] *US–1916 Act* (Article 22.6) (DSR 2004:IX, 4269), paras. 3.10–14.

[11] See, for example, *US–Byrd Amendment* (Article 22.6) (DSR 2004:IX, 4511), paras. 2.18–22 (concluding that a retaliation request which did not set out a product list or provide details of the extent of tariff increases met the minimum specificity standard applicable in an Article 22.6 arbitration).

[12] See *EC–Hormones (US)* (Article 22.6) (DSR 1999:III, 1105), para. 19; *US–Gambling* (Article 22.6) (DSR 2005:XXIII, 11637), para. 5.9.

always been consistent. The arbitral panel in *EC–Hormones* (Article 22.6) stated that 'the United States *has to* – and did – identify the products that may be subject to suspension' (emphasis added).[13] However, in practice, WTO members have refused to provide lists of products in their retaliation requests and arbitral panels have not objected to this.[14]

In cases where authorisation to cross-retaliate is sought from the DSB the reasons for this must be set out in the request.[15] The violating state has the right to object to the request on the ground that that the authorisation sought by the retaliating state involves retaliatory measures of an excessive magnitude and/or an improper form. The DSB then refers the matter to arbitration under Article 22.6 of the DSU.[16] During the course of the arbitration the right to retaliate remains suspended.[17]

(b) *The Article 22.6 arbitration process*

(i) Mandate of the arbitrator

Article 22.7 sets out the mandate of the arbitral panel. It provides that the arbitral panel must determine whether the level of suspension of concessions and other obligations 'is equivalent to the level of nullification and impairment'[18] and whether the 'principles and procedures' (regulating cross-retaliation) set out in Article 22.3 'have been followed'.[19]

Article 22.7 also imposes a significant limitation: it provides that the arbitral panel cannot 'examine the *nature* of the concessions or other obligations to be suspended' (emphasis added). As the arbitral panel in *US–Gambling* noted, this limitation means that an arbitral panel cannot 'question the complaining party's choice of specific obligations to be suspended (other than in the context of considering a claim that the

[13] *EC–Hormones (US)* (Article 22.6), para. 21. The arbitral panel provides no legal reasoning in support of its ruling.

[14] See, for example *Recourse by Brazil to Article 22.2 of the DSU*, WT/DS217/20, 16 January 2004. To date, twenty-two retaliation requests have been filed without product lists. See also, Minutes of the DSB Meeting, 19 April 1999, WT/DSB/M/59, 5, 8 (statements by the EC, Mexico and the United States noting that the DSU does not require the submission of product lists).

[15] DSU, Article 22.3(e). [16] DSU, Article 22.6. [17] DSU, Article 22.6.

[18] As noted above, different standards apply under Articles 7.9 and 4.10 of the SCM Agreement.

[19] Article 22.7 also states that arbitral panels may examine whether any proposed suspension of concessions or other obligations is allowed under a covered agreement. In practice, this question does not arise. Although Article 22.5 refers to prohibitions on the suspension of concessions or other obligations, explicit prohibitions are not found in the WTO agreements.

principles and procedures of Article 22.3 have not been followed)', instead it must 'assess the level of the proposed suspension, rather than its form'.[20] In that case, the arbitral panel refused to require Antigua to specify precisely how it would implement its authorisation to suspend obligations under the TRIPs on the basis that such a ruling would exceed its mandate.[21] The limitation has also been understood to prevent any scrutiny of the products targeted by retaliatory measures or the extent of proposed tariff increases.[22]

A further implication of this limitation is that arbitral awards are usually rendered in abstract terms. Often they contain only an aggregate figure for annual trade that can be affected by the retaliatory measures and the sector/agreement under which the retaliation must occur, but no further specifics on products that can be targeted or the magnitude of tariff increases.

The terms of reference of the arbitral panel are set by the initial request for authorisation to retaliate[23] and the objections made to that request at the time of referral.[24] Thus, arbitral panels have indicated that, in principle, they would not consider later supplemental requests made by the retaliating state to enlarge the amount sought[25] or requests to suspend obligations in sectors/agreements that are not specifically set out in the initial request for authorisation to retaliate.[26] Likewise, objections by the violating state that were not raised during the DSB meeting at which the referral was made will not be considered.[27] Measures that are not mentioned in the initial request for authorisation to retaliate are also outside the terms of reference.[28]

The arbitral panel must determine whether the initial request for authorisation to retaliate meets the disciplines on form and magnitude. If the request fails to comply with the disciplines on magnitude, the arbitral panel will proceed to make its own estimate of the proper level of suspension of concessions and other obligations.[29] If the request fails to

[20] *US–Gambling* (Article 22.6), para. 5.9. [21] *Ibid.*

[22] *EC–Hormones (US)* (Article 22.6), para. 19.

[23] *EC–Bananas III (Ecuador)* (Article 22.6), para. 20.

[24] *Brazil–Aircraft* (Article 22.6) (DSR 2002:I, 19), para. 3.15.

[25] *EC–Bananas III (Ecuador)* (Article 22.6), para. 24; *Brazil–Aircraft* (Article 22.6), para. 3.14.

[26] *EC–Bananas III (Ecuador)* (Article 22.6), para. 29.

[27] *Brazil–Aircraft* (Article 22.6), para. 3.15.

[28] *US–1916 Act* (Article 22.6), para. 3.19.

[29] See *US–Gambling* (Article 22.6), para. 2.8 and footnote 14.

comply with the disciplines on form, the arbitral panel will specify the extent, if any, to which concessions and other obligations can be suspended in other sectors or under other agreements.[30]

(ii) Burden of proof

The burden of proof in Article 22.6 proceedings is allocated in the same way as in ordinary dispute settlement proceedings. The violating state, as the party referring the matter to arbitration, bears the burden of demonstrating that the complaining state's request for authorisation to retaliate does not conform to the requirements of the DSU.[31] However, each party bears the burden of proving the specific factual allegations that it makes.[32]

(iii) Precedential effect of prior awards

Prior arbitral awards (like ordinary panel reports) do not bind future panels. Nevertheless, arbitral panels frequently quote and rely on prior awards. Given the scant guidance provided in the treaty text, prior awards assume particular importance in these cases.[33] It should be noted that arbitral panels have been reluctant to rely on awards rendered under different legal standards. Panels applying the Article 22.4 equivalence standard have distinguished and refused to rely on awards rendered under the appropriateness standard applicable in export subsidy cases and vice versa.[34]

(c) The post-award request for authorisation to retaliate

After the issuance of the arbitral award the DSB must approve any request for authorisation to retaliate that 'is consistent with the decision of the arbitrator'.[35] In most cases this occurs without any incident. Nonetheless, there may be cases where there is disagreement as to whether or not the post-award request is consistent with the arbitral award. To give one (and the only known) example, following the issuance of the arbitral

[30] See, for example, *EC–Bananas III (Ecuador)* (Article 22.6), para. 173.

[31] See, for example, *EC–Hormones (US)* (Article 22.6), paras. 9–11; *US–Gambling* (Article 22.6), para. 2.22.

[32] See, for example, *US–1916 Act* (Article 22.6), para. 2.5.

[33] See *US–Gambling* (Article 22.6), para. 2.5.

[34] See, for example, *Brazil–Aircraft* (Article 22.6), footnote 49; *US–Byrd Amendment* (Article 22.6), para. 3.70; *US–Gambling* (Article 22.6), footnote 9.

[35] DSU, Art. 22.7.

award in the *US–Byrd* case, the United States objected to the post-award requests filed by some of the co-complainants on the ground that the requests 'may not' be consistent with the arbitral award. The United States blocked the adoption of the agenda of the DSB meeting until its concerns were addressed through a diplomatic compromise brokered by the chairperson.[36]

(d) *Ensuring that retaliatory measures remain within the bounds of DSB authorisation*

If a complaining state takes retaliatory measures that exceed the bounds of what has been authorised by the DSB, the violating state can invoke normal dispute settlement procedures to challenge the WTO-consistency of those measures.[37] Although concerns have been expressed regarding the WTO-consistency of retaliatory measures,[38] to date, no challenge to retaliatory measures has been brought on the basis that they are *ultra vires* the relevant DSB authorisation.

(e) *Termination of retaliatory measures*

Article 22.8 of the DSU provides that retaliatory measures can only be 'applied until such time as the measure found to be inconsistent with a covered agreement has been removed'. This provision imposes an obligation to terminate retaliatory measures when the violating state brings itself into compliance. Often there will be a disagreement about whether the violating state has actually brought itself into compliance. In this situation, the complaining state is permitted to maintain its retaliatory measures until the disagreement is resolved through multilateral dispute settlement.[39] The disagreement should ordinarily be resolved through arbitration under Article 21.5 of the DSU,[40] but it is open to the parties to agree on alternative means of dispute settlement.[41] If it is established through such dispute settlement procedures that the violating state has brought itself into compliance, the authorisation to retaliate lapses

[36] See, *World Trade Online*, 'U.S. Blocks Byrd Retaliation Requests, Insists on Changes' (26 November 2004); *World Trade Online*, 'WTO Members Get Authorization to Retaliate Against U.S. Byrd Law' (3 December 2004).

[37] See, for example, *US–Gambling* (Article 22.6), para. 5.12.

[38] See, *World Trade Online*, 'USTR Examining Whether Byrd Retaliation Consistent with WTO' (5 August 2005).

[39] See, Appellate Body Report, *United States–Continued Suspension*, para. 306.

[40] *Ibid.*, para. 345. [41] *Ibid.*, para. 340.

automatically.[42] However, if compliance is not established the complaining state may maintain its retaliatory measures.

3. Magnitude I: the general equivalence standard

(a) *The equality-of-harm approach*[43]

In all cases decided under the general Article 22.4 equivalence standard, arbitrators have adopted what can be termed the 'equality-of-harm' approach.

The equality-of-harm approach was developed in the first Article 22.6 case, the *EC–Bananas III (US)* (Article 22.6) case. In that case the arbitral panel had to determine whether the retaliatory measure proposed by the United States (the imposition of increased duties on products imported from the EC) was equivalent to the continuing violation of WTO law by the EC (a discriminatory banana import regime in which Latin American exporters of bananas and US providers of distribution services were placed at a competitive disadvantage). In broad terms, the solution that they adopted was to compare these two measures in terms of their detrimental effects. Therefore, a retaliatory response is equivalent within the meaning of Article 22.4 when:

{Detrimental effect on state V of retaliatory response by state R} =
{Detrimental effect on state R of underlying violation by state V}

The equality-of-harm approach is sometimes restated in the form of a rule against 'punitive retaliation', with punitive retaliation being defined as 'any suspension of obligations in excess of the level of nullification or impairment'.[44]

The textual basis for choosing such an approach is the reference in Article 22.4 to 'nullification and impairment'. In effect, the *EC–Bananas III (US)* (Article 22.6) panel interpreted equivalence to require that the nullification and impairment caused by the underlying violation be equal to the nullification and impairment caused by the retaliatory response. Thus, perhaps a better term for the approach would be the 'equality-of-nullification-and-impairment approach', but I have avoided this term as it is somewhat unwieldy.

[42] *Ibid.*, para. 310.

[43] For an economic analysis of this approach see Bown and Ruta, 'The Economics of Permissible WTO Retaliation', Chapter 6, below, part 3.

[44] See, *US–1916 Act* (Article 22.6), para. 5.22; *US–Gambling* (Article 22.6), para. 3.24.

The *EC–Bananas III (US)* (Article 22.6) panel did not attempt to expressly justify its choice of approach; justification may not have been necessary because the approach appears to have been impliedly supported by both parties.[45] The approach is also broadly consistent with the methods followed by the GATT contracting parties when assessing the withdrawal of substantially equivalent concessions under Article XXVIII of the GATT.[46] The equality-of-harm approach has been followed by arbitral panels in *all* of the seven cases decided under the Article 22.4 equivalence standard. In five of these seven cases *both* parties to the dispute endorsed the use of this approach.

In order to apply this approach, arbitral panels determine the level of nullification and impairment arising from the underlying violation. This figure then provides the upper bound for the level of nullification and impairment that can arise from the retaliatory response and hence the limit of any authorisation to retaliate granted by the DSB.

(i) Calculation of nullification and impairment arising from the underlying violation

During GATT times, panels did not have to quantify the level of nullification and impairment (although they were called upon to make binary decisions about whether or not nullification and impairment were present) with any frequency. Article XXIII:2 of the GATT 1947 used a much looser 'appropriate in the circumstances' standard and, in practice, this authority was invoked only rarely.[47] As Pauwelyn points out in his contribution to this volume (Chapter 2),[48] arbitral panels acting under Article 22.6 were,

[45] The arbitral panel set out its approach in an initial decision that was circulated to both parties. The parties criticised certain aspects of the initial decision but neither party objected to the basic approach adopted by the arbitral panel. See *EC–Bananas III (US)* (Article 22.6), paras. 2.10–11 (discussing the initial decision), 4.10–15 (discussing certain EC objections to the initial decision), 6.19 (discussing certain US objections to the initial decision). It appears that the United States may have based its retaliation request on a similar approach. The United States was statutorily obliged to ensure that the retaliation in the *EC–Bananas III (US)* (Article 22.6) case affected foreign imports 'in an amount that [was] equivalent in value to the burden or restriction imposed ... on U.S. commerce'. See Trade Act of 1974, § 301(a)(3), 19 U.S.C., § 2411(a)(3) (2000).

[46] See, Anwarul Hoda, *Tariff Negotiations and Renegotiations under the GATT and the WTO: Procedures and Practices* (Cambridge University Press, 2001), 95–7; GATT Panel Report, *Canada–Lead and Zinc*, adopted 17 May 1978, BISD 25S/42; GATT Panel Report, *US/EEC–Poultry*, 21 November 1963, unadopted, L/2088.

[47] See, Minutes of Meeting, 4 May 1988, 35, GATT Doc. C/M/220.

[48] Joost Pauwelyn, 'The Calculation and Design of Trade Retaliation in Context: What is the Goal of Suspending WTO Obligations?', Chapter 2, section 5, above.

therefore, on relatively unexplored territory when developing methods for measuring nullification and impairment.

To calculate the nullification and impairment arising from the underlying violation, arbitrators have compared the current WTO-inconsistent situation with a 'counterfactual' WTO-consistent situation in which the violation is removed. The difference between these two situations (along some dimension) is used to gauge the effect of the underlying violation.

To make this calculation, arbitrators have to: (1) specify the counterfactual or baseline from which to assess the effects of the measure; (2) settle on a metric for measuring these effects; (3) specify the entities whose position is relevant to the analysis; (4) determine which detrimental effects will be considered; (5) resolve any empirical issues that may arise; and (6) account for changes over time. The remainder of this section will use this framework to analyse how arbitrators have made this calculation in the cases decided to date.

(i) **Choice of counterfactual** In order to assess the detrimental effects resulting from an illegal measure, an arbitrator must have a sense of the situation that would prevail if the illegality were removed. This, in turn, means that the arbitrator must utilise some sort of counterfactual regime as a comparator.

The *EC–Hormones* (Article 22.6) arbitrations provide an illustration of the use of counterfactuals. In the *EC–Hormones* (Article 22.6) cases, the underlying violation of WTO law was the EC's scientifically unsupported ban on imports of hormone-treated beef. The arbitrators decided to measure the detrimental effect caused by this violation by calculating 'the trade forgone due to the ban's continued existence'.[49] In order to make this calculation, the arbitrators compared, on an annual basis, (a) the value of beef exports under the current WTO-inconsistent EC regime, with (b) the value of beef exports which would have occurred in a WTO-consistent EC import regime.[50] However, in theory, the EC could have brought itself into compliance with WTO law in at least two ways: that is, by withdrawing the import ban altogether, or by keeping the import ban in place and taking steps to support it with an adequate risk assessment.

[49] *EC–Hormones (Canada)* (Article 22.6) (DSR 1999:III, 1135), para. 41; *EC–Hormones (US)* (Article 22.6), para. 42.

[50] *EC–Hormones (Canada)* (Article 22.6), para. 42; *EC–Hormones (US)* (Article 22.6), para. 43.

The choice of either of these two scenarios as the relevant counterfactual critically affects the calculations of arbitrators. In the *EC–Hormones* (Article 22.6) cases, the arbitrators opted for the first scenario and this was not contested by the EC.[51]

Every case involves an implicit or explicit counterfactual. In the *EC–Bananas III* (Article 22.6) cases, the arbitrators explicitly selected one counterfactual from among several possible options without providing any reason for their choice.[52] Just as in the *EC–Hormones* (Article 22.6) cases, this choice made a critical difference to the calculation of the amount of blocked trade. As Holger Spamann has explained, it is arguable that if another counterfactual were used (that is, a regime where banana import licences are auctioned off to the highest bidder) the level of impairment experienced by the United States would be calculated as zero (a sharp contrast from the $191.4 million per year figure that the arbitrators derived).[53] In the *US–1916 Act* case, the implicit counterfactual was a situation in which the United States refrained from imposing fines on exporters through the 1916 Act process, and in the *US–Byrd Amendment* case the implicit counterfactual was a situation in which the United States refrained from making payments to affected domestic industries. Finally, in *US–Gambling* the arbitrator explicitly selected a counterfactual in which only the horseracing sector of the US remote gambling market was opened up to foreign suppliers.[54] Here again, the choice of counterfactual was critical. On the counterfactual used by the arbitrators the level of nullification and impairment was found to be US$21 million per year, while on the counterfactual proposed by Antigua (at least in Antigua's view) the level would have been more than $3 billion a year.

On what principle is a counterfactual selected? In cases prior to *US–Gambling*, arbitrators did not even attempt to justify their choice of counterfactual.[55] But in *US–Gambling* the question of counterfactual

[51] *EC–Hormones (Canada)* (Article 22.6), para. 37; *EC–Hormones (US)* (Article 22.6), para. 38.

[52] *EC–Bananas III (US)* (Article 22.6), paras. 7.4–7.8; *EC–Bananas III (Ecuador)* (Article 22.6), paras. 166–7.

[53] See, Holger Spamann, 'The Myth of "Rebalancing" Retaliation in WTO Dispute Settlement Practice', *Journal of International Economic Law*, 9 (2006), 31, 52–3 (hereinafter Spamann).

[54] *US–Gambling* (Article 22.6), paras. 3.16–60.

[55] See, Bernard O'Connor, 'Remedies in the World Trade Organization Dispute Settlement System – The Bananas and Hormones Cases', *Journal of World Trade*, 38 (2004) 245,

choice could not be swept under the carpet. Given the positions adopted by the parties, some justification had to be provided for the counterfactual chosen.

In that case the arbitrators had to choose between three proposed counterfactuals:

(1) A counterfactual in which the entirety of the US remote gambling market was opened up to foreign suppliers. This was proposed by Antigua and formed the basis of its retaliation request.
(2) A counterfactual in which the United States implemented a ban on the provision of remote gambling services in all sectors. This was mentioned by the United States but not actually proposed by it as the basis for the calculation.
(3) A counterfactual in which the United States permitted the provision of remote gambling services in the horseracing sector but not in other sectors. This was proposed by the United States.

The majority opted for counterfactual (3) but a dissenting arbitrator opted for counterfactual (1).

The majority and dissenter agreed that the relevant principle to be applied is whether the counterfactual used is a 'plausible or reasonable compliance scenario',[56] but disagreed on the application of this principle to the facts. The majority ruled that counterfactual (1) was unreasonable because it did not 'take into account US policy objectives'[57] and opted for counterfactual (3). The dissenter found that counterfactual (3) was unreasonable because it was difficult to reconcile with the *very same* US policy objectives.[58]

The test set out by the arbitrators for what is a 'plausible or reasonable compliance scenario' is that it 'accurately reflects the level of nullification and impairment'[59] and does not 'lead to an implausible high level of nullification and impairment of benefits that would lead to a suspension in excess of the nullification and impairment actually suffered'.[60] This is perfectly circular. Any assessment of the level of nullification and impairment presupposes a particular counterfactual.

What is perplexing about the majority's choice of counterfactual in *Gambling* is that they opted for a counterfactual (counterfactual (3)) that was, as Antigua noted,[61] arguably WTO-inconsistent (in contrast, the

254–5; Spamann, 59–60; WTO, *World Trade Report*, 2005, 184 (hereinafter *World Trade Report 2005*).

56 *US–Gambling* (Article 22.6), para. 3.27. 57 *Ibid.*, para. 3.43. 58 *Ibid.*, para. 3.67.

59 *Ibid.*, paras. 3.23, 3.31. 60 *US–Gambling* (Article 22.6), para. 3.27.

61 *Ibid.*, para. 3.55.

other two counterfactuals on offer were admittedly WTO-consistent). It would appear that a threshold requirement for a counterfactual is that it is indisputably WTO-consistent. Counterfactual choice questions should arise only when there is more than one *WTO-consistent* means of coming into compliance. It is by no means clear that the US position that remote gambling must be banned in order to protect public morals can be reconciled with, at the same time, permitting remote gambling on horse races. This incoherence could be used to argue that the ban on non-horseracing related remote gambling is not necessary within the meaning of Article XIV of the GATS[62] or that the requirements of the chapeau to Article XIV are not met.

The majority and dissenter took the position that an enquiry into the WTO-consistency of the counterfactual was outside their mandate and *assumed* that counterfactual (3) would be WTO-consistent.[63] It is submitted that this approach is in error. An arbitral panel can and should satisfy itself that the counterfactual applied is WTO-consistent rather than simply assume that it is (as the majority and dissenter did in this case).[64] A comparison of the current WTO-inconsistent situation with another *WTO-inconsistent* counterfactual simply cannot yield an estimate of nullification and impairment. It is noteworthy that the arbitral panel provides no authority for its assertion that it cannot examine an issue which must be resolved in order to assess equivalence.[65]

Moreover, even accepting for the sake of argument that an assessment of the legality of the counterfactual used is outside the arbitral panel's mandate, we are still left with the question of why the arbitral panel made the assumption that the proposed counterfactual was *WTO-consistent* rather than *WTO-inconsistent*. The arbitral panel provides no reasoning in support of its choice of assumption.

[62] See, Appellate Body Report, *Korea–Various Measures on Beef* (DSR 2001:I, 5), para. 172 (noting that the use of less trade restrictive measures in certain contexts suggests that the use of stricter measures in other contexts may not be necessary).

[63] *US–Gambling* (Article 22.6), paras. 3.56–8, 3.67. [64] *Ibid.*, para. 3.67.

[65] Resolution of this issue must be an implicit part of the mandate of an arbitral panel to assess nullification and impairment under Article 22.6, DSU. For a ruling to the effect that an Article 22.6 arbitrator has the power to assess the WTO-consistency of an *implementation measure* because such an assessment is presupposed in the determination of nullification and impairment, see *EC–Bananas III (US)* (Article 22.6), paras. 4.3–15. This ruling was controversial because the EC argued that the proper forum to resolve this question was an Article 21.5 proceeding. No such argument can be made here. The WTO-consistency of a *counterfactual* cannot be resolved in Article 21.5 proceedings (which are limited to *actual* measures taken to comply/implementation measures).

Once the threshold of WTO-consistency is passed it is difficult to articulate a principle that can be used to choose between various WTO-consistent counterfactuals. Indeed, a GATT panel once concluded that the existence of multiple WTO-consistent options vitiates any attempt to measure trade effects.[66]

For now the only principle that is available is that the counterfactual must constitute a reasonable or plausible compliance scenario.[67] We also know that the 'most likely' form of compliance that would have been chosen by the implementing state is irrelevant.[68] Beyond that not much guidance is provided on this crucial issue.

In theory one could articulate a rule under which the counterfactual which generates the least amount of nullification and impairment must be preferred. This is the position adopted in English contract law. The rule is that where a contract contains a promise that can be performed in alternative ways, damages for breach are assessed on the assumption that the party in breach would have performed in the manner least advantageous to the party seeking compensation.[69] The underlying principle behind this approach could be that the retaliating state should not get more than it bargained for.[70] A different rule would be that the counterfactual which generates the highest amount of nullification and impairment must be preferred. The underlying principle could be that as long as the counterfactual used is WTO-consistent the choice of the retaliating state should not be disturbed. Arguably, the fact that this magnitude of retaliation is more likely to induce compliance could also support this rule.[71] The

66 In the *US–Superfund* case, the GATT panel observed that the existence of several possible options by which WTO members could come into compliance entailed that 'it is ... not logically possible to determine the ... trade impact from non observance of [the national treatment obligation]'. See GATT Panel Report, *US–Superfund*, L/6175 (adopted 17 June, 1987), GATT B.I.S.D. (34th Supp.), 136, para. 5.1.9.

67 *US–Gambling* (Article 22.6), para. 3.27. 68 *Ibid.*, para. 3.26.

69 See, Guenter Treitel, *The Law of Contract*, 11th edn. (London: Sweet & Maxwell, 2003), 958.

70 Compensation rationales are difficult to reconcile with the structure of the DSU, which does not allow for monetary remedies or practical means to obtain reparation. See, Thomas Sebastian, 'World Trade Organization Remedies and the Assessment of Proportionality: Equivalence and Appropriateness', *HILJ* 48 (2007), 337, 367–70 (citing many others).

71 I say 'arguably' because an inducing compliance rationale requires a focus on the incentives of the violating state and is difficult to reconcile with setting an upper bound on the level of retaliation derived from the harm suffered by the retaliating state. See, Robert Howse and Damien Neven, 'United States – Tax Treatment for "Foreign Sales Corporations" – Recourse to Arbitration by the United States Under Article 22.6 of the DSU and Article 4.11 of the SCM Agreement (WT/DS108/ARB) – A Comment', *World Trade Review*, 4 (2005), 101, 107.

arbitrators in *US–Gambling* simply refused to articulate a rule either way. In essence, they have chosen to leave the issue to the discretion of the arbitrators with all of the attendant uncertainty this creates. Concrete principles to guide this discretion are still to be developed.[72]

(ii) Choice of metric to measure nullification and impairment Arbitrators need to use a metric to measure the detrimental effects of the underlying violation. In theory, detrimental effects can be assessed using a variety of metrics, such as loss of profits, decreases in market share, number of jobs lost, increases in the burden of customs duties, etc.[73] In the leading *EC–Bananas III (US)* (Article 22.6) case, the arbitrators opted for a 'value-of-trade-blocked' metric[74] which derives the gross value of trade flows that are prevented on account of the measures in question.[75] Under this metric, an action that blocks a high value of trade causes more nullification and impairment than an action that blocks a low value of trade. Actions that block identical values of trade are equivalent.

The value-of-trade-blocked metric has been extraordinarily popular with arbitrators and WTO members. In the ten Article 22.6 arbitrations conducted to date, at least one party to the arbitration has argued for the use of this metric in one form or another. Arbitrators have applied this metric in all but one of the cases where the equality-of-harm approach was adopted.[76] In the *US–Byrd Amendment* (Article 22.6) case, the United States went so far as to argue that detrimental effects must always be measured by the 'trade effect' approach (that is, the value-of-trade-blocked metric). The arbitrators rejected the US argument, although they adopted the value-of-trade-blocked metric for the purposes of that case.

[72] To suggest one such principle: on practical grounds arbitrators should prefer WTO-consistent counterfactuals which have been previously implemented by the violating country over hypothetical counterfactuals which have never been implemented. In cases where a period of WTO-compliance preceded the violation arbitrators should use this historical experience as a baseline from which to construct the counterfactual. This 'historical worsening' approach reduces the need to make extensive assumptions about trade flows (which are inevitable when a counterfactual which has never been implemented by the violating country is used).

[73] *See*, Spamann, 37; Joel Trachtman, 'Bananas, Direct Effect and Compliance', *European Journal of International Law*, 10 (1999), 655, 673–4.

[74] *EC–Bananas III (US)* (Article 22.6), paras. 7.1, 6.12.

[75] Spamann terms this metric the 'trade effects comparator': Spamann, 39. The WTO Secretariat uses the phrase 'trade effects approach'. *World Trade Report 2005*, above, note 55, 180.

[76] The exception is the *US–1916* (Article 22.6) case, discussed below.

The arbitrators ruled that while the value-of-trade-blocked metric is *a* valid means of assessing detrimental effects, it is not the *only* means of assessing detrimental effects.[77] This ruling confirms that arbitrators are entitled to resort to alternative metrics.

Such an alternative metric was used in the *US–1916 Act* (Article 22.6) case, in which the arbitrators were asked to evaluate a proposal to apply legislation that mirrored the violation of WTO law. The arbitrators appear to have measured the violation in terms of an 'amount-of-monetary-costs-imposed' metric rather than the value-of-trade-blocked metric.[78] In the *US–Section 110(5) of the US Copyright Act* arbitration, the arbitrators measured the nullification and impairment caused by a US measure 'in terms of the royalty income forgone by EC right holders'.[79] They calculated this royalty income net of collection costs. This implies that the arbitrators were effectively using lost profits as the relevant metric.[80] In the *US–Softwood Lumber* cases, Canada's retaliation requests use excess antidumping duties collected as the relevant metric.[81]

An arbitral panel's choice of metric has significant effects on the structure of its equivalence analysis. Indeed, more than anything else, it is the choice of metric that tells us 'what' is being equalised under Article 22.4 of the DSU.

(iii) Nullification and impairment experienced by third countries

Arbitral panels also have to specify the entities whose position is relevant to their analysis of nullification and impairment. Do arbitrators have to limit themselves to the effects experienced by nationals of the retaliating state or can they consider the position of third country entities?

The arbitral panel in the *US–Byrd Amendment* (Article 22.6) case had to consider this question. In *Byrd*, the United States objected to what it viewed as an attempt by the complainants (with the exception of Chile) to include effects on third countries in the assessment of nullification and impairment. The United States argued that what was relevant to the task

[77] *US–Byrd Amendment* (Article 22.6), para. 3.70

[78] See, *US–1916 Act* (Article 22.6). paras. 5.58, 5.61 (calculating nullification and impairment in terms of 'cumulative dollar or monetary value').

[79] Award of the arbitrators, *United States–Section 110(5) of the US Copyright Act – Recourse to Arbitration under Article 25 of the DSU*, WT/DS160/ARB25/1 (9 November 2001) (DSR 2001:II, 667), para. 3.19.

[80] Spamann, 42.

[81] See, for example, *Recourse to Article 22.2 of the DSU by Canada*, WT/DS264/17, 20 May 2005.

of the arbitrator was the nullification and impairment experienced by the particular member seeking retaliation rather than third countries.[82] The arbitral panel accepted the US argument ruling that 'a Requesting Party may only request suspension of concessions or other obligations with respect to the trade effect caused by disbursements under the CDSOA *relating to its own exports*' (emphasis added).[83] As we shall see, this bilateral focus distinguishes the equality-of-harm approach from the amount-of-subsidy approach adopted in prohibited subsidies cases.

The principle that arbitrators must derive a value for the nullification and impairment suffered by the retaliating state, not third parties, will sometimes require allocation of the detrimental effects of a violation between multiple WTO members.[84] In practice, this is not always straightforward. In *Byrd* the reduced imports attributable to transfer payments under the Byrd Amendment were allocated among WTO members 'on the basis of the share of CDSOA disbursements attributable to duties collected on their particular exports'.[85] However, given that the effect of a transfer to a domestic firm is felt by *all competing exporters*, not just exporters located in countries subject to antidumping duties, it is at least arguable that this method of allocation is inaccurate and delivers excessive retaliation rights to the complainants. In *US–Gambling*, the arbitrator had to make a factual determination of which revenues from remote gambling activities could be deemed to be exports of Antigua rather than exports of other WTO members.[86]

(iv) Causation, remoteness and quantifiability In determining nullification and impairment, arbitrators also have to make assessments of whether there is a sufficient *causal link* between a claimed loss and the underlying violation. Only losses caused by the violation will be considered in the calculation of nullification and impairment. Losses attributable to other factors can be ignored. The following cases are instructive:

(1) In *Canada–Aircraft* (Article 22.6), Brazil argued that if Canada had withdrawn the export subsidies at issue a customer (Air Wisconsin) would have switched its sourcing and purchased aircraft from

[82] *US–Byrd Amendment* (Article 22.6) Panel, para. 3.147.

[83] *US–Byrd Amendment* (Article 22.6), para. 4.16. See also para. 3.147.

[84] The arbitrators in *EC–Bananas III (US)* can be read to have allocated the reduction in imports of bananas into the EC market to banana suppliers located in Latin American countries and away from agricultural input suppliers located in the United States.

[85] *US–Byrd Amendment* (Article 22.6), para. 3.148.

[86] *US–Gambling* (Article 22.6), paras. 3.96–8.

a Brazilian manufacturer. The arbitral panel concluded that, on the evidence presented, there was no demonstrated causal link between this loss and the grant of export subsidies by the Canadian government.[87]

(2) In *US–Gambling*, the United States argued that Antigua's estimates of nullification and impairment improperly attributed all of the revenue lost by Antiguan suppliers to the effects of the US measures without factoring in the impact of increased competition from suppliers located in other countries.[88] Based on the evidence before it, the arbitral panel agreed with this objection.[89] Estimates of remote gambling revenues lost by Antiguan suppliers were adjusted to account for losses that could not be attributed to the US measures but instead to increased competition from non-Antiguan suppliers.[90]

(3) In *EC–Hormones (US)* (Article 22.6), the United States argued that if the EC had lifted its import ban, US exporters would have embarked on marketing and promotional efforts and that these promotional efforts would have led to increased exports of edible beef offal worth $20.1 million. The arbitral panel refused to include these 'marketing effort driven' additional exports in its calculations, reasoning that taking these exports into account would be too 'speculative'.[91]

These causal link assessments are ultimately questions of fact and the result reached depends on the evidence presented to the panel regarding the impact of the underlying violation.

Distinct from this type of assessment, is the assessment of whether a claimed loss (which admittedly arises from the underlying violation) is too *remote* a consequence of the underlying violation to be included in the calculation of nullification and impairment. Arguably, *EC–Bananas III (US)* (Article 22.6), provides an illustration of this type of assessment. In that case, the United States contended that the EC's discriminatory measures had the effect of reducing its exports of agricultural inputs to certain Latin American countries and that these blocked exports should also be included in the arbitrator's calculations of nullification and impairment.[92]

[87] *Canada–Aircraft* (Article 22.6) (DSR 2003:III, 1187), paras. 3.22–3.

[88] *US–Gambling* (Article 22.6), paras. 3.127–8. [89] *Ibid.*, paras. 3.135–9, 3.170–1.

[90] *Ibid.*, paras. 3.181–3. [91] *EC–Hormones (US)* (Article 22.6), para. 77.

[92] The United States argued that if the EC removed its discriminatory measures, banana exports from Latin America would have increased and in turn exports of agricultural inputs from the United States to Latin America would have correspondingly increased. See, *EC–Bananas III (US)* (Article 22.6), para. 6.6.

Although other readings of the award are plausible, the result can be explained on the principle that the EC's measures did not worsen the conditions of competition between US agricultural input manufacturers and agricultural input manufacturers from other origins, and therefore could not be a *proximate* cause of the claimed losses.[93] The refusal to consider 'marketing effort driven' additional exports in *EC–Hormones (US)* (Article 22.6) could also be placed in this category as the arbitrators in that case made an alternative finding that those additional exports were too 'remote'.[94] The law on this point is still in its infancy. It is simply too early to extract general principles.

A final type of assessment is whether a claimed loss is capable of quantification. In the *US–1916 Act* (Article 22.6) case, the arbitrators were faced with the question of how to deal with two alleged effects of the underlying violation: (1) 'litigation costs' borne by European defendants while contesting proceedings under the 1916 Act; and (2) deterrent or 'chilling effects' on the commercial behaviour of European companies. The arbitral panel refused to include both of these effects in its calculations.[95] The arbitrators' ruling seems correct for the so-called 'chilling effect' on trade because it is impossible to quantify this effect using the 'amount-of-monetary-costs-imposed' metric it used in that case, but the ruling on litigation costs is difficult to understand. Litigation costs *are* capable of quantification in monetary terms.[96] Similarly, in *US–Gambling*, the arbitrator refused to include multiplier effects of the underlying violation on 'internal transactions within the Antiguan economy'[97] apparently on the ground that this was not measurable using the value-of-trade-blocked metric.[98] The answer to the question of quantifiability ultimately depends on the metric adopted by the arbitral panel and whether the claimed losses can be gauged by the adopted metric.

(v) Empirical issues Arbitrators have had to resolve a heterogeneous set of empirical questions when determining nullification and

[93] *Ibid.*, paras. 6.11–12. [94] *EC–Hormones (US)* (Article 22.6), para. 77.

[95] *US–1916 Act* (Article 22.6), para. 5.69.

[96] *Ibid.*, para. 5.76. The arbitrators fail to explain how the payment of fines can be understood as a loss of benefit accruing to a WTO member, while the payment of litigation costs cannot. The arbitrators also stated that the EC had not meaningfully quantified these effects because it did not provide 'an overall verifiable tabulation'. *Ibid.*, para. 5.77. The need for 'tabulation' is unclear given that the arbitrators themselves did not resort to any sort of historical tabulation of fines or settlements when they included claims relating to those items in their calculations. *Ibid.*, paras. 5.58–.63.

[97] *US–Gambling* (Article 22.6), para. 3.119. [98] *Ibid.*, para., 3.123.

impairment. I do not propose to describe how arbitrators have dealt with these types of questions in the cases decided (some are dealt with in other contributions to this volume, such as that by Bown and Ruta (Chapter 6)).[99] An early article stated that arbitrators' preferred extremely simple methods for assessing trade effects 'even if that means sacrificing some accuracy in determining the exact amount of damages'.[100] This statement, although completely accurate at the time it was made, needs to be revised in the light of the *US–Byrd Amendment* (Article 22.6) case where the arbitrators employed a complex econometric model to estimate the total decrease in exports that would result from cash transfers to the domestic industry, and the *US–Gambling* case which involved detailed discussion of empirical issues and extensive efforts to arrive at the most accurate results possible in the light of the data presented.

(vi) Changes over time Arbitrators derive an annual[101] figure for the level of nullification and impairment arising from the underlying violation as of the expiry of the RPT.[102] It is possible that the character of the underlying violation or the magnitude of its consequences can change after that date. For example, in a year following the expiry of the RPT, the amount of domestic support granted can increase radically or the impact of an import prohibition may increase with increased demand for the relevant commodity in the importing state. To accommodate subsequent changes of this type, retaliating states have on occasion requested a variable level of retaliation that takes into account subsequent changes. The arbitral panel in the *Byrd Amendment* case approved such a request and its award involves an equation that is updated on the basis of the most recent annual data.[103] A similar approach was adopted in the *US–1916 Act* case.[104]

[99] A good account is contained in *World Trade Report 2005*, above, note 55, 183–9.

[100] Jacob Bernstein and David Skully, 'Calculating Trade Damages in the Context of the World Trade Organization's Dispute Settlement Process', *Review of Agricultural Economics* 25 (2003), 385, 396.

[101] Arbitrators do not calculate the net present value of trade blocked over an extended time horizon. This is consistent with the view of retaliation as a temporary measure pending compliance rather than a final measure that fully resolves the dispute.

[102] See, for example, *US–Byrd Amendment* (Article 22.6), para. 4.21.

[103] *Ibid.*, paras. 4.20–3.

[104] See, *US–1916 Act* (Article 22.6), paras. 8.1–2, 9.1.

(ii) Calculation of nullification and impairment arising from retaliatory measures

Arbitral panels arrive at a figure for the nullification and impairment caused on account of the underlying violation. This figure prescribes the limit of nullification and impairment (in terms of the metric adopted by the arbitral panel) that can be caused through any retaliatory measures adopted by the retaliating state. The authorisation to retaliate from the DSB is also based on this figure.

If there is a future disagreement about whether subsequent retaliatory measures applied are within the scope of the authorisation granted by the DSB this matter can be referred to a panel. In those proceedings, the panel will have to make an assessment of whether the retaliatory measures are within the scope of the DSB authorisation *using the metric reflected in that authorisation*. The *EC–Bananas III (US)* case stands for the proposition that the same metric should be used to measure the effects of the underlying violation and the retaliatory response.[105]

This is easily done if the measure takes the form of an import prohibition or prohibitive duties on goods that block an annual value of trade equal to or lower than the value of trade blocked set out in the DSB authorisation. However, for retaliatory measures that take a different form, for instance, non-prohibitive tariffs on a value of trade larger than that set out in the DSB authorisation, the panel would have to assess annual nullification and impairment utilising the complex methods discussed above. Thus far, no such case has been brought but panels have often suggested to retaliating members that they opt for measures whose trade effects can be assessed fairly transparently.[106]

As Schropp points out in his contribution to this volume (chapter 20), it is procedurally more efficient to assess the nullification and impairment caused by the proposed retaliatory measures in the original Article 22.6 proceeding rather than in a subsequent and separate DSU proceeding.[107] Arbitral panels have interpreted Article 22.7 as preventing this type of assessment in certain cases but not in others.[108]

[105] See, *EC–Bananas III (US)* (Article 22.6), para. 7.1.

[106] See, for example, *US–Gambling* (Article 22.6), para. 5.10.

[107] Simon Schropp, 'The Equivalence Standard under Article 22.4 DSU: A "Tariffic" Misunderstanding?', chapter 20, below, part D.2.1.

[108] Compare *US–1916 Act* (Article 22.6), para. 7.4 (extreme version of the hands-off approach) with *EC–Hormones (US)* (Article 22.6), paras. 80–2 and Annex II (assessing components of the proposed retaliation).

(b) Other approaches

In two cases decided under the Article 22.4 equivalence standard, the *1916 Act* and *Byrd Amendment* cases, the complainants asked the arbitral panels to depart from the equality-of-harm approach. In both instances their attempts were rejected.

In the *US–1916 Act* (Article 22.6) case, the EC proposed an alternative 'qualitative' approach under which equivalence was to be assessed in terms of the *nature* of the measures themselves rather than their *effects*.[109] Using this approach, the EC argued that it was entitled to apply measures which mirrored the illegal measures taken by the United States. The US objection to this approach was that it provided no guarantee that the detrimental effects of the underlying violation of WTO law (the 1916 Act) and the proposed retaliation (the EC's mirror legislation) would be equal.[110] In essence, the United States argued that equivalence can be assessed *only* in terms of detrimental *effects*. The arbitrators accepted the US argument. In their view, the use of the term nullification and impairment in Article 22.4 of the DSU implies that an *effects-based* analysis is required.[111] Accordingly, because the qualitative approach provided no guarantee that the detrimental effects of its mirror legislation would not be greater than the detrimental effects caused by the US 1916 Act, the arbitrators refused to apply it.[112] This ruling raises the question of how to respond to illegal measures that do not result in adverse trade effects.

In the *Byrd Amendment* case, the complainants proposed to impose additional duties on US exports that were equal to the amount of impermissible subsidies that the United States granted to petitioners of successful antidumping actions (effectively the complainants requested the arbitral panel to treat the US measure like a prohibited subsidy and apply the amount-of-subsidy approach described below).[113] Here again, the arbitral panel refused to depart from the traditional equality-of-harm approach on the basis that what is relevant is the detrimental *effect* of the impermissible disbursements provided to US petitioners.[114]

A different approach to equivalence could ask the question: what magnitude of retaliatory measures would suffice to compensate for the

[109] *US–1916 Act* (Article 22.6), paras. 5.9–12, 5.17. [110] *Ibid.*, paras. 5.13–15.
[111] *Ibid.*, para. 5.23. [112] *Ibid.*, paras. 5.31–2, 5.34.
[113] *Byrd Amendment* (Article 22.6), paras. 3.10, 3.44
[114] *Ibid.*, paras. 3.53–5.

nullification and impairment suffered on an annual basis? In other words, the retaliatory response is equivalent as long as it does not generate compensatory rents that exceed the annual level of nullification and impairment. Cannizarro describes this type of countermeasure as an executive countermeasure where the 'respondent state ... produces by itself, through the breach of a different rule, the beneficial effect expected from its performance'.[115] Under this approach, the fact that retaliatory measures inflict greater nullification and impairment, measured in terms of value of trade blocked, on the violating state than that experienced by the retaliating state is irrelevant. All that matters is that the amount of additional duties or rents collected from nationals of the violating state does not exceed the level of nullification and impairment measured in terms of lost profits. The retaliation request filed by the EC in the *US–Section 110(5) Copyright Act* case contains traces of such an approach.[116] Whether this type of approach will be approved remains to be seen.

4 Magnitude II: the appropriateness standard in prohibited subsidies cases[117]

(a) *The amount-of-subsidy approach*

(i) Description of the approach

In prohibited subsidies cases decided under the Article 4.10 appropriateness standard, arbitrators have adopted what can be termed the 'amount-of-subsidy' approach.

This approach first emerged in the *Brazil–Aircraft* case.[118] The underlying violation in that case was the grant by the Brazilian government of prohibited export subsidies to its regional aircraft industry. In response, Canada requested authorisation to impose duties on exports of goods from Brazil of an amount equal to the total annual value of prohibited export subsidies that the Brazilian government granted to its regional

[115] Enzo Cannizarro, 'The Role of Proportionality in the Law of International Countermeasures', *European Journal of International Law*, 12 (2001), 888, 911.

[116] Recourse by the European Communities to Article 22.2 of the DSU, WT/DS160/19, 11 January 2002.

[117] For an economic analysis of this approach see Bown and Ruta, 'The Economics of Permissible WTO Retaliation', Chapter 6, below, part 4.

[118] *Brazil–Aircraft* (Article 22.6), para. 3.60.

aircraft industry. Thus, on the approach proposed by Canada, a retaliatory response is 'appropriate' within the meaning of Article 4.10 of the SCM Agreement when:

> {Value of trade from state V affected by state R's retaliatory response} = {Amount of subsidy involved in the underlying violation by state V}

Brazil vigorously contested Canada's approach and argued for the use of the equality-of-harm approach.[119] The arbitrators rejected Brazil's position and endorsed Canada's approach. The amount-of-subsidy approach was followed in two later cases, *US–FSC* and *Canada–Aircraft*.

The starting point of the calculation is the amount of the prohibited subsidy. In the *Brazil–Aircraft* case, the arbitral panel based its calculations of the amount of subsidy on the value of the *grants* provided by the Brazilian government under the PROEX scheme to the airlines purchasing the aircraft produced by Embraer.[120] In *US–FSC* the arbitral panel based its calculations on the amount of the *revenue forgone* by the US government to its enterprises pursuant to the ETI scheme.[121] In the *Canada–Aircraft* case, the arbitral panel calculated the amount of the subsidy on the basis of the *benefit* provided to Bombardier through the loan programmes offered by the Canadian government.[122] In all of these cases, calculations are based on the benefit to the recipient. In cases involving grants, such as *Brazil–Aircraft* and *US–FSC* the benefit to the recipient is equal to the value of the grant,[123] while in cases of loans on preferential terms, such as *Canada–Aircraft*, the benefit to recipient has to be calculated separately. Arbitral panels generate figures for the amount for the subsidy on the date of expiry of the reasonable period of time for implementation.[124]

Arbitrators applying this approach have the discretion to vary their award to adapt countermeasures 'to the particular case at hand'.[125] This discretion was used in *Canada–Aircraft* to add a 20 per cent top-up to the calculated subsidy amount in response to Canada's acknowledgement that it did not intend to withdraw the subsidy. The arbitral panel based this adjustment on what it called 'the "inducing compliance"

[119] *Ibid.*, paras. 3.23–6, 3.30. [120] *Brazil–Aircraft* (Article 22.6), para. 3.66.

[121] *US–FSC* (Article 22.6) (DSR 2002:VI, 2517), paras. 6.18–20 and Annex A.

[122] *Canada–Aircraft* (Article 22.6), paras. 3.52–64. [123] *Ibid.*, para. 3.61.

[124] See *Brazil–Aircraft* (Article 22.6), para. 3.93; *US–FSC* (Article 22.6), Annex A, para. A.1; *Canada–Aircraft* (Article 22.6), para. 3.90.

[125] *Ibid.*, para. 3.91.

function of countermeasures').[126] They reasoned that an upward variation of the level of countermeasures would assist in inducing compliance by Canada. The arbitrators acknowledged that this adjustment 'cannot be precisely calibrated'[127] or derived from a 'scientifically based formula'.[128]

Finally, arbitrators utilising this approach have permitted the retaliating state to respond for the entire amount of the subsidy. When confronted with the argument that the implication of this approach in cases involving more than one complainant is that a violating state may suffer retaliation in amounts that are multiples of the amount of the subsidy, they have responded that the issue was merely hypothetical and need not be resolved in the abstract. Arbitrators have indicated that if a concrete case arose the total amount of the subsidy would be allocated between complainants.[129] This is very different from the equality-of-harm approach in which considerable effort is invested in ensuring that only detrimental effects specifically experienced by the complaining state are considered in setting the magnitude of retaliation.

(ii) Justification of the approach

In the three cases decided to date, one party to the proceeding has argued against the amount-of-subsidy approach and requested the arbitral panel to adopt the equality-of-harm approach. However, these attempts have been unsuccessful (although it should be noted that the *Canada–Aircraft* panel did partially apply the equality-of-harm approach). In rejecting these attempts, arbitrators have latched on to two textual contrasts between Article 4.10 of the SCM Agreement and other provisions: (1) the absence of any reference to the concept of nullification and impairment in Article 4.10 of the SCM Agreement in contrast to Article 22.4 of the DSU;[130] and (2) the difference between Article 7.9 of the SCM Agreement, where the drafters used specific language to install a strict requirement of proportionality between the countermeasure and the detrimental effects of the subsidy, and Article 4.10 of the SCM Agreement, where no such language is to be found.[131] The arbitrators imply from these contrasts that the equality-of-harm approach need not be applied under Article 4.10 of the SCM Agreement.[132]

[126] *Ibid.*, para. 3.102. [127] *Ibid.*, para. 3.122. [128] *Ibid.*

[129] *US–FSC* (Article 22.6), paras. 6.26–29.

[130] *Brazil–Aircraft* (Article 22.6), paras. 3.46–47.

[131] *Ibid.*, para. 3.49. [132] *Ibid.*, paras. 3.51, 3.57.

Having concluded that the equality-of-harm approach is not *necessary*, arbitrators still needed to resolve the issue of what the standard of appropriateness demands and how the adoption of the amount-of-subsidy approach ensures that the resulting retaliation is somehow 'appropriate'. On this fundamental issue the reasoning of these arbitral panels is muddled and ultimately unconvincing.

In *Brazil–Aircraft*, the arbitrators provided only one comment about the substantive content of the term 'appropriate': 'We conclude that a countermeasure is "appropriate" *inter alia* if it *effectively* induces compliance.'[133] However, the award contained no further reasoning as to why, in general terms, countermeasures affecting trade of value equal to the total amount of the prohibited subsidy would be sufficient to induce Brazil to withdraw the subsidy. The inducing compliance standard, therefore, does not provide an adequate justification for the approach proposed by Canada and used by the arbitrators. The arbitrators did not attempt to provide any further legal justification for the approach adopted, but they may have been influenced by the argument that the trade effects of the subsidies are presumptively greater than the amount of the subsidy itself and, therefore, the amount-of-subsidy approach generates a lower number than the equality-of-harm approach.[134]

In *US–FSC*, the arbitral panel framed the issue in an incredibly obtuse way: that is, whether countermeasures become appropriate if 'they are aimed at neutralising the original wrongful action, its effects or both'.[135] Based on the language of footnote 9 of the SCM Agreement, the arbitrators arrived at the conclusion that the countermeasure need not aim at neutralising *the effects* of the measure.[136] In what sense countermeasures '*neutralise*' an 'original wrongful action' and how this justifies countermeasures which inflict detrimental effects on the violating state that are wholly out of proportion to the detrimental effects experienced by the complaining state is simply not explained. The convoluted reasoning in *US–FSC* does not inspire any confidence.[137]

[133] *Ibid.*, para. 3.44.

[134] See, *Brazil–Aircraft* (Article 22.6), para. 3.20. The arbitral panel also noted that the amount-of-subsidy approach was easier to apply than alternative approaches.

[135] See *US–FSC* (Article 22.6), paras. 5.6, 5.13, 5.19, 5.23, 6.11.

[136] See *US–FSC* (Article 22.6), para. 5.23, last sentence.

[137] See Robert Howse and Damien Neven, 'United States – Tax Treatment for "Foreign Sales Corporations" – Recourse to Arbitration by the United States Under Article 22.6 of the DSU and Article 4.11 of the SCM Agreement (WT/DS108/ARB) – A Comment', *World Trade Review* 4 (2005), 101, 109.

Moreover, the *Canada–Aircraft* panel did not develop any new reasoning on this question. The divergence in the approaches adopted by arbitral panels appears to be driven by a desire to avoid difficult empirical questions. However, one can expect that this divergence will come under pressure in future cases. A reconfiguration of the jurisprudence and the adoption of consistent approaches across Article 22.4 of the DSU, Article 4.10 of the SCM Agreement and Article 7.9 of the SCM Agreement is possible.

(b) Other approaches

It is important to note that the equality-of-harm approach can be used under Article 4.10 of the SCM Agreement. Indeed, in *Canada–Aircraft*, the arbitral panel first attempted to use the equality-of-harm approach before it eventually opted for the amount-of-subsidy approach.

5. Magnitude III: the commensurate standard in serious prejudice cases

Article 7.9 of the SCM Agreement specifies that in cases involving actionable subsidies countermeasures must be '*commensurate*' with the degree and nature of the adverse effects determined to exist. This standard has not yet been applied by an arbitral panel. The request filed by Brazil in the *US–Cotton* dispute is expected to proceed to arbitration shortly[138] and will be the first case in which an arbitral panel will have to apply the commensurate standard.

6. Form: the disciplines on cross-retaliation

(a) Overview: no hop, one hop, two hops

Under the scheme developed in Article 22.3 of the DSU, every violation of WTO law involves a particular 'agreement' and 'sector(s)'. If the retaliatory measure involves suspension of obligations under the same agreement and the same sector(s) as the underlying violation no difficulty arises. However, when a WTO member seeks to suspend obligations under a different sector or a different agreement, the disciplines of Article 22.3 are relevant. To illustrate: if the underlying violation is a measure which denies patent

[138] *Recourse to Article 7.9 of the SCM Agreement and Article 22.2 of the DSU by Brazil*, WT/DS267/26, 7 October 2005.

rights in breach of Article 28 of the TRIPS Agreement (agreement: TRIPS, sector: Section 5 of TRIPS) and the retaliatory response takes the form of a measure which limits the term of protection granted to patent holders in breach of Article 33 of the TRIPS Agreement (agreement: TRIPS, sector: Section 5 of TRIPS) this is not a case of cross-retaliation and the requirements of Article 22.3 are irrelevant. However, if the retaliatory response takes the form of a measure imposing an import ban on goods in breach of Article XI:1 of the GATT 1994 (agreement: GATT 1994, sector: all goods) then a question of cross-retaliation arises and the requirements of Article 22.3 must be complied with.

The disciplines on cross-retaliation seek to control the circumstances under which WTO members can 'hop', so to speak, across sectors and agreements when imposing retaliation. Article 22.3(b) permits retaliation in a different sector within the same agreement (one hop) only if retaliation in the same sector is considered not to be 'practicable or effective'. Moreover, under Article 22.3(c), retaliation is permitted under another agreement (two hops), only if retaliation in a different sector within the same agreement is considered not to be 'practicable or effective' and 'the circumstances are serious enough'. For every 'hop' across sectors or agreements Article 22.3(d) requires members to take into account certain matters enumerated therein.

(b) Scope of review

Article 22.3 contains language which implies that this provision does not establish substantive obligations. It refers to 'principles and procedures' rather than to obligations. The use of the term 'if that party considers' in the operative subparagraphs (b) and (c) implies that they have a self-judging character. Subparagraph (d) imposes a requirement to 'take into account' certain matters rather than a constraint on the content of retaliatory action. It is not surprising, therefore, that retaliating states have argued that Article 22.3 imposes 'no substantive conditions' and that an arbitral panel has only a limited remit of ascertaining whether the retaliating state has taken into account specified matters and whether it has arrived at certain conclusions but cannot query the basis for those conclusions.[139]

[139] *EC–Bananas III (Ecuador)* (Article 22.6), para. 47. In contrast, the EC, the violating state in the *EC–Bananas III* case, took the position that 'objective and reviewable evidence' must be provided to demonstrate that same sector/agreement retaliation is 'not practicable or effective' and the 'circumstances are serious enough'. *Ibid.*, para. 48.

Arbitral panels have not accepted this line of argument. Instead, they have carved out a limited but nonetheless significant jurisdiction for themselves. While they have recognised that the retaliating state has a 'certain margin of appreciation', arbitral panels have reserved the 'authority to broadly judge whether the [retaliating state] has considered the necessary facts objectively and whether on the basis of these facts, it could plausibly arrive at the conclusion that it was not practicable or effective to seek suspension within the same sector under the same agreements, or only under another agreement provided that the circumstances were serious enough'.[140] As a consequence, arbitral panels can review conclusions reached by a retaliating state regarding the practicality or effectiveness of alternative retaliatory measures. This review is limited to the question of whether the conclusion reached by the retaliating state is a plausible one (in the light of an objective consideration of the necessary facts).[141]

The power to draw the line between plausible and implausible conclusions is by no means trivial. Ecuador discovered this in the *EC–Bananas III (Ecuador)* case when its conclusion that the suspension of concessions on consumer goods was not practicable and effective was deemed by the arbitral panel to be one that 'Ecuador could not plausibly arrive at' given the absence of 'further argumentation' regarding welfare losses to end-consumers.[142] But this is the only instance to date in which a request to cross-retaliate was rejected, albeit only in part.

(c) Practicability and effectiveness

In the *EC–Bananas III (Ecuador)* case, the arbitral panel examined the criteria of 'practicability' and 'effectiveness' in subparagraphs (b) and (c) of Article 22.3. The arbitral panel noted that the 'practicability' assessment involves the question of whether an alternative suspension is 'available for application in practice, as well as suited for being used in a

[140] *EC–Bananas III (Ecuador)* (Article 22.6), para. 52; *US–Gambling* (Article 22.6), paras. 4.15–18.

[141] At least some of the parties to the negotiations that yielded Article 22.3 would be troubled by the scope of review that arbitral panels have accorded to themselves on these matters. The language of Article 22.3(b) and (c) of the DSU clearly reflects an attempt by the parties to leave the question of whether the conditions described in subparagraphs (b) and (c) are met to the retaliating state and no one else. See Minutes of the DSB Meeting, 7 April 2000, Statement by the United States, paras. 44–5.

[142] *EC–Bananas III (Ecuador)* (Article 22.6), para. 100.

particular case',[143] while the 'effectiveness' assessment involves the question of whether 'the impact of [the alternative suspension] is strong and has the desired result, namely to induce compliance by the member which fails to bring WTO-inconsistent measures into compliance with DSB rulings within a reasonable period of time'.[144] These observations were endorsed by the arbitral panel in the *US–Gambling* (Article 22.6) case.[145] In practice, arbitral panels do not segregate the 'practicability' assessment from the 'effectiveness' assessment.[146]

The following is a listing of some of the factors that arbitral panels have considered relevant to the assessment of whether alternative suspension is effective and/or practicable:

(a) *Absence of obligations*: if the retaliating state has no commitments in a particular sector this indicates that suspension in that sector is not effective and/or practicable.[147] In practice, this will rarely, if ever, be the case.[148]
(b) *Detriment to the retaliating state*: the fact that alternative suspension entails detriment to the retaliating state suggests that it is likely to be ineffective and/or impracticable.[149] Suspension which increases the cost of goods and services or restricts their availability causes detriment.[150] The same holds true for measures that distort the investment climate.[151] Status as a developing country or a small economy will be relevant in assessing detriment.[152]
(c) *Practical difficulties in implementation*: alternative suspension that cannot be given effect to, for instance, because of administrative and technical difficulties,[153] or conflicts with rights conferred under domestic law and other international treaties[154] can, for this reason, be deemed to be ineffective and/or impracticable.

[143] *Ibid.*, para. 70. [144] *Ibid.*, para. 72. [145] *US–Gambling* (Article 22.6), para. 4.29.
[146] See, for example, *EC–Bananas III (Ecuador)* (Article 22.6), paras. 96, 100, 104, 120; *US–Gambling* (Article 22.6), paras. 4.56, 4.60, 4.99.
[147] *EC–Bananas III (Ecuador)* (Article 22.6), para. 103.
[148] See *US–Gambling* (Article 22.6), paras. 4.44–5. Henning Grosse-Russe Khan, 'A Pirate of the Caribbean? The Attraction of Suspending TRIPs Obligations', *Journal of International Economic Law*, 11 (2008), 313, 344–5.
[149] See *EC–Bananas III (Ecuador)* (Article 22.6), para. 73; *US–Gambling* (Article 22.6), para. 4.89.
[150] *EC–Bananas III (Ecuador)* (Article 22.6), paras. 91–102; *US–Gambling* (Article 22.6), paras. 4.89–99.
[151] *EC–Bananas III (Ecuador)* (Article 22.6), paras. 110–12.
[152] *Ibid.*, paras, 94, 110; *US–Gambling* (Article 22.6), paras. 4.89, 4.98.
[153] *EC–Bananas III (Ecuador)* (Article 22.6), paras. 114–17.
[154] *Ibid.*, para. 113; *US–Gambling* (Article 22.6), para. 4.98.

(d) *Limited impact on the violating state*: alternative suspension that has no perceptible impact on the violating state, for instance, because the value of trade affected by it is insignificant,[155] or far less than the magnitude of retaliation authorised[156] or accounts for a negligible proportion of the violating state's overall exports[157] can, for this reason, be deemed to be ineffective and/or impracticable.[158]

While arbitral panels have relied on these factors to arrive at particular outcomes, there is little clarity on the weight to be attributed to individual factors or the relationship between these factors. For instance, Ecuador was required to suspend concessions on consumer goods on the basis that detriment to Ecuador was not established.[159] However, it seems apparent that suspension of concessions on consumer goods, like the suspension of concessions on primary goods and investment goods, would have only a marginal impact on the EC (Ecuador probably accounts for a 'negligible proportion'[160] of EC consumer goods exports). No attempt was made to explain why, in that instance, no weight was placed on the absence of impact on the violating state (the EC), while dispositive weight was placed on the absence of detriment to the retaliating state (Ecuador).

It is worth noting that arbitral panels do not assess whether the proposed cross-retaliation is *more* effective or practicable than retaliation in the same sector/agreement. Nor do they assess whether the proposed cross-retaliation will be effective and practicable for the complaining party.[161] Thus, there is no comparative dimension in the analysis.

(d) 'Circumstances are serious enough'

Article 22.3(c) provides that before suspending concessions or obligations under another agreement, the retaliating state must consider that the 'circumstances are serious enough'. As the arbitral panel in *US–Gambling* recognised, the text of Article 22.3(c) 'provides no express guidance [on] how this aspect of the determination is to be understood'.[162] It noted that whether the circumstances are serious enough must be assessed on a case-by-case basis and what is relevant will vary from case to case[163] and that the factors

[155] *US–Gambling* (Article 22.6), paras. 4.55–60. [156] *Ibid.*, paras. 4.24, 4.78, 4.82.
[157] *EC–Bananas III (Ecuador)* (Article 22.6), para. 95.
[158] *US–Gambling* (Article 22.6), paras. 4.934, 4.97.
[159] *EC–Bananas III (Ecuador)* (Article 22.6), paras. 100–2. [160] *Ibid.*, para. 95.
[161] *Ibid.*, para. 127. [162] *US–Gambling* (Article 22.6), para. 4.107. [163] *Ibid.*, para. 4.108.

listed in Article 22.3(d) may be relevant.[164] It is apparent that it is not possible to give determinate content to this wholly undefined requirement. In the cases decided to date, arbitral panels have simply accepted that the factors put forward by retaliating states allow them to 'plausibly make' a determination that 'the circumstances are serious enough'.[165]

Nevertheless, arbitral panels have signalled that they can rule – in a future case – that 'circumstances' have not reached the required 'degree or level of importance' to be considered 'serious enough' within the meaning of Article 22.3(c).[166] On what basis this assessment will be made remains a mystery.

(e) *Matters to be taken into account*

Article 22.3(d) provides a list of factors that the retaliating state 'shall take into account' while applying the principles set out in Article 22.3(a)–(c). Compliance with this requirement can be demonstrated without much difficulty. In *US–Gambling* the arbitral panel ruled that the arguments presented by Antigua on practicability and effectiveness demonstrated that it had considered the factors listed in Article 22.3(d).[167] In *EC–Bananas III (Ecuador)* assertions made by Ecuador to the arbitral panel regarding the importance of the banana sector to its economy, the economic situation in Ecuador and the limited consequences of retaliation for the EC sufficed to demonstrate that Ecuador had considered the factors enumerated in Article 22.3(d).[168]

To summarise, despite self-judging language in Article 22.3, arbitrators have assumed (or perhaps usurped) the jurisdiction of assessing whether the conclusions reached by retaliating states are 'plausible'. In carrying out this assessment they have not followed a single rule or methodology but have preferred to rely on a loose assortment of factors. In the two cases decided to date panels have been deferential but reserved their ability to intervene in future cases.

7 The purpose of retaliation

In general, arbitrators have refused to enter into means–ends calculations about whether retaliation suffices to bring about a particular outcome;

[164] *EC–Bananas III (Ecuador)* (Article 22.6), paras. 121–2; *US–Gambling* (Article 22.6), para. 4.107.

[165] See *US–Gambling* (Article 22.6), paras. 4.109–15.

[166] *Ibid.*, para. 4.108.

[167] *Ibid.*, paras. 4.61–4, 4.101–4.

[168] *EC–Bananas III (Ecuador)* (Article 22.6), paras. 128–37.

for instance, compliance while setting the magnitude of retaliation. Notwithstanding the frequent references to the inducing compliance rationale in the jurisprudence,[169] this rationale has had little influence on the calculations of the magnitude of equivalent or appropriate retaliation. The only exception to this statement is the *Canada–Aircraft* case where the objective of inducing compliance was utilised to add a 20 per cent increase over the figure generated by the amount-of-subsidy approach. However, in general, arbitrators have adopted a comparative rather than an instrumental approach to proportionality. Thus, while the case law frequently refers to inducing compliance as the purpose of retaliation, the actual methods used by arbitrators do not depend on a view of the proper purpose of retaliation.

In *US–Byrd Amendment*, the arbitral panel observed that 'it is not completely clear what role is to be played by the suspension of obligations in the DSU and a large part of the conceptual debate that took place in these proceedings could have been avoided if a clear "object and purpose" were identified'.[170] The implication here is that clarification of a single object and purpose of retaliation would help to resolve the issues confronted in particular cases. This is doubtful. If WTO members miraculously agreed to endorse an authoritative interpretation that clarified that the objective of retaliation is to (1) induce compliance, or (2) provide compensation, or (3) rebalance the bargain, or (4) facilitate efficient breach, arbitral panels would still confront significant difficulties.[171] Conceptual clarification is unlikely to radically simplify the task of arbitrators for a variety of practical reasons.

169 In the early Article 22.6 cases, arbitrators stated that *the* function of retaliation is to 'induce compliance'. *EC–Bananas III (US)* (Article 22.6) para. 6.3; *EC–Hormones (US)* (Article 22.6), para. 40; *EC–Hormones (Canada)* (Article 22.6), para. 76; *EC–Bananas III (Ecuador)* (Article 22.6), para. 76. In subsequent prohibited subsidies disputes, arbitrators observed that *one* of the functions of retaliation is to induce compliance. See, for example, *Brazil–Aircraft* (Article 22.6), para. 3.44; *US–FSC* (Article 22.6), para. 5.52; *Canada–Aircraft* (Article 22.6), paras. 3.47, 3.105, 3.107. This position was reiterated in the *US–1916 Act* (Article 22.6) case where the arbitrator noted that although other purposes may exist, inducing compliance is 'the key objective' of retaliation. *US–1916 Act* (Article 22.6), para. 5.5. By contrast, in the *US–Byrd Amendment* (Article 22.6) case, the panel observed that it was not persuaded that inducing compliance is the sole function of retaliation and noted that this may be 'only one of a number of purposes' in authorising retaliation. *US–Byrd Amendment* (Article 22.6), para. 3.74. Most recently, in *US–Gambling* (Article 22.6), the arbitral panel described 'inducing compliance' as '*the* purpose' of retaliation. *Ibid.*, para. 2.7.

170 *US–Byrd Amendment* (Article 22.6), para. 6.4.

171 An account of possible purposes of the WTO remedial regime is developed in Thomas Sebastian, 'World Trade Organization Remedies and the Assessment of Proportionality: Equivalence and Appropriateness', *Harvard International Law Journal*, 48 (2007), 337, 364–81.

Consider the following practical difficulties. If retaliation is to be set on the basis of an *inducing compliance rationale* the arbitrator would need information about the magnitude of retaliatory measures that would just suffice to force another WTO member to bring itself into compliance. This information cannot be obtained.[172] Similarly, in order to *rebalance the bargain*, arbitrators would, in theory, need precise information about a particular bilateral exchange of promises between the violating state and the retaliating state – they would need to know what obligation the retaliating state undertook in exchange for the promise by the violating state that has been breached on account of the underlying violation. Again, this information is simply not available because trade negotiations are not carried out in a manner that generates this type of bilateral bargain.[173] In order to *facilitate efficient breach* (understood as creating precise incentives to maximise joint political welfare) arbitrators would need to know 'political exchange rates' so to speak which would enable them to convert trade effects of measures into political welfare. These exchange rates are impossible to determine. As far as the *compensation rationale* is concerned, apart from the considerable difficulty in arriving at an amount of compensation in monetary terms for a sector as a whole, there is also the almost insurmountable difficulty of obtaining payment through trade sanctions (in contrast to a system that does provide for monetary awards enforceable though domestic courts).

It is submitted that particular theories about the purposes of the WTO remedial regime should not be used to evaluate individual arbitral awards unless: (1) arbitrators can give effect to the prescriptions of the theory; and (2) the theory is coherent with the structure of the DSU. If a theory does not meet these conditions then one is effectively criticising arbitrators for failing to achieve the impossible. In the absence of theoretical benchmarks, arbitral awards can be assessed only according to fairly minimalist standards. These include whether an award respects process norms, whether the approach adopted is justified by the text and whether the award is internally consistent. Beyond this, one must accept that arbitrators have a good deal of discretion. As we have seen, the treaty texts are ambiguous on crucial issues and effectively leave it to arbitrators to craft their own solutions.

172 See *Canada–Aircraft* (Article 22.6), para. 3.48.

173 Thomas Sebastian, 'World Trade Organization Remedies and the Assessment of Proportionality: Equivalence and Appropriateness', *Harvard International Law Journal* 48 (2007), 337, 370–4.

All too often, WTO members and commentators fail to acknowledge the inescapable discretion involved in the arbitrator's task. Consider the reaction to the arbitral panel's decision in the *Canada–Aircraft* (Article 22.6) case to award a 20 per cent premium in response to Canada's declaration that it did not intend to withdraw the illegal export subsides it had granted to its regional aircraft industry. This premium was subject to scathing criticism by Canada,[174] the United States[175] and the academic community.[176] However, Canada itself had requested the same arbitral panel to exercise discretion and *lower* its award, that is, to award a discount rather than a premium.[177] In light of its posture in the case, it was disingenuous for Canada to contend that an arbitral panel has no discretion to vary its award in the light of broader circumstances. The further objection that the 20 per cent figure was based on a subjective choice by the arbitrator fails to acknowledge the reality that, given the gaps left in the treaty text by the negotiators, arbitrators must invariably make subjective assessments regarding almost every aspect of an Article 22.6 award from the choice of approach, to the counterfactual, choice of metric, etc. The reality is that the arbitrators are exercising a discretionary authority that has been conferred on them by the drafters of the DSU. The process is more like a judge exercising sentencing discretion than an accountant preparing annual accounts for a company. In public international law it has long been recognised that 'judging the proportionality of counter-measures is not an easy task and can at best be accomplished by approximation'.[178] WTO members appear to be less willing to recognise this reality.

Conclusion

As this survey has shown, arbitral panels have been broadly consistent in the basic approaches that they have adopted under specific provisions of the DSU and the SCM Agreement. The equality-of-harm approach has

[174] See, Dispute Settlement Body Minutes of Meeting, 18 March, 2003, WT/DSB/M/145, paras. 45–7.

[175] *Ibid.*, para. 49 (statement by the United States).

[176] See, for example, Robert Lawrence, *Crimes and Punishments? Retaliation under the WTO* (Washington, DC: Peterson Institute, 2003), 58.

[177] *Canada–Aircraft* (Article 22.6), paras. 3.91, 3.93.

[178] See *Air Services Agreement of 27 March 1946 (United States* v. *France)*, R.I.A.A, vol. XVIII (1979), 416, para. 84.

been utilised in all cases conducted pursuant to the Article 22.4 equivalence standard, while the amount-of-subsidy approach has been utilised in all cases conducted pursuant to the SCM Agreement's Article 4.10 appropriateness standard. However, it is likely that arbitrators will come under some pressure in future cases to adopt uniform approaches across these provisions (notwithstanding differences in the wording used in the DSU and the SCM Agreement).

As far as the magnitude of retaliation is concerned, arbitrators have been reluctant to grant extensive retaliation rights. In all but one case, arbitrators have reduced the amount of retaliation authorised by more than 50 per cent. These reductions have been accomplished by a variety of means, including altering the basic approach advocated by the requesting state, varying the counterfactual used, excluding certain claimed losses from the calculation or arriving at different empirical results. One marked tendency over time has been to render awards with increased amounts of transparency regarding empirical issues. While the *EC–Bananas III* awards contain a result and not much else, the *US–Gambling* award presents calculations in considerable detail. One can expect that more sophisticated empirical methods will be used in future cases.

As far as the form of retaliation is concerned, arbitrators have been fairly deferential and have permitted almost all requests for cross-retaliation. However, the fact remains that even this deferential review arguably goes beyond what was envisaged by the negotiators of the DSU.

Ultimately the awards to date reflect an attempt by arbitrators to make sense of an open-ended mandate and develop a series of principles to guide their assessments of proportionality. Given the open texture of the standards involved and the limited number of awards so far, there remains considerable room for refinement and development in this area of law. As a consequence, the snapshot of the law developed in this chapter will certainly require revision in the years to come.

Comment on chapter 4

NICOLAS LOCKHART*

1 Introduction

This Comment was prepared for the workshop on trade sanctions, which represents another excellent initiative of the Graduate Institute, organized by Chad Bown, Joost Pauwelyn and Simon Schropp. The workshop turnout – mixing academics, delegates to the WTO and WTO Secretariat staff, as well as lawyers and economists – shows that the topic is one of considerable practical importance, and also one that raises many difficult legal and economic questions.

Tom Sebastian has presented us with a superb chapter introducing the case law to date. Describing the case law under Article 22 in a comprehensive and systematic way, as Tom does, is no mean feat. First, the treaty text is, as Tom puts it, 'sparse', and does not offer either a clear structure or clear rules, and, second, many difficult questions arise: what do we mean by harm or, in the words of the treaty, 'nullification or impairment'? What types of harm are relevant? How do we measure harm? Which time period matters? What is the relevance of the nature of the measure? What is the relevance of the nature of the violated obligation? The list goes on.

In sum, it is often easier to decide that a measure is contrary to a WTO obligation than it is to decide on a very precise amount of harm resulting from that measure. Yet, that is the task of arbitrators – to quantify exactly, in numerical terms, the amount of harm or, in subsidy cases, typically the amount of a subsidy. Tom's chapter does a great job of providing a structure for sorting our thoughts, answering many of the questions and highlighting new approaches that might be taken in future cases.

* The views expressed are the personal views of the author, as of the time of writing. I appreciate the comments that I have received from Jan Bohanes, Todd Friedbacher, Yves Renouf and Simon Schropp.

In my comments, I plan to address four topics: (1) the current state of development of Article 22; (2) the considerations influencing the arbitrator's choice of methodology (or metric) for measuring harm; (3) the WTO-consistency of the arbitrator's chosen counterfactual; and (4) straightforward steps that could be taken to improve the flow of information to arbitrators.

2 Article 22.6 of the DSU: still in the early stages of development

I would like to begin with a comment on where we are in the development of Article 22. To date, the dispute settlement system has been very successful at resolving disputes. Although there have been hundreds of formal complaints, there have been Article 22.6 arbitrations in just ten separately numbered WTO disputes, and these have involved a narrow group of only eight measures.[1] Seven of those eight arbitrations involved 'as such' measures, and just one involved an 'as applied' measure. Three of the eight arbitrations involved prohibited export subsidies.[2] This is a tiny number of cases from which to draw firm conclusions.

As a result, I believe that we are still in the early stages of development under Article 22.6. In a sense, we are probably a bit like early cartographers. We have more or less traced the outlines of the territory, we have identified the major rivers and we know, roughly, in what direction they flow. But we have too little experience to complete the map at the moment because there are still major questions that have not been posed – far less resolved. For example, none of the disputes has, as yet, addressed a very basic measure involving excessive customs duties. I will return to this example in a moment.

A second point about today's map is that arbitrators seem to approach each case very much on its own merits. They seem to be more interested in reaching an outcome they think is equitable on the facts than in establishing perfectly coherent case law. As a result, the outlines of the map have not been traced in a uniform way.

[1] *Brazil–Aircraft*, *Canada–Aircraft II*, *EC–Bananas III*, *EC–Hormones*, *US–1916 Act*, *US–Byrd Amendment*, *US–FSC* and *US–Gambling*. In *EC–Hormones* (WT/DS26 (DSR 1999:III, 1105) and WT/DS48 (DSR 1999:III, 1135)) and *US–Byrd Amendment* (WT/DS217 (DSR 2004:IX, 4591) and WT/DS234 (DSR 2004:IX, 4425)), separate WTO disputes examined the same measure. In addition, in *US–Section 110* (DSR 2001:II, 667), nullification or impairment was assessed in an arbitration conducted pursuant to Article 25 of the DSU.

[2] *Brazil–Aircraft*, *Canada–Aircraft II* and *US–FSC*.

What does this mean? My own conclusion is that we should read the case law with an open mind, recognizing that there is still a lot of unknown territory out there. We may well find that in 5 or 10 years' time the map looks different. Indeed, the map may never be complete.

3 Choice of metric for assessing nullification or impairment: the punishment should fit the crime

In four arbitrations, arbitrators assessed nullification or impairment using a metric based on 'lost exports'.[3] In two arbitrations,[4] the metric was based on the direct 'economic cost' sustained by commercial operators.[5] This immediately raises questions: when is 'lost exports', rather than 'economic cost', the appropriate metric? Are these metrics mutually exclusive alternatives or can they be applied cumulatively? Are there other metrics that could be appropriate?

Nothing in the covered agreements specifies how nullification or impairment should be measured. 'Lost exports' is not blessed as the default option; 'economic cost' is not prescribed as an alternative; and no other metrics are excluded. Arbitrators, therefore, have a degree of discretion to select an appropriate metric.

So far, how have arbitrators decided what is an appropriate metric? To some extent, the approach may be captured by the maxim that the 'punishment should fit the crime'. The crime scene here comprises the nature of the measure at issue and the nature of the obligation violated. Together, these two factors seem to influence the choice of metric.

In cases where the WTO-inconsistent *measure restricted the volume of exports* from the retaliating member, the metric was based on the value of the lost exports. The four measures were: an import ban (*Hormones*); a quota (*Bananas*); disbursements of duties to domestic producers (*Byrd Amendment*); and a ban on cross-border services (*Gambling*).

In cases where the *measure resulted in direct economic costs* for commercial operators, the metric was based on the amount of those costs. The two measures were: judicially sanctioned or litigation settlement

[3] *EC–Bananas III*, *EC–Hormones* (WT/DS26 and WT/DS48), *US–Byrd Amendment* (WT/DS217 and WT/DS234) and *US–Gambling*.

[4] *US–1916 Act* and *US–Section 110* (nullification or impairment was assessed in an arbitration conducted pursuant to Article 25 of the DSU).

[5] In prohibited subsidy cases the metric has so far been the 'amount of subsidy' (*Brazil–Aircraft*, *US–FSC* and *Canada–Aircraft II*). However, arbitrators have indicated that other metrics may be appropriate for assessing 'appropriate countermeasures'.

payments by exporters (*1916 Act*); and lost royalties by copyright holders (*Copyright*). In these cases, there was no evidence provided to demonstrate that the measures had resulted in lost exports.

In the circumstances of these cases, in view of the nature of the measures, the obligations violated and the evidence submitted, these metrics seem appropriate. However, given that the cases address just six measures, it is unlikely that these metrics exhaust the universe of appropriate metrics.

For example, there may be situations where it is appropriate to *combine* the two metrics. Imagine that a member has a zero-rated bound tariff, but imposes a 10 per cent duty. In that case, the violation of the bound tariff engenders two consequences. First, the higher tariff will restrict export volumes by a quantifiable amount that should be part of the calculus of nullification or impairment. This is a measurement of harm in terms of *trade that does not occur* because of the measure. Second, despite the 10 per cent tariff, some imports may take place. Nonetheless, harm is sustained because duties are paid on this *trade that does occur.* The overpayment of duties is very much part of the nullification or impairment resulting from violation of the tariff binding, and must be included in the calculus. Thus, in this situation, the two metrics used separately in previous cases – lost exports and economic cost – should be combined in some way.

Given that such a basic tariff measure leads us to rethink how we apply the existing metrics, it is very likely that other measures will also make us look beyond the metrics that arbitrators have so far developed. In sum, different types of harm flow from different types of measure, violating different types of obligation. The metrics arbitrators have used so far are unlikely to capture all of these different situations.

4 The choice of counterfactual: the arbitrators temporary solution must be WTO-consistent

My second comment concerns the choice of counterfactual. This choice is crucially important because it sets the benchmark for assessing the level of harm caused by a WTO-inconsistent measure. I agree fully with Tom that the benchmark for assessing harm must be a WTO-consistent counterfactual, and that the arbitrators in *Gambling* committed a serious error of law in refusing to ensure that their chosen counterfactual was WTO-consistent.

If an implementing member fails to comply with WTO law, the retaliating member is entitled to suspend concessions (or other obligations) up to the amount of nullification or impairment. The term nullification or impairment simply describes the amount of harm resulting from the violating member's *failure to respect its WTO obligations.* Unless the benchmark used to assess that harm is itself premised on market access under an unquestionably WTO-consistent counterfactual, the application of the benchmark will inevitably understate the value of market access in a WTO-consistent situation.

Unless arbitrators adhere to this principle, the DSB risks authorizing a solution to a dispute that understates the harm resulting from non-compliance because it is based on WTO-inconsistent market access. Common sense and the treaty text in Articles 3.6 and 21.5 of the DSU and Article XVI:4 of the WTO Agreement tell us that solutions to disputes *must* involve WTO-consistency. To this observer, the outcome in *Gambling* is, therefore, contrary to the treaty and represents bad policy.

I would suggest that the burden of proof has a role to play here. Because the *violating member* formally challenges the proposed level of suspension of concessions, arbitrators have stated that that member bears the burden of proving that the proposed level is not consistent with Article 22.4.[6] Given that the choice of counterfactual is, at least in part, a factual matter, the burden of proof should rest with the violating member to demonstrate that its proposed counterfactual is appropriate. The violating member must, therefore, bear the consequences of any doubts regarding the counterfactual. This seems eminently sensible, because the retaliating member has already proved once, and probably twice, that the violating member is acting inconsistently with its WTO obligations, and the violating member has failed to use the implementing period to comply. Any doubts should redound to the benefit of the retaliating member.

I also strongly disagree with the arbitrator in *Gambling* that the arbitrator has no legal authority to resolve questions of the consistency of a counterfactual. The DSU vests arbitrators with a responsibility to find a temporary solution to a dispute; that solution must be based on a WTO-consistent assessment of the level of nullification or impairment caused by the violating member. It is also hard to reconcile the decision in *Gambling* with the decision in *Bananas*, where the arbitrator found it

[6] Award of the arbitrator, *EC–Hormones (US)*, para. 9; Award of the arbitrator, *EC–Bananas III* (DSR 1999:II, 725), para. 38; Award of the arbitrator, *US–1916 Act* (DSR 2004:IX, 4269), para. 3.3; Award of the arbitrator, *Brazil–Aircraft* (DSR 2002:I, 19), para. 2.8; Award of the arbitrator, *US–Byrd Amendment*, para. 2.25.

could rule on the WTO consistency of an actual measure, and not merely a counterfactual.

5 Institutional considerations: improving the information available to arbitrators

The arbitrator in *Gambling* famously described its approach as being built on 'shaky grounds solidly laid by the parties'.[7] It described inadequacies in the data submitted, and lamented that the parties had 'retained extreme positions, and failed to propose alternative solutions'.[8] These uncommonly trenchant statements suggest a breakdown in the arbitral process: the arbitrator was not given the information considered to be necessary.

The reasons for this failure may lie, partly, in the way that arbitrations are conducted. Generally, although not always, the retaliating member provides a brief 'methodology' paper justifying the requested level of suspension; each party then submits one written submission, followed by a hearing, and a single round of questions, answers and comments on the opposing party's answers.

Compared with a panel process, which is much more drawn out in terms of time and exchanges of submissions,[9] an Article 22.6 arbitration moves fast. There are fewer opportunities, and much less time, for the parties to develop new methodologies or substantially revise their proposed methodologies. The shortness of time makes it more difficult for the parties to make major changes to their position in the later stages of the process.

In particular, under the current process, parties are unlikely to have either the time or inclination to change position dramatically in response to questions posed at the hearing for written reply thereafter. Further, even if wholly new positions were advocated at that stage, arbitrators would have no further chance to explore their questions regarding these new positions, nor would the opposing side have much time to respond to a wholly new position. Organizing the process in this way does not, therefore, provide the arbitrator with the surest foundations for its decision.

[7] Award of the arbitrator, *US–Gambling* (DSR 2005:XXIII, 11637), para. 3.173.

[8] Award of the arbitrator, *US–Gambling*, para. 3.173.

[9] A panel process typically involves a first written submission, first opening statement (provided in writing), response to the panel's first set of questions, second written submission; second opening statement (provided in writing), responses to the panel's second set of questions and comments on the opposing side's second set of answers.

However, small changes to the current process may provide arbitrators with less 'shaky' foundations for their decisions and, in turn, improve the consistency and quality of the decision making. Because the DSU does not prescribe required steps in the process, the arbitrators control the process themselves, and can give the parties more time to address their concerns regarding methodologies and data. By being proactive at an earlier stage, arbitrators would also stymie efforts by parties to play tactical games.

For example, the arbitrators can – and, I believe, should – pose a first set of questions to the parties for written answer *before* the hearing. Developing a methodology involves numerous methodological choices. At a fundamental level, choices have to be made on the overall approach used to assess harm. When an overall approach has been defined, many questions arise on the data to be used and how that data should be manipulated.

In short, arbitrators will inevitably have a long list of questions. It makes no sense for the arbitrator to hold these questions until the hearing, given that the hearing comes rather late in the process. By asking questions sooner, arbitrators can clarify the positions taken by the parties and communicate their own concerns earlier, without adding much time to the process. This would promote a better exchange of information and argument throughout the arbitration proceedings, thereby facilitating better decision making.

Many of the questions that arise in an arbitration concern issues on which perfectly reasonable people – including the parties and the arbitrator – may differ. The positions taken by the parties may not, therefore, be 'extreme'.[10] Yet, where arbitrators would like the parties to move from 'extreme positions', and consider alternative methodologies – as seems to have been the case in *US–Gambling* – asking direct questions earlier in the process can only help to provide the arbitrators with a better basis for their decisions. Finally, if the arbitrators do not receive satisfactory answers, they should have the courage to draw adverse inferences and apply the burden of proof rigorously.

[10] Award of the arbitrator, *US–Gambling*, para. 3.173.

5

From *Bananas* to *Byrd*: damage calculation coming of age?

YVES RENOUF*

The issue

The role of countermeasures in the Dispute Settlement Understanding (DSU) as it has evolved in practice is not easily summarized. Even assuming that the purpose of countermeasures is to induce compliance, as has been stressed by a number of arbitrators, the impact of their level to achieve such compliance may vary. As acknowledged by the arbitrator in the *Byrd* case:

> the general obligation to comply with DSB recommendations and rulings seems to imply that suspension of concessions or other obligations is intended to induce compliance, as has been acknowledged by previous arbitrators.[1] However, exactly what may induce compliance is likely to vary in each case, in the light of a number of factors including, but not limited to, the level of suspension of obligations authorized.[2]

And the arbitrator added in footnote 131 to that paragraph:

> While the value of the suspension or concessions or other obligations easily comes to mind as a relevant factor in inducing compliance, it must also be acknowledged that the actual role of the value of such suspension in securing compliance or not may vary from one case to the next. In some cases, even a very high amount of countermeasures may not achieve compliance, whereas in some others a limited amount may.

* The views expressed are those of the author and do not represent a position, official or unofficial, of the WTO Secretariat or WTO members. The author wishes to dedicate this brief contribution to the memory of his former colleague, Bijit Bora, who provided invaluable assistance to several Article 22.6 arbitrators.

1 *EC–Bananas III (US)* (Article 22.6 – EC) (DSR 1999:II, 725), para. 6.3.

2 *Byrd* arbitration, WT/DS217/ARB/BRA (DSR 2004:IX, 4341), para. 6.2.

Whereas the role of countermeasures in dispute resolution has been enhanced in the DSU compared with the situation under GATT 1947, the DSU grants Article 22.6 arbitrators limited flexibility in the assessment of countermeasures. As stated in Article 22.7:

> The arbitrator [footnote omitted] acting pursuant to paragraph 6 shall not examine the nature of the concessions or other obligations to be suspended but shall determine whether the level of such suspension is equivalent to the level of nullification or impairment.

Of course, arbitrators may rule on whether the principles and procedures of Article 22.3 of the DSU have been complied with, but this will be the case primarily if the prevailing party wants to retaliate in another sector or under an agreement other than that in which nullification or impairment occurred and if the party requesting arbitration alleges that the principles of Article 22.3 have not be complied with. Arbitrators cannot normally take the initiative by suggesting countermeasures in different sectors or agreements than the one(s) in which nullification or impairment occurred.[3]

As a result, arbitrators' impact on compliance is in practice limited to one factor: the amount of the countermeasure to be awarded. And even this role is somewhat constrained by the terms of the DSU, which requires the arbitrator to award countermeasures only *equivalent* to the level of nullification or impairment. This may have been intentional or related to the fact that the object and purpose of countermeasures is not clearly defined, as is underlined by other contributors to this volume.

This chapter focuses primarily on issues related to the calculation of countermeasures. However, as some trends have emerged as to how Article 22.6 arbitrators have perceived their task in this respect, the chapter also identifies some features of these trends *en vrac*.

1 The arbitrators' choice to make their own calculation of the amount of countermeasures

Article 22.6 arbitrators could have remained quite passive and limited their awards to stating whether the amount of countermeasures proposed by the prevailing party was equivalent or not to the level of nullification or impairment, without venturing into setting what they believed was a level

[3] On suspensions of concessions or other obligations under other sectors or agreements, see *EC–Bananas* (Article 22.6 arbitration), WT/DS27/ARB/ECU (DSR 2000:V, 2237).

of countermeasures equivalent to the level of nullification or impairment within the meaning of Article 22.4 of the DSU. Yet, even though such a possibility was hinted at by the *EC–Bananas* arbitrator[4] and highlighted by the *EC–Hormones* arbitrator, all arbitrators proceeded to calculate the maximum permissible amount of countermeasures they deemed commensurate with Article 22.4 of the DSU or Article 4.10/11 of the Subsidies and Countervailing Measures (SCM) Agreement. In this regard, arbitrators did not feel compelled to follow the methodologies proposed by the parties. In a number of cases, arbitrators used a methodology that was either a variation of the methodology proposed by one party or by both, or even their own methodology.[5]

The fact that the *EC–Hormones* arbitrator deemed it necessary legally to justify the decision to proceed with the recalculation of the amount of countermeasures is not merely another sign of the usual prudence of GATT and WTO dispute settlement adjudicators and arbitrators. It is also symbolic of the uncertainty surrounding the role of Article 22.6 arbitration even to this day. Indeed, in order to justify its decision to depart from the 'classical' approach of panels, which basically request the Dispute Settlement Body (DSB) to recommend that the measure be brought into conformity with WTO obligations, the *EC–Hormones* arbitrator found no express language in the DSU, and could rely only on 'the basic DSU objectives of prompt and positive settlement of disputes' and argue that this approach was *implicitly called for* in Article 22.7 of the DSU.[6]

2 The bold yet generally prudently applied concept of 'inducing compliance'

The term 'inducing compliance' is found nowhere in the relevant provisions of the DSU. Like a number of other fundamental concepts in Article 22.6 arbitrations, it is based on the arbitrators' perception of the object and purpose of countermeasures in the WTO. This concept was first used in the *EC–Bananas* arbitration in the US case[7] and applied

4 See, for example, *EC–Bananas*, WT/DS47/ARB/ECU, para. 12.

5 See, *US–FSC*, *1916 Act*, *Byrd*.

6 Article 22.6 arbitration on *EC–Hormones* (DSR 1999:III, 1105), para. 12. See also *EC–Bananas*, WT/DS47/ARB/ECU, para. 12.

7 *EC–Bananas* (Article 22.6 arbitration) (WT/DS27/ARB), para. 6.3:

> We agree with the United States that this *temporary* nature [of suspensions of concessions or other obligations] indicates that it is the purpose of

as an interpretation and assessment tool in the majority of subsequent arbitrations, even though some arbitrators highlighted other possible objects and purposes (*US–FSC*) and some even questioned whether this was merely one purpose among others (*Byrd*). The first prohibited subsidy case (*Brazil–Aircraft*), relying on the term 'appropriate' in 'appropriate countermeasures' in Article 4.10/11 of the SCM Agreement, even concluded that countermeasures in the case of export subsidies were intended to induce *effective* compliance.[8]

However, arbitrators, when applying their jurisprudential concept of 'inducing compliance', were confronted with the terms of Articles 22.4 and 22.7 of the DSU, which provide that the level of suspension of concessions and other obligations shall be *equivalent* to the level of nullification or impairment. While noting that 'equivalent' does not mean 'equal', arbitrators made sure that countermeasures would remain within certain limits so as not to be punitive, thus probably making the concept of inducing compliance more acceptable to members. That countermeasures should not be 'punitive' is another concept not expressly found in the DSU. Although the requirement of equivalence may be interpreted as an implicit obligation not to impose 'punitive' countermeasures,[9] it more certainly finds its origin in general international law and is formalized in the Articles on State Responsibility.[10]

Arbitrators under Article 4.10/11 of the SCM Agreement generally considered that the language 'appropriate countermeasures' in Article 4.10/11 and footnotes 9 and 10 of the SCM Agreement, as well as the specific constraints attached to prohibited subsidies (including the obligation to withdraw the subsidy 'without delay' (Article 4.7 of the SCM Agreement) provided more leeway in assessing the level of countermeasures than the term 'equivalent' in Article 22.6 of the DSU. However, in those cases, too, the arbitrators ensured that the level of countermeasure awarded to the

> countermeasures to *induce compliance*. But this purpose does not mean that the DSB should grant authorization to suspend concessions beyond what is *equivalent* to the level of nullification or impairment. In our view, there is nothing in Article 22.1 of the DSU, let alone in paragraphs 4 and 7 of Article 22, that could be read as a justification for counter-measures of a *punitive* nature.

[8] *Brazil–Aircraft* (DSR 2002:I, 19), para. 3.44.

[9] See, *EC–Bananas*, WT/DS27/ARB, para. 6.3.

[10] Article 51 of the Articles on Responsibility of States for Internationally Wrongful Acts (2001) provides that: 'Countermeasures must be commensurate with the injury suffered, taking into account the gravity of the internationally wrongful act and the rights in question.'

prevailing party was not 'punitive' and they often underlined, apparently as an additional justification for their choice, that the amount of the subsidy was probably less than its trade effect.

It is, however, interesting to note the position taken by the arbitrator in *Canada–Aircraft* to adjust the level of countermeasures in order to take into account the specificities of the case.[11] In this particular arbitration, the arbitrator accepted the Canadian approach of using the amount of subsidy as the basis for countermeasures. However, Canada argued that the circumstances of the case justified a downward adjustment of the level of countermeasures, whereas Brazil advocated an upward adjustment. After having considered the arguments of each party, the arbitrator decided to adjust the amount of countermeasures upward in order to take into account Canada's statement that it did not intend to withdraw the subsidy at issue (that is, probably not request its reimbursement by the Canadian aircraft manufacturer, Bombardier), but the arbitrator refused to consider the risk of future subsidization by Canada and the potentially disproportionate impact of the subsidy on the market.

Taken in isolation, this decision may look like one of the boldest rulings by an Article 22.6 arbitrator. Nonetheless, it finds its roots in the arguments of the parties, who themselves advocated 'tempering' the amount of the subsidy. Moreover, to reach its decision, the arbitrator relied heavily on the reasoning of the arbitrator in *US–FSC* and on the object and purpose of countermeasures to induce compliance. However, the arbitrator's strongest legal basis was probably the absence of definition of what constitutes 'appropriate countermeasures' under Article 4.10/11 of the SCM Agreement.

Another related question is the use of the full amount of the subsidy as the basis for the calculation of 'appropriate countermeasures'. In two of the three prohibited subsidies arbitrations (*Brazil–Aircraft* and *Canada–Aircraft*), the subsidy was granted to an industry where the subsidy recipient had only one competitor, so it could be considered that the whole amount of the subsidy affected exclusively the competitor, thus justifying the use of the full amount of the subsidy as a basis for calculation. In *US–FSC*, however, the subsidy was a tax exemption granted to US exporters irrespective of the countries to which they exported. It was argued that, if the arbitrator granted to the EC the right to retaliate up to the full amount of the subsidy, this would be equivalent to giving it the right to retaliate on behalf of other members affected by the subsidy. Yet, the

[11] *Canada–Aircraft* (DSR 2003:III, 1187), paras. 3.91–122.

arbitrator considered, *inter alia*, that the illegal nature of the subsidy and the requirement that it be withdrawn without delay justified allowing the EC to retaliate up to the full amount of the subsidy granted by the United States under the Foreign Sales Corporation regime.[12]

3 The use of economic models and data, and its limits

A number of arbitrators have used counterfactuals, the accuracy of which depends on the availability of trade data.[13]

Countermeasure calculations in the early arbitrations, even though they involved adjustments for various factors, were relatively simple in the principles applied by the arbitrators, probably because the nature of the case (for example, quantitative restrictions in the *EC–Hormones* case) was also relatively straightforward. However, the complexity of countermeasure calculations has increased with the increasing factual complexity of the cases over time.

The calculations in the two *Aircraft* subsidy cases and in the *US–FSC* subsidy case were more sophisticated than those in the *EC–Bananas* and the *EC–Hormones* cases, but this sophistication essentially resulted from the identification and allocation of the subsidy which the arbitrators had, in those cases, decided to use as the basis for the calculation of 'appropriate countermeasures'. Whereas calculation of the subsidies was complex, it did not necessitate economic modelling of the type used in other cases, for example, in *Byrd*.

In *US–FSC*, the arbitrator was confronted with two alternative approaches: one based on the total amount of the subsidy, and the other based on its trade effect on the EC. The *US–FSC* case was not the first arbitration where these alternative methodologies were suggested, but in the other two cases dealing with prohibited subsidies the arbitrators did not deem it necessary to engage in a detailed review of the merits of the two alternatives.[14] In *US–FSC*, the arbitrator considered it important to

[12] *US–FSC* arbitration (DSR 2002:VI, 2517), paras. 6.18–32.

[13] The issue of the legality of the counterfactual is addressed in other contributions to this volume.

[14] In *Brazil–Aircraft*, both parties agreed to use the amount of the subsidy as the basis for the calculation of the appropriate countermeasures, see para. 3.27. Brazil made an argument related to the trade effect of the subsidy when it claimed that only the prohibited portion of the subsidy had to be taken into account and that only the sales where the Canadian manufacturer, Bombardier, could have successfully competed (that is, where it proposed aircraft models similar to those of the Brazilian manufacturer, Embraer) should be taken into account in the calculation of the amount of the subsidy.

carry out an analysis of the trade effect of the subsidy in order to compare the results with those of the subsidy-based calculation. This was the first instance of discussion of economic models, but they did not directly support the final award of the arbitrator, except to comfort the arbitrator in the conviction that the amount of the subsidy expended by the United States constituted 'appropriate countermeasures'. An economic model was also used in *Byrd*, this time to determine the actual level of trade loss for the purpose of the calculation of the award.[15]

Recourse to economic models has the main advantage of providing the arbitrator with a reasonably objective and scientifically-based methodology, and of taking into account the economic complexity of the impact of the measure. For instance, whereas the arbitrator in *Brazil–Aircraft* had assumed that export subsidies had 'multiplying effects'[16] on trade, thus suggesting that countermeasures based on the amount of the subsidy would not be 'punitive', the discussion by the arbitrator in *US–FSC* showed that a 'pass through' effect should be taken into account and that any tax saving may not always translate into lower prices and increased exports.[17]

This said, recourse to economic models has its limits. One of them is the fact that not all economic models enjoy unanimous support among economists. Arbitrators have to make sure that the model they apply is sufficiently accepted, while adequately explaining why models proposed by the parties are not satisfactory.[18] Another problem is the capacity of generally accepted economic models to reflect sufficiently accurately the complexity of the impact of a WTO-inconsistent measure.

These problems, however, were dwarfed in comparison with the question of the data necessary to feed into economic models or counterfactuals. The apparent absence of reliable data in at least one case appeared to have required, *inter alia*, using more assumptions or estimates (*US–Gambling*). The cooperation of the parties in providing data is, therefore, essential and all arbitrators have insisted on the need for parties to provide the latest and most accurate data available. Arbitrators have sometimes gone as far as threatening to use publicly available (and presumably less accurate) data if the parties were not forthcoming.[19] However, arbitrators

[15] See, *Byrd* arbitration, Annex B. [16] Paragraph 3.54. [17] *US–FSC*, footnote 97.

[18] See, for instance, the discussion of the application of the Armington model by the United States in *US–FSC*, footnote 96.

[19] The related question of access to confidential data held by one party has also been an important aspect of calculation of countermeasures. In *Canada–Aircraft*, the arbitrator, faced with the reluctance of Canada to provide the actual selling price of the aircraft at

have generally been conservative in their calculations and have refused to take into account claims that are 'too remote', 'too speculative' or 'not meaningfully quantified', thus probably leading to an underestimate of the trade effect of a given measure (for example, in terms of the 'chilling effect' of legislation irrespective of its application).[20]

4 The reliance on trade loss as a benchmark for nullification or impairment

In the non-subsidy cases, there has been a general practice in the WTO and the GATT before it to equate nullification on impairment with trade loss and, thus, to use trade loss as a basis for compensation.[21] The first cases (*EC–Bananas*, *EC–Hormones*) concerned a loss of exports to the territory of the losing party and, thus, the calculation of nullification or impairment naturally relied on trade loss or, more specifically, on loss of exports to the member applying the WTO-inconsistent measure at issue.[22] The notion of lost trade was set aside in the three prohibited subsidy arbitrations, even though the trade effect of the tax exemption was discussed in *US–FSC*. In *US–1916 Act*, the arbitrator used the broader concept of 'economic effects',[23] and relied on the monetary value of amounts payable further to judgments entered into under the 1916 Act or of settlements reached in the context of cases initiated under the 1916 Act. As mentioned above, trade loss was generally expressed in terms of lost exports to the country imposing the WTO-inconsistent measure at issue, even when other aspects, such as lost sales in third country markets, could perhaps also have been taken into account.

issue even though the communication of such information was in the interest of Canada, decided to use the higher list price (para. 3.76).

[20] See, *US–1916 Act* (DSR 2004:IX, 4269), paras. 5.54–7.

[21] See, *Byrd* arbitration:

> In this arbitration, we have interpreted the concept of nullification or impairment, *inter alia*, from the terms of Article XXIII of GATT 1994 and Article 3.8 of the DSU. We believe, however, from the extensive discussion of this concept by the parties, that the actual meaning of this provision is disputed and needs to be addressed in the appropriate forum.

[22] See, for example, *EC–Hormones (Canada)* (DSR 1999:III, 1135), para. 41:

> What we have to do is to estimate the nullification and impairment caused by it (and presumed to exist pursuant to Article 3.8 of the DSU). To do so in the present case, we have to focus on trade flows. We must estimate trade forgone due to the ban's continuing existence beyond 13 May 1999.

[23] See, for example, para. 7.5.

One consequence is that, in cases other than the prohibited subsidies cases where it has been accepted that countermeasures could be calculated on the basis of the subsidy, absence of trade affected by the measure implies absence of countermeasures, at least until some trade is affected by the measure and damage actually occurs (*US–1916 Act*). In *Byrd*, the arbitrator also acknowledged the limits of a calculation system based on actual trade loss:

> The WTO dispute settlement system authorizes Members to challenge a law as such, i.e. irrespective of whether it has been applied or not. The 'classical' approach based on an assessment of the trade effect of a given measure may not always contribute to the identification of the actual level of nullification or impairment, in particular if no instances of application had arisen at the time. This may be because the trade effect of a measure may be difficult to assess due to the lack of verifiable figures. We are of the view that, while parties share a duty to cooperate with the Arbitrator in the establishment of the facts, there is no reason *a priori* to sanction the requesting party or the respondent if supporting figures are difficult or impossible to find. We believe that this is a situation that has to be addressed in order to reach a decision on what may be achievable through recourse to suspension of obligations in such cases.

The arbitrator in *Byrd* also identified the limits of a system based on individual trade loss, a problem also touched upon in *US–FSC* where the EC was allowed to counteract the whole amount of subsidy even though this subsidy adversely affected the trade of a number of countries and not exclusively trade of the EC (both EC exports to the United States and to third country markets).[24] In fact, the *Byrd* decisions implicitly suggested that individual countermeasures could fail to secure the removal of the measure *erga omnes*.

5 The form of countermeasures

Since retaliation is generally measured in terms of trade loss, it is logical to formulate countermeasures in terms of value of trade. This is why arbitrators' awards have been expressed in terms of value of imports upon which members could impose restrictive measures of their choice, up to total import prohibition. This is because the purpose of countermeasures is to make the exporting member suffer a loss in the value of its exports equivalent to the level of nullification or impairment. Countermeasures

[24] *US–FSC*, paras. 6.61–4.

are generally assessed on a yearly value of imports. Some, however, have been limited to a maximum amount to be allocated or not over a number of years (*Canada–Aircraft*), while some have been limited to a yearly amount over a defined period of time (*Brazil–Aircraft*). In *Byrd*, no value of trade was given; rather, the parties receiving the arbitrator's award were expected to use the most recently published yearly amount of disbursement under the Continued Dumping and Subsidy Offset Act (CDSOA) derived from the imposition of antidumping and countervailing duties on their exports as the basis for determining the extent to which their WTO benefits had incurred nullification or impairment and, thus, for calculating the value of US exports to them upon which they could impose countermeasures. One specificity of the *Byrd* awards was that, if the United States did not make any disbursement under the CDSOA in a given year, no retaliation could be taken by the prevailing parties in relation to that year.

It is possible to foresee multiple problems in the implementation of such measures. One is the risk of over-retaliation, since the values of imports are based on statistics. Arbitrators underlined this risk very early.[25] Over-retaliation is also possible in relation to suspensions of obligations other than tariff concessions, since the value of trade affected might be more difficult to quantify. Surprisingly, members who have in the past battled in a determined fashion over the amount of countermeasures seem to have shown limited concern for those risks until the most recent cases. Nonetheless, arbitrators have generally deemed it necessary to warn parties intending to suspend obligations other than tariff concessions or to cross-retaliate in non-goods sectors of the risks of over-retaliation, while implicitly admitting that they are quite powerless in this respect, *inter alia*, because they cannot rule on the proposed nature of the countermeasures.[26] Indeed, the only specific suggestion actually made was that a party affected by over-retaliation might have recourse to dispute settlement, which is a pretty cumbersome option.

Conclusion

The points highlighted above are merely a somewhat random selection of issues faced by Article 22.6 arbitrators over the past 10 years. Nonetheless, they suggest two interesting features, which probably have

[25] See, for example, *EC–Hormones (US)*, para. 82.
[26] See, *inter alia*, *US–Gambling* (DSR 2005:XXIII, 11637), paras. 5.2–13.

to be considered in the light of the actual efficiency of countermeasures in the WTO:

(1) The first is the 'idealistic' belief of some arbitrators, mostly in the first half of the above-mentioned period, that, for the system to operate, countermeasures had to induce compliance. In that context, to a certain extent, a higher level of countermeasures was more likely to lead to the losing party bringing its WTO-inconsistent measures into conformity with its WTO obligations than lower countermeasures. And, indeed, in certain subsidy cases, arbitrators have some leverage in this regard. The specific language of Article 4.10/11 of the SCM Agreement undeniably played a role in this regard, and some arbitrators have been particularly proactive, if in a somewhat prudent manner.
(2) The second feature, by contrast, has been that of a certain 'realism', which appeared more clearly in the second part of the above-mentioned period. This 'realism' shows, probably with the benefit of hindsight, some disillusion, or at least scepticism, about the efficiency of countermeasures, the objectivity of their calculation, their purpose and, above all, their role in inducing compliance. Arbitrators in that second period underlined the lack of precision of the relevant DSU provisions and the difficulties in applying economic models, and accordingly either adopted conservative approaches or invited WTO members to go back to the negotiating table in order to clarify the DSU provisions in question.

Figuratively speaking, the Article 22.6 arbitration mechanism has grown up and undoubtedly lost some of its illusions and innocence in the process. Perhaps arbitrators have now, with experience, fully grasped that the impact of countermeasures authorized in a given case – assuming they are implemented – may or may not lead to the withdrawal of the WTO-inconsistent measures which led to the imposition of such countermeasures in the first place and that other factors, including primarily political factors, may be more important. If one excludes the Article 25 arbitration in the *US–Copyright Act*, authorized countermeasures have ranged from little more than Can$10 million (*EC–Hormones (Canada)*) to more than US$4 billion (*US–FSC*). The authorization of US$4 billion in retaliation in *US–FSC* did not lead to the 'unravelling' of the WTO dispute settlement system, contrary to some predictions. It was not evidence of the failure of the system either, especially since the US Congress ultimately repealed the FSC regime even though the EC never applied the full amount of authorized retaliation. This suggests that skilful targeting of economic sectors in the losing party may ultimately have more impact than the total amount of countermeasures. The WTO system of countermeasures has, in a sense, come of age. Article 22.6 arbitrations have made members aware of its limits.[27] One question now is whether there is a need to modify it. This question is conditioned by another one: what is the actual purpose(s) of countermeasures in the WTO?

[27] See, for instance, Article 22.6 Arbitration award in *Byrd*:

> As mentioned above, the DSU does not expressly explain the purpose behind the authorization of the suspension of concessions or other obligations … the requirement that the level of such suspensions remain equivalent to the level of nullification or impairment suffered by the complaining party seems to imply that suspension of concessions or other obligations is only a means of obtaining some form of temporary compensation, even when the negotiation of compensations has failed … In other words, it is not completely clear what role is to be played by the suspension of obligations in the DSU and a large part of the conceptual debate that took place in these proceedings could have been avoided if a clear 'object and purpose' were identified.

PART III

An economic assessment after ten arbitration disputes

6

The economics of permissible WTO retaliation

CHAD P. BOWN AND MICHELE RUTA*

1 Introduction

In the 12 years following the WTO's 1995 inception, ten formal Dispute Settlement Understanding (DSU) cases reached the stage in which the respondent member's failure to comply with WTO obligations compelled DSU arbitrators to *authorize* the complaining member to retaliate and apply countermeasures. This chapter uses the lens provided by these ten cases to examine how arbitrators employ economic analysis at this critical stage of the DSU process. In order to lend an intellectual coherence to the arbitrators' approach, we first motivate the basis for DSU arbitrations in the WTO trade agreement via use of economic theory, as theory supplies a framework that complements the legal approach and allows arbitrators to put disputes into perspective.[1]

We begin by developing a theoretical approach that facilitates examination of the countermeasure construction for each of the two major categories of prevalent cases in WTO dispute settlement – that is, disputes over WTO-inconsistent import-restricting and export-promoting

* Chad Bown, Department of Economics and International Business School, MS021, Brandeis University, Waltham, MA 02454–9110, USA. Michele Ruta, Economic Research and Statistics Division, World Trade Organization, Centre William Rappard, rue de Lausanne 154, CH-1211 Genève 21, Switzerland. Chad Bown wrote this chapter while he was the visiting scholar in the Economic Research and Statistics Division at the WTO Secretariat. Nevertheless, neither author was formally involved in any of the WTO dispute settlement activity described in this chapter, and thus any views expressed are based on research alone and should not be attributed to the WTO, its members, or any of its legal or economic staff. For helpful discussions and comments, the authors thank Marc Bacchetta, Kyle Bagwell, Alex Keck, Marion Jansen, Patrick Low, Petros Mavroidis, Joost Pauwelyn, Robert Staiger, Robert Teh, and our discussant Alan Winters, as well as participants at the Graduate Institute Workshop on the Calculation and Design of Trade Sanctions in WTO Dispute Settlement in Geneva. Chad Bown thanks the German Marshall Fund of the United States for financial support of this project.

[1] Sebastian, also in this volume (Chapter 4, above), describes the legal framework affecting the calculation and design of trade sanctions in the WTO dispute settlement process.

policies. This is an important initial categorization given that DSU arbitrations have been conducted under two different mandates: that is, those that involve WTO-inconsistent trade restrictive measures and those that involve WTO-inconsistent government subsidies (WTO 2005). In the first, pursuant to DSU, Article 22.7, the duty of the arbitrators is to determine whether the level of suspensions sought by a complaining member is "equivalent to the level of nullification and impairment" that resulted from the breach of WTO obligations. The second mandate, pursuant to Articles 4.10 and 4.11 of the Subsidies and Countervailing Measures (SCM) Agreement, requires arbitrators to evaluate whether proposed countermeasures by a complaining member are "appropriate" in response to a prohibited export subsidy implemented by another member.[2]

We adopt a theoretical approach for determining the limits to permissible DSU countermeasures that derives simply from the Bagwell and Staiger (2002) interpretation of the WTO principle of *reciprocity*.[3] A particular benefit of this approach is that it fits more broadly within one fundamental political-economic understanding of the purpose of the WTO as a trade agreement. We first adapt their interpretation of reciprocity in order to analyze separately the economic theory behind permissible retaliation for WTO-inconsistent import-restricting versus export-promoting measures. Within these two broad categories, we focus on subsets of WTO-inconsistent measures disputed in practice. For import restrictions, we examine theoretical differences in the determination of countermeasures when the violation and/or WTO-consistent measure is a tariff, quota, other non-tariff measure on foreign exporters, or a domestic subsidy to import-competing firms. For export-promoting policies, we examine theoretical differences in the determination of retaliation limits when the WTO-inconsistent policies involve export subsidies in two-country and three-country models. Table 6.1 documents the ten DSU arbitrations that took place between 1995 and 2007 and allocates each one to the appropriate theoretical subsection of our analysis below.

Starting from the lens that the Bagwell and Staiger reciprocity formulation for countermeasure retaliation provides, we then turn to the specific arbitration cases. We first examine evidence from actual DSU reports to assess the extent to which the arbitrators' methods conform

[2] Note that we do not use our framework to examine the *US–Section 110(5) of US Copyright Act (EC)* case, which fell under the DSU, Article 25 arbitration that is an "alternative means of dispute settlement" (DSU, Article 25.1).

[3] Bagwell (2008) applies this theory to analyze several recent proposals aimed at improving the WTO dispute settlement system.

Table 6.1. *WTO DSU, Article 22.6 arbitrations, 1995–2007*

Case title	Agreements/ provisions infringed	Award by the arbitrators	Discussed in section
	Import-restricting measures		
EC–Bananas (US)	GATT, Article XIII	US$191.4 million	3.2
EC–Bananas (Ecuador)	GATT, Article XIII	US$201.6 million	3.2
EC–Hormones (US)	SPS Agreement	US$116.8 million	3.2
EC–Hormones (Canada)	SPS Agreement	Can$11.3 million	3.2
US–Antidumping Act of 1916 (EC)	GATT, Article VI, Antidumping agreement	No specific amount	3.3
US–Continuing Dumping and Subsidy Offset Act (Byrd Amendment) (Brazil, Canada, Chile, EC, India, Japan, Korea, Mexico)	GATT, Article VI, Antidumping agreement, SCM Agreement	0.72 * value of payments	3.4
US–Internet Gambling (Antigua and Barbuda)	GATS, Article XVI	US$21 million	3.2
	Export-promoting measures		
Brazil–Aircraft Subsidies (Canada)	SCM Agreement	US$344.2 million	4.1 and 5.1
Canada–Aircraft Subsidies (Brazil)	SCM Agreement	Can$247.796 million	4.1 and 5.1
US–Foreign Sales Corporations (FSC) (EC)	SCM Agreement	US$4.043 billion	4.1 and 4.2

to the Bagwell and Staiger reciprocity formula. In some of the DSU cases that we examine, such as the arbitrations over WTO-inconsistent quantitative restrictions, the arbitrators' actual approach appears quite consistent with this theory. In other cases, the arbitrators explicitly signal in their report a preference to use such an approach despite the practical inability to do so for procedural, computational, or data limitation reasons. Furthermore, in other types of disputes involving export subsidies, arbitrators clearly deviate from this reciprocity approach in favor of alternatives. Nevertheless, even in such instances, analyzing the retaliation determination question from a theoretically-motivated perspective allows us to compare the arbitrators' actual approach with one that might occur under this particular formulation of reciprocity.

The basic theoretical framework to examining such DSU arbitrations allows us to identify the three crucial elements to the arbitrators' decision-making process: (i) the *formula* that they decide to adopt for evaluating appropriate countermeasures, as well as its potential relationship to the theoretically-motivated Bagwell and Staiger reciprocity approach that is our benchmark; (ii) their political-legal-economic decision on a WTO-consistent *counterfactual* policy necessary to use the formula that they provide; and (iii) the *quantitative methods* they choose to use to necessarily construct the (unobserved) WTO-consistent counterfactual in reality.[4] After we introduce the simple graphical analysis that forms our basic theoretical approach, we then describe elements of the quantitative methodologies used by arbitrators to evaluate the maximum allowable level of suspension of concessions.[5]

Finally, note that we restrict attention to the economics that arbitrators use to determine the maximum limits to retaliation. We do not examine other retaliation-related issues in which the arbitrators play a lesser role, especially questions such as: given the level of permissible retaliation set by the arbitrators, what are the political-economic determinants of the target lists that complainants draw up? In which sectors do complainants choose to implement retaliation? When does it make sense for a complainant to choose GATT, GATS, or TRIPs retaliation? While these are interesting questions, we focus on the core issues to determining the *limits* to arbitrator-permitted retaliation because such questions are examined elsewhere in this volume and they are less relevant to the decisions made by the arbitrators.

The rest of this chapter proceeds as follows. In section 2, we present the basic underlying model, the motivating, underlying Bagwell and Staiger

[4] We also choose not to pursue more normative questions such as whether particular arbitration decisions "make sense" from the perspective of economic theory or techniques. Furthermore, we leave untouched the question of the economic rationale and the proper design of WTO rules governing arbitrations and, hence, the issue of whether decisions made by arbitrations enhance the WTO dispute settlement performance more generally.

[5] On this issue, see also WTO (2005) and Keck (2004). Nevertheless, because this particular element of the dispute process has received substantial discussion elsewhere, we do not focus on it here. See also Bernstein and Skully (2003) and Breuss (2004). For a broader economic analysis of the WTO system of retaliation, see Lawrence (2003).

political-economic theory behind the WTO, as well the role and interpretation of the reciprocity principle that we use to identify a theoretical formula for the arbitrators' allowances for countermeasures. In section 3, we apply the theory to cases in which WTO-inconsistent policies involved import-restricting measures, and we examine the relationship between actual DSU arbitrations over import-restricting measures in light of this theory. In section 4, we apply the theory to cases in which WTO-inconsistent policies involved export-promoting measures. Section 5 identifies other potential areas of theoretical interest given the DSU arbitrations that have occurred thus far, and section 6 concludes.

2 The Bagwell–Staiger theory of trade agreements and the "reciprocity approach"

We start by providing an economic model to organize thoughts on the actual arbitration cases. The basic political-economic model is in the spirit of Bagwell and Staiger (2001a), who show that the major principles of reciprocity and non-discrimination of the WTO system allow countries to escape a terms-of-trade driven prisoners' dilemma.[6]

To begin, we assume that there are two large countries – the respondent (R) and the complainant (C) – and we note that the complainant's variables will be denoted by *. Let good x be the natural import (export) good of the respondent (complainant) country and let y be the natural import (export) good of the complainant (respondent) country, and we assume that these goods are traded in perfectly competitive markets. For example, the markets for good x are illustrated in figure 6.1. The model is thus a two-country, two good, partial equilibrium model, and one in which we assume governments use the policy tools at their disposal to maximize an objective function consisting of a "politically" weighted sum of consumer surplus, producer surplus, and tariff revenue across their two sectors.[7]

[6] Bagwell and Staiger (2001a) is the partial equilibrium version of the model they originally introduced in a general equilibrium framework in Bagwell and Staiger (1999). The Bagwell and Staiger (2001a) model can be interpreted as a general equilibrium model by introduction of a numeraire good whose trade is determined by a requirement of overall trade balance. For a book-level synthesis of these theories, see Bagwell and Staiger (2002).

[7] If "political" weight were all equal to unity, the objective function of governments would correspond to social welfare. As it is well understood from the theory of collective action (Olson 1965) and confirmed by a large body of empirical evidence (Gawande and Krishna, 2003, present a survey), governments tend to give a higher weight in their objective function to organized special interests, such as import-competing industries, relative to diffuse consumer interests. The Grossman and Helpman (1994) lobbying model provides a micro-analytic foundation to this political economy representation.

In such an environment, Bagwell and Staiger provide important interpretations for the WTO core principles of reciprocity and non-discrimination through most-favoured-nation (MFN) treatment. In the presence of large countries that are able to affect their terms of trade (and thus world prices), reciprocity can be shown to neutralize an important internationally transmitted externality that occurs when one country's use of a unilateral trade measure redistributes surplus from its trading partner to itself. The WTO principle of MFN treatment ensures that externalities associated with trade intervention travel through world prices only. In this way, these principles work in concert to deliver *efficient* trade policy outcomes from the multilateral trading system: that is, outcomes that do not distort trade more than if each government were motivated by domestic political-economy considerations only.[8]

Our theoretical analysis begins from such a politically efficient trade agreement between symmetric countries: that is, an agreement that eliminates the trade restrictions associated with the terms-of-trade externality. While the trade agreement may not necessarily result in free trade – that is, government preferences might be such that their "politically optimal" (efficient) trade policies in this Bagwell and Staiger framework are not zero – it is efficient in light of each government's potential political preferences.

Following the approach adopted in Bown (2002, 2004), we then introduce an unanticipated "political" shock that stimulates a desire by one of the governments – the respondent – to *change* the terms of the existing agreement. The intuition is simply that the political shock creates new preferences by changing the relative weights the government in the respondent faces vis-à-vis its various sectors, therefore, its existing policies are no longer efficient. Because the nature of the shock we examine is "political," it leaves unaltered domestic demand and supply.[9] A concrete example of this type of shock would be the election of a new government that gives more weight to the producer interests of the import-competing sector, which creates an incentive for the government to move away from

[8] As discussed in Bagwell, Mavroidis and Staiger (2002), the terms-of-trade rationale for trade agreements corresponds to the market access emphasis found in the WTO articles. An increased (reduced) export price, that is an improved (diminished) terms of trade, is just the price effect induced by the corresponding increase (reduction) in export volumes that augmented (restricted) market access implies.

[9] This is certainly not the only type of shock that might trigger such a policy change, though it is perhaps most simple to use in the model to examine the questions of interest here. Nevertheless, we identify and discuss other types of shocks in section 5.

the trade policy commitments previously negotiated with its trading partner in an earlier round.

In section 3 we explore the most simple case of a government in the respondent reacting to this preference shock by imposing more import *restrictions* either directly via trade policy (for example, tariffs, quotas or other non-tariff barriers) or by providing its domestic producers with a WTO-inconsistent subsidy that leads to a similar effect of limiting trade. The key from the WTO's perspective is that these policies all restrict market access and change the conditions of competition between domestic and foreign producers away from those that could have reasonably been expected based on earlier negotiated commitments. In section 4, we explore a second set of cases in which respondent policymakers react to preference shocks that cause them to expand export *promotion* activity – for example, export subsidies – above WTO commitments.

Given the respondent country's change in policies, we then use the basic rules of the WTO's DSU to examine how the setting plays out: that is, after the respondent reacts to this "shock" by changing some policy that affects its WTO market access commitments, we assume that the adversely affected complainant country files a formal trade dispute. The parties then go through the DSU judicial process of legal argumentation, the respondent's policy is found by the panel and Appellate Body to be WTO-inconsistent, and we finally reach the stage of DSU arbitration. Assuming that the respondent has thus far refused to bring its measure into conformity with DSU rulings, it is the task of the arbitrators to define the limits of the complainant country's permissible retaliation as a response to the respondent country's initial WTO-inconsistent measure.

The DSU states that "the level of the suspension of concessions or other obligations authorized by the DSB shall be equivalent to the level of *nullification or impairment*" (GATT 1994, Article 22:4, emphasis added). In each of the cases described below in sections 3 and 4 corresponding to a different WTO-inconsistent policy, our approach is to provide a simple graphical model to evaluate the level of nullification or impairment that arises. While there is not a single interpretation of the "proper" level of nullification or impairment,[10] we adopt the Bagwell and Staiger (2002) view that this level corresponds to the *suspension of trade that is designed to stabilize the value of export and import trade volumes between countries*. For instance, in the case of a trade restrictive measure, the complainant's permissible retaliation is to reduce the volume of the exports by

[10] For a discussion, see Pauwelyn in this volume (Chapter 2).

an amount equal to the respondent's reduction of imports, both measured at original export prices: that is, before the breach of WTO commitments. We refer to this as the "reciprocity approach." Howse and Staiger (2005), for example, argue that this approach approximates a system of remedies that facilitates a form of "efficient breach" of the optimal trade treaty in the presence of uncertainty.[11] Furthermore, they show that allowing the complainant to retaliate at a level equal to trade effects calculated at original export prices preserves the terms-of-trade and is close to an efficient response for "small" shocks.[12]

3 WTO disputes and retaliation over import-restricting measures

In this section we study the process of arbitrator determination of countermeasures when the WTO-inconsistent policies are those that excessively restrict imports. We first describe the simple theoretical approach to this question and then examine how the arbitrators in the relevant DSU caseload have approached the question in practice. Our methodology relies on the Bagwell and Staiger interpretation of reciprocity to provide a theoretical framework to identifying the appropriate level of countermeasures. We then use this framework to identify three crucial elements in the arbitrators' decision-making process: (i) the formula that they decide to adopt for evaluating appropriate countermeasures, (ii) their political-legal-economic decision on a WTO-consistent counterfactual to use in the formula, and (iii) the quantitative methods they choose to use to necessarily construct the (unobserved) WTO-consistent counterfactual.

For illustrative purposes, we start our discussion of import-restricting measures with the case of tariffs. While none of the actual arbitration cases deals exclusively with this most simple trade policy measure, tariff analysis constitutes a valuable benchmark. Once we have established how the approach works to understand the basic tariff case, we then modify it appropriately to examine WTO-inconsistent quotas, which is relevant for five DSU arbitrations: the two *EC–Bananas* disputes (US, Ecuador), the two *EC–Beef Hormones* disputes (US, Canada), and the *US–Internet*

11 For a discussion of trade agreements as incomplete contracts and the analogy between the reciprocity approach to calculate appropriate trade sanctions and the concept of "expectation damages" in private contract law, see Sykes in this volume (Chapter 16) and the references therein.

12 Nevertheless, there are also some limitations to such an approach that we also identify and describe in substantial detail below, especially when it comes to the question of *implementation* of such an approach in practice.

Gambling dispute. We then also extend the approach to consider the case of WTO-inconsistent domestic subsidies and other non-tariff measures, which are relevant for the arbitrations in *US–Continuing Dumping and Subsidy Offset Act (Byrd Amendment)* and *US-Antidumping Act of 1916*.

3.1 *Import tariffs*

In our benchmark case, we assume that governments have a single policy tool – import tariffs – at their disposal. At the initial WTO-type agreement between the two countries and before we introduce any shocks, the efficient level of the policies embedded in the agreement are given by τ^E, τ^{*E}, that is, the efficient tariffs on imports of x (y) imposed by the respondent (complainant) country.

Panels (a) and (c) of figure 6.1 illustrate the demand (D_x and $D_x{}^*$) and supply (S_x and $S_x{}^*$) schedules for good x in the responding country and the complaining country, respectively, while figure 6.1(b) shows the export supply ($X_x{}^*$) and import demand (M_x) schedules in international markets. As we assume that the world is composed of these two countries only, export supply and import demand are entirely determined by the domestic conditions in the respondent's and the complainant's markets. In particular, notice that for the relevant price range, the complainant produces more of the good than it consumes and thus exports the rest, so that $X_x{}^* = S_x{}^* - D_x{}^*$, which is strictly positive for any price level larger than the equilibrium price in the complainant's market. On the other hand, the respondent consumes more than it produces and thus imports the rest, so that $M_x = D_x - S_x$, which is strictly positive for any price lower than the respondent's equilibrium price under autarky. At the initial (efficient) tariff, the world price and the volume of trade are determined by the intersection of the export supply ($X_x{}^*$) and import demand ($M_x{}^0$) schedules at point E^0 in figure 6.1(b), which we denote with $P_x{}^0 \equiv P_x(\tau^E)$ and $Q_x{}^0 \equiv Q_x(\tau^E)$.

Now assume that the respondent (R) country experiences a shock and unilaterally alters its policy from this initial level to some (non-prohibitive) level τ^I. The introduction of a higher non-prohibitive tariff ($\tau^I > \tau^E$) in country R increases its domestic price and lowers the price in the international market, as the reaction of exporters to the increased cost creates an excess demand for the good in the respondent's market and excess supply in the international market. Because of these price changes, producers in R supply more of the good and consumers demand less (see figure 6.1(a)), while in country C producers supply less and consumers demand

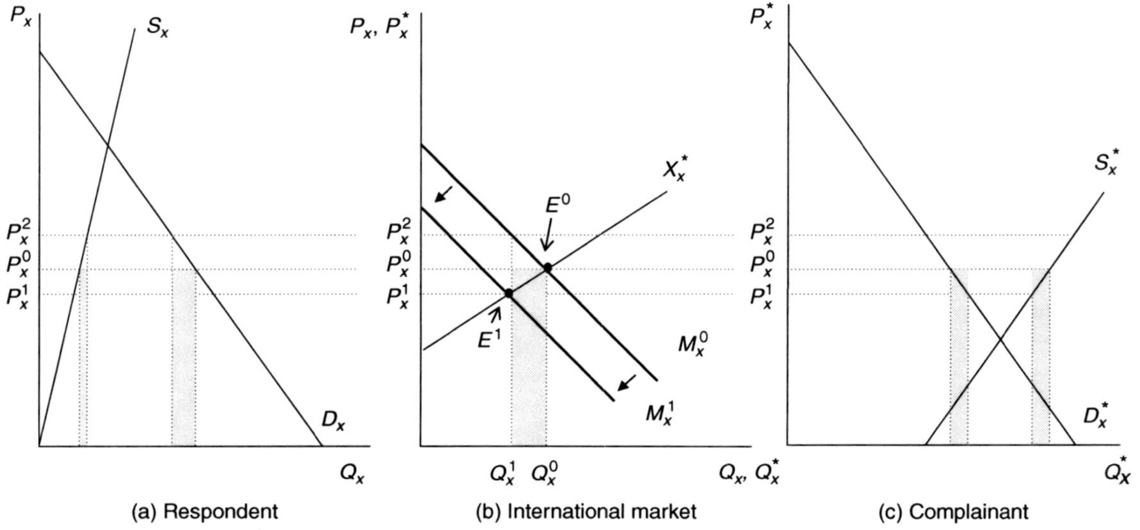

Figure 6.1. Reciprocity compensation when the respondent implements a WTO-inconsistent tariff

more (see figure 6.1(c)). This implies a shift down in the import demand schedule in figure 6.1(b) from its original position M_x^0 to the new level M_x^1. In the new equilibrium (E^1), imports and exports are lower. The effect of the restrictive measure on the volume of trade corresponds to a fall from Q_x^0 to $Q_x^1 \equiv Q_x(\tau^1)$. The introduction of this new and more restrictive measure in country R will affect the price of good x which falls from its initial level $P_x^0(\tau^E)$ to the lower level $P_x^1(\tau^1)$.

We next turn to the key question facing WTO arbitrators: what is the level of retaliation to which the complainant is entitled? That is, what is C's permitted retaliatory response via a change of its tariff policy τ^* on imports of y from the respondent?

We use the principle of reciprocity to determine the limits the arbitrators set for C's permissible retaliation. Under the reciprocity approach, the complainant is allowed to introduce a retaliatory policy measure (call it τ^{*Ret}) – that is, a trade restrictive measure on the imports of good y from country R – such that the value of export and import trade volumes between the two countries is stabilized, that is:

$$P_x^0\left(\tau^E\right)\left[Q_x^0\left(\tau^E\right)-Q_x^1\left(\tau^1\right)\right]=P_y^0\left(\tau^{*E}\right)\left[Q_y^0\left(\tau^{*E}\right)-Q_y^{Ret}\left(\tau^{*Ret}\right)\right], \tag{1}$$

where $P_y^0(\tau^{*E})$ is the initial export price of good y, $Q_y^0(\tau^{*E})$ are initial imports and $Q_y^{Ret}(\tau^{*Ret})$ is the volume of imports under the more restrictive measure.[13]

Figure 6.1(b) provides a graphical interpretation of the level of retaliation that the arbitrators accord to the complainant under the reciprocity approach defined by equation (1). The reciprocal retaliatory response that would preserve the terms-of-trade between the respondent and the complainant corresponds to the volume of lost trade ($Q_x^0 - Q_x^1$) evaluated at the original export price (P_x^0) – that is, the left-hand side of the reciprocity condition equation (1). The value of the trade effect corresponds to the

[13] As in Bagwell and Staiger (2001a, 300), when introducing a numeraire good z, the general equilibrium condition for reciprocity can be defined as:

$$P_x^0\left(\tau^E\right)\left[Q_x^0\left(\tau^E\right)-Q_x^1\left(\tau^1\right)\right]+Q_z^1\left(\tau^1,\tau^{*Ret}\right)-Q_z^0\left(\tau^E,\tau^{*E}\right)=P_y^0\left(\tau^{*E}\right)\left[Q_y^0\left(\tau^{*E}\right)-Q_y^{Ret}\left(\tau^{*Ret}\right)\right],$$

where Q_z denotes domestic country imports of the numeraire. It is easy to verify that condition (1) in the text continues to hold in this general equilibrium model for small shocks – that is, for small effects of tariff changes on domestic imports of the numeraire good.

shaded area in figure 6.1(b). Not surprisingly, this area is equal to the sum of the shaded areas in figure 6.1(a) (that is, the value of lost imports at original export price) and the sum of shaded areas in figure 6.1(c) (that is, the value of lost exports at the original export price).

3.1.1 Actual DSU arbitrations over import tariffs

While no arbitrations to date have involved purely WTO-inconsistent tariff restrictions, insights from this section will be important in helping us to understand some elements of the two *EC–Beef Hormones* arbitrations described in section 3.2.1 below.

3.2 Import quotas

While none of the arbitrations we examine focused solely on a breach of a tariff commitment, we can apply the logic just discussed to evaluate the level of nullification or impairment in the case of a WTO-inconsistent quota. Five out of ten arbitrations between 1995 and 2007 have dealt with this kind of trade restricting measure.

We begin our analysis of WTO-inconsistent quotas with all of the same modelling assumptions in section 3.1 – with the sole exception that the respondent country is now assumed to have access only to an import quota policy on good *x* instead of an import tariff. Again, we start from a politically efficient trade agreement reflecting the government's politically-weighted objective function, which implies a trade restrictive quota binding in country R.[14] This situation is depicted in figure 6.2(a), which focuses figure 6.1(b) only, illustrating the equilibrium in the international market. Differently from the tariff, the quota directly limits the amount of imports to the initial level Q_x^0, which explains the kinked shape of the import demand function in figure 6.2(a). The kink reflects the binding nature of the quota as, for prices lower than the initial export price P_x^0, country R is willing to import larger quantities of the good, as in the dotted line, but this is prevented by the existence of the quota limit.

Suppose now that the respondent experiences the same sort of political shock and responds by changing its politically optimal quota from the WTO-consistent volume Q_x^0 to the more restrictive and WTO-inconsistent volume Q_x^1. As a consequence of the imposition of this new

[14] We stress again that the quota is also "politically optimal" and is thus efficient in light of the government's objective function.

measure, import demand from country R shifts in from M_x^0 to the new level M_x^1. The effect of the lower quota is to increase the consumer price for the respondent to P_x^1 as the quantity demanded will exceed the quantity supplied by domestic and foreign producers. Furthermore, the price received by the complainant's exporters falls to P_x^2.

Before we define the reciprocity condition used to determine the level of retaliation that the arbitrators accord to the complainant, we note one additional complication for the instances in which a quota is used in lieu of a tariff, due to the question of how the import quota licenses are allocated. Because the quota limits competition in the respondent market, the price of good *x* in the respondent market is higher than the world price that the exporters would receive for sales of the same good in other markets, and thus merely the right to export to this market – what we refer to as the quota license – is something of value that can be bought and sold. Thus, in order for the arbitrator to determine the complainant exporter's received price for its sales of *x* in the respondent market, the arbitrator must know the form of the quota license-allocation regime as well as its WTO consistency. In figure 6.2(a), the value of the quota licenses – or what is frequently referred to as the "quota rent" – is given by the hatched rectangle.

Consider the range of extremes for potential WTO-consistent licensing schemes. First, if a party within the *complaining* country (for example, exporting firms or their government) receives the quota licenses directly without payment and quota rent benefits, then the relevant original exporter price is P_x^0, and thus, modifying equation (1), the reciprocity defined level of retaliation permitted to the complainant country is given by:

$$P_x^0\left[Q_x^0 - Q_x^1\right] = P_y^0\left(\tau^{*E}\right)\left[Q_y^0\left(\tau^{*E}\right) - Q_y^{Ret}\left(\tau^{*Ret}\right)\right]. \tag{2a}$$

Graphically in figure 6.2(a), the permitted level of retaliation corresponds to the combined shaded and hatched areas.

At the other extreme, if the WTO-consistent licensing regime allows for *non-complaining* country parties only to receive licenses, then the effective foreign export price under the WTO-consistent quota is P_x^3 (and not P_x^0), since the foreign exporters would have to pay a price (equivalent to $P_x^0 - P_x^3$) simply to acquire a license, therefore driving down the effective price they receive for their exports. In this event, the modification to equation (1) results in a reciprocity condition given by:

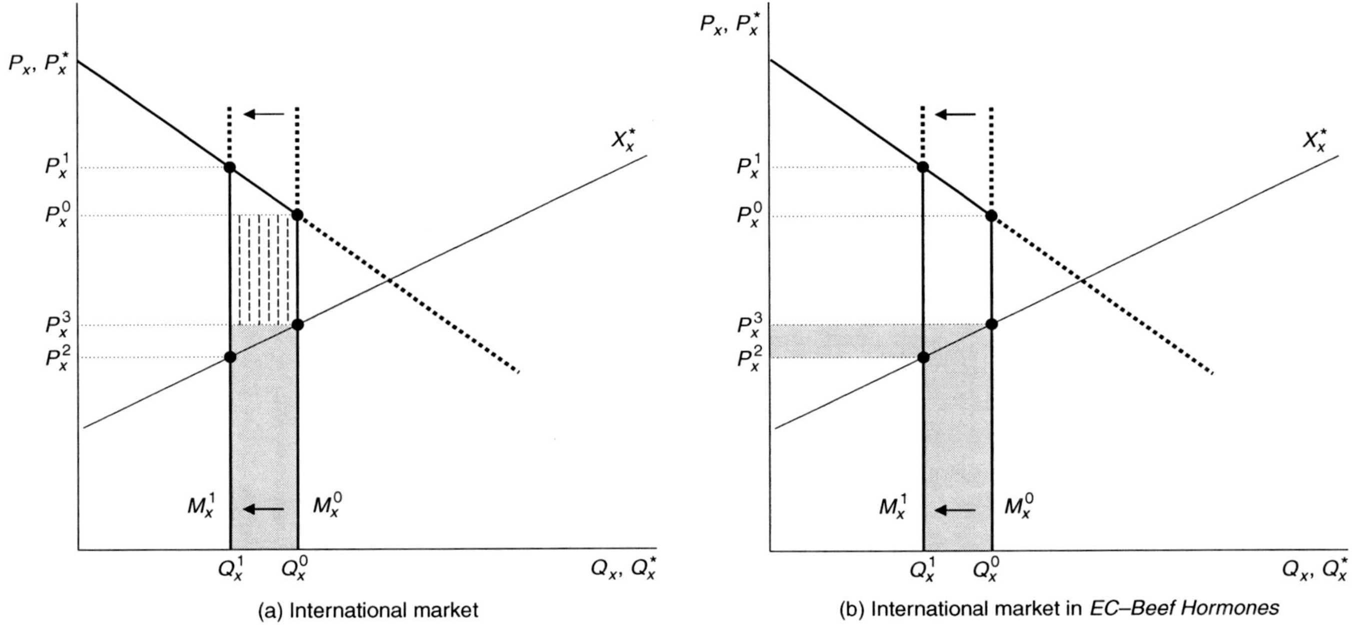

Figure 6.2. Reciprocity compensation when the respondent implements a WTO-inconsistent quota and/or implements an inconsistent licensing scheme

$$P_x^3\left[Q_x^0 - Q_x^1\right] = P_y^0\left(\tau^{*E}\right)\left[Q_y^0\left(\tau^{*E}\right) - Q_y^{Ret}\left(\tau^{*Ret}\right)\right]. \tag{2b}$$

In this case, the appropriate level of nullification or impairment in figure 6.2(a) corresponds to the fraction of the shaded area below the price P_x^3 only.

These are the two extreme cases, and it is also possible to allocate some of the licenses to foreign entities directly and some to non-foreign entities which the foreign exporter would then have to acquire through payment to export. In this instance a portion of the quota rent rectangle in figure 6.2(a) would be allocated to each group which increases the effective price received by foreign exporters above P_x^3 but still below P_x^0. What is important to note is simply that information on the WTO-consistency of the quota licensing scheme itself is a necessary condition for determining the exporter's received price, an element necessary to implement the reciprocity formula of either equation (2a) or (2b).

Before turning to the actual DSU arbitrations involving quotas, we make a final remark on the relationship between quota licenses, retaliation, and the reciprocity conditions of equations (2a) and (2b). If the *only* WTO-inconsistency associated with a quantitative restriction is the way in which import licenses under the quota were distributed, the reciprocity approach of equations (2a) or (2b) implies zero retaliation for the complainant country. This result is because there was no trade volume effect ($Q_x^0 - Q_x^1 = 0$) of the respondent's WTO-inconsistent measure.

3.2.1 Actual DSU arbitrations over import quotas: *EC–Bananas*, *EC–Beef Hormones*, and *US–Internet Gambling*

In this section we use the methodological framework of section 3.2 to help interpret what the arbitrators have done in practice. Five out of the ten arbitrations that took place between 1995 and 2007 were challenges to WTO-inconsistent quantitative restrictions: the two *EC–Banana* disputes (US, Ecuador), the two *EC–Beef Hormones* disputes (US, Canada) and the *US–Internet Gambling* dispute. As the model presented in figure 6.2 suggests, the arbitrators require three pieces of information to implement equation (2b) if they seek guidance from the reciprocity approach to determining the level of countermeasures that the complainant parties can impose: the actual level of exports under the WTO-inconsistent regime (Q_x^1); the counterfactual level of exports under a WTO-consistent regime (Q_x^0); and the counterfactual exporter price under a WTO-consistent regime (for example, P_x^3).

EC–Bananas Consider first the initial *EC–Bananas* arbitration, in which the complainant was the United States.[15] This is an interesting and precedential dispute in its own right as it was the first ever Dispute Settlement Body (DSB) case to proceed to the stage of arbitration. Since the *EC–Bananas* dispute involving Ecuador as a complainant had the same arbitrators and process for determining the appropriate level of countermeasures, we focus our discussion on the US arbitration.[16]

Evidence from the *EC–Bananas* Arbitrators' Report is broadly consistent with the idea that they followed a "reciprocity approach" formula analogous to equation (2b) to determine the limit to permissible US countermeasures. First, the arbitrators determined the actual volume of US banana exports under the WTO-inconsistent regime (Q_x^1) from data on wholesale services trade for bananas sold in the EC market, and the US share of this EC import market derived from the US share of allocated import licenses to the overall EC banana market. Then, the arbitrators sought information on the counterfactual level of exports (Q_x^0) and exporter price (P_x^3) that would occur under a WTO-consistent policy.

However, even if the arbitrators follow the reciprocity approach, the politically and economically challenging part of the arbitrators' exercise is, of course, to construct the appropriate counterfactual to deduce information on Q_x^0 and P_x^3.[17] While the arbitrators' exact methodology and data used are not publicly available from their report, their logic appears

15 *EC–Regime for the Importation, Sale and Distribution of Bananas*, Recourse to Arbitration by the European Communities under Article 22.6 of the DSU, Decision by the arbitrators, WT/DS27/ARB, April 9, 1999. For the Ecuador arbitration, see *EC–Regime for the Importation, Sale and Distribution of Bananas*, Recourse to Arbitration by the European Communities under Article 22.6 of the DSU, Decision by the arbitrators, WT/DS27/ARB/ECU, March 24, 2000.

16 A separate and interesting issue for the Ecuador dispute was not on how the level of countermeasures was constructed, but the question of how Ecuador would have been authorized to implement them – that is, via a potential withdrawal of TRIPs commitments, instead of via a withdrawal of tariff commitments under the GATT.

17 The process was politically challenging in this instance as the arbitrators first had to decide on what would have been a WTO-consistent EC banana import policy – that is, a policy itself that had never been in place. The process was also economically challenging as the arbitrators had to then take the WTO-consistent policy as given and then potentially use quantitative economic tools to determine the US export response under such a policy. We do not comment here on whether their political or economic approaches were appropriate in this case, as the information provided in the report was not sufficient to allow us to form such an assessment.

to have been the following. First, to determine the relevant exporter price, they essentially assumed that a WTO-consistent regime would leave the overall volume of imports (from all foreign sources) unchanged, and that EC production would also remain unchanged. Under this set of assumptions, the exporter price under the counterfactual that would need to be known is the same as the current exporter price, which is a statistic available in the current year's data. In terms of figure 6.2(a), this implies that in the relevant range the export supply schedule of the United States is flat (that is, infinitely elastic) at the current export price (that is, $P_x^3 = P_x^2$). Second, the arbitrators requested that the United States provide them with information on US exports of bananas from four different counterfactual regimes that might be considered to be WTO-consistent. While it is unclear what caused the arbitrators to choose one of these proposed scenarios over the others, the arbitrators used those submissions to construct their own measure for the counterfactual level of exports under a WTO-consistent regime, that is, Q_x^0.[18]

A final item to note from this dispute is the role of quota licenses, again with reference to figure 6.2(a). As highlighted in the theoretical section, whenever a trade restriction is imposed as a quota, arbitrators subsequently require additional information on the WTO-consistent license-allocation scheme in order to determine the export price to implement the reciprocity formula. For instance, if a WTO-consistent scheme is such that quota licenses are attributed to the US exporters, then the relevant counterfactual exporter price would be P_x^0 rather than P_x^3. As shown in figure 6.2(a) (the hatched area), the maximum admissible retaliation in the quota cases crucially hinges on the appropriate counterfactual export price which, in turn, depends on the decision on the WTO-consistent licensing scheme. From the information available in the report, however, it is difficult to assess the arbitrators' decision on this issue.

EC–Beef Hormones The next set of disputes involves the EC imposing WTO-inconsistent quantitative restrictions over hormone-treated beef imported from the United States and Canada.[19] While we again find

[18] In order for the arbitrators to implement the reciprocity approach, they require information on the volume of US exports under the counterfactual and not the value. Nevertheless, given their assumptions discussed above which led them to separately determine exporter prices under a WTO-consistent counterfactual regime, they could easily use those prices and the proposed value of exports to back out a volume number.

[19] *EC–Measures Concerning Meat and Meat Products (Hormones)*, Original Complaint by the United States, Recourse to Arbitration by the European Communities under Article

that the arbitrators' process of determining the US and Canadian level of countermeasures is related to the reciprocity approach, the arbitrators deviated from the exact formulation along a number of dimensions. For space constraints, we focus here on the arbitrators' methodology in the US case as the Canadian case was similar.

As relevant background information, the dispute involved two differentiated products. The arbitrators necessarily separated the two products for the reason that each product faced its own counterfactual WTO-consistent regimes: that is, one was a quantitative restriction and the other was a tariff. The first product was EC imports of high quality beef (HQB) that had been banned because it had been treated with hormones, but a product for which the WTO-consistent policy was for the EC to have a defined quota programme of an 11,500 tonne limit per year. The second product was edible beef offal (EBO), also treated with hormones and to which the EC applied a ban, but which, in the absence of a ban, would have faced an EC tariff and not a quota. The implication is that for the arbitrators, for one product (HQB) the approach would be based on the insights from section 3.2 and figure 6.2, and for the other product (EBO), the approach would be based on a combination of insights from this section and section 3.1 on tariffs and thus figure 6.1. Thus, we follow the arbitrators and analyze the two products separately. After separately calculating retaliation limits associated with the ban of each product, the arbitrators then summed their total.

First, consider HQB, for which the WTO-consistent regime was a quota, and the arbitrators' determination of the counterfactual prices and quantities that would have occurred under the WTO-consistent regime – once again referring to figure 6.2(a) and equation (2b). Here, the volume (Q_x^0) was relatively easy to calculate as it was the US share of a previously determined EC quota of 11,500 tonnes per year.[20] While the logic of the counterfactual

22.6 of the DSU, Decision by the arbitrators, WT/DS26/ARB, July 12, 1999; *EC–Measures Concerning Meat and Meat Products (Hormones)*, Original Complaint by Canada, Recourse to Arbitration by the European Communities under Article 22.6 of the DSU, Decision by the arbitrators, WT/DS48/ARB, July 12, 1999.

[20] The arbitrators did also have to determine how much of the share of the EC's 11,500 tonne quota would be allocated to the United States versus Canada, and they relied on data on the relative size of US and Canadian HQB exports to common third markets to determine shares within the quota had the ban not been in place – resulting in 92 per cent for the United States and 8 per cent for Canada. Second, the EC quota would have actually been implemented as a tariff rate quota and not a pure quota – that is, the in quota tariff rate was 20 per cent *ad valorem*, and the out of quota tariff rate was reportedly prohibitive. With respect to figure 6.2, the tariff rate quota grants the quota rents (hatched rectangle) to the government via tariff revenue, and the price received by US exporters would be P_x^3.

price that would have occurred under a WTO-consistent regime (P_x^3) is not articulated in the report, the arbitrators accepted a US proposed price of US$5,342 per tonne and thus found it straightforward to obtain.

Thus far, the arbitrators follow the reciprocity approach of equation (2b) as modified to fit the facts for HQB. The potential deviation from this approach occurs in the arbitrators' determination of the *actual* volume of US and Canadian beef exports under the WTO-inconsistent regime: that is, Q_x^1 in figure 6.2(a).[21] Unlike the *EC–Bananas* case, the arbitrators deviated from equation (2b) because they relied on an estimate of the current *value* of EC imports of HQB from the United States, that is, $P_x^2 * Q_x^1$ from figure 6.2(b), and not the current *volume* (Q_x^1).[22]

What are the implications to using this formulation of reciprocity that differs slightly from equation (2b)? Instead of using the shaded area below P_x^3 on figure 6.2(a) and thus $P_x^3 * (Q_x^0 - Q_x^1)$, the arbitrators used a formula given by $P_x^3 * Q_x^0 - P_x^2 * Q_x^1$, which corresponds to the shaded area in figure 6.2(b). As is clear from a comparison of the figures, this formula change allows for a *higher* level of countermeasures provided $P_x^2 < P_x^3$, that is, the current price received by US exporters was *lower* than the counterfactual exporter price that would be received under a WTO-consistent regime.

In the case of the second beef product (EBO) the arbitrators were required to make a determination similar to that which they had done for the HQB product retaliation, although in important ways the determination was more complex because the WTO-consistent regime was a tariff and not a quota. First, note that when it came to EBO, the arbitrators followed their own HQB formula and calculated the EBO retaliation limit given by the $P_x^3 * Q_x^0 - P_x^2 * Q_x^1$ formula instead of the reciprocity approach given by $P_x^3 * (Q_x^0 - Q_x^1)$ and equation (2b).[23] When the time

[21] Calculation of this exercise was controversial in *EC–Beef Hormones*, although for reasons not central to our topic. The argument between the EC and the United States focused on the degree to which the EC ban on hormone-treated beef had reduced current exports of HQB. The United States argued that it was effectively a ban and thus the value of imports should be zero, while the EC disagreed and presented information on imports from the United States of HQB that had been allowed entry into the EC because, after testing, they were found not to have been treated with hormones. The arbitrators chose some middle ground and determined the value of US current exports of non-hormone treated HQB to be US$23,853.584. The issue is one that could arguably have been resolved and addressed using quantitative economic techniques that we discuss in more detail below.

[22] See paras. 43 and 62 in the report. Interestingly, had the arbitrators adopted the approach taken in the US submission, the value and volume of current imports would have been the same – that is, zero – and thus the question of whether the arbitrators were using the appropriate price to precisely implement the reciprocity formula would not arise.

[23] See para. 72 in the report.

came to implement this formula, the first item to note is that for the case of EBO, the arbitrators once again simply chose a counterfactual price, P_x^3, that had been submitted to them by the parties. The choice received little discussion in the report and is a decision that raises the same economic questions as we identified above in our discussion of HQB, so we won't go into it further here.

Nevertheless, the interesting *differential* element worth highlighting is the quantitative techniques that the arbitrators used to construct the values for Q_x^3 :that is, the counterfactual volume of exports for EBO under a WTO-consistent regime. Because the counterfactual WTO-consistent regime for EBO was a tariff and not a quantitative restriction, the arbitrators would have to take some methodological approach to constructing their own value for Q_x^0, since it would have been market-determined and not pre-determined by some negotiated quota limit as was the case for both HQB and *EC–Bananas*.

An economist would typically rely on knowledge of EBO producers' export supply response elasticities to construct the value for Q_x^0 that the arbitrators were forced to undertake in this exercise, even taking as given an acceptable value for P_x^3: that is, the counterfactual exporter-received price, perhaps under the assumption that the exporter is "small" and unable to affect world prices by changing the quantities supplied.[24] While the arbitrators were aware of the market forces that would affect the level of imports under the WTO-consistent counterfactual (see paragraph 70 of the report), there is no mention of such elasticities in the report. Instead, the description of their approach suggests that the arbitrators made their determination for Q_x^0 by simply relying on historical trends in the data and making adjustments for EC demand-side changes during this time period.

US–Internet Gambling The final DSU arbitration involving a WTO-inconsistent quota is the case Antigua and Barbuda brought against the US import ban on Internet gambling services.[25] Compared with the arbitrations discussed thus far, at least two additional items from this case are worth highlighting: the formula the arbitrators adopted and the empirical difficulty the arbitrators confronted in order to implement the formula in this application.[26]

[24] See, for example, Francois and Reinert (1997). See also Armington (1969).

[25] *US–Measures Affecting the Cross-Border Supply of Gambling and Betting Services*, Recourse to Arbitration by the United States under Article 22.6 of the DSU, Decision by the arbitrators, WT/DS285/ARB, December 21, 2007.

[26] We do not comment on the question of the appropriateness of the arbitrator's choice of actual WTO-consistent counterfactual, but we simply focus on the formula for its

First, the arbitrators appear to have followed an approach that is quite close to the reciprocity formula and equation (2b). If the US measure in question essentially resulted in a ban on Internet gambling services from Antigua, the current volume of exports (Q_x^1) needed to implement the formula is equal to zero.[27] Next, the arbitrators then attempted to calculate the counterfactual value of exports ($P_x^3 Q_x^0$) under a WTO-consistent US policy toward imports of Internet gambling services from Antigua. When $Q_x^1 = 0$, calculation of equation (2b) simply reduces to calculation of $P_x^3 Q_x^0$.

While the Arbitrators' Report in this dispute is particularly transparent in that it makes clear the formula they were attempting to follow, the actual computation of $P_x^3 Q_x^0$ appears to have been extremely challenging – both for reasons of data availability and the need to implement relatively sophisticated quantitative economic techniques. First, it is a well-known general problem that trade flow data on the provision of services are typically very poor and difficult to obtain – data collection agencies have not simply not devoted sufficient resources to track services flows at the same level of detail as is the case for goods trade. Thus, the arbitrators were constrained by the relatively poor data which they were given to use. Second, even after the WTO-consistent counterfactual decision, determining an actual value for $P_x^3 Q_x^0$ relied on quantitative techniques in order to transform information on the most recently available and useful data (from the pre-2002 period) when Antigua had access to the US gambling market, to a scenario accurately reflecting what Antigua's market access at the time of the arbitration would have been in the absence of the WTO-inconsistent US measure.[28]

determination and the quantitative techniques needed to employ it in practice. As we describe elsewhere, economics could potentially play a role in the arbitrator's step 2 decision of the WTO-consistent policy – for example, if there are multiple such WTO-consistent counterfactuals, economic techniques could be used to help the arbitrators rank (and choose between) them on efficiency grounds, equity grounds, etc. See also the Sebastian discussion in this volume (Chapter 4).

27 Indeed, in other potential cases in which the WTO-inconsistent policy is not a complete ban, it may be difficult to obtain Q_x^1 since services trade data are typically reported only in values (that is, $P_x^2 Q_x^1$) and not volumes, which could result in the same sort of formula applied by the arbitrators in *EC–Beef Hormones* discussed above, with similar implications for the magnitude of the size of the retaliation vis-à-vis the formula of equation (2b).

28 In order to determine the value of Antigua and Barbuda's Internet gambling service exports at the time of the arbitration (2007), the arbitrators used quantitative economic techniques to address and control for market phenomenon such as (i) changes in US demand that had taken place since 2002, as well as (ii) supply-side changes that would have likely taken place given the evolution of the global market for such services, such as new competition by other foreign competitors that would likely have eroded Antiguan market share, given the initial level of super-normal profits in the industry and low entry barriers.

3.3 Non-tariff measures on imports that violate national treatment

In addition to traditional trade policy tools, such as tariffs and quotas, governments may impose non-tariff measures (NTMs) that ultimately alter conditions of competition between domestic and foreign producers. Examples include the introduction of new laws and regulations that discriminate by increasing costs to foreign export suppliers vis-à-vis those facing domestic firms that produce like products, thus forming some violation of national treatment. While there are many examples of such DSU cases involving national treatment violations, *US–Antidumping Act of 1916* is an example of such a dispute that went to arbitration. The case involved a piece of US legislation which potentially allowed dumped imports to be faced with treble damages, fines or imprisonment rather than tariffs authorized by the WTO's Antidumping Agreement. The EC argued that the US law thus violated national treatment as well as WTO rules on antidumping and caused a "chilling effect" on EC exports to the United States.

To begin our theoretical analysis of such NTMs that violate national treatment or otherwise increase costs for imports, we again assume an efficient initial trade agreement between the countries. After receiving the political shock, we assume that the respondent country's only available policy tool is not a new tariff or quota, but new domestic legislation that increases the costs of exporting into the respondent's market. In the central panel in figure 6.3, which shows the respondent's import demand and the complainant's export supply, this is captured by an upward shift of the export supply curve (from X_x^{*0} to X_x^{*1}), as exporters at the original price are less willing to supply the respondent's market. In the new equilibrium (E^x) the volume of exports is lower compared with the original equilibrium (from Q_x^0 to Q_x^1), and the price that the exporters receive is now higher (from P_x^0 to P_x^2).

The formulaic reciprocity approach to determining the limit to the complainant's countermeasures is straightforward to apply, as equation (1) continues to hold. Under this formula, the arbitrators allow the complainant to retaliate up to the level of lost trade calculated at the original export prices, as shown in the shaded area in figure 6.3. Therefore, in order to implement the formula, the arbitrators again require information as to the current level of exports (Q_x^1), and the counterfactual level of exports (Q_x^0) and export price (P_x^0) under a WTO-consistent regime.

Nevertheless, an important practical implication arises in these types of case, and is very similar to what we observed in the *EC–Beef Hormones*

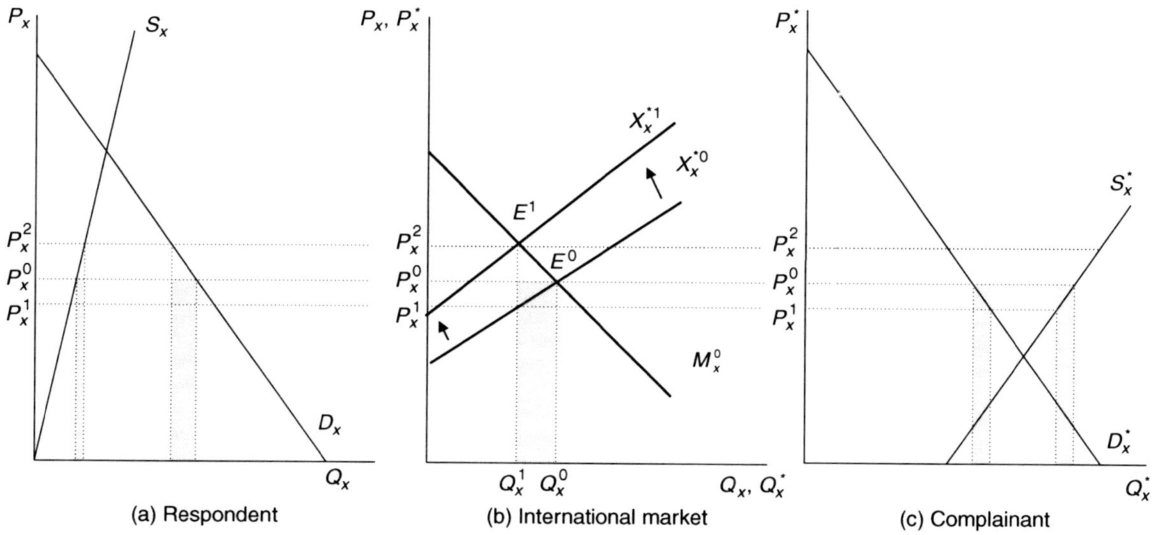

Figure 6.3. Reciprocity compensation when the respondent imposes a WTO-inconsistent non-tariff measure on a trading partner's exports (for example, violating national treatment)

arbitration and the construction of a WTO-consistent counterfactual for EBO described above. The exact quantification of the effects of national treatment violations relies on an uncertain counterfactual: that is, the inward movement of the complaining country's export supply curve. This fact makes the quantification of the appropriate response more complex than the analogous problem in the presence of applied measures such as import tariffs. Here, the quantification requires information on the size of the non-tariff measure: that is, how much the export supply curve shifts back – as well as information on the expected import demand elasticity response if that non-tariff measure were removed.

3.3.1 Actual DSU arbitrations over NTMs on imports that violate national treatment: *US–Antidumping Act of 1916*

In this particular dispute, the United States was found to have a piece of domestic legislation – the Antidumping Act of 1916 – that permitted the imposition of penalties that were inconsistent with obligations set out in the WTO's Antidumping Agreement.[29] A DSU arbitration thus determined the appropriate level of countermeasures that the EC could impose, finding that it could retaliate up to the level of damages that US courts had imposed on EC firms ("entities") under the 1916 Act as well as settlements agreed to by EC firms being prosecuted under the Act.[30]

While such a retaliatory determination is unrelated to the reciprocity approach described in the last section, we do point to one particular element of the arbitration that is relevant to such an approach. In particular, the EC made the argument to the arbitrators that the US Antidumping Act of 1916 legislation imposed a "chilling effect" on European exporting firms. In the context of our economic model and figure 6.3, such an effect can be represented as an extra cost facing foreign exporters that is not borne by domestic, import-competing firms in the United States. Thus, this piece of US legislation shifts in the EC's export supply curve in figure 6.3(b). From this theoretical perspective, it is possible for arbitrators to use

[29] *US–Antidumping Act of 1916*, Original Complaint by the European Communities, Recourse to Arbitration by the United States under Article 22.6 of the DSU, Decision by the arbitrators, WT/DS136/ARB, February 24, 2004.

[30] This led to zero retaliation in this instance as there had been no penalties imposed on EC firms, and neither party provided verifiable evidence of settlements involving EC firms that had been prosecuted under the Act. Nevertheless, the arbitrators did allow for future retaliation should such damages be incurred in the future before the United States brought the 1916 Act into WTO compliance.

the reciprocity formula approach to determine permissible EC retaliation for the trade effects illustrated there.

In practice, of course, it would have been extremely challenging for arbitrators to calculate the trade effects associated with the Antidumping Act of 1916 legislation. Quantification of the chilling effect requires the determination of the WTO-consistent counterfactual equilibrium Q^0, and thus the counterfactual export price ($P_x^{\ 0}$) as well as level of exports ($Q_x^{\ 0}$). An accurate assessment requires the calculation of the chilling effect on a product-by-product basis for all EC products that had had their exports diminished by the WTO-inconsistent policy. Individual calculations for thousands of such products may make such an approach infeasible to implement in practice, if we learn lessons from the *US–Byrd Amendment* arbitration discussed below, which similarly failed to produce product-by-product calculations despite the fact that there were many fewer such products in that instance to assess. Nevertheless, it should be pointed out that a number that is difficult to calculate is not necessarily equivalent to zero, which is the amount both the arbitrators as well as the two parties quantitatively attached to the chilling effect in the actual arbitration in *US–Antidumping Act of 1916*.

3.4 Domestic subsidies to import-competing firms

In this section we examine domestic production subsidies. Unlike the export subsidies that are the focus of section 4, domestic production subsidies are not, in principle, a trade policy measure. However, such government transfers can affect expected market access to foreign firms that WTO commitments are designed to protect. We illustrate this case in figure 6.4.

Assume that the government in R departs from an efficient agreement by providing an illegal production subsidy, *s*, to its import-competing sector.[31] As usual, a political shock, such as the increased weight on producers' surplus, may rationalize the underlying government decision to impose the new measure. Provided the domestic producers utilize at least part of the subsidy to expand domestic supply, as is the case for production subsidies by definition, then we expect an outward shift of the

[31] An important point to note is our assumption that the subsidy to import-competing producers is tied to production. On the other hand, if the transfer is just redistributed lump-sum to share holders, we should not observe any relevant effect on production and trade. However, if domestic producers utilize at least part of the subsidy to expand domestic supply this will affect the import demand curve and reduce market access to the foreign exporting firms.

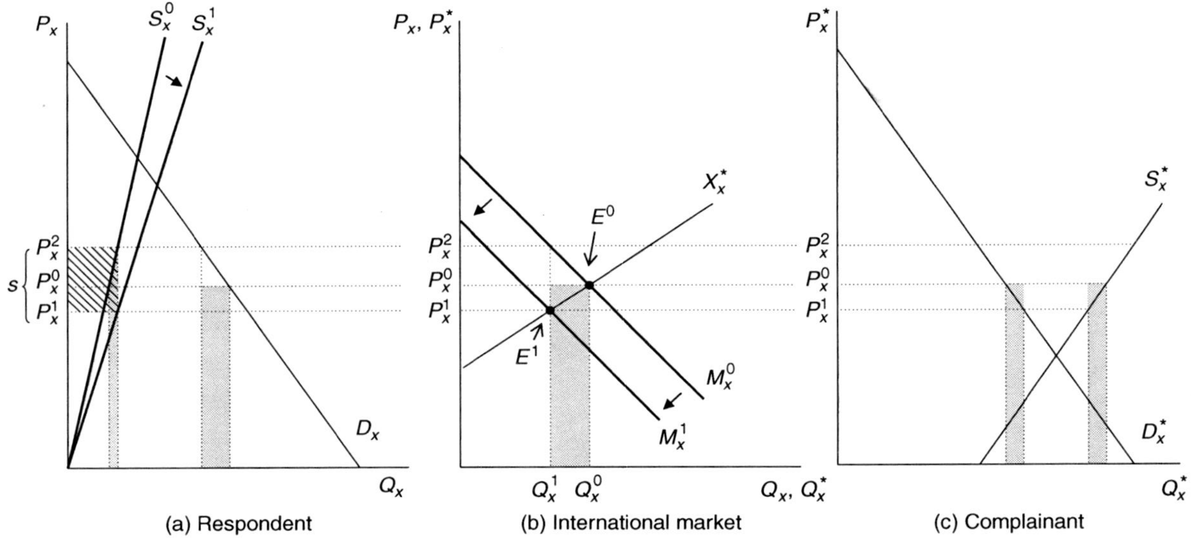

Figure 6.4. Reciprocity compensation when the respondent implements a WTO-inconsistent production subsidy to an import-competing industry

supply schedule in the respondent's market (from S_x^0 to S_x^1), depicted in figure 6.4(a). As the respondent is a net importer of the good, increased domestic production leads to a reduction in import demand from M_x^0 to M_x^1 in figure 6.4(b). In the new equilibrium (E^1), the export price falls from P_x^0 to P_x^1, which is a terms-of-trade deterioration for the complainant, and the volume of imports falls from Q_x^0 to Q_x^1.

Figure 6.4(b) illustrates how the impact of the WTO-inconsistent domestic production subsidy is analogous to an import restricting measure, such as the import tariff illustrated in figure 6.1 and described in section 3.1 – the volume of trade is lower than in the absence of such a measure. Under the reciprocity approach, the complainant is entitled to a level of retaliation equal to the shaded area in figure 6.4(b), once again permitted to impose a retaliatory tariff that restricts its imports from the respondent under the formula given by equation (1).

3.4.1 Actual DSU arbitrations over domestic subsidies to import-competing firms: *US–Continuing Dumping and Subsidy Offset Act (Byrd Amendment)*

The *US–Byrd Amendment* case involved US firms that had petitioned for antidumping and countervailing measures and subsequently received the revenue from the duties collected. We use the theoretical framework described in the last section to analyze the actual arbitration that took place.[32]

Because the Arbitrators' Report clearly signals a preference for the methodology of the US approach in the actual arbitration, we begin with a brief description of it. The US approach broadly corresponds to the reciprocity formulation developed above and the shaded area in figure 6.4(b), and it focused on three substantial points. First, the effect that the revenue remittances had on domestic production should be estimated at the product level. Second, the trade effect should be calculated by using estimates of the elasticities of US export supply and of the complaining party's import demand at the product level. Third, the calculation of the appropriate limit for the retaliatory countermeasures would then need to result from the sum of these individual values. Based on this model, the United States concluded that the trade effect of the WTO-inconsistent measure is null, as the payments did not result in any increase in production. In

[32] *US–Continued Dumping and Subsidy Offset Act of 2000*, Original Complaint by the European Communities, Recourse to Arbitration by the United States under Article 22.6 of the DSU, Decision by the arbitrators, WT/DS217/ARB/EEC, August 31, 2004.

terms of figure 6.4(a), this is equivalent to saying that the effect of the Byrd Amendment payments to US firms led to no shift in the domestic supply curve (from S_x^0 to S_x^1).

While the arbitrators indicated sympathy to the proposed US methodology for establishing the retaliation limits (paragraph 3.114 of the report), they ultimately disagreed with how the United States implemented the model and based their reasoning on two fundamental arguments. First, the arbitrators felt that the effect of the revenue remittances on domestic production would be generally different from zero. Second, the United States had chosen not to implement the model for a number of products covered by antidumping or countervailing duties that the arbitrators decided should have been part of the calculation. Therefore, while the arbitrators signaled in their report a preference to use an approach that appeared consistent with the reciprocity formula that would be implemented at the product level, they were constrained to adopting a more aggregated approach that utilizes a less data-intensive methodology.

The arbitrator's actual approach relied on an "economically determined" coefficient (72 per cent) that is then multiplied by the level of the subsidy (see figure 6.4(a) under the assumption that – a fraction of – the remittances worked as a production subsidy) to provide an estimate of the value of lost trade (in figure 6.4(b)). This coefficient is meant to capture the value of the trade effect of the WTO-inconsistent measure: each dollar paid to petitioning firms reduces the value of exports of the complainant by 72 cents. A key issue is, therefore, how such value was calculated. The broad idea is that the aggregate trade effect would be the product of three elements: the price reduction caused by the payment ("pass-through," in the language of the report); a substitution elasticity of imports; and import penetration. Arbitrators used adjusted data provided by the parties to estimate an annual value of the trade-effect coefficient for each year between 2001 and 2003 and calculated the average for the period.

As an empirical matter, it is admittedly difficult to assess whether the actual level of retaliation proposed by the arbitrators is consistent with the reciprocity approach discussed in the previous section. The two levels in figures 4(a) and 4(b) are related, but they can be generally quite different when evaluated on a product-by-product basis. The coefficient attempts to average out these effects by providing a single number is an imperfect substitute for a more detailed and disaggregated approach. However, we do note that the aim of the arbitrators' approach in this case is quite clearly to utilize available data to evaluate the *trade effect* of the subsidy.

As we discuss in the next section, this is not necessarily the case for WTO-inconsistent *export* subsidies.

4 WTO disputes and retaliation over export-promoting measures

We now turn our attention to WTO-inconsistent policy measures that a respondent country R implements that have the effect of excessively promoting exports. Examples of such policies include government transfers to the export sector, such as export and production subsidies. The theory of trade policy clearly documents how such measures have fundamentally different effects on trade volumes and the terms of trade when compared with import restraining policies. However, we show that, in a number of instances that are relevant for DSU cases and arbitrations, the logic of the reciprocity approach still delivers interesting insights. Namely, such instances rely on the presence of an export market in a third country in which both the complainant and the respondent jointly sell their goods.[33]

4.1 Export subsidies in a three-country model

We begin our investigation of the role for retaliation by looking at export subsidies. Bagwell and Staiger (2001b) show how a subsidy agreement that limits government payments and avoids subsidy escalation can be of value to governments of exporting firms. Without such an agreement, each government is tempted to subsidize its exporters so as to create a competitive advantage in a third market: that is, a prisoners' dilemma problem.

Here we extend the theoretical model of section 3 that examined import-restricting measures in two important directions. First, we introduce a third good (that we call z) which both the complainant (C) and the respondent (R) export to a third country that we refer to as the rest of the world (ROW), again under the assumption of competitive market conditions. Second, we allow the governments of countries R and C access to an export-promoting policy tool (s) that affects good z, in addition to the tariff policies (τ, τ^*) that they can implement on one another's imports of x and y, respectively.[34] For simplicity, ROW does not use any policies to

[33] Absent this assumption, as we discuss in a later section, it is unclear why export-promoting policies are a problem in the first place, which suggests that we may need a different model to rationalize existing rules.

[34] Note for clarity that this good z is different from the numeraire good introduced in the general equilibrium version of the Bagwell and Staiger (2001a) model discussed in footnote 13.

interfere with trade flows. This framework is a straightforward extension of Bagwell and Staiger (2001b). Furthermore, we begin from an efficient international agreement which binds the level of both import-restricting and export-promoting policy measures. We denote these levels with τ^E, τ^{*E} and s^E, s^{*E}, under the simplifying assumption that they are symmetric across countries and across goods.

Now assume that the government of the respondent country receives a political shock, such as an increase to the political weight on exporters' interests, so that it seeks to increase its export-promoting policy for sector z to $s^I > s^E$. The introduction of this new measure in country R will affect the volume of its export of good z to the rest of the world. As a result of excess export supply, the price of good z in international markets falls, thereby reducing country C's producers' market access in ROW as well as the price of their exports.

Figure 6.5(a) illustrates this by focusing on the ROW import market for good z from the complainant country only, thus abstracting from the respondent. It portrays ROW's net import demand from the complainant (M_z^0) and the export supply from country C (X_z^*). Before the shock in R, the equilibrium is at point E^0, which implies an export price P_z^0 (s^E, s^{*E}) and a volume of trade between the complainant and the ROW equal to Q_z^0 (s^E, s^{*E}). The effect of the subsidy in R is to shift downward ROW's net import demand curve toward products deriving from exporters in C. Intuitively, the export subsidy in R allows its exporters to supply goods in international markets at a lower price, which reduces the demand for exports from country C. In the new equilibrium, denoted with E^I, the price received by C's exporters P_z^I (s^I, s^{*E}) is lower and the quantity of exports of the complainant into the ROW market falls from Q_z^0 to Q_z^I (s^I, s^{*E}). This policy change in R hurts the exporting sector in C by lowering its market access in the rest of the world and worsening its terms of trade.

We adopt the reciprocity approach to determine the level of complainant retaliation in response to its loss of market access in the ROW. Formally, under the reciprocity approach the complainant is allowed to introduce a retaliatory trade restrictive measure (τ^{*Ret}) on the imports of good y from country R that is equal to the value of lost trade volumes at original export prices, that is:

$$P_z^0\left(s^E, s^{*E}\right)\left[Q_z^0\left(s^E, s^{*E}\right) - Q_z^1\left(s^1, s^{*E}\right)\right] = P_y^0\left(\tau^{*E}\right)\left[Q_y^0\left(\tau^E\right) - Q_y^{Ret}\left(\tau^{*Ret}\right)\right]. \quad (3)$$

The retaliation that the complainant is entitled to under the reciprocity approach corresponds to the shaded area in Figure 6.5(a). The left-hand side

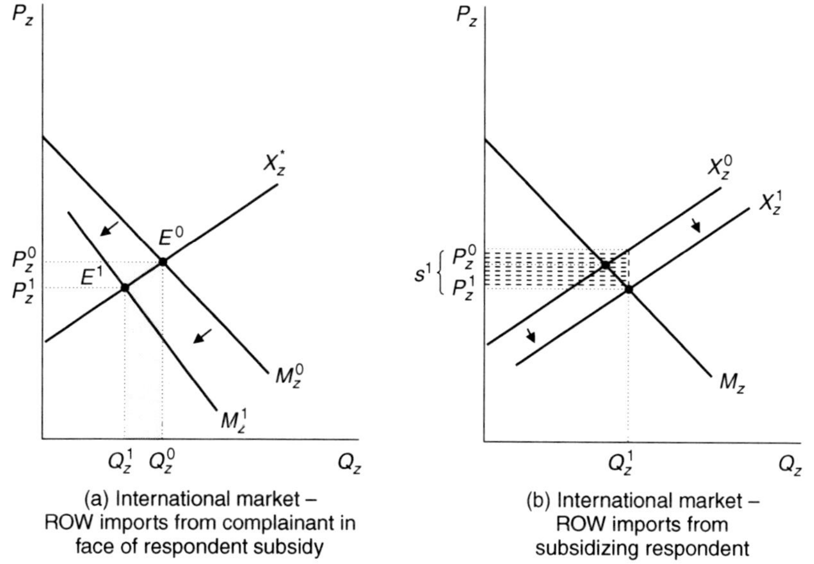

Figure 6.5. Reciprocity compensation when the respondent imposes a WTO-inconsistent export subsidy (three-country model)

of the reciprocity condition above is the volume of lost trade for the complainant $(Q_z^0 - Q_z^1)$ evaluated at the original export price, that is, $P_z^0(s^E, s^{*E})$. Similar to the case of import-restricting measures, the reciprocity approach allows for a level of retaliation which preserves a balance of concessions.

Finally, compare the effects of export-promoting policies with those of import-restricting measures analyzed in the previous section. While the higher export subsidy in R leads to a contraction in complainant trade volume with the ROW just as was the case with import-restricting measures, the *overall* effect of this subsidy policy on trade is to *expand* trade volumes. The subsidy thus *creates* more trade between R and the ROW than is lost between C and the ROW, and for this reason, the terms of trade improve for the consuming importers in the rest of the world.

4.1.1 Actual DSU arbitrations over export subsidies and third country effects: *Canada–Aircraft Subsidies, Brazil–Aircraft Subsidies, and US–Foreign Sales Corporations (FSC)*

Before describing actual DSU arbitrations over export subsidies, it is worth using this economic model to make one additional point regarding GATT/WTO treatment of export subsidies. Under the countervailing duty provisions that have been part of the GATT/WTO since 1947, if a foreign government offers a subsidy to exporting firms that leads to injury in a domestic, import-competing industry, the government of the import-competing producers can unilaterally impose a countervailing duty. However, the magnitude of the response has been limited to *no larger than the amount of the subsidy.*[35]

In the context of our earlier model, Figure 6.5(b) now presents a second illustration of the ROW import market, but this time from the perspective of the respondent's export supply curves in the face of the respondent country's export subsidy (s^1) which shifts out the X_z^0 curve to X_z^1.[36] Note that in the model, the value of the respondent's export subsidy is given by the hatched area in Figure 6.5(b). It is clear from the figure that the size of the subsidy is related to its trade effect as a larger subsidy expands R's export supply schedule. However, it is not obvious that the size of the subsidy's value corresponds to the *trade effect* that we have been examining under the reciprocity formulation. The relationship between the sizes of shaded area in Figure 6.5(a) and the hatched area in Figure 6.5(b) ultimately depends on the elasticities of the ROW's import demand and R's export supply.

Naturally, one can make an argument, which may be relevant on practical grounds, that the size of the transfer may be easier to calculate than the value of the market access effect. Nevertheless, this is different from the reciprocity formula based on a theoretical approach to understanding the purpose of retaliation from a trade-balancing effect perspective (Bagwell and Staiger 2002). We return to a discussion of this issue as it arises in the actual arbitrations on export subsidies discussed below.

Canada–Aircraft Subsidies* and *Brazil–Aircraft Subsidies The first two DSU arbitrations are the *Canada* (Bombardier) and *Brazil* (Embraer) aircraft subsidy cases.[37] These disputes fit the model as they relate to export subsidies given to firms that compete in third markets. In the first dispute that Canada brought against Brazil, Brazil was found to have provided WTO-inconsistent export subsidies via its export financing program for

[35] See, for example, the discussion in Sykes (2005).

[36] In this figure we abstract from the complainant's export supply curve, which is assumed to remain unchanged.

[37] See *Canada–Export Credits and Loan Guarantees for Regional Aircraft*, Recourse by Canada to Article 22.6 of the DSU and Article 4.11 of the SCM Agreement, Decision by the arbitrator, WT/DS222/ARB, February 17, 2003; and *Brazil–Export Financing Programme for Aircraft*, Recourse to Arbitration by Brazil under Article 22.6 of the DSU and Article 4.11 of the SCM Agreement, Decision by the arbitrators, WT/DS46/ARB, August 28, 2000.

Embraer regional jet aircraft that competed with Bombardier sales in third markets. In the second case, Canada was found to have implemented similar WTO-inconsistent policies – constructed as export credit and loan guarantees – to Bombardier's export sales of regional jets. In terms of timing, the Article 22.6 arbitration in the *Brazil* case was announced in August 2000, while the *Canada* case was announced in February 2003.

It is instructive to lump together the discussion of these cases for two reasons. First, they are clearly related in the sense of one country's WTO-inconsistent export subsidy scheme likely being in existence because of the other country's similar policy. Second, the arbitrators' logic in each dispute was similar. The arbitrators did not attempt to implement a reciprocity formula that would follow the trade-effects approach that we introduced in the theoretical section. Instead, in each case, the arbitrators sought to establish a permissible level of retaliation simply commensurate with the size of the value of the export subsidy, that is, the hatched area of Figure 6.5(b) given by $s^I\ Q_z^I$.[38] As we have noted, the size of this area is not necessarily a good proxy for the size of the *trade effects* of the export subsidy – that is, the volume of lost trade for the complainant ($Q_z^0 - Q_z^I$) evaluated at the original export price: that is, $P_z^0\ (s^E, s^{*E})$. While there are a number of potential explanations behind why the arbitrators chose a different formula (the size of the export subsidy) than the reciprocity formula based on the trade impact of the measure,[39] it is also worth pointing out that the arbitrators discussed the trade impact of the subsidies and recognized that it might differ from the size of the actual subsidy itself.[40]

38 In the arbitration over Canadian subsidies in which Brazil was permitted to retaliate, the arbitrators added 20 per cent to the size of the estimated Canadian subsidy under the argument that "the 'appropriate' level of countermeasures should reflect the specific purpose of countermeasures. Keeping this in mind, we are aware of the view that Canada's statement that, for the moment, it does not intend to withdraw the subsidy at issue suggests that in order to induce compliance in this case a higher level of countermeasures … would be necessary and appropriate" (para. 3.107, pp. 30–1).

39 These would include arguments that the arbitrators pick the size of the subsidy in third market cases because: (1) this is the analogue to the response under WTO permitted countervailing duty laws in two-country models; (2) calculating trade effects in a third market model would require data and elasticities from third country markets (the importer) which do not face the same economic incentive to rein in the use of the subsidies since they benefit from lower import prices when they are in place; (3) for "lumpy" products, such as aircraft, it may be difficult to construct the trade impact of an export subsidy precisely; (4) some of these subsidies may have dynamic (long-run) effects, especially when they are allocated in markets with high fixed costs of entry.

40 In the *Canada–Aircraft* case, the arbitrators indicated that "We agree in principle with Brazil that, in a market as competitive as the market for regional jets, even a limited difference in interest rates, if it allows a manufacturer to win a contract, may have a

Since the only WTO-consistent regime for export subsidies for these aircraft was zero, the only remaining task to implement the chosen formula is to use quantitative economics to compute the size of the subsidies. Computation of the size of the export subsidy in each of the arbitrations appears to have relied on standard techniques from financial economics. The arbitrators in each of the disputes took the basic approach of calculating the total discounted present value of the subsidy based on sales data and information on financing terms (interest rates) provided by the parties.

US–Foreign Sales Corporations (FSC) The final DSU arbitration that we consider is the retaliation the EC was authorized in response to US imposition of WTO-inconsistent subsidies in the *US-Foreign Sales Corporation (FSC)* dispute.[41] An export subsidy such as that found in the *US–FSC* case has the potential not only to have trade effects on exporting firms from complaining countries in third markets, but it is also quite possible that such a subsidy might also adversely affect the complaining countries' firms' sales in its own domestic market. In this section we limit discussion to the third-market effect and return to the latter effect after having introduced a two-country model of export subsidies in the next section.

Similar to the approach in the two aircraft subsidy disputes, the arbitrators' formula for establishing appropriate countermeasures was based on the size of the estimated subsidy that the United States gave its firms and not the trade effects embodied in the modified Bagwell and Staiger reciprocity formula.[42] Nevertheless, the arbitrators in the *US–FSC* dispute also did not rule out consideration of the trade effects approach, although nowhere in the report is there a description of either the parties or the arbitrators considering the formula, counterfactual, or quantitative techniques that would be needed to construct such a countermeasure limit in the same way that we observed and noted in *EC–Bananas*, *EC–Beef Hormones*, or *US–Internet Gambling*, for instance.[43]

disproportionate impact, calculated on the basis of the trade impact, compared with the amount of subsidy granted" (para. 3.115, p. 32).

41 *US–Tax Treatment for Foreign Sales Corporations*, Recourse to Arbitration by the United States under Article 22.6 of the DSU and Article 4.11 of the SCM Agreement, Decision of the arbitrator, WT/DS108/ARB, August 30, 2002.

42 See also the discussion in Howse and Neven (2005).

43 Indeed, the arbitrators state "We ... do not rule out *a priori* that trade effects of the measure on the affected Member can enter into consideration in a particular case, as a relevant factor, in determining the 'appropriate' amount of countermeasures within the meaning of Article 4.10 of the SCM Agreement. Indeed, as we have previously noted, the expression 'appropriate countermeasures', in our view, would entitle the complaining Member

In terms of implementing the formula once it has been decided, the choice of the WTO-consistent counterfactual was relatively straightforward in this dispute since the subsidy was prohibited. Thus, the remaining task for the arbitrators is to use quantitative economic techniques to determine the size of the US subsidy. In this particular case it was complicated by a number of factors – including the fact that, like the *US–Byrd Amendment* and *US–Antidumping Act of 1916* cases discussed above, the subsidy applied to many different firms, sectors, and products. Instead of doing a product-by-product approach to constructing the subsidy from the micro level and aggregating it upward, both of the parties relied on relatively aggregated models to construct estimates of the size of the subsidy – indeed, the EC even presented results based on a model used by the US Treasury Department in an unrelated report that it gave to the US Congress in 1997 on the trade effects of the US FSC policy. Nevertheless, in this particular instance, in order to make a decision on the size of the subsidy, the arbitrators were ultimately forced to confront and make assessments on a number of key inputs required to generate output from the models, including the parties' proposed values for "the reduction in the price of the good benefiting from the subsidy; the export response of producers benefiting from the subsidy; and the price elasticity of demand for US exports" (footnote 90, pp. 27–28 of the report).

4.2 *Export subsidies in a two-country model*

Consider again the two-country model of section 3.1, but now assume that in addition to import tariffs, governments have another policy tool in their arsenal in the form of export subsidies. The initial situation corresponds, as before, to an efficient agreement and, in response to a political shock, the government in R increases its export subsidy to domestic producers of good y to the new politically optimal level. We study the effect of this policy change on the volume of trade and on the price, and use this to infer the appropriate level of retaliation under the reciprocity approach.

Figure 6.6 illustrates the consequences of increased export subsidies in R. The central panel illustrates the equilibrium in the international market. This figure portrays the export supply schedule of the respondent and the import demand schedule of the complainant. Both curves can be obtained (*mutatis mutandis*) with the same methodology described above for the tariff analysis.

to countermeasures which would at least counter the injurious effect of the persisting illegal measure on it" (para. 6.33, pp. 25–6).

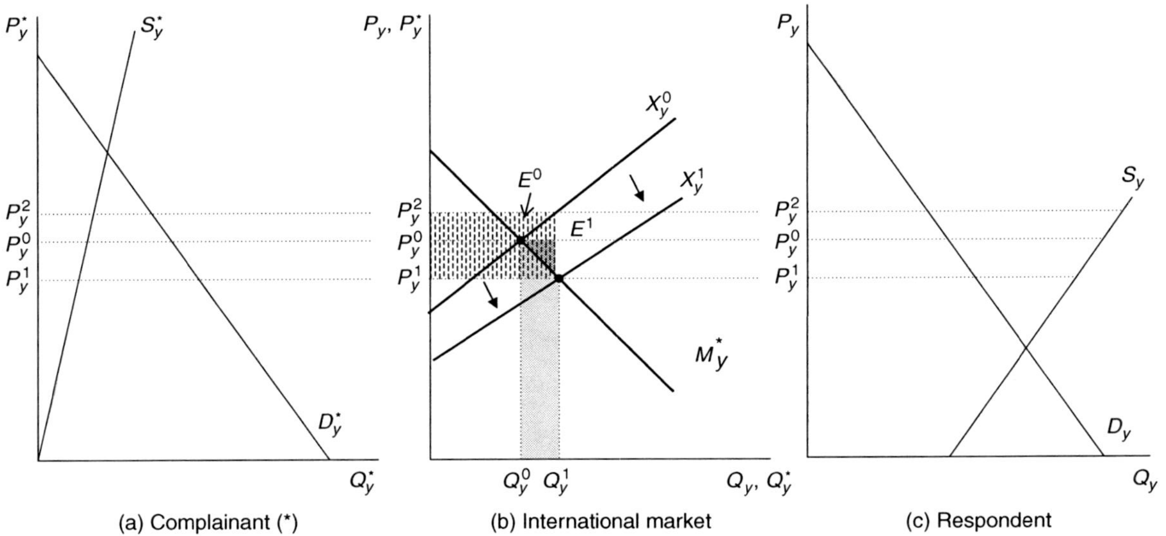

Figure 6.6. Reciprocity compensation when the respondent imposes a WTO-inconsistent export subsidy (two-country model)

The effect of the increased export subsidy is to create incentives for producers in R to export more for any given price, thus shifting downward the export supply schedule in Figure 6.6(b) from X_y^0 to X_y^1. As a result, an excess supply is created in the international (and the complainant's) market and an excess demand in country R, which causes the price to fall in the international and the complainant's market (from P_y^0 to P_y^1) and to increase in the domestic market of the respondent (from P_y^0 to P_y^2), which in turn implies a higher quantity of exports (from Q_y^0 to Q_y^1).[44]

The fundamental implication of the policy change is that the respondent *increases* its market access in the international market (that is, in country C's import market) at the expense of producers in the complainant country. Figure 6.6(b) illustrates the reciprocity formula's level of retaliation as equal to the volume of trade distorted relative to the initial agreement ($Q_y^1 - Q_y^0$) calculated at original export price (P_y^0). This area is shaded in Figure 6.6(b) and is equal to each of the shaded areas in figures 6(a) and 6(c). Note finally in Figure 6.6(b) how, similar to the three-country model export subsidy case derived in the last section, there is not necessarily an equivalence between the size of the value of the export subsidy (the hatched rectangle) and the trade effect under reciprocity (the shaded rectangle).

While the intuition of the reciprocity approach remains unaltered in this model of export subsidies vis-à-vis the model with import-restraining policies – that is, the retaliation is one that stabilizes the value of exports and imports between countries – this theoretical case also identifies an important limitation. Here we have a major departure from the previous section, in which the complainant experienced a *negative* terms-of-trade effect as a consequence of the higher export subsidy in the respondent. In this example of a two-country model, the complainant experiences a *positive* terms-of-trade effect. From the perspective of pure social welfare, it is well understood that the subsidy lowers welfare for the respondent and increases welfare for importing country C. From an aggregate welfare sense, the complainant should have little to complain about.

4.2.1 Actual and potential DSU arbitrations over export subsidies in a two-country model: *US–Foreign Sales Corporations (FSC)*

This discussion on WTO-inconsistent subsidies in two-country models suggests a novel reflection on the *US–FSC* case. As observed in section

44 Even if in our notation (both in the text and in the figure) we do not show functional arguments, the reader should keep in mind that, relative to section 3, prices and quantities are now functions of both tariffs *and* subsidies.

4.1.1 and shown above, this form of export subsidy has the potential to adversely affect the complaining countries' firms' sales in its own domestic market in addition to any third-market effect. For example, if these are multiproduct firms that produce different varieties, an export subsidy by the respondent may affect the complainants' sales in a third country export market as well as its own domestic market. Thus, while the theoretical case in this section is often thought to be most easily and efficiently dealt with outside of a DSU case via the use of (WTO-permitted) countervailing measures, in the case that export subsidies have a trade effect in both third markets and domestic markets, there may be some efficiency arguments for considering all these elements together in one DSU proceeding.

5 Other issues

In this section we briefly discuss issues that are also potentially important in light of specific DSU cases but that we could not address with the theoretical models presented thus far.

5.1 *Imperfectly competitive markets: strategic trade policy*

Each of the models introduced thus far has assumed that firms trade in perfectly competitive markets. Given that the two arbitrations over export subsidies between Canada and Brazil clearly involve aircraft-producing firms (Bombardier and Embraer) that compete in imperfectly competitive markets, here we present a simple refinement of the underlying model to check on the sensitivity of our results.

As discussed in the strategic trade policy literature, when export markets are not competitive, an export subsidy can be appealing to the exporting firm's government for reasons that are independent of any political-economy motive. The classic example is Brander and Spencer (1985), who present a model with many of the same characteristics as the three-country model of section 4. Brander and Spencer's primary departure from the model in section 4 is that there are only two firms – that is, one is the respondent and one is the complainant – and the exporting market in the ROW where producers compete is thus not competitive, but is assumed to have a Cournot oligopolistic market structure. Notwithstanding these differences, the effects of an export subsidy in this environment are remarkably similar. A key insight is that such subsidies can represent a means through which a government can give its exporters an advantage. If only one government uses such a subsidy, it can change the nature of the game to one in which its subsidy policy credibly commits its firms to a production level that effectively gives it a first-mover (Stackelberg leadership) advantage. Of course, if both governments have access to such subsidies, both may implement them and the result is a prisoner's dilemma outcome: that is, while both would be better off removing the subsidies, neither country has a unilateral incentive to do so. Hence, from these two countries' perspective, there is an incentive to craft a subsidy limitation agreement to help them to jointly escape the prisoner's dilemma outcome.

Therefore, assume we begin with such a (bilaterally) "efficient" export subsidy agreement and that government R suddenly increases the subsidy to its firm. What are the effects on the trade volume between country C and the ROW? What is the appropriate level of retaliation that an arbitrator should allow under the reciprocity approach? Similar to the earlier export subsidy model of perfect competition, the effect of a subsidy is to reduce the effective import demand of the ROW faced by the producer in C. As depicted in Figure 6.5, the downward shift of import demand in world markets leads to a contraction of export volumes for the complainant's firm. Under the reciprocity condition, the level of retaliation corresponds to the shaded area in Figure 6.5. Independently of the mode of competition in export markets, export subsidies in one country distort trade flows against exporters in the other country which results in a negative terms-of-trade effect for the complainant.

Nevertheless, it is still the case that the overall outcome of export subsidies is an increase in trade volume and a terms-of-trade (and welfare) improvement for the importing country, ROW. This positive effect is particularly strong in the case of oligopolistic markets where, notably, firms have an incentive to keep the level of production inefficiently low to increase profits. In this set of models, export subsidies may, therefore, lead to a welfare improvement for the world as a whole. This reinforces the idea expressed elsewhere that we may require a different theoretical framework to analyze agreements that limit export subsidies altogether.[45]

5.2 *Non-political shocks*

In this section we alter a second assumption of the model by considering how our analysis would change if the respondent experienced a technology

[45] See the discussions in Bagwell and Staiger (2006, 2001b). Furthermore, see Ossa (2008) who presents an alternative theory of trade agreements when markets are imperfectly competitive.

or a demand shock instead of the "political" shock we have used thus far. The main question that we need to address is whether the evaluation of the appropriate retaliation under the reciprocity approach would be substantially different in the presence of other types of shocks.[46]

To illustrate this case we use our graphs that represent the market for good x in the two-country model with import tariffs discussed in section 3.1. Figure 6.7 depicts the case of a negative technology shock to the import sector in country R. We start from an efficient trade agreement in which tariffs are initially bound at τ^E, τ^{*E}, which implies an equilibrium in international markets in figure 6.7(b) at E^0, where the export price is $P_x^{\,0}$ and the corresponding volume of trade is $Q_x^{\,0}$. The negative technology shock in R causes a reduction in domestic supply and thus an inward shift of the supply curve from $S_x^{\,0}$ to $S_x^{\,1}$. This leads to a flatter respondent import demand curve (from $M_x^{\,0}$ to $M_x^{\,1}$) in the international market. The post-shock equilibrium in figure 6.7(b) is denoted with E^1 and corresponds to a higher export price $P_x^{\,1}$ and volume of trade $Q_x^{\,1}$. Intuitively, the negative technology shock reduces domestic supply in country R and thus creates an excess demand for the good in the international market, which results in a higher price and larger imports.

In the context of this model and our discussion thus far, the supply shock has not produced anything that would result in a WTO dispute, as we have assumed that R's government did not make any policy changes in response to the shock. With no government policy response, there would be no dispute, as country C's market access and its terms of trade have improved in the face of the shock. However, there are important reasons to believe that the government in R may respond to an adverse technology shock. One possibility is that the import-competing producers of good x negatively affected by the shock increase lobbying pressure on the government, which responds by increasing its politically optimal tariff from the WTO binding of τ^E to some level τ^1 that, while non-prohibitive, violates its WTO commitments.[47] Notice that this is not a political shock, as the preferences of the government (that is, the weights on producers' surplus versus consumer welfare) have not changed. Absent the supply shock, the policymaker would not have

[46] Note that a similar analysis could be done for the equally important case of foreign (positive) technology shocks which expand market access but may, at the same time, endogenously induce the imposition of new trade barriers in response. The question of the permissible level of retaliation in the face of these two events (foreign shock and new domestic trade barrier) will also arise in such a setting.

[47] For a formal political economy model that shows why declining industries can be particularly effective in receiving protection from the government, see Baldwin and Robert-Nicoud (2007).

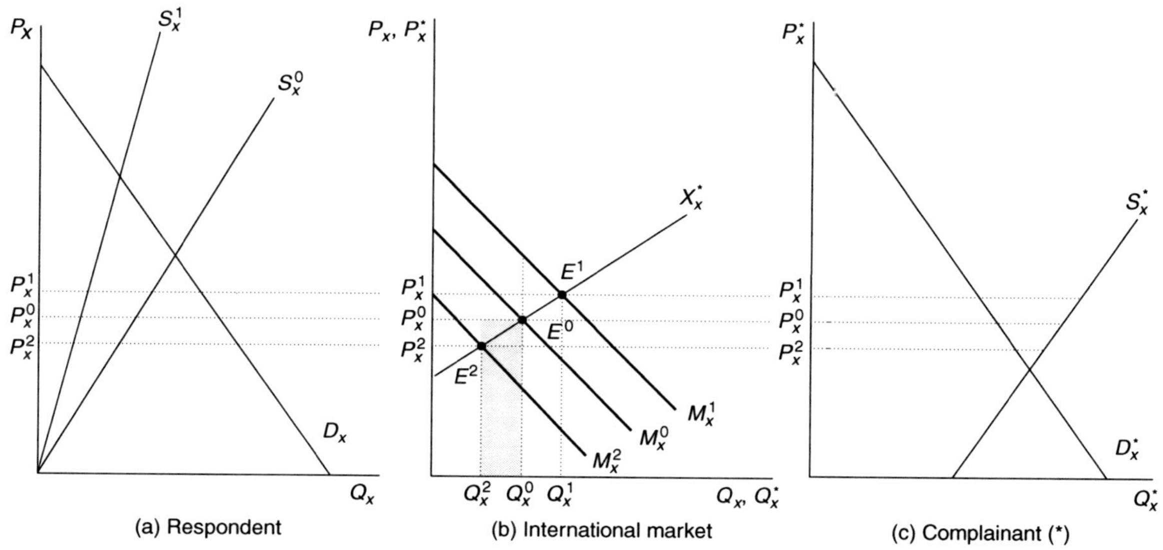

Figure 6.7. Reciprocity compensation when the respondent implements a WTO-inconsistent tariff after a supply shock

changed its policy. However, the practical effect of such a shock is no different, as both a political and a technology shock may well result in an increase of a trade-restricting measure. In what follows, we first study the effects of the higher tariff on market access in the context of a negative technology shock and then discuss the issue of appropriate retaliation.

A new (and higher) tariff in country R causes a contraction of market access and a negative terms-of-trade effect for the complainant that is similar to what we observed in figure 6.1 and discussed in section 3.1. More precisely, the higher tariff increases the domestic price of the good in R and reduces R's import demand from M_x^1 to M_x^2 in Figure 6.7(b). In the new equilibrium E^2, imports fall from Q_x^1 to Q_x^2 and the export price is at the lower level P_x^2. In the figure, market access for the complainant is not only reduced compared with equilibrium in the absence of the tariff increase in the respondent, but also relative to the pre-shock situation.[48]

What is the level of retaliation under the reciprocity approach in this instance? As the answer to this question is not trivial, we do not attempt to be exhaustive and instead limit our consideration to the two extreme cases that establish a range of possibilities. A first option is to consider the effect of the tariff only, which is equivalent to what we examined in the case of a political shock. Here the value of lost trade evaluated at the initial export price corresponds to the rectangle $P_x^1(Q_x^1 - Q_x^2)$ in Figure 6.7(b). This neglects the fact that the tariff increase was triggered by a negative supply shock in R which increased market access for producers in country C and thus may *overestimate* the prejudice to the complainant. A second possibility is the pre-shock equilibrium and assessing the value of lost trade induced by a higher tariff relative to that counterfactual. This would suggest a smaller permissible retaliation for the complainant equal to the area $P_x^0\ (Q_x^0 - Q_x^2)$: that is, the shaded area in Figure 6.7(b). In this special case in which the new equilibrium falls in between the pre- and the post-shock levels, the permissible retaliation for the complainant would be zero. Hence, the risk here may be to *underestimate* the prejudice caused by WTO-inconsistent policy actions.

6 Conclusions

The DSU gives WTO arbitrators the mandate to establish the permissible retaliation limits that aggrieved complainant countries can implement

[48] This is not necessarily the case as there is also a special case in which the new equilibrium falls between the pre- and the post-shock equilibriums.

in response. Arbitrators, therefore, set the retaliation limits that ultimately serve to enforce the overall WTO agreement. We have examined how WTO arbitrators have used theoretical and quantitative economic analysis in this stage of the DSU process for the ten disputes that reached the stage of arbitration between 1995 and 2007. Our approach also illustrates a template for many additional types of arbitrations likely to take place under the DSU going forward, in a number of different areas.

We organized the analysis by adopting the Bagwell and Staiger interpretation of the WTO principle of reciprocity to provide a theoretical framework that arbitrators can apply to identify the maximum level of retaliatory countermeasures. We have identified, characterized, and categorized the major classes of disputes – for example, those affecting import protection versus export promotion – that typically occur under the WTO and the implications of the Bagwell and Staiger approach for each type of likely dispute. Our framework has also allowed us to identify three crucial elements to the arbitrators' decision-making process for each case: (i) the formula that they decide to adopt for identifying appropriate countermeasures; (ii) their political-legal-economic decision on a WTO-consistent counterfactual to use to implement the formula; and (iii) the quantitative methods they use to necessarily construct the (unobserved) WTO-consistent counterfactual. We then analyzed each of the ten DSU arbitrations taking place between 1995 and 2007 by comparing the arbitrators' actual approach with the theory.

In many of the DSU cases that we have examined, such as the arbitrations over WTO-inconsistent quantitative restrictions that limit imports, the arbitrators' actual approach appears quite consistent with the Bagwell and Staiger reciprocity formulation theory. Furthermore, in a number of other cases, the Arbitrators' Report explicitly signals their preference to use such an approach despite the practical inability to do so for procedural, computational, or data limitation reasons related to the quantitative methods they are forced to employ in practice. Even in the arbitrations over WTO-inconsistent subsidies in which the arbitrators have departed from the trade-effects approach to establishing retaliation limits in favor of a number that is arguably easier to calculate (that is, the size of the subsidy), using theory to analyze the retaliation determination question allowed us to compare the arbitrators' actual approach to one that might occur under this particular formulation of reciprocity. Finally, in the disputes in which this reciprocity approach has not been used, we identified the procedural difficulties that arbitrators confront, thus highlighting the constraints that hinder their use of economic analysis in practice.

References

Armington, Paul S. 1969. "A Theory of Demand for Products Distinguished by Place of Production," *IMF Staff Papers*, 16(1): 159–77.

Bagwell, Kyle 2008. "Remedies in the WTO: An Economic Perspective" in Merit E. Janow, Victoria J. Donaldson and Alan Yanovich (eds.), *The WTO: Governance, Dispute Settlement & Developing Countries* (Huntington, NY: Juris Publishing), 733–70.

Bagwell, Kyle and Robert W. Staiger 1999. "An Economic Theory of GATT," *American Economic Review*, 89(1): 215–48.

2001a. "Reciprocity, Nondiscrimination and Preferential Agreements in the Multilateral Trading System," *European Journal of Political Economy*, 17(2): 281–325.

2001b. "Strategic Trade, Competitive Industries and Agricultural Trade Disputes," *Economics and Politics*, 13(2):113–28.

2002. *The Economics of the World Trading System* (Cambridge, MA: MIT Press).

2006. "Will International Rules on Subsidies Disrupt the World Trading System?" *American Economic Review*, 96(3): 877–95.

Bagwell, Kyle, Petros C. Mavroidis and Robert W. Staiger 2002. "It's a Question of Market Access," *American Journal of International Law*, 96(1): 56–76.

Baldwin, Richard and Frederic Robert-Nicoud 2007. "Entry and Asymmetric Lobbying: Why Governments Pick Losers," *Journal of the European Economic Association*, 5(5):1064–93.

Bernstein, Jason and David Skully 2003. "Calculating Trade Damages in the Context of the World Trade Organization's Dispute Settlement Process," *Review of Agricultural Economics*, 25(2): 385–98.

Bown, Chad P. 2002. "The Economics of Trade Disputes, the GATT's Article XXIII and the WTO's Dispute Settlement Understanding," *Economics and Politics*, 14(3): 283–323.

2004. "Trade Disputes and the Implementation of Protection under the GATT: An Empirical Assessment," *Journal of International Economics*, 62(2): 263–94.

Brander, James A. and Barbara Spencer 1985. "Export Subsidies as International Market Share Rivalry," *Journal of International Economics*, 17: 83–100.

Breuss, Fritz 2004. "WTO Dispute Settlement: An Economic Analysis of Four EU–US Mini Trade Wars," *Journal of Industry, Competition and Trade*, 4(4): 275–315.

Francois, Joseph F. and Kenneth A. Reinert (eds.) 1997. *Applied Methods for Trade Policy Analysis: A Handbook* (Cambridge University Press).

Gawande, Kishore and Pravin Krishna 2003. "The Political Economy of Trade Policy: Empirical Approaches" in E. K. Choi and J. Hartigan (eds.), *Handbook of International Trade*, vol. I (Oxford: Blackwell).

Grossman, Gene M. and Elhanan Helpman 1994. "Protection for Sale," *American Economic Review*, 84(4): 833–50.

Howse, Robert and Damien J. Neven 2005. "United States – Tax Treatment for 'Foreign Sales Corporations' Recourse to Arbitration by the United States under Article 22.6 of the DSU and Article 4.11 of the SCM Agreement (WT/DS106/ARB): A Comment" in Henrik Horn and Petros C. Mavroidis (eds.), *The WTO Case Law of 2002* (Cambridge University Press).

Howse, Robert and Robert W. Staiger 2005. "United States – Antidumping Act of 1916 (Original Complaint by the European Communities) – Recourse to Arbitration by the United States under Article 22.6 of the DSU," *World Trade Review*, 4(2): 295–316.

Keck, Alexander 2004. "WTO Dispute Settlement: What Role for Economic Analysis?" *Journal of Industry, Competition and Trade*, 4(4): 365–71.

Lawrence, Robert Z. 2003. *Crimes and Punishment? Retaliation under the WTO* (Washington, DC: Institute for International Economics).

Olson, Mancur 1965. *The Logic of Collective Action* (Cambridge, MA: Harvard University Press).

Ossa, Ralph 2008. "A 'New Trade' Theory of GATT/WTO Negotiations," LSE, unpublished manuscript, May.

Sykes, Alan O. 2005. "The Economics of WTO Rules on Subsidies and Countervailing Measures" in A. Appleton, P. Macrory and M. Plummer (eds.), *The World Trade Organization: Legal, Economic and Political Analysis*, vol. II (New York: Springer Verlag).

World Trade Organization (WTO) 2005. "Quantitative Economics in WTO Dispute Settlement" in *World Trade Report 2005* (Geneva: WTO), 171–212.

Comment on chapter 6

L. ALAN WINTERS*

This excellent contribution plays two roles. First, it offers an analysis of the WTO dispute arbitration process from an explicitly economic and quantitative point of view. This is unique. Second, and less important to the authors, it offers some insight into the role of reciprocity and, in particular, the use of reciprocity as a solution to the terms-of-trade externality in the GATT/WTO. The literature on this latter issue is voluminous, but Bown and Ruta offer a potentially unique insight to it by locating it firmly in a theoretical context and confronting the theory with facts. I have very little to add to the authors' excellent and detailed analysis of the economics of the arbitration process, but I do wish to explore the second issue. I shall argue that support for the maintained theory is relatively weak, but that this is not a fundamental problem for either economic science or our understanding of the GATT/WTO, because a different approach to the GATT/WTO explains practice equally well.

To summarise the argument, Bown and Ruta show that the WTO articles on retaliation aim basically to ensure that 'the punishment fits the crime' – that retaliation is 'equivalent' to the damage done by the initial violation, or, for subsidies, is 'appropriate', which they and I take as basically the same thing. Bown and Ruta appeal to Bagwell and Staiger's (2002) pioneering work to define equivalence as the two events (violation and retaliation) having an equal effect on the volume of trade when it is valued at pre-violation prices. That is, equivalence requires that:

$$p'dq^R = p'dq^V$$

Where p is the vector of initial prices, dq the vector of changes in trade quantities induced by policy changes and R refers to retaliation and V to the violation.

* Thanks are due to Chad Bown for comments on an earlier draft of this comment

Bown and Ruta assume that the initial vectors of tariffs or other trade policies in each trading partner reflect a political equilibrium, and that this is disturbed by a *political* change that makes the original (bound) policies non-optimal for one party. That party's consequent change in policy is the violation.

With this framework Bown and Ruta ask what the arbitration panels actually decide about the size of an equivalent retaliation for proven violations, how they decide (where possible) and whether their decisions meet the $p' \, dq$ rule. This is an admittedly narrow objective which evades the question of whether the arbitrations are sensible or fair, even by their own yardstick, let alone the question of whether this is a sensible yardstick. These latter questions are important, but it is no criticism of the authors that they leave them for another occasion.

The exercise highlights an eternal dilemma that the WTO raises for a liberally-inclined economist. The institution is mercantilist through and through, and we believe that this is the wrong model. Reciprocity seems misconceived for most countries – I will stop hurting my economy (that is, will reduce my protection) if you will stop hurting yours! Yet the GATT/WTO has harnessed reciprocity to preside over a massively welfare-increasing liberalisation of international trade.[1] At times the two conceptions – mercantilism and welfare maximisation – are diametrically opposed, as in this chapter in the export subsidies cases, and yet reciprocity seems to have such deep human behavioural resonance that the whole thing has more or less worked.

Reciprocity is difficult to pin down precisely, as former GATT Director General, Arthur Dunkel, stated: '[it] cannot be determined exactly, it can only be agreed upon' (GATT Press Release 1312, 5 March 1982). Even for trade negotiations, where the ultimate indicator of reciprocity is agreement, the GATT rapidly developed a convention to guide reciprocity; this was to measure the level of concessions – that is, of trade liberalisation – by the sum across tariff headings of the product of trade and the percentage tariff reduction. For disputes, agreement was much more difficult to observe, although recall that under the GATT a dispute ruling was not binding until both parties (as well as everyone else) had at least tacitly accepted it. Thus, it seems entirely consistent with the notion of the GATT that something like the $p' \, dq$ rule should emerge as an operationalisation of equivalence and fairness.

[1] '[T]he GATT was able to hitch the mercantilist tractor to the welfare-maximizer's plough', Winters (1987)

The theory that Bown and Ruta adopt is Bagwell and Staiger's interpretation of the GATT as a means to solve the terms-of-trade spillover – the fact that country A's tariff increase, designed independently to meet A's internal political needs, imposes costs on country B. They showed that the combination of reciprocity and non-discrimination allowed the internalisation of this externality if reciprocity was interpreted in *p'dq* sense. Bown and Ruta imply, if they do not state, that if dispute arbitrations are found to adhere to the *p'dq* rule we are accumulating evidence that Bagwell and Staiger are right and that, indeed, curing the terms-of-trade externality is the purpose of the GATT.

The Bagwell and Staiger thesis is by a long way the most elegant, complete and powerful theory of the GATT. But that does not make it true. There is remarkably little explicit evidence that the terms of trade motivated the founders of the GATT, or the early users of it.[2] Moreover, although there is suggestive evidence of terms-of-trade effects in some tariff policy, there is plenty of trade policy that appears to fly in the face of terms-of-trade considerations; mostly notably, voluntary export restraints explicitly give away the terms-of-trade gains stemming from import restrictions, and preferences also do so, although perhaps in return for a reciprocal gift of terms-of-trade gains from one's partners.[3] It is, however, possible that terms-of-trade considerations do significantly influence trade policy even if the players do not realise it, and if, on occasion, the terms of trade are dominated by other considerations. Thus, the chance of an empirical test is attractive.

Bown and Ruta do not offer such a test as their first objective, but there would be a temptation to conclude from an observation that Bagwell and Staiger could explain dispute arbitrations, that their theory did explain the GATT. In fact, I would argue that such a conclusion is impossible from the results in Bown and Ruta because, as I have argued above, the GATT's traditions understood in purely mercantilist terms could explain the *p'dq* rule. But a negative finding would still be informative, for if dispute arbitration, which is conscious and explicit, were not governed by the terms-of-trade theory, one might reasonably conclude that the theory was incomplete.

[2] See, for example, Irwin, Mavroidis and Sykes (2008).

[3] Two pieces of partial evidence that terms-of-trade considerations matter are Bagwell and Staiger (2006), who study the cuts in tariffs as countries enter the WTO and find that they are larger where potential terms-of-trade gains would have made the pre-WTO non-cooperative tariffs higher, and Broda, Limao and Weinstein (2008), who argue that non-WTO countries' tariff structures are consistent with their having terms-of-trade objectives.

Table 6.2. *Does Bagwell–Staiger describe dispute arbitration?*

Case	**Consistency with *p'dq* rule**
EU–Bananas	Broadly consistent
EC–Hormones	Related, but inconsistent
US–Internet Gambling	Close
US–Antidumping Act of 1916	Unrelated
US–Byrd Amendment	Broadly consistent
Canada–Aircraft Subsidies	Not applied
Brazil–Aircraft Subsidies	Not applied
US–Foreign Sales Corporation	Not applied

Thus, it is interesting to summarise the cases discussed in Bown and Ruta and ask how they match up against the *p'dq* rule. Table 6.2 rehearses the arbitration cases in the order that Bown and Ruta introduce them and uses the authors' own words to assess their consistency with the rule. The conclusion is that there is some consistency with the Bagwell–Staiger approach, but that it is far from universal.[4] While Bown and Ruta have provided an extremely rich chapter, which I heartily commend, it does not help us conclude whether or not the Bagwell–Staiger approach to the GATT is factually accurate.

References

Bagwell, Kyle and Robert W. Staiger 2002. *The Economics of the World Trading System* (Cambridge, MA: MIT Press).

2006. 'What Do Trade Negotiators Negotiate About? Empirical Evidence from the World Trade Organization', NBER Working Paper No. 12727, December.

Broda, Christian, Nuno Limao and David E. Weinstein 2008. 'Optimal Tariffs and Market Power: The Evidence', *American Economic Review*, 98(5): 2032–65.

Irwin, Doug, Petros C. Mavroidis and Alan O. Sykes 2008. *The Genesis of the GATT* (Cambridge University Press).

Winters, L. Alan 1987. 'Negotiating the Abolition of Non-tariff Barriers', *Oxford Economics Papers*, 39: 465–80.

[4] Bown and Ruta note that the arbitrations all reached for some kind of reciprocity, but this is not the same as applying precisely the *p'dq* rule. As I noted above, GATT/WTO is clearly reciprocal in a generalised sense.

7

Sticking to the rules: quantifying the market access that is potentially protected by WTO-sanctioned trade retaliation

SIMON J. EVENETT*

Introduction

Most empirical studies of the effect of implementing the multilateral agreements negotiated during the Uruguay Round pointed to the potential for small positive, but nonetheless economically significant, gains for the members of the World Trade Organization (WTO) (Brown, Deardorff and Stern 1994; Schott 1994). Many factors will determine whether these potential gains are fully realised and perhaps one of the most important is whether WTO members actually implement their commitments and do not renege on them subsequently. Since these latter actions reflect explicit choices by governments after the Uruguay Round was signed, one is entitled to ask what incentive do WTO members have to stick to the rules, so to speak? This question is pertinent when mercantilistic reasoning[1] is still thought to pervade the corridors of power.

The drafters of the Uruguay Round agreements were cognisant of the need to encourage WTO members to fulfil their obligations and introduced into the WTO architecture an enhanced dispute settlement

* Professor of International Trade and Economic Development, Department of Economics, University of St. Gallen, and Co-Director, International Trade and Regional Economics Programme, Centre for Economic Policy Research (CEPR). Professor Evenett's writings can be downloaded from www.evenett.com. The author thanks Benno Ferrarini for excellent assistance in assembling the data for this project. Comments from Chad Bown, Bernard Hoekman, Damien Neven and Gary Hufbauer were gratefully received. All errors are his own.

[1] One crude characterisation of the implications of such thinking is that a nation's exports are viewed by its policymakers as good and that its imports are bad (or undesirable).

procedure. Others are far better qualified to describe and to analyse the legal aspects of this reformed procedure (see, for example, Jackson 1998a, b). Here, however, I will focus on the implications of the bilateral nature of sanctions on trade in goods and services for the strength of incentives supplied to a country to adhere to its market access commitments.[2] This is not to suggest that other forms of retaliation are unimportant (as the discussion of the 'cross-retaliation' issue makes clear). Indeed, if my analysis found that only weak compliance incentives were created by the potential threat of trade sanctions, then this might suggest a greater role for non-trade-based sanctions.

I recognise that an assessment of the amount of overseas market access that a WTO member could lose if it fails to adhere to its WTO commitments is not the only factor that will determine the deterrent value of the WTO's Dispute Settlement Understanding (DSU).[3] Other factors are germane, too, such as whether an aggrieved WTO member is willing and able to bring a case to the DSU, the probability that a case results in the sanctioning of retaliation and the length of time between the initial violation of WTO obligations and the implementation of WTO-authorised sanctions. Each of these three factors is important in its own right and scholars and practitioners have had, and continue to have, much to say about them. Their relevance for this chapter is twofold. First, even if the current WTO DSU provisions with respect to these three factors were flawless, the deterrent value of the DSU would still turn on the magnitude of the overseas market access that a nation can expect to lose as a result of violating its WTO obligations. Secondly, and taking a very different tack, to the extent that my analysis shows that the incentives created by potential trade sanctions are weak, any flaws in the three factors mentioned above will further undermine the deterrent value of the DSU system. Therefore, one can interpret the estimates presented here – of the market access protected by trade sanctions – as being overestimates of the actual extent of market access protection under the DSU.

[2] Such trade-related sanctions can be expected to reduce exports of the affected good(s) from the sanctioned nation to the sanctioning nation, and may reduce the profits and employment levels in the sanctioned economy.

[3] Bown (2004a), for example, has emphasised the potential increase in foreign market share that follows from a WTO member successfully winning a dispute settlement case against another WTO member. Bown's analysis rightly points to one of the factors that contributes to countries bringing cases against others. In this chapter the emphasis is slightly different. I examine the loss in exports that a country may face by breaking WTO rules and, therefore, the emphasis here is one of incentives to deviate from WTO rules. Surely both factors are important in understanding the propensity to break WTO rules *and* for that violation to manifest itself in a complaint by another party.

Turning to specifics, for each of the twenty largest exporters in the developing world, together with Japan and the United States, the overall goal is to estimate the percentage of an economy's imports in the year 2000 that were shipped from those trading partners that also bought sizeable amounts of goods from the economy in question: that is, from the trading partners which have sizeable clout or leverage over the economy in question. As I explain in section 3 below, this involves a number of intermediate steps. The first involves differentiating between exports that are more or less prone to effective trade sanctions. In doing so, I will distinguish between a nation's total exports and its 'actionable' exports; and in some cases the latter are much smaller than the former.

The second step is to identify which of a nation's trading partners individually imports enough of a nation's actionable exports so that the potential for trade sanctions by those trading partners might induce the nation to adhere to its market access commitments. Each nation, then, is said to have a set of bilateral 'enforcers' of its WTO commitments. Furthermore, it is possible to identify those nations that are enforcers of many trading partners' WTO commitments; and the former can be thought of as forming the 'WTO enforcement club'.

The principal empirical finding is that across the twenty-two economies considered here the percentage of these nations' market access (as measured by their imports) that comes from their respective bilateral enforcers varies markedly from 5 per cent (Nigeria) to 95 per cent (Malaysia.) Thirteen of these twenty-two economies imported 80 per cent or more of their imports from trading partners that had enough clout to act as bilateral 'enforcers', a term I define precisely later. However, for many of the economies considered here, a considerable proportion of market access is protected by the potential for sanctions by developing economies, especially those developing country enforcers in East Asia. To the extent that those economies are unwilling or unable to bring cases against WTO members – including other developing economies – and, given the current pattern of bilateral trade flows, the deterrent value of DSU-permitted trade sanctions could be quite seriously compromised. Put another way, without any of the developing economy enforcers identified in this study, in the year 2000 none of the twenty-two economies (including Japan and the United States) sourced more than 80 per cent of their imports from industrial country enforcers.[4] More worryingly, this percentage falls below 50 per cent for ten of the economies studied

[4] In this study, the industrialised world is said to consist of those economies that are members of the OECD. The remaining economies are classified as developing economies.

here – including Japan. From the perspective of maximising compliance with existing WTO obligations, these findings highlight the need to ensure that effective participation in the DSU extends beyond the industrialised world.

This chapter's empirical results also shed light on the asymmetries that result from the effective implementation of the current DSU system. I show how some of these asymmetries arise from differences in the composition of each nation's exports (which influences the amount of actionable exports) and in the distribution of those exports across trading partners (which determines how many such trading partners have enough clout to become potential enforcers.) For example, for the twenty-two economies considered here, the number of potential enforcers varies from two to fourteen (with the United States and Japan having twelve and thirteen potential enforcers, respectively).[5] Another interesting finding is that for eight out the twenty largest exporters in the developing world, the percentage of their total imports that comes from their respective enforcers exceeds that of the United States. Again, however, much of this protected market access results from the potential for sanctions by developing economy enforcers – stripping out the contribution of the latter reduces from eight to three the number of large developing economy exporters that are under pressure from bilateral trading partners to protect more market access than the United States. If one's view is that industrialised economies, such as the United States, should face stronger incentives to comply with their WTO obligations than developing economies and if the finding (stated above) that eight out of twenty leading developing economies face stronger incentives than the United States confirms one's fears about asymmetries in the operation of the current DSU, then one might be surprised to learn that it is developing countries' own potential participation in the DSU that is responsible for the creation of this asymmetry in five out of eight cases. Essentially, the growth and prevalence of so-called South–South trade in the 1990s has meant that the deterrent value of the DSU is more dependent on developing economies holding other developing economies to account.

This chapter is organised as follows. Section 1 contains a selective overview of the economic literature on the deterrent value of the DSU. This literature provides additional motivation for the questions asked in, and the scope of, this study. Section 2 describes the empirical analysis conducted here and the results. Section 3 offers some conclusions.

[5] As I discuss in section 3, the EU is taken to be one trading entity. Therefore, the United States has eleven non-EU enforcers.

1 Further motivation provided by elements of the existing literature

International trade economists were quick to spot the implications of game theoretic analyses of sanctions for the enforcement of WTO and GATT disciplines (see Staiger 1995 for a survey.) The threat of sanctions was said to reinforce the incentives for compliance that flowed from the benefits of acquiring, and sustaining, a reputation for good conduct (Bhagwati 1990; Bown 2004b; Hoekman and Mavroidis 1999; Hudec 1993).

These game theoretic arguments have been thought to best apply to economies with larger markets – a term which more often than not is taken to be synonymous with industrialised economies (Hoekman and Mavroidis 1999; Horn and Mavroidis 1999). Indeed, it is often claimed that the deterrent value of DSU-sanctioned trade measures is said to be weaker in developing economies for three reasons.[6] First, to the extent that export interests abroad encourage governments to bring WTO DSU cases, the gains to the former from doing so are likely to be attenuated in economies with small markets.[7] This implies that some developing economies may have little DSU-related incentive to comply with their WTO commitments because – in the terminology employed in the Introduction – they have few enforcers of those commitments.

Second, economies with smaller markets may find that the clout wielded by any sanctions that they might impose is tiny, so they may feel 'powerless' to respond to violations by the 'big players' in the world trading system. Horn and Mavroidis (1999) contains an example where, it is argued, Costa Rica's ability to sanction cars made in the EU is limited because European automobile producers can easily redirect the small amount of lost sales (that Costa Rican sanctions might cause) to new markets. In contrast, it is asserted that the EU is such a large market for Costa Rican coffee that sanctions by the EU against this Costa Rican export would be quite damaging. In the terminology of the Introduction, then, perhaps the conclusion we are to draw is that there is an asymmetry in the enforcers facing the EU and Costa Rica; with the former acting as an enforcer

[6] Bown (2004b) puts the matter slightly differently, distinguishing between cases of bilateral 'powerlessness' and other cases. The empirical evidence presented in that paper is consistent with the hypothesis that the credible capacity to retaliate influences the behaviour of a nation's WTO partners.

[7] Of course, there may be other factors which determine whether an export interest encourages its government to pursue a DSU case. For example, the export interest may believe that the successful winning of a dispute may have value as a precedent in subsequent disputes with other trading partners.

for the latter while the opposite is not true. Examples such as these have led some to propose 'collectivising' or 'multilateralising' sanctions in the WTO (see Hoekman and Mavroidis 1999, among others.)

Third, to the extent that developing economies import large quantities of capital equipment and the like from industrialised economies, the former are unlikely to put sanctions on goods that are thought to promote their development. Of course, arguing from first principles, economies can retort that the imposition of trade sanctions by any economy – whether as result of a DSU case or not – is, under most circumstances, welfare reducing (see Anderson 2002, for a recent restatement of this view in the context of the operation of the DSU). Such arguments further diminish the deterrent value of DSU-sanctioned trade remedies if a nation fears that the harm done to its economy by imposing sanctions is unlikely to be sufficiently compensated by the potential benefits of improved behaviour by its trading partners.

The emphasis in the literature on the differences across industrialised and developing economies in the deterrent effect of the DSU motivated my decision to develop (perhaps crude) measures of the strength of those incentives for the United States and Japan; and to compare them with several developing economies. The developing economies I chose to focus on were the twenty largest exporters and this was to see whether the quite plausible conjectures concerning the DSU's incentives for developing economies with relatively smaller markets (the Costa Ricas of this world) carried over to those developing economies with the greatest participation in the world trading system. If so, this might strengthen the arguments – and policy recommendations – advocated in papers such as Hoekman and Mavroidis (1999). If not, and there are distinctions between different types of developing economies, then further nuance may be required in assessing the impact of the DSU on the developing world and in devising policy recommendations.

My analysis was also motivated by another factor that has tended to be overlooked in the economic literature on DSU enforcement, but has received more attention in the literature on the more general question of the effectiveness of trade sanctions (of which Hufbauer, Schott and Elliott 1990, and Haass and O'Sullivan 2000 are leading examples.) The key argument that I wish to advance is that the impact of trade sanctions on the target economy and on the sanctioning economy is likely to be different across goods. For relatively homogeneous goods which are traded on organised exchanges, sanctions by any one economy against the supplier of such a good are likely to be met by a straightforward reshuffling of trade flows – whereby the exports of the sanctioned homogeneous good are shipped elsewhere and replaced by shipments of the same good from a non-sanctioned economy. This reshuffling of trade flows will have no effect on prices unless the sanctioning economy's purchases from the sanctioned economy of the good in question constitute a large share of the worldwide transactions in that good. The fulfilment of these latter conditions is likely to be the exception and not the rule, and, in general, one can expect sanctions on homogeneous goods to have no effect on the price and the quantity that the sanctioned economy can export abroad.[8] This argument suggests that the amount of a nation's exports that are at risk of trade sanctions (whether DSU-related or not) can be smaller than their total exports, potentially eroding the deterrent value of those sanctions and any incentives for compliance created by these measures.

Another potentially important consideration is that mercantilistic (and perhaps other types of) policymakers are almost certainly loath to impose trade sanctions on the very parts and components purchased by their own export industries. With the spread of international outsourcing throughout the 1990s (Feenstra 1998; Hummels, Ishii and Yi 2001), more industries rely on the fast and efficient importation of parts and components to sustain their export competitiveness. Such outsourcing has increased partly because of trade liberalisation in the developing world, and the growth of trade in parts and components has regularly exceeded the overall growth of world trade in the 1990s. Nowhere has this phenomenon been more pronounced than in East Asia, an outcome that derived great impetus in the early 1990s with the decisions by Japanese multinational firms to source more of their parts and components offshore. Governments are well aware of these changes – in particular the link between export competitiveness and international outsourcing – and are thus highly unlikely to sanction such parts and components trade; further reducing the amount of international commerce at risk of trade sanctions, or in the terminology of this chapter, further reducing the amount of actionable exports.

To sum up, in addition to the bilateral asymmetries mentioned in the existing literature, I have advanced two arguments as to why the amount of actionable exports is likely to be smaller than previously thought, which in the context considered here may further undermine the deterrent

[8] This is not to deny that there may be some transitory disruption to markets that results from the imposition of the sanctions. However, private agents have strong incentives to keep these disruptions to a minimum.

value of the DSU system. The primary goal of the remainder of this chapter, using data on international trade flows, is to assess the quantitative importance of these arguments and examine the extent to which they reduce the amount of market access that, in principle, can be protected by DSU-permitted trade sanctions.

2 Empirical implementation

The principal data source for this study was Statistics Canada's *World Trade Analyzer*. Based on international trade flows data reported to the United Nations, this database includes observations on bilateral trade in goods between just under 200 territories and nations for the 20 years from 1980 to 2000.[9] This international trade data can be disaggregated into broad product groupings, down as far as the four-digit Standard International Trade Classification (SITC) of products and commodities. Statistics Canada performs a number of adjustments to the United Nations trade data, including carefully separating out an entrepôt's own imports from those goods that are re-exported to other destinations. Other adjustments follow from attempts to reconcile substantial differences in the reported exports of (say) nation A to nation B and the imports reported by nation B that originated in nation A. The widespread use of this database by academic economists is a testament to its quality. Having said that, its principal weakness derives from its dependence on the underlying United Nations' trade data. As has been argued elsewhere, there is believed to be substantial misreporting of certain exports of commodities, most notably oil, and considerable underreporting of trade between African economies (for details see Rozanski and Yeats 1994). The misreporting of oil exports is a cause for concern here as four of the developing economies whose trade flows I analyse in some detail below are major oil exporters. I looked for anomalies in the import and export data of these four oil-producing economies, and the data for Nigeria looks particularly suspicious.

The first step in my empirical analysis was to identify the twenty economies that exported the most goods in 2000 and that were not members of the OECD. (Here a country that is a member of the OECD is said to be industrialised; all others are said to be developing countries. It is worth noting that Korea and Mexico are currently OECD members and,

[9] Note, trade in services is not included in this database. As a rule, trade in services is much more poorly measured than trade in goods.

therefore, were not classified as developing economies for the purposes of this study.) Using the current membership information of the OECD and calculating total exports of each nation and territory in the Statistics Canada database in the year 2000, I located the twenty largest exporters that are also developing economies. This procedure identified the following twenty top exporting economies in the developing world: Algeria, Argentina, Brazil, Chile, the People's Republic of China (PRC), Hong Kong, India, Indonesia, Iran, Kuwait, Malaysia, Nigeria, the Philippines, Saudi Arabia, Singapore, South Africa, Taiwan, Thailand, United Arab Emirates and Venezuela. To obtain a sense of the magnitudes at stake, in 2000 Kuwait exported US$19.528 billion and the PRC exported US$270.574 billion: the smallest and largest exports recorded by these twenty exporters. Meanwhile, Japan exported US$504.719 billion and the United States exported US$802.580 billion. (All of these numbers were expressed in current 2000 US dollars.)

The second step was to assemble the bilateral matrices for all of the economies in the world in 1990 and in 2000.[10] (These matrices contain all of the recorded imports and exports between every economy in the given years.) It is well know that the trading patterns of small island economies, such as the Bahamas, tend to deviate from the norm, and so I eliminated from the trade matrices any trade involving economies whose populations are less than 1 million people and whose gross domestic product was less than US$5 billion in 1999 (the last year for which internationally comparable gross domestic product data was available on the World Bank's *World Development Indicators 2001* database).[11] Note that each bilateral trade matrix is constructed so that the bilateral trade flows can be broken down into four-digit SITC product categories.

The third step was to compute the amount of 'actionable' exports that each of the twenty developing economies selected above, and Japan and the United States, exported in 1990 and in 2000. As I argued earlier, there are reasons for believing that trade in relatively homogeneous goods and in parts and components are not likely targets for sanctions whose aim is to seriously punish a trading partner – either because they are likely to compromise the export competitiveness of the sanctioning economy or because the sanctions will merely reshuffle trade flows in the affected product. The goal then is to strip out of national export flows those trade

[10] Data on 1990 was collected as well as for 2000 so as to permit certain intertemporal comparisons to be made (as will become clear later).

[11] In studies of bilateral trade flows, eliminating the trade associated with small economies in the manner described here is standard practice.

flows associated with homogeneous goods, parts and components and it is here that the data on trade in distinct product categories is employed.

First, I employed James Rauch's well-known classification of the four-digit SITC product categories into three types: those goods traded on organised exchanges; those goods that are 'reference priced'; and the remaining products that are considered to be 'differentiated'.[12] Products traded on organised exchanges or markets, such as lead, come closest to the definition of homogeneous goods. That is because one market price tends to prevail for such commodities and, by implication, the price is quoted irrespective of the identity and location of the supplier. Rauch identified another set of products which do not trade on organised markets, however, buyers and sellers find it useful to list prices of such products in industry magazines and the like. These so-called reference prices also do not refer to a given manufacturer or product, which suggests that the products of different manufacturers must be sufficiently similar in the eyes of buyers and sellers. Rauch employed industry sources to classify products into these three groups, and, to be safe, produced a 'liberal' and a 'conservative' classification of the four-digit SITC categories.[13] For my purposes, I considered only the goods traded on organised markets as homogeneous; probably underestimating the amount of trade in such goods. Using the bilateral trade matrices described earlier, I computed for each nation the total amount of exports in each of the goods traded on the organised exchanges that Rauch identified. I performed this calculation using his liberal and conservative classifications and for the years 1990 and 2000. The calculations are reported in table 7.1.

Turning now to trade in parts and components, I took advantage of the reclassification of the SITC categories in the mid-1990s to identify those product categories where 'parts' and 'components' were included in the descriptor of the product category and where a related final good could also be identified.[14] Unfortunately, the latest year for which I have parts and components data is 1997 and so I computed the total exports of these goods by each of the twenty-two economies considered here in 1990 and in 1997. The 1997 trade data is, of course, reported in 1997 US dollars, so

[12] Rauch (1999).

[13] As the descriptors suggest, the latter included fewer four-digit categories of goods classified as traded on organised exchanges and as traded with reference prices than the former.

[14] Essentially, this involved checking that for each product category involving parts and components (for example, 'automobile parts') there exists a final goods category in which the parts and components were plausibly used in production ('automobiles' to complete the example).

Table 7.1. *Calculating the amount of non-actionable exports for each country*

Economy	1990 exports (US$ millions)					2000 exports (US$ millions)				
		Homogeneous goods					Homogeneous goods			
	Total exports	Liberal definition	Conservative definition	Parts	Parts plus liberal definition of homogeneous goods	Total exports	Liberal definition	Conservative definition	Parts (1997 exports in 2000 prices)	Parts plus liberal definition of homogeneous goods
Algeria	11.024	2.250	2.232	11	2.262	23.171	3.358	3.293	6	3.364
United Arab Emirates	23.789	688	580	0	688	39.145	4.795	4.333	0	4.795
Kuwait	8.236	2.083	2.039	0	2.083	19.528	5.052	5.031	0	5.052
Argentina	12.932	3.164	2.972	237	3.401	28.261	5.030	4.314	906	5.936
South Africa	25.086	5.402	3.624	246	5.648	28.000	5.617	2.677	1.199	6.816
Philippines	8.437	1.189	840	634	1.823	40.506	1.376	1.231	6.307	7.683
Chile	9.031	5.127	4.034	30	5.157	19.704	10.007	5.824	147	10.154
India	18.545	3.744	819	394	4.138	47.829	9.343	2.249	1.272	10.615
Thailand	23.801	536	194	1.559	2.094	72.765	2.013	1.397	8.694	10.707
Indonesia	28.066	5.512	1.963	300	5.813	65.529	9.334	4.138	2.250	11.584
Hong Kong	83.830	2.245	984	8.119	10.363	206.332	4.534	1.865	8.630	13.163

Brazil	33.437	7.629	6.498	1.642	9.271	59.748	11.666	8.965	4.108	15.774
Malaysia	30.508	4.336	2.248	2.716	7.052	104.436	5.882	4.955	16.978	23.860
Iran	16.664	15.520	15.488	0	15.520	29.609	25.106	26.052	0	26.106
Venezuela	13.025	10.407	10.242	92	10.499	33.411	29.600	29.386	248	29.848
Taiwan	71.298	829	491	8.550	9.379	167.214	991	774	29.691	30.682
Singapore	53.209	9.994	9.565	5.724	15.718	138.699	12.240	11.788	21.933	34.173
PRC (excluding Hong Kong)	64.897	2.723	2.083	3.095	5.818	270.574	6.825	5.357	31.299	38.124
Nigeria	13.525	12.891	12.777	0	12.891	39.018	38.888	38.873	0	38.888
Saudi Arabia	45.904	39.983	39.786	115	40.097	83.336	76.361	76.222	520	76.881
Japan	293.632	2.106	1.675	58.449	60.555	504.719	4.001	3.045	89.569	93.570
United States	413.384	27.761	11.242	64.740	92.501	802.580	35.180	17.538	127.008	162.189

I converted these reported trade flows into 2000 US dollars using the US price deflator: this ensures that the data on trade in parts and components is expressed the same year's dollars as the bilateral trade data described earlier and the trade in homogeneous goods described in the last paragraph. The amount of trade in parts and components in 1990 and in 2000 is reported in table 7.1.

On the assumptions made earlier about the effectiveness of trade sanctions against homogeneous goods, parts and components, I calculated the total value of essentially non-actionable trade that each economy exports. These calculations are reported in the sixth and final columns of table 7.1; and this table is sorted according to the amount of non-actionable exports in 2000. Large amounts of exports in parts and components account for most of the reported levels of non-actionable exports in East Asia, whereas oil exports account for Iran's, Venezuela's, Nigeria's and Saudi Arabia's large recorded amounts of non-actionable exports.

Further interpretation is possible in table 7.2, which reports the percentage of each nation's exports that are neither homogeneous goods, nor parts, nor components. Thus, this table indicates what percentage of a nation's exports are actionable – or at risk from trade sanctions. This table is sorted by the proportion of actionable exports in 2000. Several findings emerge; some surprising, some not. Notice, first, that in 2000 four oil producers (Nigeria, Saudi Arabia, Venezuela and Iran) had the least actionable exports (as a percentage of total exports.) Notice, also, how only 48 per cent of Chile's exports are actionable in 2000, thanks in large part to sizeable copper exports. In the other seventeen economies, however, the share of exports that is actionable is 74 per cent or more. This latter finding suggests that most of the economies considered here have substantial amounts of exports at risk of sanctions. Moreover, eight of the developing economies considered have proportionally more exports at risk of sanctions than the United States and nine have less, suggesting perhaps that endowments of oil and raw materials provide better indicators of the extent of actionable exports than the level of development. Figure 7.1 provides another way to visualise the results in table 7.1. As can be seen here, parts and components trade plays an important role in reducing actionable exports in East Asia, the United States, and less so in Brazil. Other than the oil exporters, trade in homogeneous goods reduces actionable exports in Argentina, India, South Africa, Brazil and Chile.

Given the substantial growth in trade during the 1990s, it is worth asking whether actionable exports grew as quickly as total exports from 1990 to 2000. Table 7.3 sheds light on this issue. The results for Nigeria are

Table 7.2. *Calculating the proportion of exports that are 'actionable' by country*

Economy	% of 1990 exports that are NOT				% of 2000 exports that are NOT			
	Homogeneous goods				Homogeneous goods			
	Liberal definition	Conservative definition	Parts	Parts or homogeneous goods (liberal definition)	Liberal definition	Conservative definition	Parts (1997 data)	Parts or homogeneous goods (liberal definition)
Nigeria	5	6	100	5	0	0	100	0
Saudi Arabia	13	13	100	13	8	9	99	8
Venezuela	20	21	99	19	11	12	99	11
Iran	7	7	100	7	12	12	100	12
Chile	43	55	100	43	49	70	99	48
Brazil	77	81	95	72	80	85	93	74
Kuwait	75	75	100	75	74	74	100	74
Singapore	81	82	89	70	91	92	84	75
South Africa	78	86	99	77	80	90	96	76
Malaysia	86	93	91	77	93	95	84	77
India	80	96	98	78	80	95	97	78
Argentina	76	77	98	74	82	85	97	79

Table 7.2. (*cont.*)

Economy	% of 1990 exports that are NOT				% of 2000 exports that are NOT			
	Homogeneous goods			Parts or homogeneous goods (liberal definition)	Homogeneous goods			Parts or homogeneous goods (liberal definition)
	Liberal definition	Conservative definition	Parts		Liberal definition	Conservative definition	Parts (1997 data)	
United States	93	97	84	78	96	98	84	80
Philippines	86	90	92	78	97	97	84	81
Japan	99	99	80	79	99	99	82	81
Taiwan	99	99	88	87	99	100	82	82
Indonesia	80	93	99	79	86	94	97	82
Thailand	98	99	93	91	97	98	88	85
Algeria	80	80	100	79	86	86	100	85
PRC (excluding Hong Kong)	96	97	95	91	97	98	88	86
United Arab Emirates	97	98	100	97	88	89	100	88
Hong Kong	97	99	90	88	98	99	96	94

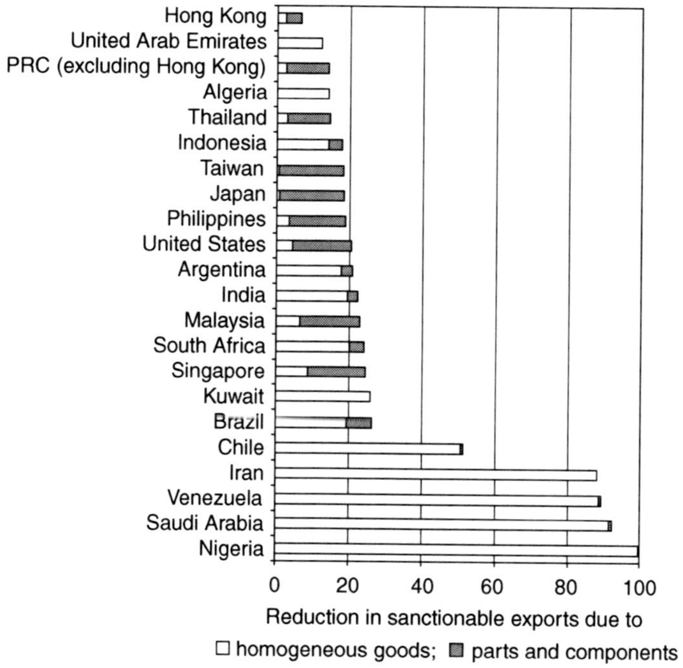

Figure 7.1. Not all exports are sanctionable and the proportions vary considerably across countries

bizarre and should probably be ignored (recall, the remark I made earlier about this economy's trade). Other than that, there is a wide variation across countries in the growth of actionable exports; which, by and large, is higher in economies where total export growth is faster. The growth of actionable exports (see also figure 7.2) could be seen as encouraging, if one takes the perspective that countries are more likely to adhere to their multilateral commitments if they have more exports at risk of sanctions.

Two further aspects of the growth of actionable exports are worth noting. First, as figure 7.2 makes clear, the top four economies in terms of actionable export growth are in East Asia (Hong Kong, Singapore, Thailand and the Philippines). Each of these four economies saw their actionable exports double during the 1990s. Second, there is little evidence of convergence across economies in the percentage of exports that are actionable. One indication of such convergence is if the percentage increase in actionable exports during the 1990s is negatively correlated with the percentage of actionable exports at the beginning of the decade

Table 7.3. *Growth of actionable exports varies greatly across countries: 1990s*

	Actionable exports				Comparator
Economy	1990 (current US$)	1990 (2000 US$)	2000 (current US$)	Real percentage change	Real percentage change in total exports
Nigeria	634	767	129	−83	140
South Africa	19.438	23.521	21.184	−10	−7
Saudi Arabia	5.806	7.026	6.455	−8	51
Venezuela	2.527	3.057	3.563	17	113
United Arab Emirates	23.101	27.953	34.350	23	37
Japan	233.077	282.031	411.149	46	43
Brazil	24.166	29.241	43.974	50	49
United States	320.883	388.279	640.392	65	62
Taiwan	61.918	74.923	136.532	82	95
Algeria	8.763	10.603	19.806	87	75
Argentina	9.531	11.533	22.325	94	82
Kuwait	6.152	7.444	14.476	94	97
Indonesia	22.253	26.927	53.945	100	94
Chile	3.874	4.688	9.550	104	82
India	14.406	17.432	37.214	113	115
Hong Kong	73.467	88.897	193.168	117	105
Singapore	37.491	45.365	104.526	130	117
Thailand	21.706	26.265	62.058	136	154
Iran	1.144	1.385	3.503	153	48
Malaysia	23.456	28.383	80.576	184	185
PRC (excluding Hong Kong)	59.079	71.487	232.450	225	247
Philippines	6.614	8.003	32.823	310	299

(1990). In fact, as shown in figure 7.3, there is a positive rather than a negative correlation between these two variables, suggesting divergence across economies in the percentage of exports at risk of sanctions.[15] This highlights one difficulty in designing incentives to comply with WTO

[15] The simple correlation coefficient between these two variables is 0.39.

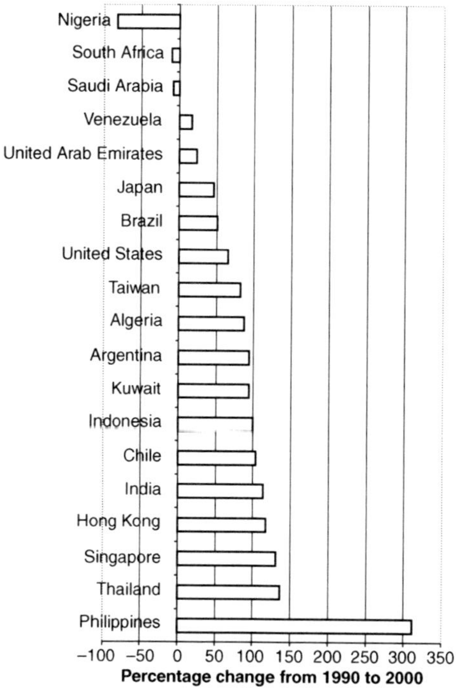

Figure 7.2. Although most nations saw a growth in actionable exports in the 1990s, the variation across countries is substantial

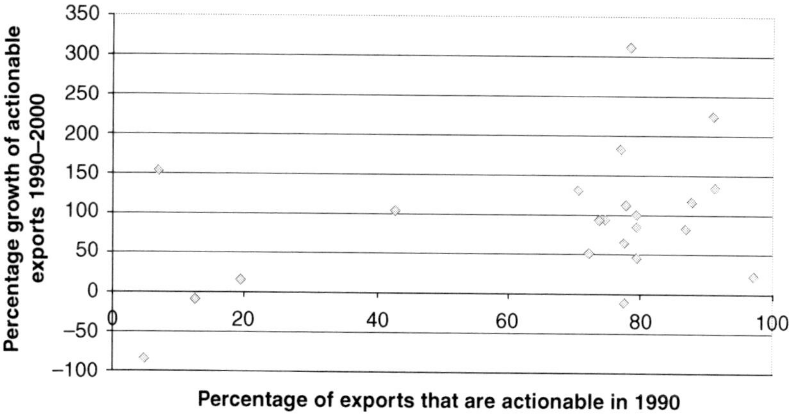

Figure 7.3. There is little evidence of convergence in the percentage of actionable exports in the 1990s

obligations: namely, that the composition and growth of exports varies considerably over economies and over time. This, in turn, suggests that the incentives supplied by trade-based sanctions are unlikely to be symmetric or to remain constant over time.

The fourth step of the empirical analysis was to identify for each exporter the trading partners that have enough clout to potentially influence the exporter's commitments to adhere to its WTO obligations. These trading partners are those that buy a substantial amount (or proportion) of an exporter's goods. I employed three thresholds for identifying such trading partners: the so-called 'enforcers' that I referred to in the Introduction. First, I located those trading partners which bought more than US$1 billion of the exporter's goods in 2000. Second, I found those trading partners that bought more than 1 per cent of the exports of the economy in question in 2000. The third threshold is like the second, except that a 0.5 per cent cut-off was used. Furthermore, given my emphasis on actionable exports, for every economy and for the three thresholds mentioned above, I calculated the number of trading partners which bought more than the respective threshold of actionable exports.[16] For all of these calculations, I took the members of the European Union (EU) to be a single trading partner, reflecting their joint representation at the WTO. The results are presented in table 7.4.

Comparing across the three thresholds, it is apparent that the US$1 billion of trade threshold is far more restrictive than the 0.5 per cent of exports threshold; as every developing economy has far fewer potential enforcers among its trading partners on the former than on the latter. The 1 per cent of exports threshold tends to provide results that lie between the other two; and employing this criterion on actionable exports reveals that the number of enforcers varies from three (Venezuela) to fourteen (South Africa and the Philippines.) In fact, only the latter two nations have more enforcers than Japan and the United States, while eleven developing economies have fewer enforcers.

Based on the 1 per cent threshold for identifying enforcers, figure 7.4 highlights the importance of distinguishing actionable exports from total exports. In only three economies (the PRC, Taiwan and Argentina) is the

[16] That is, for a given economy considered here, first I calculated the number of trading partners who purchased more than US$1 billion of actionable exports. Second, I calculated the number of trading partners whose purchases of actionable exports exceeded 0.5 per cent of the total exports of the economy in question. Third, I calculated the number of trading partners whose purchases of actionable exports exceeded 1 per cent of the total exports of the economy in question.

Table 7.4. *Identifying the number of potential 'enforcers' that each nation faces*

	Number of trading partners who import more than:						Percentage of total exports that are accounted for by trading partners who import more than:					
	US$ 1 billion		1% of the given economy's exports		0.5% of the given economy's exports		1% of the given economy's exports			0.5% of the given economy's exports		
Economy	All exports	Actionable exports	All exports	Actionable exports	All exports	Actionable exports	All exports	Actionable exports	Difference	All exports	Actionable exports	Difference
Venezuela	3	1	9	3	17	7	92	8	84	98	10	87
Nigeria	5	1	11	2	17	2	94	17	78	99	17	82
Saudi Arabia	12	6	16	8	19	10	96	23	73	98	24	74
Iran	5	2	12	6	15	9	94	26	69	96	27	69
Chile	5	3	13	9	18	13	90	40	50	94	43	51
South Africa	3	3	17	14	29	25	85	59	26	94	67	26
Brazil	7	6	12	10	23	18	84	61	23	92	66	25
India	6	3	16	13	22	21	90	64	26	94	70	25
Argentina	4	4	14	9	23	15	86	66	20	92	71	22
Kuwait	6	4	9	7	12	11	96	68	28	98	71	27
Singapore	15	14	13	12	18	16	91	71	20	94	74	21
Indonesia	12	11	14	12	17	16	92	74	18	93	77	17

Table 7.4. (*cont.*)

	Number of trading partners who import more than:						Percentage of total exports that are accounted for by trading partners who import more than:					
	US$ 1 billion		1% of the given economy's exports		0.5% of the given economy's exports		1% of the given economy's exports			0.5% of the given economy's exports		
Economy	All exports	Actionable exports	All exports	Actionable exports	All exports	Actionable exports	All exports	Actionable exports	Difference	All exports	Actionable exports	Difference
Malaysia	14	13	13	13	16	15	93	74	18	95	76	19
Thailand	12	11	14	13	22	19	88	76	13	94	80	14
PRC	18	18	9	9	16	15	86	76	10	92	80	11
Taiwan	14	14	13	13	15	14	95	80	15	96	81	15
Philippines	9	8	11	10	13	13	96	81	15	97	83	14
United Arab Emirates	9	6	15	14	18	17	95	81	14	97	84	14
Algeria	4	4	5	5	8	8	95	81	14	98	84	14
Hong Kong	18	16	11	9	18	16	91	84	6	95	89	6
Memo:												
United States	39	38	13	12	22	18	87	67	20	93	71	18
Japan	27	27	15	13	19	17	92	74	18	94	76	18

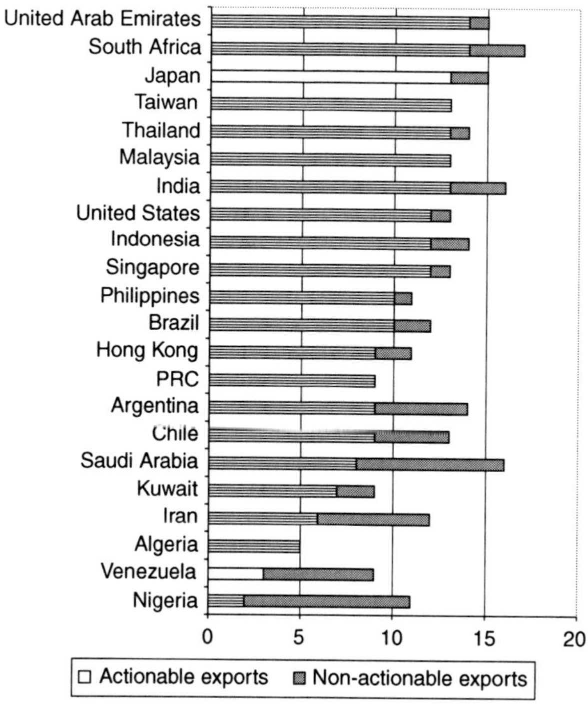

Figure 7.4. Countries differ in the number of trading partners that can act as 'enforcers'

number of enforcers the same after eliminating non-actionable exports. In contrast, focusing on those exported goods where sanctions are more likely to have an effect reduces the number of enforcers considerably for South Africa, India, Argentina, Chile, Saudi Arabia, Iran, Venezuela and Nigeria. In fact, in six of these economies eliminating non-actionable exports reduces the number of enforcers to below ten each. The findings in figure 7.4 can be put bluntly: in terms of impact on their exports, nine of the economies considered here probably fear retaliation from only ten of the 130 or so WTO members; begging the question of how well they treat imports from the other members of the WTO.

Table 7.5 provides a different cut on the results (again using the 1 per cent threshold on actionable exports) and reports how often each economy is an enforcer to the twenty-two economies considered in this study. In reporting the results, I have stated the number of developing economies that a country is an enforcer to, and whether or not the country is an enforcer to the United States and Japan. For example, Mexico is an enforcer to four of the top twenty exporters in the developing world, as well as to the United States and Japan. Looking across the candidate enforcers, not surprisingly, the EU and the United States are enforcers to almost all of the top twenty exporters in the developing world. More interesting is the fact that six East Asian economies (Korea, Japan, Singapore, the PRC, Hong Kong and Taiwan) are enforcers for at least half of the developing economies considered here; and all are enforcers for the United States and Japan.[17] Indeed, the top thirteen enforcers of the leading exporters of the developing world come from Europe, North America or East Asia. Not a single Latin American, African or South Asian economy is an enforcer of more than four of these exporters. Even more striking, only three of the economies in Latin America, Africa and South Asia are enforcers to the United States or Japan. This demonstrates just how few economies are effective members of what might be called the WTO enforcement club.[18]

The right-hand panel of table 7.4 computes the percentage of each economy's exports which are accounted for by their respective enforcers. This provides one measure of the amount of leverage that each economy's enforcers have over its exports. For example, on the 1 per cent threshold with actionable exports only, 67 per cent of America's exports are shipped to its enforcers. This table shows that nine of the top twenty exporters in the developing world have proportionally fewer exports at risk of sanctions from enforcers than the United States, casting doubt on any sweeping claims that developing economies as a rule are more exposed to sanctions from WTO dispute settlement than industrialised economies.

In the analysis pursued here, two factors are responsible for reducing the percentage of a nation's exports that are potentially exposed to sanctions from leading trading partners. The first is that not all exports are actionable. The second is that some trading partners buy only a small

[17] Obviously, Japan is not an enforcer of itself.

[18] Having a small number of members in the WTO enforcement club may be appealing on the grounds that few economies will have to bear the costs of participating fully in the WTO DSU. This argument may be all the more compelling at a time when concerns about the implementation costs of multilateral trade agreements resonate widely. However, to the extent that members of the WTO enforcement club decide not to bring actions against one another (on the grounds that 'everyone's a sinner') – essentially creating a cabal of non-enforcers – then, this clearly undermines the pressures to comply with WTO obligations. Another worrying alternative is that club members treat each other honourably however they direct any non-compliance towards non-members. Indeed, it would be interesting to see if, for a given member of the WTO enforcement club in, say, 1995, whether the share of its markets supplied by economies that are outside the WTO enforcement club fell during 1996–2000, controlling for all of the other determinants of bilateral trade flows.

Table 7.5. *Can only OECD nations play a credible enforcement role? No*

	Target of enforcement		
	Twenty developing economies considered in this paper		
Candidate enforcer	Number of trading partners that import enough 'actionable' exports to make them a credible enforcer	United States	Japan
EU members	18	1	1
United States	18		1
Korea, Republic of	14	1	1
Japan	14	1	
Singapore	11	1	1
PRC	11	1	1
Hong Kong	10	1	1
Taiwan	10	1	1
Australia	10	1	1
Canada	8	1	1
Thailand	7		1
Malaysia	6		1
Philippines	5		
Mexico	4	1	1
India	4		
Indonesia	4		
Brazil	3	1	
Pakistan	3		
Argentina	2		
Chile	2		
Colombia	2		
Paraguay	2		
Peru	2		
Uruguay	2		
Venezuela	2		
Iran	2		
Saudi Arabia	2		
United Arab Emirates	2		
Turkey	2		
Egypt	1		

Table 7.5. (*cont.*)

	Target of enforcement		
	Twenty developing economies considered in this paper		
Candidate enforcer	Number of trading partners that import enough 'actionable' exports to make them a credible enforcer	United States	Japan
Kenya	1		
Malawi	1		
Mozambique	1		
Zimbabwe	1		
Zambia	1		
Oman	1		
Nepal	1		
Vietnam	1		
Panama	0		1
Switzerland	0	1	

Notes: (a) Nation X is said to be a potential enforcer of nation Y if the latter's actionable exports to X constitute more than 1 per cent of Y's total exports. (b) Nations that are enforcers to the United States and Japan are indicated by a '1' in the table.

proportion of a nation's exports. Using the data reported in table 7.4, figure 7.5 decomposes the reduction in the total amount of exports that are sanctionable by enforcers into these two component parts. Consider Singapore, on the 1 per cent criterion; exports to non-enforcers accounted for only 9 (= 100 – 91) per cent of her total exports in 2000. In contrast, after stripping out non-actionable exports and recalculating the number of enforcers that still buy more than 1 per cent of Singapore's total exports, 71 per cent of her exports are potentially subject to sanctions from enforcers. Stripping out non-actionable exports has, therefore, reduced her exposure to sanctions by 20 (= 91 – 71) per cent and is more than twice the reduction due to exports to non-enforcers. The overwhelming message from figure 7.5 is that exposure to sanctions is reduced far more by non-actionable exports than it is by exports to relatively small export markets (non-enforcers).

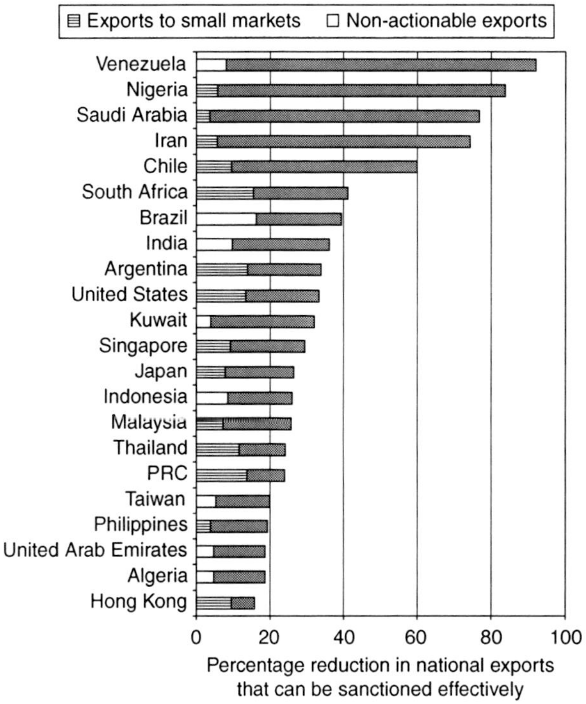

Figure 7.5. Non-actionable exports tend to erode deterrent value of the DSU more than exports to lesser markets

Pursuing the Singaporean example a little further, we know from table 7.2 that Singapore's actionable exports account for 75 per cent of its total exports. As noted in the last paragraph, Singapore's twelve enforcers already import 71 per cent of her exports. This implies that a move from collective sanctions by these twelve enforcers to multilateral sanctions would increase by a mere four percentage points the share of Singapore's exports at risk of sanctions. In terms of increasing clout, therefore, there appears to be little to be gained from enfranchising the non-enforcers; a finding that is by no means limited to Singapore in the economies considered here. In fact, calculations such as these suggest that, as far as strengthening the incentives for WTO compliance is concerned, ensuring that each member of the WTO enforcement club is active might be more promising than moving toward multilateral sanctions.

Now that the enforcers have been identified for each economy, the fifth step is to calculate what percentage of each economy's imports is sourced from its respective enforcers. This provides one measure of how much of an economy's market access is potentially protected by trading partners that, in turn, have considerable clout against the exports of the economy in question. I performed this calculation using the enforcers that were identified using the 1 per cent and 0.5 per cent thresholds on trade in actionable exports; the results are reported in table 7.6. In addition, I have broken out the market access that is potentially protected by OECD nations and by developing economies (non-OECD economies). The data in table 7.6 are sorted by the percentage of imports from all enforcers when the 1 per cent threshold is used to identify the enforcers. The first observation is that in all but three of the economies, two-thirds or more of imports are sourced from their respective enforcers.[19] Second, there is no apparent relationship between the level of development and the amount of market access that is potentially protected by WTO dispute settlement. Having said that, there does appear to be an important regional dimension to the results. On the 1 per cent threshold, the economies with the six largest percentages of market access protection are all from East Asia. Earlier I observed that six East Asian economies are potential enforcers to more than half of the leading exporters in the developing world. Here, they are subject to more potential pressure to enforce their WTO commitments. This symmetry does not carry over to other developing economies, however. Consider South Africa: according to table 7.5, it is not an enforcer to any of the top twenty exporters in the developing world; nor is it an enforcer to the United States or Japan. Yet, in table 7.6, on the 1 per cent threshold, three-quarters of its imports come from its enforcers.[20] Maybe this is a desirable outcome as South Africa feels pressure to comply with WTO obligations without having to bear the costs of engaging fully in WTO dispute settlement. However, if the WTO obligations being enforced are not conducive to its development or if it has little leverage over trading partners that might impair market access to its exporters, then it casts this finding in a different light.

[19] All three economies are oil producers.

[20] More generally, future research might be devoted to identifying which countries – developing and industrial – share South Africa's plight. That is, identifying countries that have many enforcers of their obligations but are enforcers to no (or a small number of) economies. I suspect that some analysts will find this type of asymmetry violates certain norms of fairness. Others may doubt that it can be healthy for the perception of the DSU that (what could be a) large number of WTO members are likely to be only defendants in the dispute settlement system and rarely plaintiffs.

Table 7.6. *What percentage of each economy's imports come from the potential enforcers?*

	Trading partners which:							
	Account for more than 1% of an economy's exports				Account for more than 0.5% of an economy's exports			
		% of economy's imports supplied by major trading partners				% of economy's imports supplied by major trading partners		
Economy	Number	All enforcers	OECD enforcers	Non-OECD enforcers	Number	All enforcers	OECD enforcers	Non-OECD enforcers
Nigeria	2	5	0	5	2	5	0	5
Saudi Arabia	8	33	27	7	10	70	62	8
Iran	6	63	50	13	9	63	53	15
Venezuela	3	67	59	8	7	73	63	10
India	13	72	49	23	21	94	53	42
Chile	9	75	46	28	13	80	49	31
South Africa	14	75	63	12	25	85	63	22
Japan	13	75	44	31	17	90	44	45
Brazil	10	78	60	18	18	88	64	24
Indonesia	12	80	56	24	16	85	58	28
Argentina	9	80	48	33	15	89	53	36

Table 7.6. (*cont.*)

	Trading partners which:							
	Account for more than 1% of an economy's exports				Account for more than 0.5% of an economy's exports			
		% of economy's imports supplied by major trading partners				% of economy's imports supplied by major trading partners		
Economy	Number	All enforcers	OECD enforcers	Non-OECD enforcers	Number	All enforcers	OECD enforcers	Non-OECD enforcers
Kuwait	7	81	71	9	11	83	71	12
United States	12	82	67	15	18	90	67	22
Philippines	10	83	53	30	13	86	56	30
Algeria	5	83	79	4	8	86	81	4
United Arab Emirates	14	84	48	36	17	92	48	44
Thailand	13	84	54	31	19	92	55	37
PRC	9	87	46	41	15	93	46	47
Singapore	12	87	51	36	16	89	51	38
Hong Kong	9	87	42	45	16	95	43	51
Taiwan	13	93	70	23	14	95	70	25
Malaysia	13	95	48	47	15	96	49	47

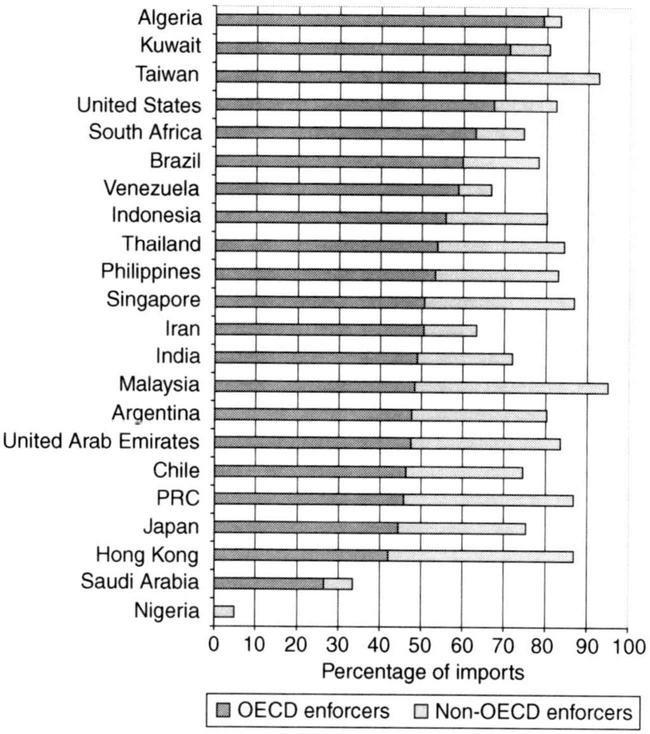

Figure 7.6. Imports from nations that are potential enforcers, or the amount of each nation's market access that can be defended through WTO dispute settlement

Figure 7.6 emphasises the important contribution that non-OECD enforcers can play in strengthening the incentives to adhere to WTO obligations. The economies are ranked in this figure according to the market access that is potentially protected by enforcers from the OECD nations. Without the developing economy (non-OECD) enforcers, ten of the economies considered here – including Japan – would find imports from the remaining enforcers to be less than half of their total imports. This shows that, after a decade of considerable growth in so-called South–South trade and North–South trade, the pressure to adhere to WTO commitments is critically dependent on the role that developing economies, especially those from East Asia, play in WTO dispute settlement. If developing economies are unwilling or unable to participate in the WTO's dispute settlement system, then the incentive for WTO members to stick to the rules will be considerably eroded. This finding also suggests that certain

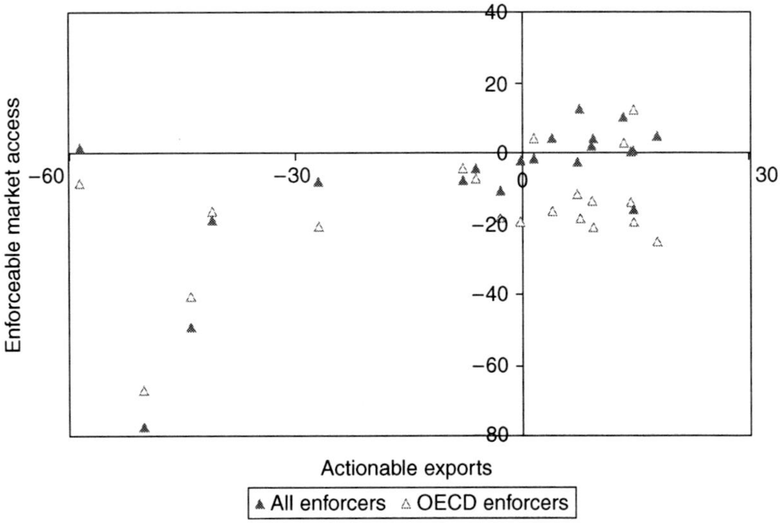

Figure 7.7. Are developing economies exposed to greater potential sanctions than the United States?

developing economies may have considerable leverage in negotiations over how to reform the DSU.

Taking account of the importance of the potential contribution of developing economies to WTO dispute settlement is, it turns out, also a central factor in assessing whether the leading exporters from the developing world face greater pressures to conform to WTO disciplines than the industrialised economies. Figure 7.7 shows that, compared with the proportion of market access the United States is under pressure to enforce, and in terms of the proportion of exports potentially at risk of sanctions, eight of these leading developing country exporters face more pressure. However, this is largely a function of enforcement pressure from other developing economies! Strip out the latter, and only three of these leading exporters face more pressure (along both dimensions considered in figure 7.7) than the United States. The irony here is that complaints from leading exporters in the developing world about asymmetric pressures to conform with WTO obligations are, on this analysis, largely created by other developing economies enforcing their market access rights.

Figure 7.8 reinforces the point that there is a wide variation in the developing world in the pressures to conform to WTO rules. Figure 7.8 is identical to Figure 7.7 except that the comparator country is now India, not the United States. With all enforcers taking part, ten of India's peers face more pressure to enforce their market access obligations and have

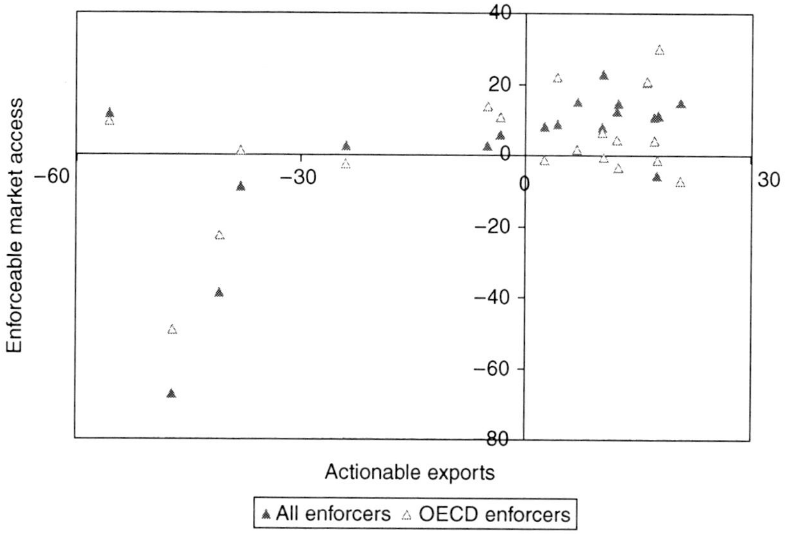

Figure 7.8. Are developing economies exposed to greater potential sanctions than India?

proportionally more exporters to enforcers than India does. Moreover, this number drops to seven only if the non-OECD economies cease to enforce their market access rights. It would be interesting to explore whether the variation in the pressure to conform to WTO disciplines is greater within the developing world than it is between the developing world and the industrial world. Without coming to any definite conclusion, the findings presented here point to the former rather than the latter. This, in turn, has implications as to whether developing economies should seek reforms to the DSU that are intended to bolster compliance in the industrialised world or among their peers.

3 Concluding remarks

One key component of the WTO DSU is, under certain circumstances, its reliance on bilateral trade sanctions. To date, there has been little analysis of how the actual pattern of bilateral trade flows and the composition of bilateral trade influences the incentive to comply with WTO obligations. In this chapter I have computed, for over twenty economies that engage in considerable amounts of international commerce, the percentage of their exports that are actionable (or at risk from sanctions from trading partners), the number of trading partners that import a substantial portion of each economy's exports and so have some clout over the exporter's behaviour (the so-called enforcers) and the percentage of each economy's imports that are potentially protected by those enforcers. The latter can be thought of as a proxy for the pressure to protect market access that is induced by the potential for DSU-authorised bilateral sanctions. The results showed a wide variation in such pressure across economies. This variation is better accounted for in differences in endowments of oil and raw materials and by differences in the amount of parts and components trade than by differences in the level of development. Indeed, the variation among developing economies in what might be thought of as the pressure to conform to WTO disciplines appears to be greater than the variation between these developing economies and Japan and the United States. It would seem, then, that straightforward North versus South characterisations of the potential impact of bilateral sanctions under the DSU are misplaced. Furthermore, the analysis revealed, after decades of relatively faster export and import growth, the important role that middle income nations in East Asia can play in encouraging developing and industrialised economies to comply with their WTO obligations.

References

Anderson, Kym 2002. 'Peculiarities of Retaliation in the WTO Dispute Settlement', *World Trade Review*, 1(2): 123–34.

Bhagwati, Jagdish 1990. 'Aggressive Unilateralism: An Overview' in Jagdish Bhagwati and Hugh Patrick (eds.), *Aggressive Unilateralism: America's Trade Policy and the World Trading System* (New York: Harvester-Wheatsheaf).

Bown, Chad P. 2004a. 'On the Economic Success of GATT/WTO Dispute Settlement', *Review of Economics and Statistics*, 86(2): 811–23.

2004b. 'Trade Disputes and the Implementation of Protection under the GATT: An Empirical Assessment', *Journal of International Economics*, 62(2): 263–94.

Brown, Drusilla, Alan Deardoff and Robert Stern 1994. 'Economic Effects of Quota and Tariff Reductions' in Susan Collins and Barry Bosworth (eds.), *The New GATT: Implications for the United States* (Washington, DC: Brookings Institution), 7–39.

Feenstra, Robert 1998. 'Integration of Trade and Disintegration of Production in the Global Economy', *Journal of Economic Perspectives*, 12(4): 31–50.

Haass, Richard and Meghan O'Sullivan 2000. *Honey and Vinegar: Incentives, Sanctions, and Foreign Policy* (Washington, DC: Brookings Institution).

Hoekman, Bernard and Petros C. Mavroidis 1999. 'Enforcing Multilateral Commitments: Dispute Settlement and Developing Economies', Paper presented at the WTO/World Bank Conference on Developing Countries in a Millennium Round, World Trade Organization, Geneva, 20–21 September 1999.

Horn, Henrik and Petros C. Mavroidis 1999. 'Remedies in the WTO Dispute Settlement System and Developing Country Interests', Mimeo.

Hudec, Robert 1993. *Enforcing International Trade Law* (Salem, NH: Butterworths).

Hufbauer, Gary, Jeffrey Schott and Kimberly Elliott 1990. *Economic Sanctions Reconsidered*, 2nd edn. (Washington, DC: Institute for International Economics).

Hummels, David, Jun Ishii and Kei-Mu Yi 2001. 'The Nature and Growth of Vertical Specialization in World Trade', *Journal of International Economics*, 54(1): 75–96.

Jackson, John H. 1998a. *The World Trade Organization: Constitution and Jurisprudence* (London: Royal Institute of International Affairs).

1998b. 'Designing and Implementing Effective Dispute Settlement Procedures: WTO Dispute Settlement, Appraisal and Prospects' in Anne Krueger (ed.), *The WTO as an International Organization* (University of Chicago Press), ch. 5.

Rauch, James 1999. 'Networks Versus Markets in International Trade', *Journal of International Economics*, 48: 7–35.

Rozanski, Jerzy and Alexander Yeats 1994. 'On the (In)accuracy of Economic Observations: An Assessment of Trends in the Reliability of International Trade Statistics', *Journal of Development Economics*, 44(1): 103–30.

Schott, Jeffrey 1994. *The Uruguay Round: An Assessment* (Washington, DC: Institute for International Economics).

Staiger, Robert W. 1995. 'International Rules and Institutions for Trade Policy' in Gene Grossman and Ken Rogoff (eds.), *Handbook of International Economics*, vol. 3 (Amsterdam: North Holland).

PART IV

The domestic politics and procedures for implementing trade retaliation

8

The United States' experience and practice in suspending WTO obligations

SCOTT D. ANDERSEN* AND JUSTINE BLANCHET†

1 Introduction

Despite being one of the most active and successful complaining parties in the history of the WTO dispute settlement, the United States has suspended concessions in only two disputes – both against the European Communities (EC) in the *Bananas* and *Hormones* disputes. Set out below is a description of the legal and procedural framework used by the United States to suspend concessions in those two disputes. Various reasons that could explain the United States' limited resort to this implementation-forcing mechanism are also offered below.

2 US procedures for suspension of concessions

The United States Trade Representative (USTR) is granted the authority to suspend concessions following multilateral determinations of non-compliance with WTO rulings and recommendations under section 407 of the Trade and Development Act 2000 which amended the Trade Act 1974. As the suspension of concessions practice has developed since the mid-1990s, the first step is for the USTR to request public comment on a broad preliminary list of products. This generally occurs shortly after the expiration of the reasonable period of time if, in the USTR's view, the losing member has not fully implemented the rulings and recommendations. After analysing those comments and consulting internally within the US government, the USTR then requests public comment on a narrow final list of products. Products chosen for this smaller (final) retaliation

* Managing Partner, Sidley Austin LLP, Geneva, Switzerland.
† International Trade Analyst, Sidley Austin LLP, Geneva, Switzerland. The views expressed herein are solely those of the authors and should not be attributed to Sidley Austin LLP, or any clients of Sidley Austin LLP.

list, pursuant to section 407 of the Trade and Development Act 2000, must include, where possible, at least some reciprocal goods of the industries affected by the failure of the foreign country or countries to implement the recommendation.

Given the commercial interests involved, it is not surprising that there has been very active input from US importers and users of products on the initial list of possible products used to develop the final list of products. In both the *Bananas* and *Hormones* disputes, it is reported that the USTR received many hundreds of comments from potentially affected US companies and trade associations who purchase and use products that were on the initial (larger) list of products. Most of the comments emphasized the potential harm to the US economy and to their particular industry from the imposition of larger tariffs on particular potentially targeted products.

The concessions suspended by the United States in *Hormones* and *Bananas* involved the imposition of 100 per cent tariffs on each of the products in the final list. To date, the United States has not suspended concessions in the form of initially slightly increased tariffs that graduate to higher tariffs as non-compliance continues (such as the EC suspension in the *FSC* dispute). Nor has the United States sought to suspend concessions in the form of non-tariff measures with respect to goods such as the suspension of the material injury test in trade remedy disputes, or the imposition of monetary penalties on companies of the losing party found to have dumped products into the US market. Finally, the United States has not sought or had the opportunity in any case to date to suspend concessions with respect to services or intellectual property rights.

In 1999, the US Congress provided the USTR with an additional tool designed to allegedly enhance its ability to encourage more rapid implementation. Known as the 'carousel' provision in section 407 of Public Law 106–200, it required the USTR to revise the retaliation list every 180 days. However, no such revisions were required if the USTR determined that a settlement was imminent, or if the USTR and the petitioning party agreed not to revise the list. The USTR was directed by section 407 to revise the list in ways that would most likely result in implementation or a satisfactory solution. Finally, the amended section 407 mandated that the retaliation list include the reciprocal goods of affected US industries.

The legislative intent behind the 'carousel' was to exert more pressure on losing WTO members to comply with WTO rulings. In practice, this was directed at the EC. Press reports suggested that it resulted from political pressure by US banana and hormone-treated beef exporters who were frustrated with the lack of implementation by the EC in *Hormones* and *Bananas*. However, there were other voices in the debate, most notably many US businesses that did not agree with carousel provisions. They claimed that a carousel would create confusion and hardship for retailers and small and mid-sized businesses by continually raising and lowering tariffs. On 31 May 2000, the USTR published a request for comments on a possible modification of the retaliation lists in *Bananas* and *Hormones*, pursuant to the carousel provisions of the 2000 Trade Act.[1] On 19 June 2000, the USTR announced a revision to the list of products in the *Bananas* dispute.[2]

However, the United States has never changed the products on the final lists in either the *Hormone* or *Bananas* disputes under the carousel (or any other) provision. This may be explained by the fact that hundreds of US businesses and Members of Congress petitioned the USTR in both the *Bananas* and the *Hormones* case to avoid imposition of sanctions on particular industry sectors. Another reason may be that US trading partners, most notably the EC, claimed that the carousel was a 'dangerous game' for the United States to play because it could be used against it by its trading partners, most notably the EC in the *FSC* dispute. Nevertheless, the mere existence of the carousel provision in the USTR arsenal induced then US Trade Representative, Robert Zoellick, to assert that the carousel provision had been successful in inducing compliance and could be used as leverage in other instances.[3] As such, the carousel remains a potential, but commercially and politically unwieldy, tool for the USTR to use in the future.

3 US Suspension of tariff concessions in *Hormones* and *Bananas*

As noted, the United States has suspended concessions in only two instances which are discussed below in relation to the WTO *Bananas* and *Hormones* disputes. The possible suspension of concessions in the ongoing *Biotech* litigation is also addressed.

1 US Federal Register Notice, Vol. 65, No. 105, 31 May 2000, 34786–96.

2 'USTR Announces Plans to Modify EU Beef, Bananas Measures', 26 May 2000, available at: http://useu.usmission.gov/Dossiers/Bananas/May2600_USTR_Modify.asp.

3 'U.S. Will Use "Carousel" Law as "Leverage" to Open Foreign Markets, USTR Zoellick Says', *International Trade Reporter*, 31 May 2001.

EC–Bananas

On 14 January 1999, the United States requested authorization to suspend concessions under Article 22.2 of the DSU in the amount of US$520 million. The arbitrator determined the level of nullification suffered by the United States to be equal to US$191.4 million. Upon the formal authorization by the Dispute Settlement Body (DSB) to suspend concessions, the USTR notified, on 19 April 1999, the imposition of a 100 per cent *ad valorem* rate of duty on a list of nine products[4] originating from certain EC member states.[5]

The nine non-agricultural products selected appeared designed to put pressure on EC member states that supported the banana regime.[6] This included the United Kingdom and France. For example, one product was 'bath preparations, other than bath salts', where the United States had a previous duty of 4.9 per cent *ad valorem*, which was applied, in 1998, to US$7.6 million in imports from the United Kingdom and US$7.5 million in imports from France (two leading banana supporters). The imposition of 100 per cent tariffs had an immediate impact. In the fourth quarter after the imposition of 100 per cent tariffs, US imports fell to US$1.3 million – an 83 per cent decline – and to US$4.1 million – 45 per cent decline – respectively.[7] The tariff lines selected appeared to have caused considerable trade losses for the EC as well as uncertainty as to whether EC exporters could recover their lost market shares in the future.

Ultimately, the suspension of concessions probably contributed to the EC entering into an agreement in April 2001 with the United States. In that agreement, the United States agreed to terminate the suspension of 100 per cent tariffs on the nine products in exchange for an EC commitment to shift to a tariff-only regime for bananas no later than 1 January 2006. However, when the EC finally made changes to its banana regime in late 2005, the United States determined that they were not WTO-consistent and initiated a second set of compliance proceedings on 29 June 2007.

The second compliance panel report, circulated to members on 7 April 2008, concluded, *inter alia*, that the current EC regime for the

[4] Products under subchapter III of chapter 99 of the US Harmonized Tariff Schedule, such as 'bath preparations', handbags, bed linen or coffee/tea makers.

[5] Austria, Belgium, Finland, France, Germany, Greece, Ireland, Italy, Luxembourg, Portugal, Spain, Sweden and the United Kingdom. Federal Register Notice, Vol. 64, No. 74, 19 April 1999, 19209–11.

[6] See, for example, *Inside US Trade*, 1999, 9–10.

[7] Lenore Sek, 'Trade Retaliation: The "Carousel" Approach', *Congressional Research Service Report*, RS20715, updated 5 March 2002, 2–3.

importation of bananas failed to implement the recommendations and rulings of the DSB. As the original DSB recommendations and rulings in this dispute remained operative through the results of the current compliance proceedings, the panel made no new recommendation. The panel's conclusion was confirmed on appeal (albeit with different reasoning).[8] It remains to be seen whether the United States will eventually re-suspend concessions in the *Bananas* dispute.[9]

EC–Hormones

Following the circulation of the panel and Appellate Body Report finding that the EC ban on hormone-treated beef violated the SPS Agreement, on 25 March 1999 the USTR published a Federal Register Notice requesting 'comments on the action that the USTR should take to exercise US rights under Article 22 of the WTO Dispute Settlement Understanding' (DSU).[10] In an Annex, the USTR proposed a list of products on which a 100 per cent *ad valorem* duty could be imposed. The list included meat products, certain vegetables, fruits, nuts and cereals among others, and tariffs could be imposed on any of the products classified in those Harmonized Tariff Schedule (HTS) headings and subheadings. Furthermore, the USTR indicated that such duties could target particular EU member states.[11]

On 3 June 1999, the United States, pursuant to Article 22.2 of the DSU, requested authorization from the DSB for the suspension of concessions to the EC in the amount of US$202 million. The EC requested arbitration under Article 22.6 of the DSU. The Arbitrator Report was circulated on 12 July 1999 and authorized the suspension of concessions by the United States in the amount of US$116.8 million. On 26 July 1999, the DSB authorized the suspension of concessions for the two complaining parties.

[8] Appellate Body Report, WT/DS27/AB/RW/USA (United States), 26 November 2008, para. 478, USA-161–2.

[9] An attempt to solve this long-standing dispute also failed during the Doha Ministerial Conference held in Geneva in July 2008. The EU maintains the agreement was dependent on the WTO members reaching an overall agreement in the talks, while Ecuador considers that the agreement on bananas was a stand-alone. The other Latin American member states have expressed 'extreme disappointment'. See, for example, 'EU Appeals Ruling on Banana Import Regime', Vol. 12, No. 28, 4 September 2008, available at: http://ictsd.net/i/news/bridgesweekly/27660/.

[10] US Federal Register Notice, Vol. 64, No. 57, 25 March 1999, 14486.

[11] US Federal Register Notice, Vol. 64, No. 57, 25 March 1999, 14486–92.

Thereafter, the United States turned down an EC offer to settle by providing the United States with additional market access to the EC for hormone-free beef. Thereafter, the United States imposed 100 per cent *ad valorem* duty rates on thirty-four different products. These were primarily beef and pork-related products from France, Germany, Italy and Denmark. Media reports suggested that these countries were selected because they were perceived to be the biggest supporters of the hormone ban. Almost a year later, the USTR announced that it was considering changes to that list of EC products and published a combined Federal Register Notice on 31 May 2000 for comments on retaliation lists in *Bananas* and *Hormones*.[12] However, this 'carousel' provision was never used and the United States continued to suspend concessions to the original thirty-four different products.

At the 7 November 2003 DSB meeting, the EC announced that it had complied with the DSB's recommendations and ruling by adopting a new Directive and, therefore, requested the lifting of the sanctions imposed by Canada and the United States. The United States disagreed with the EC and considered that there was no basis for removing the sanctions. The EC requested and secured the establishment of a panel on 17 February 2005 to challenge the continued suspension of concessions by the United States. The EC claimed the United States should have immediately withdrawn the suspension of concessions in November 2003, and would have to start new compliance proceedings and a new Article 22.6 proceeding because of the alleged compliance by the EC.[13]

The *Hormones* panel found, *inter alia*, that when imposing retaliation on the new European regime, the United States had failed to have recourse to the DSU and, therefore, breached paragraphs 1 and 2 of Article 23 of the DSU. However, because the EC had not completely brought its measures into conformity with the DSB recommendation and rulings, the panel also concluded that the United States had not breached Article 22.8 of the DSU. On 29 May 2008, the EC notified its decision to appeal the panel decision. The Appellate Body reversed the panel on many grounds but ultimately could not complete the analysis on whether the new EC regime on hormone-treated beef remains WTO-inconsistent.[14] Most importantly for present purposes, in a crucial finding, the Appellate Body

[12] US Federal Register Notice, Vol. 65, No. 105, 31 May 2000, 34786–96.

[13] Following normal procedure, the USTR requested comments on the issues raised in the dispute. US Federal Register Notice, Vol. 70, No. 34, 22 February 2005, 8655–6.

[14] Appellate Body Report, WT/DS320/AB/R, 19 September 2008, paras. 736–7, 316–19.

reversed the panel's conclusion that the United States, by continuing to retaliate after November 2003, violated Article 23 of the DSU. Instead, the Appellate Body found that until EC compliance was multilaterally established under the DSU, the United States had the right to continue to suspend concessions. Throughout the entire time since 1999 to the present, the United States has continued to suspend concessions of 100 per cent tariffs for the original thirty-four products.

EC–Biotech: *proposed suspension of concessions*

On 21 November 2006, the DSB adopted reports finding that the EC had failed to comply with WTO rules regarding approval of biotech products. Following a 14-month reasonable period of time, the United States requested, on 17 January 2008, authority from the DSB to suspend concessions under Article 22.2 of the DSU.

On 24 January 2008, the USTR published a request for comments 'with respect to the specific products of the EC or EC member states, and/or with respect to the specific member states of the EC, that should be subject to a suspension of concessions, such as through increases of rates of duty above current rates'.[15] The notice also informed that the comments received would serve as a basis for the preliminary product list. This suspension of concessions, however, was suspended pursuant to the sequencing agreement of procedure under Articles 21 and 22.

As in *Hormones* and *Bananas*, it can be expected that there will be very active comments from industry on the USTR's preliminary list of possible products to suspend concessions. Based on the prior experience in *Bananas* and *Hormones*, it is likely that the United States, if it receives authorization from the DSB, will impose 100 per cent *ad valorem* rates of duty – as opposed to other trade sanctions – on products from the EC members who have failed to approve biotech products.

4 Analysis and conclusion

Since the WTO began in 1995, the United States has been quite successful in encouraging its trading partners to implement their WTO-inconsistent trade measures in a manner which has apparently satisfied both the US government and its private sector stakeholders. Of the twenty-nine disputes where the United States claims to have prevailed, sanctions have been

[15] US Federal Register Notice, Vol. 73, No. 16, 24 January 2008, 4289.

imposed only in *Bananas* and *Hormones* (and are currently being prepared in *Biotech*).[16] This likely reflects the calculation of WTO members who lose a dispute with the United States that fairly rapid implementation is preferable to losing a significant portion of their exporters' access to the large and prosperous US market. As a result, the considerable majority of disputes in which the United States has prevailed have resulted in implementation before any Article 22.6 proceedings were necessary.

It is perhaps not surprising that the EC is the only WTO member to date that has failed to implement all of its disputes involving the United States and is thus the only one to suffer the consequences of a suspension of concessions. This may reflect the relatively huge size of the EC economy and market and its ability to withstand US$200–300 million annual suspension of concessions (combining those authorized in *Bananas* and *Hormones*). Nevertheless, there is some evidence that the suspension of concessions in the *Bananas* dispute from 1999 to 2001 was an impetus for the EC to enter into an agreement with the United States to change its bananas regime in 2001.

Yet, the size and value of the US market alone does not explain the limited use of suspension of concessions by the United States. There is a well recognized systemic reluctance of many WTO members to suspend concessions. This is because, at least with respect to the suspension of concessions involving goods, suspension normally involves imposing trade restrictions in the form of higher tariffs (or other non-tariff measures) on the consumers of goods originating from the losing WTO member. Presumably, those consumers and industrial producers of the winning WTO member originally purchased the goods of the losing WTO member because they represented the best value at the best price compared with like products from other WTO members. Such consumers and industrial users are reluctant to part with proven, cost-efficient supplies. This explains why there has been such a complex and difficult process for the USTR to select the goods in the *Hormones* and *Bananas* disputes to suspend concessions. It also explains why the so-called 'carousel' provision has not been used, to date, by the USTR.

Even where the United States has been a *defending* party, there have been only a limited number of instances in which winning WTO members have suspended concessions. In only six out of the thirty-four disputes in

[16] 'USTR Snapshot of WTO Cases Involving the United States', 1, available at: www.ustr.gov/assets/Trade_Agreements/Monitoring_Enforcement/Dispute_Settlement/WTO/asset_upload_file562_5696.pdf.

which the United States acknowledges not to have fully prevailed on core issues as a respondent[17] have other WTO members taken, or been authorized to suspend concessions against the United States (*Byrd*, *Gambling*, *1916*, *FSC*, *Cotton* and *Zeroing*). This evidence suggests that losing WTO members normally take appropriate and timely steps to implement their WTO obligations. This is consistent with the conclusion that WTO members recognize that they have much more to gain from a stronger WTO system than by weakening it through failing to take steps to implement. And the evidence raises some doubts about the assertion that developing countries have no leverage to encourage implementation by developed country members. That said, it is obviously much easier for the EC to withstand US$300 million in withdrawn exports to the US market than it is for a smaller member such as Peru.

[17] 'USTR Snapshot of WTO Cases Involving the United States', 2, available at: www.ustr.gov/assets/Trade_Agreements/Monitoring_Enforcement/Dispute_Settlement/WTO/asset_upload_file562_5696.pdf.

9

The European Community's experience and practice in suspending WTO obligations

LOTHAR EHRING*

1 Introduction: the EC's experience and the objectives of trade sanctions

As is known, the European Community (EC) joined relatively late the club of WTO members obtaining an authorisation from the Dispute Settlement Body (DSB) to suspend obligations, after starting the WTO era as the WTO member against which such suspension was authorised in two cases. Since then, however, the EC has accumulated relevant experience. To date, the EC is among the few WTO members having obtained DSB authorisations to suspend obligations, and one of even fewer WTO members to also use such authorisations. In addition, the EC has been following the developments in this area with great attention.

There is much debate over the precise objective of the trade sanctions in WTO dispute settlement, namely whether they are to serve to induce compliance or whether they are intended to redress the imbalance in reciprocal benefits[1] created by the breach (or other nullification or impairment), or both, and to what extent exactly. While the debate over this question so

* The author serves in the Legal Unit of the European Commission's Directorate General for Trade. He formerly worked in the Legal Affairs Division of the WTO Secretariat and the Appellate Body Secretariat. The present chapter is an expanded version of the author's contribution to the Workshop held the Graduate Institute of International Studies in Geneva on 18 and 19 July 2008 with the title 'The Calculation and Design of Trade Sanctions in WTO Dispute Settlement'. The views expressed in this article do not necessarily coincide with positions of the EC.

[1] Economists will, of course, have great doubts about this reference to reciprocal *benefits* accruing under the WTO Agreement, in light of the true benefits accruing from trade liberalisation and the absence of WTO-incompatible distortions. However, it would not be more correct to speak about the rebalancing of mutual *rights and obligations* because the responding party is legally obliged to bring itself into line with the WTO obligation it is breaching, whereas the complaining party is temporarily relieved from an equivalent obligation through the authorised suspension of that obligation pursuant to Article 22 of

far has not resulted in an unequivocal answer accepted by all actors, or at least authoritatively declared by the WTO's judicial instances, one can say with more confidence that the EC leans toward the view that the main or predominant purpose of trade sanctions is to induce compliance.

This question of the purpose of trade sanctions can also be viewed less from the central perspective of the WTO as an institution and an agreement between more than 150 members, and more from the individual perspective of individual complainants in cases where non-compliance persists. The EC, one can safely say, has invariably adopted trade sanctions for the *sole* purpose of inducing the responding party (in all cases so far, the United States) to bring about compliance. Rebalancing the overall level of reciprocal benefits, in contrast, was not the EC's objective, neither was obtaining damages. Further, the EC did not pursue the objective of protecting a domestic industry with the measures it adopted pursuant to the suspension of concessions on the basis of the Dispute Settlement Understanding (DSU).[2]

Finally, there may also have been no intention to 'punish' the responding member that continued to act inconsistently with the WTO Agreement. This analogy to the purpose of criminal prosecution, however, opens an interesting perspective on the other very important purpose of prosecution, namely prevention, in which one *can* find an objective which retaliating WTO members pursue. The EC is probably not the only WTO member which, when it suspends obligations in a WTO dispute, does so not only to induce compliance in the instant case, but equally to deter future WTO breaches by the same member (special prevention), as well as by other WTO members (general prevention). Indeed, just by bringing a WTO dispute and later by enforcing the obtained condemnation, the complaining party signals to the responding party, and also to other WTO members, that it is not willing to tolerate and leave unchallenged/unpunished a particular type of WTO breach or WTO breaches in general. In this sense, a WTO member's recourse to WTO dispute settlement and, as the last resort, its recourse to trade sanctions, sends a signal to other WTO members that they have to take their WTO obligations

the DSU. In that sense, a balance of rights and obligations therefore exists, whether these are respected or not, before the DSB's authorisation to suspend obligations and definitely not afterwards.

[2] Whereas the suspension of concessions under Article 8 of the Agreement on Safeguards in *US–Wheat Gluten*, see below, note 6. Which occurred in the same sector in which the safeguard had been applied, may well have had a component of helping the domestic industry whose exports to the United States were subject to safeguard measures.

seriously because non-observance will not remain without negative consequences. Thus, by using the dispute settlement system, including its last resort, WTO members strengthen the legal discipline in general and the value and quality of the WTO as a legal order.

A final comment on 'inducing compliance' versus 'rebalancing' as the objective of trade sanctions: it is relatively apparent that other WTO members, like the EC, apply trade sanctions not for the purpose of rebalancing benefits but in order to induce compliance. This was apparent not only from statements made at the Workshop that gave rise to this book by delegates from the WTO members which have applied sanctions to date. It is also very plausible if one considers that WTO members initiate dispute settlement proceedings with the aim of achieving WTO-compliance on the respondent's side. This objective does not suddenly change when the respondent has failed to achieve compliance within the reasonable period of time, and the complainant resorts to the measures which the DSU provides for such situations.[3] This actual objective pursued by WTO members resorting to the DSU's final recourse may well be relevant practice to take into consideration when examining the interpretative question of the purpose of trade sanctions from the perspective of the WTO Agreement.

2 The cases in which the EC applied sanctions

The EC acquired its experience with the application of trade sanctions through practice. Apart from Articles 12–14 of the Trade Barriers Regulation,[4] which apply only if the WTO dispute was initiated under the Regulation,[5] the EC does not have specific procedures for the design of trade sanctions. Articles 12–14 of the Trade Barriers Regulation also do not determine the design of trade sanctions (Article 12(3) is merely illustrative), but rather specify the procedure between the Commission

[3] This can be presumed to also include the United States, although its occasional statements to the contrary give rise to some uncertainty in this regard. See, for example, DSB, Minutes of Meeting, 24 and 26 November 2004, WT/DSB/M/178, 17 January 2005, para. 73.

[4] Council Regulation (EC) No. 3286/94, 22 December 1994, laying down EC procedures in the field of the common commercial policy in order to ensure the exercise of the EC's rights under international trade rules, in particular those established under the auspices of the World Trade Organization, as amended by Council Regulation (EC) No. 356/95, 20 February 1995, and Council Regulation (EC) No. 125/2008, 12 February 2008.

[5] None of the WTO disputes in which the EC resorted to retaliatory measures so far falls into that category.

and the Council of the European Union (where the member states are represented). In the majority of cases which the EC submits to dispute settlement in the WTO, and in all cases where the EC actually applied sanctions to date, Article 133 of the EC Treaty served as the legal basis.

(a) *Retaliation against safeguards: the* Wheat Gluten *and* Steel *disputes*

The first cases to mention from the perspective of the EC's experience with trade sanctions are *US–Wheat Gluten Safeguards* and *US–Steel Safeguards*. It may seem surprising to mention these cases because the suspension of GATT obligations under Article 8 of the Agreement on Safeguards does not belong to 'trade sanctions in dispute settlement' (the title of the conference). Also, it did not actually come to retaliation in *Steel* (in 2003). In *Wheat Gluten*, the countermeasures applied to very few products[6] during the several months between the DSB's adoption of the Appellate Body and panel reports and the expiry of the safeguard measure (between January and June 2001).

Yet it is important to mention these cases for at least four reasons. First, it is useful to broaden the focus beyond Article 22 of the DSU to also include other rules which permit retaliation, such as Article 8 of the Safeguards Agreement, Article XXVIII of the GATT 1994 or Article XXI of the GATS. These non-DSU retaliation bases are an interesting context for the classical question of whether DSU retaliation serves for enforcement or for rebalancing.

Second, one can even question the proposition that retaliation under Article 8 of the Agreement on Safeguards is not related to dispute settlement. The last phrase of Article 8.3 requires a WTO breach in the event of an absolute increase in imports, a WTO breach that may be established only in WTO dispute settlement (Article 23 of the DSU).

Third, *Steel* was a highly successful case of enforcement of a WTO ruling. The imminent threat of sanctions in the form of additional import duties starting from the fifth day after adoption of the panel and Appellate Body reports in the DSB[7] arguably played a role in President Bush's

[6] Council Regulation (EC) No. 1804/1998, 14 August 1998 establishing an autonomous duty applicable for residues … of maize … and introducing a tariff rate quota.

[7] Article 4 of Council Regulation (EC) No. 1031/2002, 13 June 2002, establishing additional customs duties on imports of certain products originating in the United States.

decision to abrogate the safeguards even prior to the DSB's adoption of the reports.

Fourth, *Steel* was the EC's first real experience of designing sanctions (whereas the sanctions in *Wheat Gluten* applied to a narrow product in the same sector). The products were selected with a certain degree of political targeting, which at the time meant selecting US industries with domestic political leverage, as well as industries located in politically critical states for the 2004 US presidential elections. The EC adopted suspension measures which would have become effective automatically five days after the DSB adoption of the panel and Appellate Body reports, and which could have been terminated in the event of the United States' withdrawal of the safeguards.

(b) US–Foreign Sales Corporations (FSC)

The EC built on the *Steel* experience in *US–FSC*, where the EC obtained an authorisation to retaliate to the tune of US$4.043 billion. This enormous amount, however, required the compilation of a new product list as opposed to that used in *Steel*, as well as an effort to minimise the damage that would be inflicted on the EC's economy. The European Commission, therefore, resorted to a very thorough, open consultation, in which not only EU member states, but also the general public, that is, companies and their associations including US companies established in the EU, were consulted. The first step was the consultation of the public regarding a first, broad list of potential products for the imposition of sanctions,[8] which had been selected from the categories notified to the WTO.[9] Companies could contact the European Commission directly and request the removal from the list of certain products, by indicating the total value of their worldwide purchases as well as the share of products originating in the United States. Six months later, the European Commission submitted to the member states a draft list of products for countermeasures, which gave potentially affected industries another opportunity to request (via the member states) the exclusion of certain products. At that time, legislative work for the repeal of the *FSC* subsidies had already been initiated in the United

[8] Notice No. 2002/C 217/02 relating to the WTO dispute settlement proceeding concerning the US tax treatment of Foreign Sales Corporations (FSC), 'Invitation for Comments on the List of Products that Could be Subject to Countermeasures', *Official Journal of the European Communities*, No. C217, 13 September 2002, 2.

[9] *US–Foreign Sales Corporations*, Recourse by the EC to Article 4.10 of the SCM Agreement and Article 22.2 of the DSU, WT/DS108/13, 17 November 2000.

States. As these efforts did not bear fruit within another period of ten months, the Council of the European Union adopted a regulation foreseeing the imposition of sanctions from 1 March 2004, until the United States implemented the DSB's recommendations and rulings.[10]

One of the tools for minimising the damage on the European economy was the selection of products for which there were sufficient alternative sources of supply.[11] Obviously, this (statistical) enquiry took place at the level of tariff classifications, and could not exclude the fact that more narrowly defined individual products deviated in their supply pattern from the broader product category in which they fell. Thus, as the EC realised only when the sanctions came into effect, they caused severe problems for suppliers of cheerleader pom-poms to American football teams in Europe. There is obviously no separate tariff line for this product, and thus the absence of alternative sources of supply for this product outside the United States was not visible in the process of selecting the products which were to be the subject of the sanctions. Nor had the affected retailer(s) requested the exclusion of the respective product category during the prior consultation process. Quite understandably, small and medium-sized enterprises do not follow such matters as closely, nor are they in as regular contact with trade administrations at the national or European levels as large industrial companies or their associations.

The EC's chosen form of retaliation was arguably also cleverer than the 100 per cent duties which the WTO had mostly seen until then (notably in sanctions imposed by the United States against the EC). Instead, countermeasures were applied in the form of a 5 per cent additional import duty, to be increased by 1 per cent every month for a period of one year, until the level of 17 per cent was reached. From 1 May 2004, the sanctions applied to the US imports into the enlarged EU.

Presumably, the impressive number of US$4.043 billion as the total awarded amount of permitted countermeasures was instrumental in creating significant political attention in the United States, with the result

[10] Council Regulation (EC) No. 2193/2003, 8 December 2003, establishing additional customs duties on imports of certain products originating in the United States.

[11] This is admittedly a static exercise based on past trade flows, and may ignore potential dynamic effects mitigating the negative effects of sanctions on the domestic economy based on production relocation away from the country subject to sanctions (a point made at the conference by Lars Anell). The likelihood and extent of such relocation may, however, often be difficult to predict because they depend not only on the share of the retaliating country's demand for the product in question and on the industry's geographical flexibility, but also on the duration of the sanctions, which is unknown at the outset. Yet, it may at times occur that trade sanctions affect such investment decisions.

that there was a relatively quick adoption of implementing legislation. Although the EC did not consider that implementing legislation to be fully in line with WTO disciplines, it suspended the sanctions with effect from 1 January 2005, initiated compliance proceedings under Article 21.5 of the DSU, and foresaw the automatic reintroduction of the sanctions sixty days after the DSB's adoption of panel and Appellate Body reports confirming the implementation deficiency (notably the generous grandfathering of subsidies).[12] The EC's suspension of sanctions incidentally sharply contrasted with the approach of the United States and Canada shortly thereafter in *EC–Hormones*, resulting in a new WTO dispute brought by the EC against the United States' and Canada's continued suspension of obligations after the EC's adoption of a compliance measure.[13] On 14 March 2006, the DSB adopted panel and Appellate Body reports confirming the US implementation failure in *FSC*, and the Commission, therefore, published a notice on 3 May 2006 stating that an additional duty of 14 per cent would become applicable again on 16 May 2006. In the short time period between this notice and the date of the scheduled reintroduction of sanctions, the US Congress adopted a bill repealing the provisions of the FSC/ETI legislation and the Jobs Act for the following tax years and thereby removed the most important implementation deficiency. The EC, therefore, extended the suspension of the sanctions by an additional two weeks, giving the US President ten days to sign the bill, which he did. The same regulation foresaw the repeal of the sanctions in that event, and their reintroduction in the opposite scenario, both to be confirmed through a Commission notice in the *Official Journal*.[14]

(c) US–Byrd Amendment

The *US–Byrd Amendment* dispute followed the EC's experience in *US–1916 Act* which will be discussed in the next section. A common aspect of the two cases was the US allegation that the caused nullification or

[12] Council Regulation (EC) No. 171/2005, 31 January 2005, amending and suspending the application of Regulation (EC) No. 2193/2003 establishing additional customs duties on imports of certain products originating in the United States.

[13] *US–* and *Canada–Continued suspension of obligations*, WT/DS320 and 321, where the latest state is the Appellate Body Report of 16 October 2008, which contrary to the panel report of 31 March 2008 vindicates the unilateral continuation of sanctions if the complainant considers the implementing measure insufficient.

[14] Council Regulation (EC) No. 728/2006, 15 May 2006, suspending and conditionally repealing Regulation (EC) No. 2193/2003 establishing additional customs duties on imports of certain products originating in the United States.

impairment was zero (somewhat questionably, the arbitrators rejected this possibility based on the panel's nullification or impairment finding that was based on a presumption). During the arbitration, the EC countered this zero allegation and advanced a model according to which the disbursements under the *Byrd Amendment* resulted in 150 per cent trade effects. The arbitrators, however, developed a methodology under which the effect happened to amount to 72 per cent of the disbursement amounts – roughly the average between the opposing positions.

Leaving aside the numbers, methodologies and economics, the experience in *Byrd* impressively illustrates how useful it is for complainants to act jointly in a coalition, in this case of eleven co-complainants. The reason is not so much the increased resulting overall level of retaliation (each complainant was allowed to retaliate only within the amount of its exports that result in disbursements). Rather, the political message emerging from that coalition was important, particularly when considering that many WTO members took the step of applying sanctions in the *Byrd Amendment* dispute for the first time. Despite the strong domestic constituency in support of the Byrd Amendment (both inside and outside Congress), the coalition's political momentum brought about the eventual elimination of the Byrd Amendment, even if this elimination takes full legal effect only in the future (and sanctions continue to date). There was, and is, quite some controversy within the DSB regarding the sanctions in *Byrd*. First, the United States tried to oppose the authorisation of the suspension of obligations in the DSB despite the decision-making rule of negative consensus in Articles 22.6 and 22.7 of the DSU, arguing that the complainants' intentions were not in line with the arbitrators' decision.[15] Second, for some time and at every DSB meeting, the complainants criticise the United States' failure to periodically publish status reports under Article 21.6 of the DSU as it is required to do until implementation is achieved or the issue is otherwise resolved.[16] Recently, the United States has complained in the DSB about the EC's continuation of sanctions, although they are tied to the continuation of disbursements under the Byrd Amendment over the years until their full elimination.[17] Both controversies have so far remained at the diplomatic level, with no party

[15] Dispute Settlement Body, Minutes of Meeting, 24 and 26 November 2004, WT/DSB/M/178, 17 January 2005, paras. 47, 78.

[16] See the Minutes of the DSB throughout the years 2006, 2007 and 2008.

[17] DSB, Minutes of Meeting, 24 June 2008, WT/DSB/M/253, 28 July 2008, para. 44; see also the Minutes of subsequent meeting of the DSB on 1 August 2008, WT/DSB/M/254, 22 October 2008.

resorting to dispute settlement (the United States against the form, level or continuation of sanctions; the co-complainants because of the non-filing of status reports pending the full coming into effect of compliance).

As far as the precise form of the EC's sanctions is concerned, the arbitrators endorsed a methodology of a varying level of nullification or impairment from one year to the next, which for the EC means broadening or reducing the product scope from year to year within the initially notified product list. The sanctions have applied since 1 May 2005 and take the form of a 15 per cent additional duty applied to a list of products, which the Commission adjusts every year in order to ensure equivalence of the sanctions to the latest annual disbursements under the Byrd Amendment.[18] The comprehensive product list has been chosen based on consultations with the EU member states, with a view to minimising economic harm in the EC and to strengthening the political leverage on the US side.

If one looks back at the developments in this dispute to date, one has to note in particular the fact that the United States managed to take legislative action despite the strong support which the Byrd Amendment enjoyed in the US Senate. On the other hand, the implementation continues to be imperfect and sanctions as well as diplomatic haggling continue between the United States and other WTO members. These two facets demonstrate ably both the strength and the weakness of the WTO dispute settlement system.

3 Cases in which the EC has so far not applied sanctions

(a) US–1916 Act

The EC's experience in the dispute *US–1916 Act* contrasts sharply with that in *US–FCS*. The EC ultimately applied no sanctions (the EC adopted only a blocking statute). The arbitrators considered that sanctions needed to be equivalent to the amount of damages to which EC companies would be condemned (which never happened for an EC company, and only later for a Japanese company), or to the amount of settlements which

[18] Council Regulation (EC) No. 673/2005, 25 April 2005, establishing additional customs duties on imports of certain products originating in the United States, subsequently amended by Commission Regulation (EC) No. 632/2006, 24 April 2006, Commission Regulation (EC) No. 409/2007, 16 April 2007, and Commission Regulation (EC) No. 283/2008, 27 March 2008, replacing Annexes I and II to Council Regulation (EC) No. 673/2005 establishing additional customs duties on imports of certain products originating in the United States.

EC companies had to sign (that information tends to be confidential). However, given that the US Congress abrogated the law quickly, the application of sanctions did not become necessary.

The arbitrators' measurement was doubtful because the exclusive focus on actual condemnations to damages or settlements ignored the potentially significant chilling effect of the 1916 Act, as well as the considerable expenses for legal defence incurred by foreign companies due to the law. The arbitrators also rejected the EC's proposal to ensure equivalence by adopting mirror legislation, and insisted on a quantitative, not a qualitative equivalence. The arbitrators' approach was doubtful because it is entirely conceivable to see the impaired benefit in a legal advantage or guarantee existing under the WTO Agreement[19] – in this case the absence of remedies that breach the Antidumping Agreement. Of course, it is inherently difficult to measure a deterrent or chilling effect with precision. Insurance premiums could be a correct approach, but still unworkable if there is no market for the insurance in question. Economic modelling is similarly difficult or imprecise for measuring the effects of a law.

A positive outcome of this arbitration, however, was, first, that the amount of the permitted retaliation was recognised to vary from year to year. Accordingly, the arbitrators did not fix a single number, but instead provided a methodology for the calculation of sanctions, a point which the arbitrators in the *US–Byrd Amendment* dispute case (discussed above) subsequently confirmed. Until the *1916 Act* arbitration, there had always been a single amount and no possibility of adaptation over time, which is rather questionable given that the value of, for example, potential exports affected by a WTO-incompatible measure can vary significantly over time. Second, it was accepted that the impaired benefit could be measured not only in lost trade, but also in broader economic effects.

(b) US–Section 110(5) of the Copyright Act (*the* Irish music *case*)

The dispute *US–Section 110(5) of the Copyright Act* was a significant success in that the parties were able to negotiate compensation,[20] which remains very exceptional in WTO dispute settlement. The United States and the EC agreed to use an arbitration procedure under Article 25 of the

[19] Like the benefit of equal competitive opportunities accruing under Article III of the GATT 1994, see below, footnote 29 and accompanying text.

[20] See the Notification of a Mutually Satisfactory Temporary Arrangement, WT/DS160/23, 26 June 2003.

DSU in order to set the appropriate level of compensation for the WTO breach in question.[21] This avoided a prior request that the DSB authorise sanctions, which is a prerequisite for determining with binding force the permitted level of retaliation through an arbitration under Articles 22.6 and 22.7. In the agreed arrangement, lost royalties served as the benchmark for calculating the level of nullification or impairment, which was intuitive in a TRIPS context. The arbitrators, however, took a narrow approach to the determination of damages, discarding any constructions aimed at determining the economic effects of the measure beyond mere immediate and quantifiable damage.

The first compensation deal concluded between the EC and the United States after the arbitration was valid for three years only and has not been renewed since. The amount of US$1 million per year may be small, and if the EC retaliated to that amount it is not certain how much this would add to the diplomatic pressure in the DSB where the United States every month faces criticism for not complying with the TRIPS Agreement. Yet, the application of retaliatory measures, irrespective of their magnitude, can serve a useful purpose in keeping an issue more alive in the internal implementation debate. In that sense, one should not consider small amounts to be necessarily irrelevant, even if they are not capable of inflicting painful economic harm on the non-complying WTO member.

(c) US–Section 211 of the Omnibus Appropriations Act (Havana Club)

Havana Club is another EC victory, again against the United States, that has so far not resulted in the application of sanctions, and where the EC is still waiting for implementation. The fact that the WTO breaches in question result in the nullification or impairment of benefits accruing to Cuba does not necessarily mean that no such nullification or impairment could exist to the disadvantage of the EC. The findings of the arbitrator in *US–1916 Act*, and the Appellate Body's remarks regarding nullification or impairment in *Bananas III*[22] and (so far) those of the panel in *Bananas III, Article 21.5 (US)*[23] suggest that indirect benefits and effects are also relevant.

[21] Award of the arbitrators, WT/DS160/ARB25/1, 9 November 2001 (DSR 2001:II, 667).

[22] Panel Report, *EC–Bananas III* (DSR 1997:II, 943), para. 7.50; Appellate Body Report, *EC–Bananas III* (DSR 1997:II, 591), para. 136.

[23] Panel Report, *EC–Bananas III (US)* Article 21.5 (DSR 1999:II, 725), paras. 8.7, 8.10.

4 Tentative lessons

(a) *Sanctions applied by the EC*

The EC's experience with the application of sanctions may be more extensive than that of most other WTO members, but it is nevertheless limited to a handful of cases. Any conclusion one may wish to draw at this stage is, therefore, inevitably tentative and will be subject to deeper or different insights gained from future practice.

A first aspect that one can already highlight based on the small sample of cases in the EC's experience is that numbers may matter, but the political message does not depend on numbers alone. In other words, it is useful for inducing compliance if the awarded amount of permitted sanctions is astronomic, but small amounts, too, can work to this effect. One tentative conclusion, therefore, is that despite all the unattractive aspects of applying sanctions (which for a big trading nation in most cases inevitably means erecting trade barriers that harm the domestic economy), it can be very useful to use retaliation rights no matter how large or small the amount. The fact that sanctions are applied sends a signal to the implementing WTO member that the complaining party is serious in its demand for compliance. The momentum which this political message, as well as some degree of economic harm to internal constituencies, creates in the political instances of the implementing member can be instrumental in bringing about implementation.

Second, there are methods that allow the minimising of the economic harm which the sanctions cause for the economy of the member imposing them, and of maximising their effectiveness in the country subject to the sanctions. The two objectives may not always relate one to another in full harmony; it is then unavoidable that trade-offs are found and compromises struck. For minimising domestic economic harm, it has proven useful to design sanctions in an inclusive internal process where affected stakeholders can voice their interests. As much internal consensus as possible should be achieved as this protects some of the potential victims. In the internal process, the avoidance of domestic economic harm is likely to receive political priority, but the retaliating WTO member should not lose sight of the effectiveness of the sanctions; also long-term ineffective sanctions can over time cause more domestic harm than short-term effective sanctions.

'Smart sanctions' in the form of increased import duties that are not prohibitive offer an important advantage not only for the economy of the member applying sanctions, but potentially also in terms of impact on the member that should implement. Such sanctions can become irritants without however blocking trade flows entirely. They can be useful politically in the long run as they maintain the pressure: a frustrated exporter can have a more powerful voice domestically than an eliminated exporter that has gone out of business entirely or that has lost a certain export market without hope of re-conquering it quickly. In contrast, at least prohibitive sanctions can reach a point where they are no longer very useful if there is no implementation over a long period of time. It can then be that they fail to keep the issue of implementation alive, that exporters have found other markets (or ways around the sanctions) or that the sanctions merely cause economic losses that are not noted much any more.

(b) Sanctions applied against the EC

The latter effect (sanctions are not noted much any more) has partly been the case in relation to the sanctions applied against the EC for several years in *EC–Bananas III* and to date in *EC–Hormones*. While some of the targeted products continue to be denied entry into the US market and EC producers endure the corresponding losses, the actual effects are more difficult to measure in relation to those other products where export numbers have remained stable or even increased after the imposition of the sanctions.

Certainly, the application of sanctions against EC exports to the United States (and Canada) has influenced the EC's efforts to achieve compliance or (in *EC–Bananas III*) to negotiate a solution in 2001 under which sanctions came to an end. This is not to say that the EC would have been less active or less in a hurry in these efforts had there been no sanctions. In order to improve its compliance record the EC would have kept as short as possible the period until the adoption of compliance measures, during which time it also had to file status reports in every DSB meeting; the unenviable situation in which the United States now finds itself in a long list of cases. On the other hand, certain compliance actions are complex and take time, be it for negotiations (*EC–Bananas III*), or for a new and improved scientific risk assessment (*EC–Hormones*); tasks that are not easy to accelerate at will. Certainly, however, a trade administration cannot, and does not, ignore the fact that domestic economic operators are facing retaliatory measures in their trade with another WTO member. The economic losses which these operators incur are known, if not in precise numbers then at least in principle, and these operators often press for relief in their contacts with trade administrations at the national or European level. At some point, however, an administration cannot do much more than it has done: namely, when it has taken a measure which it considers in good faith achieves WTO-compliance. When sanctions continue in that scenario, as they do in *EC–Hormones*, they not only constitute a breach of the ban on unilateralism stipulated in Article 23 of the DSU,[24] but they also will not press the implementing member to do more than it has already done before there is a compliance ruling from the WTO. In the situation where the United States refused to suspend the sanctions, to initiate a compliance review or to agree on an arbitration procedure to resolve the dispute, the remaining option for the EC in order to defend the interests of exporters affected by sanctions was to challenge these sanctions directly as illegal under the WTO Agreement. In the future and based on the Appellate Body reports in *United States/ Canada–Continued suspension of obligations*, an implementing member will in that situation initiate a compliance panel procedure under Article 21.5 of the DSU.[25]

In the EC, operators affected by sanctions have also attempted to achieve satisfaction through the courts. Despite the failed early attempts of banana importers to challenge in domestic lawsuits the legality of EC measures that had been found inconsistent with the WTO Agreement, exporters affected by sanctions in the United States later sought damages or compensation from the EC, arguing that the EC had caused their losses by not implementing within a reasonable period of time. Again, these attempts had to fail as far as damages for illegal action (Article 288(2) of the EC Treaty) were concerned, because WTO law does not enjoy direct internal effect in the EC's legal order. The recent *FIAMM* judgment of the European Court of Justice sets a provisional endpoint to the affected exporters' attempts to seek compensation through the courts by also ruling out the EC's liability for legal action (legal because the WTO-inconsistency does not create an illegality in

[24] As convincingly established by the panels in *US–* and *Canada–Continued suspension of obligations*, WT/DS320/R, WT/DS321/R, 31 March 2008. The Appellate Body, however, reversed this finding in its reports of 16 October 2008, WT/DS320/AB/R, WT/DS321/AB/R. The Appellate Body's approach of considering continued sanctions permitted under Article 22.8 of the DSU even beyond the point where WTO-compliance has actually been achieved, as well as the Appellate Body's reasoning regarding Article 23 of the DSU are less than fully convincing. From a policy perspective, the Appellate Body's approach, however, makes good sense and is in line with the post-retaliation proposals under discussion in the DSU review.

[25] See the Appellate Body reports, 16 October 2008.

the internal legal order), based on special and unusual damage suffered by the exporters.[26]

Had the latter basis for damages or compensation been retained, it should have applied equally to other cases of retaliation permitted in the WTO, including in response to *legal* action (under Article XXVIII of the GATT 1994 or Article 8 of the Safeguards Agreement), as well as another WTO member's increase of applied duties, if this action was somehow caused by the WTO member in question. Accepting governmental liability for the losses incurred by exporters who are subject to sanctions would have had far-reaching implications. It is easy to understand the appeal and apparent fairness of the idea; after all, the affected exporters typically bear no responsibility whatsoever for what caused the sanctions. This, however, does not mean such compensation is necessarily a good idea from a policy perspective. Some would be attracted to such compensation because of the financial fine element for the WTO non-compliant government, but it is certainly not useful to discourage affected exporters from finding alternative export markets and to encourage them to fill out damages applications instead. The obligation of damage mitigation could in theory solve this moral hazard, but in practice it is certainly not possible for an administration to prove to an exporter what quantities of what product could have been sold at what prices on other markets.

An alternative idea for compensating affected exporters has been proposed[27] in the form of an unjustified enrichment claim against producers in the country applying sanctions if these result in undeserved rents in the form of increased sales and higher prices as a result of the border protection provided by retaliatory tariffs. As interesting and appealing as this idea may be, it at first glance seems questionable whether the proposed legal basis will actually work and be operational before domestic courts.

5 A few additional remarks

(a) Terminology

The DSU uses very convoluted terminology when it refers to the 'suspension of concessions or other obligations'. Expressing, writing and reading this entire phrase not only takes a lot of space and time, it also adds nothing when compared with 'suspension of obligations'. Both in the legal

[26] European Court of Justice, judgment, 9 September 2008, Joined Cases C-120/06 P and C-121/06 P, *Fiamm* v. *Council* and *Commission*.

[27] By Robert Howse.

framework of the WTO Agreement and in the logic of the construction 'concessions or *other* obligations' it is absolutely clear that concessions are just a subtype of WTO obligations. Despite the fact that tariff concessions happen to be the most frequently suspended WTO obligation, it is sounder to use the more efficient terminology of 'suspension of obligations'. The name of the disputes *United States–* and *Canada–Continued suspension of obligations* is an example worth following.

(b) The difference between the suspension of WTO obligations and the actual sanctions

A seemingly fine distinction hardly ever seems to be acknowledged in relation to trade sanctions, namely their dual nature. The 'suspension of obligations' operates at the level of the WTO Agreement because the DSB permits the suspension of obligations contained in the WTO Agreement. 'Suspension' means the temporary deactivation of the international obligation in question; it legally opens the way for conduct that would not be permitted had the obligation not been suspended. Therefore, the suspension of obligations is not identical to the retaliatory measures which a suspending member may take, for example, import duties that exceed bound tariffs in the sense of Article II in the case of suspended tariff concessions. The suspension of Article II as a WTO obligation means that the increased duties are not illegal for the duration of the suspension. Legally, the suspension of the Article II obligation at the WTO level and the imposition of higher import duties at the national level are two distinct steps, even if they can coincide temporally.

This distinction between the suspension of obligations and the imposition of sanctions reveals that a WTO member can perfectly well suspend tariff concessions *without* subsequently increasing any duties. Specifically, this distinction has some relevance for the several WTO members who did not use their right to suspend obligations, as well for WTO members who consider that they are not capable, without causing undue economic harm to their own economies, of imposing sanctions. Obviously, this is not a panacea to overcome all difficulties faced by small or developing country economies in relation to the limited impact of the sanctions they can impose. On the other hand, the problem of harm caused to one's own economy largely disappears when a country limits itself to suspending WTO obligations and does not use the additional legal margin of manoeuvre thereby opened. One also should not think that such suspension would remain completely without effect and that the other party will be entirely indifferent: a suspended tariff concession makes the respective tariff lines temporarily unbound and the applied duties subject to greater flexibility and lower predictability. This fact and the interest which WTO members often have in reducing the bound levels of other members' tariffs suggests that the mere suspension of obligations would not necessarily leave the responding party indifferent.

(c) The need for appellate review of arbitration decisions under Article 22.6

It is generally acknowledged that arbitrators have struggled with their task of determining the appropriate level of retaliation that is permitted under Article 22.4 of the DSU (whereas the parameters of the Agreement on Subsidies and Countervailing Measures may have been applied in a more straightforward manner). These difficulties of arbitrators were by no means limited to factual questions, such as the underlying economics. Rather, the very core, legal questions of procedure and substance have caused difficulty, and have resulted in the unsatisfactory quality of the reasoning in arbitration decisions, as well as stark inconsistency between various decisions. For an evaluation and criticism of the unsatisfactory state of the jurisprudence, one can refer to the excellent analysis by Holger Spamann.[28] A recent example is the *Gambling* arbitration, in which one arbitrator even resorted to writing a sound dissenting opinion, for which there is no precedent, nor an explicit basis in the DSU, and where the majority gave a highly troubling reasoning that is affected by serious legal mistakes, as will be explained in the following section.

The best remedy to that situation probably is the introduction of appellate review of arbitrators' decisions, obviously for legal questions only. This could quickly result in a higher level of discipline when it comes to legal reasoning, and it would improve the quality, accuracy and consistency of the decisions. This accuracy is by no means unimportant: after perhaps five rounds of litigation over perhaps 4 to 5 years, the winning party certainly deserves a decision that correctly sets the level of permitted retaliation, not least because the resulting numbers can have an important effect on the following compliance efforts. Appellate review could also bring about improvements through the stronger legitimacy and authority of the Appellate Body as a permanent institution, compared with arbitrators

[28] Holger Spamann, 'The Myth of "Rebalancing" Retaliation in WTO Dispute Settlement Practice', *Journal of International Economic Law*, 9 (2006), 31–79.

serving in individual disputes where they know that they make a final decision with potentially serious economic consequences. The proposal to add appellate review to arbitrations under Articles 22.6 and 22.7 of the DSU is now included in the July 2008 text of the Chairman of the Special Session of the Dispute Settlement Body that negotiates the DSU, albeit in bracketed form.

(d) The US–Gambling *arbitration: a judicial disaster*

In the meantime, arbitrators should, even in the absence of the threat of reversal by the Appellate Body, take great care when they interpret and apply the law. *Gambling* is a relevant case where the core legal question should have been the identification of the 'benefit' which the United States' inconsistent measure impaired or even nullified. The past jurisprudence has already given indications about the nature of this benefit. For instance, it is recognised that the benefit accruing under Article III of the GATT 1994 is not the expectation of trade flows, but the equal competitive relationship between imported and domestic products.[29] The benefit accruing under Article XI:1 of the GATT 1994 could similarly be, *inter alia*, the absence of quantitative and other restrictions outlawed by that provision. Obviously, all GATT obligations are subject to exceptions under Article XX. Yet the right to invoke an exception exists only when *all* conditions of Article XX are satisfied – just like an Article III breach only exists when all conditions for a violation are met. In *Gambling*, this enquiry into the 'benefit' should have led to the conclusion that the impaired benefit was the entirety of the market access prevented by the Article XVI-inconsistent barrier because that barrier was in its entirety GATS illegal. If an exception like Article XX of the GATT 1994 or Article XIV of the GATS fails to justify a measure, it is irrelevant whether this is because the exception does not apply to a measure, whether that measure fails to satisfy one or many, important or less important, conditions for justifying a measure.

Of course, these questions matter for whether and how it *would be* possible for the losing party in the future to adopt a measure that complies with the WTO Agreement. However, as long as no such WTO-consistent measure replaces the existing measure, the latter is illegal, not just 'partly illegal' or 'somewhat illegal'. Unlike non-discrimination rules, provisions like Article XI of the GATT 1994 and Article XVI of the

[29] GATT Panel Report, *US–Taxes on Petroleum and Certain Imported Substances*, adopted 17 June 1987, BISD 34S/136, para. 5.1.9.

GATS do not permit any part of a measure that contravenes these provisions without being justified under an exception. Thus, if a WTO member 'nearly succeeded' in terms of satisfying the applicable conditions of an exception, it should consider itself fortunate to face a relatively easy task in achieving compliance. Until it does so, however, 'nearly legal' nevertheless remains illegal.

The *Gambling* arbitrators were, therefore, wrong to calculate the impaired benefit 'only in respect of horseracing gambling and betting'.[30] Incidentally, this reliance on the point on which the Appellate Body found a discrimination in the sense of the Article XIV chapeau is all the more surprising given that the same arbitrators had, as recently as nine months earlier when they sat as a compliance panel, pinpointed the fact that the US measure discriminated also by not banning intrastate remote gambling,[31] thereby proving wrong relatively explicitly the Appellate Body's assertion that 'these measures, on their face, do *not* discriminate'.[32]

The approach of considering the entire market access prevented by the illegal barrier as the impaired benefit avoids questions to which there can easily be no answer in an arbitration. Such was also the approach in past disputes, for example, *EC–Hormones*, where the sanctions arbitration was not concerned with whether the EC could adopt an SPS-consistent ban on hormones based on an SPS-consistent risk assessment, nor with how much hormone-treated beef the United States and Canada could then import into the EC (obviously zero). It has recently taken a panel 3 years to come to a view on this question after the EC had conducted a new risk assessment and modified its measure.[33] It would certainly not have been possible to sort this out within the short time frame of an arbitration and when the question is merely hypothetical. Instead of trying to come to terms with such a tricky question, the arbitrators in *EC–Hormones* calculated the impairment based on the hypothetical that hormone-treated beef would be sold in the EC (not necessarily a 'plausible' counterfactual).

The *Gambling* arbitrators (majority opinion) were also mistaken in calculating the level of nullification or impairment in relation to a

[30] Decision of the arbitrator, *US–Gambling* (DSR 2005:XXIII, 11639), para. 3.74.

[31] See Panel Report, *US–Gambling*, Article 21.5, para. 6.123 and footnote 184.

[32] Appellate Body Report, *US–Gambling* (DSR 2005:XII, 5663), para. 357. This inconsistency with a *res judicata* prior decision in the same dispute is also a procedural legal error.

[33] See the Panel Report, above, footnote 24.

'plausible' compliance scenario. A WTO-illegal compliance scenario certainly cannot qualify as a relevant counterfactual and the same goes for a counterfactual the legality of which is uncertain.[34] There also cannot be freedom of choice for the arbitrators to pick one of several counterfactuals, as this would imply that differing levels of nullification or impairment would exist simultaneously. Further, as explained above, the question of the legality of a counterfactual is often not suitable for a reliable resolution within a sanctions arbitration. The existing panel and Appellate Body decisions condemning the challenged measure in the given dispute are inherently unreliable for finding an answer to the question of what would constitute a hypothetical legal measure other than the simple removal/abrogation of the WTO-inconsistent market access barrier. Panels and the Appellate Body in their reports only establish that the existing measure is WTO-inconsistent; except perhaps when they make a suggestion under Article 19.1, second sentence, of the DSU, they do not give a list of potential measures that would not breach any of the manifold obligations in the WTO Agreement. It would obviously be hazardous for a panel or the Appellate Body to do so. Thus, it should be no surprise that the WTO-legality of the hypothetical scenario of permitted cross-border horserace betting was very questionable, to say the least, because: (i) of the already-mentioned dimension of intrastate gambling; (ii) horserace gambling may result in a bias in favour of domestic suppliers; and (iii) a number of other issues have not been resolved in the *Gambling* dispute, such as whether online casinos and physical casinos provide like services. Nor did such questions have to be resolved at the substantive stage of the *Gambling* dispute, given that there was sufficient material to find the US remote gambling restriction WTO-inconsistent. Any tribunal and any complainant reasonably exercise some judicial economy in selecting the points they advance as evidence of a legal breach, without suggesting that everything else is, therefore, legal.

The *Gambling* arbitrators' approach of trying to work with a WTO-consistent counterfactual other than the hypothetical situation where the illegal market access restriction does not exist is also wrong at a more fundamental level. There are nearly always many ways in which a losing WTO member can bring itself into compliance. To return to the *EC–Hormones* case and leaving aside the contentious option of an SPS-compliant hormone ban, the EC could certainly, without breaching WTO obligations,

[34] This point was pertinently made by Nicolas Lockhart at the conference.

ban all beef (or, if necessary because of Article III of the GATT 1994, all meat), impose labelling which would deter most consumers from buying hormone-treated beef, or withdraw the tariff concession under Article XXVIII of the GATT 1994 and impose a prohibitive import duty. In other cases, the option of a waiver may come into play, and breaches of the most-favoured-nation (MFN) treatment obligation can often be rectified by concluding a free trade agreement. The trade flows which the winning party would obtain in these scenarios will vary greatly; in the given product they will often be zero. Non-discrimination obligations can typically be complied with without improving market access conditions for the successful complainant: should these fundamental WTO obligations be enforceable only if a removal of the discrimination margin is sufficiently plausible? Also, what on one day may seem an 'implausible' option may soon after become the chosen route. These legal options may exist for the implementing party which, of course, enjoys sovereign discretion in making that choice. Conversely, however, until compliance is achieved, the successful complainant deserves nothing less than a meaningful, uncrippled right to suspend obligations. In sum, one can only hope that the serious legal mistakes committed by the *Gambling* arbitrators (majority) will not be repeated in future cases.

(e) Retaliation under the TRIPS Agreement and conventions administered by the WIPO

Cross-retaliation under the TRIPS Agreement is known to be important for developing countries because it is perhaps the only area where obligations can be suspended without erecting trade barriers (subject to the qualification made above in section 5(b) on the difference between the suspension of WTO obligations and the actual sanctions). Ever since the Ecuadorian *Bananas* arbitration,[35] however, the argument circulated that parallel obligations under conventions administered by the WIPO would continue to stand in the way of using TRIPS suspensions. The non-scholarly trade press has regularly recalled this argument over the years,[36] in most cases without rebuttal, but also without much reasoning. In the context of the *US–Gambling* dispute, a WIPO official even made public

[35] See Decision by the arbitrators, *EC–Bananas III*, Recourse to Arbitration by the EC under Article 22.6 (Ecuador), WT/DS27/ARB/ECU (DSR 2000:V, 2237), paras. 148, 152.

[36] In particular *Inside US Trade* repeatedly referred to this apparent argument.

statements about the Berne Convention standing in the way of Antigua's use of TRIPS cross-retaliation.[37] These arguments are not only damaging for the credibility of the WTO dispute settlement system, they are also mistaken as a matter of correct application of the law. One way of explaining this incorrectness is that the DSU's express permission to cross-retaliate under the TRIPS Agreement prevails over the respective convention administered by the WIPO in such cases where parallel obligations exist.[38] This is a perfectly plausible explanation, but it is quite simple and straightforward and is, therefore, unlikely to be new to, and convince, the proponents of the mentioned arguments of an obstacle to cross-retaliation. They could probably not be convinced in the light of the fact that the DSU does not specifically address parallel obligations that may exist under non-WTO instruments, and that the TRIPS Agreement expressly leaves untouched members' obligations under conventions administered by the WIPO (Article 2.2) and permits higher levels of protection (Article 1.1). Therefore, the more powerful explanation may be that the parallel obligation under the WIPO Convention (where there is no formal and exclusive form of dispute settlement) can simultaneously be suspended as a countermeasure under general international law against the same WTO breach which has given rise to the right to suspend obligations in the WTO.[39] The double remedy does not breach the requirement that countermeasures be proportionate ('commensurate' in the language of Article 51 of the ILC Articles on State Responsibility), if the same substantive obligation of intellectual property protection is suspended in both cases, and to the same extent.[40] As a result, it can be concluded that the proposition of conventions administered by the WIPO preventing TRIPS cross-retaliation appears to be bereft of a sound legal basis. In the interests of the reputation of the WTO dispute settlement system and also its perceived effectiveness for smaller or developing countries, the proponents

[37] See Jorgen Blomqvist's interview in the *Antigua Sun*, 16 January 2008, quoted in *Bridges Weekly*, Vol. 22, No. 2, 23 January 2008, from which the WIPO Secretariat distanced itself, see *Bridges*, *ibid.*

[38] See, in particular, Frederick Abbott, quoted in *Bridges Weekly*, Vol. 22, No. 2, 23 January 2008.

[39] Henning Grosse Ruse-Khan, 'Conflicting Obligations in WTO Retaliation – The Case of Overlapping Layers of Intellectual Property Protection' (draft paper on file with the editors of this book), takes the same position, based on a detailed analysis.

[40] Interestingly, in the scenario at hand, that is, when the retaliating WTO member simultaneously takes a countermeasure under a non-WTO international agreement, it becomes *a legal requirement* that the objective be the inducement of WTO-compliance. See Article 49(1) of the ILC Articles on State Responsibility.

of this argument should reconsider their position, or support it with legal arguments based on a proper enquiry into the applicable law.

It should also be mentioned that this question of retaliation obstacles pursuant to other international agreements is relevant not only in the context of cross-retaliation under the TRIPS Agreement. Parallel obligations can exist in all areas of the WTO Agreement and, in fact, increasingly do exist notably in the form of free trade agreements, which in significant part repeat WTO obligations (for example, national treatment, the prohibition of non-tariff border restrictions or the requirement of proportionality of TBT and SPS measures). Where they do not repeat WTO obligations, but go beyond them (for example, tariff elimination), the 'distance' to relevant WTO obligations (for example, the MFN tariff binding) may be, or in the future become, exceedingly small for the purpose of allowing any, or any meaningful, retaliation under the dispute settlement systems of either agreement. In these cases, too, the above explanations can be offered in order to avoid the situation where retaliation becomes impossible or ineffective due to a limitation to MFN duty snap-back.[41]

[41] The best is, of course, to stipulate this expressly, as some FTA parties do by stipulating that nothing in the WTO Agreement shall prevent the parties from availing themselves of their retaliation rights under the FTA and vice versa. Of course, no one can at this stage give a legal guarantee that the WTO dispute settlement system would uphold such a stipulation of a bilateral agreement, just as this uncertainty (to say the least) also exists in relation to the general international instrument of the countermeasure (in *Mexico–Soft Drinks* (DSR 2006:I, 3), the Appellate Body did not decide this question given that Mexico refrained from relying on the justification of countermeasures under public international law, yet it puzzlingly stated that it could not 'adjudicate' non-WTO disputes, see para. 56 of the report). However, an express stipulation that sanctions are permitted irrespective of (partly) parallel obligations under other agreements is a step forward in terms of clarity, and it may already be effective by preventing (abusive) WTO litigation against FTA-authorised sanctions and vice versa.

10

The politics of selecting trade retaliation in the European Community: a view from the floor

HÅKAN NORDSTRÖM*

1 Introduction

Since the beginning of the WTO in 1995, the European Community (EC) has taken procedural steps toward trade sanctions in seven trade disputes and introduced sanctions in two cases.[1] The seven cases are reviewed in this volume by Lothar Ehring of the Directorate General for Trade (DG Trade) (Ehring, Chapter 9, above). In my commentary on the politics of selecting and implementing trade sanctions in the EC, I highlight some political and legal problems and suggest an alternative default strategy for the EC.

2 Splitting the bill

There is no question that as far as the EC is concerned the purpose of trade sanctions is to induce compliance. Other motives suggested in the literature – such as 'rebalancing' the exchange of trade concessions after a unilateral breach of the WTO agreement[2] – have no currency in EC trade policy circles.[3] The best strategy to induce compliance is arguably to aim at politically influential sectors and goods made by marginal constituents.[4]

* The author is the chief economist of the National Board of Trade (Kommerskollegium), the central administrative body in Sweden dealing with foreign trade and trade policy. This chapter is written in a personal capacity and should not be attributed to the Swedish government.

[1] *US–Wheat Gluten Safeguards, US–Steel Safeguards, US–Foreign Sales Corporations, US–Byrd Amendment, US–Antidumping Act of 1916, US–Section 110(5) of the Copyright Act, US–Section 211 of the Omnibus Appropriations Act ('Havana Club').*

[2] See Sykes, Chapter 16, below.

[3] See Ehring , Chapter 9, above.

[4] This strategy is used also by the United States, Canada and Mexico.

This strategy was used in the *US–Steel Safeguards* dispute that took aim at 'swing states' in the 2004 elections, such as steel from Pennsylvania and orange juice from Florida. While all member states would seem to agree with this strategy in the abstract, splitting the bill has been more problematic because of domestic opposition.

The consultations held in Sweden revealed, for example, a strong opposition to inclusion of orange juice on the product list. The food industry argued that they could not navigate around the sanctions by buying from other sources since brands are based on a certain quality and origin. A producer of tablecloths submitted that there was no alternative supplier of the kind of fabrics it needed, nor could it pass on the additional duty to its clients since the market was very competitive. The importer and dealer of Harley-Davidson motorbikes feared that the entire season would be destroyed. Other agents of brand-name products concurred. Orders for barbeques, sunglasses, apparel and furniture were already in place and profit margins would be wiped out by the additional duties.

What became clear during these consultations was that the aggregate impact on the Swedish economy was not very large. However, the design of the trade sanctions that imposed high tariffs on a short list of products meant that the damage would be highly concentrated. It would hit hardest on importers and retailers of certain brand-name products, as well as producers that that could not find alternative suppliers for their inputs at short notice. The Ministry of Foreign Affairs decided to make a pledge in Brussels for the most pressing cases; as did other member states.

Faced with this opposition, DG Trade agreed to revise the list but insisted that the total value should remain the same. New products had to be added to the list to make up for the shortfall. This triggered new demands for revisions by member states that could not accept the substitutes. At this stage DG Trade became rather impatient with the member states' efforts to keep the sanctions out of their own backyard. Any new demands had to be followed by suggestions for substitutes that *were* acceptable.[5] The response time was also shortened in order to force a convergence. When the bell tolled, seventy-nine products had been taken off the list and 144 had been added.

The outcome of this zero-sum game is shown in figure 10.1. The grey bars are the historical import shares of the covered products on the final

[5] Whether this helps the process along is questionable since country A may be no happier with the substitutes proposed by country B than by the substitutes proposed by DG Trade.

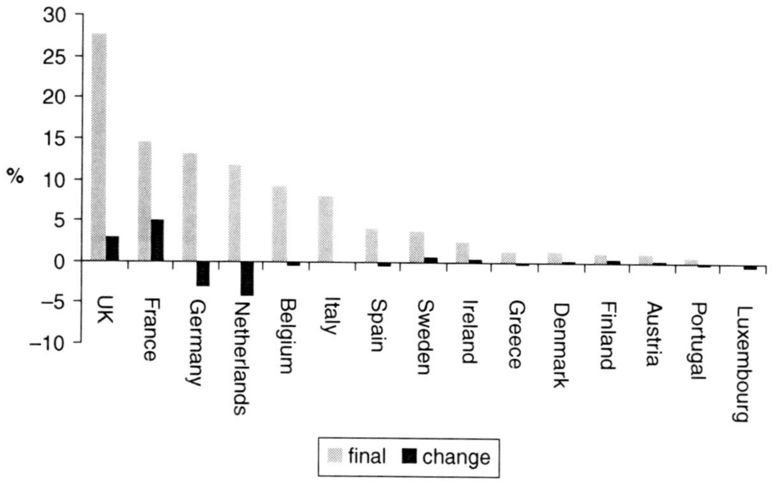

Figure 10.1. Splitting the bill for *US–Steel Safeguards*

list.[6] It is not surprising to find the big economies at the top of the list, with the United Kingdom at the first spot since trade between it and the United States is particularly intense for historical and geographical reasons. But the individual shares also depend on the composition of the list, which is a factor that the member states *can* influence by asking for strategic exemptions – and some member states played this game better than others.[7] The revisions of the list resulted in a higher share for the United Kingdom and France and lower shares for Germany and the Netherlands (the black bars). Also Belgium, Spain, Greece, Portugal and Luxembourg came out ahead.

In the *US–Foreign Sales Corporation (FSC)* dispute illustrated in figure 10.2, DG Trade changed tactics to avoid the substitution mess. The list submitted to the member states was about three times larger than the amount awarded by the arbitrators. Of the 2,556 items on the initial list, 956 items were taken off after requests by the member states, EC companies and trade associations. No substitutes had to be called in.

The composition this time around was even more tilted against products imported by the United Kingdom. In fact, more than 50 per cent of the EU-15 imports of the products on the final list were destined for the United Kingdom in the reference period, compared with 33 per cent

[6] The base year for these calculations is 2000.

[7] The most cynical strategy is to ask for an exemption of a product that you import and propose a substitute that others import.

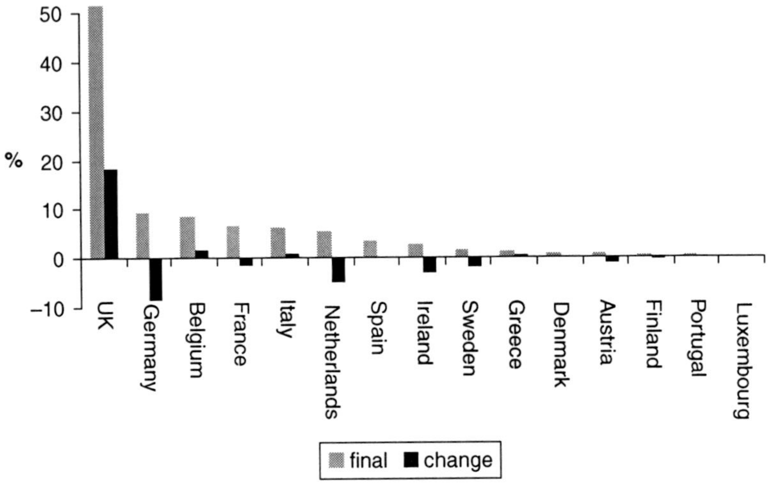

Figure 10.2. Splitting the bill for *US–Foreign Sales Corporations*

of the initial list submitted by DG Trade. The burden shifted toward the United Kingdom because other countries were more successful in unloading imports that were important for their own economies. Germany, the Netherlands, Ireland, Sweden and Austria were all able to cut their shares by at least a half.

The United Kingdom certainly has a lesson to learn from this exercise, but is it a problem also for the EC? I would say so. The manoeuvring to keep the sanctions out of each member state's own backyard shows that the targeting strategy does not work politically in the EC. What was supposed to be a carefully laid out strategy became a free-for-all party, not unlike the current fight over the distribution of the CO_2 emission cuts. Everyone agrees with the objective, but no one wants to pay the bill.

3 Non-contractual liability

The splitting of the bill is not the only problem facing the EC. If push comes to shove, there *will* be casualties at home among importers, retailers and producers that use the foreign supplies on the sanction list. The manoeuvring to keep the sanctions out of one's own backyard does not eliminate this problem; it only shifts the burden to different sectors and member states.

These causalities are not only an ethical problem but also a legal problem insofar as the EC can be held responsible for the damage incurred. Firms that are harmed may not accept their fate as 'pawns' in this game, but may sue the EC at the European Court of Justice (ECJ) for the losses incurred. Such claims are brought under Article 288 of the EC Treaty, second paragraph:

> In the case of non-contractual liability, the Community shall, in accordance with the general principles common to the laws of the Member States, make good any damage caused by its institutions or by its servants in the performance of their duties.

The most recent case law in this area is *Fiamm and Fedon* v. *The Commission and the Council* (C-120/06 P and C-121/06 P). The case concerns a claim for compensation by two Italian firms that were damaged by the sanctions imposed by the United States against the European firms in the *EC–Bananas* dispute, that is, the mirror image of the situation we have discussed thus far (EC firms suing for compensation for the harm caused by EC sanctions).[8] The US sanctions took the form of a 100 per cent duty on selected products, including cases for eye-wear produced by *Fedon* and stationary batteries produced by *Fiamm*. The sanctions lasted between April 1999 and June 2001.

The requests were referred to the Court of First Instance (CFI). The first plea of the plaintiffs was that the Commission and the Council had acted unlawfully by failing to comply with the WTO ruling in *EC–Bananas*. This provoked the US countermeasures that caused the damage to the producers.

The CFI accepted the argument that there was a direct link between the EC's failure to comply and the trade damage suffered by the consequential sanctions imposed by the United States. However, the CFI did not accept the argument that the EC had to make good the damage. The court noted that the WTO Agreement has no *direct effect* in the EC but for two recognized exceptions that were not applicable in this case. The CFI further noted that the Dispute Settlement Understanding (DSU) of the WTO does not impose an absolute requirement to comply, although this was the preferred solution. Other options were available to the respondent, including compensatory tariff reductions to restore the balance of trade concessions (the 'rebalancing' argument). A right to compensation for EC exporters would put undue pressure on the Commission and the Council to comply in cases where the general interest may speak for another solution of the dispute.

[8] See Mavroidis (2007) for a critical review of this case.

Having lost this argument, the plaintiffs pleaded that the EC was in any event liable since, under EC law, the EC can be held responsible for the damage of lawful acts if the nature of the damage is unusual and special. The court concurred that the EC can, *exceptionally*, be held responsible even for lawful acts. Previous case law had established three criteria that, at the very minimum, must be satisfied:

(1) evidence of damage;
(2) a causal link between the damage and the lawful act (in this case, the decision not to implement the WTO ruling); and
(3) unusual and special nature of the damage.

The first two criteria were satisfied in the current case. The claims for compensation turned on the issue of whether the nature of the damage was 'unusual and special', in essence, if trade sanctions were a normal business risk in international trade. The CFI argued that it *was* a normal business risk. The argument was not based on the possibility of predicting trade sanctions but simply that it *could* happen, being a permissible response to a breach of the WTO Agreement. The claims for compensation were, therefore, dismissed.

The ruling was appealed. The ECJ asked the Advocates General[9] for a legal opinion, which was issued on 28 February 2008.[10] The Advocate General took issue with the CFI and argued that trade sanctions caused by a dispute in an unrelated sector (bananas) could not be viewed as a normal business risk for manufacturers of cases for eye-wear (Fedon) and stationary batteries (Fiamm). The Advocate General consequently recommended that the Italian firms should be compensated for the losses incurred.

However, this opinion was set aside by the ECJ, which has the final word.[11] While non-contractual liability for *unlawful* conduct was firmly established in EC case law, the ECJ argued that no such principle had been recognized for *lawful* conduct, especially not for legislative acts. Earlier case law had established only that, '*if the principle of such liability came*

[9] The role of the Advocates General is to propose to the court, with complete independence, a legal solution to the cases that are referred to them. The Advocate General's opinion, although often in fact followed, is not binding on the court.

[10] Opinion of Advocate General Poiares Maduro, 20 February 2008, Joined Cases C-120/06 P and C-121/06 P, *Fiamm and Fedon* v. *Council of the European Union and Commission of the European Communities.*

[11] Judgment of the Court (Grand Chamber), 9 September 2008, Joined Cases C-120/06 P and C-121/06 P, *Fiamm and Fedon* v. *Council of the European Union and Commission of the European Communities.*

to be recognized, at the very least three conditions, comprising the fact of damage, the existence of a causal link between it and the act concerned and the unusual and special nature of the damage, would all have to be satisfied in order for liability to be incurred' (emphasis added).[12] Moreover, non-contractual liability could be incurred by the EC only 'in accordance with the general principles common to the laws of the Member States'. The court agreed with the defendants' view (the Commission and the Council) that, while some member states provided for such extracontractual liability, there was no convergence between the laws of the member states in this regard. The conditions for non-contractual liability in Article 288 were, therefore, not satisfied and the claims for compensation were dismissed.

It remains to be seen whether this ruling also closes the door to compensation for the damage caused by the sanctions *adopted by* the EC. I am not a lawyer, but I would imagine that the ECJ would find it more difficult to deny such claims because of the direct link between the EC's decision to place a product on a sanction list and the damage incurred by EC firms that trade in these goods. If the EC put orange juice on the sanction list, importers, processors and retailers of orange juice will be harmed. The court would have to make an assessment of whether this is a normal business risk (*political risk*) that firms must accept when they engage in international trade.

In other contexts, governments will have to make good the damage caused by lawful acts that have a *disproportionate* impact on individual members of society. A case in point is expropriation of land to build a public highway. Such a decision can be motivated by the general interests of society, but this does not give the government the right to take the land without due compensation. It is not unreasonable, in my opinion, to compensate individual firms that carry a disproportionate burden of a trade dispute on behalf of the EC. The common burdens should be carried equitably and not distributed at will. This principle is enshrined in the legal order of, for example, France ('l'égalité des citoyens devant les charges publiques') and Germany ('Sonderopfer').

My preferred option is not the compensation route, however, since that would swamp the legal system with claims that are difficult to evaluate. Moreover, it may have undesirable trade effects that could possibly undermine the objectives of the sanctions (that is, to induce compliance). My preferred choice is to look for alternatives that would avoid both

[12] Para. 169.

the political problem of splitting the bill and the potential problem of non-contractual liability. In the next section, I outline such a strategy.

4 The 'long list' approach

The DSU leaves considerable discretion to the complaining party in the selection of trade sanctions. Article 22.7 DSU provides that 'the arbitrator ... shall *not examine the nature* of the concessions or other obligations to be suspended but shall determine whether the level of such suspension is equivalent to the level of nullification or impairment' (emphasis added). The nature only becomes an issue for the arbitrators if the defendant claims that the complaining party has not followed the principles and procedures set forth in Article 22.3, which recommend suspensions in the same agreement and sector as the offending act if 'practicable and effective'.

In particular, there is nothing in the DSU that requires the plaintiff to impose 100 per cent duties on a short list of products whose combined import value in a representative period (the last three years of available statistics) adds up to the level of suspension awarded by the arbitrators. This is a convention and not a legal requirement. Any combination of products and tariff rates that suppresses the same value of trade is consistent with the trade suppression criteria used by arbitrators in the equivalence assessment.

My preferred alternative to the short list approach is to impose a small uniform tariff on *all* goods. The admissible tariff rate would be calculated by the following formula:

$$\text{tariff} \leq \frac{\text{level of suspension}}{\text{import value} \times \text{average import elasticity}}.$$

The average import elasticity would have to be estimated on historical import data since it depends on the product composition of the bilateral trade in the particular case. For example, in the *US–FSC* dispute, where the award was US$4.043 billion and the import in the reference period US$199 billion, the uniform duty would be 1 per cent if the average import elasticity is 2.

The long list approach would address the political and legal problems discussed before:

(1) there would be no need to consult on which products should be on the list; *all* goods are on the list by default; and

(2) the burdens are shared equitably, which avoids the potential liability problem.

To these advantages one could add two more benefits. The threat of sanctions would be *credible* since the harm to the country's own economy would be minimal. The sanctions would also have a positive revenue side. In the case of *US–FSC*, since imports from the United States would have fallen only marginally, these alternative sanctions would have improved the budget by approximately US\$2 billion a year (1 per cent × US\$199 billion) for the duration of the dispute. In contrast, prohibitive tariffs on a short list of goods generate very little, if any, revenue since the tax base is destroyed. Indeed, it is quite likely that a small uniform tariff would improve the welfare of the EC because of a positive terms-of-trade effect (a marginal reduction of the export prices of the targeted country).

These advantages should be weighed against the benefits of the short list approach which may be more efficient in inducing compliance. Indeed, this was the argument made by the Swedish Ministry of Foreign Affairs when I submitted a proposal along these lines in 2003.[13]

I agree with this objection. But I also believe that the power of trade sanctions is over-rated. Some 90 per cent of the disputes in the GATT era were resolved without trade sanctions being authorized. The track record has not improved in recent years when trade sanctions have become more automatic. Economic coercion can certainly add some extra pressure to comply, but the decisive factor is often the legal ruling *per se* and the bad reputation it would earn a government who refused to stand by its international obligations. Even a 'small' punishment would signal the resolve of the EC, and the additional tariffs, however small, would be an irritant for the export industry in the targeted country, and hence also a problem for the government concerned.

5 But . . .

The long list approach is not the best response in all types of dispute. For example, in *US–Antidumping Act of 1916* and *US–Byrd Amendment*, it was reasonable in my view to suspend obligations in a way that mirrors the wrongful act (had it been permitted by the arbitrators). Likewise, in disputes regarding GATS and TRIPS, it may be more appropriate and effective to respond within the ambits of these agreements. Indeed, the

[13] See Nordström (2003).

EC may have little choice but to do so since the DSU mandates a response in the same agreements and the same sector (category for TRIPS) if 'practicable and effective'.

References

Mavroidis, Petros C. 2007. 'It's Alright Ma, I'm only Bleeding' in Astrid Epiney, Marcel Haag and Andreas Heinemann (eds.), *Challenging Boundaries, Festschrift für Roland Bieber* (Baden Baden: Noms Verlag), 548–58

Nordström, Håkan 2003. 'Reflections on the Community's Trade Sanction Strategy', Dnr 112 2962–2003, National Board of Trade.

11

Canada's experience and practice in suspending WTO obligations

VASKEN KHABAYAN

Since the establishment of the WTO in 1995 Canada has been involved in at least thirty disputes as a complainant.[1] Of these thirty complaints, only seven have resulted in Canada seeking authorization from the Dispute Settlement Body (DSB) of the WTO to suspend tariff concessions or other obligations against another WTO member: *EC–Hormones*;[2] *Australia–Salmon*;[3] *Brazil–Aircraft*;[4] *US–CDSOA*;[5] *US–Softwood Lumber III*;[6] *US–Softwood Lumber V*;[7] and *US–Softwood Lumber IV*.[8] Of these seven cases, only three cases reached the stage where Canada received the authorization to suspend tariffs or other obligations,[9] and in only two of those cases did it actually impose the retaliation rights it received (*EC–Hormones* and *US–CDSOA*).

Like many other WTO members, when a request for authorization to retaliate is being considered, Canada prepares its list for retaliation after a series of consultations has been completed. As a first step, the Government of Canada will conduct its own research into the products imported from the target member. Once Canada has compiled this list according to HS codes, it will select a list of possible goods to target based on its analysis

[1] Canada has requested consultations in thirty cases, but has requested panel establishment in only eighteen cases in which seventeen original panel reports have been issued.

[2] *EC–Measures Concerning Meat and Meat Products*, WT/DS48/17.

[3] *Australia–Measures Affecting Importation of Salmon*, WT/DS18/12.

[4] *Brazil–Export Financing Program for Aircraft*, WT/DS46/16.

[5] *US–Continued Dumping and Subsidies Offset Act of 2000*, WT/DS234/25.

[6] *US–Final Countervailing Duty Determination regarding Softwood Lumber*, WT/DS257/16.

[7] *US–Investigation of the International Trade Commission in Softwood Lumber*, WT/DS277/9.

[8] *US–Final Dumping Determination on Softwood Lumber*, WT/DS264/17.

[9] In the remaining four cases, Canada reached a mutually agreed solution with the respondent prior to the completion of an Article 22.6 arbitration.

of the value of trade that could fit within the requested level of retaliation. The second step is to publish and notify to the likely industries that Canada may be seeking to raise the bound rates of certain targeted goods. A period of time is provided for the public to comment on the proposed list, and often a large amount of comments are received from importers looking to exempt their products from the list. After the consultations are completed, a final list of goods is prepared.

As much as possible, Foreign Affairs and International Trade Canada (DFAIT), the institution in charge of this matter, seeks to avoid hurting domestic importers and consumers by targeting goods that have either alternative sources of importation from another country that is not subject to the retaliation request, or by domestic sources. However, this is not an easy task. Canada has a very large trading partner to its south from which it receives about 75 per cent of its imports. Despite the fact that Canada does almost Can$2 billion in trade a day with the United States, the trade relationships are so long-standing and profound that many importers cannot easily find equally priced alternatives to goods originating in the United States, so compiling targeted goods is not an easy task. Canada, therefore, has to be very conscious of these supply lines in the selection of targeted goods so that the trade retaliation does not end up causing as much economic pain to our own domestic constituents.

However, in the one case where we have retaliated against the United States, sometimes it seems that the opposite problem occurs. How do you target such a large economy with very little retaliation and still be effective? In the *US–CDSOA* case, Canada was awarded retaliation by the arbitrator based on a formula where the amount of duties disbursed pursuant to the CDSOA would be multiplied by a factor of 0.72. In the one year (2005) that Canada retaliated against the United States under this authorization, the amount of retaliation was only US$11.2 million. Not very much in terms of real trade between the two countries; in fact, one would think it would barely cause a ripple in the overall trade between these two economies. The products chosen from the final retaliation list included live swine, ornamental fish, oysters and cigarettes. These products were selected because the supporters of the offending legislation were from Virginia and Maine, and the chosen products were from their districts. In addition, it was believed that other sources could be easily found for the import of these products, although this did not stop some domestic importers from complaining. With such little retaliation, the product targets appear to have more to do with sending a political message to the US Congress rather than having a real economic impact. But the political message was underscored by the fact that several of the co-complainants in this case sought retaliation authorization nearly concurrently. Furthermore, there was the underlying threat that Canada's retaliation would balloon considerably if the United States were to disburse the nearly US$4 billion in duties collected on softwood lumber over the years.

The same considerations apply to Canada's other large trading partner, the European Union (EU), which represents roughly 10 per cent of our total world trade. In the one case in which Canada was granted retaliation rights against the EU, *EC–Hormones*, the award was only Can$11.3 million per annum, a tiny fraction of the annual trade between Canada and the EU.[10] Again, trade retaliation at this amount would not cause much disruption of two-way trade and, therefore, one may question the efficacy of retaliation that may not cause economic harm to the targeted country. However, Canada did consider it important to use this retaliation right to send a clear message to the offending WTO member that it was violating the rules. Retaliation on this scale may lack the economic impact to enforce compliance, but it could still send a message to others that the dispute settlement mechanism of the WTO is an important tool. Therefore, it was important for Canada to follow the process to its final conclusion, even though, in the end, it selected some apparently innocuous products, like Spanish pickles and Danish pork. These were products that were quite easily sourced from other markets.

Finally, Canada obtained significant retaliation rights against Brazil in the case *Brazil–Aircraft*. Brazil is a significant world market, but less so for Canada, as it represents about 0.567 per cent of Canada's total external merchandise trade or about Can$2 billion in 2002. This posed a different problem in establishing a list for retaliation: Canada just did not have enough products from Brazil that could be sourced from elsewhere if it used its full level of Can$344.2 million per annum. There would have been some products, such as orange juice, that would have been very difficult to replace at that level of importation if total trade in that sector was eliminated through a 100 per cent increase in tariffs. However, retaliation was never finally implemented in this case. A likely critical point in the decision not to implement retaliation was the fact that Brazil also was awarded the right to suspend concessions against Canada in the amount of about US$250 million as a result of the *Canada–Aircraft II* case shortly

[10] Bilateral Canada–EU trade was Can$84 billion in 2007, of which Can$49 billion were in imports from the EU. Available at: www.international.gc.ca/eet/pocket-facts-en.asp.

thereafter. With both parties facing potential sanctions, and in particular having a firm value of the level of retaliation available to both, certain external conditions made it easier for both parties to not proceed with the actual use of the retaliation rights.

In conclusion, even for an economy the size of Canada, it is not easy to come up with a list of products for retaliation that would cause less harm to the home market than the potential gain from eliminating a targeted import. The small amounts of sanctions that have been put in place by Canada to date have been more symbolically significant than economically important.

12

Is retaliation useful? Observations and analysis of Mexico's experience

JORGE A. HUERTA-GOLDMAN*

This contribution is about Mexico's decisions on whether or not to use those provisions in international trade law, both multilateral and regional (WTO and preferential trade agreements), allowing it to retaliate. I analyse only cases where Mexico is the complainant.[1] It has been faced with a decision five times on whether or not to take retaliation.

Section 1 presents the observations and provides the relevant data. Those cases where Mexico decided to retaliate allow us to measure the extent to which this choice enhanced the complainant's bargaining power. Also, it presents the selection of goods Mexico chose for retaliation. The cases where Mexico decided not to retaliate complement the picture by providing the political economy considerations. Section 2 presents our analysis of the data. We argue that the chocolate cake scenario – the defendant retains more chocolate by facing retaliation than by complying with the law of the contract or compensating otherwise – significantly diminishes the effectiveness of retaliation and provides negative economic incentives for compliance and compensation. The sensitivity of the goods/services subject to the dispute influences the position of the defendant and this has a direct impact on the use or otherwise of retaliation and on the outcome of the case. But more data would be needed to better understand how far this conclusion can be taken.

* The author is currently working for the Mexican Ministry of Economy. The opinions expressed in this work are entirely those of the author and he alone is responsible for the accuracy of the information. I should like to thank Petros Mavroidis, Cesar Guerra Guerrero, Sol Leal Campos, Carlos Vejar, Ilaria Accorsi, Yannick Palacios and Peter Bennett for their comments and guidance in writing this chapter.

[1] There is one case where Mexico was procedurally close to eventually facing retaliation, but it withdrew the measure after a report in favour of the complainant by an Article 21.5 panel, as modified by the Appellate Body. See *Mexico–High Fructose II* (DS132) (DSR 2001:XIII, 6675).

Also, Mexico decided not to resort to retaliation in a number of cases, preferring a more amicable position, where the defendant has greater control of the outcome. The contribution also touches upon the selection of the goods subject to retaliatory measures and presents some relevant considerations.

1 Some observations

*1.1 Observation one: only some portions of the chocolate cake were taken into account for retaliation (*Byrd*)*

The WTO case *US–Byrd* (217/234) was initiated on 21 May 2001 by Mexico, Canada, Australia, Brazil, Chile, the EC, India, Indonesia, Japan, Korea and Thailand. They challenged a legislative measure relating to countervailing duties (CVD) and antidumping duties (AD) imposed by the United States whereby the US government distributed to domestic companies the ADs/CVDs collected if they had participated in the investigation and supported the petition. The panel and the Appellate Body (AB) sided with the complainants, finding violation of the Antidumping Agreement and the Agreement on Subsidies and Countervailing Measures (SCM Agreement).[2] But no case was taken under Article 21.5 of the Dispute Settlement Understanding (DSU), since there was no disagreement, at the time, on the lack of compliance by the United States. The co-complainants reverted to arbitration under Article 22.6 of the DSU on nullification or impairment, as requested by the defendant. The products protected by the United States were general goods (those subject to ADs and CVDs) and these included many that were highly sensitive for US industry.

The co-complainants were allowed to retaliate only for a value of up to 72 per cent of the ADs/CVDs collected and disbursed relating to their exports from the previous year. The United States published the yearly disbursements, and this served as the basis for the retaliatory measures in the subsequent year.[3]

Mexico initiated retaliatory measures in a decree published on 17 August 2005 with a validity of twelve months. Japan, Canada and the EC had already imposed retaliatory measures at the time. In a decree

[2] The Offset Act was held to be a non-permissible specific action against dumping or a subsidy.

[3] See award under Article 22.6, *US–Offset Act* (WT/DS234/ARB/MEX) (DSR 2004:X, 4931), 5.2.

published on 13 September 2006, Mexico imposed a second set of retaliatory measures, which expired on 31 October 2006.

For purposes of simplification, the example of a chocolate cake is used. Assume 'member X' illegally gets one chocolate cake a year from other WTO members. Only four WTO members are able to recover, through retaliation, four pieces of the cake, representing in total 54 per cent of the entire cake. From a purely chocolate point of view, to put it simply, 'member X' would be better off facing retaliation (it keeps 46 per cent of the cake) than complying with the WTO contract (where it does not have the right to take the cake) and perhaps even better off than if it compensated otherwise: it keeps more chocolate by facing retaliation.

The CDSOA Annual Report for Fiscal Year 2004 documents the percentage of 2004 disbursements which were not subject to retaliation in 2005.[4] The United States faced retaliation over 54 per cent of its disbursements, since only four WTO members were able to retaliate (Canada with 5 per cent of the disbursements, Japan with 25 per cent, the EC with 14 per cent and Mexico with 10 per cent). The remaining 46 per cent of the disbursements were not subject to retaliation in 2005. These came from WTO members that were not able to retaliate, even though some of them were co-complainants.

The reality in *Byrd* was very similar to our chocolate cake example. The United States did not face retaliation in respect of 46 per cent of its 2004 disbursements – disbursements in 2004 constituted the basis for retaliation in 2005. Hence, it could also be argued that, from an economic point of view, the United States was better off not complying with the recommendations of the DSB in this case since a large portion of its disbursements – the illegal measure – was untouched by retaliation. It was a lesser economic burden to face retaliation than to comply, since it got a large part of the cake for free.

1.2 *Observation two: there was no negotiation on compensation (*Byrd*)*

Even though the DSU provides for compensation as a second legal remedy for the parties to a dispute, the record of the WTO case in *Byrd* does not show any attempt to negotiate such compensation. Perhaps this was because the bargaining power of the co-complainants was low relative to

[4] See www.customs.gov/xp/cgov/trade/priority_trade/add_cvd/cont_dump/cdsoa_04/ (accessed January 2009).

that of the defendant, even if there were eleven of them, and it was not worth the negotiating effort. Perhaps retaliation was not considered a credible threat.

1.3 Observation three: compliance came late, notwithstanding the strength of the co-complainants (Byrd)

Byrd is probably the WTO case with the highest number of co-complainants (eleven WTO members). It is difficult to imagine a stronger coalition of co-complainants than three members of the quad (the EC, Canada and Japan),[5] Australia and seven of the largest developing countries (Mexico, Brazil, Chile, India, Indonesia, Korea and Thailand). But only four of them believed that retaliation was useful (the three quads plus Mexico). Notwithstanding the fact that the co-complainants constituted a powerful group, the measure remained in force from 2000 to 2007 and its effects continued to be felt after that.[6] The reasonable period of time to comply expired on 27 December 2003.

1.4 Observation four: rules on early retaliation were followed by earlier compliance (Brooms)

This observation derives from the NAFTA Chapter 20 case in *US–Brooms Safeguard*, where Mexico challenged the imposition of a safeguard measure imposed by the United States on Broom Corn Brooms (industrial goods).[7] Consultations were requested on 21 August 1996. Mexico instituted retaliatory tariffs against the United States on 12 December 1996, arguing that the measure affected trade to the value of approximately US$1.4 million in the first year.[8] The panel report was issued on 30 January

[5] The Quad or Quadrilateral group is an informal group composed of the trade ministers of the United States, the EC, Japan and Canada.

[6] Antidumping and countervailing duties charged on goods imported into the United States up to 30 September 2007 were still being distributed. This means that disbursements continued even after that date. See WT/DSB/M/205.

[7] On 28 April 1997 Colombia challenged the same measure (Presidential Proclamation 6961) under the WTO dispute settlement mechanism. The case did not go beyond the consultations stage in the WTO and never went to a panel. Mexico did not seek to be joined in those DSU consultations. See WTO Dispute Settlement Database by Horn and Mavroidis http://go.worldbank.org/X5EZPHXJY0 (accessed January 2009).

[8] See the report of the panel in USA-97-2008-01 United States Safeguard Action Taken on Broom Corn Brooms from Mexico, 16.

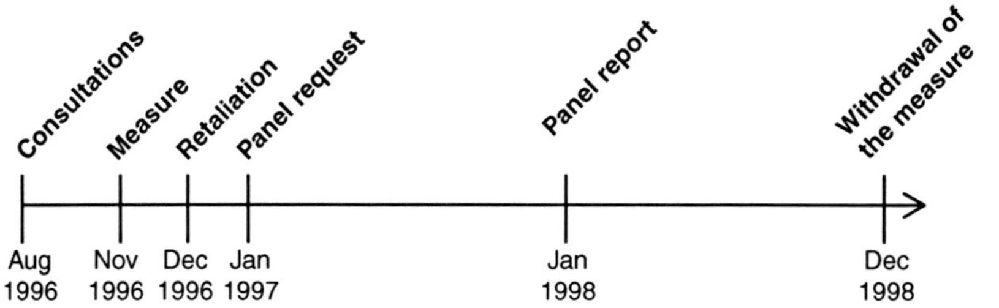

Figure 12.1. Time-line for *US–Brooms Safeguards*

1998 and it came out in favour of Mexico.[9] The safeguard measure was withdrawn on 8 December 1998,[10] eleven months later, even though the NAFTA panel ordered immediate compliance.

In the NAFTA case *US–Brooms Safeguard*, the NAFTA law on safeguards gave Mexico the opportunity to retaliate at an earlier procedural stage. NAFTA, Articles 801.4 (bilateral safeguards) and 802.6 (global safeguards) provide for compensation, and if not agreed, retaliation against safeguards without imposing any time frame for these legal remedies. In other words, they allow for early retaliation (as is the case under Article 8 of the WTO safeguards agreements, as discussed in Ehring's contribution to this volume (Chapter 9) where he examines the EC retaliation against US safeguards in *Wheat Gluten* and *Steel*). Finally, retaliation under these NAFTA rules continues for the minimum period necessary to achieve the substantially equivalent effects.

Figure 12.1 shows the time-line of the case. We note that Mexico retaliated immediately after the imposition of the final safeguard measure and before the panel request.

*1.5 Observation five: the selection of goods subject to retaliation involved consideration of the impact on domestic consumers (*Byrd *and* Brooms*)*

Mexico retaliated twice, once under WTO rules (in *Byrd*) and once under NAFTA (in *Brooms*). It did no more than suspend concessions negotiated

[9] It concluded that the United States had failed to provide 'reasoned conclusions on all pertinent issues of law and fact'.

[10] See 'Termination of the Safeguard Measure: Presidential Proclamation 7154, to Terminate Temporary Duties on Imports of Broom Corn Brooms', 63 Fed. Reg. 67761 (8 December 1998).

in the two contracts, that is, tariffs. Mexico has never suspended any other obligations such as the application of rule-oriented provisions.[11] There is no clear information on how Mexico selected the tariff lines subject to retaliation. But we can make some assumptions.

Mexico issued two decrees covering the specifics of retaliation in the WTO case in *Byrd*. The first was published in the *Federal Official Journal* on 17 August 2005, and it entered into force the next day.[12] It had a validity of 12 months. Mexico retaliated with additional import tariffs in the following US goods: 9 per cent on chewing gums (1704.10.01, 1704.90.99); 30 per cent, below a quota of 29,400 tonnes per year, on certain dairy products (1901.90.05); and 20 per cent on certain wines, champagnes and other sparkling wines (2204.10.01, 2204.21.01, 2204.21.02, 2204.21.03, 2204.21.04, 2204.21.99, 2204.29.99).

The second decree relating to the same case was published on 13 September 2006.[13] It was in force from 14 September 2006 to 31 December 2006 and imposed a 110 per cent import duty on certain dairy products (1901.90.05). Thus, it had a short validity but a strong impact by imposing a high tariff.

In the other case where Mexico imposed retaliatory measures, the NAFTA Chapter 20 dispute on *Brooms*, Mexico imposed retaliatory tariffs against the United States on 12 December 1996,[14] just a few days after the safeguard measure had entered into force on 4 December 1996.[15] NAFTA safeguards law allows for early retaliation, as explained above. According to Mexico, the US measure affected trade to the value of approximately US$1.4 million in the first year.[16] The retaliatory tariffs covered high

[11] The WTO agreements refer to retaliation as suspension of concessions or other obligations. The concept is not very clear, but concessions refer more to tariffs and other obligations than to rule-oriented provisions such as national treatment.

[12] See DECRETO por el que se modifica temporalmente el artículo 1 del Decreto por el que se establece la Tasa Aplicable durante 2003, del Impuesto General de Importación, para las mercancías originarias de América del Norte, publicado el 31 de diciembre de 2002, por lo que respecta a las mercancías originarias de EE.UU.

[13] See DECRETO por el que se modifica temporalmente el Artículo 1 del Decreto por el que se establece la Tasa Aplicable durante 2003, del Impuesto General de Importación, para las mercancías originarias de América del Norte, publicado el 31 de diciembre de 2002, por lo que respecta a las mercancías originarias de los EE.UU.

[14] See DECRETO por el que se aumenta la tasa aplicable a la importación de mercancías originarias de los Estados Unidos de América.

[15] See Proclamation No. 6961, 61 Fed. Reg. 64431-33 (4 December 1996) (to facilitate positive adjustment to competition from imports of Broom Corn Brooms).

[16] See the report of the panel in USA-97-2008-01 US Safeguard Action Taken on Broom Corn Brooms from Mexico, 16.

fructose corn syrup, wine, wine coolers, brandy, Tennessee whiskey, notebooks, flat glass and wooden furniture.[17] The decree does not have an expiry date and we were unable to find information on when the retaliatory tariffs were withdrawn. The preamble of the decree states that the Mexican domestic industry would not be affected by the retaliation since there were alternative suppliers, both national and foreign (non-US), of these goods.

1.6 *Observation six: an amicable approach was preferred to retaliation* (Bananas)

The WTO case *EC–Bananas III* (DS27) was originally initiated by Mexico, Ecuador, Guatemala, Honduras and the United States on 5 February 1996. It relates to trade in agricultural goods and trade in services (importation, sales and distribution of bananas). The measures challenged were the EC regime for the importation, sale and distribution of bananas and related instruments. The panel and the AB sided with the complainants, finding violations of different provisions (GATT, Agreement on Licensing and GATS). The EC faced retaliation by the United States only, even though Ecuador also obtained authorisation to retaliate for a value of almost US$200 million a year. As mentioned, Mexico did not seek retaliation.

At the time, Mexico decided not to pursue its procedural rights at the Article 21.5 panel stage and abandoned the case after requesting an Article 21.5 panel on 18 August 1998 – perhaps because a free trade agreement (FTA) between Mexico and the EC which entered into force one year later, on 1 July 2000, was under negotiation. Mexico could have eventually requested retaliatory rights, but it appears that for political-economy reasons it decided not to do so. Instead, it used its bargaining power to negotiate amicably with the EC for an FTA.

On 19 May 2008 a new Article 21.5 panel report was distributed in *EC–Bananas III*.[18] It concluded that the duty-free quota granted to

[17] These goods are classified under the following HS numbers in Mexican law: 1702.40.01; 1702.40.99; 1702.50.01; 1702.60.01; 2204.10.01; 2204.21.01; 2204.21.02; 2204.21.03; 2204.21.04; 2204.29.99; 2206.00.01; 2208.20.02; 2208.30.04; 4820.20.01; 7005.29.02; 7005.29.03; 7005.29.99; 9403.30.01; 9403.50.01.

[18] See the Article 21.5 Panel Report, *EC–Regime for the Importation, Sale and Distribution of Bananas*, WT/DS27/RW/United States, Recourse by the United States (DSR 1997:II, 943).

African, Caribbean and Pacific (ACP) countries only,[19] violated the most-favoured-nation treatment (MFN) provision (Article I) of the GATT and that no waiver affecting that provision was in force. Also, the panel found violation of the provisions on 'Non-Discriminatory Administration of Quantitative Restrictions' (Article XIII) of the GATT. Mexico played a passive role in this new phase. The AB confirmed the panel on appeal (albeit with different reasoning).

*1.7 Observation seven: negotiation on implementation was preferred to retaliation (*Trucking*)*

Mexico also decided not to retaliate in the NAFTA case *US–Trucking* either. The measure at issue was a US moratorium on the processing of applications by Mexican-owned trucking firms for authority to operate in the US border states: that is, market access for trucking services and investment. Mexico initiated this procedure based on the dispute settlement mechanism of NAFTA Chapter 20. Consultations were requested on 18 December 1995 and the panel report was issued on 6 February 2001. The United States did not implement the measure with respect to services.[20] On 23 February 2007, the United States and Mexico started a provisional programme aimed at opening the border to cross-border trucking services. The programme is ongoing, but it has encountered difficulties and it is partial and provisional. It has recently been extended for two more years.[21]

1.8 Observation eight: no retaliation occurred when MFN market access eroded Mexico's tariff preference subject to dispute

Finally, Mexico decided not to retaliate in a case under the auspices of the Asociación Latinoamericana de Integración (ALADI): this is, *Peru–Computers*. In that case, Mexico challenged Peru's refusal to grant preferential treatment to Mexican computers (industrial goods). It initiated this case based on the dispute settlement mechanism of the *Acuerdo de*

[19] See Council Regulation (EC) No. 1964/2005, 29 November 2005, in particular its duty-free tariff quota for bananas originating in ACP countries.

[20] Apparently, investment is already open to Mexicans but not for cross-border trucking services.

[21] See Continúa el proyecto demostrativo de autotransporte transfronterizo de carga, *Boletín de prensa No. 74*, available at: www.economia.gob.mx/?P=125 (accessed January 2009).

Cooperación Económica (ACE) No. 8 between Mexico and Peru under ALADI.[22] Consultations were requested on 16 January 2002 and the panel report was issued on 11 March 2004. The panel sided with Mexico on the origin of the computers. With respect to implementation, we note that the MFN applied tariff used by Peru as of 2007 for the goods subject to dispute was zero. Hence, Mexico's preferential tariff was eroded. But we do not have information on whether Mexican exports between 2004 and 2007 were ultimately given preference.

2 Analysis

The observations in section 1 are significant in helping to understand how retaliation worked in Mexico's cases. Some of them could apply to all or other WTO cases. This section explores some possible implications.

2.1 *The decision of whether or not to retaliate*

2.1.1 The chocolate cake scenario

The chocolate cake scenario – set up above – where the defendant carries a lesser economic burden from facing retaliation than from complying with the report or even from compensating otherwise, could potentially apply to many WTO cases. It is applicable to all those cases where the WTO-illegal measure affects more than one WTO member, but only some members are able to retaliate. The exception is countermeasures under the SCM Agreement, since case law there suggests that a given complainant may retaliate for the whole amount of the subsidy, regardless of the number of members affected.[23]

This scenario could easily apply in many other WTO cases – any violation of WTO law has the potential to affect trade or the conditions under which traders compete in the market of more than one WTO member. The EC regime on bananas is one clear example. But the cost, both political and financial, of taking litigation under the dispute settlement process of the WTO is high. Depending on the defendant's position, the complainant normally has to go through five procedures before it can obtain authorisation to retaliate: consultations; panel/AB;

[22] The ACE No. 8 between Mexico and Peru, negotiated under the umbrella of ALADI, contains a dispute settlement mechanism between the two countries. See www.aladi.org (accessed January 2009).

[23] See award under Article 22.6, *US–Foreign Sales Corporation* (WT/DS108/ARB) (DSR 2002:VI, 2517), A 34.

reasonable period of time; panel/AB under Article 21.5 of the DSU; and arbitration under Article 22.6 of the DSU on nullification or impairment. For instance, Mexico requested consultations on 21 May 2001 in *Byrd* and was able to retaliate only on 17 August 2005. This was still a relatively fast case since it did not have to go through the procedure on compliance (Article 21.5 of the DSU). But the cost was high and this could deter many WTO members from pursuing retaliation. There will certainly be many more obstacles to achieve retaliation but this chapter is not the place to explore them.

The chocolate cake scenario would be a disincentive for the defendant to comply with the report of the panel/AB. If the benefit gained by the illegal measure is greater than the costs of facing retaliation – plus 'other costs' – the defendant would have no incentive to comply, but on the contrary would have strong reasons to maintain the illegal measure. The 'other costs' mentioned above may include political pressure to comply, the cost of litigation and the disruption of trade relations with the complainants among others. Giving that each country is different, it is hard to determine what weight each individual WTO member would give to these 'other costs'. But they constitute a fundamental element which has to be taken into account in any negotiation/litigation on WTO violations.

The chocolate cake scenario directly affects compensation. The incentive to compensate is very low if the defendant continues to want to maintain the illegal measure. The defendant may prefer to face a low cost retaliation rather than the full cost of compliance or something in between as compensation. It is not likely to be very willing to pay, as compensation, anything higher than the cost of retaliation.

This incentive pushing a defendant toward retaliation would serve to reduce the number of cases of efficient breaches of WTO law (as referred to in Sykes, Chapter 16, below).[24] It narrows down the options that the defendant is willing to provide as compensation in exchange for allowing the illegal measure to continue, because a DSB report finding a WTO violation has a diminished real value.

[24] This refers to cases where the parties would be in a better situation politically and economically by violating WTO law rather than complying with it, because the defendant pays for its WTO violation with something of greater value to the complainant than that which is protected under WTO law. See Warren F. Schwartz and Alan O. Sykes, 'The Economics Structure of Renegotiation and Dispute Resolution in the WTO/GATT System', *Journal of Legal Studies*, 31:1(2) (2002), available at: www.law.uchicago.edu/Lawecon/WkngPprs_126-150/143.AOS.wto.pdf (accessed January 2009). Also, see Petros C. Mavroidis, *Trade in Goods* (Oxford University Press, 2007), 430–1.

2.1.2 Duration of the retaliation

In *Byrd*, the United States was able to maintain the illegal measure for almost 7 years. In 2005, four members retaliated. The United States stopped the disbursements of ADs/CVDs charged on goods imported after 30 September 2007, though duties collected before that date were still distributed. It took two years from the initiation of the retaliatory measures to the withdrawal of the Offset Act.

In *Brooms* under NAFTA, it also took the United States two years from the imposition of early retaliation (December 1996) to the withdrawal of the illegal safeguard measure (December 1998). The United States complied with the report within eleven months. But in practice, as compared with the WTO, compliance eleven months after the issuing of the report can be considered as prompt and within an acceptable period of time.[25]

In both cases retaliation was followed by implementation, which suggests that retaliation influences implementation to a certain degree. But as we saw, the chocolate case scenario diminishes the impact of retaliation. The following section adds one more variable to our analysis on retaliation.

2.1.3 Level of sensitivity of the products

This section clusters the products subject to the dispute (goods or services) on a scale of sensitivity for the defendant/violator: that is, the pressure from the domestic constituency in the violating country with respect to that product. Our classification is limited to the data from section 1 of this chapter. This makes table 12.1 speculative to a certain extent, but the analysis is revealing.

We reach the following conclusions from table 12.1:

- Retaliation was followed by implementation when either the level of sensitivity of the product in the violating country was low or when the political environment was soft (the protection offered to industry under the *Byrd Amendment* was not crucial but extra).
- Implementation occurred without retaliation when the level of sensitivity of the product in the violating country was low.
- Implementation did not take place in two cases where the level of sensitivity of the product in the violating country was high and retaliation did not occur.

[25] The average of the reasonable period of time to comply in the WTO in cases involving arbitration under Article 21.3(c) of the DSU is 11.69 months. See www.worldtradelaw.net (accessed January 2009).

Table 12.1. *Level of sensitivity of the products subject to the dispute*

(1) Product	(2) Level of sensitivity	(3) Political environment	(4) Retaliation	(5) Implementation
Goods subject to the *Byrd Amendment*	High[26]	Second remedy applied (ADs/CVDs are in effect)[27]	Yes	Implemented
Brooms	Low[28]	The US President had already been re-elected at the time of implementation of this case[29]	Yes	Implemented
Bananas	High[30]	No further information	No	Not implemented
Cross-Border Trucking Services	High[31]	Strong opposition exists to the provisional programme	No	Not implemented
Computers	Low[32]	No further information	No	Implemented

[26] These goods had already been selected by the petitioners of ADs/CVDs in the United States. They are as a result almost by definition industry sensitive.

[27] The distributions under the Byrd Amendment were held to be additional remedies against dumping and subsidies by the Appellate Body, as mentioned above. Hence, the Byrd Amendment was not crucial for the industry since the products were already protected through the ADs/CVDs.

[28] During the year 1996, the US imports of brooms (classified under subheading 9603.10) from Mexico amounted to US$10.1 million, whereas total imports from Mexico were US$74.1 billion (data from UN Comtrade, HS1992). The US imports of brooms from Mexico were marginal with respect to total imports from Mexico during 1996. Furthermore, the trade loss estimated by Mexico was US$1.4 million, as mentioned above.

[29] During 1997 the Democrats in the United States were seeking a second term in the US presidency with Bill Clinton. Perhaps they needed to send the right message to domestic industry by, among other things, imposing a safeguard. If that were the case, the Democrats did not need the safeguard any longer for political reasons in December 1998.

[30] The EC maintained a defensive position for a very long time with respect to its imports of bananas. The request for consultations in *EC–Bananas III* was issued on 5 February 1996. There are three GATT cases relating to imports of bananas where the defendant has been the predecessor to the EC–EEC – or one of its member states: (i) *EC–Member States' Import Regimes for Bananas* ('*Bananas I*'), DS32/R, 3 June 1993; (ii) *EC–Import Regime for Bananas* ('*Bananas II*'), DS38/R, 11 February 1994; and (iii) *United Kingdom Waivers (Application in Respect of Customs Duties on Bananas)*, L/1749, 11 April 1962.

[31] Trades unions oppose the opening of trucking services from Mexico to the United States, arguing environmental and trade concerns.

[32] Peru is not a major producer of computers. It is not a member of the Information Technology Agreement (ITA) which provides a zero tariff for information technology goods. The product coverage of the ITA covers computers. See WT/MIN(96)/16.

2.1.4 Amicable approach for something of comparable value

Mexico decided not to pursue its procedural rights in *EC–Bananas III* in favour of negotiating an FTA with the EC. At that time (1998), there was no experience in the WTO on requests/authorisation to retaliate. But as noted above, Mexico had already taken retaliatory measures against the United States in a NAFTA case. The first WTO experience on retaliation came one year after Mexico abandoned the case. The United States was the first WTO member authorised to retaliate, in the same case, *EC–Bananas III*, but further down the road.

At the time of writing, the EC had not eliminated the discrimination in that case – as confirmed by the new Article 21.5 WTO panel and AB report mentioned above. We can speculate that if Mexico had decided to continue with the case on bananas, it would have probably ended up like Ecuador and the United States, waiting to gain something out of bringing the case. On the other hand, it is obvious that an FTA has greater economic and political impact than an agreement/compliance by the EC on bananas. However, we cannot know whether it was crucial for Mexico to accommodate its WTO rights on bananas in order to achieve an FTA with the EC. It could be argued that the FTA is a standalone agreement with its own set of incentives for both parties, and Mexico could still have kept the bananas issue alive during the negotiations of the FTA. Perhaps Mexico negotiated a better deal on other concessions with the EC through the FTA by using bananas as a bargaining tool. But all this is speculation since we do not have the means to know. What is clear, however, is that Mexico did not want to take the risk of losing the FTA.

The other case where Mexico decided to adopt an amicable position was *US–Trucking (NAFTA)*. Free flow of trucking services between Mexico and the United States is fundamental for NAFTA integration. Since time is a valuable element for most traders, an inefficient cross-border system can delay the delivery of inputs for different industries. NAFTA industries would become more competitive if they had better integrated lines of production, but this requires an efficient cross-border system for road transportation. The use of road transport for Mexico's trade with its NAFTA partners increased significantly from 1995 to 2006, going from less than US$100 billion to almost US$250 billion in value.[33] Perhaps Mexico believed that the United States would eventually comply with its

[33] See North American Transportation Statistics Database, Chart 6–1b at http://nats.sct.gob.mx/nats/sys/index.jsp?i=3 (accessed January 2009).

NAFTA obligations on trucking services because of the importance of the value protected. Perhaps, Mexico did not see retaliation as a valid option and opted for a negotiated outcome that is yet to see the light of day.

2.2 *The goods subject to retaliation*

2.2.1 Three considerations for product selection

From the data available, we can distil three considerations for the selection of goods to be subject to retaliatory measures. First, the retaliating government may have defensive interests at play with respect to certain goods. For instance, in *US–Brooms* Mexico retaliated on high fructose corn syrup from the United States. We note that it imposed two defensive measures relating to trade in these products that created several WTO and NAFTA litigations.[34] Hence, it had some defensive interests and used its retaliatory rights to protect them.

The Mexican sugar industry has successfully exerted a heavy influence on decision makers, even though trade in sugar does not represent a large share of Mexico's GDP. We note that the percentage of GDP represented by agriculture, forestry and fisheries fluctuated between 4 per cent and 6 per cent in the period 1995 to 2007. The contribution of the sugar industry would be included in these figures, but it is not clear what the exact percentage is.[35] The Mexican Ministry of Agriculture, however, indicated, in a report dated 2008, that sugar represented 0.4 per cent of national GDP.[36]

Second, the retaliating member needs to consider the potential effects of retaliation on those domestic consumers that benefit from the imports of the goods subject to retaliation. Mexico did this when it analysed which

[34] The Mexican administration imposed final AD duties on high fructose corn syrup from the United States on 23 January 1998. The order was challenged in the WTO twice and once through Chapter 19 of NAFTA, and was revoked on 21 May 2002 through the resolution to comply with the binational NAFTA panel. At the same time, the Mexican Congress applied a tax on soft drinks and other beverages that use any sweetener other than cane sugar. On 16 March 2004, the United States initiated a WTO case. The panel, as modified by the AB, found violation of national treatment. The same measure (the tax law) was the basis for a case resting on investor–state procedures. Mexico implemented the measure on 27 December 2006, but it litigated the case up to the Appellate Body of the WTO.

[35] Source: *INEGI*. See http://dgcnesyp.inegi.gob.mx/cgi-win/bdieintsi.exe/NIVA 05001000150005#ARBOL (accessed March 2008).

[36] See www.sagarpa.gob.mx/cmdrs/sesiones/2008/2a_sesion/4_cana.pdf (accessed March 2008). However, the Ministry of Agriculture did not specify any period for this figure.

other entities were supplying the domestic market in *Brooms*, as indicated in the preamble to the decree mentioned above. But the decree provides no further detail with respect to this analysis.

Finally, the retaliating member may seek to put pressure on policy makers in the other country who support the illegal measure subject to dispute. This is simply an assumption, since there is no indication in the material that we have analysed that in Mexico's case this consideration was at the forefront in selecting goods subject to retaliation. But it can be taken for granted that the complainants in *Byrd* would be interested in applying pressure on key US senators to repeal the Byrd Amendment. But they would need to know which US exports are produced in the states represented by those senators who support the Byrd Amendment, and which of those goods have one of the co-complainants as a significant foreign market. Under the most favourable scenario, the targeted producer would be so seriously affected by the retaliation that it would put pressure on key senators to repeal the Byrd Amendment and eliminate the retaliation. As mentioned above, it took the United States more than four years from the end of the reasonable period of time to repeal the Byrd Amendment. The measure was in force for a period of more than seven years. What yardstick can we use to determine whether the complainants retaliating in this case were effective in putting the right pressure on the US Congress?

2.2.2 The clarity of the data

A policy maker considering the selection of goods to be subject to retaliation is handicapped if he or she does not have a comprehensive set of trade data available. There are reliable sources of information on international trade flows, and they can play a substantial role in the selection process. However, the HS classification may cluster the goods being considered under a wider classification of goods, so trade data may present part of the picture, but not provide the necessary detail.

Production data may also be useful. Assume that exports of widgets from the United States to Mexico amount to US$10 per year. A retaliatory tariff of 20 per cent may impact differently where the production of the exporter/producer is worth US$100 per year rather than where it is worth US$15. The problem is that it may not be easy to acquire reliable data on production in all the countries.

Information on domestic consumption is vital to any analysis of the effect of retaliation on those domestic consumers who benefit from imports of the goods in question. An assessment of the elasticity of the products concerned is also fundamental in determining the effects of the retaliatory measures. Information available to a policy maker may not be sufficient for him or her to be able to paint a clear and detailed picture of the situation, and the level of detail available regarding the domestic markets of defendants/violators varies from country to country.

3 Conclusions

The limited data analysed in this contribution on Mexico's experience with trade retaliation suggests that retaliation may not always be effective in every situation. The effectiveness of retaliation is diminished in the chocolate cake scenario and this has a negative effect on incentives for compliance or compensation. It also reduces the scope for efficient breach of international trade law. The effectiveness of retaliation is directly connected to the level of sensitivity of the goods/services subject to dispute.

The dispute settlement mechanisms adjudicating international trade law are in constant evolution. There are many strengths and weaknesses. Retaliation as a legal remedy is not very effective, but it is preferable to have a system which offers these mechanisms, as deficient as they may be, rather than not to have any such system at all. The track we are on is positive and it is evolving.

13

Procedures for the design and implementation of trade retaliation in Brazil

LUIZ EDUARDO SALLES*

1 Introduction

Brazil is one of the most active participants in WTO dispute settlement proceedings and one of the few to ever have been granted authorization to suspend obligations under Article 22 of the DSU.[1] However, it is also just one among the many WTO members that have never actually resorted to suspension of WTO obligations.[2] Given this lack of experience, one might ask why it is important to expend ink to introduce Brazil's domestic procedures to that effect.[3] Abstract intellectual curiosity aside, the justification for this exercise is twofold. First, although optimistic, Brazil's lack of experience in suspending WTO obligations will certainly not last forever: the ongoing arbitration in the *Cotton* dispute immediately comes to mind, for example.[4] Indeed, the looming retaliation against the United States in the *Cotton* case has triggered a quest within Brazil for domestic instruments that would facilitate a response

* Barretto Ferreira, Kujawski, Brancher e Gonçalves, São Paulo, Brazil. I would like to thank Lauro Locks for an insightful conversation about PL 1893/2007 and Marcelo Varella for comments. The views expressed herein are strictly personal.

[1] See *Canada–Aircraft (*Article 22.6 DSU, 4.11 SCM Agreement*)* (DSR 2003:III, 1187) and *US–Byrd Amendment (*Article 22.6 DSU, Brazil*)* (DSR 2004:IX, 4591).

[2] The *Byrd Amendment* dispute involved eleven co-complainants, and the EC has applied sanctions against the United States. Brazil has not. See L. Ehring, 'The European Community's Experience and Practice in Suspending WTO Obligations', Chapter 9, above.

[3] Compare the Brazilian inexperience with the experience of the United States and the EC, described, respectively, by S. Andersen and J. Blanchet, 'The United States' Experience and Practice in Suspending WTO Obligations', Chapter 8, above, and L. Ehring, Chapter 9, above.

[4] See WTO docs. WT/DS267/38 and WT/DS267/39, where Brazil requested the resumption of the arbitration under Article 22.6 of the DSU and Article 4.11 of the SCM Agreement.

to non-compliance.[5] In particular, legislators have been pushing forward a bill regulating retaliation under the TRIPS agreement which, to my knowledge, is unparalleled among WTO members. Hence, Brazil's endeavour provides an interesting test case on the creation of instruments to suspend intellectual property rights in domestic legal systems based on WTO rules. It also illustrates the strong connection between domestic law instruments and the ability to implement trade retaliation, a link all the more interesting when it comes to the uncharted waters of 'cross-retaliation'.[6]

Second, and related to the first reason, the very threat of sanctions is one factor that promotes compliance with WTO rules and rulings.[7] Depending on the way in which proceedings related to the design and implementation of sanctions are structured, a country may minimize the need to actually resort to such sanctions.[8] Therefore, from the perspective of inducing compliance it is in a country's interest to have a credible arsenal of measures at hand to implement potential Dispute Settlement Body (DSB) authorizations to suspend obligations. Cross-retaliation in TRIPS ranks high on that account in the light of the likely

[5] Thus, the Brazilian Ambassador to the WTO in Geneva, Roberto Azevedo, has reportedly stated that 'we have not decided that we will use it [referring to cross-retaliation]... the important thing is to have the instrument to do so, if we so decide'. S. Leo, 'País Estuda Suspensão de Direito de Propriedade Intelectual Para Retaliar EUA', *Valor Econômico*, 24 August 2007. See also Opinion by Deputy A. Lupion on PL 1893/2007, Commission of Agriculture of the Chamber of Deputies (2008) and Opinion by Deputy M. Corrêa Jr. on PL 1893/2007, Commission of Economic Development of the Chamber of Deputies (2008), available in Portuguese at: www2.camara.gov.br/proposicoes, accessed 14 January 2009.

[6] On cross-retaliation more generally, see F. Abbott, 'Cross-Retaliation in TRIPS: Issues of Law and Practice', Chapter 22, below.

[7] Retaliation or the threat thereof, of course, fulfils not only the role of inducing compliance with the findings and recommendations in WTO disputes. It has also a more general role of deterring rule violations.

[8] On the importance of the threat of sanctions in inducing compliance, see also S. Charnovitz, 'Should the Teeth Be Pulled? An Analysis of WTO Sanctions' in D. Kennedy and J. Southwick (eds.), *The Political Economy of International Trade Law: Essays In Honor of Robert Hudec* (Cambridge University Press, 2002), 602 at 618–19; R. Hudec, 'Broadening the Scope of Remedies in WTO Dispute Settlement' in F. Weiss (ed.), *Improving WTO Dispute Settlement Procedures: Issues and Lessons from the Practice of Other International Courts and Tribunals* (London: Cameron May, 2000), 369 at 387–8; and S. Andersen and J. Blanchet, Chapter 8, above (noting the threat of 'carousel' as a factor to induce compliance). Of course, one has to be careful here. Retaliation, let alone the threat thereof, is not a panacea in promoting compliance with rules and rulings. See, generally, J. Pauwelyn, *Optimal Protection of International Law: Navigating Between European Absolutism and American Voluntarism* (Cambridge University Press, 2008). But at any rate, the credibility of the threat definitely has a role in the compliance riddle.

and justifiable outcry from intellectual property-dependent industries, and of the self-destructive impact of other means of retaliation, such as raising tariff barriers.[9] Here again, the developments underway in Brazil are worthy of notice.

The present chapter aims to describe the institutional and legislative landscape for the design and implementation of suspension of WTO obligations in Brazil, and to discuss the central aspects of the 'TRIPS retaliation bill' under congressional consideration at the time of writing (hereafter PL 1893/2007).[10] Section 2 outlines the existing procedure for the design and implementation of suspension of obligations. Section 3 briefly analyses the main aspects of PL 1893/2007. Section 4 concludes.

2 Procedures for designing and implementing trade sanctions: an outline

(a) *Design*

In Brazil, the Foreign Trade Chamber, that is, Câmara de Comércio Exterior (CAMEX) is granted authority to *propose* measures following non-compliance with international trade agreements,[11] such as in the case of trade sanctions under the WTO's Dispute Settlement Understanding (DSU). By implication, the design of a potential trade sanctions regime is under the auspices of CAMEX.

CAMEX is an executive agency linked to the presidency.[12] Its deliberative body is the Council of Ministers.[13] The Council's voting rule encourages consensus, but ultimately provides that decisions can be taken by simple majority.[14] The composition of the Council is such that different branches of the executive have an input,[15] and theoretically most potential

[9] See F. Abbott, Chapter 22, below.

[10] The project was presented on 28 August 2007 by Deputy Paulo Teixeira and is available in Portuguese at: www2.camara.gov.br/proposicoes, accessed 14 January 2009.

[11] Article 2.2, Decree 4.732/2003 (10 July 2003); Article 5.2, CAMEX, Council of Ministers Resolution 11/2005 (25 April 2005).

[12] See Decree 4.732/2003 (10 July 2003).

[13] Decree 4.732/2003, Article 4:I–VII. Seven ministers participate in the Council. They are the ministers of development (the Council's chair), foreign relations, economy, agriculture, planning and budget, agrarian development and the presidency (through the Head of Cabinet: Ministro Chefe da Casa Civil).

[14] Article 11, CAMEX, Council of Ministers Resolution 11/2005 (25 April 2005).

[15] See above, note 13.

stakeholders would be at least indirectly represented in the design process. Moreover, under the Council of Ministers operates an inter-agency, the Executive Managing Committee.[16] The Committee is responsible for most of CAMEX's business in practice and is assisted by a consultative council from the private sector, which consists of up to twenty representatives from various segments: for instance, producers and traders and workers.[17] All in all, this diversity should lead to increased input legitimacy in the process of elaborating trade sanctions.[18]

CAMEX can also establish technical working groups to deal with questions such as suspension of WTO obligations. There is currently a group working on potential measures to follow the decision in the *US–Cotton* arbitration under Article 22.6 of the DSU and Article 4.11 of the SCM Agreement. The work of this group remains, at the time of writing, confidential. Confidentiality, as a general proposition, goes against the idea that sanctions – which are potentially harmful to domestic stakeholders and to the broader economic environment in Brazil – should be subject to inclusive public discussions and participation so as to guarantee optimality. In effect, the option for confidentiality can subtract from the theoretical input legitimacy referred to above if it is taken to its extreme. Moreover, if confidentiality is kept throughout the design process, Brazil's experience will contrast with the practice in the United States and Europe, where public participation is normally sought.[19] In any event, the CAMEX working group is meant to take into account the legal, economic and political aspects of retaliation and will likely have an important role in shaping measures to be possibly taken against the United States in *Cotton*. It is hoped that the outcome of the group's work makes up for the lack of public participation, and will be subject to further debate with civil society after the arbitrators' decision in *US–Cotton*.

[16] Article 5, Decree 4.732/2003 (10 July 2003); Articles 14–24, CAMEX, Council of Ministers Resolution 11/2005 (25 April 2005).

[17] Article 5, Decree 4.732/2003 (10 July 2003); Articles 25–34, CAMEX, Council of Ministers Resolution 11/2005 (25 April 2005).

[18] See, generally, S. Meunier, 'Trade Policy and Political Legitimacy in the European Union', *Comparative European Politics*, 1:1 (2003), 67. It could be questioned whether consumers should be better represented under the decision-making structure of the Chamber. Nevertheless, since Brazil, at the time of writing, has neither designed nor implemented sanctions, this is hardly verifiable. It can be argued that, given the varied input to the process (through different ministries and, for instance, traders through the Private Council), the output would reflect consumers' interest to some extent.

[19] See S. Andersen and J. Blanchet, Chapter 8, above and L. Ehring, Chapter 9, above.

(b) Implementation

While the procedures for the design of sanctions are fairly straightforward, actual implementation of the sanctions could face significant complexity. Questions about implementation will, of course, influence the design process: the easier it is to run a given sanctions regime, the better – especially taking into account the temporary nature of such a regime. Hence, as a general proposition one can expect that measures falling under CAMEX's own regulatory authority, which consequently do not require further legislative action, will be privileged. An example in point is the raising of import tariffs applied on products from the WTO non-compliant member, since CAMEX has the authority to manage import duties.[20] Such measures would be similar to previous sanctions applied by the United States and the EC.[21] CAMEX could also suspend most-favoured-nation (MFN) obligations toward the WTO violator and, conversely, reduce applied import tariffs for all other members.[22] At the domestic level, these procedures would be facilitated because they would take place under CAMEX and through its simplified decision-making processes.

The existence of parallel obligations under MERCOSUR acts as a complicating factor for the implementation of most types of sanctions, even where they could be implemented under CAMEX authority from a purely domestic law perspective.[23] To return to the two examples just mentioned (higher import tariffs or MFN suspension), MERCOSUR's common external tariff implies that Brazil would have to negotiate ad hoc exceptions with its MERCOSUR partners when resorting to WTO retaliation.[24] This added layer of procedural complexity is also likely to

[20] Article 1, Law 8.085/1990 (23 October 1990); Article 2:XIV, Decree 4.732/2003 (10 July 2003).

[21] See references in note 19, above.

[22] The possibility of applying WTO sanctions by reducing tariffs for other members, thus suspending MFN obligations toward the violating member, is somewhat counterintuitive (in that it may actually increase foreign trade) and is often neglected. This possibility was, for instance, overlooked by the arbitrators in *EC–Bananas III* (Article 22.6 Ecuador) (DSR 2000:V, 2237), para. 71 (but see *US–Gambling* (Article 22.6), paras. 4.52–8). From an economic perspective, the suspension of MFN obligations would increase overall welfare, while at the same time setting the mechanics of reciprocity vis-à-vis the WTO non-compliant member in motion.

[23] Unless one were to argue that the DSB authorization to apply sanctions trumped potentially conflicting obligations under MERCOSUR. I would not adhere to this view.

[24] At present, there are only three possibilities for a temporary modification of MERCOSUR's common external tariff: its inclusion on a common list of reduced rates (see Decree 5901/2006; MERCOSUR Common Market Council, Decision 40/05); supply shortages (see CAMEX Resolution 9/2002 (25 April 2002), MERCOSUR Common Market Group,

influence the design process, and ideally Brazil should anticipate the reaction of other MERCOSUR members in elaborating its own sanctions regime.

Besides the MERCOSUR factor, sanctions outside CAMEX's regulatory authority would require more convoluted domestic procedures for implementation. Notably, statutory changes require standard legislative procedures to take place. In particular, if CAMEX proposes that Brazil implements the suspension of WTO obligations under the TRIPS agreement, as is currently expected in relation to *US–Cotton*, statutory derogation from Brazil's intellectual property law will be required.[25] And as it happens, the more complex and the slower it becomes to design and implement sanctions, the less effectively and promptly can retaliation induce compliance. Likewise, the very threat of retaliation becomes less credible. From this perspective, the lack of an instrument to suspend WTO obligations relating to intellectual property would reduce Brazil's leverage against WTO non-compliant countries.

To this effect, PL 1893/2007 would simplify the procedure for implementation of suspensions in intellectual property rights in Brazil. The bill was presented in August 2007, and procedures for approval have gained new impetus after Brazil's request to resume the arbitration proceedings in *US–Cotton* in August 2008.[26] Interestingly, WTO and cross-retaliation awareness in Brazil's legislative debate has risen in tandem with the evolution of the *Cotton* dispute and the broader debate on agricultural subsidy disciplines. Indeed, the axis of that debate has quickly swung from an eminent 'intellectual-property-perspective' to a predominantly 'inducing-compliance-perspective'.[27] This shift makes it possible and

Resolution 69/2000); and inclusion on a list of exceptions (see MERCOSUR Common Market Council, Decision 59/2007). However, the list of exceptions is currently limited to 100 tariff lines under the common nomenclature of the MERCOSUR and will be limited to fifty by the end of 2010.

[25] See, especially, Law 9.279/1996 (14 May 1996).

[26] See above, note 4.

[27] Thus, in 2006 a project with the same objective as the PL 1893/2007 (see PL 5489/2005) was unanimously rejected by the Commission on Economic Development of the Chamber of Deputies, essentially based on concerns with domestic intellectual property law. In 2008, PL 1893/2007 was unanimously approved by the same commission, essentially based on the need to simplify domestic procedures for retaliation and so as to induce compliance more effectively. Compare Opinion by Deputy M. Corrêa Jr. on PL 1893/2007, Commission of Economic Development of the Chamber of Deputies (2008) with Opinion by Deputy Nelson Marquezelli on PL 5489/2005, Commission of Economic Development of the Chamber of Deputies (2006). The documents are available in Portuguese at: www2.camara.gov.br/proposicoes, accessed 14 January 2009.

arguably probable that PL 1893/2007, or an improved version of it, will see the light of day in the short-term future.

3 Boosting Brazil's capacity to 'induce compliance': the TRIPS retaliation bill

PL 1893/2007 seeks to establish a legislative framework for the suspension of TRIPS obligations by Brazil. It grants discretion to the executive power to suspend compliance with parts II, III and IV of TRIPS and to suspend the application of corresponding domestic legislation.[28] The project also envisages the suspension of TRIPS-*plus* rights.[29] The reason for including this possibility is that TRIPS' national treatment and MFN obligations (set out in part I of TRIPS) apply broadly to the *protection* of intellectual property, and protection may go beyond the obligations established in parts II, III and IV of the TRIPS.[30] Therefore, if and when TRIPS-*plus* rights are granted domestically the TRIPS' national treatment and MFN disciplines remain applicable to those rights. Similarly, from a WTO perspective the suspension of both TRIPS and TRIPS-*plus* rights at the domestic level would require DSB authorization.

One caveat might exist to the very possibility of suspending domestic TRIPS-*plus* rights as a means of retaliation under WTO law and, since PL 1893/2007 would allow suspension of such rights, it is important to mention it. As we know, Article 22(3)(f)(iii) of the DSU, in defining a 'sector' subject to suspension of obligations under the TRIPS Agreement, includes parts II, III and IV of the TRIPS. By contrast, it does not include part I of that agreement – where the obligations on national treatment and MFN are established.[31] This, of course, does mean that WTO members cannot suspend MFN/national treatment obligations under the TRIPS at all: retaliation necessarily involves discrimination against the WTO

[28] Article 3, PL 1893/2007. Notice that while PL 1893/2007 includes TRIPS, parts II, III and IV (thus, theoretically including section 8, part II of the TRIPS), DSU, Article 22(3)(f)(iii) does not include section 8, part II of TRIPS. However, section 8, part II does not, strictly speaking, refer to obligations under the TRIPS. Arguably, it grants WTO members certain *rights* to control anticompetitive practices when it comes to contractual licences.

[29] Article 2:V, PL 1893/2007 (establishing the possibility of suspension of 'other intellectual property rights established by Brazilian legislation in force').

[30] Footnote 3, TRIPS Agreement: ' "protection" shall include matters affecting the availability, acquisition, scope, maintenance and enforcement of intellectual property rights as well as those matters affecting the use of intellectual property rights specifically addressed in this Agreement'. Note that only the second part of footnote 3 restricts the notion of 'protection' to rights specifically addressed in the Agreement. The first part does not.

[31] Articles 3–4, TRIPS Agreement.

non-compliant member. The absence of the MFN and national treatment provisions of TRIPS from the text of Article 22(3)(f)(iii) of the DSU would simply mean that retaliation under TRIPS, which implies a departure from MFN/national treatment obligations, should *target* the 'sectors' explicitly defined therein. Yet, the suspension of TRIPS-*plus* rights, from the standpoint of the TRIPS agreement, would target the MFN/national treatment obligations of TRIPS as such, instead of the obligations under the sectors specified in Article 22(3)(f)(iii) of the DSU. And because MFN/national treatment are not as such included in Article 22(3)(f)(iii), one could be led to the awkward result whereby TRIPS-*plus* rights enjoy *stronger* protection (that is, they cannot be suspended on a discriminatory basis because they are protected by MFN/national treatment disciplines) than the rights explicitly foreseen in parts II, III and IV of the Agreement (which can be suspended on a discriminatory basis following DSB authorization). One way to avoid this contradiction is to consider that the lack of explicit mention of part I of the TRIPS agreement in the DSU is a drafting mistake.[32] This way, MFN/national treatment obligations could be considered a 'sector' for the purposes of TRIPS retaliation and, thus, be subject to suspension. The question, however, remains open and it is difficult to say with certainty whether the possibility envisaged in PL 1893/2007 to suspend TRIPS-*plus* rights would be completely WTO-consistent.[33]

The authority to suspend intellectual property rights, if PL 1893/2007 enters into force, is likely to be granted to CAMEX through presidential decree. This would make implementation of retaliation under TRIPS simpler, in line with the procedures presented above.[34] Executive discretion under PL 1893/2007 is triggered by the WTO DSB's authorization to suspend obligations under Article 22 of the DSU and is conditioned by other Article 22 requirements, such as the temporary nature of suspensions, which could remain in force only until the WTO-inconsistent measure is removed.[35] The explicit incorporation of Article 22 of the DSU in PL 1893/2007 is one of its core elements and is essential to guarantee the consistency of the project with Brazil's WTO obligations.[36]

[32] See N. P. de Carvalho, *TRIPS Regime of Trademarks and Designs* (The Hague: Kluwer, 2006), 414–15.

[33] It should be noted that, since PL 1893/2007 would be legislation granting discretion to executive authorities, it could be covered by the 'mandatory vs discretionary legislation' dichotomy.

[34] See above, section 2. [35] Article 6.1, PL 1893/2007. See Article 22.8, DSU.

[36] Article 4, PL 1893/2007. Thus, for instance, the level of suspensions implemented in domestic law will be linked to the DSB-authorized level of suspensions.

PL 1893/2007 applies to intellectual property rights of individuals of the WTO non-compliant state[37] related to that state through a link of nationality or domicile.[38] For corporate entities, the draft refers to a link of domicile or effective establishment.[39] The suspension of intellectual property rights is temporary and conditional on the continuation of the violation along the lines of Article 22.8 of the DSU. Once the suspension is lifted, PL 1893/2007 would preclude liability possibly arising from acts covered by the executive measures taken to implement the suspension.[40] Eight specific suspension measures are envisaged which can be applied alternatively or cumulatively: (1) temporary rejection of requests for the registration of intellectual property rights; (2) interruption of the proceedings on pending applications for registration of rights; (3) blocking of international payments of royalties and technical assistance resulting from the exploitation of intellectual property rights; (4) granting of compulsory licences; (5) discriminatory increasing of fees for the processing of applications related to the registration of intellectual property rights or to the exploitation of those rights; (6) refusal of registration to exploit economically the object of protection of the right; (7) public domain over intellectual property rights; and (8) extinction of intellectual property rights.[41]

Some of these suspensions would be of less importance or less effective from the viewpoint of 'inducing compliance', at least if taken individually. For instance, (1) temporary rejection of requests and (2) interruption of proceedings would not be particularly strong instruments to induce compliance. The slowness in the processing of requests related to intellectual property rights in Brazil is well known to the economic operators in the intellectual property field. Moreover, expectations arising from the simple request for registration do enjoy some legal protection

[37] PL 1893/2007 refers to states as opposed to separate customs territories or WTO members. If this language is not reviewed and in cases where the WTO non-compliant member is not a 'state', an extensive interpretation would be required.

[38] Besides the question of nationality at the WTO level, which needs to be taken into account to avoid WTO-inconsistent implementation of sanctions as against other members, there is the question under Brazil's constitutional law of whether discrimination against aliens is possible when it comes to intellectual property rights. See Article 5 of Brazil's Constitution (granting equal rights to all Brazilians and foreigners residing therein).

[39] Article 3, PL 1893/2007. Article 3, Paris Convention (incorporated in Article 1, TRIPS), defines nationals in terms of domicile or real and effective industrial or commercial establishment. See also Article 3, Berne Convention (incorporated in Article 1, TRIPS), which assimilates 'habitual residents' to residents; Article 2, Rome Convention (incorporated in Article 1, TRIPS); Article 5, Washington Treaty (also incorporated in Article 1, TRIPS, but note that Brazil is not a party to the Washington Treaty).

[40] Article 6.2, PL 1893/2007. [41] Article 5, PL 1893/2007.

despite the possibility to 'temporarily reject' (*sic*) the request or stay proceedings. Moreover, (5) increasing application fees, might not generate strong incentives to comply. These three measures also provide significant room for circumvention, given the nationality requirements. It could be argued that the strength of these measures would be multiplied if they were cumulatively applied as irritating factors against the WTO non-compliant member. Still, the administrative burden in applying several measures at once should not be underestimated.

Other forms of suspension face important drafting problems or risk backfiring in terms of the WTO consistency of a sanctions regime. For instance, the proposal to refuse 'registration to exploit economically the object of protection of the right' (6) is at odds with the idea that the TRIPS agreement does not generally provide for 'positive rights'. The registration of intellectual property rights normally guarantees exclusivity to the right holder, but it has no bearing on the use by the holder of the right as such.[42] The purpose of registration of a patent, for instance, is to prevent others from freely exploiting the object of the patent during the patent's life. Contrary to the proposition in PL 1893/2007, the patent holder is not impeded from exploiting its own creation because it has not registered it. Put briefly, proposal (6) as currently drafted is a *non sequitur.*

The possibility of putting intellectual property rights into the public domain (7) and the proposal on extinction of rights (8)[43] are hard to square with the temporary character of suspensions as required under Article 22 of the DSU and incorporated in PL 1893/2007. It is difficult to see how public domain or extinction of intellectual property rights could be reversed in case the WTO violation underlying the sanctions is removed and Brazil has to lift the suspension. It would also be complicated to manage the quantum of retaliation in cases of putting IP rights in the public domain.[44] Finally, those measures could generate vexing questions

[42] See also Panel Report on *EC–Trademarks and Geographical Indications (US)* (DSR 2005:VIII–IX, 3499), para. 7.210: 'the TRIPS Agreement does not generally provide for the grant of positive rights to exploit or use certain subject matter, but rather provides for the grant of negative rights to prevent certain acts'.

[43] These two hypotheses largely coincide. The practical effect of say a patent being extinguished or falling in the public domain is the same: exclusivity lapses.

[44] One alternative would be to establish a government-sanctioned licensing system, taking up the remarks by the arbitrators in *EC–Bananas III* (Article 22.6 – Ecuador), paras. 159–65. Apart from the hypothesis of 'compulsory licensing' discussed below, and which could be interpreted as a hypothesis of licensing, PL 1893/2007 does not clearly foresee this possibility. See infra, notes 47–50 and accompanying text.

under Brazil's criminal law relating to the retroactivity of the extinction of intellectual property rights. All these problems would undermine Brazil's ability to properly administer the sanctions regime domestically and to guarantee the WTO consistency of retaliatory measures.

The options of blocking international payments of royalties and technical assistance (3) or of compulsory licensing (4) seem to be the most attractive and promising – at least from the perspective of inducing compliance without incurring overwhelming administrative burdens.[45] Outgoing payments of royalties and technical assistance are normally subject to registration and monitoring, and it would be simple to freeze transfers.[46] Likewise, compulsory licensing would allow significant governmental control and precision in the application of the sanctions, while potentially benefiting public programmes.

As a matter of fact, compulsory licensing is already permitted under the TRIPS Agreement.[47] One could question whether this is really a case of 'suspending' obligations – if the conditions specified in Article 31 were to be respected, there would be no 'suspension' in the first place. Thus, in my view, compulsory licensing as a retaliatory measure in PL 1893/2007 would provide for an exceptional hypothesis of licensing that 'suspends' the normal conditions for the issuing of licences under both WTO and domestic law,[48] subject to the discretion of the executive agency designing the sanctions regime and to the general conditions in PL 1893/2007.[49] For instance, the need to make efforts to obtain authorization from the

[45] See also M. Basso and E. Beas, 'Cross-Retaliation Through TRIPS in the *Cotton* Dispute?', *Bridges*, 5 (May 2005), 19.

[46] As DSB authorization to retaliate under TRIPS obligations would allow the use of intellectual property rights without payment of remuneration and without authorization of the rights holders (see, for example, *EC–Bananas III* (Article 22.6 – Ecuador), para. 160) the transfers could arguably even be cancelled under WTO law. However, in my view, these measures would have too drastic an impact on business relations. Even the freezing of the transfers would require careful administration in the light of the potential impact on the investment environment. However, undeniably this option would cause significant nuisance in the WTO non-compliant member.

[47] Article 31, TRIPS Agreement.

[48] Another way to interpret the provision on compulsory licensing is to consider it purely as a new hypothesis of compulsory licensing under domestic law, which would still need to respect the other conditions for the granting of licences. But this would neither mean a 'suspension of WTO obligations' nor 'suspension of' domestic intellectual property disciplines as they stand. In short, this interpretation would make the provision for compulsory licences in PL 1893/2007 redundant.

[49] Notably, it would be linked to the conditions under Article 22, DSU and on nationality under PL 1893/2007.

right holder could be waived.[50] However, in order to avoid abuses and guarantee coherence in the application of the sanctions, it would be advisable that the provision on compulsory licensing be clarified in relation to the existing domestic disciplines on licensing (that is, to what extent are these derogated from?). At any rate, a margin of appreciation has to be granted for the executive authority to design a government-sanctioned licensing system that fits the peculiarities of each case. The general provision on licensing should, therefore, be complemented by more specific instruments designing the specific sanctions regime, which is a matter for future development.

4 Concluding remarks

When Brazil will finally enter the club of WTO suspenders is anyone's guess. The key to that question lies not only in the existence of domestic procedures as such, but in the intricacies of domestic and international trade politics.[51] But it is crucial that the domestic mechanisms for retaliation be ready when that day comes. It is also fundamental to have those mechanisms on stand-by as one more element to induce compliance with WTO rules and rulings even if only as a threat without the need for actual retaliation to be triggered. This chapter has shown that Brazil's procedures for the design and implementation of WTO sanctions are fairly established. The development of a legislative framework concerning TRIPS retaliation would add an important element in terms of 'credibility of the threat'. The current project under congressional consideration, PL 1893/2007, would meet that objective. On the other hand, especially the

[50] Article 31(b), TRIPS Agreement.

[51] See, for example, the remarks by former Deputy Secretary of State, Robert Zoellick, at a joint press conference with former Brazilian Minister of Economy, Antonio Palloci, when Zoellick was asked of his opinion of Brazil's threat to retaliate against the United States following the *Cotton* dispute (7 October 2005):

> There's always a danger in trade relations – these things start to slip out of control. You know, keep in mind, Brazil sells about two and half billion dollars under a special preference program to the United States, under the Generalized System of Preferences. We have been working with Brazil because of problems of intellectual property violations here, which could lead to their removal. It did in the case of Ukraine. So, I think it is dangerous for people to go down these paths because one retaliates, and all of a sudden you might find that something else happens. We have felt – in the case of intellectual property rights – that Brazil is trying. We've decided to give time to work, to try. But, [if] one decides to retaliate, well, who knows, maybe others will too.

hypotheses of suspension foreseen could be further elaborated. Overall, the pioneer endeavour in PL 1893/2007 could represent an important step toward cross-retaliation seeing the light of day for the first time in the WTO's history. To Brazil, it might also signify increased leverage against the United States in the aftermath of *US–Cotton*, as well as against WTO members with strong intellectual-property-dependent industries more generally.

14

Retaliation in the WTO: the experience of Antigua and Barbuda in *US–Gambling*

MARK E. MENDEL*

The experience of Antigua and Barbuda (Antigua) with the sanctions process at the World Trade Organization (WTO) has been, like all other aspects of its dispute with the United States over the cross-border supply of gambling and betting services (*US–Gambling*), very much a mixed bag. This chapter will briefly summarise Antigua's experience, assess the efficacy of the system and posit some important questions for dispute resolution at the WTO going forward.

The award of the arbitrators

As was true with other reports and decisions in this case, the award of the arbitrators in the arbitration under Article 22.6 of the DSU bears many of the features of an essentially political approach to what should have been a relatively straightforward application of WTO legal principles to a largely undisputed body of facts. Although the United States stridently contested the factual basis for the Antiguan claimed level of nullification and impairment, a careful review of all materials submitted makes it clear that Antigua's evidence was not met by any substantive contrary evidence.

The arbitrators nonetheless made a number of unsupported assumptions and tenuous conclusions in order to trim Antigua's claim from billions of dollars down to the low hundreds of millions. Apparently not satisfied that the number was yet low enough, two of the arbitrators greatly minimised Antigua's claim by reaching three astonishing conclusions:

* Mark Mendel is a lawyer engaged by Antigua to handle the *US–Gambling* case at the WTO, and has led the legal effort throughout the course of the dispute. Mr Mendel lives in County Cork, Ireland. The views presented in this paper are his own and do not necessarily reflect the position of the Antiguan government.

(1) it was unreasonable for Antigua to apply a counterfactual which assumed the United States would observe the letter of its treaty obligations;
(2) rather, subjective, domestic political considerations had to be taken into account in determining what the United States would be more likely to do with respect to compliance;
(3) hypothetical Antiguan access to the American domestic remote gambling market on horse racing would constitute compliance with the Appellate Body decision in *US–Gambling*.

The United States had pressed for this kind of ruling during the course of the arbitration, and Antigua had argued very forcefully against it. Unfortunately, Antigua did not really expect that the arbitrators would go off in this direction, as there was no support for them to do so and plenty of reasons why they should not.

The primary reason against the two arbitrators taking this exceptional deviation is the most fundamental: a nation's treaty obligations can be measured only by the unambiguous language and effect of the treaty itself. If all treaty partners are relegated to measuring the expectations of others against subjective facts and circumstances of domestic politics and other factors, then most treaties would prove to be meaningless. To conclude that it is unreasonable of one treaty partner to expect that the other will perform its obligations as written is simply unsupportable, and so clearly contrary to international law that there is really very little more to be said about it.

A second major error in the decision of the two arbitrators was in essence to give the United States the benefit of its defence under Article XIV of the WTO's General Agreement on Trade in Services (GATS) even though, as the very same panel had ruled in the proceeding under Article 21.5 of the DSU, a successful defence under Article XIV requires the party asserting it not only to establish the applicability of one of the paragraphs of Article XIV but also compliance with the chapeau. In this decision, the two arbitrators essentially reversed themselves and wrote the chapeau out of the equation.

The US defence under Article XIV was predicated on the assertion that it prohibited *all* remote gambling to protect the health and welfare of its citizens. When it was established that the United States did not, in fact, prohibit all remote gambling, but rather prohibited most remote gambling that crossed state or international borders, the whole predicate for its defence was rendered baseless. In point of fact, the chapeau worked perfectly in the case to unmask a prohibition on the cross-border supply of gambling and betting services that, indeed, is nothing more than a 'disguised restriction on trade'.

At no time during the case did the United States argue that *some* remote gambling was 'safer' than others, or that some product offerings were acceptable while others were not. Therefore, for the arbitrators to fashion a hypothetical method of compliance by the United States based on Antiguan access to remote gambling on horse races was nothing short of absurd. Among the errors made by the arbitrators in this regard were not only ignoring the plain meaning of a full commitment to the provision of a service, but in practical effect imposing some kind of national treatment limitation over market access. Further, the United States got the benefit in the arbitration of asserting a line of argument that it very obviously consciously decided to avoid in the original proceeding for strategic reasons.

Antigua had argued during the proceeding that an Article 22.6 arbitration was not the proper place to determine what would constitute compliance with an Appellate Body decision, particularly when it was obvious that the parties themselves were very much in disagreement over the issue. From Antigua's perspective, if the United States believed that giving Antigua access to the remote horse race gambling market in America would put the United States into compliance, then it should do just that. If Antigua disagreed, it would then have the ability to have the issue assessed by a panel under Article 21.5 of the DSU and, importantly, reviewed by the Appellate Body.

Further, Antigua had noted that Article 22.6's basic purpose is to induce compliance by an offending member. For Article 22.6 arbitrators to concoct a level of nullification and impairment based upon a hypothetical method of compliance most favourable to the offending member would seem to work against the objective of inducing compliance.

But perhaps the most egregious aspect of this decision was that by deciding that the United States could comply with the Appellate Body decision under this hypothetical means of compliance, the arbitrators denied Antigua the ability to have the ruling reviewed by the Appellate Body. This was a severe error, and should not be allowed to stand – or to be followed – if the DSU is to remain viable.

As observed earlier, the award of the Article 22.6 arbitrators could be viewed as 'political' in nature – as it left both parties very unhappy. As outraged as Antigua was by the rendering of a multi-billion dollar industry down to a US$21 million one, the United States appeared to be equally upset, if not more so, by the arbitrators' decision to permit cross-agreement retaliation under the WTO's Agreement on Trade-Related Aspects of Intellectual Property Rights (TRIPS). Actually, the decision to allow the cross-agreement retaliation was the most straightforward part of the arbitration. If ever the facts and circumstances of an arbitration were going to fit the principles for the cross-agreement remedy under Article 22.3 of the DSU, this was the case. As incomprehensible as the two arbitrators' assessment of the level of nullification and impairment was, it would have been virtually impossible for them to disallow the cross-agreement remedy to Antigua. Each of the Article 22.3 'boxes' was thoroughly and methodically ticked without real contradiction, establishing that Antigua had no effective remedy under the GATS. Although the United States may not have been happy with this part of the ruling, it could hardly have been surprised.

Application of the TRIPS remedy

Antigua has not, at the time writing, chosen to apply any of the sanctions awarded it under Article 22 of the DSU. Instead, it has elected to pursue a lengthy process of engagement with the United States in the hope of reaching some kind of agreed accommodation. While this process continues, the ultimate application of the sanctions should not be ruled out. Even at the low level approved by the two arbitrators, the application of the authorised sanctions might prove to be effective. Antigua has a strategy for the application of its remedies which could very well have the intended effect. The intended effect is, of course, the exertion of sufficient domestic political pressure to induce the United States to comply with its treaty obligations, or at least to engage with the Antiguan government on effecting a reasonable compromise.

A major consideration for Antigua is, however, uncertainty over the greater effects, if any, of the imposition of the sanctions. In what is a recurring theme in *US–Gambling*, the undercurrent of a small, delicate economy juxtaposed against a global trade and political superpower raises some concerns. The reaction of the United States to the authorisation of the cross-agreement retaliation was perhaps telling. Despite the fact that the sanctions were approved by an international body to which the United States has fairly and consistently adhered, the public position of the US government was essentially that resort by Antigua to its sanctioned remedies would itself be a violation of international law and somehow put Antigua beyond the pale of acceptable conduct.

This position could be viewed as exceptional in many ways, not the least of which is ironic, given that the United States continues to apply its laws aggressively (and, some might argue, even *over*-apply its laws) to deny Antiguan service providers access to American consumers in a clear and unambiguous violation of international law as found by an international tribunal – the WTO – after a full, lengthy consideration of the issue on its merits. However, there can be little doubt that the aggressive posture of the United States has had an effect. Facing an intransigent US government that has made no attempt to comply with the adverse ruling and has arguably shown very little appetite for settling it either, it would be natural for the Antiguan government to wonder if the imposition of sanctions might have a broader and more adverse impact on the tiny country. Any such concerns, which would not be felt by a less dependent, more diverse economy, could have a pronounced chilling effect on a country's willingness to utilise its full remedies under the WTO agreement, and highlights a real and pernicious weakness of the WTO system.

Massive inequalities between two economic and political systems had never, until *US–Gambling*, been tested in a dispute at the WTO. Antigua was hopeful that the rules-based system of the WTO, combined with the apparent attachment of the United States to the dispute resolution system, would go a long way toward neutralising these innate inequities and provide Antigua with a level playing field and a fair result and remedy. This is very much in question at present.

GATS, Article XXI and its implications

If all that preceded were not enough, the remarkable decision by the United States to revoke its cross-border gambling and betting commitment moved the *US–Gambling* dispute to a different level entirely. Antigua had, of course, considered the use of Article XXI before bringing the case, but concluded that this inartfully drafted, obscure provision was probably unlikely to come into play. In particular, the provision allowing all 'affected members' to submit a claim and requiring 'compensatory adjustments … to maintain a level of mutually advantageous commitments not less favourable to trade' than that which existed before the withdrawal would prove to be an insurmountable barrier to withdrawal of a commitment in a case like this one where the volume of trade was, is and could be enormous. Antigua did, in fact, consider Article XXI to be purposefully draconian – a disincentive to restricting trade in the face of the WTO's repeatedly stated objective of further trade liberalisation.

The United States cast its unprecedented effort to withdraw the commitment as a way of achieving compliance in *US–Gambling*. Simply and disingenuously stated, if the United States no longer has a commitment, it can no longer be in violation of the GATS by prohibiting trade in the withdrawn sector. Simple, tidy and absurd. Antigua does not believe that the withdrawal of a commitment can be a method of complying with an adverse WTO decision. This is particularly so where the harmed member is not provided with compensation or adjustments that truly make the member whole. Surely, destroying a multi-billion dollar industry in one small member country, in violation of international law, cannot be compensated by scattering a number of other concessions around the globe in a way that nullifies the rights of the small country given by the GATS and the DSU. If this is to be the case, then developing countries will be unable to reap any effective remedy from the DSU. An offending major economy will simply withdraw the commitment in every case, leave the complaining member with no recourse and buy its way out of an adverse ruling through accommodations – political *and* economic perhaps – with other trading partners.

Using *US–Gambling* as an obvious example, Antigua has established that the United States is in violation of its obligations under the GATS by prohibiting the cross-border provision of gambling and betting services. Antigua has received the right to induce American compliance with its treaty obligations by the imposition of sanctions under Article 22 of the DSU. The failure of the United States to comply, and its relentless efforts to destroy the remote gambling industry in Antigua has caused Antigua to suffer billions of dollars in damage (a point which Antigua believes subsequent arbitrators will affirm, notwithstanding the opinion of the two arbitrators in the recent Article 22.6 proceeding).[1] Antigua, a nation of less than 100,000 people and extremely limited natural and economic resources, is not positioned to compete in, say, international express delivery and warehousing services.

So, how would a compensation package which, even assuming on a global basis adds up to the trade lost by withdrawal of the commitment,

[1] For a number of reasons, including location, culture and historical development, the Antiguan industry was fashioned almost exclusively to service the Northern American gaming markets. Remote gambling and betting services are not exactly a fungible product, and the decision of the United States to prevent Antiguan service providers from offering their services to consumers in America has had a materially deleterious effect on the Antiguan industry that is not susceptible to replacement by directing services into other jurisdictions.

offers absolutely nothing to Antigua go to serve as 'compliance' in *US–Gambling*? It cannot. If, as currently appears inevitable, this dispute continues on to arbitration under GATS, Article XXI, Antigua will press just this point – that a withdrawal or modification of a commitment cannot be an acceptable method of complying with an adverse WTO ruling, at least not without providing real and effective compensation to the member that prevailed in the underlying case.

PART V

Problems and options for reform

15

Evaluating the criticism that WTO retaliation rules undermine the utility of WTO dispute settlement for developing countries

HUNTER NOTTAGE*

1 Introduction

It has often been observed that a fundamental disadvantage of the WTO dispute settlement system for developing countries is the inability of many of them to enforce positive rulings against larger WTO members. When there is an asymmetry in the market size of the developing country and the non-complying WTO member, the WTO's enforcement measures have been characterised as 'virtually meaningless'.[1]

The WTO legal system envisages a right of retaliation through the suspension of trade concessions or obligations as well as countermeasures.[2] The criticism of these retaliation rules, from a developing-country perspective, is that developing countries with small domestic markets are not able to impose sufficient economic or political losses within the larger WTO members to generate the requisite pressure in order to induce compliance. In fact, the suspension of trade concessions may be more detrimental to the developing country than the non-complying member. Consequently, there is a common perception that shortcomings in the WTO retaliation

* Counsel, Advisory Centre on WTO Law. Many thanks to Chad Bown, William Davey, Simon Evenett, Jorge Huerta-Goldman, Niall Meagher, Mark Mendel, Cesar Montano Huerta, José Ackell Zavala, Joost Pauwelyn, Frieder Roessler and Thomas Sebastian for helpful comments and discussions. The views expressed reflect those of the author.

1 M. Footer, 'Developing Country Practice in the Matter of WTO Dispute Settlement', *Journal of World Trade*, 35:1 (2001), 55 at 94.

2 Article 22 of the Understanding on the Rules and Procedures Governing the Settlement of Disputes (DSU) and Articles 4.10 and 7.9 of the Agreement on Subsidies and Countervailing Measures (SCM Agreement). This chapter refers to these enforcement options, collectively, as 'retaliation rules'.

rules undermine the utility of WTO dispute settlement for developing countries.

This chapter critically evaluates this widely held criticism of the WTO retaliation rules. It observes that while legal and economic *theory* illustrates the potential shortcomings of WTO retaliation for developing countries, GATT and WTO dispute settlement *practice* demonstrates high rates of compliance with dispute settlement rulings. Thus, the chapter queries whether the ability to retaliate effectively is a key determinant for WTO members complying with dispute settlement rulings. It ponders Robert Hudec's observation that 'enforcement is a more complex process than mere retaliation'[3] and puts forward the proposition that governments comply with WTO dispute settlement rulings for a multitude of reasons of which retaliation is often not a key ingredient. Thus, the chapter argues that the theoretical shortcomings of the WTO retaliation rules for developing countries should not significantly affect developing countries' decisions to utilise the WTO dispute settlement system. The chapter concludes with an overview of developing-country experience with WTO retaliation to date and the embryonic potential of cross-retaliating in areas such as intellectual property rights or services.

2 The criticism that WTO retaliation rules undermine the utility of WTO dispute settlement for developing countries

The widely held criticism that shortcomings in WTO retaliation rules undermine the utility of WTO dispute settlement for developing countries is based on the following four arguments.

(a) Developing-country sanctions are not able to generate sufficient pressure to induce compliance

Trade retaliation under the GATT and WTO has typically envisaged the withdrawal of tariff concessions with the effect of raised tariffs for specific imports from the non-complying member. The theory being

[3] R. Hudec, 'The Adequacy of WTO Dispute Settlement Remedies: A Developing Country Perspective' in B. Hoekman, A. Mattoo and P. English (eds.), *Development, Trade and the WTO* (Washington, DC: World Bank, 2002), 81.

that by raising tariffs to inflict economic harm on exporters in the non-complying member the respondent government will be placed under domestic pressure to remove the measures inconsistent with WTO law.

This ideal scenario, however, is dependent upon the size of the domestic market of the retaliating member in relation to that of the non-complying member. The first concern with WTO retaliation rules is that developing countries with small domestic markets are not able to impose sufficient economic or political losses within larger WTO members to generate the requisite pressure to induce compliance. The retaliation request of Antigua and Barbuda (Antigua), one of the smallest WTO members with approximately 80,000 inhabitants, against the United States provides an illustration of retaliation difficulties where there is an asymmetry in market size. As Antigua stated in its request for retaliation, 'ceasing all trade whatsoever with the United States (approximately US$180 million annually, or less than 0.02 per cent of all exports from the United States) would have virtually no impact on the economy of the United States, which could easily shift such a relatively small volume of trade elsewhere'.[4] A similar statement was made by the arbitrator examining the ability of Ecuador to retaliate effectively against the European Communities (EC) by withdrawing tariff concessions. Ecuador imports less than 0.1 per cent of total EC exports, leading the arbitrator to observe that 'given the fact that Ecuador, as a small developing country, only accounts for a negligible proportion of the EC's exports of these products, the suspension of concessions is unlikely to have any significant effect on demand for these EC exports'.[5] The arbitrator queried whether the objective of inducing compliance 'may ever be achieved where a great imbalance in terms of trade volume and economic power exists between the complaining party seeking suspension and the other party'.[6]

For these reasons, it has been observed that developing countries with small markets are unlikely to be able to induce compliance by larger trading members. As one commentator stated, retaliation through the suspension of tariff concessions 'therefore cannot offer a realistic option

[4] Recourse by Antigua and Barbuda to Article 22.2 of the DSU, *United States–Measures Affecting the Cross-Border Supply of Gambling and Betting Services* (*US–Gambling*), WT/DS285/22, 22 June 2007, para. 3.

[5] Decision by the arbitrator, *EC–Bananas III (Ecuador)* (Article 22.6 – EC), DSR 2000:V, 2237, para. 95.

[6] *EC–Bananas III (Ecuador)*, DSR 2000: V, 2237, para. 73.

to enforce WTO obligations if performed against considerably larger economies'.[7]

(b) Developing countries harm themselves by imposing sanctions

A further concern with retaliation through the withdrawal of tariff concessions is that the remedy may, in fact, have detrimental effects on consumers and economic welfare in the retaliating member. It has been commented that '[p]erhaps the biggest disadvantage of WTO sanctions is that they bite the country imposing the sanction'.[8] Others rue that the suspension of concessions goes 'against the very trade liberalising principles the GATT/WTO system stands for' and is 'bad policy' that amounts to 'shooting oneself in the foot'.[9]

These criticisms were raised by Antigua and Ecuador in their respective requests for retaliation against the United States and the EC. Antigua is a small island with negligible natural resources making it heavily reliant on imports. As 50 per cent of those imports are from the United States, Antigua expressed concern that retaliating through import restrictions would have a 'disproportionate adverse impact on Antigua and Barbuda by making these products and services materially more expensive to the citizens of the country'.[10] Retaliatory restrictions on goods or services from the United States were argued to have 'a much greater negative impact on Antigua and Barbuda than it would on the United States'.[11] Similarly, the arbitrator examining Ecuador's request for retaliation against the EC noted that 'in situations where the complaining party is highly dependent on imports from the other party, it may happen that the suspension of certain concessions or certain other obligations entails more harmful

[7] H. Grosse Ruse-Kahn, 'A Pirate of the Caribbean? The Attractions of Suspending TRIPS Obligations', *Journal of International Economic Law*, 11:2 (2008), 313–64, at 332.

[8] S. Charnovitz, 'Should the Teeth Be Pulled? An Analysis of WTO Sanctions' in D. L. M. Kennedy and J. D. Southwick (eds.), *Political Economy of International Trade Law: Essays in Honor of Robert E. Hudec* (Cambridge University Press, 2002) 602–35 at 621.

[9] See M. Bronkers and N. van den Broek, 'Financial Compensation in the WTO: Improving Remedies of WTO Dispute Settlement', *Journal of International Economic Law*, 8:1 (2006), 101–26 at 103; P. Mavroidis, 'Remedies in the WTO Legal System: Between a Rock and a Hard Place', *European Journal of International Law*, 11:1 (2000); and B. Hoekman and P. Mavroidis, *WTO Dispute Settlement, Transparency, and Surveillance* (Washington, DC: World Bank, 1999), 6.

[10] Recourse by Antigua and Barbuda to Article 22.2 of the DSU, *US–Gambling*, paras. 2–3.

[11] *US–Gambling*, paras. 2–3.

effects for the party seeking suspension of concessions than for the other party'.[12]

(c) *WTO retaliation rules are skewed against developing countries*

These two arguments have led commentators and developing countries to contend that the WTO retaliation rules are skewed against developing countries.

In the context of DSU review negotiations, the LDC Group has commented that the 'lack of an effective enforcement mechanism and the potential impact of retaliatory measures for poor economies is well documented'.[13] The African Group, similarly, has observed that one of the 'major problems' African WTO members face in utilising the WTO dispute settlement is that 'the means provided for enforcement of findings and recommendations (trade retaliation) are skewed against and disadvantage African Members'.[14] According to the African Group, the 'realities are such that developing-country Members cannot practically utilise this ultimate sanction' as 'they would probably suffer further injury if they adopted retaliatory measures'.[15]

Commentators appear to agree. It has been observed that the WTO 'sanctioning power tends to favour large economies over smaller ones',[16] that 'as a practical matter' trade sanctions 'can probably only be adopted by developed country Members, or large, advanced developing countries'[17] and that 'the adoption of countermeasures is simply not an option for the poorer WTO Members'.[18] Trade retaliation by developing countries against industrialised countries has been characterised as 'not available to them, with the possible exception of the largest among them',[19] and 'counterproductive' as they 'would mostly harm the former, not induce compliance by the latter'.[20] For all these reasons, it has been argued that

[12] Decision by the arbitrator, *EC–Bananas III (Ecuador)* (Article 22.6 – EC), para. 73. See also para. 86.

[13] TN/DS/W/17, paras. 12 and 15.

[14] TN/DS/W/15, paras. 2 and 6.

[15] TN/DS/W/15, paras. 2 and 6.

[16] S. Charnovitz, see above, note 8, 625.

[17] Y. Renouf, 'A Brief Introduction to Countermeasures in the WTO Dispute Settlement System' in R. Yerxa and B. Wilson (eds.), *Key Issues in WTO Dispute Settlement* (Cambridge University Press, 2005), 118

[18] P. Mavroidis, see above, note 9, 763–813.

[19] M. Bronkers and N. van den Broek, see above, note 9, 102.

[20] J. Pauwelyn 'Enforcement and Countermeasures in the WTO: Rules are Rules – Towards a More Collective Approach', *American Journal of International Law*, 94:2 (2000), 335–47 at 338 (albeit that Pauwelyn merely poses the question).

'countermeasures are a more or less ineffective instrument in the hands of smaller players'[21] and that 'there is indeed a practical problem for small countries and developing countries when they attempt to carry through with effective retaliation within the WTO system'.[22] The WTO *World Trade Report* for 2007 synthesises these various critiques in the following manner:

> In applying retaliatory measures, large countries can cause economic harm to the party found not to be in compliance with its obligations … conversely, small countries, in view of their limited size are unable to exert sufficient pressure on larger Members to alter their behaviour.[23]

(d) WTO retaliation rules undermine the utility of WTO dispute settlement for developing countries

The final element in the criticism is that these shortcomings in WTO retaliation rules undermine the utility of the WTO dispute settlement system for developing countries.

This linkage between the WTO retaliation rules and the utility of WTO dispute settlement is based on the premise that one of the 'main attractions' of WTO dispute settlement system is that 'it explicitly envisages remedies in the event of continued non-compliance when a country loses a dispute settlement procedure'.[24]

The premise results in what has been characterised as the 'conventional wisdom' that it is 'a waste of time and money for developing countries to invoke the WTO's dispute settlement procedures against industrialised countries' because 'the developing country has no effective way to enforce the ruling'.[25] The inability of developing countries to retaliate effectively has been argued to mean that their access to WTO dispute settlement 'is not equal to that of developed countries, and [is] in fact largely illusory'.[26]

Certainly, in the context of DSU review negotiations, the LDC Group noted that 'the question of little or no utilisation of the dispute settlement system by developing and least-developed country Members has been linked to the inadequacies and structural rigidities of the remedies

[21] K. Bagwell, P. Mavroidis and R. Staiger, 'The Case for Tradable Remedies in WTO Dispute Settlement' (Washington, DC, World Bank Policy Research Paper No. 3314, 2004), 14–15.

[22] P. Mavroidis, see above, note 9, 763–813. [23] *World Trade Report 2007*, WTO, 284.

[24] M. Bronkers and N. van den Broek, see above, note 9, 101.

[25] R. Hudec, see above, note 3, 81.

[26] M. Bronkers and N. van den Broek, see above, note 9, 106.

available to poor countries'.[27] The LDC Group has recommended that changes are required in order to 'enable LDCs to use the dispute settlement system meaningfully'.[28]

The concern that shortcomings in the WTO retaliation rules for developing countries undermine the utility of the WTO dispute settlement for those countries may explain the various proposals by developing countries for review of those enforcement provisions. DSU review proposals include promoting the use of compensation,[29] introducing collective retaliation[30] and tradable retaliation rights.[31]

3 An evaluation of the criticism

(a) Even skewed WTO retaliation rules do not undermine the utility of WTO dispute settlement for developing countries

The arguments that the current WTO retaliation rules are skewed against developing countries have merit. The positions articulated by Antigua and Ecuador in the WTO regarding the economic costs of trade sanctions on developing countries are economically sound. It is also logical that traditional trade sanctions imposed by developing countries with small markets are unlikely to generate significant economic or political losses in larger non-complying members.

The consequential argument that these deficiencies undermine the utility of the WTO dispute settlement system for developing countries is, however, more controversial. Two differing perspectives can be discerned.

On the one hand, a number of studies and commentaries contend that the capacity to retaliate *is* a critical component in ensuring that WTO members comply with dispute settlement rulings. These analyses suggest that, if developing countries do not have the capacity to retaliate credibly, the likelihood of developing countries achieving successful outcomes through WTO dispute settlement is undermined. One empirical analysis of all GATT and WTO disputes between 1973 and 1998 finds 'substantial evidence that the threat of retaliation is an

[27] TN/DS/W/17, para. 12. [28] TN/DS/W/17, para. 12.

[29] For example, TN/DS/W/33 (Ecuador), TN/DS/W/17 and TN/DS/W/37 (LDC Group) and TN/DS/W/15 and TN/DS/W/42 (African Group).

[30] For example, TN/DS/W/47 (India, Cuba, the Dominican Republic, Egypt, Honduras, Jamaica and Malaysia).

[31] For example, TN/DS/W/23 (Mexico).

important influence determining a defendant country's ability to credibly commit to liberalisation'.[32] Its results were interpreted to 'suggest that the successful economic resolution to disputes is influenced by the concern for retaliation'.[33] Another study finds that 'implementation is much more likely in a developed against developing country scenario than vice-versa'.[34] As a result, that study concludes that 'there is indeed a problem in the functioning of the DSU in this respect' and that proposals to reform the retaliation rules to address these failings 'are addressing a real issue and not a ghost'.[35] The WTO *World Trade Report* for 2007 reflects the view that small countries are 'unable to exert sufficient pressure on larger Members to alter their behaviour' and that this retaliation impotence 'fails to deter economically powerful countries from committing a violation against small countries'.[36]

On the other hand, other evaluations of the GATT and WTO dispute settlement data demonstrate a high rate of compliance with dispute settlement rulings. One analysis of the first ten years of the WTO dispute settlement system indicates a successful implementation rate of adopted panel and Appellate Body reports of 83 per cent.[37] Only ten of the 181 initiated disputes examined resulted in no implementation or disagreement over implementation.[38] As the author of that analysis concluded, 'it is the case that most reports are eventually implemented'.[39] A separate study, covering the period until March 2007, describes the 'generally positive record of Members in complying with adverse rulings'.[40] That study notes that of 109 panel and Appellate Body reports adopted, 90 per cent found violations of WTO law, and that in 'virtually all of these cases the WTO Member found to be in violation indicated its intention

[32] C. Bown, 'On the Economic Success of GATT/WTO Dispute Settlement', *Review of Economics and Statistics*, (2004) 86 at 17.

[33] Bown, note 32, above.

[34] K. Bagwell, P. Mavroidis and R. Staiger, see above, note 21, 4.

[35] K. Bagwell, P. Mavroidis and R. Staiger, see above, note 21.

[36] World Trade Report 2007, WTO, 284.

[37] W. Davey, 'The WTO Dispute Settlement System: The First Ten Years', *Journal of International Economic Law*, 8:1 (2005), 17 at 46–8.

[38] W. Davey, see above, note 37, at 47. The figure of 83 per cent was derived from the implementation of forty-eight out of the fifty-eight disputes that resulted in findings of violation of WTO law. *Ibid.* at footnotes 114 and 115.

[39] W. Davey, 'The WTO: Looking Forwards', *Journal of International Economic Law*, 9:1 (2006), 3 at 12.

[40] B. Wilson, 'Compliance by WTO Members with Adverse WTO Dispute Settlement Rulings', *Journal of International Economic Law*, 10:2 (2007), 397 at 397.

to bring itself into compliance and the record indicates that in most cases it has already done so'.[41]

A key finding for the purposes of this chapter is that these high compliance rates with adverse WTO dispute settlement rulings are not limited to those disputes brought by developed countries. Similar compliance rates have been observed when smaller and developing countries have obtained favourable rulings. As one study recently found:

> WTO dispute settlement experience to date does not suggest that responding Members have a manifestly worse record of compliance with DSB rulings in cases where the complaining Member was a small or developing country than in cases where the complaining Member was another type of developing country or developed country.[42]

This practice of high compliance with dispute settlement rulings, even when the complainant is a small or developing country, is hard to reconcile with the above-mentioned perspective that the capacity to retaliate is an 'important influence' in the resolution of WTO disputes. If retaliation were a significant factor for compliance with adverse rulings, one would expect low rates of compliance in those disputes where smaller or developing countries were complainants.

Based on the high compliance rates with dispute settlement rulings, even when the complainant is a small or developing country, this chapter puts forward the proposition that the capacity to retaliate effectively is often not a significant factor for government compliance with adverse panel and Appellate Body rulings.

GATT practice supports this proposition. One of the key distinctions between dispute settlement under the GATT and the WTO was that GATT dispute settlement procedures required consensus permitting the defendant to veto both adverse rulings and any request for retaliation. As the defendant had the ability to veto retaliation, under the GATT regime complainants effectively did not have the capacity to retaliate against countries that did not wish to comply with adverse rulings.[43] Thus, GATT

[41] B. Wilson, see above, note 40.

[42] R. Malacrida, 'Towards Sounder and Fairer WTO Retaliation: Suggestions for Possible Additional Procedural Rules Governing Members' Preparation and Adoption of Retaliatory Measures', *Journal of World Trade* 42:1 (2008), 3–60 at 20.

[43] In fact, in GATT practice retaliation was only authorised on one occasion. See Determination by the Contracting Parties of 8 November 1952, *Netherlands Measures of Suspension of Obligations to the United States*, BISD 1S/32–33. On four other occasions, the requests for retaliation authority were vetoed. See, for example, the request vetoed by

practice appears to provide an environment to test the extent to which the capacity to retaliate induces compliance with adverse rulings.

GATT practice suggests that retaliation capacity is often not a necessary component for compliance. Hudec's comprehensive study of GATT disputes found 'almost a 100 percent success rate' in producing satisfactory responses to legal rulings in the first three decades of the GATT.[44] While this fell to 81 per cent in the following period it was characterised as 'still a very impressive performance for an international legal regime'.[45] Significantly, ten of the eleven GATT panel rulings in favour of developing countries had a successful outcome. Hudec's interpretation of this data was as follows:

> The paradoxical contrast between the voluntary procedures and weak remedies of the GATT dispute settlement system, on the one hand, and its rather strong record of success, on the other, contains a lesson. It teaches that the enforcement of international legal obligations cannot be explained by superficial analysis of dispute settlement procedures and remedies.[46]

While the lesson from this GATT practice ought to be tempered somewhat when applied to the WTO environment,[47] the practice nonetheless suggests that there are factors other than retaliation capacity that result in governments complying with adverse dispute settlement rulings.[48]

According to Hudec, these other factors include that: (i) some parts of the defendant government and its constituents usually want the conduct found inconsistent with WTO law to be removed simply because it is good policy; (ii) the defendant government is likely to see a long-term value in preserving the legitimacy of the legal system for when it may need to rely on it for its own purposes; and (iii) the shaming pressure caused by other governments wishing to preserve the legitimacy of the legal system

the United States following the adverse ruling in the GATT Panel Report, *United States–Taxes on Petroleum and Certain Imported Substances*, L/6175, adopted 17 June 1987, BISD 34S/136.

44 R. Hudec, see above, note 3 at 82. 45 R. Hudec, see above, note 3.

46 R. Hudec, see above, note 3.

47 It has been observed that as the GATT dispute settlement regime permitted defendants to block both the establishment of panels and the adoption of adverse panel reports 'it is not surprising that if and when a contracting party accepted an adverse panel report ... that contracting party then ordinarily went on to implement the ruling'. R. Malacrida, see above, note 42 at 8.

48 If not, why was it that 'the great majority of [GATT] violation rulings were in fact adopted' and that 'the bulk of these violation rulings, including many of those not adopted, did produce a satisfactory correction of the practice at issue'. See R. Hudec, above, note 3 at 82.

should not be underestimated.[49] These factors would appear to apply equally in the WTO environment (Pauwelyn, for example, Chapter 2, above prominently refers to them as 'community costs' which, in his view, play a crucial role in explaining the high compliance rate with WTO dispute settlement rulings).

WTO practice also demonstrates that the high compliance rates observed in WTO dispute settlement to date have not required members to regularly request or impose retaliatory measures. Of the sixty WTO disputes where retaliation was possible, as the reasonable period of time to comply had expired without compliance being achieved, members only requested the right to retaliate in seventeen disputes.[50] The complainant pursued and gained retaliation rights from the WTO Dispute Settlement Body (DSB) in only nine of those disputes, with retaliatory measures being imposed in only five of them.[51] Thus, while the DSB has authorised retaliation on occasion, it is seems fair to say that 'retaliation has been the exception rather than the rule'.[52] From these figures one might extrapolate that, even in the WTO environment where retaliation can no longer be vetoed, in the vast majority of disputes the catalyst for compliance does not appear to have been the threat of retaliation.[53] As one observer noted, 'the overall positive record of Members in complying with adverse rulings is reflected in, and confirmed by, the low number of cases where Members have sought and received authorisation to impose retaliatory measures'.[54]

The above analysis permits certain conclusions. First, that in both the GATT and the WTO there have been high rates of compliance with adverse dispute settlement rulings. Second, that these high rates of compliance occurred even in situations where the complainant had little capacity to retaliate effectively (whether because a developing country or because retaliation was subject to a veto under the GATT). Thus, the practice to date suggests that, even without effective retaliation capacity, WTO dispute settlement often can be an effective mechanism for developing countries wishing to bring the illegal measures of larger members into conformity with WTO law.

[49] R. Hudec, see above, note 3 at 82–3.

[50] See R. Malacrida, above, note 42, table at Appendix B (with the addition of the request for authorisation to retaliate in *US–Upland Cotton*).

[51] R. Malacrida, above, note 42. [52] R. Malacrida, above, note 42.

[53] On the other hand, it might also be noted that on a number of occasions mutually agreed solutions were apparently reached after authorisation to request retaliation was made. See R. Malacrida, above, note 42, table at Appendix B.

[54] B. Wilson, see above, note 39 at 397.

Of course, on those occasions where a defendant is a larger economy and does not voluntarily comply with adverse rulings, the weaknesses of WTO retaliation rules for developing countries with small domestic markets are real and will undermine the utility of dispute settlement. The purpose of this chapter, however, is to highlight that voluntary compliance has occurred in the vast majority of disputes. Consequently, in the majority of disputes brought by developing countries in the WTO,[55] shortcomings in retaliation capacity have not undermined the utility of WTO dispute settlement.

(b) Developing-country practice with retaliation

This section briefly examines developing-country experience with WTO retaliation to date (more detailed assessments of country-specific experiences in Antigua, Brazil and Mexico are included elsewhere in this volume). It observes that developing countries appear to have seen merit in requesting WTO retaliation on those occasions where compliance had not been achieved. It also notes that developing countries have imposed retaliatory measures on only one occasion. However, this apparently alarming statistic may be due to circumstances particular to the relevant disputes as opposed to concerns that retaliatory measures would be both ineffective for, and harmful to, the relevant developing countries.

As noted above, members have requested authorisation from the DSB to retaliate in seventeen disputes. The first observation that can be made is that of the thirteen members that made these requests, eight were developing-country members.[56] These developing countries had varying market sizes and trade shares.[57] This suggests that a spectrum of developing countries saw utility in at least requesting retaliation. Of these requests, nine disputes led to arbitration proceedings under Article 22.6

[55] Acknowledging that the conclusions of this chapter are based on statistics regarding disputes initiated by developing countries. The chapter does not account for any disputes that developing countries may not have *initiated* due to concerns that successful rulings would not result in compliance in the absence of retaliation. Evidence of this nature is hard to document accurately. It would affect the conclusions of this chapter only if it could be demonstrated that defendants would not have complied in the absence of retaliation. Otherwise it would only illustrate the assumption, often inaccurate and at the centre of this chapter's analysis, that retaliation is a requirement for compliance in dispute settlement.

[56] Antigua and Barbuda, Argentina, Brazil, Chile, Ecuador, India, Korea and Mexico.

[57] Antigua and Barbuda, Argentina, Brazil, Chile, Ecuador, India, Korea and Mexico.

of the DSU on the level of suspension of concessions or other obligations. Here again, developing countries pursued their right to retaliate through to the arbitration stage in five of those disputes, suggesting that developing countries have seen merit in pursuing actual DSB authorisation to retaliate.[58] This data illustrates that developing countries have been at least as active as developed countries in requesting authorisation from the DSB to retaliate. These are results that may come as a surprise when one considers the conventional argument that WTO retaliation is seen as 'virtually meaningless' for developing countries.

The area where there has been a marked discrepancy between developing-country practice and developed-country practice, however, has been in the imposition of retaliatory measures. While four developed countries have imposed retaliatory measures (developed countries imposed measures on eight of the ten occasions where they were granted authorisation), only one developing country (Mexico, as discussed by Jorge Huerta-Goldman, Chapter 12, above) has imposed retaliatory measures (developing countries consequently imposed measures on only one of the eight occasions where they were granted such authorisation).[59] The question arises whether this difference in track record in the imposition of retaliatory measures is due to the limitations of the WTO retaliation rules for developing countries. In particular, was the decision not to impose trade sanctions due to a realisation that (i) the developing-country sanctions would be ineffective at generating sufficient pressure to induce compliance and/or (ii) the developing-country sanctions would create greater harm to the developing country than the non-complying member?

It is difficult to determine with certainty the motivations behind the decisions of governments not to retaliate in disputes where they were granted such authorisation. The four occasions being *EC–Bananas III (Ecuador)* (Article 22.6 – EC), *Canada–Aircraft Credits and Guarantees* (Article 22.6 – Canada), *US–Offset Act (Byrd Amendment)* (Article 22.6 – US) (Brazil, Chile, India, Korea, Mexico) and *US–Gambling* (Article 22.6 – US). Nonetheless, the following tentative observations might be made for each of the disputes.

[58] The disputes pursued by developing countries being: *US–Upland Cotton* (Article 22.6 – US); *US–Gambling* (Article 22.6 – US); *US–Offset Act (Byrd Amendment)* (Article 22.6 – US) (Brazil, Chile, India, Korea, Mexico); *Canada–Aircraft Credits and Guarantees* (Article 22.6 – Canada); and *EC–Bananas III (Ecuador)* (Article 22.6 – EC).

[59] Mexico imposed retaliatory measures in *US–Offset Act (Byrd Amendment)* (Article 22.6 – US).

The first dispute where a developing country was granted the right to retaliate was in *EC–Bananas III (Ecuador)* (Article 22.6 – EC), where Ecuador obtained authorisation to suspend concessions or other obligations up to US$201.6 million annually as a result of the WTO-inconsistent aspects of the EC import regime for bananas. It appears that the decision not to utilise this right of retaliation was directly influenced by the sense that sanctions would be ineffective at generating sufficient pressure to induce compliance and that they would cause greater harm to the Ecuadorian economy than that of the EC. As Ecuador stated in subsequent DSB meetings, applying sanctions 'would cause even greater injury to the economy of the complaining Member' and that '[t]his did not happen in Ecuador precisely because it did not apply the retaliation measures authorized by the DSB'.[60] Similarly, a lawyer who has acted for the commercial banana industry for many years made the observation that 'Ecuador never made use of the possibility of applying sanctions against the European Communities on the basis that the harm to the Ecuadorian economy would outweigh the possible benefit of persuading the European Communities to comply with its commitments.'[61] Nonetheless, the motivations behind the Ecuadorian government not imposing retaliatory measures are hard to isolate from the context that the United States had also been granted the right to retaliate against the EC in the same dispute with the consequence that Ecuadorian retaliation would have only added incremental pressure on the EC to comply.[62] Furthermore, the award of the arbitrator was circulated in March 2000 and by June 2001 Ecuador and the United States appeared to have obtained a pathway toward future settlement of the disputes through the Bananas Understandings signed with the EC.[63] The Bananas Understanding signed between Ecuador and the EC provided that upon full implementation of a new banana import regime, 'Ecuador's right to suspend concessions or other obligations of a level not exceeding

[60] Communication from Ecuador, Contribution of Ecuador to the Improvement of the DSU, 28 June 2002, TN/DS/W/9, 2.

[61] B. O'Connor, 'Remedies in the World Trade Organization Dispute Settlement System – The Bananas and Hormones Cases', *Journal of World Trade*, 38:2 (2004), 245–66 at 249.

[62] Decision of the arbitrator, *EC–Bananas III (US)* (Article 22.6 – EC).

[63] Understanding on Bananas between Ecuador and the EC, *EC–Regime for the Importation, Sale and Distribution of Bananas*, 3 July 2001, WT/DS27/60 and Communication from the United States, *EC–Regime for the Importation, Sale and Distribution of Bananas*, 26 June 2001, WT/DS27/59.

US$201.6 million per year vis-à-vis the EC will be terminated.'[64] Thus, having achieved a negotiated settlement by June 2001, the incentive to apply the retaliatory measures no longer existed.[65]

The second dispute where a developing country was granted a right to retaliate was in *Canada–Aircraft Credits and Guarantees* (Article 22.6 – Canada), where the arbitrator decided that Brazil's imposition of countermeasures against Canada covering trade up to US$247,797,000 would be appropriate within the meaning of Article 4.10 of the SCM Agreement. Brazil never imposed the countermeasures. However, this does not appear to be due to Brazil's status as a developing country but because Brazil had managed to achieve a negotiated solution with Canada.

The extent to which Brazil's right to retaliate in *Canada–Aircraft Credits and Guarantees* (Article 22.6 – Canada) motivated a negotiated solution has to be examined in the particular context that Canada had been granted the right to retaliate against Brazil in *Brazil–Aircraft* (Article 22.6 – Brazil). It has been observed that the amount awarded to Brazil was 'very close to the amount awarded to Canada'[66] and that this may explain why retaliatory measures were not imposed by either member and a negotiated solution preferred.[67] Certainly, it has been commented that 'it is likely that, by awarding to Brazil an amount of countermeasures close to the amount of countermeasures awarded to Canada in the Brazil–Aircraft Article 22.6 arbitration, the arbitrator was attempting to create an incentive for parties to go back to the negotiating table'.[68] The concluding paragraph of the award in *Canada–Aircraft Credits and Guarantees* (Article 22.6 – Canada) supports such an interpretation of the motivations behind the Arbitrator's award, providing that:

> the Arbitrator understands that the parties have been holding consultations. The Arbitrator is of the opinion that, given the particular

[64] See note 63, above.

[65] Ecuador considered the Banana Understanding as a potential pathway to *future* settlement but never accepted the understandings as a mutually agreed solution within the meaning of Article 3.6 of the DSU. *Ibid.* at 1 ('... it must be made clear that the provisions of Article 3.6 of the DSU are not applicable in this case'.).

[66] Y. Renouf, see above, note 17 at 120.

[67] K. Bagwell, P. Mavroidis and R. Staiger, see above, note 21 at 13 ('Canada did not impose countermeasures against Brazil most likely because Brazil could do the same in the same dispute (export subsidies in regional aircraft where Bombardier and Embraer, Canadian and Brazilian producers respectively hold a join dominant position in the market).').

[68] Y. Renouf, see above, note 17 at 121.

> circumstances of this case, a mutually satisfactory agreement between the parties addressing the issues dealt with in this case *in their broader context* would be the most appropriate solution. (original emphasis)[69]

Brazil's experience in *Canada–Aircraft Credits and Guarantees* (Article 22.6 – Canada) appears to provide a further example where a developing country was able to negotiate a solution with a developed-country defendant in the shadow of its authorised right to retaliate. As José Akcell Zavala, of the Brazilian Mission to the WTO in Geneva, confirmed in his statements at the Workshop which was the origin of this book: 'the Brazilian experience shows that at least in one case the recourse to retaliation proved to be useful in stimulating parties to pursue negotiations, as it was the case in the disputes concerning civil aircraft, that resulted in a mutually satisfactory resolution'.

The third dispute where developing countries were granted the right to retaliate was in *US–Offset Act (Byrd Amendment)* (Article 22.6 – US). In this dispute, five developing countries (Brazil, Chile, India, Korea and Mexico) and three developed countries (EC, Japan and Canada) obtained the right to suspend concessions or other obligations. The fact that all three developed countries imposed retaliatory measures while only one developing country, Mexico, did so might suggest that developing countries are more hesitant to enforce rulings through trade sanctions. On the other hand, it could be argued that the need for these developing countries to impose sanctions was mitigated by the fact that the other larger economies were already applying pressure on the United States to comply through their retaliatory measures.

The fourth dispute where a developing country was granted the right to retaliate was in *US–Gambling* (Article 22.6 – Antigua and Barbuda), where the arbitrator determined that Antigua may request authorisation from the DSB to suspend obligations under the WTO Agreement on Trade-Related Intellectual Property Rights (TRIPS Agreement) up to US$21 million annually. So far, Antigua has not imposed retaliatory measures. This decision may be due to the complicating factor that the United States decided to modify its services commitments through the procedures of Article XXI of the General Agreement on Trade in Services (GATS). By modifying its scheduled commitments, it could be argued that Antigua's right to retaliate under the DSU is no longer legally justified. Of course, Antigua might have rights under the GATS regarding compensatory

[69] Award of the arbitrator, *Canada–Aircraft Credits and Guarantees* (Article 22.6 – Canada) (DSR 2003:III, 1187), para. 4.4.

adjustments to the extent that it is affected by the modification. The possibility that a member brings itself into compliance through the modification of scheduled commitments, as opposed to its domestic laws and practices, raises a number of questions of developing-country relevance as many will not fulfil the criteria for compensatory adjustments as a result of schedule modifications.

The factual circumstances of these disputes illustrates that generalisations regarding the motivations behind the decisions of developing-country governments not to impose retaliatory measures are difficult. Retaliation may no longer have been necessary in two disputes as solutions had been negotiated (Ecuador in *Bananas*; Brazil in *Aircraft*), of limited incremental purpose in two disputes as other larger WTO members were already imposing retaliatory measures (*Byrd* and *Bananas*) and, potentially, no longer justified in one dispute as the member may have brought itself into compliance by modifying its schedule (*Gambling*).

(c) Conventional wisdom may need to be revisited where developing countries cross-retaliate with intellectual property rights or services

An interesting development in developing-country practice with retaliation has been requests to cross-retaliate through the suspension of obligations under the TRIPS Agreement and the GATS. Article 22.3 of the DSU permits retaliation across agreements where retaliation under the same agreement would not be 'practicable or effective'.

The possibility of cross-retaliation was first requested, and obtained, by Ecuador in *EC–Bananas III (Ecuador)* (Article 22.6 – EC) and has continued to gain momentum with similar requests by Antigua in *US–Gambling* (Article 22.6 – Antigua and Barbuda) and Brazil in *US–Upland Cotton* (Article 22.6 – US). The option has been explored with respect to obligations under both the TRIPS Agreement (see the contributions by Salles, Chapter 13, above and Abbott, Chapter 22, below) and, most recently, the GATS (see Appleton, Chapter 23, below).

Suspending obligations under the TRIPS Agreement has been argued to be of particular interest to developing countries in disputes against developed countries.[70] It will be recalled that the main concerns

[70] A. Subramanian and J. Watal, 'Can TRIPS serve as an Enforcement Device for Developing Countries in the WTO?', *Journal of International Economic Law*, 3 (2000), 403–16. H. Grosse Ruse-Kahn, see above, note 7 at 313–64.

with retaliation through the suspension of tariff concessions voiced by developing countries are: (i) that retaliation will be ineffective in inducing compliance in larger WTO members where the developing countries have small domestic markets; and (ii) that the suspension of concessions may be more detrimental to the developing country than the non-complying member. Cross-retaliation by suspending obligations in the field of intellectual property rights is seen by many to address both concerns.

Regarding the first limitation of traditional trade retaliation, it is argued that the intellectual property obligations contained in the TRIPS Agreement are of significant value for politically and economically important companies in a number of industrialised countries.[71] There is a view that 'developing countries have undertaken serious commitments on TRIPS from which large, multinational corporations based in industrialised countries stand to benefit enormously'.[72] For this reason, even the threat of, or minimal, retaliation by developing countries in the area of intellectual property rights is seen as likely to generate a significant industry lobbying response placing industrialised governments under considerable political pressure to comply.

With respect to the second limitation, various commentators have argued that 'retaliation in TRIPS can be genuinely welfare enhancing in a way that conventional retaliation … is not'.[73] The theory is that intellectual property protection tends to serve the interests of developed countries with a comparative advantage in innovation. If correctly selected and applied, suspending this protection is seen as providing greater benefits to developing countries than burdens.[74]

Nonetheless, the extent to which cross-retaliation in the field of intellectual property rights may accurately be hailed as the perfect retaliatory weapon in trade disputes for developing countries is an open question. The arbitrator in *EC–Bananas III (Ecuador)* (Article 22.6 – EC) cautioned that even TRIPS retaliation will involve distinctive legal, practical and economic difficulties for the retaliating member.[75] Furthermore, despite Ecuador and Antigua being granted the right to cross-retaliate by suspending TRIPS Agreement obligations in *EC–Bananas III (Ecuador)* (Article 22.6 – EC) and *US–Gambling* (Article 22.6 – Antigua and Barbuda) they have not taken such measures. Thus, there is still no practice permitting

[71] H. Grosse Ruse-Kahn, see above, note 7 at 334.
[72] A. Subramanian and J. Watal, see above, note 70 at 406.
[73] A. Subramanian and J. Watal, see above, note 70 at 405.
[74] H. Grosse Ruse-Kahn, see above, note 7 at 313–64.
[75] Decision by the arbitrator, *EC–Bananas III (Ecuador)* (Article 22.6 – EC), paras. 130–65.

an assessment of the effectiveness, or benefits, of suspending TRIPS Agreement obligations.

At this stage, cross-retaliation in the field of intellectual property rights or services will need further analysis and use before its capacity to mitigate developing-country concerns with the current WTO retaliation rules can credibly be determined.

4 Conclusion

There is a common perception that shortcomings in WTO retaliation rules undermine the utility of WTO dispute settlement for developing countries.

This chapter evaluated that perception. It segregated the criticism into distinct arguments agreeing with the theoretical proposition that WTO retaliation rules are skewed against developing countries as a means of inducing compliance by WTO members of asymmetrical market size. In such situations retaliation may be more detrimental to the developing country than the non-complying member.[76]

However, the consequential argument that shortcomings in WTO retaliation rules undermine the utility of the WTO dispute settlement system for developing countries is questionable.

GATT and WTO dispute settlement *practice* demonstrates high rates of compliance with adverse dispute settlement rulings *even when smaller and developing countries are complainants*. This practice suggests that governments comply with rulings for a multitude of reasons (including what Pauwelyn, Chapter 2, above refers to as 'community costs') of which the fear of retaliation is often not a necessary ingredient. Historically, the majority of disputes brought by developing countries have resulted in compliance.

This trend of high rates of compliance supports the perspective that, even where a developing country lacks retaliation capacity, WTO dispute settlement may nonetheless often provide an effective policy option for developing countries wishing to remove illegal trade barriers of WTO members. Of course, on those occasions where a defendant does not voluntarily comply, weaknesses in the WTO retaliation rules for developing countries are a genuine constraint. Solutions to this constraint, such as

[76] These arguments would apply equally to smaller developed countries attempting to induce compliance by WTO members with larger economies. See S. J. Evenett, 'Sticking to the Rules: Quantifying the Market Access Protected by WTO Retaliation', Chapter 7, above.

cross-retaliation and new enforcement paradigms, deserve continuing attention. It may be a disservice, however, to overplay the magnitude of this constraint as voluntary compliance occurs in the majority of disputes brought by developing countries.

The chapter also examined developing-country experience with WTO retaliation to date. The results do not support the common perception that developing countries see little utility in the current WTO retaliation rules. The data illustrate that developing countries have been at least as active as developed countries in requesting authorisation from the DSB to retaliate and in pursuing those requests through to DSU Article 22.6 arbitrations. The area of discrepancy with developed-country practice is in the imposition of retaliatory measures. Only one developing country has done so. The extent to which this permits wider conclusions is limited, however, as the factual circumstances of the four relevant disputes demonstrate that actual retaliation may no longer have been necessary or of limited incremental purpose.

The chapter, therefore, concludes that the conventional wisdom that the current WTO retaliation rules undermine the utility of the WTO dispute settlement system for developing countries deserves re-evaluation. There is considerable evidence that retaliation is not the key ingredient for compliance with GATT and WTO rulings. Developing countries should not be overly dissuaded from using WTO dispute settlement to achieve their trade objectives due to a lack of retaliation capacity.

16

Optimal sanctions in the WTO: the case for decoupling (and the uneasy case for the *status quo*)

ALAN O. SYKES*

My contribution to this volume falls under the rubric "problems and options for reform." As shall quickly become clear, however, I am not an advocate of any particular improvements or new approaches. In general, I believe that the WTO dispute resolution system has evolved in a reasonably defensible and satisfactory fashion in response to a number of competing pressures. The overall level of compliance with WTO obligations is high (though by no means perfect), disputes are reasonably modest in number and formal sanctions are comparatively rare. The system is not broken and does not require fixing.

I do not mean to suggest that everything about the WTO dispute system functions perfectly. Certainly, one can quibble with the details of dispute resolution in individual cases, as a number of other contributors to this volume do quite persuasively. No doubt more can be done in cases that proceed to a formal suspension of concessions, for example, to devise better compliance counterfactuals and to measure their trade implications more accurately.[1] But nothing in these thoughtful critiques makes out a case for any fundamental change in the design and operation of the dispute resolution process.

Rather than advocate for particular reforms, therefore, I take this opportunity to raise doubts about some that have been proposed. In particular, the burgeoning commentary on the dispute settlement system includes much criticism of trade sanctions as the "punishment" for breach

* James and Patricia Kowal Professor of Law, Stanford University. I have received thoughtful comments on earlier versions of this chapter from Chad Bown, William Davey, John Jackson, Petros Mavroidis, Joost Pauwelyn, Robert Staiger, and from the participants in the conference on the Calculation and Design of Trade Sanctions in WTO Dispute Settlement at the Graduate Institute of International Studies, Geneva, July 2008.

[1] See, for example, the contributions to this volume by Sebastian (Chapter 4), Evenett (Chapters 7 and 25), and Bown and Ruta (Chapter 6).

of WTO obligations. Among other things, critics point out that trade retaliation is economically costly and may harm the nation that retaliates. Some critics further observe that trade sanctions do not compensate the victims of breach, taken to be the injured exporters, but instead insulate other import-competing firms from competition at the expense of consumers while harming the "innocent" exporters targeted by sanctions. Such thinking often leads to the suggestion that, in one fashion or another, monetary compensation should replace or supplement trade sanctions.[2]

A system of monetary compensation must address a range of issues. Would exporters have a private right of action? How would monetary damages be calculated? Who would receive the monetary compensation: the treasury of the complaining nation(s), the injured exporters, or someone else? Would compensation extend to all harm caused by the violation ("retroactive compensation"), or just to the prospective harm that occurs after a violator nation refuses to comply with an adverse ruling within a reasonable period of time? What would happen if a WTO member refused to pay a monetary judgment against it? This list of issues is no doubt incomplete.

I will not take on all of these matters in this brief chapter, but instead will focus on the narrower question of whether it would be desirable for exporters injured by a violation to receive financial compensation for their losses.[3] The current system of sanctions in the WTO may be characterized

[2] See, for example, Davey (Chapter 17), below and also Joost Pauwelyn, "Enforcement and Countermeasures in the WTO: Rules are Rules – Toward a More Collective Approach," *American Journal of International Law*, 94 (2000), 335–47; Steve Charnovitz, "Rethinking WTO Trade Sanctions," *American Journal of International Law*, 95 (2001), 792–832; Robert Lawrence, *Crimes and Punishments: Retaliation under the WTO* (Washington, DC: Institute for International Economics, 2003); William J. Davey, "The Sutherland Report on Dispute Settlement: A Comment," *Journal of International Economic Law*, 8 (2005), 321–8; Marco Bronckers and Naboth van den Broek, "Financial Compensation in the WTO: Improving the Remedies of WTO Dispute Settlement," *Journal of International Economic Law*, 8 (2005), 101–26; and Kyle Bagwell, Petros C. Mavroidis, and Robert W. Staiger, "Auctioning Countermeasures in the WTO," *Journal of International Economics*, 73 (2007), 309–32.

[3] Such compensation might be provided through a variety of mechanisms. One can imagine a system that requires violator nations to compensate exporters harmed by a violation, a system in which violators simply choose to negotiate compensation for exporters in lieu of some other penalty (in principle possible now, although not employed to date outside of the *US–Copyright* case), or a system in which complainant governments use retaliatory tariffs to raise revenue to provide compensation to injured exporters. Each of these possibilities raises both distinct and common issues. The analysis to follow will elide these details to a considerable degree, but is aimed primarily at proposals to make financial compensation mandatory in lieu of the existing system of trade sanctions.

as "decoupled" in the sense that recalcitrant violator nations may pay a price in the form of trade sanctions, but the exporters injured by violations do not receive compensation for the harm caused by violations (except indirectly if sanctions eventually induce compliance). The purpose of this contribution is to examine the wisdom of moving away from a decoupled system in the direction of a system that provides direct compensation to exporters. Although the analysis is not conclusive, decoupling has a number of virtues that may counsel in favor of retaining it. The remainder of this chapter will explicate those virtues and, along the way, lay out the basic argument for the system as is, or what one might term the somewhat "uneasy case" for the *status quo*.

1 The expectation damages analogy

As other participants in this volume have noted,[4] it is difficult to assess the effectiveness of WTO sanctions without a conception of their purpose. A long and inconclusive debate exists in the literature in this regard, with some commentators taking the view that the purpose of formal sanctions is to induce compliance with WTO obligations, and others taking the view that centralized oversight of sanctions is intended to ensure that the price for deviation from WTO obligations is not "too high." Efforts to resolve this debate based on the treaty text seem inconclusive because the text is confused and contradictory. Snippets of text can support a variety of perspectives.[5] Arbitrators seeking to ascertain "purpose" from the text have noted these inconsistencies as well. See *United States–Byrd Amendment* arbitration (DSR 2004:IX, 4591), paragraphs 6.2–7.

In my view, much more can be learned about the purpose of sanctions from a thoughtful examination of the history and structure of WTO dispute settlement, assisted by some basic economic observations about the challenges of designing an optimal treaty mechanism under

[4] See, for example, the contribution to this volume by Pauwelyn (Chapter 2).

[5] Judith Hippler Bello, "The WTO Dispute Settlement Understanding: Less is More," *American Journal of International Law* 90 (1996), 416–18; John H. Jackson, "The WTO Dispute Settlement Understanding – Misunderstanding on the Nature of Legal Obligation," *American Journal of International Law*, 91 (1997), 60–4; Alan O. Sykes, "The Remedy for Breach of Obligations under the WTO Dispute Settlement Understanding: Damages or Specific Performance?" in Marco Bronckers and Reinhard Quick (eds.), *New Directions in International Economic Law: Essays in Honor of John H. Jackson* (The Hague: Kluwer Law, 2000); and Warren F. Schwartz and Alan O. Sykes, "The Economic Structure of Renegotiation and Dispute Resolution in the World Trade Organization," *Journal of Legal Studies*, 31 (2002), S179–S204.

conditions of uncertainty. Following this approach, one quickly comes to an appreciation of how, in a limited and imperfect sense, the system of sanctions under the WTO Dispute Settlement Understanding (DSU) plays a role somewhat akin to that of expectation damages in private contracts, in that it facilitates arguably desirable deviations from the letter of the bargain under politically exigent circumstances (what economists often term "preference shocks"). This observation is not new, but it is useful to review the basis for it here as it serves as a building block for consideration of decoupling.

(a) Sanctions during the GATT years

The WTO dispute settlement system is now 13 years old, but it was preceded by 48 years of disputes under GATT. During that time, collectively authorized sanctions played no material role in the system. Disputes were resolved (if at all) through diplomacy, often aided by GATT panel reports. Despite the absence of a dispute resolution system with "teeth," however, the GATT held together well and brought about dramatic reductions in average tariff rates around the world, particularly among the developed economies.

GATT members respected most of their commitments, most of the time, for two reasons. First, it is in the interest of nations that seek international cooperation on trade (and other matters) to demonstrate their reliability to other nations by adhering to their commitments. Nations that fail to do so, at least with sufficient frequency, will be deemed unreliable and other nations will not cooperate with them in the future. In economic parlance, nations adhere to commitments because it is in their interest to develop a *reputation* for cooperative behavior.[6]

Second, and related, GATT members harmed or threatened by violations could employ "self-help" by engaging, or threatening to engage, in unilateral retaliation against violators. It is well known in both the theoretical and experimental literature on game theory that threats of retaliatory defection can (though they need not) sustain cooperation over time when strategic interaction is open-ended ("infinitely repeated") and when parties to strategic interaction are sufficiently patient so that the short-term gains from cheating do not outweigh the long-term costs of undermining cooperation. Previous commentators have made the

[6] See, for example, Andrew Guzman, *How International Law Works: A Rational Choice Theory* (Oxford University Press, 2008) and Pauwelyn earlier in this volume (Chapter 2).

argument that unilateral self-help was a useful part of the "glue" holding the GATT system together[7] and, indeed, the now standard economic models of trade agreements presuppose that mutual threats of retaliatory defection are key to sustaining cooperation.[8]

If the incentives created by reputational concerns and unilateral retaliation enabled GATT to flourish without formal sanctions, what was the role of dispute resolution under GATT? The answer lies in the fact that informal methods for sustaining cooperation can function well only if cooperative behavior can be identified accurately. Disputes can arise over the question of whether actions breach the agreement due to differences of opinion about the facts or the law. GATT panels (and the consultations that preceded them) provided an opportunity for the disputants to clarify the facts regarding the conduct at issue and to seek legal interpretations of ambiguous obligations. The fact that panel formation could be "blocked" over much of the history of GATT did little to undermine this role, in that concerned parties could generally draw a (correct) adverse inference from the decision by a disputant to block the panel process.

In short, the role of dispute resolution during the GATT years was to provide the information necessary for cooperation to be sustained through informal mechanisms grounded in reputation and self-help. Centrally administered sanctions played no role, and their absence was of no great consequence.

(b) The WTO innovation

Why did the parties to the Uruguay Round negotiations see fit to replace the GATT dispute system with the DSU, which introduced a real prospect of centrally authorized sanctions which, indeed, has resulted in the imposition of sanctions in a number of cases? A naive and incorrect answer is that the GATT suffered from too much "cheating," so that a new system was needed to introduce tougher penalties for breach. A moment's reflection will reveal that the new system did no such thing.

As under GATT, WTO disputes are initiated by signatories who claim to have been harmed by a violation (to have had their benefits from the

[7] See Alan O. Sykes, "Constructive Unilateral Threats in International Commercial Relations: The Limited Case for Section 301," *Law and Policy in International Business*, 23 (1992), 263–330; and Chad P. Bown, "On the Economic Success of GATT/WTO Dispute Settlement," *Review of Economics and Statistics*, 86 (2004), 811–23.

[8] For example, Kyle Bagwell and Robert W. Staiger, *The Economics of the World Trading System* (Cambridge, MA: MIT Press, 2002).

bargain "nullified or impaired"). There is no "public prosecutor." And just as under GATT, if a respondent loses its case and declines to comply with the ruling against it, it suffers two adverse consequences: damage to its reputation, and the costs of any trade (or other) sanctions that the complaining nation(s) may impose. Nothing in the WTO system augments the ability of complaining nations to impose sanctions, and there is no authority for collective retaliation by other nations. If a complaining nation is weak and lacks the ability to impose meaningful retaliation, therefore, it must content itself with the favorable ruling alone, just as under the old GATT system. It cannot fairly be said that the DSU enhances the penalties for breach.

So what has really changed? Aside from an appellate process to review disputed legal interpretations, the primary change lies in the fact that the magnitude of trade (or other) sanctions is now subject to central oversight through an arbitration process under DSU, Article 22. The systematic effect of this arbitral process – both in its design and in practice – has been to *reduce* the magnitude of the trade (or other) sanctions that the complaining nation(s) may impose.

This innovation was, as argued elsewhere, a response to the "aggressive unilateralism" that developed during the waning years of GATT.[9] Under GATT, nations aggrieved by an actual or alleged breach of obligations would employ self-help remedies to a degree of their own choosing because nothing in the GATT dispute system offered any practical constraint on the magnitude of those measures. The United States, through section 301 of the Trade Act of 1974, was particularly aggressive in this regard. Reputational concerns were at best an imperfect constraint on unilateral sanctions because it was difficult for other nations to observe when sanctions were "excessive" – indeed, GATT itself did not establish any clear principle for determining what level of self-help was acceptable (consider GATT, Article XXIII, which provided for the suspension of "such concessions or other obligations under this Agreement as the [Contracting Parties collectively] determine to be appropriate in the circumstances"). Likewise, it was questionable whether excessive retaliation could be adequately disciplined by counterretaliation, and the worry instead was that such scenarios could escalate into trade wars that might unravel cooperation.

[9] See, generally, Jagdish Bhagwati and Hugh T. Patrick (eds.), *Aggressive Unilateralism: America's 301 Trade Policy and the World Trading System* (Ann Arbor, MI: University of Michigan Press, 1990); and Warren F. Schwartz and Alan O. Sykes, note 5, above, S179–S204.

Consequently, toward the end of GATT, many signatories came to believe that some mechanism was needed to rein in unilateral retaliation. This proposition is, I believe, quite widely accepted. But implicit in the proposition is the notion that retaliation can be "excessive." This observation raises a core issue that has proven to be a source of controversy through the years: why might retaliation be "excessive?"

To frame the issue, suppose that a WTO member breaches its obligations. The facts and the law clearly establish the breach, and the violator refuses to change its behavior. Why should the sanction for such recalcitrance be limited at all? If the complaining nation wants to engage in "massive" retaliation for the purpose of inducing the violator to comply with its commitments, why should the system object? Indeed, why not permit all WTO members to retaliate collectively for the purpose of coercing compliance, even the members whose interests are not impaired by the breach?[10] Two ostensibly different answers have been offered through the years, although as I will suggest below, they actually collapse into a single logical point.

Economically-oriented commentators offer an answer grounded in familiar ideas from the literature on contracts. Contracts are entered into under conditions of uncertainty and positive transactions costs. It is prohibitively costly for the parties to contracts to anticipate every possible contingency that may materialize and to write down the optimal response to every such contingency. Accordingly, even contracts that include built-in flexibility mechanisms will generally fail to anticipate every situation in which deviation from the bargain is desirable. The parties can thus benefit from alternative mechanisms that facilitate deviation. Renegotiation is always an option, but it may be subject to bargaining failure and hold-up problems that in turn have unfortunate *ex ante* consequences. As an alternative, contracting parties may limit the remedies for breach, as by subjecting themselves to a legal system that awards only expectation damages. Such a system requires the breaching party to compensate the party harmed by breach, and thus encourages parties to breach precisely when net gains arise.

An essentially identical story may be told about many treaties, and the WTO in particular. The set of issues addressed by the WTO is vast, and WTO agreements are negotiated in the face of enormous uncertainty about the future. Even with built-in flexibility mechanisms, such as GATT,

[10] See Giovanni Maggi, "The Role of Multilateral Institutions in International Trade Cooperation," *American Economic Review* 89:1 (1999), 190–214.

Articles XIX, XX, XXI, and XXVIII, it is unlikely that the negotiators can anticipate all of the circumstances in which deviation from the agreement is jointly optimal (for purposes of this argument, the welfare metric is arbitrary). Renegotiation is not an attractive way to deal with this problem given the vast number of WTO members. Hold-up problems become all the more acute as the number of parties to renegotiation increases, a problem compounded by the most-favored-nation obligation. Thus, some other device is needed to allow deviation from commitments that are not optimal *ex post*. A mechanism akin to the expectation damages regime for private contracts can strike a sensible balance. Of course, the task of designing such a mechanism is immensely more complex here, but the observation that WTO agreements are analogous to "incomplete contracts" offers a clear rationale for a system that does not penalize breach "excessively."[11]

Some commentators, however, balk at the claim that compliance with international law generally, or WTO law in particular, may at times be "inefficient." When asked why the WTO should nevertheless constrain the magnitude of retaliation for breach, these commentators typically answer that a need arises to cabin retaliation to maintain the stability of the system – to prevent trade wars that might cause an unraveling of cooperation. This argument for limited retaliation, of course, is simply another account of efficient breach. It says, in effect, that the parties to the arrangement are jointly better off by limiting retaliation so as to sustain greater cooperation over time, even if the result is long-term deviation from the law by some parties in some situations – *a fortiori*, violations are sometimes efficient.

In sum, a strong theoretical case can be made for limiting the penalty for breach of obligations under GATT and other WTO agreements. If signatories can deviate from the bargain without paying an excessive price, the bargain becomes more valuable and more trade concessions can be expected *ex ante*. It thus comes as no surprise that when the DSU introduced a serious prospect of formal sanctions into the dispute settlement system, it concurrently limited their magnitude: DSU, Article 22.4 states that such measures should be "equivalent to the level of nullification or impairment." As under GATT, aggrieved parties can still penalize violations with trade sanctions, but those sanctions are subject to the

[11] See Henrik Horn, Giovanni Maggi and Robert W. Staiger, *Trade Agreements as Endogenously Incomplete Contracts* (2006), Mimeo, for more on the incomplete contract perspective on trade agreements.

ceiling implied by "equivalence" (putting aside the prohibited subsidies cases[12]), to be enforced by an arbitral process.

As argued elsewhere, this particular innovation in the DSU may be understood as a crude analog of expectation damages under private contracts. Just like expectation damages, the ceiling on retaliation associated with Article 22.4 can work to prevent the price of breach from becoming too high.[13]

To be sure, the analogy to expectation damages fails in other respects. Expectation damages in the private contract setting not only ensure that the price of breach is not too high, but also that it does not become too *low*. Neither Article 22.4 nor any other part of the DSU addresses the latter issue – if a complaining nation lacks the capacity to retaliate in a meaningful way, nothing in the DSU strengthens its hand.[14]

The analogy to expectation damages is imperfect in other ways as well. Most importantly, the question of how to measure and operationalize "equivalence" is much less clear than in the private contract setting. The next section discusses this issue further, and explains why it is unnecessary for injured exporters to be compensated for the system to achieve a reasonable calibration of sanctions.

2 "Equivalent" trade sanctions

In the private contract setting, the measurement of expectation damages is conceptually straightforward. The court determines the monetary value of what the promisee would have received if the contract had been performed, and deducts the value of the promisee's position following breach. What is the analogous calculation in the WTO setting?

To answer that question, one must first specify who is to be conceived of as the injured promisee. On one view, the promisees are the exporters whose market access (or some other right) has been impaired by a violation. This line of thinking leads quickly to the idea that payment of compensation to exporters for economic losses might be a sensible mechanism

[12] Three arbitral panels have ruled that the countermeasures available in prohibited subsidies cases need not satisfy the "equivalence" standard that applies to other cases, relying on language in Article 4.10 of the WTO Agreement on Subsidies and Countervailing Measures. See John H. Jackson, William J. Davey, and Alan O. Sykes, *International Economic Relations*, 5th edn. (Minneapolis, MN: Thompson West, 2008), section 7.5.

[13] Warren F. Schwartz and Alan O. Sykes, see note 5, above, S179–S204.

[14] Of course, as in the days of GATT, reputational considerations may do much to protect the interests of weaker nations. And the addition of TRIPs to the WTO system may empower weaker nations considerably with a prospect of cross-retaliation.

for imposing sanctions for breach, an idea to which we will return in the next section.

But it is not obvious that the "promisees" in the WTO bargain are properly viewed as private actors. Treaties are entered by political officials, and the field of public choice teaches that such officials commonly behave in such as a way as to maximize their political interests, as measured by votes, campaign contributions, and the like. An "optimal" treaty, therefore, might be expected to maximize the joint welfare of signatory officials in a rough sense. Those same officials may also be viewed as the beneficiaries of the treaty bargain, and from this perspective, the cost of violations arises in the form of a loss of political welfare for officials in nations harmed by the violation. The connection between the loss suffered by political officials, and the loss suffered by private actors, may be close or attenuated, depending on such factors as whether the private actors in question are well organized politically.[15]

This line of thinking implies that sanctions might ideally take the form of measures that allow aggrieved political officials to restore their political welfare in the face of a breach. Of course, compensation to exporters may serve that function, but it is by no means the only option.

In particular, if officials in a nation harmed by a violation may impose trade sanctions, they can use them to pursue one of two politically valuable strategies. One option is to target the sanctions at foreign exporters who seem likely to lobby their own governments to cure the violation in order to end the sanctions. Political officials who pursue this strategy successfully will reap political rewards from exporters harmed by the original violation. A second option is to employ trade sanctions to protect import-competing firms that value such protection, and that will directly reward their officials for providing it. Savvy political actors may be expected to choose between these two strategies according to which one benefits them the most. Plainly, trade sanctions also impose political costs on officials in the violator nation. Exporters harmed by trade sanctions may be expected to withdraw political support from the domestic officials whose policies result in the violation that begets the sanctions.

Thus, if one shifts the focus to political officials and treats them as the beneficiaries of the bargain, trade sanctions seem a perfectly plausible enforcement mechanism.[16] Trade sanctions impose political costs

[15] See Alan O. Sykes, "Public versus Private Enforcement of International Economic Law: Standing and Remedy," *Journal of Legal Studies*, 34 (2005), 631–66.

[16] In this respect, one must distinguish investment agreements from trade agreements. As to the former, I have argued elsewhere that a private right of action for damages

on violators, and allow officials in nations harmed by a violation to reap political benefits. *If* the sanctions are calibrated properly, they would seem to have as much potential to create proper incentives for compliance or breach (in relation to the political welfare "maximand" in the background) as any monetary compensation mechanism.[17]

But the last statement contains a big "if." How can the WTO ensure that trade sanctions are calibrated properly: that is, large enough to encourage an appropriate degree of compliance, and not so large as to discourage efficient (in the political sense) deviation from the bargain?

The modern theory of trade agreements suggests some useful principles. Bagwell and Staiger[18] develop the concept of "reciprocity" in trade agreements. Roughly, reciprocity refers to a process whereby trade concessions are exchanged in a manner that expands the volume of trade but holds the terms of trade constant. Although they do not explicitly consider how reciprocity might work in the event of a breach of a trade agreement,[19] Howse and Staiger[20] extend the basic idea to consider the optimal response to changed circumstances (a "preference shock") that lead a party to a trade agreement to contemplate breach. In their model, each government maximizes a welfare function that is quite general in its specification, and allows political considerations to enter in the form of arbitrary preferences regarding local prices (which reflect the distribution of rents among interest groups). A regime of "expectation damages" – that is, a regime that restores the welfare of the government harmed by a

suffered by individual investors (as is common in bilateral investment treaties, for example) makes good sense. If a capital-importer wishes to lower its cost of capital most effectively, a promise of compensation to private investors for acts such as "expropriation" is a more effective mechanism than a right of retaliation vested in the investor's home government. For elaboration of this argument and an analysis of why it does not apply to trade agreements, see Alan O. Sykes, note 15, above, 631–66.

[17] Of course, the political welfare maximand will not in general correspond to economic welfare conventionally defined. Some of us may lament the disparity, but there is nothing that we can do about it. For this reason, I view efforts to ground the dispute settlement mechanism in conventional welfare economics as futile or counterproductive.

[18] Kyle Bagwell and Robert W. Staiger, see note 8, above.

[19] In the basic Bagwell–Staiger model, cooperation is sustained by a mutual, reciprocal threat to withdraw trade concessions and return to the non-cooperative (Nash) equilibrium that precedes the agreement. The withdrawal of reciprocal concessions is thus an "off equilibrium" threat that does not occur when cooperation is sustained.

[20] Robert Howse and Robert W. Staiger, "United States – Anti-Dumping Act of 1916 – Recourse to Arbitration by the United States under Article 22.6 of the DSU" in Henrik Horn and Petros C. Mavroidis (eds.), *The WTO Case Law of 2003* (Cambridge University Press, 2006).

violation – can be approximated in this framework with a rule whereby breach is followed by trade sanctions that reduce the exports of the breaching party in an amount equal to the reduction in exports caused by the violation (valued at the pre-violation prices). This analysis offers a rough theoretical defense of the approach that has been used in WTO arbitrations to date (again putting aside the prohibited subsidies cases): calculate the export trade lost as a result of the violation by the complaining nation(s), and then permit sanctions in an amount that would reduce the violator's exports by the same amount.

To be sure, the real world is more complicated than the simple Howse and Staiger model, which involves trade in two goods with four countries, and in which the only policy variables are tariffs. The WTO involves trade in thousands of goods and services, among over 150 countries, with many different border and domestic policy instruments in play. Nevertheless, their analysis suggests how a principle of "equivalence" that seeks to calibrate the trade effects of sanctions to the trade effects of the original violation may represent a sensible, simple rule of thumb that explains the basic approach seen in a number of WTO arbitrations.

3 Compensating exporters as an alternative

Even if trade sanctions linked to the trade effects of the violation are a plausible mechanism, might a system of monetary compensation for aggrieved exporters be better yet? Such a system, one might argue, could also restore the political welfare of officials harmed by a violation by alleviating the injury suffered by their exporters. It would also arguably facilitate efficient breach (if a nation wishing to deviate from its commitments can compensate injured exporters and still remain better off itself, breach seems efficient). Further, as others have noted, a system of compensation for exporters would have the advantage of avoiding the deadweight costs of protection associated with sanctions.

Such thinking is open to question for a variety of reasons. First, it is important to recall a well-known inefficiency associated with expectation damages. Although expectation damages may in principle induce breach when and only when it is desirable, they also insure promisees against the loss of their expectancy. By compensating promisees for breach even when breach is efficient, "over-reliance" will result – promisees will make excessive irreversible investments that enhance the value of performance to them. This is why, as a general matter, it cannot be shown that expectation damages are superior to a rule that excuses liability for breach altogether.[21] The inefficiency that results from expectation damages disappears, however, if damages are decoupled. If the breaching promisor must bear the cost of breach to the promisee, but the promisee does not receive that cost, both the breach decision and the reliance decision can be optimized.

How might excessive "reliance" manifest itself in the international trade setting? Firms assured of market access to a particular market or full compensation for its withdrawal might well sink excessive costs in anticipation of serving that market. These could include investments in customizing goods or services for the market, or investments in production, sales, and distribution arrangements for that market. The notion that international trade can entail significant relationship-specific investments of this sort is well established in the literature.[22]

Second, the costs of measuring the economic losses caused by violations could be enormous. It is one thing to do the analysis to construct a counterfactual to measure the aggregate trade volume effects of a violation, as is done now. To take that analysis to the next level, and calculate the economic losses for every exporting firm affected by the violation, would add another layer of complexity. Among other things, the costs for each firm would be needed to determine lost profit, along with an examination of opportunities in each firm to mitigate losses. Furthermore, the lost profits of exporting firms do not capture the full costs of a violation. Rather, the loss is borne by all factors of production that earn rents or quasi-rents from the export opportunity, including the owners of all specific capital involved in the export industry (such as workers with specific human capital). The task of valuing such losses, and aggregating across what might be many firms, workers, and others, would be error prone and quite expensive.

Of course, this problem could be averted by a system of "liquidated" damages (as some commentators have proposed, see Broncker and van den Broek[23]), whereby a violator pays a fixed amount per period regardless of the nature and extent of the violation. But such a system forfeits almost all of the benefits of a sensibly designed sanctions mechanism. The price

[21] See Steven Shavell, "Damage Measures for Breach of Contract," *Bell Journal of Economics* 11 (1980), 466–90.

[22] See, for example, Beth V. Yarbrough and Robert M. Yarbrough, *Cooperation and Governance in International Trade: The Strategic Organizational Approach* (Princeton University Press, 1992); and Pol Antras and Robert W. Staiger, *Offshoring and the Value of Trade Agreements* (2007), Mimeo.

[23] Marco Bronckers and Naboth van den Broek, see note 2, above, 101–26.

of breach would be unrelated to the harm it causes, leading to situations in which the price of breach is excessive and to others in which nations could buy out of their obligations too cheaply.

A third caution regarding the compensation of exporters concerns the claim that monetary compensation is more efficient because it avoids the deadweight costs of protection. This is at best a misleading claim for it ignores the deadweight costs of the tax system that would raise the funds to pay compensation. Once we put the economists' fiction of lump-sum taxation to the side,[24] it becomes apparent that all tax systems in practice generate deadweight costs. It is possible that the taxes imposed to raise funds for compensation will have smaller deadweight costs than trade protection, but one cannot be sure.

A fourth concern regarding the compensation of exporters relates to the cost and volume of litigation. How would a prospect of compensation affect the number of cases filed in the WTO and the resources invested in them? Simple economic theory suggests that as the returns to litigation increase, the number of cases filed and the resources invested in each case will increase. If exporters were given the equivalent of a private right of action, one can imagine legal entrepreneurs searching far and wide for compensable violations and filing numerous cases on something akin to a contingency fee basis. And even if the right of action remains with governments alone, the prospect of compensation for harm suffered might well ratchet up the political pressure on governments to bring actions (especially if compensation were extended to past harm and not simply to the future harm that follows from a nation's refusal to comply with an adverse ruling).

Of course, the fact that litigation and litigation costs might increase is not undesirable *a priori*. Perhaps current levels of litigation and enforcement are too low from a social perspective. But violations of trade agreements often result in private losses that exceed social losses. Protection for domestic industries diverts profits from foreign firms to domestic firms, and the loss suffered by foreign firms may greatly exceed the deadweight

[24] Nuno Limao and Kamal Saggi, "Tariff Retaliation versus Financial Compensation in the Enforcement of International Trade Agreements," *Journal of International Economics*, 76 (2008), 48–60, analyze a formal model of a trade agreement in which cooperation can be sustained either by retaliatory defection on tariff commitments, or by a monetary fine (paid to the other government). They conclude that both mechanisms are capable of sustaining the same degree of tariff cooperation, but that the monetary enforcement mechanism Pareto dominates retaliatory tariffs because fines create no deadweight losses. That result, however, depends on the assumption that the money to pay fines is raised by lump-sum taxation. See *ibid.*, 53.

costs of protection. Violations can also shift business among foreign firms in ways that cause a loss of profits to some of them which far exceed the social costs of the trade diversion. Indeed, some violations of WTO law (such as export subsidies) may actually enhance global economic welfare. These considerations lead to the distinct possibility of excessive litigation in the WTO system, whereby the amount spent on the pursuit of compensation exceeds the social value of discouraging non-compliant practices.[25]

I do not wish to overstate the case here. It is also possible that the mere threat of litigation will induce a higher level of compliance in many settings such that actual litigation is unnecessary, and the gains from greater compliance might exceed the costs of the occasional cases. The point is simply that the net costs and benefits of an increased incentive to litigate and to invest resources in litigation are very much uncertain, and will depend on the balance of various empirical considerations.[26]

Fifth, and finally, any consideration of compensation for exporters must take into account the situation facing developing countries. With regard to developing countries as potential defendants, compensation requirements might represent a worrisome threat to their public sector budgets, doubly so when "violations" may be more accidental than deliberate due to limited compliance capacity. To be sure, these issues might be addressed by yet another form of "special and differential treatment," but exemptions for developing countries would weaken the utility of the system and complicate the politics of agreeing on any sort of reform.

As for developing-country plaintiffs, by contrast, compensation requirements are sometimes thought to be potentially useful because of the limited capacity of developing countries to retaliate with trade sanctions.[27] Such arguments are not fully convincing, however, given the ability of small nations to obtain authority for cross-retaliation on matters such as TRIPs rights (as in *EC–Bananas* and *United States–Gambling*).

Furthermore, it is a mistake to imagine that substantive rights can be divorced from the remedies that enforce them. If developing countries lack retaliatory capacity, it is because they have not made concessions of value to trading partners that they can take back. And if that is the case, it is not necessarily in the interest of developing countries to make the

[25] See Steven Shavell, "The Social versus the Private Incentive to Bring Suit in a Costly Legal System," *Journal of Legal Studies* 11 (1982), 333–9.

[26] See, generally, Alan O. Sykes, note 15, above.

[27] See, for example, Kyle Bagwell, Petros C. Mavroidis, and Robert W. Staiger, note 2, above.

obligations running in their direction more "enforceable." In particular, if developing countries receive concessions for which they have not "paid" with meaningful concessions of their own, a prospect of stiffer sanctions for breach of those concessions may lead the countries that would otherwise make the concessions to withhold them in the first place, leaving developing countries worse off rather than better off.[28]

4 Conclusion

For the reasons developed above, I believe that the case for replacing the current system of trade sanctions with some form of direct compensation to injured exporters is a weak one. Despite its imperfections, the current "decoupled" mechanism of trade sanctions has a number of considerable virtues. It is also noteworthy that WTO members could always agree to compensate aggrieved exporters presently in settlement of cases, but do not elect to do so (putting aside the *United States–Copyright Act* case, which involved the payment of a modest sum to an entity that already existed for the purpose of distributing such monies among the relevant private actors). This "revealed preference" on the part of the WTO membership as a whole suggests further reason to question whether an exporter compensation system would be an improvement over the current state of affairs.

Of course, it is possible to design monetary compensation mechanisms that remain decoupled and do not compensate exporters. Some of the objections above would not apply to such a system and, indeed, there are many moving parts in any monetary compensation mechanism that would have to be considered as noted in the introduction. But once any system to provide monetary "compensation" for harm caused by WTO violations was introduced, the political pressure for governments to turn those funds over to injured exporters might become considerable. This observation raises a further caution about any sort of remedial system grounded in monetary compensation.

[28] Gene M. Grossman and Alan O. Sykes, "A Preference for Development: The Law and Economics of GSP," *World Trade Review* 4 (2005), 41–67.

Comment on chapter 16

Money talks the talk (but does it walk the walk?)

PETROS C. MAVROIDIS*

1 The author's thesis

In his chapter, Professor Sykes dismisses the thesis that introducing monetary compensation into the WTO dispute settlement system should be the preferred option over the current regime. It is probably equally important to clarify *ex ante* what the chapter does *not* state: it does not state which is the first best option, nor does it discuss issues relating to the quantification of the damage; it simply provides a response to the question, should the current regime be dropped in favor of monetary compensation.

2 No direct effect

In my comment, I will also start with what I am not stating here: in what follows, I am not advocating standing for private parties in front of the WTO adjudication system. Monetary compensation can occur in two ways:

(1) as an agreement between the parties to the dispute. Indeed, this is what happened in *US–Section 110(5) Copyright Act*. The parties to the dispute (the EC, the United States), following the finding by a panel that the defendant was in violation of its obligations under the WTO, submitted a joint request to an arbitrator (Article 25 of the DSU) who was mandated to set the amount of money that the defendant should be transferring to the complainant in order to address the damage inflicted through the commission of the illegal act;[1]

* Petros C. Mavroidis, is Edwin B. Parker Professor of Law at Columbia Law School, New York, Professor of Law at the University of Neuchâtel and Research Fellow at CEPR.

[1] See on this score, Gene M. Grossman and Petros C. Mavroidis, "Would've or Should've? Impaired Benefits Due to Copyright Infringement" in Henrik Horn and Petros C. Mavroidis (eds.), *The American Law Institute Reporters' Studies on WTO Case Law* (New York: Cambridge University Press, 2007), 294–314.

(2) by acknowledging standing to private parties who can in turn sue before the WTO and request monetary compensation.

Monetary compensation, thus, is not necessarily linked to option (2) above. Yet, it is often referred to in literature as the preferred option of private parties, assuming, of course, that they had their say as to the means to address illegalities. This is, of course, not the case as things stand, since the WTO is a government-to-government contract with no standing before its adjudicating bodies provided for private parties.

It is probably warranted that I clarify at the outset that assuming that monetary compensation were to be retained as an option, I would not support standing for private rights. For a number of reasons eloquently explained, *inter alia*, in a short paper by Levy and Srinivasan,[2] it is probably unwise to introduce direct effect in the WTO dispute settlement system: in short, private interests might diverge from state interests, and were private parties allowed standing before the WTO this might provide state actors with a disincentive to make commitments.

3 Collateral damage?

A good case to discuss Sykes' thesis is the recent *Fedon* judgment by the European Court of Justice (ECJ). Following the lack of implementation of the Appellate Body (AB) report on *EC–Bananas III*, the United States requested authorization to impose countermeasures against products originating in the EC. In the absence of agreement among the two interested parties as to the level of countermeasures, their dispute was submitted to arbitrators. So far, countermeasures in the WTO have taken one form only: suspension of concessions, whereby the injured state imposes trade harm on the author of the illegal act.

The arbitrators revised the US request downwards and, subsequently, the WTO (through the Dispute Settlement Body (DSB)) authorized the United States to impose countermeasures of US$191.4 million against products originating in the EC. The United States included in the list of products the concessions on which they suspended products by Fedon, an Italian company producing articles of a kind normally carried in the

[2] See Phil Levy and T. N. Srinivasan, "Regionalism and the (Dis-)advantage of Dispute Settlement Access," in Jagdish Bhagwati, Pravin Krishna, and Arvind Panigariya (eds.), *Trading Blocks* (Cambridge, MA: MIT Press, 1999), 531–40.

pocket or in the handbag, with an outer surface of plastic sheeting, or of reinforced or laminated plastics (cases for eyewear). In April 1999 the United States imposed duties of 100 percent *ad valorem* on Fedon products.[3] Following negotiations between the EC and the United States, the latter agreed to suspend provisionally the high duties imposed on June 30, 2001.[4] During this period, the product market where Fedon participates suffered considerable damage.[5] Fedon requested that the Commission reimburse the damage suffered during that period as a result of the extra duty imposed on its products.[6]

The European Court of First Instance was not sympathetic to Fedon's complaint, and the company appealed its judgment. Following an encouraging, at least in part, opinion by the Advocate General, the ECJ confirmed the view that Fedon could not claim compensation for the damage suffered. In short, Fedon has done nothing wrong but still has to pay for the EC decision to violate its WTO obligations in a sector totally unrelated to Fedon's realm of activity.[7] In equilibrium, in other words, the EC preferred to protect the interests of one lobby (banana distributors) over another (Fedon).[8]

The current regime does not address similar issues. Indeed, as Sykes implicitly at the very least argues, this should not be a WTO concern: it should be for the EC in this case to compensate losers from the trading game. Since I have dismissed the appropriateness of private rights, would the introduction of monetary compensation help Fedon? Yes, is the short answer: had the EC *agreed* to pay its way out of its WTO obligations, Fedon would not have had to suffer higher duties (and the resulting reduced market access) in the lucrative US market. It is quite likely, of course, that some of its income will be taxed in order to compensate the

[3] See the European Court of First Instance (CFI) judgment, T-135/01, on *Fedon* v. *Council and Commission*, December 14, 2005. By moving it to 100 percent *ad valorem*, the United States had imposed an extra duty of 95.4 percent on *Fedon* products, section 34.

[4] CFI, T-135/01, *Fedon* (note 5), section 45.

[5] As evidenced in the EC Commission's own statistics, see CFI, T-135/01, *Fedon* (note 5), section 46.

[6] The exact quantification of the damage by *Fedon* is included in CFI, T-135/01, *Fedon* (note 5), section 56 (€289,242,07 million, plus interest rate).

[7] See the analysis in Petros C. Mavroidis, "It's Alright Ma, I'm Only Bleeding" in Astrid Epiney, Marcel Haag and Andreas Heinemann (eds.), *Challenging Boundaries, Festschrift für Roland Bieber* (Baden Baden: Nomos Verlag, 2007), 548–58.

[8] On this score, see Gene M. Grossman and Elhanan Helpman, *Special Interest Politics* (Cambridge, MA: MIT Press, 2001).

United States, but costs will usually be spread sufficiently for Fedon to feel this is the better option.

So far I have painted a rosy picture of the situation. The issue is, however, what if the EC refuses to pay? This is a likely scenario. Indeed, if the EC agrees to pay, then why not implement in the first place? Sure, one can imagine scenarios where the EC might wish to redistribute wealth across segments of its society using trade policy as an instrument to this effect. Sure enough, one can also imagine scenarios to the opposite. If the EC refuses to pay, we are back to square one. In short, the introduction of monetary compensation is not a step forward unless one assumes cooperative behaviour by the defaulting state. This assumption is unrealistic when trade policy is not used as means to redistribute wealth across national producers.

There is one area where monetary compensation might make sense: government procurement. Assume a case like *Trondheim*,[9] where a public work has been offered without competition and in violation of all relevant rules. What to do next? In WTO practice, remedies are *de facto* prospective,[10] but crucially, in this scenario there is a problem of identification of the injured party, since, in principle, all companies of all signatories could have won the competition.[11] Agreeing to pay a lump sum, a function of the worth of the public work emerges as a reasonable candidate for remedying this situation.[12]

4 Discrepancy no more

Sykes' chapter is very timely. There is no more discrepancy between academia and the negotiating table regarding the issue of remedies.

[9] See Petros C. Mavroidis, "Government Procurement Agreement; The Trondheim Case: The Remedies Issue", *Aussenwirtschaft*, 48 (1993), 77–94.

[10] See Joost Pauwelyn, "Enforcement and Countermeasures in the WTO: Rules Are Rules – Toward a More Collective Approach", *American Journal of International Law*, 94 (2000), 335–47.

[11] This is an exaggeration. Quantifying the probability to win, however, is a task most WTO panels would happily do away with.

[12] Some of these concerns have been removed with the introduction of the so-called *challenge procedures*. Nonetheless, we have yet to see a study on the effectiveness of this instrument. If at all, accounts post-dating its introduction show that, even in integrated regimes such as the EU, buy national continues to dominate national procurement markets, see Patrick Messerlin, *Measuring the Cost of Protection in Europe* (Washington, DC: Institute of International Economics, 2001).

Indeed, during the Doha Round we have experienced a flurry of proposals regarding the reform of the current regime emanating especially from developing countries. Many of these proposals address real concerns and are meritorious. Before moving any further, negotiators will be well advised to keep in mind Sykes' words of caution: first do no harm.

17

Sanctions in the WTO: problems and solutions

WILLIAM J. DAVEY*

This brief contribution on sanctions in the WTO attempts to do three things. First, it overviews the current state of compliance with WTO dispute settlement decisions in order to set the stage for considering how important effective sanctions are to the successful operation of that system. Second, it comments on chapter 16 by Professor Sykes, above and proposes an alteration to the current system of sanctions. Third, it discusses several topics relevant to the calculation and implementation of sanctions in specific cases. The issues treated are: (1) timing considerations; (2) the use of counterfactuals to set the level of sanctions; (3) the use of so-called carousel provisions; (4) causation issues; and (5) how to handle changed circumstances, such as a claim that the violation has been corrected after the sanctions were imposed.

1 Compliance in WTO dispute settlement: how much of a problem? What role for sanctions?

Overall, the WTO dispute settlement system has an excellent compliance record. An examination of the implementation record for the first 10 years of WTO dispute settlement found a compliance rate of 83 percent.[1] That is an impressive record, but it does not consider the quality and timeliness of compliance. The idea of "quality" of compliance concerns the extent to which the complainant obtained useful redress for the violation as a result of compliance. This is an issue because in certain kinds of cases compliance occurs, but may not be very meaningful. For example, in

* Professor of Law (Retired), University of Illinois College of Law.

[1] William J. Davey, "The WTO Dispute Settlement System: The First Ten Years," *Journal of International Economic Law* 8:17 (2005), 46–8. Several of the "problem" cases outstanding at that time have since been resolved.

safeguard cases the compliance record is excellent in the sense that safeguards found to violate WTO rules have generally been removed within the reasonable period of time set for compliance. However, given the time it takes to process a case through the WTO system, the objectionable safeguards have typically remained in effect for 3 years or so, which means that their intended trade effect was achieved.[2] This is what some have called a "three-year free pass" to violate WTO agreements since any remedy for non-compliance is available only prospectively[3] and only if the violator fails to implement within the reasonable period of time.[4] Another example is found in antidumping and countervail cases. In most of these cases, the measure is not removed, but is only modified. And many of the modifications do not result in a significant change in the duty rate, even though they may technically bring the measure into compliance.[5] In other words, technical compliance may not really remedy the damage caused by the WTO-inconsistent measure.

The quality-of-compliance problem is exacerbated by the timeliness-of-compliance problem. But the timeliness problem is a broader problem. It encompasses failures to implement within the reasonable period of time and questionable implementation measures that are challenged (almost always successfully) in DSU, Article 21.5 actions, as well as failures by panels and others to make serious attempts to stay within the time frames established by the Dispute Settlement Understanding (DSU). Timely compliance occurred in only about 60 percent of the cases.[6] As to the overall timeliness of the panel and appellate process, panels usually

[2] William J. Davey, "Evaluating WTO Dispute Settlement: What Results Have Been Achieved Through Consultations and Implementation of Panel Reports?" in Yasuhei Taniguchi, Alan Yanovich and Jan Bohanes (eds.), *The WTO in the Twenty-First Century: Dispute Settlement, Negotiations, and Regionalism in Asia* (Cambridge University Press, 2007), 98, 110.

[3] There is no retrospective aspect to WTO remedies. The offending nation, in other words, does not owe any reparations for the injuries caused by its actions.

[4] In many cases, the violator will take some action and assert that it has brought its non-conforming measure into compliance with WTO rules. To establish non-compliance, the prevailing WTO member must then start an Article 21.5 compliance panel proceeding following the expiration of the reasonable period of time and will be authorized to take remedial action only after that proceeding (and any ensuing appeal) is completed and the level of retaliation has been set by an arbitral proceeding. As noted in the next paragraph, these proceedings take considerable time to complete.

[5] William J. Davey, "Implementation of the Results of WTO Remedy Cases" in Mitsuo Matsushita, Dukgeun Ahn and Tain-Jy Chen (eds.), *The WTO Trade Remedy System: East Asian Perspectives* (London: Cameron May, 2006), 33–61.

[6] William J. Davey, see above, note 2, 137–8.

exceed the targets set in the DSU by many months, especially in Article 21.5 compliance proceedings and Article 22 arbitrations.[7] While the Appellate Body usually issues its report within 90 days of an appeal,[8] the overall time taken by the WTO dispute settlement process, particularly when the overly generous "reasonable" periods of time for implementation are taken into account, is quite long.[9]

Interestingly, the countries that failed to comply in a timely manner in the first decade included the United States, the European Union (EU), Canada, Japan and Australia.[10] These countries often failed to comply in cases against each other.[11] The trends observed during the first decade have continued during the succeeding years, although trade remedy cases now predominate in contested dispute settlement proceedings,[12] and the United States has become the main source of untimely implementation.[13]

Taken together, the foregoing suggests that while the WTO dispute settlement system may have an admirable record overall, there appears to be considerable room for improving the quality and timeliness of compliance. Indeed, many cite concerns about non-compliance and delays as reasons not to use the system.[14] Thus, it is legitimate to ask whether the current WTO remedy for non-compliance – prospective sanctions – is adequate.

[7] William J. Davey, "Expediting the Panel Process in WTO Dispute Settlement" in Merit E. Janow, Victoria Donaldson and Alan Yanovich (eds.), *The WTO: Governance, Dispute Settlement and Developing Countries* (Huntington, NY: Juris, 2008), 409, 415–18, 420–1.

[8] William J. Davey, note 7, above, 418.

[9] William J. Davey, note 7, above, 419–20.

[10] William J. Davey, see above, note 2, 113, 138.

[11] William J. Davey, see above, note 2, 113, 138.

[12] See Appellate Body Report, *Annual Report for 2007*, WT/AB/9, 42–7 (January 30, 2008).

[13] There are currently three cases where the United States has been reporting monthly to the DSB for many years on its failure to implement. Moreover, there is one case where the EU and Japan comment monthly on the failure of the United States to implement or report. See, for example, DSB, *Minutes of Meeting held on March 14, 2008*, 2–9, WT/DSB/M/248 (April 30, 2008). In addition, the United States has recently lost several Article 21.5 compliance actions (*US–Gambling; US–Cotton* and various *Zeroing* cases). See latest *Update of WTO Dispute Settlement Cases*, WT/DS/OV/, available at: www.wto.org/english/tratop-E/dispu-e.htm).

[14] See Gary G. Yerkey, "U.S. Poultry Producers Do Not Plan to Urge U.S. to File Case at WTO over EU Import Ban," *BNA International Trade Daily*, June 9, 2008 (noting EU failure to comply in the *Hormones* case). In the DSU reform negotiations, Mexico has been particularly critical of what it calls the "'fundamental problem' of the WTO dispute settlement system, namely the 'period of time which a WTO-inconsistent measure can be in place without the slightest consequences' to the offending party." Daniel Pruzin, "Mexico Presents 'Radical' Proposal for WTO Dispute Resolution Reform," 19 *BNA International Trade Reporter* 1984 (November 21, 2002).

2 Comments on Sykes, chapter 16 and a proposal to modify WTO sanctions practice

(a) Comments

In general, I agree with most of the points made by Professor Sykes in Chapter 16. My principal disagreements are as follows. First, I do not agree that we need to worry about making breach more costly or too costly. As noted in the foregoing section, the consequences of breach are often not very costly at all, compared with the damage done by the rule violation because remedies are prospective and available only after a very long legal process is completed and no compliance is achieved. This situation combined with the Article 22.4 requirement that the level of retaliation should not exceed the level of nullification ensure that breach is, if anything, cheap. Given that the WTO promotes a rules-based system in order to ensure security and predictability in trade flows, it needs to ensure that breaches are not too cheap.

Second, the current system's reliance on retaliation as the only remedy means that as a practical matter most WTO members have no effective remedy for non-compliance available to them. It is true as noted above that developing countries have usually obtained compliance and that most of the major non-compliance problems have arisen in disputes between developed countries, but there have been exceptions, such as *EC Bananas* and *US Gambling*, and, potentially, *US Cotton*. Thus, while the system's reliance on retaliation as the sole remedy may not yet have resulted in many serious problems, it is of concern because (1) developing and smaller developed countries cite the situation as evidence that the WTO system is fundamentally unfair and tilted against them and (2) this belief may cause them to undervalue the WTO and underuse its dispute settlement system. Moreover, it is important to realize that these countries are unable to retaliate effectively because their economies are relatively small, not because they have failed to make significant concessions in multilateral negotiations. To suggest that smaller WTO members must just accept their fate (that is, they have no remedy because they cannot retaliate effectively) will undermine the general attractiveness of WTO membership and breed resentments on the part of members in that position, and ultimately slow trade liberalization.[15]

[15] It is true that developing countries may be able to retaliate in the TRIPS sector under circumstances that might result in effective pressure for compliance being brought to bear on the United States or the EU by lobbyists for powerful IP interests, but to date this has not in fact worked out. Ecuador did not use the authorization it obtained to retaliate in

(b) A proposal

In light of the existing compliance problems noted in part 1 and the need to craft a more effective remedy for the typical WTO member noted in part 2(a), some form of monetary remedy should be available in WTO dispute settlement. While the precise details of such a remedy would need to be worked out, the following offers some general guidelines:

- *Choice of remedy / differential treatment.* The normal WTO remedy is retaliation in the sector where the violation occurred, subject to the possibility of retaliation in other sectors if the inadequacy of same-sector retaliation is shown. The possibility of a monetary remedy should be similarly available, that is, when same-sector retaliation would be inadequate. This would effectively allow smaller countries to demand monetary compensation, while the United States and the EU would not be able to do so. As such, there would probably be no need for special and differential treatment to govern the right to compensation.[16]
- *Enforceability of compensation.* If the matter is thought to be in doubt, it could be agreed in the DSU that Article 22 arbitral awards are enforceable under the New York Convention on the Enforcement of Arbitral Awards, which on its face seems to apply to awards against governments.
- *No private right to compensation.* Many of the problems with creating private rights in this situation, which are the main focus of Sykes, Chapter 16, seem well founded. Obviously, once money is received by a government, there may be pressures by those claiming to have been injured by the WTO-illegal action to receive part of the compensation. Individual governments should decide how to deal with that problem independently of any WTO rule.
- *Increased levels of nullification and impairment.* It is appropriate to maintain the link between the level of nullification and trade flows. But as discussed in part 3(a), the current approach should be modified so that the trade effect is measured from an earlier point in time. In addition, in the event that the defaulting country does not bring its measure

the TRIPS sector in *EC Bananas* and Antigua has not even sought authorization to do so from the DSB, even though such a possibility was approved in an Article 22 arbitration in *US Gambling*.

[16] The situation where a poor country is required to pay compensation could also be avoided or moderated by having a rule that adjusted the level of compensation set under normal procedures in light of the relative GNP per capita of the country in question with a standard GNP per capita or, possibly, the GNP per capita of the prevailing country.

into conformity with WTO rules, the level of permitted retaliation/compensation should be increased annually on the theory that a continued failure to implement is in itself a justification for concluding that the original level of nullification has increased, with the result that the permitted level of retaliation would also increase.

- *Reparations*. The standard international law remedy is reparations.[17] To adopt such a rule for WTO violations would represent a major change in approach and should be considered only after the foregoing reforms have been tried and found to be inadequate. In this regard, it is worth noting that the proposal to increase levels of nullification contains an element of reparations, but it would be owed only in the event of failure to comply within the reasonable period of time, as opposed to being owed in all cases and at the level of actual damage.

The adoption of the proposal would result in higher levels of retaliation/compensation, which hopefully would improve the WTO dispute settlement system's compliance record. While it would not solve the quality of compliance problem (except, of course, by increasing the consequences of losing an Article 21.5 proceeding in cases of questionable compliance), it would probably greatly encourage timely compliance. But even if these changes do not greatly improve compliance, they would provide some relief for countries harmed by WTO rule violations who would be able to claim compensation. Since both compliance and rebalancing are appropriate goals of retaliation/compliance, the changes will certainly result in some improvement compared with the current situation.

3 Specific topics: the calculation and implementation of sanctions

This part examines five important topics related to the calculation and implementation of sanctions: (1) the appropriate time period to use for calculating the level of nullification; (2) the appropriate use of counterfactuals; (3) the legitimacy of carousel provisions; (4) issues related to causation; and (5) procedures for dealing with changed circumstances.

[17] See James Crawford, *The International Law Commission's Articles on State Responsibility: Introduction, Text and Commentaries* (2006), 201–6 (noting that Article 31(1) of the International Law Commission's Articles on State Responsibility provides: "The responsible State is under an obligation to make full reparation for the injury caused by the internationally wrongful act").

(a) *Time period for calculating nullification*

Whether one views the WTO dispute settlement system's goal as (a) rebalancing concessions following a nullification of benefits or (b) promoting implementation of compliance action, the time period covered by retaliation/compensation should start sooner, so as not to encourage foot-dragging in the dispute settlement process and to provide a fairer remedy for successful complainants adversely affected by the violation. As proposed above, the time period for calculating nullification should be changed. The time period should, as a minimum, start as of the adoption of the initial reports. Consideration should be given to starting the time period as early as the time of the consultation request. Also as proposed above, to the extent that the system's goal is promoting compliance, the level of nullification should be deemed to have increased over time in the event of continuing non-compliance – since the failure to comply is in itself a violation of the rules and is deserving of some sanction.

How precisely would such changes be applied? In the case of an earlier starting point for measuring the beginning of the period of nullification or impairment, the calculation method would be the same as now and would involve setting, for example, in the typical case, an annual level of nullification.[18] To take a concrete example, suppose the level of nullification is determined to be US$100 million annually. At present, the prevailing party would be authorized to apply retaliatory measures in that amount on an ongoing basis, such as has been the case in *EC Hormones*. Under the proposal, assuming that non-compliance was admitted at the end of a 12-month reasonable period of time (that is, 12 months after adoption), there would be an additional US$100 million of nullification. A decision would have to be made on how this amount should be allocated over time. For example, the rule could be that it is all added to the annual retaliation level or one could add a percentage of it to that annual level. Thus, in the hypothetical case, if all were added, the annual retaliation rate would be US$200 million; if 50 percent were added, the retaliation rate would be US$150 million. Note that in cases where there is an Article 21.5 proceeding, the time taken by that proceeding, because it is subsequent to the adoption date, would mean a significant increase in the authorized retaliation level unless the defaulting party established that its new measure was WTO-consistent. This is because Article 21.5 proceedings typically take more than a year. This would encourage prompt compliance and

[18] In cases where there is a lump sum nullification – such as might arise in a subsidies case – instead of a continuing nullification, current rules would still apply. The proposal would affect those cases where there is a continuing violation causing ongoing nullification.

discourage questionable implementation measures, as opposed to the current situation where the completely prospective nature of retaliatory measures actually encourages delay. It is important to bear in mind that these additional levels of retaliation are applied only to those who fail to comply within the reasonable period of time, which is a fundamentally different approach than requiring payment of reparations for all damages caused.

In the event of continuing non-implementation, the proposal would provide first that the level of authorized retaliation would never decline. Thus, in the above example, assume that the US$100 million "extra" retaliation is all allocated to the first year of retaliation, such that the level of retaliation permitted would be US$200 million. Although it could be argued that in the second year, the level should drop to US$100 million, which is the ongoing level of nullification, the proposal foresees keeping the level at US$200 million, with the additional US$100 million being considered to offset continuing nullification arising from non-compliance – a separate problem from the underlying violation. If non-implementation continues for more than a few years (3 to 5 years or some other agreed period), then the proposal would provide for a percentage increase in the level of authorized retaliation on the theory that the continuing non-implementation continues to increase the level of nullification of benefits suffered by the adversely affecting complaining party.

Two other issues should be mentioned. First, the same rules could be used to set the level of monetary compensation. Second, as to special or differential treatment, it is not clear that it is needed, since experience to date indicates that it is the major players that are the problem in non-compliance. However, it would be possible as a practical matter to have more favorable rules applicable to developing countries in default for any aspects of the proposal. For example, the "extra" retaliation could be allocated over a longer period; the rate of increase in retaliation levels over time could be lower.

As noted, this proposal does not solve the "three-year-pass" problem, in that if a country violates WTO rules and implements within the reasonable period of time, it would suffer no penalty. Only a system of reparations can solve that, and the WTO's membership is probably not ready to adopt such a system. The proposal outlined would, however, significantly increase pressure on countries to implement promptly and in good faith.

(b) Counterfactuals

The use of counterfactuals in the calculation of the level of nullification seems unavoidable, but some standards are needed, in particular with respect to (a) how to choose among alternative counterfactuals and (b) how to ensure that the needed information is obtained by the arbitrator.

As to how to choose among counterfactuals, the complaining party should have the right to choose its preferred counterfactual, so long as it is WTO-consistent, in its initial request for retaliation authority and it should be for the respondent to come up with a plausible WTO-consistent alternative if it objects to the complainant's counterfactual. If the respondent can meet that burden, then the respondent's alternative should be used. That will lead to a lower level of nullification being calculated, but that is appropriate as long as the respondent meets its burden of demonstrating plausibility and WTO consistency.[19] In that regard, it is obvious that the counterfactual used by the arbitrators must be WTO-consistent, and as the *US Gambling* case indicates, the determination of such consistency may be difficult. Nonetheless, consistency must be carefully considered, even if that means a regular panel-like consideration of that issue. As to the plausibility issue, that will be difficult to assess and it may be best viewed as a requirement that the proposed counterfactual should not be clearly implausible.

It is obviously essential for the arbitrator to obtain all information necessary to assess the proposed counterfactuals and to use the chosen one to set the appropriate level of retaliation. The only reason why it might currently be difficult to obtain all of the needed information is the very tight time frame set in the DSU for the arbitrator's decision. Since that deadline has never been met (not even close) and since the current procedures were set in a very unusual and complicated case where there were intense pressures to act very quickly (that is, *EC Bananas*), it would seem appropriate to reconsider the standard procedures used in Article 22 arbitrations and, as a minimum, expand the briefing and question-and-answer opportunities in these proceedings. A second meeting between the arbitrators and the parties would probably be useful.

(c) Carousel provisions

The use of carousel provisions, which result in the targets of the retaliation being changed periodically, does not raise any particular concerns (that is, there is no reason not to allow it), so long as (a) there are procedures for ensuring that the level of retaliation does not exceed the level of nullification and impairment and (b) the uncertainty associated with a plan to

[19] It is well established that, as the wrongdoer, the respondent bears the burden of proof in challenging the complainant's proposed level of retaliation.

use a carousel approach is considered in the setting of the level of retaliation. This latter issue was raised by the arbitrators in *EC Hormones*, but not explored since the United States indicated that it did not intend to use a carousel approach. While the existence of the US carousel provision has engendered much controversy, particularly because the EU thought it would be a target of its use in the *Bananas* and *Hormones* cases, it is difficult to understand why. Certainly, there is no reason that a defaulting member is entitled to have retaliatory measures against it frozen in time. That is particularly true given that one goal of such measures is to bring about compliance.

(d) Causation

There are a number of difficult causation issues that arise in Article 22 arbitrations. In respect of establishing the level of nullification, which is in essence concerned with determining the trade effects of the non-conforming measure, there is the question of how to treat indirect or intangible effects. An example of the former arose in the *Bananas* case. The United States claimed that its exports of fertilizer to banana-exporting countries in Latin America were reduced because the EC measures at issue reduced the banana exports of those countries. The arbitrators rejected that claim, largely because of the potential for double-counting if those banana exporters later sought to retaliate on their own behalf based on their banana exports. In fact, Ecuador did later seek authorization to retaliate. While one could argue that the US claim should have been accepted and that Ecuador's level of authorized retaliation should have been reduced to reflect the existence of imported inputs in its exports (so as to ensure, per Article 22.4, that the level of retaliation does not exceed the level of nullification), such result would unnecessarily complicate the calculation of trade effects.[20] Given the imprecision resulting from using counterfactuals to begin with, such a complication would make arbitration results even more speculative.

Intangible effects would include the chilling effects of a non-conforming measure (such as were claimed by the EC in the *US–1916 Act* case) or lost trade opportunities (such as raised in the *EC–Hormones* case). The arbitrators in both of those cases refused to consider those effects because they

[20] The double-counting problem was inappropriately ignored by the arbitrators in the *US–FSC* arbitration where the EU was permitted to retaliate at a level several times the level of its own nullified benefits.

were too speculative.[21] This seems to be appropriate, although the line may be sometimes difficult to draw.[22]

The concern raised in these cases is that the level of nullification not be underestimated. But it is necessary to avoid making the process too speculative. It is worth noting that if the retaliation-enhancing aspects of the above-discussed proposal are adopted, it would greatly alleviate these concerns that current retaliation levels may be too low.[23]

There is a related causation issue that arises in the setting of the appropriate level of retaliation. So far, all retaliatory measures that have been implemented have consisted of tariff increases applied to products whose dollar trade volume has added up to the level of nullification that was set in the case. However, Ecuador was authorized to suspend certain TRIPS obligations owed to the EU, and Brazil was authorized to suspend application of import licensing rules owed to Canada. Other completed arbitrations where Dispute Settlement Body (DSB) authorization for retaliatory action has not yet been requested have also involved measures other than tariff increases (for example, *US–1916 Act*; *US–Gambling*). While it is clear that such retaliatory actions are possible under the DSU, it is not clear how the effect of such actions should be calculated so as to ensure that the level of nullification is not exceeded. In some cases, this may not be so difficult. For example, the country suspending TRIPS obligations could establish a registration system so that it could keep a running count of royalty payments otherwise owed but not paid. Once the level of such payments equaled the level of nullification, further "counterfeiting" would have to cease (until the beginning of the next appropriate time period).

In other cases, it may be much more difficult to establish the effect of the retaliatory measure. Trying to assess the impact of less favorable licensing rules on exports or the impact of less favorable procedural rules in safeguard or antidumping cases would be very difficult. It would essentially involve the sort of speculation that was criticized above. If the possibility of monetary compensation is adopted, the desire to utilize these difficult-

[21] *EC–Hormones (US)* (Article 22.6) (DSR 1999:III, 1105), para. 41; *US–1916 Act (EC)* (Article 22.6) (DSR 2004:IX, 4269), paras. 5.54–79.

[22] In *US–1916 Act* arbitration, the problems of trying to assess the precise extent of a "chilling" effect were obvious; they were less clear in respect of increased legal costs, which arguably could have a trade impact through increased prices.

[23] As noted in the discussion of the proposal, it would be necessary to have agreement on rules for increasing the level of retaliation over the base level. For arbitrators to engage in attempting to do this on their own would undoubtedly result in much controversy among the WTO membership. *Cf. Canada–Aircraft Credits and Guarantees.*

to-evaluate retaliation measures would probably decline significantly, since they seem to be largely of interest to small and developing countries. If that is the case, it would support taking a non-speculative approach to the evaluation of such measures in line with the approach favored above for causation issues related to setting the level of nullification.

(e) Changed circumstances (implementation after retaliation)

The DSU currently has no clear mechanism for dealing with the situation that arises when a country subject to retaliatory action claims that it has brought its offending measure into conformity with its WTO obligations. Needless to say, the DSU needs to be amended to provide such a procedure, and there have been proposals to do so, although when any changes to the DSU will finally be agreed is unclear.

This issue was considered in detail for the first time in the 2008 *Hormones* case, where the EU claimed that the United States and Canada were violating the DSU by keeping their retaliatory measures in place after the EU had enacted new, WTO-consistent measures. The panel decision in the case concluded that the retaliating member must remove the retaliatory measures and re-establish its right to impose those measures if the targeted member simply claims that it has taken appropriate implementing action. This result obviously did not provide the appropriate balance between the rights of the targeted and retaliating members and was reversed on appeal.

According to the Appellate Body's decision in *Hormones*, when the targeted member believes that it has brought the defaulting measure into conformity with its WTO obligations, it should initiate an Article 21.5 proceeding to verify its claim. During the course of the proceeding, the retaliating member would be entitled to maintain the retaliatory measures.[24] As to the difficult issue of burden of proof, the Appellate Body concluded:

> 362. Since the suspension of concessions is a remedy of last resort imposed after an elaborate multilateral dispute settlement process, in our view, it is appropriate that the Member whose measure has brought about the suspension of concessions should make some showing that it has removed the measure found to be inconsistent by the DSB in the original proceedings, so that normality can be

[24] The Appellate Body was of the view that both parties should initiate an Article 21.5 action, although it seems that the only party with a real incentive to do so is the respondent.

lawfully restored. This requires that the original respondent will have an onus to show that its implementing measure has cured the defects identified in the DSB's recommendations and rulings. The quantum of proof entailed by this is a clear description of its implementing measure, and an adequate explanation regarding how this measure rectifies the inconsistencies found in the original proceedings, so as to place the Article 21.5 panel in a position to make an objective assessment of the matter and, in the absence of rebuttal, to rule in favour of the original respondent ...

364. In respect of all other issues, the burden of proof rests upon the original complainant. Such issues may include a claim that the implementing measure is otherwise inconsistent with the covered agreements or that the implementing measure remains wanting for reasons not traversed by the original respondent in discharging its burden of proof.

If the original respondent prevailed, the conditions in Article 22.8 for continuing application of the retaliatory measures would be met and those measures would have to be removed.[25]

The Appellate Body's decision effectively establishes a procedure for dealing with cases where the continued application of retaliatory measures is challenged on the grounds that the defaulting measure has been brought into conformity with WTO rules. While it would be useful to have a clear DSU provision dealing with this issue, the urgent need for such a provision no longer exists. Unfortunately, the Appellate Body's decision on burden of proof is not crystal clear and may well lead to problems if panels misapply it. Nonetheless, it clearly provides a framework for dealing with these cases.

Conclusion

The WTO dispute settlement system has worked relatively well, although there are problems with timely compliance with DSB recommendations. A change to a system where monetary compensation is an alternative to trade retaliation, and where sanctions are more onerous where there is non-compliance within the reasonable period of time would help alleviate that problem.

[25] Article 22.8 provides that retaliatory measures may "only be applied until such time as the measure found to be inconsistent with a covered agreement has been removed."

18

WTO retaliatory measures: the case for multilateral regulation of the domestic decision-making process

RETO MALACRIDA*

The present contribution argues that the domestic decision-making process WTO members use to prepare and adopt WTO retaliatory measures is a legitimate concern for the WTO and that there would be merit in regulating this process at the multilateral level.

The importance of the domestic process

One of the key differences between dispute settlement under the GATT and dispute settlement under the WTO has been the frequency of recourse to retaliation. During the close to 50 years of the GATT there was but one single dispute in which the GATT Council authorized a 'suspension of concessions or other obligations'.[1] On the other hand, under the WTO, which has been in existence only since 1995, there have so far been six disputes in which the DSB has granted authorization to retaliate.[2] Moreover, there currently are an additional two WTO disputes in

* Counsellor, WTO Legal Affairs Division. The views and ideas expressed in this contribution are those of the author acting in a personal capacity and do not represent a position, official or unofficial, of the WTO Secretariat. The author wishes to thank Bruce Wilson for useful comments. The contribution draws on, and develops, an earlier publication by the author entitled 'Towards Sounder and Fairer WTO Retaliation: Suggestions for Possible Additional Procedural Rules Governing Members' Preparation and Adoption of Retaliatory Measures' and published in *Journal of World Trade*, 42:1 (2008), 3–60. Data referred to in this contribution are up to date as of the end of 2008.

1 See Determination by the Contracting Parties, 8 November 1952, *Netherlands Measures of Suspension of Obligations to the United States*, BISD 1S/32–33.

2 The six disputes are: (1) *EC–Bananas III* (authorization granted to the United States, and later Ecuador, against the EC); (2) *EC–Measures Concerning Meat and Meat Products (Hormones)* (authorization granted to the United States and Canada against the EC), (3)

which authorization to retaliate might be granted in the future.[3] If retaliation remains a recurrent feature of international trade relations under the WTO, and the indications are that it will, it becomes pertinent to ask whether existing DSU rules deal with all aspects of retaliation adequately. To determine whether existing Dispute Settlement Understanding (DSU) rules on retaliation are adequate, it is necessary first to consider what factors determine the success and acceptance of WTO retaliation as a remedy. It would seem that three factors in particular are key: namely, effectiveness, cost and fairness.

Effectiveness concerns the extent to which a retaliatory measure can induce compliance by the responding member. Retaliation is fundamentally about restricting trade on a discriminatory basis. Most world trade nowadays is conducted by, and between, private parties. Therefore, if a complaining member wishes to retaliate, it effectively has no choice but to try to target the export interests of private parties of the responding member.[4] Even then, however, doing so can be successful only if the targeted private parties are both able and willing to put pressure on their policy- and/or lawmakers to take appropriate action to comply with the relevant adverse Dispute Settlement Body (DSB) ruling.

The *ability* of private parties of the responding member to mobilize politicians and government officials into action is linked to their ability to organize and form coalitions with political weight. The *willingness* of private parties of the responding member to devote time and effort to solving the retaliating member's problem is linked to their ability to avoid the effect of, or circumvent, a retaliatory measure. Thus, a targeted private party may be able to export to third-country markets on similar terms, or it may be able to carry out origin-conferring operations in a third country

Brazil–Export Financing Programme for Aircraft (authorization granted to Canada against Brazil); (4) *US–Tax Treatment for 'Foreign Sales Corporations'* (authorization granted to the EC against the United States); (5) *Canada–Export Credits and Loan Guarantees for Regional Aircraft* (authorization granted to Brazil against Canada); and (6) *US–Continued Dumping and Subsidy Offset Act of 2000 (Byrd Amendment)* (authorization granted to Canada, the EC, Japan and Mexico against the United States).

3 The two disputes are: *US–Subsidies on Upland Cotton* (request by Brazil against the United States); and *US–Gambling* (request by Antigua and Barbuda against the United States).

4 To avoid misunderstanding, it should be made clear that ordinarily complaining members select particular tariff lines in respect of which they decide to apply a 100 per cent 'killer' duty. As a result, private parties are not being targeted as such, that is, as companies or individuals, but rather indirectly, by virtue of the fact that they are exporters or producers of targeted products. The situation could be different where a retaliatory measure targets service suppliers rather than services, or in the case of suspension of intellectual property rights, which are private rights.

before exporting to the retaliating member, or it may be able to enter into joint ventures with producers of the retaliating member.

Effectiveness is important for another reason also, and this leads to the cost factor. A measure that brings about prompt compliance contributes to limiting any cost retaliation imposed on the economy of the retaliating member. A discriminatory restriction on trade tends to entail a cost for the economy of the retaliating member, particularly in the case of countries with small, open economies.[5] For example, retaliation disrupts existing supply chains, and producers and consumers in the retaliating member might not be able to obtain goods or services of comparable quality, or at a comparable price, from alternative sources. Also, a retaliatory measure may need to remain in place for several years.[6] For it to be credible as an enforcement measure, it is important that it be sustainable in cost terms.[7]

The third factor is fairness. As indicated, retaliatory measures usually target private parties of the responding member. Furthermore, the targeted private parties frequently are 'innocent', in the sense that they did not lobby for the adoption of the WTO-inconsistent measure at the origin of the relevant dispute, nor are they beneficiaries of the continued maintenance of that measure. It is arguably not by accident, but rather by design, that retaliating members often target innocent private parties.[8] Indeed, targeting the domestic beneficiaries of the underlying WTO-inconsistent measure is uncertain to succeed since, by definition, they have a vested interest in maintaining the measure. Conversely, targeting domestic opponents of the WTO-inconsistent measure (for example, a downstream industry that is denied access to cheaper imported inputs) may likewise be ineffective since they are likely to have already used whatever influence they have to prevent the adoption or maintenance of the WTO-inconsistent measure, quite apart from the fact that they are also the customers to whom the retaliating member wishes to export its

[5] For retaliating members with small economies retaliation is unlikely to result in positive terms-of-trade effects.

[6] Note that the retaliatory measures in the *EC–Measures Concerning Meat and Meat Products (Hormones)* dispute have been in place since the second half of 1999.

[7] In this regard, note that the DSB in *US–Tax Treatment for 'Foreign Sales Corporations'* authorized retaliation of up to US$4.043 billion per annum The EC implemented a retaliatory measure that affected much less trade in value terms. There is an argument to be made that retaliating up to the full authorized amount would not have been a sustainable strategy for the EC, and to that extent, might not have been considered credible.

[8] See, for example, Solomon Major and Anthony J. McGann, 'Caught in the Crossfire: "Innocent Bystanders" as Optimal Targets of Economic Sanctions', *Journal of Conflict Resolution*, 49:3 (2005), 348 and 350–1.

products once the responding member complies with the relevant DSB ruling.

It would seem, therefore, that retaliating members do not target innocent private parties out of malice, but for lack of more effective alternatives. It must also be remembered that they need to be mindful of their own private parties who are adversely affected by the failure of the responding member to comply with its WTO obligations. Nonetheless, it is understandable that innocent private parties who are targeted by a retaliatory measure generally find it unfair that they should be made to pay for the 'sins' of their government.[9] The message they often hear from the retaliating member who targets them is that although they are not part of the problem, they must, willy-nilly, be part of the solution.[10] As a result, in the eyes of innocent private parties, the retaliating member who targets them is likely to suffer reputational damage.[11] In addition to the retaliating member, the WTO as an organization might also suffer reputational damage, as the relevant retaliatory measure would have been authorized by the WTO. More seriously, a perceived lack of fairness might cause the underlying dispute to escalate. For instance, retaliation could trigger a privately organized boycott of products originating in the territory of the retaliating member, or of products produced in the territory of

[9] See Aaron Lukas, 'Brussels Sins, Cheese Lovers Do Penance', *Journal of Commerce*, 2 (August 1999).

[10] To illustrate, the well-known French activist and farmer José Bové is reported to have compared the targeting of innocent private parties of the responding member with the taking of hostages and the bombing of civilians. See 'Pascal Lamy promet à José Bové de plaider pour un meilleur fonctionnement de l'OMC', *Le Monde*, 15 August 2001. In a similar vein, the Director of Trade Policy of the Confederation of Swedish Enterprise wrote that politicians 'still treat trade as a kind of surrogate war, where perceived state interests (i.e. short-term political advantage) rule supreme' and in which '[c]onsumers and companies are treated as mere pawns who should be happy to sacrifice themselves for the narrow electoral interests that fuel [protectionism in countries] around the world'. See Hans Ekdahl, 'Suffering Citizenry Continues Enriching the Trade War Lords', *Financial Times*, 21 June 2002.

[11] Thus, in response to plans by the US government to impose 100 per cent duties on EC motorcycles in retaliation for EC non-compliance in the *EC–Measures Concerning Meat and Meat Products (Hormones)* dispute, Edward W. Moreland, representative of the American Motorcyclist Association, wondered: 'Where's the beef in motorcycles?' See 'U.S. Agriculture Reps Urge Rotating Products on Beef Hormone Retaliation List', *International Trade Reporter*, 16:16 (1999), 662. Similarly, in the *EC–Bananas III* dispute, the United States initially targeted Italian manufacturers of a sheep's milk cheese called 'pecorino'. They similarly found it hard to comprehend the reason for being drawn into an intergovernmental trade dispute, reportedly asking: 'What do we have to do with bananas?' See 'Italian Cheese Gets Caught in Grinder of Banana Dispute', *Wall Street Journal*, 1 March 1999.

the responding member by producers owned or controlled by nationals of the retaliating member.[12]

The issue of fairness would arise in respect of all innocent private parties who are potential targets of a retaliatory measure. However, within this class of private parties, there usually are potential targets in respect of whom the concern about fairness would apply with even greater force and justification. They notably include those exporters and producers of the responding member who have little or no ability to form part of the solution (for example, due to lack of political weight or connections),[13] and those who would suffer disproportionate or irreversible harm.[14]

The foregoing highlights the importance of the design of a retaliatory measure. The design determines whether a retaliatory measure will be effective, and whether or not it will entail a significant cost for the economy of the retaliating member. The foregoing also suggests that, particularly (but not exclusively) in relation to the element of fairness, the nature and type of the domestic decision-making process used to prepare retaliatory measures matters a great deal.

In relation to the DSU the question thus presents itself whether existing DSU rules adequately deal with these two aspects of retaliation: that is, the design of retaliatory measures and the domestic process that leads to such a design. As far as the design of retaliatory measures is concerned, under current DSU rules, members are subject to relatively few multilateral disciplines.[15] In relation to the domestic process for designing retaliatory

[12] Apparently, certain French cafe owners in regions affected by US retaliatory measures in the *EC–Measures Concerning Meat and Meat Products (Hormones)* dispute decided to 'counter-retaliate' by pricing bottles of Coca-Cola at the equivalent of £50. Others replaced Coca-Cola by Pepsi-Cola because the latter was made in France under licence by a French company. See 'French take their revenge with £50 Coca-Cola', *Daily Telegraph*, 9 August 1999. Also, the town council of St. Pierre-de-Trivisy, a town in France, decided to levy a 100 per cent tax on bottles of Coca-Cola sold at the town campground and recreation centre for as long as the United States maintained its retaliatory tariff on Roquefort cheese. See 'A Roquefort David Strikes a Coke Goliath', *International Herald Tribune*, 23 August 1999.

[13] To illustrate, in the *EC–Bananas III* dispute, the United States decided to target, among many other private parties, a French exporter of bed-sheets and other linens. The press reported this exporter as saying that '[i]f I complain to the French government, nobody is going to care about it because we are too small'. See 'What Bananas? Tariff Fight Baffles Europe', *Washington Post*, 18 March 1999.

[14] For example, according to news agency reports, a (subsequently reversed) US decision to target Scottish cashmere sweaters might have caused the loss of 4,000 jobs in rural Scotland. See 'US groups want cashmere on EU retaliation list', *Reuters*, 10 July 2000.

[15] Articles 22.3, 4 and 5 of the DSU impose constraints, in terms of the circumstances under which cross-retaliation is permissible, equivalence of level of suspension and level of

measures, the current DSU contains no multilateral rules at all.[16] In other words, the DSU leaves the domestic process for designing such measures unregulated. Each member, therefore, proceeds in accordance with its own domestic legal procedures and requirements.

It is understandable that members wish to minimize any *substantive* constraints on their ability to design retaliatory measures as they see fit.[17] In contrast, the absence of multilateral rules governing the domestic decision-making *process* deserves rethinking now that the enforcement tool of retaliation has been repeatedly used. In view of this change in circumstances, there would appear to be a case for introducing appropriate rules in the DSU to regulate the domestic process for designing retaliatory measures. As will be explained further below, establishing such rules would not only serve the interests of retaliating members and members retaliated against, but also the systemic interests of all members.

Before commenting on possible new DSU rules, it is important to note that no suggestion is made here that introduction of such rules should have priority over agreeing on other possible improvements of, or alternatives to, WTO retaliation as we know it.[18] The suggested new DSU rules could complement other possible reforms. Equally, in the absence of other possible reforms, they could effect useful standalone reform.

How to regulate the domestic process and at what level

Turning now to the question of how possible new DSU rules could regulate the domestic process for designing retaliatory measures, the first point to be noted is that such rules could be added to the DSU only by a consensus decision.[19] Hence, any new DSU rules would need to be largely

nullification or impairment, and obligations not to be suspended (although it is not clear what they are). Importantly, however, Article 22.7 of the DSU makes clear that the selection of the tariff concessions or other obligations to be suspended is the prerogative of the complaining member and is not subject to question by the DSB or an Article 22.6 arbitrator, subject to Article 22.5 of the DSU which, as mentioned, refers to obligations that may not be suspended, though none are identified.

[16] The only requirement is to prepare a written request for authorization to retaliate.

[17] In fact, in the context of the ongoing DSU reform negotiations proposals have been tabled that would remove existing substantive constraints, for example, in relation to the conditions that must be met before recourse can be had to cross-retaliation. See, for example, WTO documents TN/DS/W/19 and TN/DS/W/47.

[18] A number of relevant proposals are being discussed by members in the framework of the DSU negotiations. They include collective retaliation, auctioning of retaliation rights, enhancing the role of trade compensation and mandatory financial compensation.

[19] Article X:8 of the WTO Agreement.

uncontroversial and easy for all members to implement. Arguably the best way to demonstrate that possible new DSU rules meet these conditions is to point to other WTO rules by which members have already agreed to abide and which correspond, in terms of their type and nature, to the suggested new DSU rules. In this regard, the SPS and TBT agreements as currently in force contain rules regulating the domestic process for designing SPS measures and technical regulations, respectively.[20] That is, they regulate the process to be followed in preparing and adopting such measures. The particular type of process that is prescribed in the SPS and TBT agreements is known in US administrative law as a 'notice-and-comment' decision-making procedure. For brevity and convenience, this contribution also uses that term.

Accordingly, for purposes of regulating the domestic process for designing retaliatory measures, members could draw inspiration from the SPS and TBT agreements. In other words, possible new DSU rules could, likewise, prescribe a domestic notice-and-comment decision-making procedure. More specifically, possible new DSU rules could require that as part of its domestic decision-making process a retaliating member conduct an administrative procedure under which (1) public notice would be given by the government of the retaliating member of any proposed retaliatory measure, (2) interested domestic and foreign private parties would have the right to submit to the government comments or information relevant to the proposed measure and (3) the government of the retaliating member would have to take any comments or information into account before adopting a final retaliatory measure to be submitted to the DSB for multilateral authorization.[21]

Alternatively, possible new DSU rules might require that the same three-step domestic notice-and-comment decision-making procedure be conducted *after* the DSB has granted authorization to retaliate, but *before* any specific retaliatory measure is imposed. The DSB would then need to grant its authorization on the basis of a request which describes only the basic parameters of a possible future retaliatory measure.[22]

[20] For example, Article 2.9 of the Agreement on Technical Barriers to Trade and Annex B.5 of the Agreement on Sanitary and Phytosanitary Measures.

[21] The Annex to this contribution contains a suggestion as to how Article 22 of the DSU could be amended so as to require the conduct of a domestic notice-and-comment decision-making procedure.

[22] Such a basic request would not provide information on the specific goods or services in relation to which concessions would be suspended. See, for example, WTO document WT/DS291/39 concerning the dispute *EC–Measures Affecting the Approval and Marketing of Biotech Products*.

Under this alternative, it would be necessary to create the possibility for a WTO arbitrator to examine, on request, a claim by a responding member that the retaliating member did not follow the prescribed procedure.[23] Furthermore, it would be necessary to provide that if (but only if) a WTO arbitrator determines that the procedure has not been followed correctly, imposition of a retaliatory measure is to be suspended until such time as the procedure has been properly conducted. In case a different retaliatory measure is adopted as a result of conducting the procedure, imposition of the old retaliatory measure would need to be discontinued for good.

A few points are worth highlighting in relation to the proposed three-step notice-and-comment decision-making procedure. First, not each and every domestic or foreign private party could legitimately claim to be an 'interested' party. Among the private parties with a fairly obvious interest in participating in the proposed procedure are foreign exporters or producers of a good targeted by a proposed retaliatory measure, or domestic importers or industrial users of the same targeted good, or, if the good is a consumer good, a representative domestic consumer organization.[24] Other private parties who could claim a legitimate interest would appear to include domestic exporters or producers of a good the sale of which is adversely affected by the underlying WTO-inconsistent measure of the responding member, and 'upstream' suppliers of such domestic exporters or producers. Thus, the most relevant interests, whether on the export or the import side, whether foreign or domestic, would be given an opportunity to provide relevant input.[25]

Second, regarding the obligation to 'take into account' any comments and/or information received, it should be noted that this constitutes an obligation of conduct, not of result. Thus, the government would not be required to modify a proposed measure in a particular way, or to modify it at all, merely because domestic or foreign private parties object to, or find fault with, it. The government would, however, be under a duty to consider in good faith, and with an open mind, any comments and information submitted and to make appropriate changes, provided that doing

[23] Such arbitration could be carried out by the arbitrator referred to in Article 22.6 of the DSU. Since an assessment of whether a straightforward three-step notice-and-comment procedure has been conducted does not seem to involve particularly complex analysis, it should be possible for such arbitration to be completed within a short period of time.

[24] Similar categories of interested private parties could be identified in cases where the underlying WTO-inconsistent measure and/or the retaliatory measure affect trade in services or the protection of intellectual property rights.

[25] This would help to avoid regulatory capture and possible biases resulting from imbalanced information gathering.

so would not conflict with other, overriding considerations, such as considerations of public policy.

Finally, under the suggested procedure, the government would not be required to prepare a public report supporting its ultimate decision. In that sense, the suggested notice-and-comment procedure would be an informal decision-making procedure.[26] Nor would a requirement to conduct a notice-and-comment procedure preclude governments from imposing reasonable limits on interested private parties, for example, by setting deadlines for the submission of comments or information, or by imposing page limits and/or language requirements.

It would seem from the above that the suggested domestic notice-and-comment procedure would be easy to implement and would not be overly burdensome. The bigger question, of course, is whether the mandatory use of such a procedure could be reasonably expected to produce benefits which justify any associated administrative burdens. The answer, it is submitted, is in the affirmative.

Two substantial benefits can be readily identified. To begin with, it is important to bear in mind that designing a retaliatory measure is a process fraught with uncertainties. By nature, this process involves predicting the likely impact of, or response to, a particular retaliatory measure in a foreign country. Access to information in sufficient quantity and of sufficient quality is, accordingly, a critically important factor. Typically, retaliatory measures are designed by government officials. As such, they do not inherently have ready access to relevant information about foreign private parties (companies) who might be targeted. Relevant information would include information about these private parties' ability to avoid the impact of a retaliatory measure; the risk that a retaliatory measure would inadvertently cause damage to nationals of the retaliating member (for example, in cases where companies of the retaliating member depend on supplies by a targeted foreign company, or where a targeted foreign company is supplied to a significant extent by a company of the retaliating member); and the political weight and influence of potentially targeted parties. While some of this information may, in principle, be obtainable, there would normally be a significant search cost associated with any attempt to obtain it.

A notice-and-comment decision-making procedure would help governments to avoid, or limit, the search cost associated with information

[26] In US administrative law, notice-and-comment rule making is also referred to as 'informal' rule making.

gathering. Indeed, a government soliciting comments and information about a proposed retaliatory measure would not receive such information cost-free from the interested private parties submitting them. Moreover, it is arguable that, by conducting a notice-and-comment procedure, governments could obtain more and better information due to the underlying incentive structure. To explain, a foreign private party singled out for retaliation has an incentive to supply the government of the retaliating member with information that is relevant to deciding whether it should remain on a target list. More particularly, it is in a potential target's interests to indicate to the government, for example, what action it could take to avoid the effect of the proposed retaliatory measure; whether it is an important supplier of companies in the retaliating member and whether it has sufficient political influence to contribute to corrective action by the member retaliated against. Similarly, domestic private parties interested in tough retaliatory measures have an incentive to pass on to their government information to which they have access and which would assist the government in maximizing the effectiveness of a retaliatory measure. Last, but not least, domestic private parties whose interests would be adversely affected by a proposed retaliatory measure have an incentive to inform their government about some of the cost likely to be associated with the proposed measure. In so doing, they would assist the government in minimizing the cost of a retaliatory measure. Thus, the conduct of a notice-and-comment decision-making procedure may be expected to enhance the soundness of whatever retaliatory measures governments adopt.[27]

The other benefit of conducting a notice-and-comment procedure is no less important. By conducting a notice-and-comment decision-making procedure, a retaliating member would go a long way toward ensuring that any retaliatory measures it adopts are the outcome of a fair domestic process. It has to do with the fairness of the domestic decision-making procedure. Under such a procedure, government decision makers

[27] It may be the case that certain interested parties, by virtue of being 'interested', might be tempted to overstate the impact of a proposed retaliatory measure. However, in anticipation of this, a government could ask that any assertions of adverse impact should be duly substantiated. Moreover, this would not be a problem that is specific to the design of retaliatory measures. Rather, this problem arises in relation to many measures that a government proposes to adopt. Also, even though it is true that governments might need appropriately to 'discount' the value of certain assertions by interested private parties there is little doubt that through the conduct of a notice-and-comment procedure governments would get access to information that they could not otherwise have obtained or would have had to obtain at high cost.

would need to accept representations from any and all interested parties, including from those with adverse interests (that is, domestic exporters as well as domestic importers, domestic interests as well as foreign interests, etc.).[28] In addition, interested parties would have equal access to government decision makers, irrespective of their political weight or connections. Also, the conduct of a notice-and-comment procedure would ensure that targeted foreign private parties have a fair opportunity to present their case to, and plead with, government decision makers to remove them from their target list, for example, on account of the likely disproportionate or irreparable harm that they would suffer.

The significance of this should not be underestimated.[29] As pointed out earlier, the targeted foreign private parties are often 'innocent bystanders'. They are not caught up in the crossfire merely by accident, however. Rather, their economic interests are intentionally harmed by the retaliating member who targets them. Furthermore, there is asymmetry in bargaining power as between the retaliating member and the targeted foreign private parties. The latter find themselves in a vulnerable position not just because, like most private parties, they may have limited resources to defend their interests, but also because they lack the right to vote in political elections in the retaliating member.[30] As there thus is no significant 'check' on the government of the retaliating member, there is an inherent risk that a retaliatory measure is adopted which would cause excessive harm to the economic interests of a foreign private party. Given all of this, it would seem that, as a matter of basic procedural fairness, targeted foreign private parties ought to be given an opportunity to seek to persuade the retaliating member to refrain from targeting them.

The fact that, as argued above, members could expect to derive substantial benefits from the conduct of a domestic notice-and-comment decision-making procedure does not necessarily support the view that it would be appropriate to prescribe at the multilateral level, through an amendment to the DSU, that members conduct such a procedure. In fact, the DSU as it currently stands does not preclude members from regulating

[28] Again, as noted, this would not preclude the imposition of reasonable limits necessary to maintain efficiency of administration.

[29] Indeed, one need only put oneself in the shoes of a potential target to realize that an opportunity to present one's case is invariably welcomed, and in fact expected, by a targeted private party.

[30] Herein lies an important difference between foreign and domestic private parties whose economic interests would be harmed by a proposed retaliatory measure. The former appear to have an even stronger case for seeking a right to participate in the domestic decision-making process.

the domestic process for designing retaliatory measures as they deem fit. Accordingly, the current DSU does not prevent members from using a domestic notice-and-comment decision-making procedure at the domestic level, through provisions of domestic law. Moreover, as explained, the use of such a procedure would make for better informed government decision makers and, thereby, for better designed retaliatory measures. It is arguable, therefore, that members would have an incentive to use this type of procedure.[31]

Nonetheless, there would appear to be good reasons for requiring at the multilateral level that retaliating members conduct a domestic notice-and-comment decision-making procedure. It is one thing to say that, in principle, there exists an incentive for potential retaliating members to use such a procedure at the domestic level. It is another for members actually to do so. Legislative action is associated with high transaction costs, and so a WTO requirement to provide for the procedure in question would undoubtedly contribute to ensuring that the procedure would be in place when it is needed: that is, when the member concerned decides to resort to retaliation. Also, a WTO requirement is the only means by which a member can secure for its private parties opportunities for direct interest representation in a retaliating member in case they are targeted by a proposed retaliatory measure. Finally, there would appear to be little reason for justifiable concern about a lock-in effect resulting from regulation at the multilateral level. As noted previously, the SPS and TBT agreements already impose on members an obligation to conduct domestic notice-and-comment procedures. Furthermore, as also explained, the main obligation imposed would be an obligation of conduct, and so no particular substantive outcomes would be predetermined.

The foregoing considerations suggest that both retaliating members and members who are retaliated against – and this group would potentially seem to include most members – would have an interest in the WTO regulating the domestic process for designing retaliatory measures. The former are looking to enhance the soundness of their retaliatory measures; the latter are looking to assure the fairness of the domestic process in the retaliating member. But even if the view were taken that the foregoing considerations provide insufficient grounds for regulating the domestic

[31] It is not apparent that the same incentive would be created by the prospect of achieving the second benefit of such a procedure – ensuring procedural fairness. However, if a member introduced a notice-and-comment procedure in order to achieve the first benefit, it would automatically realize the second benefit, since both are inherent in the procedure.

process for designing retaliatory measures at WTO level, there are other interests of a systemic nature that would seem to support such regulation. In other words, there is an argument to be made that the domestic process for designing retaliatory measures would still be a legitimate concern for the WTO. Indeed, even members who do not expect ever to be retaliating members, or members retaliated against, would appear to have a systemic interest in the creation of new DSU rules.

To see why, it needs to be remembered that such members, like all members, are represented in the DSB which, subject to relevant requirements being satisfied, is mandated to authorize retaliatory measures at the request of a retaliating member. When the DSB authorizes a retaliatory measure, it effectively grants a licence to the retaliating member to discriminate against the responding member and, thus, to depart from the fundamental WTO principle of most-favoured-nation treatment. Moreover, since a retaliating member ordinarily targets private parties of the responding member, the DSB in authorizing a retaliatory measure in effect also grants the retaliating member a licence to harm the commercial interests of private parties of the responding member, who often have nothing to do with the underlying dispute. It is important to recall in this connection that, subject to two limited exceptions,[32] the DSB cannot review the nature of the concessions or other obligations to be suspended by a retaliating member.

Under these circumstances, it seems somewhat odd, from a systemic perspective, that under current DSU rules the DSB in effect grants authorization to discriminate and to inflict harm on private economic interests without requiring as a precondition that retaliatory measures for which DSB authorization is sought should be the outcome of a domestic decision-making process which is fair and conducive to sound choices. After all, the DSB is the WTO body charged with preserving the integrity of the rule-based multilateral trading system, as well as the security and predictability of that system. From a systemic point of view, intentional discrimination and intentional imposition of harm on private parties are highly anomalous actions, even if it is true that they do not breach any WTO rules when they are resorted to for purposes of WTO retaliation. Now that the DSB has been called on to actually grant authorization of the aforesaid

[32] Articles 22.5 and 22.3 of the DSU confer on the DSB, or a WTO arbitrator, a limited right of review. The former article provides that the DSB may not authorize the suspension of concessions or other obligations if a covered WTO agreement prohibits their suspension. The latter article provides that members may cross-retaliate only if certain conditions are present.

type, it seems legitimate to ask whether it would not be desirable for the DSB to begin to assert greater control and impose procedural conditions on the grant of a relevant 'licence'. As suggested in this chapter, one way of conditioning a DSB authorization appropriately would be to require a retaliating member to conduct a domestic notice-and-comment procedure prior to adopting a retaliatory measure and submitting it to the DSB for authorization. This would provide at least some assurance to the DSB that any retaliatory measure it authorizes is the result of a domestic process which promotes sound outcomes and guarantees a minimum of procedural fairness.

There is a further reason why all members may be said to have a systemic interest in the creation of new DSU rules regulating the domestic process for designing retaliatory measures, and more specifically in prescribing the conduct of a domestic notice-and-comment decision-making procedure. By guaranteeing rights of participation for interested domestic and foreign private parties, retaliating members would not only enhance their ability to design retaliatory measures which are effective and/or entail a lower cost for their economy, but they would also demonstrate that they take the legitimate expectations and concerns of interested private parties very seriously.[33] Over and above promoting good governance and administration, this would no doubt contribute a great deal to maintaining the support of interested private parties for the WTO dispute settlement mechanism and, indirectly, the multilateral trading system and further multilateral trade liberalization, which are common concerns of all members.

Conclusion

The scant treatment the current DSU gives to procedural aspects of retaliation is inconsequential as long as retaliation is a largely theoretical worst-case scenario. It seems inadequate, however, in today's world where retaliation is, and looks set to remain, a recurrent practice of members. This chapter suggests that it would, therefore, be desirable for the WTO

[33] By providing such rights of participation to interested private parties, governments would effectively enter into a compact with the private sector under which they would provide assurances to the latter that they will impose retaliatory measures, which invariably interfere with private business decisions concerning marketing, sourcing or investment, only until after having consulted with interested segments of the private sector. In other words, governments would introduce into the contentious retaliation stage of WTO dispute settlement a significant element of confidence-building and private–public partnership.

to regulate the domestic process for designing retaliatory measures. As argued above, this would not only serve the interests of retaliating members and members retaliated against, but also the systemic interests of all members. Moreover, the suggestion put forward in this chapter would essentially do nothing more than extend to the DSU, and more particularly to WTO retaliation, a concept of good governance and administration that members have already codified, and agreed to abide by, in other WTO agreements. Therefore, regulating the domestic process for designing retaliatory measures would be a small step for members to take. But it would be one which would allow members to reach a significant milestone in terms of enhancing the soundness and fairness of WTO retaliation.

ANNEX

Possible amendments to Article 22 of the DSU (providing for a new requirement that a domestic notice-and-comment decision-making procedure precede the submission to the DSB of a request for authorization to retaliate):[34]

22.3 In considering what concessions or other obligations to suspend, the complaining party shall apply the following principles and procedures:

(a) the general principle is that the complaining party should first seek to suspend concessions or other obligations with respect to the same sector(s) as that in which the panel or Appellate Body has found a violation or other nullification or impairment;
(b) if that party considers that it is not practicable or effective to suspend concessions or other obligations with respect to the same sector(s), it may seek to suspend concessions or other obligations in other sectors under the same agreement;
(c) if that party considers that it is not practicable or effective to suspend concessions or other obligations with respect to other sectors under the same agreement, and that the circumstances are serious enough, it may seek to suspend concessions or other obligations under another covered agreement;
(d) in applying the above principles, that party shall take into account:

[34] The suggested amendments are in italic type and are taken from Malacrida, 'Towards Sounder and Fairer WTO Retaliation', 39–40.

(i) the trade in the sector or under the agreement under which the panel or Appellate Body has found a violation or other nullification or impairment, and the importance of such trade to that party;
(ii) the broader economic elements related to the nullification or impairment and the broader economic consequences of the suspension of concessions or other obligations;

(d*bis*) *irrespective of whether that party decides to request authorization from the DSB to suspend concessions or other obligations pursuant to subparagraphs (a), (b) or (c), it shall:*
(i) *prepare a notice which identifies the concessions or other obligations it may wish to request to suspend in such a manner as to enable interested parties to become acquainted with the goods, services, and/or holders of intellectual property rights which may be covered by the request;*
(ii) *publish the notice at an early appropriate stage, in a manner that ensures that it can still take into account comments and information provided by interested parties, but at the same time avoids as much as possible any adverse effects on trade arising from the publication of the notice; [and notify the government of the responding party of the notice without delay;]*
(iii) *allow reasonable time for interested parties to provide comments and information in writing;*
(iv) *take into account any comments and information provided in writing by interested parties; and*
(v) *indicate in its request how the procedures set out in subparagraph (d*bis*) have been followed. The request forwarded to the DSB shall also identify the concessions or other obligations the suspension of which the complaining party requests the DSB to authorize, wherever possible in a manner that enables Members and interested parties to become acquainted with the goods, services, and/or holders of intellectual property rights which are covered by the request.*[13bis]

...

[13]*bis When an arbitrator acting pursuant to paragraph 6 determines that principles or procedures set forth in paragraph 3 have not been followed and the complaining party seeks to comply with the arbitrator's decision by submitting a new or amended request which may cover goods, services, and/or intellectual property rights, or holders of intellectual property rights, not already covered by the original request forwarded to the DSB, the complaining party shall re-apply the procedures set forth in paragraph 3(d*bis*) before submitting the new or amended request to the DSB. However, that party may limit the scope of these procedures to any new concessions or other obligations which it may wish to suspend or any new goods, services and/or intellectual property rights which may be covered by the new or amended request.*

(h) *for purposes of this paragraph, 'interested party' means:*

(i) *a foreign exporter or producer of a good, a foreign supplier of a service, or a foreign holder of an intellectual property right, where such good, service or intellectual property right is, or is proposed to be, covered by a request pursuant to paragraph 3(a), (b) or (c);*

(ii) *a domestic importer of a good, a domestic industrial user of such good, or, where such good is commonly sold at the retail level, a representative domestic consumer organization, where such good is, or is proposed to be, covered by a request pursuant to paragraph 3(a), (b) or (c); or natural or juridical persons of the complaining party consuming a service in the territory of the complaining party or the territory of the Member that must implement recommendations or rulings, or authorized domestic users of a relevant intellectual property right, where such service or intellectual property right is, or is proposed to be, covered by a request pursuant to paragraph 3(a), (b) or (c); and*

(iii) *a domestic exporter or producer of a good, a domestic supplier of a service, or a domestic holder of an intellectual property right, where the exporter or producer of such good, the supplier of such service, or the holder of such intellectual property right is adversely affected by the violation or other nullification or impairment found by the panel or Appellate Body.*[14bis]

This list shall not preclude the complaining party from allowing domestic or foreign parties other than those mentioned above to be included as interested parties.

...

6. When the situation described in paragraph 2 occurs, the DSB, upon request, shall grant authorization to suspend concessions or other obligations within 30 days of the expiry of the reasonable period of time unless the DSB decides by consensus to reject the request. However, if the Member concerned objects to the level of suspension proposed, or claims that the principles and procedures set forth in paragraph 3 have not been followed *[where a complaining party has requested authorization to suspend concessions or other obligations pursuant to paragraph*

[14bis] *Sub-paragraph (h)(iv) is not intended to preclude the complaining party from considering, or to require that party to consider, as adversely affected by the violation or other nullification or impairment found by the panel or Appellate Body, e.g., a domestic industrial supplier of a directly affected exporter, producer or supplier of a good or service.*

3[(a),] (b) or (c)], the matter shall be referred to arbitration. Such arbitration shall be carried out by the original panel, if members are available, or by an arbitrator appointed by the Director-General and shall be completed within 60 days after the date of expiry of the reasonable period of time. Concessions or other obligations shall not be suspended during the course of the arbitration.

19

The WTO Secretariat and the role of economics in panels and arbitrations

CHAD P. BOWN*

1 Introduction

The process of resolving disputes under the WTO's Dispute Settlement Understanding (DSU) involves a complex and evolving legal jurisprudence. One foundational element to the WTO legal contract is that WTO adjudicators – that is, panellists and arbitrators – issue formal rulings that might result in changes to members' *economic* policies. This tight link between WTO dispute settlement and changes to members' economic policy makes it important to understand, evaluate, and continually refine how *economic analysis* is used to influence the legal–judicial process that is a critical element of the WTO's institutional performance.

Consider two representative examples of DSU panellists' and arbitrators' direct influence on members' *economic* policies. One is the *US–Steel Safeguards* dispute in which the prospect (or realization) of a DSU arbitration and authorized retaliation induced the respondent country to comply with WTO obligations by *reforming* a policy that adversely affected another member's expected market access benefits. In this dispute, the United States responded to the threat of DSU arbitration by eliminating

* Department of Economics and International Business School, MS021, Brandeis University, Waltham, MA 02454-9110, USA. The author wrote this chapter while he was the visiting scholar in the Economic Research and Statistics Division at the WTO Secretariat. However, he was not formally involved in any of the WTO dispute settlement activity described in this chapter, and thus any views expressed are based on research alone and should not be attributed to the WTO, its members, or any of its legal or economic staff. Henrik Horn, Petros Mavroidis, Meredith Crowley, Rachel McCulloch, Reto Malacrida, Joost Pauwelyn, Morris Morkre, Niall Meagher, Scott Andersen, Todd Friedbacher, Tom Prusa, and participants at the Trade Sanctions in WTO Dispute Settlement conference at the Graduate Institute provided helpful comments. Chad Bown also thanks Marc Bacchetta, Marion Jansen, Alex Keck, Roberta Piermartini, Michele Ruta, and Robert Teh for useful background discussions. The German Marshall Fund of the United States provided generous financial support of this project.

a WTO-inconsistent safeguard and thus decreasing the US import tariff.[1] A second example is the *EC–Beef Hormones* case; even though the dispute settlement process failed to change the respondent's economic policy and induce compliance, WTO arbitrators established a level of permissible retaliation that authorized the adversely affected complainant to change *its* economic policy. In this case, the complainant policy change was an increase in the US import tariff. And while these two disputes are examples of induced changes in national trade policies, almost every dispute involves a contested government measure affecting markets or economic incentives, and thus affects some element of a nation's economic policy.[2]

When the WTO members wrote the DSU, what role did they anticipate economic analysis would play in resolving future disputes which would result in such changes to members' national economic policies? Interestingly, Article 27.1 of the DSU leaves to the WTO Secretariat the crucial decision of how to implement the provision of legal and "technical" support in DSU panels and arbitrations.[3] To my knowledge, there has been little previous analysis of Secretariat provision of the technical *economic* support that is the subject of this chapter.[4]

1 This particular dispute never reached the stage of arbitration, as the United States complied with the ruling earlier. Nevertheless, one contributing factor to the US late 2003 compliance decision was the EC's effectiveness at creating a politically sensitive list of goods produced and exported from US "swing states" expected to be contested in the upcoming 2004 presidential election, for example, oranges and other citrus products from Florida, etc. An early draft of the products on the eventual EC target list can be found in European Commission (2002). Nordström (Chapter 10, above) presents an alternative perspective of issues surrounding the drafting of the retaliation list in this particular dispute.

2 While the DSU relevance of a contested policy typically concerns an actual or potential effect on market access protected by WTO obligations, the policy changes resulting from DSU decisions may involve an explicit trade policy (for example, tariff, quota, or other non-tariff measure), or some other policy affecting economic activity (for example, taxes, environmental regulation, health, or consumer protection). Examples of DSU-permissible changes in economic policy available to the complainant include withdrawing WTO commitments under GATT, TRIPs, GATS, or another covered agreement.

3 DSU, Article 27.1 states "The Secretariat shall have the responsibility of assisting panels, especially on the legal, historical and procedural aspects of the matters dealt with, and of providing secretarial and technical support."

4 While the WTO Secretariat provides legal assistance primarily via the Legal Affairs and Rules Divisions, and these divisions' potential influence over panel and arbitration decisions are also important subjects of investigation, we do not examine them here. We also do not examine the separate issue of the Appellate Body access to formal economic "expertise," nor do we focus on questions regarding the procedural separation of panel versus Appellate Body decisions. Nevertheless, many of the arguments of this chapter would support the independent Appellate Body Secretariat having its own chief economist on staff as well.

My goal is to analyze how economists and – more importantly – *economic analysis* interact with panels, arbitrators, and WTO Secretariat legal support staff in the DSU adjudication process. The WTO is a set of voluntary, self-enforcing agreements among member states that requires their ongoing participation and commitment. Thus, understanding and improving the way economic analysis is used throughout all areas of the organization, including dispute settlement, can enhance the functioning of the institution, its long-term viability, and the trust that its members place in it.[5] Furthermore, when member litigants make arguments that are more economically advanced and submit evidence based on models and data that are more economically complex, they provide the Secretariat with a clear mandate to improve the economic sophistication of DSU adjudicators.[6]

That the members delegated to the WTO Secretariat the responsibility to provide technical economic support to DSU panels and arbitrations raises a number of broad questions that are taken up in this chapter. We begin our analysis with a normative question: How *should* the Secretariat provide this technical economic support? Rather than attempting a complete answer, we identify trade-offs that the Secretariat confronts when adopting one approach instead of another. As a second step, we turn to a positive question: how *does* the Secretariat currently provide this technical economic support?

As a third step we examine the experiences of institutions such as central banks, competition authorities, and national trade remedy investigating agencies that have allowed economic analysis to influence the ways in which they affect policy. Such institutions are useful comparators not only out of recognition that high-level economic analysis is an important input into the determinants of their long-run performance, but also because, like the DSU, such institutions operate in challenging political environments. The wide variation in experience across such institutions allows us to draw important lessons for the DSU – especially regarding

5 For a discussion of the basic underlying economic theory and principles motivating the need for the WTO as an institution, its rules, and its dispute settlement procedures, see Bagwell and Staiger (2002).

6 The Appellate Body has itself called for panels to improve along this dimension. For example, see the Appellate Body, Article 21.5 report in the *US–Upland Cotton* dispute, in which the Appellate Body states (para. 357) "[M]odelling exercises are likely to be an important analytical tool that a panel should scrutinize. The relative complexity of a model and its parameters is not a reason for a panel to remain agnostic about them. Like other categories of evidence, a panel should reach conclusions with respect to the probative value it accords to economic simulations or models presented to it."

transparency, political independence, and the quality and longevity of the role of economic analysis within the institution's operations.

Fourth, we identify areas of concern with the Secretariat's current provision of technical economic support to the DSU process. While we do not attempt a formal theoretical or empirical assessment of whether the Secretariat's current approach is achieving either its own or the members' objectives, we do identify potential areas of concern – at the institutional and individual (staff) levels – to motivate reform proposals.[7] At the institutional level, we find that WTO operations would benefit from more analysis from Ph.D.-level economists. We also consider where within the Secretariat Ph.D. economists should be housed and what specialities are needed. Second, at the level of individuals, the WTO system is evolving to one in which professional staff need a clear and sophisticated understanding of both law *and* economics. We therefore discuss the hurdles facing individual Secretariat staff members who need to become effective WTO specialists – either as economists or lawyers – as they likely require substantial cross-disciplinary competency that is scarce in the external labour market.

While we argue for the injection of more economic analysis into WTO Secretariat support of the DSU, we identify limits to the role of economics and the need for increased economic analysis to be integrated with (and not supplied at the expense of) the legal and diplomatic/political elements of the DSU. Thus, we describe the costs of introducing more economic analysis into the process, and we highlight specific qualifications of the economists that the WTO Secretariat needs. We therefore also identify the sort of economists that the Secretariat might avoid, as flawed economic analysis could lead to an institutional outcome that is worse than the *status quo*. Nevertheless, we conclude that major problems facing the WTO include the small number of economists housed in the Secretariat – that is, a staff of eight for most of the last decade – with even the minimum academic qualifications necessary to provide technical economic support, the lack of diversity to their fields of specialization, and the ad hoc manner in which they have been integrated into the DSU adjudication process thus far.

This chapter also contributes to a broader literature on the appropriate design of DSU adjudication within the WTO system. For example, Weiler

[7] Divergences between the objective functions of the Secretariat and its members may occur if, for example, the Secretariat has a shorter time horizon (discount factor) than do the members etc. Elsig (2008) considers the interplay between the Secretariat and its members from the perspective of principal–agent theory.

(2001), Janow (2004), Shaffer (2005), and Nordström (2005) provide discussions of the broader Secretariat role in support of dispute settlement and raise other fundamental questions not specifically addressed here.[8] It is taken as given the current ways panels/arbitrators are chosen and the Secretariat provides legal support to these adjudicators in order to examine questions involving the appropriate provision of technical economic support to the DSU adjudication process. Nevertheless, the key insights of this chapter would also apply to proposals for more fundamental reform of the DSU. Whether under the current or a reformed institutional framework for the DSU, the WTO needs to improve the role of economic analysis in DSU adjudication.

Before turning to the substance of the chapter, we provide two additional motives for improving the technical economic support used in the DSU process. The first is simply recognition that *how* the WTO's dispute settlement process affects members' national economic policy will become an increasingly important determinant of the institution's overall relevance and success.[9] With its role as a traditional "negotiating forum" for trade liberalization diminishing, the WTO's performance will be judged increasingly by its ability to adjudicate disputes that are politically contentious and economically complex, involve extensive claims and evidence, and are argued by the most sophisticated legal–economic teams that the members can provide. The Secretariat faces the challenge of gaining the trust of its members by meeting their expanded needs for adjudicating capacity.

The final reason to focus attention on how economic analysis is used in the DSU process is the recent call for the entire WTO to treat economics more seriously. For example, the proposals of the Sutherland Report (Sutherland *et al.*, 2004, 77) complement much of the analysis we present here: "[t]he membership should also encourage and stimulate a greater intellectual output from the Secretariat … We see no reason

[8] For example, we do not examine the process by which the parties and the Secretariat choose the three panellists in a dispute, the implications of any particular method of doing so, the influence of the Secretariat legal support team in panellist or arbitrator decisions, or whether the WTO should move to a system of a permanent roster of panellists.

[9] A certain sticking point for the Doha Round of negotiations is that, especially for many developed countries, there is little potential new market access in goods (relative to historical Rounds) "left" to negotiate over. Still, what is left to negotiate over may disproportionately affect the trade of developing countries and, thus, be important from an equity perspective. This is, however, a separate issue. Furthermore, more liberalization negotiations are taking place outside the WTO framework through preferential trade agreements.

why the status and recognition accorded to the WTO's chief economist should be any less marked than that given to his or her opposite numbers in other economic institutions – at least with respect to trade issues." Indeed, a number of the topics we identify below suggest not only an expanded and enhanced role for the WTO's chief economist, but also that the WTO Secretariat will likely require a substantially larger, more flexible, and more diversely trained economic staff than the members traditionally demanded exist.

2 The roles for economic analysis in DSU adjudication

Before describing the various potential roles for economic analysis and economists in the WTO's dispute resolution process, we explore in more detail why economic analysis is increasingly relevant and necessary. First, we describe ways in which DSU rulings, in theory, affect members' economic policy. We then appeal to research showing that WTO decisions and DSU-induced policy changes affect markets and economic incentives not only in theory but also in practice.

After concluding that there is an important role for economic analysis in WTO dispute settlement, in subsections 2.2 through 2.4 we describe the range of possible uses for economic analysis in the actual DSU process. Through this approach we identify the implicit trade-offs at the heart of the normative question of how *should* the Secretariat use economic analysis in DSU adjudication.

2.1 Theoretical and empirical arguments that the DSU process affects economic markets

While the DSU process is by definition a legal proceeding, it differs from most other legal proceedings because the purpose of many disputes is to affect some member government's implemented as well as projected *economic* policy. When a DSU decision finds one member's policy to be in violation of its WTO obligations, WTO panellists and arbitrators issue rulings that promote change to one of the nation's economic policies. For example, the panel may request that a respondent member replace its WTO-inconsistent policy with one that is WTO-consistent. Likewise, a respondent's failure to comply with requests of a panel could lead to an Article 22.6 arbitration in which WTO arbitrators authorize the complainant country to change its trade policy and retaliate.

Therefore, DSU rulings, such as those that led to changes in US tariff policy, affect members' economic policy in much the same way that policy makers at central banks determine the supply of a country's money, finance ministers contribute to fiscal policy decision making, or antitrust authorities affect conditions of market competition. From this perspective, just as it is desirable for economic expertise to be an important input into the determination of monetary, fiscal, or competition policy, economic expertise has a useful role in informing the DSU panel and arbitration process.

The above argument is that DSU rulings affect economic policy in theory. Is there evidence to suggest that these effects are "economically important" – that is, sizable – empirically?[10] If the analogy to central banks and the theory that DSU decisions affect economic policy and economic activity is not sufficiently convincing, an alternative way to highlight the economic importance of DSU rulings is to present the results of economic research and empirical evidence that DSU activity moves markets.

There is extensive research documenting how changes in trade policies, including those directly influenced by WTO decisions, affect trade flows and hence underlying economic activity in importing and exporting countries.[11] Nevertheless, and perhaps more in line with the central bank analogy, there is even evidence from papers such as Desai and Hines (2008) and Liebman and Tomlin (2008) that WTO DSU "announcements" (and member announcement of DSU-related actions) can similarly move *financial* markets via changes in stock prices, in much the same way as announcements made by policy makers at central banks.[12]

[10] If there is little evidence that DSU rulings have substantial effects on trade flows or other economic activity, then increasing the resource costs of the process by injecting more economic analysis/economists to get the economic reasoning or rulings "right" may not be an efficient use of resources.

[11] For example, Bown (2004a,2004b) examines the determinants of the changes in trade flows in GATT/WTO trade disputes from the respondent exporting and third-party exporting country perspectives, respectively. The research establishing that trade policy changes affect trade flows is too vast to summarize here, though we do note the interesting new approach of Brambilla, Porto, and Tarozzi (2008) that finds evidence of a link between foreign trade policies and micro-level activity in a developing country by studying the impact of US antidumping measures on Vietnamese catfish-producing households.

[12] Desai and Hines (2008) study the impact of government announcements in the *US–Foreign Sales Corporation (FSC)* case and Liebman and Tomlin (2008) study the *US –Steel Safeguards* case.

A final argument in favour of a more substantive role for economic analysis in the DSU process could be based on evidence that panels, the Appellate Body, or arbitrators either made economic "mistakes" in their decisions or provided decisions that were flawed in their economic reasoning or analysis. Are there examples of actual cases in which one of these three DSU actors could have gained potential insights from economic analysis? While we do not point to any particular dispute here, there is an evolving body of research to suggest that mistakes or flawed decisions have been made. For example, teams of legal and economic scholars organized by the American Law Institute (ALI) (for example, Horn and Mavroidis, 2004, 2005, 2006a) analyze the stock of evolving case law deriving from WTO Appellate Body decisions and unappealed Panel Reports, and such interdisciplinary research identifies many such shortcomings, including some of a fundamental economic nature, across a wide variety of disputes.

When we combine the theory with evidence that panellists and arbitrators make rulings under DSU auspices that affect economic policy choices and economic outcomes, it may appear obvious to most economists that this legal process is about more than "just" the law. But this is not necessarily the accepted view of those involved either in the DSU process, the WTO Secretariat, or the members themselves. In the next three sections we adopt the perspective that economic analysis has an important role to play in the DSU's adjudication process, and from this viewpoint we present a range of possibilities as to how the services of professional economists might be best used in the increasingly legalized DSU process in practice.

2.2 *One extreme: economists only as experts in interpreting evidence*

We begin by identifying and discussing the most obvious (albeit limited) role for introducing economists in the DSU process, where economics is treated merely as evidentiary input.[13] For example, in certain disputes the parties introduce "evidence" from economic studies or data on market

[13] Even more extreme, it is possible to imagine a scenario in which professional economists are not even utilized in this role, or if the WTO actually discouraged the provision and assessment of economic evidence – a scenario not out of the realm of political possibility given historical experiences of related institutional settings in which the use of economic analysis has waxed and waned for political reasons. However, a legal process that did not rely on serious economic evidence or seriously interpreting economic evidence would likely be so different from the current setting that it would not be grounded in law. In such a case, the system might be better suited to a more informal and diplomatic dispute

conditions. The evidence might address questions such as whether two goods (one imported and one domestically produced) are sufficiently similar products ("like products") to compete head-to-head; whether dumped or increasing imports are a likely determinant of injury to a domestic industry; or whether subsidized exports lead to "serious prejudice" or price suppression in foreign markets.

The legal parties that submit such evidence typically use the services of a Ph.D.-level economist to interpret data and construct economic models so as to reveal an empirically-based "story" in support of their legal arguments.[14] The creation of convincing evidence requires a professional economist who is adept at economic theory and can construct a mathematical model of the relevant market and adapt it to provide a rough approximation to the relevant market while remaining relatively simple to analyze and interpret. The party's economist typically collects and processes data and then uses complex computer software packages so as to undertake statistical, econometric, computable general equilibrium (CGE) or partial equilibrium modeling. The economist must also be able to interpret the output of the model – its econometric estimates or simulated predictions – and translate it into less technical language for use by lawyers litigating their case. Examples of such evidence abound, especially in DSU litigation such as *Japan–Alcoholic Beverages II*, *Korea–Alcoholic Beverages*, and *Chile–Alcoholic Beverages* as well as the recent *US–Upland Cotton* dispute.[15]

Given the ways in which economic evidence is typically used by parties in DSU proceedings, what would an economist "on the inside" of the adjudicating process contribute? The first and most obvious role

resolution process, perhaps one akin to the "Working Party" norm for dispute resolution of the early GATT era. For a discussion of dispute settlement in this era, see Jackson (1969), Dam (1970), and Hudec (1975).

[14] Critics of the DSU process, including the author, have identified litigation costs (which would include hiring economic experts) and the insufficient legal capacity of developing countries as significant hurdles that prevent them from more effectively using and participating in the WTO system. Nevertheless, among poor country litigants that rely on the subsidized legal assistance provided by the capable, Geneva-based, Advisory Centre on WTO Law (ACWL), even such countries are able to tap into economic expertise for their DSU needs via the ACWL's "Technical Expertise Trust Fund" (ACWL, 2008). I thank Hunter Nottage for making this point.

[15] A substantial effort to document how such evidence has been used in WTO panels and arbitrations is provided in WTO (2005) as well as Keck (2004), so we will not further delve into the topic here. See also Sapir and Trachtman (2008) for a discussion of *US–Upland Cotton*. Bown and Ruta (Chapter 6, above) also discuss how this evidence and construction in arbitrations can be more broadly reconciled with insights from economic theory.

for an economist is to help the other adjudicators (panellists/arbitrators and Secretariat-provided legal support staff) interpret or weigh the relative merits of economic evidence the opposing parties provide. For example, a Ph.D.-level economist has had the graduate training to assess the plausibility of the evidence or methodology from the perspective of accepted practice in economic science.[16] Was the evidence generated using sound statistical techniques? Are the results robust to slight changes in the testing environment, for example, slight modifications in assumptions of the model or the time period covered by the data? The economist could also suggest clarifying questions that panellists and/or arbitrators can take back to the parties to further identify the sensitivity of their results. In the next section, we argue that this is not the only useful role that an economist might provide as an insider in the adjudication process.

2.3 *The other extreme: economists as equal collaboration partners in the DSU adjudication process*

Are there other ways, beyond expertise in interpreting economic evidence, in which an economist might contribute as an active participant in the DSU adjudication process? Here we identify a number of arguments that economists are not only useful to conduct scientific studies and to thus create (and interpret) evidence relevant to a proceeding, but also provide a "way of thinking" particularly suited to efficiently processing and assessing the information at the core of DSU adjudication.

Since many of the more sophisticated legal parties now use economists to help construct and influence arguments in DSU proceedings, there is scope for the panels, arbitrators, and Secretariat support to improve their own capacity along this dimension as well. Indeed, the legal parties in a number of disputes, especially those relying on private sector law firms, increasingly turn to economists not just for "expert witness testimony" and economic studies to be used as supporting evidence, but also to help the lawyers *draft briefs* and other supporting materials

[16] Scepticism regarding evidence or methodology is acquired via Ph.D.-level training in economics and reinforced as economists continue on a research trajectory beyond the Ph.D. and attempt to publish academic-level research in professional journals. The peer review demands inherent in this discipline's publishing process serve to reinforce the skill-set of such research economists. This creates another reason for the WTO Secretariat to expand its staff of economists at the Ph.D.-research level and also to create incentives that *encourage* them to continue to work on academic-level research in addition to their DSU support duties.

to make sure the economic arguments are coherent, consistent, and concise.[17]

Second, from the perspective of a DSU panellist or arbitrator, there is an additional benefit from access to an economist's single-minded thinking about model-driven incentives. With access to such economic thinking, panellists/arbitrators are better positioned to *anticipate* many of the arguments that parties will make and the nature of the evidence they will put forward, given that well-positioned complainant and respondent parties are also likely working with economists to develop their arguments.[18] Because Ph.D.-level economists share a common training and set of available theoretical and statistical tools, they tend to "think" (reason) alike. While panellists and arbitrators are, understandably, permitted to examine evidence only on the claims presented to them, given the resource constraints of the Secretariat and time constraints of the panel and arbitration process, an important efficiency argument can be made for those on the adjudicating side to be less "surprised" by what the parties are likely to argue.[19] Just as a good judge relies on legal experience to anticipate the scope of likely legal arguments in order to focus attention on *evaluating* their relative merits, an economist is better positioned to anticipate both the economic *arguments* that parties are likely to make and the *ways* in which they will make them. Access to such economic thinking allows panellists or arbitrators to focus earlier in the process on evaluating economic evidence and ask clarifying questions or request additional probative information. Furthermore, parties' knowledge that panellists/arbitrators are accessing technical economic expertise may have an endogenous effect, inducing the parties to provide "better" (more economically sound and data-based) evidence in the first place.

Third, panellists in the DSU process inevitably use "judicial economy" and make the conscious decision to rule on some claims that come before them while not ruling on other claims. Reasons for such an approach include recognition of political constraints (the fear of being seen as

[17] A number of private law firms with a substantial presence in WTO litigation have Ph.D. or similarly trained economists on their staff in their trade litigation practice groups. Since these firms *also* frequently commission external economic studies and hire expert witnesses, an inference is that the firms' internal economists are being used for some other function, such as to help develop and refine the economic arguments presented in briefs.

[18] In section 4, below on lessons learned from other institutions, we describe how competition authorities have increasingly used Ph.D.-level economists together with legal teams to "develop case theories" collaboratively.

[19] This is important in the time-condensed arbitration process in particular, a point raised by Lockhart (in his Comment on Chapter 4, above).

"judicially active" by the members) as well as resource constraints (too little time or support for the panellists to rule on every claim). Regardless of the underlying cause, a DSU panel that invokes "judicial economy" as a reason to fail to rule on a claim generates other benefits and costs on the system. In this light, one role for an economist would be to identify some of the costs and benefits of various discretionary choices that panels make when they are forced to exercise judicial economy on a claim-by-claim basis. That is, an economist might provide data-driven information to give panellists some forecasting ability as to how their ruling – and implicitly their decision of how narrowly or broadly to shape it – has *externality* effects beyond the current case.[20] While perhaps not in the interest of any given set of panellists who may be more concerned about their decisions being appealed and overturned by the Appellate Body, there are some externality benefits to the DSU system of such an approach. Furthermore, there is also the compelling argument that panellists make better legal decisions when they receive additional and more accurate information about the political and economic implications of their rulings.

Finally, and as we identified earlier, the case for increased interaction between lawyers and economists in DSU-related activity is proceeding on other fronts. Most noteworthy, perhaps, are the teams of economic and legal scholars that the ALI (for example, Horn and Mavroidis, 2004, 2005, 2006a) has organized to analyze the evolving WTO Appellate Body case law. As this work program illustrates, there are substantial synergies associated with putting such groups together.[21] While economists, for example, might have a greater expertise in anticipating likely arguments or directions in the case because they are trained to focus on incentives, economists also, of course, have a comparative disadvantage at many other important elements of the DSU process. These would include failing to understand legal implications of the agreements, to pay attention to sufficient detail, to follow procedure and basic rules of evidence, etc. Furthermore, the research combinations of these ALI volumes raise

[20] Bown and Sykes (2008) explore some of these costs and benefits of judicial economy in the context of how the Appellate Body itself has chosen to address the issue of zeroing in an iterative fashion, resulting in a continued progression of disputes over permutations of the issue, as opposed to a more comprehensive fashion early on in the set of zeroing cases it received.

[21] Clearly this is the purpose of including economists in this academic exercise. That is, the purpose of the ALI approach is not to simply have the economists use their expertise to examine the economic evidence used in a given case, since the scholars did not have access to much of the technical evidence considered by the panels and arbitrators in the actual disputes.

other questions that will also arise for the Secretariat and that we return to below, including the difficulties that lawyers and economists have in communicating with one another, even when they are "only" attempting to do so at a scholarly level.

2.4 *The limits to the utility of economists*

While the last section identified arguments in favor of staffing WTO DSU panels and arbitrations with more economic expertise, it admittedly focused only on benefits to doing so. In this section, therefore, we describe the costs of such staffing choices, and we also identify characteristics that economists must have to work effectively in DSU adjudication, which thus implicitly also identifies some of the limits to what economists can contribute.

The first argument is that there simply may be disputes in which the marginal cost of staffing the case with an economist (a scarce input) is likely larger than the marginal benefits. Examples are perhaps disputes that are simply procedural in nature, such as those in which the core claims are whether a country followed proper investigative procedure in a trade remedy investigation. Nevertheless, even in some of these cases, what may appear to be a *prima facie* case of inappropriate procedure often has critical economic issues at its heart that are discovered only after scratching the surface and introducing economic analysis.[22] The risk is that if such a case is not staffed by an economist on the adjudicating side, many such issues would be missed opportunities for panels to provide economic clarity to the WTO agreement via the missed opportunity to address subtleties to the economic arguments that the parties make.

Thus, in the immediate term, especially in light of the data we present in the next section, it may be better to endure the cost of a minimal staff of economists on every case. The extreme case of using economics only to

[22] An example might be one of the procedural issues in the *US–Softwood Lumber (V)* dispute which was revealed to have deep economic complexities. While the procedural question was the propriety of a method used in a dumping margin calculation, the actual issue at stake involved the economically difficult question of how to allocate capital costs rationally across a conglomerate (multi-product) firm when capital costs are only available at the firm level and the antidumping investigation only targets a subset of the firm's products. The failure of a panel to explore adequately the full legal *and* economic issues in such a case implies that there both remains a "hole" in the case law and a missed opportunity for the DSU process to identify an important issue for WTO members that may be needed to "complete" the WTO contract through negotiations. For a discussion, see Bown and Sykes (2008).

interpret economic evidence might be most applicable in the context of areas of WTO law that are relatively well developed and accepted – areas in which there is little economic controversy and thus economists have little value-added outside of technical expertise. Nevertheless, while such areas within WTO law may be easier to identify and more expansive going forward as more case law develops, given the relatively nascent stage of the current institution and the case law, the DSU is a long way from using too much economic analysis.

The second argument is that not every Ph.D.-level trained economist is "appropriate" for the DSU adjudication process. Put differently, the technical training of an economics Ph.D. is a necessary, but not sufficient qualification. Equally important are a number of qualities not emphasized in Ph.D. programs but which are typically obtained only after years of practical experience. These would include understanding the overall political–legal–economic purpose of the WTO agreements, appreciating the critical *complementary* roles of lawyers and diplomats (politics) in the DSU process, knowing the limits of what technical economics can offer, as well as having the (hard-to-define) characteristic of "good judgment." And it is certainly possible that injecting additional technical economic expertise into DSU adjudication without the appropriate legal–diplomatic balance and integration could have disastrous consequences. As a lesson learned from other institutions described below in section 4, membership dissatisfaction with a Secretariat that was misusing economics as a technical excuse and providing a DSU that would become insufficiently responsive to law and politics could lead to an outcome in which *all* use of technical economic analysis is effectively taken away.

3 Economists in DSU panels and arbitrations

In current practice, economic analysis and economists can become part of DSU adjudication via one of three avenues: for example, as the panellists/arbitrators themselves; as the support staff provided by the WTO Secretariat; or through extra-Secretariat support that the panellists/arbitrators might request. We explore each of these possibilities in the next three subsections.

3.1 *The panellists and arbitrators*

If injecting more economic analysis into DSU adjudication is an important objective, then simply picking panellists from the available stock of economists is one way to do it. To what extent has the DSU process chosen this route? While a complete determination of the level or influence of economic expertise in DSU panels is a potentially interesting and important empirical exercise, it is beyond the scope of this chapter. Therefore, since this volume focuses on the more narrow set of DSU panels that have gone to the phase of arbitration, what we can learn about the subset of DSU panellists/arbitrators involved in these particular disputes?

Table 19.1 presents information on the twenty-three different arbitrators from the ten DSU disputes that have gone to the stage of arbitration. While economic "expertise" is, of course, subjective and difficult to measure, the table provides some information on the arbitrators' relevant backgrounds in this area via two pieces of information: his or her current professional position (at the time of the arbitration) as well as the highest university degrees received. Interestingly, in at least half of the disputes, one out of the three arbitrators did have university or professional studies in economics.[23] Nevertheless, in only the *EC–Banana Regime* arbitrations is it apparent that one of the arbitrators (Kym Anderson) is an individual who another economist would likely classify as an analytical research economist at the level necessary either to interpret technical economic evidence or to construct the economic counterfactuals that are of utmost importance to arbitration proceedings in particular.

Overall, while the data in table 19.1 suggest some economic "thinking" permeates the panel and arbitration process because a handful of individuals report some university or graduate training in economics, this phenomenon is not pervasive. The majority of panellists'/arbitrators' most relevant WTO expertise derives from experience in the two other core areas of DSU adjudication – law or diplomacy (politics) – as even the panellists with an academic background in economics (with the exception of Anderson) have left the analytical/technical economics profession. The implication from table 19.1 is that, while panels and arbitrations appear well selected to represent the legal and political expertise needed for DSU adjudication, panellists/arbitrators are likely to have a high level of demand for the WTO Secretariat to appropriately tailor the analytical economic support we describe in the next section.

[23] Note that all of the data on individual characteristics in this table is "self-proclaimed" – that is, what each arbitrator claims was their highest university degree received and professional position was obtained by the author via Internet searches for curriculum vitae and/or personal email contact with the arbitrator.

Table 19.1. *The arbitrators in the disputes*

Dispute	Arbitrator	Primary employer at time of arbitration	Education
EC–Banana Regime, US, 1999	Stuart Harbinson (Hong Kong)	Permanent Representative of Hong Kong to the WTO	M.A., University of Cambridge
	Kym Anderson (Australia)	Professor, University of Adelaide	Ph.D. in economics, Stanford University
	Christian Haberli (Switzerland)	Swiss Federal Department (Ministry) for Economic Affairs	Ph.D. in law, University of Basel
EC–Beef Hormones, US and Canada, 1999	Thomas Cottier (Switzerland)	Professor, University of Bern and World Trade Institute	Dr. juris. L.L.M., University of Bern Law School
	Peter Palecka (Czech Republic)	Permanent Representative of the Czech Republic to the WTO	Graduate of the University of Economics, Bratislava
	Jun Yokota (Japan)	Deputy Director-General, Economic Affairs Bureau, Ministry of Foreign Affairs, Japan	Undergraduate coursework in law, University of Tokyo
EC–Banana Regime, Ecuador, 1999	Stuart Harbinson (Hong Kong)	Permanent Representative of Hong Kong to the WTO	M.A., University of Cambridge
	Kym Anderson (Australia)	Professor, University of Adelaide	Ph.D. in economics, Stanford University

Dispute	Arbitrator	Primary employer at time of arbitration	Education
	Christian Haberli (Switzerland)	Swiss Federal Department (Ministry) for Economic Affairs	Ph.D. in law, University of Basel
Brazil–Aircraft Subsidies, Canada, 2000	Dariusz Rosati (Poland)	Professor, Warsaw School of Economics; Monetary Policy Council, Republic of Poland	Masters' in economics, Warsaw School of Economics
	Akio Shimizu (Japan)	Professor, Waseda University School of Law (Tokyo)	LL.M., Waseda University School of Law (Tokyo) and Yale Law School
	Kajit Sukhum (Thailand)	Commercial Counsellor, Permanent Mission of Thailand to the WTO	Ph.D. in agricultural economics
US–Foreign Sales Corporations, EC, 2000	Crawford Falconer (New Zealand)	Chief Trade Negotiator, New Zealand Ministry of Foreign Affairs and Trade's (MFAT)	Victoria University of Wellington, London School of Economics
	Didier Chambovey (Switzerland)	Deputy Permanent Representative to the WTO for Switzerland	Ph.D. in economics, University of Lausanne

Table 19.1. (*cont.*)

Dispute	Arbitrator	Primary employer at time of arbitration	Education
	Seung Wha Chang (South Korea)	Professor, Seoul National University	S.J.D., Harvard; LL.M. Harvard University and Seoul National University
US–AD Act of 1916, EC, 2002	Dimitrij Grcar (Slovenia)	Counsellor, Permanent Mission of Slovenia to the WTO	B.A., Law, M.A. in Social Anthropology, University of Ljubljana
	Brendan McGivern (Canada)	Senior Legal Adviser, Canadian Mission to the WTO	LL.B., University of British Columbia
	Eugeniusz Piontek (Poland)	Professor, University of Warsaw and Lawyer, Piontek, Rymar, Ślązak, Wiśniewski and Co.	NA
Canada–Aircraft Subsidies, Brazil, 2002	William J. Davey (US)	Professor, University of Illinois College of Law	J.D., University of Michigan
	Seung Wha Chang (South Korea)	Professor, Seoul National University	S.J.D., Harvard; LL.M. Harvard University and Seoul National University
	Usha Dwarka-Canabady (Mauritius)	Mission of Mauritius to the WTO	NA
US–Byrd Amendment, Brazil, Canada,	Luzius Wasescha (Switzerland)	Ambassador, State Secretariat for Economic	Dr. in Law, University of Lausanne

Dispute	Arbitrator	Primary employer at time of arbitration	Education
Chile, EC, India, Japan, Korea, Mexico, 2004		Affairs (SECO), Switzerland	
	M. Maamoun Abdel-Fattah (Egypt)	Advisor to the Minister, Ministry of Economy and Foreign Trade, Egypt	NA
	William Falconer (New Zealand)	Company Director, Meat Industry Association of New Zealand	LL.B. (Bachelor of Laws), Victoria University of Wellington, New Zealand
US–Internet Gambling, Antigua, 2007	Lars Anell (Sweden)	Research Council on Working Life and Social Science (FAS), and former Swedish Ambassador to the WTO	B.A., Stockholm School of Economics and University of Stockholm
	Mathias Francke (Chile)	Permanent Mission of Chile to the WTO	J.D., Universidad Católica de Chile
	Virachai Plasai (Thailand)	Director-General of the Department of International Economic Affairs of the Ministry of Foreign Affairs, Thailand	NA

Sources: Internet searches and personal correspondence, available from the author on request. "NA" indicates not available.

3.2 *The WTO Secretariat: legal and economic staff*

The second avenue through which economic analysis has the potential to become part of DSU adjudication is through the support staff that the WTO Secretariat provides to the panellists and arbitrators. In the next two subsections we describe the evolving Secretariat process for staffing DSU cases with legal and economic assistance and the data on the size of this Secretariat support.

3.2.1 The process of staffing panels and arbitrations with Secretariat support

In this section we provide a brief discussion of how the Secretariat currently staffs legal and economic support teams to panellists and arbitrators in disputes. We begin by attempting to shed light on the default rule for staffing.[24] The first item to recall is that under Article 27.1 of the DSU, the members abdicated the decision of how to support panels and arbitrations to the discretion of the Secretariat – therefore, such decisions are based on internal Secretariat procedures.

The primary legal support to the panellists and arbitrators in DSU cases is typically supplied by one of two divisions in the WTO Secretariat: the Legal Affairs Division or the Rules Division.[25] For historical reasons, the Rules Division handles all disputes involving trade remedies (antidumping, countervailing measures, safeguards) and subsidies unless it faces staffing shortages, which may increasingly be the case given the growing number of trade remedy disputes. In such instances, the Legal Affairs Division provides assistance if it has temporary excess capacity. Legal Affairs then provides the lead legal officer in all "other" disputes, though in "interdisciplinary" disputes covering multiple agreements (for

[24] The information in this section is based on not-for-attribution conversations and discussions with current and former WTO Secretariat staff. As far as we are able to research from public information, an explicit Secretariat practice on how it supports panels and arbitrations is not codified or written down.

[25] Assisting panels and arbitrators is not the only function of the staff in either these divisions or the Economics Research Division. The Legal Affairs Division, for example, also provides a number of annual WTO publications such as the *Analytical Index* and *Dispute Settlement Reports*, in addition to assisting with technical assistance and trade policy course (TPC) training. The Rules Division is heavily involved in committee work and rules negotiations between members (in the more "legislative" context). The economists in the Economic Research and Statistics Division also provide support to research requests submitted by the Director General, construct the annual *World Trade Report*, participate in TPC activity, as well as engage in academic-level scientific research to maintain their analytic skill-sets.

example, goods, services, agriculture, TRIPs), Legal Affairs will turn to legal staff from the other relevant divisions to also provide support and agreement-specific expertise.[26]

The legal support staff that the Secretariat provides to a panel is typically in the range of two to five attorneys from the divisions, with likely cross-case variation explained by the complexity of issues involved in the dispute, the number of WTO agreements with claims at issue, the anticipated amount of evidence involved, the number of parties involved, the resource constraints associated with limitations on available Secretariat support staff, etc.[27] The professional staff in the Legal Affairs Division is entirely made up of trained lawyers, while the professional staff in the Rules Division is a mix of lawyers and other professionals. While some of the "professionals" in the Rules Division have significant training and perhaps prior professional experience in economics, including experience in national trade remedy investigating agencies, currently none of them would be classified as an analytical "research" economist with Ph.D.-level technical preparation.

Most of the economic "expertise" housed in the WTO Secretariat, at least as measured by technical economic expertise at the Ph.D.-level equipped to make such a contribution to the DSU process, is currently found in the Economic Research and Statistics Division.[28] While the default staffing rule is that the Secretariat team to support panels always consists of a set of lawyers from the Rules or Legal Affairs Divisions, the teams have only rarely been staffed with a Secretariat-provided economist at the panel stage. Even in the instances in which an economist is brought into the support team, the context and process may differ. It may not be until sufficiently complex economic evidence is brought into a dispute that the legal support staff and/or panellists recognize the need for such economic expertise, which, of course, limits the economists' ability

[26] In addition to permanent staff, in times of peak demand for legal assistance on DSU panels and arbitrations, the Secretariat can rely on short-term contract lawyers as well as legal interns.

[27] First, using the "Legal Affairs Division Officer advising the Panel" variables from the database in Horn and Mavroidis (2006b), of the 119 disputes with adopted Panel Reports and available data, over 55 percent (sixty-five disputes) list the names of two Secretariat lawyers, 33 percent (thirty-nine disputes) list the names of three lawyers, while four (eleven disputes) and five (four disputes) Secretariat lawyers were named in fewer instances. Second, note that the statement in the text on the likely determinants of the number of Secretariat legal support staff assigned to any one case is simply a conjecture. Empirically this question could be rigorously addressed through examination of the data in Horn and Mavroidis (2006b).

[28] There are a handful of other Ph.D.-level economists located in other divisions: namely, Agriculture and Commodities, Trade in Services, and Trade Policies Review Divisions.

to fully collaborate with panellists in developing their basic case theories, which likely began much earlier in the process.

Conditional on an economist's being used to help inform adjudicators at all, the follow-up issue of how an economist is used in any given dispute also likely varies with a number of factors. These would include demand-side factors, such as the needs and expertise of the panel, the personalities involved and the various technical competencies of the Secretariat-provided legal support staff. Supply-side factors, such as the matching of the skill-set of available Secretariat economists, would certainly also affect whether economists were utilized.

A final note relates to an important distinction between the panellists versus the Secretariat-provided support staff in DSU cases that go to arbitration. While the panellist side of the process typically does not turn over (that is, the panellists in the dispute typically also serve as the arbitrators), the Secretariat support teams can take the opportunity to "re-staff" in order to bring in additional competency to disputes that proceed to arbitration. For example, Legal Affairs may re-staff the arbitration phase with lawyers with a greater facility at processing the economics inherent at this stage. Second, although Secretariat-provided economic expertise may not have been used in the panel process, an economist staff member from the Economic Research Division has been brought in to provide assistance to the arbitrators and the legal support staff in the arbitration phase of all of the recent disputes in table 19.1. This decision is likely based on learning and Secretariat recognition of their value-added for this stage of the process.

A key reform proposal motivated by our earlier discussion is to make economic analysis more available throughout the entire DSU adjudication process. If the Secretariat makes the conscious decision to treat economic analysis more seriously, a politically benign approach would be to simply change the default rule for supporting DSU panels to one in which the Secretariat provides a support team that includes at least one Ph.D.-level economist *from its inception*. The economist should then be expected to help all economics-related aspects of the legal team's support of the panel and arbitrators in the dispute – not only interpreting technical economic evidence, but also collaborating in the formulation of questions and the development of case theories.

3.2.2 The data on divisions that staff panels and arbitrations with Secretariat support

In order to examine questions related to whether the WTO Secretariat has the right level of legal and economic capacity and the right level and mix of expertise given DSU caseload coverage so as to optimally staff disputes, a researcher would like access to data. The most useful data would be the number of full-time equivalent legal support staff allocated to work on DSU matters, the full-time equivalent economic support staff that could potentially be allocated to work on the DSU, information on how they have been used historically, their personal qualifications, such as education and prior professional experience, some measure of their technical expertise, etc. Not surprisingly, such detailed data are not publicly available.

Nevertheless, table 19.2 illustrates data from publicly available sources on how the WTO Secretariat has staffed various divisions over the 2000–2007 period. The first item to note is the extremely small number of staff in both the Legal Affairs and Rules Divisions over the period. Furthermore, while the staff support in Legal Affairs is essentially flat, the Rules Division has experienced a small amount of growth. This is likely in response to the massive shift in DSU activity related to trade remedies and subsidies taking place since 2001, the increasing number of claims the parties submit in these disputes, and the increasingly complex and resource-intensive nature of the technical evidence that the parties provide.[29] Nevertheless, the fact that there is very little overall increase in legal staffing support between 2001 and 2007 is perhaps surprising, given that the stock of DSB-adopted panel and Appellate Body reports has more than tripled during this time period, increasing the amount of "institutional knowledge" per capita that is required of the staff in these divisions.[30]

The second item to note is the number of Ph.D.-level economists in the Economic Research Division between 2000 and 2007. The number is both small (8.0) and unchanging over the time period. Thus, despite the increasing demands that DSU cases have put onto its staff, in addition to their more historical supportive role that the economists provide in the Secretariat, the Secretariat has not provided additional staffing resources to the division.

[29] Indeed, Bown and Hoekman (2008) report that while 14 percent of the set of disputes initiated between 1995 and 1998 involved trade remedies, this percentage increased to nearly 50 percent in the 1999–2006 period.

[30] Sutherland *et al.* (2004, 51) document that, of the eighty-one adopted DSB panel reports by 2003, the result was more than 27,000 pages of jurisprudence. One important role for the Secretariat's legal support staff in DSU cases is to help facilitate the transmission of relevant DSB case law to panellists and arbitrators who may not be specialists or experts in the particularly detailed topic under dispute. Thus, one might expect that as the stock and complexity of case law of which panellists/arbitrators should be aware grows, so would the size of the support staff.

Table 19.2. *WTO members, disputes, and the distribution of Secretariat staff positions within various divisions, 2000–2007*

	2000	2001	2002	2003	2004	2005	2006	2007
Economic Research*	8.0	8.0	8.0		8.0	8.0	8.0	8.0
Legal Affairs Division	15.0	17.0	16.5		17.0	17.0	16.0	16.8
Rules Division	13.0	16.0	16.0		17.0	18.0	19.0	19.0
Agriculture and Commodities Division	15.0	16.0	16.0		16.0	16.0	16.0	17.0
Intellectual Property Division	12.0	13.0	13.5		15.5	14.5	14.0	13.0
Trade in Services Division	15.0	16.0	15.0		16.0	16.0	17.0	17.0
Appellate Body	9.0	13.0	13.0		14.0	15.0	15.0	15.0
Trade Policies Review Division	29.5	29.5	34.5		34.0	35.0	36.0	37.0
Informatics Division	16.0	16.5	17.5		28.0	33.0	37.0	38.0
Language Services and Documentation	137.0	138.0	138.0		144.0	147.0	160.0	162.5
Other Divisions	269.5	269	272		298.5	296	297.5	294.2
Total WTO staff	539.0	552.0	560.0		608.0	615.5	635.5	637.5

Members[†]	135	140	143	144	146	148	149	149
New requests for DSU consultations	34	23	37	26	19	12	20	13
Stock of DSB-adopted Panel reports	38	55	70	82	98	106	120	122
Stock of DSB-adopted Appellate Body reports[‡]	29	40	51	58	71	77	87	90

Sources and notes: WTO Secretariat staff data based on the table "Distribution of staff positions within the WTO's various divisions" in the *WTO Annual Report* for years 2000 through 2007. This table is missing data from 2003 because the relevant table was omitted from that year's Annual Report.

* Data is for Ph.D. economists within the "Economic Research" Division since the staff coverage changed a number of times over this period – for example, at various points including statistics, library services, and development. The implication for this table is that data from the *WTO Annual Report* tables neither reflects the number of Ph.D. research economists in the division nor is it consistently defined (and thus comparable) over time. Information on stock of adopted Panel and AB reports is taken from Horn and Mavroidis (2006b).

† WTO membership as of 1 January.

‡ Appeals of Panel reports only and not Article 21.5 actions.

Consider again our reform proposal that, out of recognition that DSU adjudicators could benefit from additional support from economists, the Secretariat could adjust the staffing "default" rule and assign one Ph.D.-level economist to each dispute that arises from the inception of the panel. Going back to table 19.2, one implication of such a staffing procedural change would be on the demand for time of Secretariat economists. Assigning a more active role to economists will require that there are many more of them than has traditionally been the case in the Secretariat.

While the levels of Secretariat staff in divisions critical to the DSU support process – Legal Affairs, Rules, and Economic Research – are essentially unchanged over the 2001 to 2007 period, the overall size of the Secretariat staff has grown by over 14 percent during this period. An interesting feature of the data in table 19.2 is that nearly 50 percent of this recent growth in WTO Secretariat staff is in two *other* divisions: that is, Informatics (IT), and Language Services and Documentation.[31] Some of this particular growth is to be expected, as the information technology revolution has increased demand for IT professionals in most similarly situated public and private institutions. Furthermore, the increased demand for staff in Language Services and Documentation is to be expected given the growth in meetings and proceedings relating both to the DSU as well as other WTO-related (for example, Doha negotiations) "business." Nevertheless, a particular irony arising from this WTO data is that the private sector is increasingly taking advantage of globalization, technological innovation, and trade to digitize much of this material and to outsource/offshore the sort of services being provided by these two divisions at lower costs, and in many instances this services trade is occurring with developing countries.[32]

As a reform proposal, such an outsourcing approach might be of interest if the institution really does find itself confronted with an overall resource/budget constraint and yet the need to substantially increase its technical economic and legal support capacity – that is, core WTO Secretariat services that may be more costly to offshore/

[31] A substantial share of the total increase has also gone to increase staffing of the Trade Policies Review Division, which also makes sense given the rise in WTO membership and the fact that more countries now need to have their policies reviewed, and that there are an increasing number of commitments to review within countries, given the full phase-in of TRIPs, the end of the Multi-Fibre Arrangement and transitional Agreement on Textiles and Clothing, the expiration of the "Peace Clause" for the Agreement on Agriculture, etc.

[32] For more on this phenomenon, see WTO (2008).

outsource – to handle an increasingly complex dispute settlement process and caseload.[33]

3.3 *The panellists, arbitrators and extra-Secretariat assistance*

In addition to economic expertise permeating the DSU process via panellists/arbitrators themselves and/or Secretariat-provided support staff, a final possibility is that panels/arbitrators recognize the need for a certain economic specialty or expertise that is not available within the support functions provided by the Secretariat and request that this expertise is provided from the outside. Obviously such requests for outside expertise occur in other evidentiary domains in the DSU process: see, for example, the role of scientific experts in sanitary or phytosanitary (SPS) disputes.[34] Thus, such an approach is a procedural possibility.

What are the costs and benefits of applying such an approach to economists? On the positive side, attracting outside technical expertise that is important to one particular dispute only would be less costly to the Secretariat, as it would not have to commit "in-house" resources to hiring permanently an individual who might not have much utility elsewhere in the institution. Indeed, subsidy cases such as *Foreign Sales Corporations (FSC)*, the Canada and Brazil *Civil Aircraft* disputes, as well as others likely require *specialized* expertise in corporate finance – a sub-discipline of economics that is not likely to be the *ex ante* specialty of the typical high quality WTO research economist.[35] Similarly, environmental or regulatory economic expertise and experience with constructing cost–benefit analysis is extremely important in a dispute such as *Brazil–Retreaded*

[33] There is, of course, a legitimate argument that the members deliberately keep the Secretariat with a small overall staff – not because of resource constraints but because of a political decision to not cede too much power. One implication of this is that how the Secretariat chooses to allocate resources across divisions is jointly determined with the members and with knowledge of the size of the overall budget.

[34] See the discussion in Pauwelyn (2002). For arguments that scientific expertise should be included into panels themselves, see Iynedjian (2008).

[35] Economists most interested in being a full-time staff member at the WTO Secretariat are likely to be trained in the fundamental economics of international trade, given that that is the Secretariat's "core" business. Professional experts in corporate finance are likely to be found in university business school programs, and are thus academics who typically attract very high salaries. Given that "finance" is not the core business of the WTO, it is not obvious that the top-level researchers in this field would be attracted to working in the Secretariat, given the lack of colleagues who would share their research interests.

Tyres.[36] Finally, even in disputes in which "trade" is the core issue, DSU adjudicators would find it useful to access specialized knowledge over competitiveness conditions of the *particular* market at issue – something that is typically the expertise of economists in subfields of industrial organization (for the case of manufactures) or agricultural economics.

There are, of course, a number of downsides to a system in which the DSU receives the bulk of its technical economic expertise from the outside. The first is that any learning (externality) that the economist generates by working on one case is not maintained within the Secretariat to be used in a subsequent dispute, given that the economist was hired one-off and will return to the private sector. The second is the issue of informational asymmetries, as it is more difficult for the Secretariat to judge the quality of outside candidates, to be able to monitor outside resources, and to ensure the confidentiality of data, relative to its own staff. Furthermore, and perhaps most importantly, just as the parties in any dispute frequently have difficulties agreeing on a set of panellists that they feel are sufficiently neutral *ex ante*, getting the parties to agree on outside experts in any given dispute would also be problematic.

4 Experiences and lessons from similarly situated institutions

In this section we examine the experience of other relevant institutions that have injected "economic analysis" into their policy-making procedures. The DSU adjudication process has many lessons to learn from central banks, trade remedy investigating agencies, and competition authorities as these institutions operate in similar, politically-sensitive environments and confront many of the same issues as the WTO Secretariat.

4.1 The lessons from central banks

While it may not seem like an obvious point of comparison, arguably there are lessons to be learned from the policy-making process of central banks such as the Federal Reserve in the United States, or more recently, the European Central Bank (ECB) for the European Union. First, out of recognition that central banks require political independence to give them credibility, successful central banks have an institutional structure that is divorced from day-to-day political pressure which allows them to better focus on their primary policy objectives – whether it

[36] See, for example, the legal–economic analysis described in Bown and Trachtman (2009).

be establishing a supply of money to the economy that keeps inflation low (ECB), or price stability combined with economic growth (Federal Reserve).

Second, central banks have recently undertaken a forceful debate about the benefits to providing additional transparency to the decision-making process that they go through to conduct monetary policy.[37] For central banks that seek to reduce costly fluctuations and volatility in financial markets, a claim is that institutional transparency improves the discipline of policy makers, as well as the public's understanding of how policy makers are conducting monetary policy. Combined, this transparency serves to increase foundational support for the underlying monetary policy regime. The policy mechanism for this additional transparency may include both the use of more consistent language in public announcements, but also providing greater accessibility to the tools that the policy makers are using in their decision-making processes via access to the minutes of their meetings etc.

From the perspective of lessons learned from central banks, it is clear that the WTO's dispute settlement system faces a difficult balancing act in terms of information, privacy, and transparency. On the one hand, DSU adjudication surely needs to maintain the privacy of individual firms that have the right to protect proprietary information, trade secrets, etc. Furthermore, the disputants in the cases are sovereign nations whose governments face political pressure and sensitivity at home – despite having signed off on the ability to delegate some of their sovereignty (perhaps for their own good) by agreeing to the terms of membership in the WTO system. Nevertheless, one public perception of the Secretariat, which lingers because of its concurrent role as a separate forum for trade liberalization negotiations, is that it is non-transparent. The Secretariat's initial reaction to any inquiry or challenge is frequently to protect its members' privacy. Surely this is not only rooted in the desire to protect and legitimize its own existence, but also to ensure that the members vest it with additional trust and responsibility going forward.

Nevertheless, when it comes to DSU adjudication, non-transparency for the WTO can create problems when the legitimacy of the system requires that the players who have the most at stake from fair use of dispute settlement understand and appreciate the *process* by which rulings are made. For example, for the firms that engage in trade, the consumers that benefit

[37] An accessible account of this debate is Blinder *et al.* (2001). See also the Svensson (2001) comments on Blinder *et al.* (2001).

from access to foreign goods and services via trade, or the governments that have to be politically responsive to various interests at home, all parties require information on how decisions are made so they can form expectations and adapt their future behavior appropriately. Transparency and fairness are also needed if we expect members and their constituencies with a trading interest to place *more* trust in the system via additional policy commitments and the delegation of power to a rules-based WTO. From the perspective of the other extreme, an opaque dispute settlement process could result in massive distrust for the way in which the DSU process "works" in the same manner that there is apprehension and misperception over how WTO negotiating rounds work (Fatoumata and Kwa, 2004).

Thus, there are important arguments that DSU adjudicators' legal and economic reasoning should be reasonably transparent so that outsiders can understand and assess them. DSU adjudication also needs to be receptive to outside "influence" – though of the intellectual (learning) and not necessarily of the political kind. Consider, in particular, the nature of formal economic analysis. While the economics field has become increasingly scientific, it is also *evolving* as a science. What economists "know" is improving over time as models become better grounded in reality, and as competing theories face more accessible and available data to test between them. Since the DSU process is fundamentally about economic policy making, DSU adjudicators must recognize not only how economic science can contribute to their task at hand, but also its limits and how it is evolving, so that they do not stubbornly refuse to change their reasoning, mode of analysis, and argumentation as the precision and insight from economics improves over time. Sometimes panellists and arbitrators rely on WTO Secretariat-provided economic support that turns out to be incorrect *ex post*, even though it may have been the best information that was available at the time. Such is the nature of economics as a science that relies on inference via statistical analysis of data and probability. It is better to be honest about it and prepared for it, rather than simply being surprised about it when it happens.

Finally, what is the track record for transparency of the economic analysis used by DSU adjudicators thus far? When it comes to Article 22.6 arbitrations in particular, it appears that some improvement is being made. Consider the measure of the number of pages of the arbitration reports, which we use as a proxy for the level of detail that the arbitrators provided when describing the methodology taken to determine the

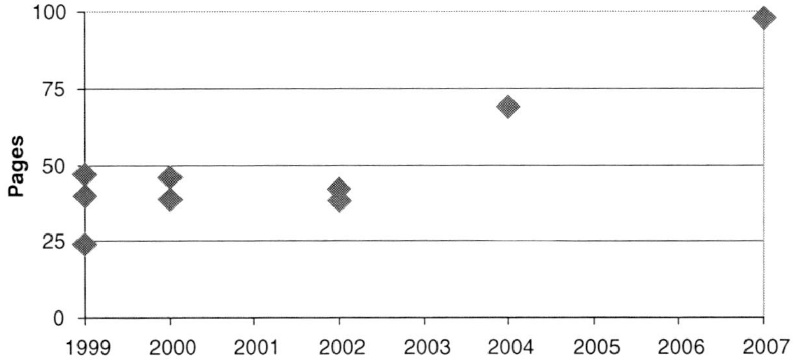

Figure 19.1. Page length of DSU, Article 22.6 arbitration reports, 1999–2007

level of permissible retaliation.[38] Figure 19.1 provides some anecdotal evidence that this has been going up over time, as the more recent cases of *US–Byrd Amendment* (2004) and *US–Internet Gambling* (2007) had public reports of sixty-nine and ninety-eight pages, respectively. Certainly, while not too much inference should be drawn from so few observations, it is worth noting that these reports are much more informative than the arbitration reports of the 1999–2002 period, which were less descriptively in the range of twenty-four (*EC–Beef Hormones, US*) to forty-seven pages (*EC–Banana Regime, US*).

Furthermore, in terms of the informative content found in the reports, there is arguably also an improvement along this dimension. For example, while the decision by the arbitrators in the most recent *US–Internet Gambling* case has become somewhat controversial among legal analysts and scholars, one of the causes of these groups' ability to be critical is because the arbitrators were transparent in their approach and methodology. When outside analysts have such information, which was not as clearly the case in some of the earlier arbitrations in table 19.1, it is possible to provide useful critical analysis to inform the process of reflection for future arbitrations. Thus, the arbitrator's transparency in this and

[38] While this is admittedly a crude measure, the number of pages of an arbitration report is a useful benchmark because each arbitration has essentially one task: that is, determine the permissible level of retaliation. On the other hand, the number of pages of a panel report would not be a useful measure because the number of tasks asked of the panellists is endogenously determined by the number of claims submitted by the parties, which is not normalized across disputes.

other recent cases is to be applauded – even if such transparency allows the external community to be more critical.

Another important insight resulting from the transparency of the reports of both *US–Internet Gambling* and *US–Byrd Amendment*, is that the arbitrators not only clearly reveal their own methodological approach, but they also identify the approach that they would have *preferred* to adopt had they not been constrained by factors as diverse as data availability, cooperation of the parties, etc. Such information is also useful, of course, to future litigating parties when seeking guidance on approaches most in line with the goals of DSU adjudicators.

4.2 *The lessons from national trade remedy investigating agencies*

The history of the antidumping investigations in the United States provides a second institution with important experiences resulting from the use of economic analysis. The US antidumping process involves a history of economic policy-making bodies that have used economists, but in a way that illustrates the dangers from misuse that have led to bumps in the road that the WTO Secretariat should anticipate *ex ante*. Two notable events stand out in particular.

First, in the late 1970s, out of concern that there was insufficient political sensitivity to antidumping investigations, the US Congress moved the dumping determination out of the US Treasury and to the Department of Commerce. Irwin (2005, 655–66) recalls the history behind this by noting that a 1979 US House Ways and Means Committee report stated:[39]

> "This Committee has long been dissatisfied with the administration of the antidumping and countervailing duty statutes by the Treasury Department ... Given Treasury's performance over the past 10 years, many have questioned whether the dumping and countervail investigations and policy functions should remain in the Treasury Department." In its report, the House (1979, pp. 6–7) committee noted (without specifically naming the Treasury Department) that "past deficient administration of these laws" was due to "low priority and inadequate staffing levels." The committee noted that the shift "will give these functions high priority within a Department whose principal mission is trade. In the past, agencies have arbitrarily set a course of administration of these statutes contrary to congressional intent."

[39] The passages quoted from Irwin (2005, 655–66) are taken from the Committee on Ways and Means, US House of Representatives, Report on the Trade Agreements Act of 1979, House Report No. 317, 96th Congress, 1st Session, July 1979. See also Finger (1993).

Second, in the period from the mid-1980s through early 2000s, the injury investigation side of the US antidumping process underwent fluctuations in how to treat economic evidence – in particular, vis-à-vis the question of attribution, or whether dumped subject imports are a cause of domestic industry injury.[40] Durling and McCullough (2005) present an interesting perspective on the early use of economics at the US International Trade Commission (USITC) via partial equilibrium simulation models.[41] Such models rely on minimal data and assumptions about elasticity parameters to identify the effect of an increase in subject imports on the price and volume of domestic shipments. It is a method able to obtain some empirical basis for understanding the likelihood of injury.

Over time and with the arrival of new Commissioners, as well as political pressure from domestic industry groups and Congress, the USITC's interest in using such models waned, as instead they switched to relying on a less rigorous (and economically satisfying) approach typically referred to as a 'trends analysis' where the USITC examines simple correlations between imports and various measures of industry injury. Durling and McCullough (2005) also describe how the use of more sophisticated econometric regression models was introduced in some steel antidumping cases in the early 2000s. After the USITC offered an initially positive response, this support decreased as well under what was perceived as renewed political pressure sceptical of the utility of formal and rigorous economic analysis and evidence.[42]

From the perspective of DSU adjudication, what lessons can be learned from the US experiences with antidumping over the last 30 years? First, the WTO Secretariat must be wary of inevitable political push-back by members; in particular, countries that have had economic analysis used against them in a dispute. Of course, the main way for the DSU process

[40] As J. Michael Finger (1981, 1270), the former Director of the Office of Trade Research at the US Treasury Department stated upon his exit with the dissolution of the office due to the political events of the period, "[F]or a year I was privileged to observe both the deliberations of the [International Trade Commission] to reach decisions and the diligent efforts of their staff to produce a staff report. But there was no relationship of one to the other. Indeed, the place where the commission's decision and the staff report came together was always the printshop. I notice that though its purpose was obscure, the staff report did serve a function – to misdirect and to obfuscate."

[41] See also the discussion in Suomela (1993).

[42] On the other hand, the USITC does at least report quite detailed information and much of the data that was used in the case, although not always fully disclosing the extent to which it relied on (some of the more rigorous forms of assessing) economic evidence in the reasoning behind its decision. While not perfect, such transparency does create some additional benefits to the system that could be usefully adopted by the WTO.

to withstand this pressure is if adjudication decisions are intellectually "right": that is, supported by strong economic evidence that will stand the test of time, as well as sound legal reasoning. This is much more likely if the DSU process is transparent and the panellists'/arbitrators' methodologies are receptive to modification in the face of informed outside scholarship.

A final lesson from both central banks and the US antidumping process is that the economic analysis used within the process needs to be independent from political influences that might arise from within the Secretariat or its members. This is not to suggest that DSU adjudication should be based only on economic analysis – it is simply recognition that if economic analysis is to used to inform DSU decisions, the best use of economics will take place when it is based on science and is as politically neutral as possible.

4.3 The lessons from competition authorities

Finally, we briefly turn to lessons from national authorities in antitrust, which typically focus on policies to maintain competitive conditions in domestic markets. While there are so many insights from antitrust that an entire chapter in this volume is needed to sufficiently expand on them (see Evenett, Chapter 25, below), here we choose to highlight one particularly interesting point.

In section 2.3 we presented a discussion of the potential benefits to DSU adjudication if economists were to become, along with lawyers and diplomats, more equal collaborators in dispute resolution. In particular, we described the contributions that economists might provide beyond simply interpreting specific technical evidence provided by the parties, but also in the process of formulating the panellists'/arbitrators' "case theories."

While such an approach has already been adopted by competition authorities in a number of countries, including the United States, it is important to point out that this has not always been the case. In describing how this evolved, former Chief Economist in the Antitrust Division of the US Department of Justice, Lawrence White, describes it as:

> economists' direct involvement in antitrust extends back at least to the beginning of the twentieth century, although their role prior to the 1970s was often limited to simple litigation support – in a sense, as "hewers of wood and haulers of water" – rather than being able to participate in the *development of case theories* and the formulation of policy (White, forthcoming, emphasis added).

White provides an interesting account of how economists – both inside and outside (via scholarship) the actual antitrust enforcement process in the United States – served to influence policy making in ways that appear to have many parallels with the current evolution of DSU adjudication that we have described throughout this chapter.

5 Providing additional economic support to the DSU via the WTO Secretariat

Thus far this chapter has proceeded in three steps. First, we identified ways in which economic analysis and expertise could be increasingly useful in DSU adjudication, and we used theory and empirical evidence to motivate why such economic expertise is necessary for the WTO system. Second, we examined how the DSU process – through panellists, arbitrators, and Secretariat-provided support staff – has historically introduced formal economic expertise and analysis. We concluded that there is an under-utilization of economic analysis, and that the Secretariat will likely need to add more going forward – for reasons including the increasing economic complexity of disputes and the fact that parties to disputes are using more sophisticated economic analysis both to construct arguments and to support them with technical economic evidence. Third, we drew lessons from other relevant institutions on some of the costs and benefits that they experienced from injecting economic analysis into their policy-making process.

Nevertheless, any infusion of economic analysis into the Secretariat, even if it is intended to improve both support for and the quality of DSU adjudication, will affect the nature of the institution. In this section, we attempt to identify issues that may arise. This section is thus intended to provoke thought and discussion about likely changes and frictions (and the sources thereof) that may evolve if more economic analysis does begin to permeate the Secretariat.

We start by considering institutional-level issues, such as what kind of economists the Secretariat should add and where they should be placed. Then, we turn to questions at the individual level that will arise as Secretariat support for panels and arbitrations starts to employ a greater mix of legal and economic resources. Finally, we raise the question of what needs to be done to make those interdisciplinary teams more effective, and we speculate as to some of the key underlying differences between economists and lawyers that need to be overcome in order to ensure the quality of a collaborative model of DSU support in the future.

5.1 *Institutional reform: staffing the Secretariat with the right economists*

As a first step, the WTO Secretariat must think critically and attempt to forecast what type of economic expertise it is most necessary to have "in-house" – given its expectations on the evolution of future dispute settlement activity. For example, the set of economic expertise in-house and the economic training required will be different depending on whether the future caseload is dominated by agricultural disputes, trade remedy disputes, TRIPs disputes, environmental disputes, SPS/TBT-type disputes, subsidy disputes, etc. While it is difficult to forecast accurately where the future frictions will arise, the WTO Secretariat can certainly take into consideration the information learned from the level of commitments undertaken in any Doha Round agreement, the contentiousness between the parties in coming to these agreements (which may manifest itself in political backlash and potential policy backsliding), and other related factors.[43]

As a second step, the Secretariat needs to make the decision of where to house any expanded capacity for analytically trained economists. If an essential skill for any Ph.D.-level economist employed by the Secretariat is his or her ability to provide technical economic support to DSU panels and arbitrations, there will be suggestions that they might be put directly into the Legal Affairs or Rules Division instead of Economic Research.

For a number of reasons, any expansion of Ph.D.-level economists within the Secretariat should continue to be through the Economic Research Division. First, other economists in Economic Research are much better positioned at evaluating the appropriate skill-set and expertise of potential hires, as well as their professional performance once they are on the job. Second, it is important that all hired economists be encouraged to spend some of their professional time engaging in academic-level research, so that they continue to upgrade their technical skills as the outside economics profession evolves. Recall, the legal–economic teams of the parties in the disputes are providing increasingly sophisticated economic models and evidence, so the Secretariat support staff need the time

[43] Furthermore it should also be noted that we can expect that trade remedies, such as antidumping and countervailing duties, are likely to remain on the DSU docket for political economy and free-riding reasons. That is, antidumping cases are more likely to be brought because they are specific to one country (even one firm), which reduces the size of positive externalities associated with getting a WTO-inconsistent measure removed and, hence, the free-rider problem of organizing a dispute in the first place.

and resources to intellectually "keep up." Third, hiring top-level economists is easier if they are in a workplace able to interact substantially with other researchers. The best people in this field are *less* likely to be interested in working in a division in which their colleagues are mostly non-economists. This should thus be avoided, as the WTO Secretariat needs to attract the best candidates in the field.

A final point to note is that an expansion of economic resource capacity within the Secretariat will likely be accompanied by a more frequent turnover in economic staff. This is an endemic feature within the economics "job market" more broadly, although it is somewhat at odds with the overall across-Secretariat staffing culture, which is historically beset by extraordinarily little staff turnover. While excessive turnover itself can be problematic (that is, losing institution-specific knowledge), turnover in a continually evolving field like economics can also have positive aspects, as it will permit the Secretariat to more routinely have openings and thus continually be able to add more recently educated economists, who are individuals most likely to have knowledge on the latest technological advances, and who are best able to pass these on to colleagues. The main point is that the Secretariat should be prepared for the fact that with a larger economic support staff there will be more turnover in this staff, and it should see this as natural and plan to deal with it effectively.

5.2 *Reform at the individual level: bridging the legal–economic communications gap*

Because economists are trained in graduate programs and lawyers are trained in law schools, they have different expertise and comparative advantage. While it would solve all problems if the Secretariat could hire an "all-inclusive" staff – that is, lawyers and economists with substantial in-depth cross-disciplinary training – unfortunately, there are very few graduate and legal programs that do an excellent job at training the *same* person in both subjects. In the short run, injecting more economic analysis and economists into the DSU support process will, therefore, also create costs, and in particular, the communications costs of two groups of people (legal staff and economic staff) who are not yet well positioned to communicate with one another.

In order to identify ways in which to address these new communications costs, we begin by undertaking the, admittedly sociological, exercise of speculating as to some of the underlying causes of these communication difficulties. As it is important for the legal and economic support teams in these disputes to be able to communicate effectively with one another, to be more certain of their own and their team mates' strengths and weaknesses, we then identify as a reform proposal the Secretariat's need to put its own resources into appropriate additional training to bridge the legal–economics communications gap.

What are the likely sources of lawyer–economist communication difficulties? First, while economists rely on models and theory to influence their statements and decisions, lawyers are not easily convinced that the "reality" at the heart of a case can be boiled down to something so simple and mechanical. Furthermore, models are based on assumptions that implicitly impose a discipline on what one can say – limits that economists are used to having to live under, but which lawyers may not be. Finally, since lawyers are trained to base arguments on evidence, they may seek reassurances that even the assumptions that an economist is willing to make can be defended empirically.

For an economist to be effective, the first step is to recognize the need to spend time explaining to the lawyers what the benefits to the modeling process are, so that they increasingly buy into what it has to offer. Nevertheless, the economist will also need to be aware of, and to clarify, to lawyer team mates the "limitations" to economic models: that is, what questions can the model not answer, or can the model only answer with a low level of certainty? Such completeness and honesty is necessary to ensure the trust of the legal partners so that they do not get blindsided by arguments presented from either of the parties' legal–economic teams, or the panellists/arbitrators themselves.

A second communications gap may be due to the differential training the team mates receive in a "research" program, such as economics versus "professional" law program. First, economists are trained to be collaborative researchers with the purpose of seeking and expanding knowledge. Thus, their method of problem-solving is typically to discuss ideas with other economists, get their ideas rejected, have to rethink them and then present them again – all through an iterative process associated with the scientific method. In an actual dispute in which the Secretariat provides support of only one Ph.D.-level economist who is not permitted legally to discuss the case with anyone outside the team of lawyers or panellists, the economist is likely to feel uncomfortable, given prior experiences in collaborative research and the fact that he or she has no other economist peer with which to (legally) discuss their ideas or questions regarding complex economic problems. This suggests an important reform to Secretariat staffing on DSU support – legally clear at least two economists from the Economic Research Division to work on each case so that they can collaborate.[44]

On the other hand, economists' training to use the scientific method may help complement the experience of lawyers on the legal–economic teams and improve the process along other dimensions. For example, research economists' experience of being at the centre of critical attention (when presenting their own research findings) may allow them to better grapple with the reality that DSU decisions establish an evolving set of law that must be continuously debated and revised, in light of many factors. From this perspective, economic scientists perceive the set of laws coming out of DSU rulings much like an ongoing expansion of knowledge that is continually being challenged by others in order that it is further refined.[45] Indeed, as the Sutherland report also notes along this dimension:

> Finally, it is interesting to note how extensively the WTO dispute settlement system is being treated in literature from non-governmental sources. There is an enormous amount of scholarly and policy-centered literature about the dispute settlement system. This is evidence of the general and public interest in the subject, and in the recognized importance and, perhaps, value of the system. Individual cases are debated at length (similar to attention received by decisions of national courts). This activity, either of scholars or of intelligent and pointed argumentation by other perceptive observers, can play a constructive and complementary role in support for a rules-based institutional framework for international trade, just as similar activity plays such a role within nations. (Sutherland *et al.*, 2004, 59)

44 There are also additional lessons to be learned from central banks along this dimension. Some central banks have external consultants (typically academics) who provide valuable advice to internal permanent staff on the process of understanding models, and the consultants answer questions related to frontier-level methodologies for modeling. Nevertheless, such consultants are never privy to any confidential information or the underlying data in the central banks' actual forecasts. It is conceivable for the WTO to adopt a similar approach for disputes that involve complex economic models submitted by the parties – the WTO's Economic Research Division might hire consultants to advise its internal staff on modeling decisions and help provide interpretations of basic questions, without having access to any of the actual underlying data submitted by the parties. I thank Meredith Crowley for making this point to me.

45 For example, given that our (broad) understanding of the fundamentals of the global economy are changing, the rules of the world trading system are evolving, the scientific techniques that allow us to evaluate policies and economic effects are changing, there is going to be an inevitable and ongoing process of revising DSU case law. It will be natural that DSU panellists, arbitrators, and Secretariat legal and economic staff who do much of the underlying support work in these cases will have their rulings challenged and criticized on intellectual grounds – by future parties, as well as academics.

Perhaps ironically, introduction of more Ph.D.-level research economists to support the DSU process may help to contribute a positive effect such as that envisioned by the Sutherland report. This derives from the fact that economists typically have much more experience in learning from this type of external "feedback" (criticism) than either their peers in the legal support staff or the panellists/arbitrators themselves.[46]

Given the resource constraints of the Secretariat, there is also the benefit of obtaining this "knowledge" from outside expertise via academics or other researchers. Looking for useful information and relying on the efforts of others is a particular strength of Ph.D.-trained economists. This may not be as common among professional lawyers who may be less familiar with the need to continually improve one's technical skills (for example, mathematical or empirical modeling) – something that is mandatory to remain relevant within the economics profession.

6 Conclusions and policy recommendations

The WTO's DSU adjudication process inherently involves bringing about changes to a member nation's economic policies. Therefore, panellists' and arbitrators' decisions and rulings should be informed by the best available economic analysis and support that the Secretariat can provide.

Our analysis concludes that the current use of economic analysis in DSU adjudication is insufficient. To that end we offer a number of proposals for reform that we summarize here. First, in each dispute, at least one of the three panellists/arbitrators should have formal graduate training in economics in order to complement the other legal and diplomatic experience that is the expertise of the majority of constituted panels. Second, the default staffing rule for WTO Secretariat support teams to panels and arbitrations should include at least one Ph.D.-level economist from the Economic Research Division, and this allocation should be made at the inception of the panel so that the economist is made an equal, collaborative partner in the Secretariat support process. Furthermore, at least one other economist from the division should be legally cleared to also work on the case, so that the lead economist has other economic peer colleagues with which to collaborate and share ideas regarding complex economic evidence and party arguments.

[46] Economists may be better prepared for this criticism, unless it were the case that either the panellists/arbitrators or legal support staff had prior judicial experience and were used to being the focus of such critical commentary. While some of this experience may have come from being a repeat panellist, it is unlikely that either of these groups' prior experience before becoming part of the DSU adjudication process was in the "judicial" realm.

In order to provide this additional staffing of economists to support DSU panels and arbitrations, our third proposal is that the Secretariat significantly expand the staff of Ph.D.-level research economists and house them in Economic Research. However, it is critical for the institution that any expansion of economic staff targets individuals with important complementary characteristics beyond simply a Ph.D. – including understanding the overall political–legal–economic purpose of the WTO agreements, appreciating the critical complementary roles of lawyers and diplomats (politics) in the DSU process, knowing the limits of what technical economic analysis can offer, as well as having "good judgment." Fourth, once this economic staff has been expanded, in order to effectively complement the legal and diplomatic expertise found in current DSU adjudication, the Secretariat will need to expend substantial resources to integrate the "legal–economic" support teams by improving their communication abilities and respective skill-sets.

Finally, the Secretariat should continue to improve transparency regarding how economic analysis is being used in DSU adjudication, following the model of central banks. After injecting more economic support into panels and arbitrations, the Secretariat should also continue to provide its economists with political independence. The Secretariat must also anticipate the likely political backlash that may arise from the membership and thus develop safeguards to prevent politics from disrupting the positive contributions that increased economic analysis can mean for the DSU process. The Secretariat staff will then be better positioned to interact with outside resources – in particular, informed critical commentary from the scholarly community – to continually refine the role of law, diplomacy, and economic analysis used in the DSU adjudication that forms the enforcement backbone of the WTO system.

References

Advisory Centre on WTO Law (ACWL) 2008. "How to Use the Services of the ACWL: A Guide for Developing Countries and LDCs," available on line at www.acwl.ch/pdf/how_to.pdf, accessed on August 12, 2008.

Bagwell, Kyle and Robert W. Staiger 2002. *The Economics of the World Trading System* (Cambridge, MA: MIT Press).

Blinder, Alan S., Charles A. Goodhart, Philipp M. Hildebrand, David Lipton, and Charles Wyplosz 2001. *How Do Central Banks Talk?* (Geneva: CEPR and ICMB), Reports on the World Economy No. 3.

Bown, Chad P. 2004a. "On the Economic Success of GATT/WTO Dispute Settlement," *The Review of Economics and Statistics*, 86(3): 811–23.

2004b. "Trade Policy under the GATT/WTO: Empirical Evidence of the Equal Treatment Rule," *Canadian Journal of Economics*, 37(3): 678–720.

Bown, Chad P. and Bernard M. Hoekman 2008. "Developing Countries and Enforcement of Trade Agreements: Why Dispute Settlement Is Not Enough," *Journal of World Trade*, 42(1): 177–203.

Bown, Chad P. and Alan O. Sykes 2008. "The Zeroing Issue: A Critical Analysis of *Softwood V*," *World Trade Review*, 7(1): 121–42.

Bown, Chad P. and Joel P. Trachtman 2009. "*Brazil–Measures Affecting Imports of Retreaded Tyres*: A Balancing Act?" *World Trade Review*, 8(1): 85–135.

Brambilla, Irene, Guido Porto, and Alessandro Tarozzi 2008. "Adjusting to Trade Policy: Evidence from U.S. Antidumping Duties on Vietnamese Catfish," NBER Working Paper No. 14495, November.

Dam, Kenneth W. 1970. *The GATT: Law and International Organization* (University of Chicago Press).

Desai, Mihir and James R. Hines, Jr. 2008. "Market Reactions to Export Subsidies," *Journal of International Economics*, 74(2): 459–74.

Durling, James P. and Matthew McCullough 2005. "Teaching Old Laws New Tricks: The Legal Obligation of Non-Attribution and the Need for Economic Rigor in Injury Analysis Under US Trade Law" in E. K. Choi and J. C. Hartigan (eds.), *Handbook of International Trade Volume II: Economic and Legal Analyses of Trade Policy and Institutions* (Oxford: Blackwell), 73–106.

Elsig, Manfred 2008. "Agency Theory and the WTO: Complex Agency and 'Missing Delegation'?" World Trade Institute unpublished manuscript.

European Commission 2002. "Proposal for a Council Regulation establishing additional customs duties on imports of certain products originating in the United States of America," Brussels, COM(2002) 202 final, 2002/0095 (ACC), April 19.

Fatoumata, Jawara and Aileen Kwa 2004. *Behind the Scenes at the WTO: The Real World of International Trade Negotiations* (London: Zed Books).

Finger, J. Michael. 1981. "Policy Research," *Journal of Political Economy*, 89(6): 1270–2

1993. "The Origins and Evolution of Antidumping Regulation" in J. M. Finger (ed.), *Antidumping: How It Works and Who Gets Hurt* (University of Michigan Press).

Horn, Henrik and Petros C. Mavroidis (eds.)

2004. *The WTO Case Law of 2001* (Cambridge University Press).

2005. *The WTO Case Law of 2002* (Cambridge University Press).

2006a. *The WTO Case Law of 2003* (Cambridge University Press).

2006b. *WTO Dispute Settlement Data Set*, available at: www.econ-law.se, accessed on June 10, 2008.

Hudec, Robert E. 1975. *The GATT Legal System and World Trade Diplomacy* (New York: Praeger).

Irwin, Douglas A. 2005. "The Rise of US Anti-dumping Activity in Historical Perspective," *The World Economy*, 28(5): 651–68.
Iynedjian, Marc 2008. "The Case for Incorporating Scientists and Technicians into WTO Panels," *Journal of World Trade*, 42(2): 279–97.
Jackson, John H. 1969. *World Trade and the Law of GATT* (New York: Bobbs-Merrill).
Janow, Merit 2004. "The Role of the WTO Secretariat in Dispute Settlement," Columbia Law School unpublished manuscript.
Keck, Alexander 2004. "WTO Dispute Settlement: What Role for Economic Analysis?" *Journal of Industry, Competition and Trade*, 4(4): 365–71.
Liebman, Benjamin and Kasaundra Tomlin 2008. " Safeguards and Retaliatory Threats," *Journal of Law and Economics*, 51(2): 351–76.
Nordström, Håkan 2005. "The World Trade Organization Secretariat in a Changing World," *Journal of World Trade*, 39(5): 819–53.
Pauwelyn, Joost 2002. "The Use of Experts in WTO Dispute Settlement," *International and Comparative Law Quarterly*, 51: 325–64.
Sapir, André and Joel P. Trachtman 2008. "Subsidization, Price Suppression, and Expertise: Causation and Precision in Upland Cotton," *World Trade Review*, 7(1): 183–209.
Shaffer, Gregory C. 2005. "The Role of the WTO Director-General and Secretariat," *World Trade Review*, 4(3): 429–38.
Suomela, John W. 1993. *Free Trade Versus Fair Trade: The Making of American Trade Policy in a Political Environment* (Turku, Finland: Institute for European Studies).
Sutherland, Peter et al. 2004. *The Future of the WTO: Addressing Institutional Challenges in the New Millennium* (Geneva: WTO).
Svensson, Lars. E. O. 2001. "Comment on Blinder, Goodhart, Hildebrand, Lipton and Wyplosz, 'How Do Central Banks Talk?'" Princeton University unpublished notes, available at: www.princeton.edu/svensson/papers/ohgen.pdf, accessed June 11, 2008.
Weiler, Joseph 2001. "The Rule of Lawyers and the Ethos of Diplomats," *Journal of World Trade*, 35(2): 191–208.
White, Lawrence J. forthcoming. "Economics, Economists, and Antitrust: A Tale of Growing Influence" in John J. Siegfried (ed.), *Living Better through Economics* (Cambridge, MA: Harvard University Press).
WTO 2005. "Quantitative Economics in WTO Dispute Settlement," in *World Trade Report 2005* (Geneva: WTO), 171–212.
WTO 2008. *World Trade Report 2008: Trade in a Globalizing World* (Geneva: WTO).
WTO various years. *WTO Annual Report,* available at www.wto.org/english/res_e/reser_e/annual_report_e.htm, accessed August 29, 2008.

Comment on chapter 19

Some reflections on the use of economic analysis in WTO dispute settlement proceedings

RETO MALACRIDA*

Professor Bown's contribution raises numerous important and interesting issues regarding the place and use of economics in WTO dispute settlement. In the interests of brevity, I shall comment on only a few of the arguments and recommendations that are contained in his contribution.[1]

A central argument Professor Bown puts forward is that WTO dispute settlement panels (hereafter 'panels') and WTO arbitrators should 'inject[] more economic analysis/economists to get the economic reasoning or rulings "right" '.[2] More particularly, he argues for a greater role to be given to what he calls 'analytical Ph.D.-trained economists' in the process of WTO adjudication. Those economists, Professor Bown recommends, should be members of the WTO Secretariat support staff assisting WTO adjudicators.[3]

* Counsellor, WTO Legal Affairs Division. The views and ideas expressed in this Comment are those of the author acting in a personal capacity and do not represent a position, official or unofficial, of the WTO Secretariat. In view of the topic of these comments it bears mentioning that the author's academic background includes economics. The author wishes to thank Bruce Wilson as well as Johann Human, Bruce McRae and Yves Renouf for very useful comments and suggestions.

[1] Since Professor Bown's contribution includes substantial discussion of the WTO Secretariat, I should note that the fact that I chose to comment on some aspects of this discussion, but not others, should not be construed to mean that I necessarily agree with those aspects on which I do not comment.

[2] Chad P. Bown, 'The WTO Secretariat and the Role of Economics in Panels and Arbitrations', Chapter 19, above, note 10. I should note that the WTO arbitrators at issue are primarily those acting pursuant to Article 22.6 of the DSU, that is to say, arbitrators whose mandate it is to determine whether the level of suspension of concessions or other obligations that a complaining member is proposing is equivalent to the level of nullification or impairment caused by a WTO-inconsistent measure that has not been withdrawn by the responding member.

[3] See Bown, Chapter 19, above, for example, sections 2.4 and 5.2.

I fully support the idea of using economics, in cases where it is appropriate to do so. A good knowledge and understanding of general, or 'conceptual', economics is useful in a substantial number of cases referred to WTO adjudicating bodies.[4] Quantitative economics (econometrics etc.) can be a useful tool, in particular in cases where an effects-based economic analysis is necessary or appropriate.[5] However, a large proportion of cases that are referred to WTO adjudicating bodies does not require, or warrant, this type of analysis simply because the WTO provisions that are to be applied do not call for this type of inquiry.[6] On the other hand, it may well be that in some of the cases where the use of quantitative economics would have been appropriate, such use by the parties and WTO adjudicating bodies was either lacking altogether or deficient.[7]

Professor Bown's view that greater reliance should be placed on economic analysis and economists leads him to make a number of specific 'policy recommendations'. I would like to make a brief comment on two of them. One is the recommendation that 'in each dispute, at least one of the three panellists/arbitrators should have formal graduate training in economics ...'[8] In my view, this recommendation sweeps too broadly. The composition of a panel is a matter for the disputing parties

[4] It is doubtful, however, whether a Ph.D. in economics, as opposed to a less advanced academic degree in economics or an interdisciplinary degree, is indispensable in all of those cases.

[5] For an overview of the type of situations in which effects-based economic analysis may be necessary or appropriate, see World Trade Organization, *World Trade Report 2005* (Geneva: WTO, 2005), 172–4 (distinguishing between analyses of the effect of policy measures on trade and analyses of the effect of imports on domestic products/producers).

[6] See also, for example, World Trade Organization, *World Trade Report 2005*, 189 and 198. Due to the difference in their respective legal mandates, there is greater scope for recourse to quantitative economics in Article 22.6 arbitrations than in typical panel proceedings. While quantitative economics has been used often in Article 22.6 arbitrations, it has not been necessary or appropriate to use it in all such arbitrations.

[7] To put this into perspective, it should be noted that the perception that quantitative economics may have been 'underutilized' is not specific, or limited, to WTO dispute settlement. Indeed, similar claims are being made in respect of other legal practice areas, including, for example, competition law. See Martin Hellwig, *Wirtschaftspolitik als Rechtsanwendung: Zum Verhältnis von Jurisprudenz und Ökonomie in der Wettbewerbspolitik* (Forschungsgemeinschaft für Nationalökonomie der Universität St. Gallen: Walter-Adolf-Jöhr-Vorlesung, 2007), 6–9, 23–32 (identifying EC competition law cases in which the European Court of Justice and the European Court of First Instance gave rulings that are alleged to be based on inadequate, or lacking, empirical economic analysis).

[8] Bown, Chapter 19, above, section 6.

to determine by mutual agreement, or for the WTO Director General to determine based on selection criteria provided by the parties.[9] If the parties consider that a particular case does not require, or warrant, any panellist with economic expertise and that there is, therefore, no need for an economist on the panel in question, the Secretariat in proposing names, or the Director General in determining a panel's composition, should, wherever possible, accommodate the parties' preference. The parties are more familiar with the facts of the case and, hence, the expertise required to adjudicate it. Also, it is their dispute that is to be adjudicated. Besides, when a panel considers that it needs expert advice from economists, it has the option of consulting independent economic experts.[10]

The other policy recommendation is that the WTO Secretariat should 'significantly expand the staff of Ph.D.-level research economists and house them in Economic Research'.[11] As an initial matter, I would note that in cases where technical economic expertise is called for, Secretariat economists can, and do, make significant contributions to the work of panels or arbitrators. For example, they can explain to panels or arbitrators the strengths and weaknesses of any economic arguments the parties may be advancing in support of their positions, or of econometric analyses the parties may have submitted.[12] As to whether a 'significant' increase in 'Ph.D.-level research economists' would be warranted, this should be considered as part of an objective and horizontal assessment of the Secretariat's human resource needs for its dispute settlement-related activities.

Conspicuously absent from Professor Bown's several 'policy recommendations' is the option of panels consulting independent economic

[9] See Article 8 of the WTO Dispute Settlement Understanding (hereafter the DSU). Similarly, arbitrations under Article 22.6 of the DSU are to be carried out by the original panel, if members are available, or else by individuals appointed by the Director General.

[10] Article 13 of the DSU specifically provides for this possibility. By 'independent economic experts' I mean experts who (i) are not members of the WTO Secretariat, (ii) are not, and have not been, working for either of the two disputing parties and (iii) do not otherwise present a possible conflict of interest.

[11] Bown, Chapter 19, above, section 6.

[12] It is worth noting in passing that WTO panellists and arbitrators are fortunate to have access to economic support staff at all, because, usually, domestic courts and international tribunals do not employ economists. At most, domestic courts and international tribunals may have some legal staff with an interdisciplinary background. If they need economic expertise, they either ask the parties to provide it or else seek the advice of independent economic experts.

experts to obtain their technical advice on specific economic issues.[13] This is somewhat surprising. If there is one thing that is striking about the use of economics in WTO dispute settlement, it is arguably the fact that up until now no panel has, as far as I am aware, found it necessary or appropriate to call on independent economic experts for their advice.[14] I do not mean to suggest that this should necessarily have been done. But the fact that there has been no instance in which economic experts were consulted is still noteworthy, not least because it contrasts with the fact that there are several cases – I can think of eight – in which panels have consulted scientific or technical experts other than economists.[15]

It is true that consulting independent experts would ordinarily entail a certain amount of delay in the completion of the relevant legal proceedings, as experts need to be selected in consultation with the parties, and they also need to be given adequate time to prepare their replies to panel questions. However, the Dispute Settlement Body (DSB) could easily create an indicative list of governmental and non-governmental economic experts, as it has done for potential panellists. This would assist panels in identifying promptly potentially suitable experts.[16]

Another potential concern about seeking advice from independent economic experts might be that, should a panel decide to consult more than one expert, those experts might give contradictory and offsetting advice, thereby making it difficult for non-expert WTO adjudicators to

[13] I should mention that 'requests for outside expertise' are mentioned in Professor Bown's contribution as a 'procedural possibility', and some discussion is offered of the 'costs and benefits' of making use of that possibility. See Bown, Chapter 19, above, section 3.3.

[14] Similarly, no panel has as yet requested the assistance of the 'Permanent Group of Experts' under Article 4.5 of the Agreement on Subsidies and Countervailing Measures.

[15] Essentially, experts have so far been consulted in one environment-related case and in cases involving claims under the Agreement on Sanitary or Phytosanitary Measures. It should be mentioned that Article 11.2 of the Agreement on Sanitary or Phytosanitary Measures says that panels 'should' seek advice from experts in cases involving scientific or technical issues.

[16] The point made by Professor Bown – that it would be difficult to get the parties to agree on any independent economic experts to be selected (Bown, Chapter 19, above, section 3.3) – appears to be based on the assumption that panels would consult experts, or select particular experts, only if the parties agree. It is certainly true that panels would make reasonable efforts to select only experts whom both parties can accept. But the ultimate decision on whether to seek any expert advice and, if so, whether to select particular experts rests with panels. Moreover, experience with past processes for the selection of scientific experts shows that party objections have sometimes been overridden where such objections were considered to be unwarranted.

reach conclusions. While this is a possibility,[17] that possibility also exists in other WTO cases in which scientific or technical experts are typically consulted.[18]

At any rate, consultation of independent economic experts would arguably present significant benefits. For instance, as independent economic experts would be consulted on an ad hoc basis, it would often be possible to call on experts who individually or collectively have the right mix of expertise and experience that is needed in a given case.[19] In addition, the advice offered by outside economic experts would be transparent to the parties, and the parties would be given an opportunity to respond to, and comment on, the experts' views.[20]

Accordingly, in cases where technical economic issues are presented and where these issues are central to the disposition of these cases, it

[17] Arguably, however, in the case of independent economic experts, the risk of receiving completely contradictory advice may be somewhat smaller than in cases where the only experts involved in the proceedings are those advising the parties. It has been remarked in this respect that 'we should not conclude that economic experts differ because they are mere advocates for their clients. Nonetheless, there is a myriad of inducements for the expert witness to become an advocate for their client.' Jeffrey K. MacKie-Mason and Richard A. Pfau, 'Inducements to Advocacy: The Economist as Independent Expert' in D. J. Slottje (ed.), *The Role of the Academic Economist in Litigation Support* (Amsterdam: Elsevier Science, 1999), 208. See also 'Dueling Experts in U.S. Courts: Overseas Lawyers Question System of Paid, Partisan Testimony', *International Herald Tribune*, 12 August 2008, 5.

[18] If a panel were to form an 'expert review group' as envisaged in Article 13 and Appendix 4 of the DSU, there would probably be less need for a panel to try to understand and assess the importance of any divergence of opinion among individual economic experts, although an expert review group's advisory report could arguably still set out minority opinions. I should note that there is, to date, no example of a case in which a panel has established an expert review group.

[19] Professor Bown makes the point that it would be more difficult to maintain the confidentiality of data in the case of independent economic experts than in the case of Secretariat economists (Bown, Chapter 19, above, section 3.3). I am not persuaded that this should factor in the decision on whether to seek advice from independent economic experts. Indeed, they would be subject to the very same rules of conduct as WTO adjudicators and Secretariat support staff. Moreover, there has already been a WTO case in which independent scientific experts were given access to strictly confidential information.

[20] These advantages might be significant from the perspective of the disputing parties, at least in those disputes whose outcome critically depends on factual determinations to be made by panels. The Appellate Body has repeatedly indicated that panels are the triers of fact in the WTO adjudicative system and that, as such, they enjoy a measure of discretion in assessing the value and weight of evidence submitted to them. See, for example, Appellate Body Report, *Australia–Measures Affecting Importation of Salmon*, WT/DS18/AB/R, 6 November 1998, DSR 1998:VIII, 3227, para. 272.

might well be appropriate and worthwhile for *panels* to seek advice from independent economic experts rather than rely exclusively on their own economic expertise and/or that of economic support staff from the Secretariat.[21] Needless to say, panels would not simply go ahead and do so, but would seek the parties' views before making a decision in this regard. Also, recourse to independent economic experts would not preclude WTO Secretariat economists from continuing to provide technical support to panels.

In the specific case of *arbitration* under Article 22.6 of the DSU, recourse to independent economic experts would present further potential issues. The first is the legal issue of whether such arbitrators would be entitled to seek technical advice from independent experts. The possibility of seeking expert advice is explicitly mentioned in the DSU in relation to panels, not arbitrators.[22] However, there is an argument to be made that if this possibility is given to panels, it should be open also to arbitrators on the grounds that they, too, may need to assess highly complex economic evidence, including the validity of, and results yielded by, econometric models.[23] The other issue relates to the requirement that Article 22.6 arbitrations are to be completed within 60 days. If an arbitrator were to consult an independent economic expert, it might in some cases be difficult to complete arbitration within this period of time. Having said this, considering that the suspension of concessions or other WTO obligations is a serious matter with potentially serious consequences, including for 'innocent' private parties of the responding member, it is important that arbitrators issue decisions that are of sufficient quality.[24] Also several past Article 22.6 arbitrations have taken significantly longer than 60 days, not least because of the complex economic issues involved.

Even if it were considered that consulting independent economic experts would be inappropriate for arbitrators, either for legal reasons or

[21] Interestingly, a US Supreme Court justice has similarly suggested that in complex technical cases lower courts might usefully retain their own experts, with the parties retaining the right to supplement the views of any such experts with expert views of their own. See Stephen Breyer, *Economic Reasoning and Judicial Review* (Washington, DC: AEI-Brookings Joint Center for Regulatory Studies, 2003), 12.

[22] See Article 13 of the DSU.

[23] Also, it is noteworthy that in the context of arbitrations conducted in non-WTO fora it is not uncommon for arbitrators to have recourse to independent technical experts (for example, valuation experts) to assist them in their task.

[24] On the impact of retaliatory measures on private party interests, see Reto Malacrida, 'WTO Retaliatory Measures: the Case for Multilateral Regulation of the Domestic Decision-Making Process', Chapter 18, above .

because of likely delays, parties could also explore another, new avenue. Thus, when an original panel is established, the disputing parties could agree that the panel should be composed of five panellists instead of the customary three.[25] The parties could further agree that the additional two panellists should be what Professor Bown calls 'analytical Ph.D.-trained economists'. Those two economists could then be excused, by mutual agreement of the parties, from participating in the original and any subsequent compliance panel proceedings, such that they would be involved only in an eventual Article 22.6 arbitration.[26] Needless to say, if the parties consider that during the panel process technical economic expertise is required, the two economic experts could be asked to participate also at the panel stage.[27]

A further comment I would like to make is in response to the assertion, attributed by Professor Bown to academics, that the Appellate Body, panels and arbitrators have made 'economic mistakes' or reached 'flawed decisions' and that they did so 'across a wide variety of disputes'.[28] Leaving aside the issue of whether this is true, it would appear that in establishing the causes behind any 'economic mistakes' account should be taken not merely of the output of WTO adjudicating bodies, but also of the input of the disputing parties. It is not apparent that ensuring proper reliance on, and correct use of, economics is, or should be, the exclusive responsibility of panels or arbitrators, much less of their Secretariat support staff. Arguably, it is also part of the responsibility of the parties to make panels or arbitrators aware of critical economic issues and adequately to explain and brief these issues in their submissions. In addition, if a panel (or arbitrators) decided to seek the advice of independent economic experts, the parties would be invited to assist in the preparation of questions to be submitted to the experts and, subsequently, to comment on the responses offered by the experts. Moreover, should a panel make a factual finding which a party considers economically unsound, the interim review process provides an opportunity to request the panel to review this particular aspect of its report.[29]

[25] Article 8.5 of the DSU provides for the possibility of having panels of five members. So far, this possibility has not been used.

[26] The two economic experts could be selected on condition that they agree not to participate in the panel process.

[27] Alternatively, as indicated above, the parties could agree that at least one of the customary three panellists should have the requisite economic expertise.

[28] See Bown, Chapter 19, above, section 2.1.

[29] See Article 15.2 of the DSU. Legal findings of a panel are in any event subject to appeal to the WTO Appellate Body. The DSU does not provide for an interim review procedure in Article 22.6 arbitrations.

To be clear, it is not my contention that panels or arbitrators should use economic analysis only if the parties are in favour of doing so, or that panels or arbitrators need not attempt to improve on the quality of any economic analyses offered by the parties if those analyses are found to be deficient. I would have equal misgivings, however, if panels or arbitrators began to assume an 'activist' stance in relation to the use of economics and to pursue complex economic issues that it is not necessary to resolve in order to dispose of a case. In this regard, I do not share Professor Bown's apparent concern about 'missed opportunities for panels to provide economic clarity to the agreement', or about leaving 'a "hole" in the case law'.[30] As I see it, clarification of the meaning of WTO provisions, or of the 'operationalisation' of concepts they contain, is a by-product of WTO dispute settlement and not an end in itself, since the primary objective of the WTO dispute settlement mechanism is to settle relevant disputes.

In any event, a healthy degree of caution seems warranted in view of the limitations of quantitative economics. Econometric analysis, or modelling, invariably proceeds on the basis of assumptions. The question, therefore, arises whether such assumptions are supported by any evidence and how sensitive the end result is to changes in the assumptions made. Econometric analysis, or modelling, is also data intensive. Relevant data may be unavailable, or it may be available, but quantitatively or qualitatively inadequate, or deliberately disregarded or withheld so as to predetermine desired results. Data, as well as modelling results, also need to be correctly interpreted.[31] An inevitable consequence of these inherent limitations is that econometric analysis, or modelling, may not always yield sufficiently reliable results. Or it may yield results that lack precision, for example, where a model provides, not a specific value/number/coefficient, but a range of equally possible values/numbers/coefficients.[32]

If, then, quantitative economics does not always provide clear and authoritative answers, what can we do to avoid situations where

[30] Bown, Chapter 19, above, section 2.1.

[31] Regarding the limitations of quantitative economics, see also World Trade Organization, *World Trade Report 2005*, 206 (stating that 'quantitative analysis is frequently beset by methodological difficulties, the existence of competing approaches of apparently equal validity but that yield different results, simplifying assumptions and data limitations').

[32] This would be a concern in cases where the relevant range of possibilities would lead to ultimate decisions that diverge, either in terms of dollars and cents or in terms of legal right or wrong. In this respect, see World Trade Organization, *World Trade Report 2005*, 206 (stating that 'economic analysis rarely, if ever, can provide clear-cut answers' and that '[e]xperience to date has confirmed that quantitative economic analysis cannot determine dispute settlement outcomes').

quantitative economics is either over- or underutilized? And how can we make disputing parties and WTO adjudicators feel more comfortable about using it? One approach is to think of quantitative economics as a tool.[33] Sometimes it is the best tool available, notwithstanding its inherent limitations. At other times, it may not be appropriate to use it.[34] This approach would support the view that quantitative economics should be used judiciously and, wherever possible, in conjunction with other evidence.[35] A further, and arguably complementary, approach which it may be worth considering would consist in the adoption by WTO members of a consensus statement for use by parties, panels and arbitrators. Yet another approach, specific to Article 22.6 arbitration, would be to provide for optional or mandatory final offer arbitration.[36] It is perhaps useful to say a few words about the latter two approaches, to explain what they might entail.

A consensus statement could take the form of a decision by the DSB. The purpose of such a decision by the DSB would be to provide non-binding guidance regarding the use of quantitative economics in WTO dispute settlement.[37] Procedurally, the DSB could follow the example of the WTO Committee on Anti-Dumping Practices and form an 'ad hoc group' which would be tasked with preparing recommendations for the DSB on issues where a consensus seems possible.[38] The members of such a group would include economic experts from members. They could study these

[33] See also, World Trade Organization, *World Trade Report 2005*, 206 (referring to a 'supporting role of quantitative economics in dispute settlement' and describing economic analysis as a 'complementary tool').

[34] For instance, in *US–Antidumping Act of 1916*, the arbitrator, based on the information provided , accepted the parties' view that it was not possible to quantify the 'chilling effect' the Antidumping Act of 1916 was allegedly producing on EC exports. See, Decision by the arbitrator, *US–Antidumping Act of 1916*, Original Complaint by the European Communities, Recourse to Arbitration by the United States under Article 22.6 of the DSU, WT/DS136/ARB, 24 February 2004, DSR 2004:IX, 4269, para. 5.72.

[35] The same point has been made by a professor of economics in relation to the use of qualitative economics in support of economic policy advice. See Gert G. Wagner, 'Gegenseitige Abhängigkeit von Ordnungspolitik und Mainstream-Ökonomie in der Politikberatung', *Wirtschaftdienst*, 7: 2009, 445.

[36] I am indebted to Bruce McRae for drawing my attention to the possibility of using final offer arbitration.

[37] As a 'consensus statement' would not be legally binding on panels and arbitrators, it would provide sufficient flexibility for panels and arbitrators to depart from the DSB's guidance whenever the circumstances of a particular case warranted.

[38] See WTO document G/ADP/W/399. The Committee on Anti-Dumping Practices has, in fact, adopted a number of recommendations that provide guidelines on various topics. See, for example, WTO documents G/ADP/5, G/ADP/6, G/ADP/7 and G/ADP/10.

issues in a systematic and horizontal fashion and, unlike panels and arbitrators, they could do so without being significantly time constrained.

Among the issues a DSB guideline could cover is that of how Article 22.6 arbitrators could go about determining the level of nullification or impairment resulting from an ongoing breach of various types of WTO obligations. In this regard, the DSB could identify acceptable methodologies for determining the relevant value (value of lost trade, lost profits, or whatever is deemed the relevant value) and, where appropriate, establish a general order of priority for such methodologies. Guidance might also usefully be given on acceptable principles for establishing the level of nullification or impairment in cases where quantitative economic analysis yields, not a precise a number, but a range of possible numbers. Furthermore, the DSB could cover the use of quantitative economics in the context of panel proceedings. This would initially involve identification of WTO provisions, application of which may call for an inquiry into the economic effects of a challenged government measure. In addition, the DSB could provide guidance on appropriate methodologies, quantitative tests and other relevant matters.

The value to panels and arbitrators of any guidance from the DSB would appear to be essentially twofold. First, it could assist panels and arbitrators in settling disputes 'promptly'.[39] If panels and arbitrators can rely on guidance from the DSB on appropriate analytical approaches and methodologies, there is no, or less, need for panels and arbitrators to analyse, by themselves and together with the parties, the propriety of using such approaches and methodologies. As a result, time savings could likely be realized. Second, there would be the 'legitimating' function of a consensus statement. Thus, by endorsing, in principle, recourse to certain approaches and methodologies, the DSB could go a long way toward putting the minds of parties, panels and arbitrators at ease over relying on those approaches and methodologies.[40]

In relation to final offer arbitration, this would probably necessitate an amendment of, *inter alia*, Article 22.6 of the DSU. Under this form of arbitration, both parties would simultaneously submit their final best 'estimates' of the level of nullification or impairment to an arbitrator. The arbitrator would then select one of the two proposed levels. That level

[39] See Article 3.3 of the DSU.

[40] Significantly, however, even if a 'consensus statement' of the DSB indicated that it would be acceptable, in principle, to use a particular approach or methodology, there might still be reasons why it would not be appropriate to use it in a given case, and so parties, panels and arbitrators would still need to make an independent assessment on a case-by-case basis.

would become the arbitrator's decision (award). In cases where an arbitrator considers that neither of the two proposed levels is appropriate, for example, because neither is based on the best methodology available, the arbitrator would select the one which is more appropriate in the light of all relevant circumstances. In other words, the arbitrator would not make an independent determination of the level of nullification or impairment.[41] Since both parties know in advance that the arbitrator will select the more appropriate estimate, they have an incentive to submit estimates that are reasonable.[42]

To conduct such final offer arbitration, arbitrators would still need economic expertise – to determine which of the two proposed levels is more appropriate. But they would not themselves need to determine the level of nullification or impairment, which, as indicated, is often difficult for arbitrators to do because of the inherent uncertainties and the time constraint involved. Also, since arbitrators would need only to select one of two proposals, it would be realistic that they could generally complete the arbitration within the 60-day time limit.

In conclusion, I would agree with Professor Bown that there is a place for economic analysis, including quantitative economic analysis, in WTO dispute settlement and that in certain categories of disputes – particularly those where effects-based economic analysis is necessary or useful – there may be room for it to be used more frequently, or extensively, than has been the case in the past. I would also agree that panels, arbitrators and the Secretariat have an important part to play in ensuring the sound use of economics and correct economic reasoning in WTO dispute settlement reports and decisions. However, as I have pointed out, it would also be worthwhile to enlist the help and contributions of others, notably of the disputing parties, independent economic experts and the DSB. Indeed, this should be a concerted effort of the many rather than an isolated quest of the few. As for the disputing parties, they are key because, quite logically, it is they who are primarily interested in, and concerned by, how economics is used in the adjudication of their dispute. Moreover, it is in the parties' own best interests to assist panels and arbitrators in carrying out their task and arriving at decisions based on the best economic

[41] It would thus be up to the parties to make sure that their proposed levels are properly based on, and supported by, economics.

[42] Currently, the parties to Article 22.6 arbitrations arguably do not have a strong incentive to stake out reasonable positions. Rather, the responding member has an incentive to argue for a low level of nullification or impairment, whereas the complaining member has an incentive to argue for a high level.

analysis possible. As for independent economic experts, they could potentially make a real difference, because they could be consulted on an ad hoc basis with a view to obtaining specialized expert advice on technical economic issues put before panels or arbitrators. Finally, the DSB could be instrumental in facilitating the use of quantitative economics by panels and arbitrators, for example, by adopting guidelines on acceptable economic approaches and methodologies.

The equivalence standard under Article 22.4 of the DSU: a 'tariffic' misunderstanding?

SIMON SCHROPP*

1 Synopsis of the argument

A systematic study of the 'equivalence standard' in WTO arbitrations under Article 22.4 of the Dispute Settlement Understanding (DSU) has so far been wanting in WTO scholarship and in the practice of Dispute Settlement Body (DSB) arbitrators.[1] Article 22.7 of the DSU mandates the WTO arbitrator to 'determine whether the level of [suspension of concessions or other obligations] is equivalent to the level of nullification or impairment'. Decomposing this standard into its constituent parts, and assessing the tasks of the arbitrator, namely:

- quantification of the level of nullification or impairment (NoI) according to the nature, form and intensity of the offending measure;
- quantification of the level of suspension of concessions or other operations (SCOO) according to the nature, form and intensity of remedial action;
- safeguarding equivalence between the two levels

we bring forth three independent claims.

* International trade analyst at Sidley Austin LLP, Geneva. The author would like to thank Chad Bown, Fritz Breuss, Gabrielle Kaufmann-Kohler, Petros Mavroidis, Joost Pauwelyn and all participants of the interdisciplinary workshop on the Calculation of Trade Sanctions that was held in Geneva on 18–19, July 2008. Special thanks go to Scott Andersen, Todd Friedbacher and Nicolas Lockhart of Sidley Austin LLP for putting up with the author's academic extravaganzas. The views expressed in this article are those of the author and shall not be attributed to his employer or clients. The same goes for all flaws, errors and lapses that may have sneaked into the text.

[1] The term 'Article 22.4 arbitration' shall be used as shorthand for 'DSU, Article 22.6 arbitrations dealing with the equivalence standard of Article 22.4 of the DSU'.

First, when assessing the level of NoI, WTO arbitrators systematically utilized an inappropriate *damage measure*, or baseline counterfactual, with which the actual situation of the complainant is to be compared. Under the current practice, arbitrators compare the actual breach-ridden situation with a counterfactual that would prevail if the illegality were removed after the reasonable period of time (RPT). This counterfactual may be apt to re-establish the *status quo ante* the breach, yet it is not suited to compensate the complainant for its true damage suffered from the violation of the contract. Contract theory would mandate that NoI be calculated based on a counterfactual that puts the injured party in as good a position as it would have been if the violating party had performed as promised ('expectation damages').

Second, arbitrators have consistently applied the direct-trade-blocked metric to approximate the unobservable trade damages suffered by the complaining party from a violation of the WTO Agreement. This metric is inapt to approximate the real trade damages suffered. Close examination of the WTO contract suggests that NoI is best measured in terms of the *economic losses* sustained by the complaining member in the affected sector(s) – not as *direct trade blocked.*

Third, arbitrators have failed to address in a meaningful manner the quantification and operationalization of the level of retaliation, or countermeasures, that is, the SCOO. This renders the equivalence standard futile, and has dramatic consequences for the entire dispute settlement system.

Each one of the three claims is self-standing, that is, mutually independent of the other two. Four significant consequences from these deficiencies of current WTO arbitrations will be highlighted:

(1) The equivalence standard of Article 22.4 of the DSU is an ambitious objective. Achievement of this goal has so far been a fiction. Under the current practice of WTO arbitrations we will hardly find a real equivalence test. The arbitrators' mandate of safeguarding equivalence between NoI and SCOO remains to be fulfilled. Worse still, on the rare occasions where arbitrators have provided substance on the calculation of the level of SCOO, their comments quite often seem to be rather counterproductive and reduced equivalence of the levels of NoI and SCOO to a mere game of chance.
(2) During the process of arbitration, the true extent of the WTO contract and the nature of WTO violations seem to have remained unseized. By measuring NoI in terms of direct trade effects, arbitrators equated

trade damage with harm from restricted market access (tariff barriers, quantitative restrictions, red-tape measures, etc.) in the industry concerned. Yet the WTO contains various other entitlements above and beyond reciprocal market access; consequently, violation of those other entitlements causes a different kind of economic harm to complainants.

As long as DSB arbitrations deal only with market access-related infringements confined to one sector at issue, the arbitrators' tariff-centric ('tariffic') blinders were merely problematic: NoI proxied by means of *direct trade effects* is undercompensatory to victims of contractual breach. With the advent of the *US–Antidumping Act of 1916* case (DS 136), however, this tariffic logic of calculating NoI collapsed entirely: given that *US–1916 Act* dealt with *cross-sectoral* and *non*-market access-related violations of the WTO, direct trade effects are a conceptually inept measurement unit of injury. No arbitration under Article 22.4 of the DSU has so far challenged this inappropriate quantification standard to calculate NoI. However, the Arbitration Report of *US–Section 110(5)*, an ad hoc arbitration under Article 25.3 of the DSU, truly is a silver line on the horizon. The arbitrator refrained from using a direct trade-effects test and used expectation damages as a baseline counterfactual.

(3) In order to fulfil the equivalence standard, arbitrators will have to enter the virgin territory of quantifying SCOO and establishing guidelines for implementing retaliation. This can be done without interfering with the complainant's choice of *nature* or *form* of retaliation (as Article 22.7 of the DSU demands). The complaining member may just as well prescribe its preferred modalities or policy mix of SCOO – such as a minor *ad valorem* tariff hike in a number of sectors, prohibitive tariffs on targeted products, suspension of intellectual property rights, etc. Yet it is for the arbitrator to judge and approve the *intensity* of such action. Importantly, equivalence between the level of NoI and SCOO can be established without retaliating in the identical *form* and *intensity* to counter the detrimental effect of the offending measure: having 'monetized' both the level of damage suffered and remedy granted *according to the same quantification methodology* suffices to make different actions *equi*-valent (of equal value). Hence, although NoI may have been triggered by an infringement of some intellectual property right (measured in terms of economic losses suffered), the SCOO could well occur in terms of imposition of retaliatory tariffs.

(4) Reform may seem organizationally simple, but it is technically challenging: to our mind, the current major deficiencies of WTO arbitration are not the result of a flawed *contract*, but rather of an incomplete contract *interpreted* in an erroneous manner by previous arbitrators. The upshot of this is finding that an agenda for reform can be implemented without having to rewrite parts of the WTO Agreement.

2 Introduction: a law and economics approach to the equivalence standard of Article 22.4 of the DSU

Enforcement is a crucial component of every contract.[2] The WTO, like any other contract, is staffed with a remedial regime aimed at establishing a fair and equitable relationship between injury and punishment. The DSU regulates the process of litigating, arbitrating and sanctioning cases of contractual breach.[3] Most violations of the WTO contract fall into the category of the 'equivalence standard' of Article 22.4 of the DSU, which states that '[t]he level of the suspension of concessions or other obligations authorized by the DSB shall be *equivalent* to the level of the nullification or impairment' (emphasis added).[4]

When the framers of the WTO Agreement authorized the arbitrator[5] to establish and safeguard this equivalence standard in Article 22.7 of the

[2] In fact, contractual enforcement is a *sine qua non* of contracts, since it gives effect to mutual commitments and deters defection. Without enforcement, a contract is likely to break down, or, more probably, will not be concluded in the first place (see WTO 2007, *World Trade Report 2007: Sixty Years of Multilateral Trading Order*, section III.E for an exhaustive introduction of enforcement).

[3] The WTO deals with issues of enforcement mainly in Article XXIII of the General Agreement on Tariffs and Trade (GATT), the General Agreement on Trade in Services (GATS), and the DSU. However, some multilateral agreements feature their own dispute settlement clauses (for example the Agreement on Safeguards and Countervailing Measures, SCM, or the Agreement on Agriculture).

[4] Alternative standards to equivalence are that of 'appropriateness', as spelled out in Article 4.10 of the SCM Agreement and 'commensurate adverse effects' in Article 7.9 of the SCM (see Thomas Sebastian, Chapter 4, above). When retaliating against prohibited subsidies (Article 4.10 of the SCM), complaining parties are allowed to enact 'appropriate', rather than 'substantially equivalent' countermeasures. Three arbitrations under the provision of Art. 4.10 SCM have so far been concluded (*Brazil–Aircraft*, *Canada–Aircraft II*, *US–FSC*, DS 46, 70, 108). The arbitration in *US–Cotton* (DS 267) dealt with 'actionable' subsidies and 'countermeasures commensurate adverse effects determined to exist', under the purview of Article 7.9 of the SCM.

[5] Footnote 16 of the DSU clarifies that '[t]he expression "arbitrator" shall be interpreted as referring either to an individual or a group or to the members of the original panel when serving in the capacity of arbitrator'.

DSU,[6] they may have seen it as a straightforward task. At face value, the equivalence standard consists of three components:

(1) determine whether the amount of NoI claimed to have been suffered by the complaining party is equivalent to the level of NoI of benefits accruing to this member as a result of the respondent's failure to bring its inconsistent measure into conformity with its obligations. If this is not the case, establish the level of NoI by assessing the detrimental effects on the complaining party caused by a violation of WTO rules;
(2) establish the level of suspension of SCOO, that is, assess the retaliation mix that the complainant may legally enact against the injurer (the responding party);
(3) safeguard equivalence between the levels of NoI and SCOO.

As this chapter will argue, the devil lies in the detail, and the practice of arbitrations in the last 14 years has shown that implementing the equivalence standard has not been a straightforward exercise, and not one that arbitrators have mastered with distinction.

A structured and coherent study of the 'equivalence standard' under Article 22.4 of the DSU has so far been wanting in the WTO literature[7] – and in the practice of DSB arbitrators. This chapter will proceed in a straightforward fashion. Decomposing the WTO's equivalence standard into its constituent parts, section 3 will deal with the law and economics (L&E) aspects of the calculation of NoI, the quantification of SCOO and ways of safeguarding the equivalence between those two components. In that section, we lay out which choices contracting parties principally have when choosing a remedial regime, and give a practical and theoretical assessment of the different options. We will discuss the remedies that rational contracting parties of a multilateral trade agreement can be assumed to craft, and the tasks this would impose on WTO arbitrators.

In Section 4, we will then compare these theoretical findings with the past 14 years of arbitration practice in the WTO. It will be argued that

[6] 'The arbitrator ... shall determine whether the level of such suspension is equivalent to the level of nullification or impairment' (Article 22.7 of the DSU).

[7] Exceptions are the works of T. Sebastian, 'World Trade Organization Remedies and the Assessment of Proportionality: Equivalence and Appropriateness', *Harvard International Law Journal*, 48:2 (2007), 337–82; H. Spamann, 'The Myth of "Rebalancing" Retaliation in WTO Dispute Settlement Practice', *Journal of International Economic Law*, 9:1 (2006), 31–79 and to some extent R. Z. Lawrence, *Crimes and Punishments? Retaliation under the WTO* (Washington, DC: Institute for International Economics, 2003). See also Thomas Sebastian's fine contribution in this volume (Chapter 4, above).

arbitrators have failed to fulfil their mandate of safeguarding the equivalence standard, because they assumed a 'hands-off' approach to the calculation of SCOO. Instead, arbitrators quantified the level of NoI, leaving the decision over the level of SCOO to the complaining party. The calculation of the level of NoI was undercompensatory for the complaining parties, arbitrary in its choice of counterfactuals and incompetent to address violations of non-market access WTO entitlements.

Section 5 will conclude, starting with a discussion of whether it is the WTO enforcement *system* that is at fault, or whether the *interpretation* of the contract by the arbitrators has caused the profound flaws in the current WTO arbitrations. After all, arbitrators might not be to blame for the failure to fulfil their mandate of safeguarding the equivalence standard; the WTO contract may have been drafted in a manner that renders the equivalence standard futile. Based on this discussion, we draw conclusions and lay out a tentative agenda for reform.

3 The law and economics of the equivalence standard

Detached from the reality of WTO arbitrations, this section will examine L&E aspects of enforcement in multilateral trading agreements. We thereby follow the instructions of Article 22.4 of the DSU (as set out in points (1) to (3) above). Subsection 3.1 is concerned with examining theoretical aspects of injury and damage assessment in a multilateral trade agreement (such as the WTO): we discuss the principal options contracting parties have when choosing damage benchmarks, measurement proxies for the unobservable harm and the scope of NoI. Subsection 3.2 will proceed to discuss the basics of remedial action: we assess theoretical aspects in connection with the calculation and operationalization of retaliation or 'trade sanctions', which is the DSU's remedy of last resort (see Articles 3.7 and 22.1 of the DSU). Finally, subsection 3.3 will discuss ways of satisfying the equivalence between the level of trade damages (NoI) and remedies (SCOO).

3.1 Calculating the level of nullification and impairment

As a matter of principle, contract injury is a function of *nature*, *form* and *intensity* of harm suffered by a victim party. If one is to assess the detrimental effects suffered by a WTO complainant from a violating measure, one has to grasp just which contractual commitment is being violated by the measure in question, how the violation took place and the extent of the violation.

3.1.1 Nature and form of injury

Since a contractual violation (partially) undoes the underlying contract, the *nature* and *form* of harm incurred by the victim are intricately intertwined with the *nature* of the contract proper. Applied to the WTO treaty, this means that any measurement of NoI presupposes a clear understanding of the reasons why sovereign countries decided to cooperate in trade affairs in the first place. We need to understand the nature of WTO commitments exchanged by contracting parties in pursuit of these underlying motivations to conclude a contract.

Siding with Irwin and Mavroidis and the WTO Trade Report 2007,[8] we believe that the WTO Agreement is a 'mixed motive game'[9] concluded by a number of quite heterogeneous countries. When signing (on to) the WTO, signatories to the WTO were probably motivated by an array of (partially conflicting) economic and non-economic contracting objectives. Governments may have wished to promote peace and stability in their regions, propel their power rank in the international system, attract direct foreign investment, fight unemployment, mitigate the influence of special interest groups or stop trade partners from engaging in excessive 'beggar-thy-neighbour' policies.[10] This multitude of objectives has given rise to an array of mutual rights and obligations (contractual commitments or 'entitlements'). We distinguish three different groups of entitlements that WTO members have agreed to exchange: (i) the reciprocal market access entitlement; (ii) various minimum standard entitlements; and (iii) auxiliary entitlements.[11]

(i) *The reciprocal market access entitlement.* This entitlement is a WTO member's right to compete fairly in the goods and services markets of its trade partners – up to the degree granted by each of them. The market access entitlement forms the backbone of the GATT and the GATS. It is composed of *substantive* and *contracting*

[8] D. A. Irwin and P. C. Mavroidis, *The Genesis of the GATT* (Oxford University Press, 2008); and WTO, *World Trade Report 2007: Sixty Years of Multilateral Trading Order*, (Geneva: World Trade Organization, 2007).

[9] P. C. Mavroidis, *Trade in Goods* (Oxford University Press, 2007), ch. 1.2.5, 20.

[10] WTO, see note 8, above, section II.B.

[11] The interested reader is referred to J. Pauwelyn, 'How Strongly *Should* We Protect and Enforce International Law?', Mimeo, 2006, subsequently published in revised version as *Optimal Protection of International Law: Navigating between European Absolutism and American Voluntarism* (Cambridge University Press, 2008), S. A. B. Schropp, *Trade Policy Flexibility and Enforcement in the WTO: A Law and Economics Analysis* (Cambridge University Press, 2009; S. A. B. Schropp, 'Revisiting the "Compliance-vs.-Rebalancing" Debate in WTO Scholarship: Towards a Unified Research Agenda', Mimeo, 2007.

obligations.[12] The *substantive* WTO obligations define the reciprocal trade liberalization commitments in the form of tariff cuts and service concessions in the four GATS service modes of supply ('schedules'). Substantive trade liberalization concessions form the core of any trade agreement. The level of market access is equivalent to the size of the promise – the number of sectors and the degree of market opening to which signatories agree to be bound. It lies in the contractual nature of the WTO that the trade entitlement is *reciprocally* owed.[13] Yet the market access entitlement consists of more than just substantive commitments to trade liberalization. Integrated into the market access entitlement are *contracting* provisions aimed at maintaining and stabilizing the initially agreed-upon mutual trade balance.[14]

(ii) *Minimum standard entitlements.* The bilaterally owed market access entitlement is crucial, albeit not the only commitment exchanged in the WTO contract. As Pauwelyn aptly states, there are other

[12] A. Schwartz, 'Relational Contracts in the Courts: An Analysis of Incomplete Agreements and Judicial Strategies', *Journal of Legal Studies*, 21:2 (1992), 271–318.

[13] To appreciate the inherently bilateral and reciprocal logic of the market access entitlement, consider the following: each contracting party enters into a *bilateral* trade liberalization deal with every other WTO member, and fixes its level of market access depending on the access to foreign markets it is granted in return. For mercantilist or welfare-economic reasons, it is in the interest of every trade negotiator to extract the most extensive trade concessions possible from other contracting parties and to 'give away' as few concessions as possible (K. Bagwell and R. W. Staiger, 'An Economic Theory of GATT', *American Economic Review*, 89:1 (1999), 215–48; K. Bagwell, P. C. Mavroidis and R. W. Staiger, 'It's a Question of Market Access', *American Journal of International Law*, 96:1 (2002), 56–76; K. Bagwell and R. W. Staiger, *The Economics of the World Trading System* (Cambridge, MA: MIT Press, 2002)). Whether or not an accord between parties A and B frustrates previous market access commitments of another third party C, is *a priori* irrelevant to the governments of members A and B, as long as doing so does not affect their respective utilities. The market access obligation is consequently organized in a web of bilateral deals. Despite the most-favoured-nations obligation of Articles I of the GATT and II of the GATS (rules geared toward reducing transaction costs and negative spillovers), the right to trade is not owed to the collective membership, but *directly* to every signatory.

[14] Examples for *contracting* provisions are non-discrimination stipulations (for example, Articles I and III GATT); a prohibition of quantitative restrictions (for example, Article XI of the GATT); codes of conduct detailing how to deal with non-tariff barriers (for example, Article III of the GATT, or the agreements on Subsidies and Countervailing Duties, Technical Barriers to Trade, or Rules of Origin). Explicit exceptions to the right to compete in foreign markets also form part of the trade entitlement (such as Articles IV, XVII, XXIV of the GATT, or the 'Enabling Clause'), as do waivers (for example, Art. IX of the Marrakech Agreement).

non-market access-related entitlements in the WTO which are inexplicable by the logic of reciprocal tariff concessions alone.[15]

Minimum standard entitlements, or *positive integration* norms, as they could also be termed, are contractual concessions that oblige every participating WTO member to adhere to an agreed core set of legal standards and abide by the same rules of the game. The objective of these minimum standard provisions is to reap positive concessions from every participating member.[16] Often, positive integration rules mandate the introduction of certain institutional features and procedures – *independently* of the state of implementation in other countries.[17] Examples of minimum standard entitlements can be found most poignantly in the multilateral TRIPS and ILP agreements.[18] The so-called 'new issue areas' of the WTO may be seen as accords in the same spirit – motivations based on a motivation quite distinct from the reciprocal exchange of market access.[19]

Minimum standard entitlements, in contrast to bilaterally owed market access entitlement, are owed to the contracting community as a whole, that is, they have a *multilateral* scope. Their *erga omnes partes* logic is distinct from a bilateral ambit of the market access

[15] J. Pauwelyn, 'How Strongly *Should* We Protect and Enforce International Law?', footnotes 91 and 93.

[16] For example, D. de Bièvre, 'Governance in International Trade: Judicialisation and Positive Integration in the WTO', *Preprints of the Max Planck Institute for Research on Collective Goods* (Bonn: Max Planck Institute for Research on Collective Goods, 2004), 1–23.

[17] Positive integration norms are based on a 'thou shalt ...' (prescriptive) logic, whereas negative integration norms are based on a 'thou shalt not ...' (prohibitive) logic. Positive norms mandate the establishment of a certain result or effect, while negative norms prohibit certain behaviour or outcomes. Take the TRIPS Agreement: Part II (Articles 9–40) is entitled 'Standards Concerning the Availability, Scope and Use of Intellectual Property Rights'. These articles lay down for each intellectual property right in succession, the applicable minimum standards for protection, and to what extent – and how – member countries are required to comply with them.

[18] Agreement on Trade-Related Intellectual Property Rights and Agreement on Import Licensing Procedures, respectively. Note, however, that other agreements, such as the Agreement on Technical Barriers to Trade, the Agreement on Sanitary and Phytosanitary Measures, the 'Agreement on Government Procurement' (GPA) or the 'Agreement on Rules of Origin' also contain numerous positive integration norms.

[19] Other 'new WTO issues', such as competition, investment, trade facilitation, labour and environment, belong to the same category of positive integration rules. These new issues have not yet been cast into WTO agreements, but have been on the bargaining table for some time (for in-depth introduction into new trade policy issues, see B. Hoekman and M. Kostecki, *The Political Economy of The World Trading System* (Oxford University Press, 1995); J. H. Jackson, *The World Trading System* (Cambridge, MA: MIT Press,), 305–18; M. Trebilcock and R. Howse, *International Trade Regulation (*London: Routledge, 2006).

entitlement:[20] as to reciprocal entitlements, the *rights* of one contracting party constitute the *obligations* of the other. A multilateral entitlement, on the other hand, is not exchanged on a *quid pro quo* basis; it is *owned by* the entire membership, as well as *owed to* the WTO community as a whole. If a member violates its multilateral obligation to, say, supply patent protection and establish a functioning patent office under TRIPS, this member impairs the competitive opportunities of all other members. It brings down the general level of operations and harms the system as a whole.

(iii) *Auxiliary entitlements.* The WTO also comprises a vast number of auxiliary entitlements – social ordering devices that supply the trade agreement with a fundamental structure necessary to facilitate the underlying exchange. Auxiliary entitlements are also phrased as positive *erga omnes partes* norms and rarely leave any degrees of freedom to transactors; they oblige all contracting parties to the same degree. We propose to distinguish four types of basic auxiliary entitlements in the WTO: (1) procedural rules;[21] (2) transparency

[20] Multilateral obligations are sometimes called *obligations erga omnes partes* (*cf.* J. Pauwelyn, 'The Role of Public International Law in the WTO: How Far Can We Go?' *American Journal of International Law*, 95:3 (2001), 535–78), since they are owed to the entire membership. This nomenclature, however, may be perceived as misleading, because *as a matter of positive law* (by virtue of Article 3.4 of the DSU), WTO rights and obligations are *de iure* applicable to *all* WTO members. Based on this insight, some scholars have argued that reciprocity and bilateral market access-related rights and obligations are a thing of the past, and that all contemporary WTO legal obligations have a multilateral ambit (for example J. Pauwelyn, 'Enforcement and Countermeasures in the WTO: Rules are Rules – Toward a More Collective Approach', *American Journal of International Law*, 94:2 (2000), 335–47; S. Charnovitz, 'Rethinking WTO Trade Sanctions', *American Journal of International Law*, 95:4 (2001), 792–832; S. Charnovitz, 'Should the Teeth Be Pulled? An Analysis of WTO Sanctions' in D. L. M. Kennedy and J. D. Southwick (eds.), *Political Economy of International Trade Law: Essays in Honor of Robert E. Hudec* (Cambridge University Press, 2002), 602–35; J. H. Jackson, 'International Law Status of WTO Dispute Settlement Reports: Obligation to Comply or Option to "Buy Out"?', *American Journal of International Law*, 98:1 (2004), 109–25). We beg to differ: as we explained in footnote 13, above, the *logic* of the market access entitlement is inherently bilateral, even though it is *de iure* owed to the all WTO members. We will henceforth use the terminology *erga omnes partes* only for those entitlements that logically have a multilateral ambit.

[21] The WTO has a whole range of procedural rules that delineate organizational issues, such as time-lines (for example those laid down in Articles 4, 8, 16, 17, 20 and 22 of the DSU), rules of decision making (Article IX of the Marrakech Agreement), voting and selection procedures (for example, Article 8.4 of the DSU on dispute panel composition), disclosure requirements (such as those in Art. XXIV.7 of the GATT, or Articles 3, 4, 10 or 25 of the DSU), or general provisions of *modus operandi* (such as Arts. XXII, XIV and XV of the Marrakech Agreement on *accession, acceptance, entry into force and deposit* and *withdrawal*, respectively).

entitlements;[22] (3) obligations owed to the Institution;[23] and (4) 'external' entitlements.[24]

The reader may prefer a different classification of WTO entitlements that the contracting parties have shaped for themselves, yet one thing seems evident: the WTO is a *multi-objective*, certainly, however, a *multi-entitlement* treaty.

Violations of the treaty can affect different entitlements (*nature* of damage) and affect single entitlements in different ways (*form* of damage). Any approach to calculation of injury or damage that fails to identify the *nature* and *form* of the entitlement that is being violated by an offending measure is prone to produce serious flaws. An infringement of a reciprocal market access entitlement, for example, a violation of a bound tariff commitment, is likely to provoke a quite different set of detrimental effects on complaining parties, as does a breach of an *erga omnes partes* commitment (say, the violation of a transparency obligation).[25]

[22] Transparency obligations are scattered across WTO agreements. Their objective is to reduce unnecessary search and error costs in connection with economic exchange (see R. Wolfe, 'Regulatory Transparency, Developing Countries and the WTO', *World Trade Review*, 2:2 (2003), 157–82 or WTO, *World Trade Report 2007*, section II.C.5).

[23] Examples for obligations owed to the Institution are yearly financial contributions by members to the WTO or the obligation to assign trade experts to serve on dispute panels.

[24] External entitlements delineate contractual freedom in the WTO. International trade has crucial ties to many other activities of international concern (J. Pauwelyn, *Conflicts of Norms in Public International Law: How the WTO Relates to Other Rules of International Law* (Cambridge University Press, 2003). Hence, public international law is the relevant 'playground', or domain, in which WTO members are free to contract. Of special importance are peremptory norms of international law (*ius cogens*), which have acceptance among the international community of states as a whole, not for WTO members only. Unlike norms of customary international law which can be modified by mutual consent or subsequent practice, WTO members must not 'contract around' *ius cogens* norms.

[25] To see the logical and practical differences between a market access-related and an *erga omnes partes*-related violation, consider the *Norway–Trondheim Toll Ring* case from 1991 (a GATT dispute). Norway failed to respect its transparency obligations under the GPA, because the municipal authorities in Trondheim assigned un-notified public works to a Norwegian company. This infringement of the GPA transparency provisions may have led to damage. Yet, who was harmed by the measure and how to quantify such damages? Note that in principle *any* company operating in the relevant field and originating from a GPA signatory country could have won the contract bid. Hence, *any* supplier could have successfully litigated against Norway (*cf.* P. C. Mavroidis, 'Government Procurement Agreement; The Trondheim Case: The Remedies Issue', *Aussenwirtschaft*, 48(I) (1993), 77–94). Contrast this with the illegal imposition of a tariff by country A against country B: the impact of the offending measure can be readily assessed due to the bilateral nature of the market access entitlement.

3.1.2 Intensity of injury

If one is to assess the degree, or intensity, of injury caused by the violation of a certain contractual entitlement, close consideration must be put on two basic issues: (i) the specification of a proper baseline or counterfactual with which to compare reality; and (ii) finding the adequate scale and scope, that is, the right unit of measurement with which to quantify NoI and the right mix of effects to consider.

3.1.2.1 Constructing the appropriate counterfactual Quantification of injury provoked by contractual violation necessarily involves the comparison between an *actual* situation – the world as it exists today in the presence of a continuing violation – and a *hypothetical* situation of what the world could look like in the absence of that unlawful measure at issue. When concluding the trade agreement, contracting parties can choose between different counterfactual scenarios against which to compare the actual violation-ridden situation. We want to distinguish between three different scenarios that have received wide attention in the L&E literature:[26]

(a) the construction of the *status quo ante* the breach, that is, the hypothetical situation that would exist if the illegality were removed (so-called *reliance* measure of damage calculation);
(b) the construction of the *status quo ante* the contract, that is, the hypothetical situation that would exist if the initial deal had never contained the obligation that was withdrawn by the responding member in the first place (*restitution* measure);
(c) the construction of the hypothetical situation that would exist if the illegality had never been committed and the injurer had always performed according the contract (*expectation* measure).

These three counterfactual scenarios differ significantly in the resulting amount of injury to which the complaining party will be authorized to retaliate.

[26] For example, S. Shavell, 'Damage Measures for Breach of Contract', *Bell Journal of Economics*, 11:2 (1980), 466–90; W. P. Rogerson, 'Efficient Reliance and Damage Measures for Breach of Contract', *Rand Journal of Economics*, 15:1 (1984), 39–53; S. Shavell, 'The Design of Contracts and Remedies for Breach', *Quarterly Journal of Economics*, 99:1 (1984), 121–48; R. Cooter and M. A. Eisenberg, 'Damages for Breach of Contract', *Californian Law Review*, 73:5 (1985), 1432–81; A. S. Edlin and S. Reichelstein, 'Holdups, Standard Breach Remedies, and Optimal Investment', *American Economic Review*, 86:3 (1996), 478–501; P. G. Mahoney, 'Contract Remedies: General' in B. Bouckaert and G. de Geest (eds.), *Encyclopedia of Law and Economics* (Ghent: Edward Elgar, University

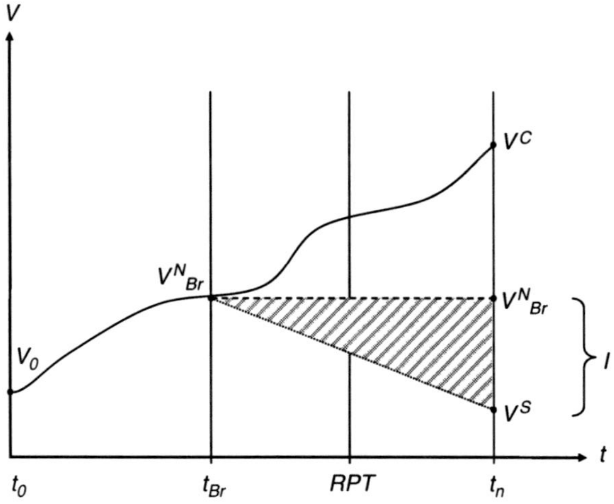

Figure 20.1. Reliance damages as baseline for the calculation of NoI

(a) The reliance measure The *reliance* remedy measure hypothesizes a world that would exist if the illegality were removed once and for all. Such a counterfactual demands that the level of damages be sufficient to restore the victim's *status quo ante* the breach.[27] To see the implications of this applied to the WTO context, consider figure 20.1, which represents a stylized cooperation scenario between two contracting parties, seen from the point of view of an injured party.

Suppose a trade agreement between two countries, *C* (for complainant) and *R* (for respondent). At some point in time (t_0), the two countries decide to conclude a trade liberalization treaty, because both countries realize that they could benefit from economic efficiencies generated from market opening, rule of law, specialization gains and trading activity. The vertical axis of figure 20.1 plots the complainant's welfare level (*V*), the horizontal axis is a time ray. Point V_0 marks the welfare level in the non-cooperative past in absence of a contract.[28] As time goes by, this mutual

of Ghent, 1999), 117–40; and S. E. Masten, 'Contractual Choice' in B. Bouckaert and G. de Geest (eds.), *Encyclopedia of Law and Economics*, 25–45.

[27] R. Cooter and M. A. Eisenberg, 'Damages For Breach of Contract'; P. G. Mahoney, 'Contract Remedies: General'; K. Mahlstein and S. A. B. Schropp, 'Optimal Design of Trade Policy Flexibility in the WTO', Mimeo, 2007.

[28] Note that point V_0 represents the Nash level of cooperation, which is the degree of cooperation with no contract in place. The cooperation at the Nash level may well be positive and different from a zero transaction level.

trade liberalization contract reaps the expected efficiencies and, hence, produces welfare gains. Signatory *C* benefits from a productive exchange of goods and services with *R*. *C*'s welfare level thereby is dependent on the frequency of interactions, the depth and breadth of initial trade liberalization commitments and the quality of the institutional design agreed to *ex ante*, that is, at the time of the conclusion of the contract.

At some point in time (t_{Br}), the respondent *R* – for whatever reason – commits a breach of the contract (for simplicity, suppose a protectionist tariff hike or tariff equivalent red-tape measure). *C* suffers damage from this violation and initiates a trade dispute. Time passes as the litigation proceeds through the different dispute stages, while *C* continues to suffer injury from the offending measure. At present (t_n), the complainant's welfare level is V^S – instead of V^C, the welfare level that *C* would enjoy under continuing performance on the part of signatory *R*.

Assuming that the two contracting parties have agreed on the design of a remedial regime such that NoI is calculated according to *reliance* damages, a WTO arbitrator is mandated to construct a counterfactual situation that would exist if the illegality were removed at t_n, and full cooperation were to resume on the same level as before the breach. It is important to notice that all the gains from continued cooperation that would have been reaped between t_{Br} (the time of the violation) and t_n (the present) are not taken into account. The time lapsed between t_{Br} and t_n is essentially treated as if it had not happened, or as if no contractual exchange had occurred meanwhile and, hence, no trade efficiencies realized. With respect to the violated obligation the arbitrator has to construct the Nash payoff at the time of the violation ($V^N{}_{Br}$), and to calculate the injury as the difference between the complainant's actual welfare level V^S and the constructed welfare level $V^N{}_{Br}$. Taking into consideration the time lapsed between the breach yields a level of damage in the amount of the hatched triangle.

(b) The restitution measure The *restitution* damage measure re-establishes the *status quo ante* of the *contract* with respect to the measure in question.[29] The level of NoI must be sufficient to restore the Nash level that persisted before the contract in the non-cooperative past with respect to the violated commitment. Restitution damages aim at reconstructing what the contract would look like if the offending measure in question had *never* been part of the initial deal. With a mandate of restitution, the WTO arbitrator has to compare reality with a counterfactual situation

[29] P. G. Mahoney, 'Contract Remedies: General'.

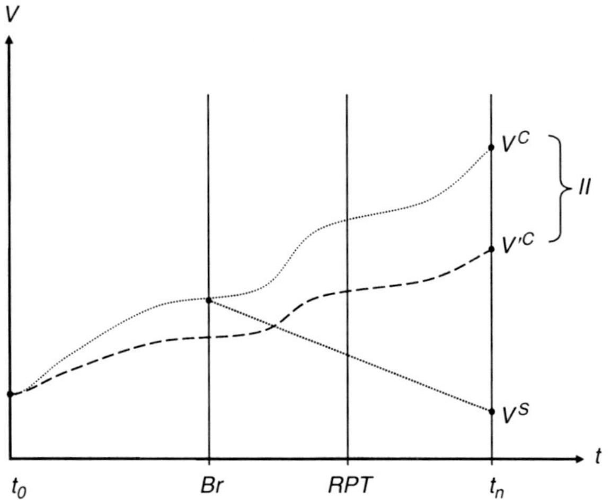

Figure 20.2. Restitution damages as baseline for the calculation of NoI

that would exist if the initial trade agreement had never contained the offending measure. The arbitrator is to re-establish the contract net of the withdrawn contractual provision: he is to *rebalance* the trade contract *at a lower level* of cooperation. Had the complainant known that the withdrawn measure was not part of the initial deal, it would have made fewer trade liberalization commitments from the start. The contract consequently would have featured fewer mutual commitments, less depth and breadth and therewith yielded fewer trade efficiencies.[30]

The outcome of calculating NoI according to the restitution measures is illustrated in figure 20.2 above. Under a restitution scenario, the arbitrator assesses how the absence of the withdrawn concession would have changed the content of the initial trade deal at time t_0 (figure 20.2). In essence, he is tasked with retracting (or retrofitting) the signatories' cooperative zeal *without* the offending measure and the measure's reciprocal commitment on the part of the complaining party, and how cooperation would have played out during the entire contract history. This hypothetical situation is then compared with C's payoff under the counterfactual of continued cooperation under the real contract at the

[30] Note that re-establishing the *status quo ante* the contractual obligation puts the arbitrator in the same situation as the one faced by WTO members when one requesting member requests permission to *modify* its concessions under Articles XXVIII of the GATT or XXI of the GATS (see S. A. B. Schropp, *Trade Policy Flexibility and Enforcement in the WTO: A Law and Economics Analysis*, ch. 5).

present t_n. The arbitrator ought to compare V^C and V'^C. The net present value of the difference between the hypothetical welfare levels V'^C and V^C then makes up the injury suffered by the complaining party.

(c) The expectation measure *Expectation* damages relate to a world in which the victim of a contractual violation is fully compensated for all its efficiency losses due to the respondent's measure in question. 'Expectation damages are designed to protect the expectation interest, and have the purpose of placing the victim of breach in the position he would have been in if the other party had performed.'[31] Expectation damages are equivalent to the replacement value that exactly makes the victim indifferent between the injurer's performance and his default. Expectation damages aim to reconstruct what the world would look like if the measure in question had never been committed. They are essentially 'commensurate damages' in game theory; they fully insure the victim against any dynamics that unfold *ex post*.[32]

To better illustrate expectation damages, consider figure 20.3: the arbitrator is essentially charged with retracting the efficiency path of cooperation that existed before the violating measure. Starting from t_{Br}, he constructs the efficiency path of the trading agreement up to the present t_n. At that time, he compares the hypothetical cooperation level V^C with the actual level V^S.

(d) Comparison of the three counterfactuals Figure 20.4 compares the three different calculation methods of NoI. It is important to realize that *all* three hypothetical scenarios are 'rebalancing' exercises of sorts: reliance (*I*) rebalances according to the pre-breach Nash level with respect to the violated obligation; expectation (*III*) rebalances mutual commitments as if breach had never happened; and restitution (*II*) rebalances

31 R. Cooter and M. A. Eisenberg, 'Damages For Breach of Contract', 1435.

32 The difference between expectation and reliance damages is that reliance compensates the victim for direct harm suffered, but leaves aside other effects and forgone opportunities. P. C. Mavroidis, 'Remedies in the WTO Legal System: Between a Rock and a Hard Place', *European Journal of International Law*, 11:4 (2000), 800 argues that expectation damages are strictly higher than *damnum emergens* (direct harm suffered). Rather, they must be interpreted as *lucrum cessans*: *all* further efficiency costs (opportunity costs or losses in value added) caused by the partial breach of the agreement over and above direct effects must be indemnified. Note that it is exactly these contractual efficiency gains that motivated transactors to conclude the contract in the first place (see also S. A. B. Schropp, 'The Case for Tariff Compensation in WTO Dispute Settlement', *Aussenwirtschaft*, 60:IV (2005), footnote 10 and accompanying text).

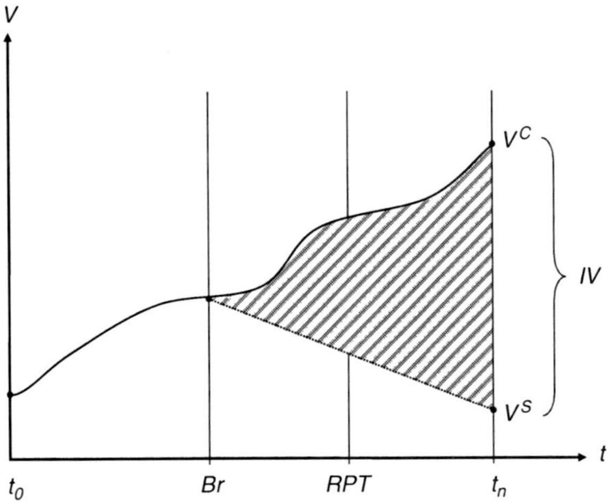

Figure 20.3. Expectation damages as baseline for the calculation of NoI

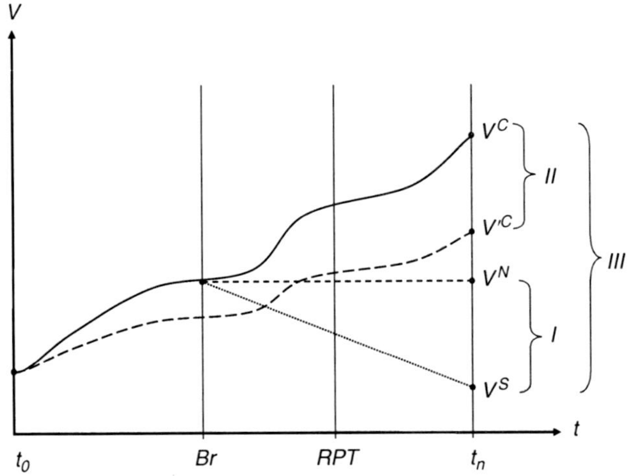

Figure 20.4. Comparing reliance (*I*), restitution (*II*) and expectation damages (*III*)

mutual obligations on a lower level, as if the offending measure had never been part of the original deal.

By definition, injury calculation by means of the reliance measure is smaller than expectation damages. Reliance is constructed using a counterfactual apt to compensate the complaining party for direct harm suffered, but leaves aside efficiency effects and forgone opportunities, such as transactional efficiency gains that would have accrued in the case of normal contractual performance. Yet it should be recalled that it is exactly these contractual efficiency gains that motivated transactors to conclude the contract in the first place.

Comparing the restitution counterfactual with reliance or expectation damages is considerably more difficult, since doing so essentially means comparing two entirely different contracts: the restitution counterfactual constructs a novel, less cooperative contract. Whether or not restitution damages are higher or lower than reliance damages cannot be generalized, since the restitution damage is forward-looking (net present value of the difference between cooperative payoffs under the real and hypothetical trade contract), whereas reliance and expectation damages are inherently backward-looking.

Let us now compare these three calculation methods from a L&E perspective: which of these three options would rational contracting parties opt for and fix contractually (if they had not forgotten to specify it, as is the case in the WTO)? We distinguish between *systemic* and *practical* evaluation criteria.

From a *systemic* point of view there is little doubt that expectation damages are the calculation benchmark of choice for rational and forward-looking signatories that conclude a trade agreement in an uncertain and volatile world. Modelling the WTO as a fully non-contingent tariff liberalization contract where contingencies (or 'states of nature') are uncertain and asymmetrically revealed, Mahlstein and Schropp[33] prove game-theoretically what Dunoff and Trachtman, Mavroidis, Sykes, and Schwartz and Sykes had already conjectured:[34] trade damages amounting to the expectation measure Pareto-dominate all other damage awards. Only NoI calculated as expectation damages yields the right incentives for contracting parties to liberalize optimally *ex ante*, and to default optimally *ex post*. In a world where complete contracts are impossible to conclude due to uncertainty about the future, trade agreements staffed with

[33] K. Mahlstein and S. A. B. Schropp, 'Optimal Design of Trade Policy Flexibility in the WTO'.

[34] J. L. Dunoff and J. P. Trachtman, 'Economic Analysis of International Law', *Yale Journal of International Law*, 24: winter (1999), 1–55; P. C. Mavroidis, 'Remedies in the WTO Legal System: Between a Rock and a Hard Place'; A. O. Sykes, 'The Remedy for Breach of Obligations under the WTO Dispute Settlement Understanding: Damages or Specific Performance?' in M. Bronckers and R. Quick (eds.), *New Directions in International Economic Law* (London: Kluwer Law, 2000), 347–57; W. F. Schwartz and A. O. Sykes 'The Economic Structure of Renegotiation and Dispute Resolution in the WTO/GATT System', *Journal of Legal Studies*, 31:1 (2002), 170–204.

an expectation damages rule replicate the outcomes of the hypothetical contracting ideal of the complete contingent contract, and thereby fulfil the criteria of 'efficient breach'.[35] Both reliance and restitution damages *under*compensate the complaining party, because they do not indemnify it for the entire injury suffered. This, in turn, invites *excessive breach* by members in violation of the Agreement, because they are not forced to internalize all the injury they are causing and, hence, benefit from abrogating their *ex ante* commitments inefficiently often. *Ex ante,* that is, before the conclusion of the contract, those WTO members expecting to ever become an injured party during the course of the contract react by liberalizing inefficiently little compared with what would be welfare-optimal.[36]

[35] The 'efficient breach' hypothesis, as formulated by contemporary WTO literature, can be summarized as follows: 'There are circumstances where breach of contract is more efficient [for the general welfare of contracting parties] than performance, and the law ought to facilitate breach in such circumstances.' (J. L. Dunoff and J. P. Trachtman, 'Economic Analysis of International Law', 31); 'According to the concept of "efficient breach" … a contract breach allows the breaching party to pay damages to redress the harm (loss of profit etc.) without performing its obligations under the contract. In most cases, the nonbreaching party will be made "whole" and, in some cases, even better-off. Thus, the breaching party has the option of refusing further performance if its compensation fully protects the nonbreaching party's reasonable economic expectations from performance of the contract' (J. H. Jackson, 'International Law Status of WTO Dispute Settlement Reports: Obligation to Comply or Option to "Buy Out"?', 122).

[36] Note that this result of Pareto-dominance of the expectation damages measure seemingly stands in contrast to the findings suggested by the 'terms-of-trade' model of trade agreements, as promoted most prominently by Bagwell and Staiger (K. Bagwell and R. W. Staiger, 'An Economic Theory of GATT'; K. Bagwell, P. C. Mavroidis and R. W. Staiger, 'It's a Question of Market Access'; K. Bagwell and R. W. Staiger, *The Economics of the World Trading System*; K. Bagwell and R. W. Staiger, 'Multilateral Trade Negotiations, Bilateral Opportunism and the Rules of GATT/WTO', *Journal of International Economics*, 63:1 (2004), 1; WTO, *World Trade Report 2007*, section II.B provides a comprehensive overview of the terms-of-trade approach to trade agreements): as the contribution by Chad Bown and Michele Ruta, chapter 6, above, shows, the terms-of-trade school of trade agreements posits rebalancing according to the *status quo ante* the breach (reliance damages). The complaining party should react to WTO violations by raising its import tariffs up to a point where the initial terms of trade are re-established (compare K. Bagwell, and R. W. Staiger, *The Economics of the World Trading System*, ch. 6). We do not believe this result to be accurate, for the following reasons: first, the terms-of-trade model is primarily concerned with explaining the reasons for the existence of the trade contract – not a model of contractual deviation and enforcement (A. Keck and S. A. B. Schropp, 'Indisputably Essential: The Economics of Dispute Settlement Institutions in Trade Agreements', *Journal of World Trade*, 45:5 (2008)). Second, the model is uniquely focused on relative world prices, or terms of trade, and neglects all other reasons for contracting (compare, for example, W. J. Ethier, 'Political Externalities, Nondiscrimination, and a Multilateral World', *Review of International Economics*, 12:3 (2004), 303–20; W. J. Ethier,

From a *practical* point of view, it seems that expectation damages prevail over both restitution and reliance as the appropriate counterfactual for NoI. It is probably fair to say that quantifying NoI according to the restitution measure overburdens any arbitrator, no matter what his level of sophistication and economic expertise. Quantifying the *status quo ante* the *contract* net of the withdrawn commitment requires the construction of not only *one* counterfactual, but of *two*: that is, the welfare level yielded in the normal course of action of the contract (V^C in figure 20.4) *plus* what the original contract would have looked like if the reciprocal level of concession had been reduced by both the withdrawn commitment and the offsetting reciprocal commitment on the part of the complainant (V'^C). As mentioned above, the arbitrator in essence would need to engage in the same exercise as members that are modifying their schedules under Articles XXVIII, GATT or XXI, GATS: he would have to divine which concession or bundles of concessions the complaining party would have initially traded in for the respondent's right to drop the very concession it violated later on. Moreover, the arbitrator then ought to sketch the efficiency trajectory that this hypothetical contract would have taken from the conclusion of the contract up to the present. This demanding task would then be topped off with a net present value calculation of the difference between the hypothetical gains of the actual contract (V^C) with the hypothetical gains of the hypothetical contract (V'^C). Somewhere along this process the arbitrator would almost certainly be confronted with the vehement opposition of both litigating parties. Not only would the arbitrator most likely 'get it wrong', that is, construct a counterfactual contract that parties would not have concluded; in addition, both parties would have an incentive to misrepresent reality *ex post facto* by stating that the withdrawn commitment would have been worth much more, or much less, in terms of reciprocal concessions at the conclusion of the contract.

Comparing the practicality of the reliance scenario with the expectation measure of quantifying NoI, we point out the following: the reliance

'Selling Protection for Sale', PIER Working Paper No. 06–14, who is very critical of that approach). Third, the Bagwell and Staiger model world is a fairly schematic neoclassical model of trade in which real-life aspects, like increasing returns to scale or imperfect competition, are neglected. Also, the terms-of-trade model characterizes the WTO as a contract, with only *reciprocal tariff concessions* exchanged. This assumption makes self-enforcement especially easy. Most importantly, self-enforcement is modelled as *immediate* adjustment behaviour, rather than as lengthy dispute settlement. Enforcement is assumed to happen instantaneously and without time-lag, in which case reliance and expectation damages collapse to one solution anyway.

measure basically constructs the hypothesis of how the world would look if the illegal measure had been withdrawn at some point in the past. The question is, just *how* should the illegality be withdrawn. The respondent has a whole arsenal of options to bring its violating measure into compliance and therewith to re-establish a *status quo ante* the breach. It could withdraw the offending measure (say, a discriminatory treatment of imports), or it could seize the discrimination by banning all goods – imported and domestic alike – that display a certain feature. It could replace the illegal measure with an alternative sanitary or phytosanitary regulation.[37] Depending upon the underlying scenario, the quantification of damages will differ quite significantly.[38]

Compare the issue of multiple competing counterfactuals with the results of the expectation method of damage calculation: for expectation damages, the relevant counterfactual is the construction of a hypothetical world that would exist if *all* contracting parties had continued to perform according to the initial agreement. As long as there is a reasonable certainty of the exact nature of the illegal measure at issue, the task for the arbitrator is relatively straightforward. He is to extrapolate welfare levels and cooperation gains from the pre-breach past into the present in order to fabricate *one single* expectation counterfactual: what would the complainant's welfare level be today if the respondent had always performed according to its initial contractual obligations? Any further discussion of the choice of counterfactual is largely futile.

Giving the arbitrator guidelines as to how to construct the relevant baseline, or counterfactual, with which to compare the current situation, is a crucial contractual design issue for contracting parties to a trade

[37] See, for example, the panel in the *US–Superfund* case which noted that several different ways could be adopted to bring the disputed measure (here: a tax on gasoline) into conformity with Article III of the GATT, including an increase in the tax imposed on US products to bring it into line with the tax imposed on foreign products, or a reduction in the tax imposed on foreign products to bring it into line with the US internal level. According to the panel, 'each of these solutions would have different trade results and it is *therefore logically not possible to determine the … trade impact between the present tax and one consistent with Art III.2* [GATT]' (para. 5.1.9, emphasis added).

[38] T. Sebastian, 'World Trade Organization Remedies and the Assessment of Proportionality: Equivalence and Appropriateness' puts it in cautious legalese: 'The key point here is that the determination of the extent of detrimental effect resulting from a violation is a comparative exercise that requires the adoption of a baseline. *Because there are no clear governing principles, the choice of this baseline could be controversial …* All calculations of detrimental effects suffer from a certain degree of arbitrariness' (added emphasis), (351, 353; see also H. Spamann, 'The Myth of "Rebalancing" Retaliation in WTO Dispute Settlement Practice', 52).

agreement. Possible candidates of injury calculation are the reliance, restitution and expectation damages measures. All three are 'rebalancing' measures of sorts, yet each counterfactual strives at rebalancing mutual concessions on different levels: before the contract (restitution); before the breach (reliance); after the breach (expectation). The choice of counterfactual has a most important impact on the functioning of a trade regime, both from a systemic and a practical point of view.

Expectation damages as a counterfactual against which to measure the actual situation seems to Pareto-dominate other institutional arrangements. Under the regime of expectation damages, signatories to a trade agreement are prone to liberalize optimally *ex ante* and to refrain from excessive breach *ex post*. Expectation damages relieve the arbitrator from having to make more or less arbitrary choices between multiple different counterfactual scenarios.

3.1.2.2 Different standards of measuring NoI: issues of scale and scope Knowledge of the appropriate counterfactual with which to compare the actual violation-ridden situation is a valuable first step in an injury calculation. Further issues arise. In principle, damage suffered from contractual breach is not only profoundly *subjective* to the victim, it is also *private information* to the affected party. This fact leads to several non-trivial problems: for any damage calculation, the arbitrator should be aware of the *identity* of the concerned party. Is the injured party the international trading system, society at large, the government (trade policy makers), companies in the affected sector or special interest groups?[39] Next, should *non-economic* dimensions, such as emotional, cultural, societal or physical distress, play any role and thus be integrated in a damage assessment?[40] Finally, self-revelation of actual damage by the affected party is not an option, since this would inevitably invite moral hazard

[39] On this topic, see Alan Sykes, Chapter 16, above.

[40] When it comes to considering *non-economic* effects, we concur with standing case law that WTO arbitrations are to deal exclusively with economic issues. It is probably fair to say that the WTO is an economic contract and its 'currency' therefore also is profoundly economic. See the arbitrator in *EC–Bananas III (US)* (Article 22.6) (DSR 1999:II, 725), para. 6.10: '[A] Member's *potential interest* in trade in goods or services and its interest in a determination of rights and obligations under the WTO Agreements are each sufficient to establish a right to pursue a WTO dispute settlement proceeding. However, a Member's *legal interest* in compliance by other Members does *not*, in our view, automatically imply that it is entitled to obtain authorization to suspend concessions under Article 22 of the DSU' (emphasis added). See also the Panel Report in *US–Byrd* (Article 22.6) (DSR 2003:II, 489), footnote 53.

behaviour on the part of the complainant. Due to hidden knowledge, victims of contractual breach are bound to overstate their actual harm so as to clock up any damage award.

Nothing in the text of the DSU reveals anything about how to deal with the above issues, or how trade damages should be measured. Article 22.4 of the DSU merely talks of a member's 'benefits' being nullified or impaired, but remains mute about whose benefits exactly are to be taken into consideration and which unit of measurement best proxies these forgone benefits. Since the text of the DSU is hardly helpful, let us resort to theory: what could be a reliable proxy for the unobservable NoI? Which metric best captures the actual injury suffered by a complaining party, is readily calculable and is fungible in the sense that it can be eventually transposed into a remedy award (read: SCOO)? In order to 'monetize', that is, monetarily quantify the injury suffered by the complaining member, issues of 'scale' and 'scope' are important.

As for the *scale*, or unit of measurement to quantify 'benefits' lost, at least three different metrics have been suggested in WTO scholarship:[41] trade effects; lost profits; and broader economic effects.

(1) A 'trade-effects test' measures trade flows blocked, that is, transactions lost or turnover not realized due to the respondent's measure in question. This is a fairly straightforward exercise in which the arbitrator assesses the quantity, or volume, of lost sales suffered by the complainant, priced in world prices for that good or service.[42]
(2) 'Lost profits'. It is assumed that the injured party could market its products somewhere else – albeit under less favourable conditions. The complainant forgoes profits due to the market-closing behaviour of the respondent, which are measured as 'deadweight loss triangles' in international economics.[43] Economists favour this way of measuring NoI, because it comes closest to their efficiency-driven worldview.

[41] J. Bernstein and D. Skully, 'Calculating Trade Damages in the Context of the World Trade Organization's Dispute Settlement Process', *Review of Agricultural Economics*, 25:2 (2003), 385–98; F. Breuss, 'WTO Dispute Settlement: An Economic Analysis of four EU-US Mine Trade Wars', *Journal of Industry, Competition and Trade*, 4:4 (2004), 275–315; J. P. Trachtman, 'Building the WTO Cathedral', Mimeo, 2006; T. Sebastian, 'World Trade Organization Remedies and the Assessment of Proportionality: Equivalence and Appropriateness'.

[42] For example, A. Keck, 'WTO Dispute Settlement: What Role for Economic Analysis?', *Journal of Industry, Competition and Trade*, 4:4 (2004), 365–71; WTO, *World Trade Report: Trade, Standards and the WTO* (Geneva: World Trade Organization, 2005), ch. III.A.

[43] J. Bernstein and D. Skully, 'Calculating Trade Damages in the Context of the World Trade Organization's Dispute Settlement Process'.

(3) A final alternative of measurement is economic gains and losses sustained by the complaining party as a result of the offending measure. This variant is considerably broader than both (1) and (2) in that it includes deadweight losses and direct trade blocked, but it also integrates other economic costs connected with losing existing markets and winning alternative ones, such as switching costs, transportation costs, warehousing costs, information-gathering costs, marketing costs or the costs of finding new outlets. It also includes economic gains that occur if other markets and outlets can be found to replace the lost profits to the respondent's market.

Concerning the *scope*, contracting parties may agree to look at only *direct* effects, that is, consequences in the affected sector. Alternatively, they may decide to consider *indirect* effects accruing in the complainant's entire economy, or even in other third-country markets. Market-closing behaviour by one country in a particular sector may provoke trickle-down, or spillover, effects in upstream or downstream industries within the domestic economy of a complaining party or in third countries. The United States in *EC–Bananas III*, for example, claimed damage in its domestic services sector stemming from the EC's ban of *Ecuadorian* bananas. Indirect effects can also occur in unaffected third-country markets. In *US–Byrd (Article 22.6)* the EC claimed that the US disbursements of antidumping and countervailing duty tariffs to its domestic operators crowded out European exports in other third-country markets.[44]

The difference between direct and indirect effects is obviously one between a *partial* and a *general equilibrium* view on the affected economy. As economists will testify, the choice between a partial and a general equilibrium set-up leads to a substantial difference in outcomes.

Figure 20.5 summarizes in a 2×3 matrix the possible standards of measuring NoI that contracting parties can opt for when they design a multilateral trading agreement below.

Let us now compare the six alternative ways of measuring NoI from a systemic and a practical point of view. From a systemic point of view a holistic examination of economy-wide effects would yield the most accurate results, if the arbitrator managed to perform a clear-cut *ceteris paribus* calculation, in which he managed to isolate and precisely separate effects caused by the violation from the 'white noise' triggered by the

[44] In the requesting parties' view, 'any analysis of trade effects should take into account the trade effects on the world market' (Arbitrator's Report, *US–Byrd* (Article 22.6) (DSR 2004:IX, 4591), para. 3.128).

Scale \ Scope	Direct (sectoral)	Indirect (economy-wide)
Trade blocked (lost turnover)	Blocked market access (volume effects)	Worldwide price and volume effects
Efficiency losses (lost profits)	Deadweight loss (partial equilibrium)	Deadweight loss (general equilibrium)
Economic losses	Economic gains/losses in sector	Economy-wide gains/losses

Figure 20.5. Different standards of measuring the intensity of NoI

normal course of economic activity. The problem with considering indirect effects, however, is one of accuracy. The more sectors that are integrated into the arbitrator's 'but for' analysis, the more difficult it becomes to attribute economic effects to the measure in question and to exclude with certainty that other social, economic, political or technical shocks are the source of the complainant's harm. 'Clinical' separation of injurious effects from other economic effects is difficult.[45] The arbitrator would commit a serious error if he attributed a certain economic effect to the offending measure while in reality it was caused by the business cycle, normal competition, a demand crisis or exchange rate volatility.[46]

[45] A. Keck, 'WTO Dispute Settlement: What Role for Economic Analysis?'

[46] Very understandably, contracting parties are keen on having arbitrators avoid *Type-I errors* (false positives). However, this comes at the cost of *Type-II errors* (false negatives). A *Type-I error* in this setting occurs whenever the arbitrator attributes a particular effect to the respondent's violation when, in fact, the effect is due to another cause or normal economic activity. With *Type-II errors*, the same arbitrator refuses to subject a particular effect to the responding party's actions when, in fact, these actions are at the core of a negative effect on the complaining party. The costs associated with each type of error may vary, but with a view to the amicability and stability of the entire dispute settlement system, it is probably the right choice for signatories to have the arbitrator avoid excessive attribution of damage to the respondent. Otherwise, inappropriate damage attribution may sour the atmosphere of the cooperation system. WTO members, instead of using the DSB in good faith, may enact retaliatory antidumping measures, or enter into retaliatory litigation. Alternatively, they may engage in *extra*-contractual means of retribution and/or aggressive self-help behaviour: they may opt for bilateral resolution outside the WTO forum, seek retaliation outside the trade realm (for example, political coercion), or engage in unilateral retaliation (for example, Section 301 of the US Trade Act of 1974).

Litigating parties in the WTO have shown a preference for curbing the arbitrator's opportunities to 'address effects that are too remote or speculative' (Arbitrator Report, *US–Byrd* at paragraph 3.129).[47] It is probably apposite for arbitrators to isolate the sector in question (in case the dispute pertains only to a single good or services sector) and to assess the direct effects in that affected industry, even if it comes at a cost of accuracy.

As for the choice of metric to approximate the unobservable damages suffered from WTO violations,[48] we contend that focusing uniquely on *lost profits* yields too small an amount to indemnify the injured complainant and to deter injuring parties from violating the WTO Agreement: calculating uniquely economic deadweight losses may satisfy a general welfare view on the global trading system, but this metric ultimately lacks realism. Not only does it assume perfect markets, infinitely elastic supply, absence of income and substitution effects, a partial equilibrium optic, etc. It also examines gains and losses from a detached, macro-economic, worldwide position, and thereby fails to attribute gains and losses to the different litigating parties: a loss of market share and competitive sales by a complaining party involves unrequited and unilateral transfer of resources from the complainant to the defendant (and possibly to third countries). Calculating deadweight losses may only proxy the resulting damage to the complainant accurately under quite abstract conditions: a two-country world with a trade barrier erected in the form of quotas (quota rents then go to the complainant); with alternative markets readily available to the complaining member; and no additional costs, such as product-switching costs, logistics costs, marketing costs or lost scale economies.

Applying a trade-effects test (blocked trade) to proxy NoI accruing to a complainant has three significant drawbacks: (1) it may *overstate* the damage incurred by the injured party, wherever alternative markets and outlets are available; (2) it *understates* injury with comparison to broader economic losses; and (3) it can only deal with traditional market access barriers such as tariffs, quotas and other import restrictions, but fails as a metric for measuring violation of other non-market access obligations.

[47] See also, Arbitration Report, *US–1916 Act* (DSR 2004:IX, 4269), para. 5.57 (citing the Arbitrators' Report, *EC–Hormones*, para. 77): 'We therefore proceed to consider the level of nullification and impairment in the present case, while avoiding claims that are "too remote", "too speculative", or "not meaningfully quantified".'

[48] J. Bernstein and D. Skully, 'Calculating Trade Damages in the Context of the World Trade Organization's Dispute Settlement Process', 389.

- Calculating bilateral trade blocked due to an offending measure is apt to overstate the true damage whenever the injured party can find alternative outlets for its goods and services. If the product at issue is in high demand and reasonably commoditized, the real damages accruing to the complainant may be much lower than forgone gross sales revenue.
- However, trade blocked (that is, turnover not generated) only partly covers the true injury suffered by the complainant and its domestic exporting industries. The complainant (or rather, industries originating in a complaining country) may face additional economic costs, such as product-switching costs, logistics, warehousing, information-gathering costs, marketing expenses and others. Moreover, the complaining party forgoes exactly those economic gains for which it concluded the trade agreement in the first place, namely, efficiencies from economic transactions, that is, trade efficiencies.
- Most importantly, blocked trade as a metric for NoI only applies to those violations that involve a partial closing of reciprocal market access. Whenever a WTO member, by means of a violating measure, forestalls reciprocal market access (be it in the form of a quantitative restriction, a trade barrier, red-tape measures or other kinds of market-closing policy), damage can be readily quantified in terms of blocked trade. But what about all the other non-reciprocal and non-market access entitlements that form a large part of WTO obligations (see subsection 3.1.1 above)? Trying to quantify NoI caused by a defection from an unreciprocated, multilateral entitlement by way of trade blocked must be seen as a futile task. It is hard to see how any rebalancing of mutual rights and obligations can be achieved through analysis of blocked trade in situations with positive, non-reciprocated commitments, such as a minimum standard obligations,[49] are infringed (think of a respondent's failure to establish a patent office).[50] In sum, as soon as a treaty obligation is violated which is not based on bilateral market access commitments, the 'trade effects' approach falters.

[49] See the earlier discussion around footnote 177 and accompanying text.

[50] See, for example, J. Pauwelyn, 'Enforcement and Countermeasures in the WTO: Rules are Rules – Toward a More Collective Approach', 342; J. H. Jackson, 'International Law Status of WTO Dispute Settlement Reports: Obligation to Comply or Option to "Buy Out"?', 121 notes: '[H]ow does one quantify a breach of a DSU norm? Rebalancing in any objective and meaningful way seems to be a fallacy in the light of the shifting perspective of the GATT/WTO system away from more quantifiable norms, such as tariff norms, toward broader rules that should arguably be shaped so as to provide benefits to all sides, not just a reciprocal "swap"'. See also our discussion around note 25, above.

Using a unit of measurement based on broader economic effects in the industry at issue may remedy the three above-mentioned shortcomings in connection with the calculation of NoI based on trade effects:[51] proper estimation of economic gains/losses should avoid the pitfall of overestimating damage in case alternative markets have been found for the complaining member's goods and services. Alternative markets and additional sales are economic gains that have to be juxtaposed to the economic losses involved in finding, capturing and marketing those new outlets, plus all the excess production that cannot be marketed. An economic gains and losses test integrates all those actually incurred economic costs that a mere trade-blocked methodology ignores (switching costs, information-gathering costs, logistics, warehousing, etc.). An economic effects test can deal with non-market access-related infringements, such as violations of patent protection, copyright standards or transparency obligations. Finally, a broader economic effects metric is comprehensive in the sense that a pure trade-effects test forms a subset of it.[52]

[51] One may argue that not only economic gains and losses *in the affected industry* should be taken into consideration, but the *general welfare* in the entire economy, including consumers, importers, and other economic actors (see Fritz Breuss' commentary on this chapter, below; see also F. Breuss, 'WTO Dispute Settlement: An Economic Analysis of Four EU–US Mine Trade Wars'; J. P. Trachtman, 'Building the WTO Cathedral'; H. Spamann, 'The Myth of "Rebalancing" Retaliation in WTO Dispute Settlement Practice'). Yet, as we stated above, *indirect* effects to other economic actors and other sectors may be accurate, but at the same time are very difficult to separate from the normal activity in a globalized economy (see I. Araki, 'Comment on Fritz Breuss "WTO Dispute Settlement"', *Journal of Industry, Competition and Trade*, 4:4 (2004), 345–64; A. Keck, 'WTO Dispute Settlement: What Role for Economic Analysis?'; W. Kohler, 'The WTO Dispute Settlement Mechanism: Battlefield or Cooperation?', *Journal of Industry, Competition and Trade*, 4:4 (2004), 317–36 in reaction to F. Breuss, 'WTO Dispute Settlement: An Economic Analysis of Four EU–US Mine Trade Wars'). Where do you draw the line? Whose benefits do you include: consumers', policy makers', customs officials', importers', import-competing industries', exporters', downstream suppliers', upstream buyers', overseas subsidiaries'? Any cut-off point here is arbitrary; we propose a simple and intuitive cut-off point in the form of the affected industry.

[52] Our rooting for broader economic effects stands in contrast to results generated by economic terms-of-trade models which measure trade damages in terms of blocked trade (see Chad Bown and Michele Ruta, Chapter 6, above). The reasons for that are straightforward: first, terms-of-trade approaches to trade agreements abstract from reality in that they model the WTO as a *tariff reduction contract*. In other words, it is assumed that the contract consists of only one entitlement, viz. reciprocal tariff concessions. Second, as was discussed in note 36, above, the terms-of-trade literature assumes instantaneous self-enforcement by the complaining party. Under these two assumptions, there is no difference between measuring NoI in terms of trade effects and economic effects. In sum, terms-of-trade models portray a special case of WTO violations and enforcement, and measuring NoI in terms-of-trade effects is valid *given the unique assumptions*

Summing up our findings on the calculation of the level of NoI in trade agreements: when it comes to assessing as accurately as possible the injury incurred by a complainant, the aspects of *nature*, *form* and *intensity* of the violation have to be taken into consideration. Any quantification of the intensity must contain an appropriate counterfactual or baseline of comparison, on the one hand, and deal with issues of scale and scope, on the other hand. We have shown that for systemic and practical reasons the *expectation* damages measure is the incentive-compatible quantification option. Calculating expectation damages Pareto-dominates both the *reliance* and the *restitution* scenarios. We have further argued that, although desirable, indirect effects are too difficult to measure. Indirect damage effects provoked by a violation in other sectors, to other domestic constituencies and in third markets are too remote and too speculative to calculate, therefore integrating indirect effects would be prone to conflicts between members and even a loss of faith in the international trading system. Finally, we argued that the right proxy, or metric, for nullification and impairment is the direct *economic gains and losses test*, which considers economic consequences of violating measures in the affected industry/industries of the complaining country. This test not only examines *trade blocked*, but also *lost profits* and other economic cost and benefit categories that a victim member incurs in case of any violation of the WTO Agreement.[53]

3.2 Calculating the level of suspension of concessions or other operations

The calculation of injury or damage is only the first step in contractual enforcement. Once parties (or in their stead, the arbitrator) have an idea of the level of NoI, they can move on to determine the remedial action.[54]

of the terms-of-trade model world. However, we would caution against the generalization of this result above and beyond the confines of the narrow model assumptions (on this issue, see S. A. B. Schropp, 'Revisiting the "Compliance-vs.-Rebalancing" Debate in WTO Scholarship: Towards a Unified Research Agenda').

[53] The choice of counterfactual and the choice of metric are not entirely independent factors: the expectation damages counterfactual, for example, cannot be constructed by means of a trade-effects test as a measurement unit of trade damages.

[54] In principle, remedies, or enforcement instruments, are as varied as contracts underlying them (A. Keck and S. A. B. Schropp, 'Indisputably Essential: The Economics of Dispute Settlement Institutions in Trade Agreements'). Contractual remedies can range from physical measures (incarceration), to economic (penalty fees) and emotional (reputation loss, withdrawal of affection) measures. Furthermore, remedies can be enacted by an independent third party (for example, the police), by the collective (for example, ostracism by a tribe or clan), or by the affected party itself ('self-enforcement').

The WTO acknowledges various remedies (bring measure into compliance, reach mutually agreed solution, tariff compensation, retaliation), and many more have been suggested in WTO scholarship.[55] However, the ultimate enforcement instrument in the WTO is the SCOO, also known as 'retaliation', 'countermeasures' or 'trade sanctions', which is regulated in Article 22 of the DSU.

Rational and forward-looking signatories to a multilateral trade agreement might be expected to provide an arbitrator with clear and unambiguous instructions as to how, in the case of conflict, he is to calculate the level of countermeasure that is to be awarded to a complainant in response to a nullification or impairment of its benefits. It is rather problematic that the drafters of the WTO Agreement in those days missed a good opportunity to specify these instructions. Hence, let us move from the DSU text (or lack thereof) to a more theoretical deliberation of how rational contracting parties would design a system of remediation. This

[55] Several reform proposals of the remedy regime in the WTO have been tabled, including making tariff compensation mandatory and automatic (Meltzer Commission to the US Congress [International Financial Institutions Advisory Commission Report, March 2000], B. Lindsey, D. T. Griswold, M. A. Groombridge and A. Lukas, 'Seattle and Beyond – A WTO Agenda for the New Millennium', CATO Center for Trade Policy Studies No. 8, 1999; J. Pauwelyn, 'Enforcement and Countermeasures in the WTO: Rules are Rules – Toward a More Collective Approach'; S. Charnovitz, 'Rethinking WTO Trade Sanctions'; S. Charnovitz, 'Should the Teeth Be Pulled?'; S. Charnovitz, 'The WTO's Problematic "Last Resort" Against Non-Compliance', *Aussenwirtschaft*, 57:IV (2002), 409–40; A. Roitinger, 'The Institutional Design of Trade Policy Flexibility in the World Trade Order – Analysis and New Direction for Reform', Thesis at Universität St. Gallen (HSG), 2004, 188); suspension of membership rights, such as the right to attend meetings, to participate in decisions, to use the DSM or other WTO provisions or to receive technical assistance (S. Charnovitz, 'Rethinking WTO Trade Sanctions'; R. Z. Lawrence, *Crimes and Punishments? Retaliation under the WTO*, ch. 5); collective retaliation (G. Maggi, 'The Role of Multilateral Institutions in International Trade Cooperation', *American Economic Review*, 89:1 (1999), 190–214; J. Pauwelyn, 'Enforcement and Countermeasures in the WTO: Rules are Rules – Toward a More Collective Approach'); tradable remedies (K. Bagwell, P. C. Mavroidis and R. W. Staiger, 'The Case for Tradable Remedies in the WTO' in S. Evenett and B. Hoekman (eds.), *Economic Development and Multilateral Trade Cooperation* (Washington, DC: Palgrave Macmillan and World Bank, 2005), 56–76, and N. Limao and K. Saggi, 'Tariff Retaliation versus Financial Compensation in the Enforcement of International Trade Agreements', CEPR Working Paper Series No. 5560, 2006); or monetary fees (WTO, *The Future of the WTO – Addressing Institutional Challenges in the New Millennium*', Report by the Consultative Board to the Director-General Supachai Panichpakdi, World Trade Organization (Geneva: WTO, 2004); M. Bronckers and N. van den Broek, 'Financial Compensation in the WTO: Improving the Remedies of WTO Dispute Settlement', *Journal of International Economic Law*, 8:1 (2005), 101–26; W. J. Davey, 'The Sutherland Report on Dispute Settlement: A Comment', *Journal of International Economic Law*, 8:2 (2005), 321–8).

will serve as a benchmark against which to measure the actual WTO arbitration practice (section 4, below).

Contractual remedies, in the WTO just as in any other contract, are a function of three constituent parameters: *nature*, *form* and *intensity*. Applied to the context of the WTO and the remedy of SCOO, these components can be explained as follows. The *nature* of SCOO is the specification of the contractual entitlement, or obligation, to be targeted and suspended by the successful complainant in response to the contractual violation found to be in existence. As our discussion in subsection 3.1.1 showed, there are three groups of entitlements that can be affected by enforcement: market access; minimum standard; and auxiliary entitlements. The *form* of SCOO indicates the modalities of retaliation: product coverage (sectors, subsectors, specific obligations), and type of suspension (*ad valorem* or *specific* tariff, copyright infringements or royalty payment suppression, etc.). Finally, the *intensity* of SCOO specifies the *degree* to which obligations are suspended or withdrawn – it is the calculative benchmark of retaliation.

The party engaging in SCOO (or in its stead, the arbitrator) must have a clear idea of the expected impact of its proposed actions, that is, of the negative effects its remedial measures will cause to the injuring member. To that end, it is of importance that any calculation of the remedial action follows a methodology that *exactly mirrors* the one utilized in the calculation of trade damages. Otherwise one ends up comparing apples with oranges and any talk of 'equivalence' of the NoI and SCOO must remain a distant ideal. The manner in which trade damages are measured in terms of (i) applicable counterfactual, (ii) scale (metric) and (iii) scope of effects, must also guide the determination of retaliatory action.[56]

This simple insight of mirror methodology does *not* mean that complaining parties cannot suspend different obligations in a different format and to a different degree as compared with the initial violation to which they were exposed. As long as the monetized dollar amount of SCOO awarded by the arbitrator is based on the same calculation standard, or methodology, complaining parties should be granted some leeway in

[56] As a practical example: it would be profoundly flawed to have in place a methodology of measuring the level of NoI using direct economic gains and losses amounting to the complainant's expectation damages, while measuring SCOO in terms of direct trade blocked by the complainant. To all intents and purposes, those two numbers would bear no logical resemblance; this again would be comparing apples with oranges. Note that this rather strange retaliation strategy was requested by the EC in *US–Byrd* (see Arbitrators' Report, para. 4.6). More on the issue of incoherence of levels of NoI and SCOO below.

selecting their retaliatory strategy of choice. It is not the *measures* of NoI and SCOO that should be identical, but rather the *methodologies* of calculating their respective level.

Yet the logical precept of mirror methodology reveals the profound myopia of using the *trade-effects metric* as the proxy of choice to measure NoI: if signatories (or in their stead, the arbitrator) measure trade damages narrowly in terms of blocked trade flows, they restrict *retaliatory action* to the same metric, that is, reduction of market access by the complaining party vis-à-vis the respondent. This limits the manoeuvring space of the complainant considerably, since it essentially forestalls all kinds of suspension of non-market access entitlements. Measuring NoI by using blocked trade flows makes suspension of intellectual property rights difficult and leaves only the choice between a rock and a hard place: either you leave the terrain of comparability, which makes retaliation arbitrary, or you jettison the possibility of cross-retaliation.

What latitude should complaining members be granted in the retaliation process? Should it fall upon the arbitrator to single-handedly decide over *nature*, *form* and *intensity* of retaliation? Conceptually, it does not matter who chooses *nature* and *form* of retaliation (rational framers of the Agreement will probably let the litigating parties negotiate over this issue, and – in case of disagreement – leave the ultimate decision to the complaining party), as long as the determination of the *intensity* of the measure resides with a neutral third party, such as the arbitrator. The complaining party can retain discretion over *nature* and *form* of retaliation: if it wishes to impose 5 per cent *ad valorem* tariffs on all goods in the HS 52 category, this should be fine as long as the *level* or *degree* of this retaliatory action – measured in the identical metric as the level of trade damages suffered – is equivalent to the initial offending measure. If the complainant favours a different policy mix with prohibitive tariffs, suspension of intellectual property rights or suspension of transparency obligations vis-à-vis the respondent, this again should be within its discretion, as long as the competence to assign the *intensity* of such action resides with the arbitrator and is coherent with the prior methodology of calculating the level of injury.

3.3 *Safeguarding equivalence between NoI and SCOO*

Theoretically, once the levels of NoI and SCOO are calibrated such that both calculations are based on the same quantification methodology and have been accordingly been 'monetized', the task of safeguarding equivalence is a mere formality: the complaining party requests authorization to suspend concessions or other obligations in a certain amount. The arbitrator then checks whether the requested amount will have an impact on the defending country that is truly equivalent to the level of NoI. He then signals the go-ahead to the complainant, who then suggests a certain policy mix (*nature* and *form* of retaliation). The arbitrator is charged with fixing the degree to which the complainant may enact its requested retaliation mix (mindful of the constraints posed by Articles 22.3 and 22.5 of the DSU).

One interesting issue with respect to equivalence has come up in the course of the arbitration in *US–1916 Act*, when the EC requested authorization to enact 'mirror legislation':[57] do the levels of NoI and SCOO have to be quantifiable at all, or may the arbitrator refrain from calculating either side of the equation, hoping that *identical* measures ('inputs') will yield *identical* outcomes? Here, we side with the arbitrator who opined that trade damages and SCOO must be 'meaningfully quantifiable' in 'numerical or monetary terms'.[58] Only in this way can the arbitrator determine the *level* of NoI and SCOO, respectively, and define equivalence. Identical measures enacted by different signatories at different points in time (that is, under different circumstances) can have strikingly different outcomes, and it is the arbitrator's mandate to safeguard the position that the measure taken in response to a violation is neither undercompensatory nor punitive for the respondent.[59] However, the arbitrator has to find ways to quantify and compare NoI and SCOO. Reliance on chance or hope is not enough.

4 The equivalence standard in the light of past Article 22.6 arbitrations

The last section was concerned with L&E theory of enforcement and the rational *ex ante* design of a remedial regime under Article 22.4 of the

[57] With 'mirror legislation', the EC planned to enact legislation identical to, and in some points less stringent than, the US Antidumping Act of 1916.

[58] Arbitrators' Reports, *US–1916 Act* (Article 22.6) at paras. 5.23 and 5.57. For a dissenting view, see H. Spamann, 'The Myth of "Rebalancing" Retaliation in WTO Dispute Settlement Practice'.

[59] Identical actions and transactions can have different subjective values for individuals (this, in fact, is the very motivation for individuals to engage in economic transactions or trades in the first place). Imputing identical effects to identical measures constitutes an inappropriate understanding of social interaction.

DSU.[60] This section is concerned with the way in which arbitrators have actually interpreted the equivalence standard and how they have executed their mandate under the DSU. Given our previous findings, we have some issues with the track record of WTO arbitrators in the last 14 years of dispute settlement.

4.1 *An assessment of arbitrators' calculation of NoI*

The first WTO arbitrations to be charged with the task of calculating the level of NoI under the purview of Article 22.4 of the DSU (*EC–Bananas III (US)* (Article 22.6), *EC–Bananas III (Ecuador)* (Article 22.6), *EC–Hormones (US)* (Article 22.6), and *EC–Hormones (Canada)* (Article 22.6)) dealt with traditional market access barriers such as tariffs, quotas and other import restrictions. This prompted the arbitrators to construct the *reliance damage measure* as the baseline hypothetical, and to measure NoI in terms of direct trade effects of the violation.[61]

In the light of the insights gathered so far, the following subsections will raise two concerns with the arbitrators' practice of calculating NoI. First, using reliance damages as the baseline against which to compare the complaining parties' actual situation resulted in *under*compensation of the complaining parties, as well as in the problem of having to choose between competing counterfactuals of 'withdrawal of the measure at issue'. Second, the *direct trade-effects test* seems to have been established as the one-size-fits-all approach of measuring trade damages. With the advent of *US–Antidumping Act of 1916* case this tariff-centric ('tariffic') logic of calculating injury should have been called into question and consequently overturned, since direct trade damages are conceptually inept to deal with cross-sectoral and/or *non*-market access-related violations. However, arbitrators have yet to engage in a proper discussion of alternatives to the trade-effects test.

[60] Note that we have not discussed whether the equivalence standard makes sense at all and whether trade sanctions, or SCOO, are a sensible contract remedy in the first place – we take those constraints as given. For a more exhaustive treatment of that question and of remedies in multilateral trade agreements in general, see S. A. B. Schropp, *Trade Policy Flexibility and Enforcement in the WTO: A Law and Economics Analysis*.

[61] P. C. Mavroidis, 'Remedies in the WTO Legal System: Between a Rock and a Hard Place', 774; S. Charnovitz, 'The WTO's Problematic "Last Resort" Against Non-Compliance', 418; R. E. Hudec, 'The Adequacy of WTO Dispute Settlement Remedies: A Developing Country Perspective' in B. Hoekman, A. Mattoo and P. English (eds.), *Development, Trade and the WTO* (Washington, DC: World Bank, 2002), 86; R. Z. Lawrence, *Crimes and Punishments? Retaliation under the WTO*, 37; WTO, *The Future of the WTO – Addressing Institutional Challenges in the New Millennium*, 243.

4.1.1 Using reliance damages as counterfactual is not appropriate

All arbitrations under Article 22.4 of DSU so far have calculated *prospective* damages amounting to direct trade effects.[62] Although the prospective nature of damages is not mentioned *expressis verbis* in any WTO provision, arbitrators have decided to calculate NoI *not* from the time when an illegality was committed, but from the end of the 'reasonable period of time' (RPT), set by the so-called 'Article 21.3-Panel'.[63] WTO arbitrators have interpreted Article 22.4 of the DSU such that the level of NoI roughly implies a counterfactual scenario apt to re-establish the *status quo ante* the breach:[64] in constructing a counterfactual situation that would prevail if the illegality were removed, WTO arbitrators have awarded damages that are appropriate to restore the trade level that would exist had the injurer brought his contravening measure into conformity after the RPT.[65] Hence, the current system of contractual remedies is probably best characterized as a remedy short of *reliance damage measure*.[66] Figure 20.6 illustrates the arbitrators' practice.

[62] See P. Grané, 'Remedies Under WTO Law', *Journal of International Economic Law*, 4:4 (2001), 755–72; K. Anderson, 'Peculiarities of retaliation in WTO dispute settlement', CEPR Discussion Paper No. 3578, 2002; W. F. Schwartz and A. O. Sykes, 'The Economic Structure of Renegotiation and Dispute Resolution in the WTO/GATT System'; I. Araki, 'Comment on Fritz Breuss "WTO Dispute Settlement"';F. Breuss, 'WTO Dispute Settlement: An Economic Analysis of Four EU–US Mine Trade Wars'; A. Keck, 'WTO Dispute Settlement: What Role for Economic Analysis?'; W. Kohler, 'The WTO Dispute Settlement Mechanism: Battlefield or Cooperation?'; S. A. B. Schropp, 'The Case for Tariff Compensation in WTO Dispute Settlement'; H. Spamann, 'The Myth of "Rebalancing" Retaliation in WTO Dispute Settlement Practice'; J. P. Trachtman, 'Building the WTO Cathedral'. An exception here may be the arbitrator in *US–1916 Act*, who did not find any NoI at all (more on the *US–1916* arbitration below).

[63] Damages awards are *ex nunc* instead of *ex tunc* (see, for example, J. Pauwelyn, 'Enforcement and Countermeasures in the WTO: Rules are Rules – Toward a More Collective Approach'; P. Grané, 'Remedies Under WTO Law'; M. Bronckers and N. van den Broek, 'Financial Compensation in the WTO: Improving the Remedies of WTO Dispute Settlement'; H. Spamann, 'The Myth of "Rebalancing" Retaliation in WTO Dispute Settlement Practice').

[64] P. C. Mavroidis, 'Remedies in the WTO Legal System: Between a Rock and a Hard Place'; R. Z. Lawrence, *Crimes and Punishments? Retaliation under the WTO*; F. Breuss, 'WTO Dispute Settlement: An Economic Analysis of Four EU–US Mine Trade Wars'; and H. Spamann, 'The Myth of "Rebalancing" Retaliation in WTO Dispute Settlement Practice'.

[65] T. Sebastian, 'World Trade Organization Remedies and the Assessment of Proportionality: Equivalence and Appropriateness', 351.

[66] We say 'short of' the reliance damage measure, because the prospective nature of arbitration awards renders impossible the exact re-establishment of the *status quo* of the market

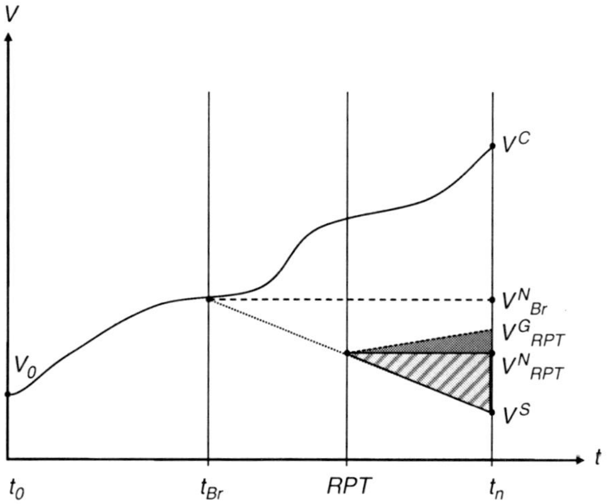

Figure 20.6. The calculation baseline according to WTO arbitrators' practice

In previous Article 22.4 of the DSU arbitration, WTO arbitrators have essentially tried to calculate the difference between the complainant's actual situation and a hypothetical situation that would prevail if the illegality were removed (in some way or other) after the RPT had lapsed. They thereby refused to consider retroactivity, indirect effects, efficiency losses, as well as litigation costs.[67] However, what the arbitrator in *EC–Bananas III (Ecuador)* actually did when constructing his counterfactual was to integrate some kind of market growth potential in the affected markets.[68] Hence, using our previous illustration, figure 20.6

access balance as it existed before the breach. Thus, the remedy applied by WTO arbitrators fails to compensate the victim for direct trade damages incurred between the enactment of the measure in question and the lapse of the RPT (*cf.* for example, J. Pauwelyn, 'Enforcement and Countermeasures in the WTO: Rules are Rules – Toward a More Collective Approach').

[67] The arbitrator in *EC–Bananas III (Ecuador)* (Article 22.6) (DSR 2000:V, 2237) set the precedent by denying the United States indemnity for lost profits resulting from the EC banana importing regime which, *inter alia*, harmed the Mexican banana industry, a major consumer of US fertilizer (paras. 6.12–14). A direct outcome of the discussion on indirect benefits is the decision by the arbitrator in the same case to compute only *value added* when calculating the level of nullification and impairment (para. 6.18). The arbitrator in *US–1916 Act (EC)* (Article 22.6) (para. 5.76) made it clear that legal fees paid cannot form part of the calculation of nullification and impairment.

[68] The arbitrator in *EC–Bananas (Ecuador)* (Article 22.6), para. 169, assumed that 'Ecuador's banana exports to the EC would increase to the level of its best-ever exports during the past decade, that the share of those bananas distributed by Ecuadorian service suppliers

shows that the arbitrators seemed to have constructed a baseline hypothetical which amounts to a level of NoI consisting of the *status quo ante* the RPT (hatched triangle), plus a market growth component (solid grey triangle). In the light of the theoretical discussion of section 3 above, we have two concerns about the use of the *reliance* counterfactual used by the *Bananas* arbitrator and all arbitrators thereafter:

(1) First, opting for reliance damages as the baseline counterfactual and taking the end of the RPT as the starting point for damage calculation results in an undercompensatory benchmark. As noted in subsection 3.1.2.1, calculating damages according to a hypothetical *status quo ante* the breach is undercompensatory for the injured party; this prompts excessive breach on the part of injuring parties and inefficiently little *ex ante* trade liberalization by prospective complainants.[69]

(2) Second, WTO arbitrators had to struggle with selecting an appropriate counterfactual that best describes the situation which would prevail if the illegality were removed. The *US–Gambling (Article 22.6)* case is an instructive example. As the arbitrator realized, the United States could have brought its illegal ban into compliance in at least three different ways:

   - by legalizing all forms of Internet gambling;
   - by banning all Internet gambling;
   - by legalizing all Internet gambling on horse races.

   The arbitrator constructed the somewhat tepid concept of a 'plausible or reasonable counterfactual' (Arbitrator's Report, paragraphs 3.26–40).[70] This concept prompted a dissenting opinion from one of the three arbitration panellists (paragraphs 3.62–73), who pointed out that 'reasonableness' can be seen from at least two perspectives: the point of view of the complainant and that of the respondent. As the majority of the arbitrators constructed a counterfactual which they deemed reasonable from the respondent's perspective ('a reasonable

would rise to 60 per cent, and that the proportion of those distributed bananas for which Ecuadorian service suppliers are given import licenses would rise to 92 per cent.'

[69] See also S. A. B. Schropp, 'Trade Policy Flexibility and Enforcement in the WTO: Reform Agenda Towards an Efficient "Breach" Contract'.

[70] The arbitrator stated (paras. 3.25–6): 'The Member concerned may have had a range of WTO-consistent options at its disposal to choose from to ensure compliance. *It is not for us to speculate on what might have been the "most likely" scenario.* Nonetheless, the counterfactual should, in our view, reflect at least a plausible or "reasonable" compliance scenario.' See also the Arbitrator's Report, *EC–Bananas III (Ecuador)* (Article 22.6), paras. 166–70.

counterfactual must take into account [the respondent's] policy objectives', paragraphs 3.51), the dissenting arbitrator begged to differ and stated:

> In the circumstances of this case, it was not unreasonable for [the complainant] to base its counterfactual on an assumption that [the respondent] would open its market to the cross-border provision of [all] remote gambling services. Such an assumption is fully compatible with the nature of the Appellate Body's findings in this case ... In a situation where different means of compliance might form the basis of a counterfactual in order to determine the level of nullification and impairment of benefits, the complaining party would not be prevented from selecting a counterfactual that may lead to a higher level of nullification or impairment than others, provided that such counterfactual is reasonable (paragraphs 3.67 and 3.70).

Whatever counterfactual the arbitrator chooses as the right counterfactual for withdrawal of the measure in question, it will always have to confront the criticism of having overstepped the line between arbitration and arbitrariness. If, however, the arbitrator chose the expectation damages counterfactual, one single appropriate counterfactual would apply: that is, the complainant's welfare level under continued and incessant cooperation by the respondent.

4.1.2 Using direct trade damages as the unit of measurement is not appropriate

With the exception of *US–1916 Act*, all arbitrations under Article 22.4 of the DSU measured the detrimental effect caused by a WTO violation in terms of the *direct trade blocked* due to the ban's continued existence.[71] Measuring NoI as *direct trade effects* was a rather unfortunate choice.

First, it does not reflect the true harm suffered by complaining members.[72] The use of direct trade effects may be a reflection of the fact 'that trade loss is generally more directly identifiable and quantifiable and that,

[71] In *EC–Bananas (US)*, the Arbitrator measured benefits nullified or impaired in the amount of the losses in US exports of goods and losses by US service suppliers (see Arbitrator's Report, para. 6.12); in *EC–Bananas (Ecuador)*, losses by Ecuador of actual trade and potential trade opportunities in bananas and loss of actual and potential distribution service supply (see Arbitrator's Report, footnote 52); in *EC–Hormones (US)* and *(Canada)*, NoI was calculated as forgone US/Canadian exports of hormone-treated beef and beef products (see Arbitrator's Reports, paras. 41 and 40, respectively); *US–Gambling* measured NoI as trade in remote gambling on horse races blocked by the United States (Arbitrator's Report, para. 3.25).

[72] See the related theoretical discussion above in section 3.1.2.2.

in such context, arbitrators preferred to rely on verifiable figures'.[73] Yet as we argued *above*, it may miss the mark of indemnifying the complainant for the real economic harm suffered from a violation of the WTO Agreement, which in turn invites overbreach by injuring members.

Second, as the proverb goes – when all you have is a hammer, everything you see looks like a nail: arbitrators in the first four Article 22.6 arbitrations set a non-sustainable and potentially misleading precedent. *Bananas* and *Hormones* were cases dealing with traditional market access barriers, such as tariffs, quotas, and other import restrictions. Measuring trade damages in terms of direct trade effects may not be a perfect proxy, but it works for violations of market access concessions. Yet as was stated above in subsection 3.2, direct trade damages are conceptually inept to deal with cross-sectoral and/or non-market access-related violations of the WTO.

The advent of the *US–Antidumping Act of 1916* case should have marked the end of this tariffic misunderstanding, that is, the tariff-centric logic of calculating NoI as a one-size-fits-all proxy. However, the Arbitrator's Report did not offer a deeper discussion.[74] On the positive side, the arbitrator in his report on *US–1916 Act* (at paragraph 7.2) recognized that the application of the 1916 Act (judicial decisions or forced settlements, as the case may be) did not automatically restrict trade and he, therefore, saw the need to examine broader 'economic effects' of the measure at issue. He explicitly acknowledged that a systemic alternative to direct trade effects exists.[75] Unfortunately, the arbitrator talked the talk but did not walk the walk; the rhetoric of 'economic effects' remained lip service.[76] The arbitrator neither engaged in a discussion concerning the nature of the entitlement infringed upon by the United States, nor in a thorough examination of the economic consequences of the measure at issue. Instead of looking for ways to quantify the economic harm resulting from forced settlements and suppressed economic activity on the complaining parties, the arbitrator awarded the EC the right to suspend obligations and concessions

[73] Arbitrator's Report, *US–Byrd*, at para. 3.39.

[74] In *US–1916 Act* the EC and Japan had successfully attacked a US regulation that threatened to sanction the import of dumped goods with criminal charges and provided compensation payments for injured US businesses. Although the 1916 Act had played little role in trade practice, the EC and Japan pointed to numerous forced settlements between EC/Japanese importers and US firms under the threat of litigation.

[75] See also Arbitrator's Report, *US–Byrd*, paras. 3.39–40.

[76] See T. Jürgensen, 'Crime and Punishment: Retaliation under the World Trade Organization Dispute Settlement System', *Journal of World Trade*, 39 (2005); and H. Spamann, 'The Myth of "Rebalancing" Retaliation in WTO Dispute Settlement Practice'.

only if and when future judgments against or settlements accepted by EC exporters disclosed the amount that EC exporters would have to pay (paragraphs 8.1–2).

Two circumstances confirm the conjecture that the arbitrator did not seriously engage in an economic gains/losses test: first, he refrained from considering clearly attributable litigation costs resulting from forced settlements. Second, the arbitrator refused to draw *adverse inferences* against the United States. The reason why payments and forced settlements were so hard to measure was that US parties to these settlements objected to disclosure of the settlement terms, including the amount of money the importers agreed to pay (paragraphs 6.8–9). The arbitrator thus could have used his discretion to draw *adverse inferences* when it became clear that the responding party was stonewalling the process.[77] The arbitrator would not have overstepped his mandate if he had constructed an economic model to calculate these (undisclosed) payments. It is not unfathomable for an arbitrator either to make conjectures and or to rely on outside expertise, as the *US–Gambling* case showed, where the arbitrator referred to datasets from the World Bank and other organizations (see Arbitrator's Report, section III.D).

WTO arbitrators have yet to engage in a proper discussion of alternatives to the trade-effects test. A positive outlier in this list of 'tariffic' blinders is the *US–Section 110(5)* case, which perceptively was conducted under an ad hoc arbitration (Article of the 25 DSU).[78] The Arbitrator's Report is a refreshing departure both from the trade effects approach and from the use of the dubious reliance counterfactual: cognizant of the *nature* of the entitlement at issue, namely, the reciprocal intellectual property rights, the arbitrator compiled economic gains and losses instead of calculating direct trade effects. Instead of trying to construct a counterfactual amounting to reliance damages, the arbitrator put the complaining party in as good a position as it would have been had the respondent performed according to the terms of the TRIPS Agreement, which is a formulation of expectation damages. The arbitrator counted only those

[77] Note that a DSB panel in the recent *Turkey–Rice* case (DS 334) did exactly that (see D. Gantz and S. A. B. Schropp, '(R)ice Age – Comments on the Panel Report Turkey–Measures Affecting the Importation of Rice' in H. Horn and P. C. Mavroidis (eds.), *The WTO Case-Law of 2006: The American Law Institute Reporters' Studies* (Cambridge University Press, 2009).

[78] In this case, bars, restaurants and small retail establishments below a certain threshold size are exempted from royalty payments to copyright holders of music. The United States and the EC decided to call on the arbitrator to put a price tag on the nullification and impairment suffered by EC right holders.

royalty payments which would actually have been collected by economically rational EC rights holders, net of collection costs (see Arbitrator's Report, paragraph 3.3).

4.2 *The WTO experience with calculating SCOO in previous WTO arbitrations*

Turning to the calculation of the level of SCOO, we find that Article 22.4 arbitrations did not appropriately take up the quantification challenge. Most arbitrators have not really engaged in calculating remedies; instead, they have consistently adopted a hands-off approach to the level of SCOO. Equivalence of two items requires the occupation with both sides of the equation. Neglect of one side frustrates the concept of equivalence. What is worse, on those few occasions where the arbitrators *did* say something about the level of SCOO, their comments were counterintuitive and even counterproductive.

4.2.1 The arbitrators' 'hands-off' approach to calculating the level of SCOO

Up to this very day, arbitrators have not developed a culture of engaging in serious deliberations over the calculation of the level of SCOO. On certain occasions, arbitration panels have demanded a detailed retaliation list from complainants (containing targeted sectors and import values), but this was not followed by any serious attempt to fix an adequate level of retaliation.[79] The reason can be found in the following passage from the Report in *EC–Hormones (US/Canada)* (Article 22.6), at paragraphs 18 and 19). It seems to us representative of all arbitrators' opinions. Interpreting Article 22.7 of the DSU, the arbitrator in *EC–Hormones* opined:[80]

[79] See for example the Arbitrator's Report, *EC–Hormones (US)* (DSR 1999:III, 1105), paras. 80–2: 'In reply to questions by the arbitrators, the US submitted for each product on the proposed suspension list the average import value of EC exports to the US over a three-year period (1996–1998). We consider the calculations thus provided to be reasonable … The US is free to pick products from the proposed list as long as the total trade value is lower than or equivalent to the amount of nullification and impairment we have found, namely US$116.8 million … We received confirmation from the US that the actual level of suspension once implemented will be equivalent to the level of nullification and impairment we have found. All we can do at this stage is to encourage the US to stand by this confirmation and to abide by Article 22.4 of the DSU.'

[80] Article 22.7 of the DSU, which reads in pertinent parts: 'The arbitrator … shall not examine the nature of the concessions or other obligations to be suspended but shall determine whether the level of such suspensions is equivalent to the level of nullification or impairment.'

> Arbitrators are explicitly prohibited from 'examin[ing] *the nature* of the concessions or other obligations to be suspended' (other than under Articles 22.3 and 22.5). On these grounds, we cannot require that [the complainant] further specify the nature of the proposed suspension ... In case a proposal for suspension were to target, for example, only biscuits with a 100 per cent tariff *ad valorem*, it would not be for the arbitrators to decide that, for example, cheese and not biscuits should be targeted; that a 150 per cent tariff should be imposed instead of a 100 per cent tariff; or that tariff increases should be levied on a product weight basis, not *ad valorem*. All of these are *qualitative* aspects of the proposed suspension touching upon the 'nature' of concessions to be withdrawn. They fall outside the arbitrators' jurisdiction. (original emphasis italics, underline added)

This interpretation of Article 22.7 of the DSU seems doubtful from a legal and a systemic perspective:

- From a legal point of view the arbitrators' interpretation of Article 22.7 of the DSU seems to confuse *nature/form* with *intensity* of retaliation. The complainant, after having won a DSU litigation, may very well be free to choose the policy mix with which to enact its righteous remedy. It may choose the *nature* of the entitlements it wishes to suspend, it may proceed with selecting the sectors, industries and products targets; it should even be free to select the *modalities* of its retaliatory action – without the interference of the arbitrator. However, as stated above in subsection 3.2, once the complaining party submits its retaliation list, the competence to determine the *intensity* of such action should reside with a neutral third party, that is, the arbitrator. Nothing, to our mind, in the language of Article 22.7 of the DSU would preclude the arbitrator from doing just that. The arbitrator in *US–1916 Act* (Article 22.6), therefore, may be right in stating that 'the arbitrators do not have the jurisdiction to approve the adoption of *measures* [in the sense of policy choices] by the complaining party' (paragraphs 5.42), yet his conclusions are disputable. The arbitrator in *US–Gambling (Article 22.6)* seemed to have understood this when stating:

> Our mandate does not allow us ... to consider the 'nature' of the obligations to be suspended. We understand this to mean that we may not question the complaining party's choice of specific obligations to be suspended (other than in the context of considering a claim that the principles and procedures of Article 22.3 have not been followed) and that *we must assess the level of the proposed suspension, rather than its form, against the level of nullification and impairment*'. (Arbitrator's Report, para. 5.9, emphasis added)

Unfortunately, this Arbitrator did not act according to this insight in due course of the *Gambling* proceedings as he simply did not address the appropriate level that would have corresponded to the complainant's proposed retaliation mix.

- From a systemic perspective, arbitrators should have engaged in the quantification of the SCOO. They have not. Not only have arbitrators therewith obliterated their mandate, in essence, they have also rendered *inutile* the equivalence standard under Article 22.4 of the DSU. If a judge, asked to establish and safeguard the equivalence between the injury caused by an offending measure and the level of retaliatory action, does not calculate the value of the right-hand side of the equation (the retaliation), the entire calculation breaks down. Without any treatment of one side of an equation, the equality sign stands for mere wishful thinking.[81]

The absurd consequence of the arbitrators' 'hands-off' approach to the quantification of SCOO is that there is nobody to check on what the retaliating complainant is actually doing. And even if someone set out to do just that, on what methodology would he or she base her or his calculation? At the present time there is *no* methodology in place to quantify SCOO. Consequently, the best advice the arbitrator can give to a respondent suspected to be victim of overzealous retaliation is to start a novel litigation.[82] This situation emerged in the latest chapter of the *Hormones* saga (*Canada/US–Hormones Suspension*, DS 320/321), in which the EC opined that the United States and had Canada illegally continued with their trade sanctions, since the EC regards itself as being in compliance.

Starting a novel DSU dispute to counter *over-retaliation* cannot be what the framers of the WTO had in mind when mandating the arbitrator to deal with Article 22.4 of the DSU. This would be very surprising indeed, since a procedure of this sort would question the fundamental principles of the WTO: stability and predictability of the world trading order (as instructed by Article XVI of the WTO Charter and Article 3.2 of the DSU).

[81] For all intents and purposes it could be a 'less-than' sign or a 'greater-than' sign – how can one know if it is only the left-hand side that is subject to scrutiny and quantification?

[82] Confer Arbitrator's Report, *US–1916* (Article 22.6), para. 3.20: 'If, in the future, the [complainant] is of the view that the actual application of the blocking regulation results in a situation where the suspension of obligations exceeds the level of nullification and impairment, the [complainant] may have recourse to the appropriate dispute settlement procedures to address this issue.' See also the Arbitration Reports, *EC–Hormones (Canada)* (Article 22.6) (DSR 1999:III, 1135), para. 71, *EC–Hormones (US)* (Article 22.6), para. 82, *US–Byrd* (Article 22.6), para. 4.27 and *US–Gambling* (Article 22.6), para. 5.12.

Furthermore, removing quantification of SCOO and equivalence from consideration risks rendering futile the calculation of the level of NoI. If you do not face the challenge of quantification of SCOO, the standalone calculation of the level of NoI is a mirror without reflection, a one-armed scale. What is the inherent value to any litigating party to know what the complainant suffered, if it remains ignorant of what are the practical implications? Both complainant and respondent will have to freely guess the composition and volume of countermeasures. For the complaining party there is no metric in which to measure retaliatory actions; in the same vein, absent any methodology on calculating the level of SCOO, how can the respondent even know whether the complainant *over-* or *under-retaliated*?

To summarize, by refusing to design a methodology of calculating and operationalizing the appropriate level of SCOO, the arbitrators have practically defied the purpose of the entire quantification exercise mandated by Article 22.4 of the DSU, and therewith have put a big question mark on their own role in the process.

4.2.2 The arbitrators' opinion on calculating the level of SCOO

Arbitrators rejected their mandate to quantify the level of SCOO, alleging that it is prohibited by law to examine the *nature* of concessions or other obligations to be suspended. Yet, despite the general 'hands-off' stance, on various occasions arbitrators have nevertheless inserted a comment on the calculation of SCOO. Some of these comments unfortunately were rather counterproductive.

Take the arbitration in *EC–Bananas III (US)* (Article 22.6), paragraph 7.1: in response to the requesting party's demand to integrate domestic firms' costs and profits in the calculation of the level of NoI, the arbitrator stated that the 'same basis' needed to be used for measuring and comparing the levels of SCOO *and* NoI, and that the basis for the former was the 'gross value of imports'.[83] This statement contains two errors: first, it is *not* a systemic prerequisite that NoI and SCOO require an identical 'basis', if by 'basis' the arbitrator understands the nature of the offending and

[83] The exact words of the arbitrator were: 'To estimate the level of nullification or impairment, the *same basis* needs to be used for measuring the level of suspension of concessions. Since the latter is the *gross value* of US imports from the European Communities, the comparable basis for estimating nullification and impairment in our view is the impact on the value of relevant EC imports from the United States (rather than US firms' costs and profits, as used in the US submission).'

retaliatory act. Second, even if the trade-effects test is assumed to be the adequate approach to measuring NoI (*quod non*), taking the '*gross* trade value' (trade affected) as the basis of retaliation is the wrong comparator against which to measure 'trade blocked' by the offending measure:

- First, as we noted above in subsection 3.2,[84] from a theoretical standpoint, it is not only unnecessary, but also counterproductive to demand the same 'basis' for SCOO and NoI, that is, to demand that the *nature*, *form* and *intensity* of the offending act have to be identical to the *nature*, *form* and *intensity* of the remedy. The arbitrator in *EC–Bananas* in essence proposed to avenge an eye for an eye and a tooth for a tooth. But requiring that violation of benefits in the form of market-closing behaviour be avenged by yet another market-closing retaliation moves the idea of 'equivalent' dangerously close to 'identical'. As suggested by the word equi*valent*, it is not necessary to retaliate a lost eye with another eye. As long as there is in place a coherent methodology of calibrating, monetizing and quantifying trade damage and SCOO, a violation of any entitlement, in any form and intensity can be retaliated against by means of, say, a suspension of certain intellectual property rights. In other words, the appropriate comparator between the level of NoI and SCOO is a *coherent methodology*, but *not* an identical measure of retaliation. Quantification according to a logical consistent method hence ensures that trade damages and suspension are being calibrated and transformed into a fungible 'currency', viz. dollar-equivalent amounts of NoI and SCOO.
- Second, indemnifying damage – measured in terms of *trade blocked* – by means of calculating *affected* or *gross* trade is an asymmetrical definition of trade effects.[85] Arbitrators have repeatedly assumed that retaliation has to take the form of a *prohibitive* 100 per cent *ad valorem* tariff on targeted goods.[86] (This is nothing short of prejudging the *form* and *intensity* of SCOO – something that arbitrators have otherwise enjoined themselves from doing.) But *lost trade* equals *affected trade* only if tariff retaliation is fully prohibitive. In all other instances, *lost trade* is a subset of *affected trade*, and hence SCOO and NoI are *not* equal. To see

[84] See the main body text following footnote 56.

[85] This section is inspired by H. Spamann, 'The Myth of "Rebalancing" Retaliation in WTO Dispute Settlement Practice', sections I.B and II.A.

[86] That this conjecture is pervasive among arbitrators can be seen by comparing *EC–Hormones (US)* (Article. 22.6), paras. 13 and 21, *US–Byrd* (Article 22.6), para. 4.11, or *Brazil–Aircraft* (Article 22.6) (DSR 2002:I, 19), para. 4.2.

this, assume an original WTO violation in the form of a 5 per cent tariff hike affecting US$100 worth of trade of good *x*. The *direct trade effect* of this measure suffered by the complainant is US$5 (for simplicity we are neglecting tariff revenues paid by the complainant's exporters here), the *affected trade* is US$100. Receiving retaliation authorization for US$5 worth of *affected trade* allows the complainant to either erect a prohibitive tariff on good *y* and to block US$5 worth of *y* produce (in which case *affected trade* equals *blocked trade*). Alternatively, the complaining party may want to institute a 10 per cent tariff hike as retaliation. Using the arbitrators' conception of SCOO, however, the complainant would be allowed to leverage only a 10 per cent tariff on US$5 worth of *affected* or *gross trade* – a measure that would block only US$0.5 worth of trade flows stemming from the responding member. Such a retaliation award would be vastly *under*compensatory to the complainant.

- *Lost trade* is an effect, that is, a transaction not made due to a measure of certain form and intensity. *Affected trade* or *gross value of trade* is a scope of application to cover all transactions affected by a measure, that is, the entire trade flow.[87] Thus, the arbitrators' notion of SCOO as gross trade is rather myopic. True equivalence of NoI and SCOO (measured in direct trade effects) can only be achieved in very special circumstances, namely, when the offending measure is a traditional market access violation, when the complainant desires to retaliate with suspension of yet another market access action and when the complainant succeeds in erecting *prohibitive* tariffs vis-à-vis the respondent's goods or services. In any other circumstances equivalence will not occur, or will occur only haphazardly. Hence, this approach of quantifying SCOO as gross trade reduces the equivalence of NoI and SCOO to a mere game of chance.

WTO arbitrators have so far shied away from quantifying SCOO. They have failed to address their core mandate, namely, to establish equivalence between the levels of NoI and SCOO. Arbitrators have mostly concentrated on calculating the level of NoI (and with dubious success, as section 3 has argued), leaving implementation issues of *nature*, *form* and *intensity* of retaliation entirely in the hands of the complaining party.[88] Given that the arbitrator has occasionally expressed his views on the quantification of SCOO (views of dubious quality, and

[87] H. Spamann, 'The Myth of "Rebalancing" Retaliation in WTO Dispute Settlement Practice', 45.

[88] To put it in slightly provoking terms, thus far, arbitrators have maintained a quite sedate attitude toward their mandate: 'Thou shalt not breach! If, for whatever reason you happen

views that rarely played in favour of the complaining party), it would seem advisable for a complainant not to lose a single word on how it intends to retaliate, and instead to remind the arbitrator of standing jurisprudence that he refrain from taking any decision on the topic of SCOO.[89]

4.3 *Safeguarding equivalence between NoI and SCOO*

In light of the findings of the previous subsection, we observe that equilibrating SCOO and NoI has been a non-existent task in WTO arbitrations. As was argued at length above, arbitrators seem only to be talking about this task, but given their continuing refusal to come forward with a calculation methodology for the level of SCOO, they have not given any meaning to the concept of equivalence.

5 Conclusions and policy reforms

This chapter deals with the law and economics of WTO enforcement. From a theoretical and practical perspective we examined how rational, forward-looking contracting parties would operationalize the equivalence standard of Article 22.4 of the DSU, given that the legal text of Article 22.4 of the DSU is rather parsimonious and does not provide concrete guidelines. Cognizant of the fact that multilateral trade agreements, such as the WTO, are concluded in a state of uncertainty and are thus necessarily incomplete contracts, rational contracting parties mandate the arbitrator to calculate injury according to direct expectation effects. In addition, contracting parties should request the arbitrator to apply a mirror methodology when calculating injury and remedies. The rationale behind direct economic gains

to breach, I'll eagerly calculate the damages your behaviour causes. Subsequently, I'll hand the case over to the complainant, leaving it at that member's discretion (and ingenuity) to implement the damage amount. If you feel maltreated by the complainant's retaliation, you may appeal to yet another arbitration. Good luck with that and see you again in two to three years.'

[89] Antigua and Barbuda have understood well these rules of the game. See *US–Gambling* (Article 22.6), para. 5.5: 'Once Antigua is given authorization to suspend concessions or other obligations, and once the level of authorization is set, then Antigua will assess its alternatives. Antigua argues that the "equivalence" is achieved by first setting the level of nullification and impairment and thereafter Antigua setting the SCOO at the same level.'

and losses amounting to expectation damages lies in the insight that damages lower than expectation *under*compensate the complainant and, in addition, pose the practical problem of choosing between competing counterfactual scenarios. The idea driving the mirror methodology for NoI and SCOO is that damage and remedies need to be measured in the same 'currency' to be comparable, but that SCOO should remain flexible as to the policy mix of sectors and entitlements retaliated against.

We then contrasted our theoretical findings to the reality of seven Article 22.4 arbitrations conducted so far. The arbitrators' conduct did not match with what L&E theory would predict, causing consequential systemic problems.

First, the arbitrator's central mandate under Article 22.7 of the DSU – to safeguard equivalence between the level of NoI and SCOO – so far remains unfulfilled. All arbitrators have to date shied away from a meaningful attempt to quantify the level of SCOO. Whenever the right-hand side of an equation remains an unknown, equality between the two sides is reduced to pure guesswork. Therefore, under the current reality of Article 22.4 arbitrations, complaining parties are more or less unconstrained in the application of retaliatory actions.

Second, arbitrators' calculation of the level of NoI is burdened by two substantial flaws:

(1) Arbitrators have relied too heavily on the 'direct trade effects' metric for quantifying NoI. This 'tariffic' logic may well function for market access-related violations, but it breaks down whenever other, *non*-market access entitlements are infringed upon. In addition, since the same quantification methodology (counterfactual, metric and scope) must be used for the calculation of NoI *and* SCOO (so as to make them comparable and ensure equivalence), focusing on a trade-effects test for NoI seriously limits the space for later retaliation rights. It forces the arbitrator to apply the identical metric for the compilation of SCOO. But since trade effects are applicable only to market access restrictions, the retaliatory option space for complaining parties is, therefore, unnecessarily narrowed down.

(2) Arbitrators used an inappropriate calculation baseline, or counterfactual. Instead of constructing an *expectation damages* counterfactual, they used a methodology that most closely resembles *reliance damages.*

These flaws result in a systematic *undercompensation* of complaining members. This is critical for the world trading system, because under-compensation invites *over-breach* on the part of injuring members and, consequently, is prone to seriously reducing members' trade liberalization commitments in ongoing trade rounds: any member in fear of ever being a complaining party in an Article 22.6 litigation will anticipate being inadequately compensated for the damage suffered. The only rational behaviour in this situation is to scale back cooperative ambition.[90]

5.1 *Discussion: car or driver – who is to blame?*

An important aspect that we ought to discuss is whether the shortcomings we detected are attributable to myopic conduct by the arbitrators or whether they are the result of a deficient Agreement upon which the arbitrators are forced to act. Are we dealing with a poorly designed car or with inadequate operation by the driver – or with both?

Four arguments might be raised against our conjecture that it was, in fact, the arbitrators' *interpretation* of the – frugal – DSU language that produced the systemic problems we discussed above. First, arbitrators, by virtue of Article 22.7 of the DSU, are barred from engaging in any meaningful discussion of SCOO. Therefore, they cannot question or challenge the level of SCOO (or its calculations) suggested by the complainant(s). Second, retroactive (*ex tunc*) damages are prohibited by the language of the DSU. Hence, remedies amounting to expectation damages cannot be granted, even if arbitrators wanted to. Third, our theoretical discussion in section 3 seemed to implicitly assume that compensation is the objective of WTO enforcement, when in fact it is not. With alternative enforcement objectives in place, such as rebalancing, inducing compliance, tit-for-tat, etc., our analysis is void, and we could at most argue that the objectives underlying the DSU are flawed, but not that the arbitrators' conduct has been at fault. Finally, with SCOO, that is, trade retaliation, as the self-enforcement tool of last resort, real compensation of the victim party can *never* be achieved. Given this constraint, arbitrators have done their best to try to rebalance the level of mutual concessions to the *status quo ante* the breach. We address each of these arguments in turn.

[90] K. Mahlstein, and S. A. B. Schropp, 'Optimal Design of Trade Policy Flexibility in the WTO'; and S. A. B. Schropp, *The Law and Economics of Trade Policy Flexibility and Enforcement in the WTO.*

5.1.1 Does Article 22.7 of the DSU bar arbitrators from checking the intensity of SCOO?

In section 4.2.1 we have already discussed why we believe that arbitrators have misinterpreted their mandate under Art. 22.7. The complainant's choice of *nature* and *form* of SCOO notwithstanding, nothing in Article 22.7 of the DSU prohibits the arbitrator determining the appropriate *level* of the proposed retaliation mix. Indeed, as argued at length above, an arbitrator denying himself any authority over the level of proposed sanctions renders *inutile* his mandate under Article 22.7 of the DSU, and therewith the equivalence standard of Article 22.4 of the DSU. There is no indication that the framers of the WTO have pursued such a nonsensical objective.

5.1.2 Is retroactivity possible under current DSU rules?

The question of whether retroactivity is possible under current DSU rules is still unresolved in WTO scholarship. It is undisputed that in the arbitrations relevant for this chapter, arbitrators have calculated NoI prospectively (*ex nunc*), that is, not from the time when an illegality was committed but from the end of the RPT.[91] Yet the prospective nature of damages is not put down *expressis verbis* in any WTO provision, and we side with the Panel Report in *Australia–Automotive Leather II* (DSR 1999:III, 951, paragraph 6.26),[92] which did not detect any constraint on retroactive remedies as a matter of positive DSU law.[93] Hence, we find it hard to blame

[91] See, for example, M. Bronckers, and N. van den Broek, 'Financial Compensation in the WTO: Improving the Remedies of WTO Dispute Settlement'; P. Grané, 'Remedies Under WTO Law'; J. Pauwelyn, 'Enforcement and Countermeasures in the WTO: Rules are Rules – Toward a More Collective Approach'; H. Spamann, 'The Myth of "Rebalancing" Retaliation in WTO Dispute Settlement Practice'. In total there were five arbitration panels that departed from the standard of prospective remedies, all of them dealing with antidumping, countervailing duties or subsidies. Panels recommended revocation and reimbursement of illegally imposed duties (P. C. Mavroidis, 'Remedies in the WTO Legal System: Between a Rock and a Hard Place', 775; R. Z. Lawrence, *Crimes and Punishments? Retaliation under the WTO*, ch. 3). However, disputes in subsidy and CVD matters are not regulated by the DSU, but by special procedures in the SCM Agreement (Articles 4 and 7 of the SCM; see note 4, above). Panels and the AB have interpreted the language of Article 4.10 of SCM to bear a more extensive meaning than Article 22.4 of the DSU. The recent WTO disputes *Brazil–Aircraft*, *Canada–Aircraft II* and *US–FSC* (DS 46, 70, 108; all subsidy cases) applied retroactive damages.

[92] See P. C. Mavroidis, 'Remedies in the WTO Legal System: Between a Rock and a Hard Place', 789; and P. C. Mavroidis, *Trade in Goods*, 584.

[93] But compare M. Bronckers, and N. van den Broek, 'Financial Compensation in the WTO: Improving the Remedies of WTO Dispute Settlement', 103 or P. Grané, 'Remedies

the framework of the WTO Agreement for lacking retroactivity in WTO arbitration practice.

5.1.3 Is compensation the objective of WTO enforcement?

The concept of injury is dependent on the purpose of enforcement.[94] Our theoretical treatment of damage calculation in subsection 3.1.2 implicitly assumed that compensation of the injured party was at the core of WTO enforcement. We found that NoI amounting to the victim's expectation Pareto-dominates all other injury benchmarks and provides WTO members with the right incentive to liberalize optimally *ex ante* and breach optimally *ex post*. But what if the object and purpose of WTO enforcement is not that of compensation after all?

Different motives of WTO enforcement have been suggested, including that of punishment, tit-for-tat, efficient breach, balancing of concessions or inducing compliance.[95] If, say, rebalancing were to be the true purpose of enforcement, our finger-pointing at arbitrators may be off the mark.

We have the following comments to make: nothing in the text of the Agreement incontrovertibly nails down what the purpose of WTO enforcement really is.[96] Therefore, the framers of the WTO can be blamed for a lack of guidance, but hardly for giving the 'wrong' objective.[97] Also, irrespective of what one believes to be the objective of WTO enforcement, measuring

Under WTO Law', 768, who claim that the *prospective* nature of WTO remedies is justified by virtue of Article 19.1 of the DSU.

94 R. Cooter and M. A. Eisenberg, 'Damages For Breach of Contract', 1435.

95 See Pauwelyn, Chapter 2, above, R. Z. Lawrence, *Crimes and Punishments? Retaliation under the WTO*; S. Charnovitz, 'Recent Developments and Scholarship on WTO Enforcement Remedies' in J. Lacarte and J. Grenados (eds.), *Inter-Governmental Trade Dispute Settlement: Multilateral and Regional Approaches* (London: Cameron May, 2004), 151–65; and T. Sebastian, 'World Trade Organization Remedies and the Assessment of Proportionality: Equivalence and Appropriateness', for good summaries.

96 There is surprising unanimity in the international trade community on this issue. WTO framers have failed to state clearly what WTO enforcement is intended to achieve. Dispute panels have been left with imputing object and purpose, and came up with conflicting opinions (see Thomas Sebastian, Chapter 4, above). When it comes to the purpose of enforcement in the WTO, the major dispute in trade scholarship is between proponents of the 'compliance' and the 'rebalancing' school of thought, represented by John H. Jackson for the compliance camp and Alan Sykes for the rebalancing view of the WTO (see Joost Pauwelyn, Chapter 2, above; see also S. A. B. Schropp, 'Revisiting the "Compliance-vs.-Rebalancing" Debate in WTO Scholarship: Towards a Unified Research Agenda' for a comprehensive review of the compliance-rebalancing dispute in WTO scholarship).

97 The absence of concrete contractual language is exactly why we resorted to L&E theory in the first place. As mentioned above, L&E theory predicts that, if confronted with the decision *ex ante*, that is, in a state of uncertainty of the future, forward-looking contracting parties will opt for a remedy regime that provides for compensation, rather than for punishment

NoI in terms of expectation damages is the most comprehensive way of quantifying harm. Calculated properly, remedies amounting to the victim's expectation will induce compliance (where compliance is efficient), fully rebalance the mutual trade liberalization concessions and compensate the victim of contractual breach. No other trade damage benchmark is as inclusive and can thus act as a sensible middle ground.[98] Given that we simply do not know the object and purpose of WTO enforcement, expectation damages would seem to be an obvious choice for WTO arbitrators.

5.1.4 Can retaliation compensate complainants at all?

A final rebuttal against the arguments brought forth in this chapter can be that the objective of compensation cannot be achieved with the legally prescribed remedy of SCOO at all. Thus, arbitrators were right in *not* quantifying the level of damages according to the expectation benchmark, because the remedy of retaliation fails to achieve the objective of compensation anyway.

Tariff retaliation as a countermeasure is a dysfunctional, some would even argue nonsensical, mechanism of remediation. Charnovitz finds at least eight serious disadvantages of the countermeasure of retaliation.[99] Most compellingly, a complaining party 'shoots itself in the foot'[100] when avenging the injurer's violation by raising trade barriers on its part, since doing so is inefficient, harms consumers and downstream industries, and, in addition, makes the beneficiaries of sanctions (import-competing industries in the complaining country) complacent and slack. By impeding the cross-border flow of trade in goods and services, less instead of more cooperation is achieved. SCOO can thus at best re-establish the *status quo ante* the breach but cannot ever place the victim member in as good a position as it would have been had the injuring party fulfilled its contractual obligations.[101] A higher retaliation award would merely enlarge the self-inflicted hole in the complainant's foot. Hence, the argument

or compliance (for example, W. F. Schwartz, and A. O. Sykes, 'The Economic Structure of Renegotiation and Dispute Resolution in the WTO/GATT System'; K. Mahlstein and S. A. B. Schropp, 'Optimal Design of Trade Policy Flexibility in the WTO').

98 Punitive damages may induce compliance, but cannot rebalance mutual concessions; reliance damages can rebalance at a lower level (the *status quo ante* the breach), but neither compensate the victim(s) adequately, nor induce compliance on the part of injuring member.

99 S. Charnovitz, 'Rethinking WTO Trade Sanctions', *American Journal of International Law*, 95:4 (2001), 792–832.

100 P. C. Mavroidis, 'Remedies in the WTO Legal System: Between a Rock and a Hard Place'.

101 R. Z. Lawrence, *Crimes and Punishments? Retaliation under the WTO.*

may continue, as a matter of principle SCOO as a remedy mechanism can hardly fulfil the ideal of expectation damages and arbitrators were right in awarding reliance damages only.

This argument confuses the issues of injury calculation, on the one hand, and of remediation mechanisms, on the other hand. SCOO may not be a perfect remedy (and, in fact, Article 3.2 of the DSU makes it clear that the withdrawal of the offending measure, a mutually agreed solution, and tariff compensation are preferred means of enforcement). Should this circumstance determine the appropriate calculation of NoI? That would be inappropriate for a number of reasons:

- As the fallback remedy of last resort, SCOO sets the yardstick for all other remedies the WTO applies.[102] Since members should be interested in *full* – not partial – withdrawal of the offending measure and *full* – not partial – tariff compensation, it is important to calculate correctly trade damages incurred by the complainant(s), regardless of whether this amount harms or benefits the complaining party later on.
- Every country entitled to SCOO can decide for itself to what extent to make use of its retaliation right.[103] The arbitrator is not to dictate to members how much retaliation is 'good for them'.
- Although from a general welfare perspective, less tariff retaliation is preferred to more, it is not at all clear whether general welfare, or rather policy-makers' well-being, is the correct 'currency' in the WTO. After all, the WTO is a political deal and it is policy makers that negotiate and conclude trade agreements.[104] If political welfare is the currency to

[102] SCOO sets the benchmark for all other (formal and informal) escape remedies in the WTO and determines the power relationship in all settlement negotiations between injurers and victims: when bartering over a mutually agreed solution or voluntary compensation, no respondent will be willing to settle above his reservation utility, that is, the expected cost of enduring retaliation.

[103] And indeed, as the contributions by Hunter Nottage (Chapter 15), Lothar Ehring (Chapter 9) and Scott Andersen and Justine Blanchet (Chapter 8) in this volume show, many successful complainants have not fully exhausted their retaliation awards.

[104] Compare the discussion around footnote 39 and accompanying text. See Alan Sykes, Chapter 16, above; see also W. F. Schwartz, and A. O. Sykes, 'The Economic Structure of Renegotiation and Dispute Resolution in the WTO/GATT System'; W. J. Ethier, 'Political Externalities, Nondiscrimination, and a Multilateral World'; T. E. Josling, 'WTO Dispute Settlement and the EU–US Mini Trade Wars: A Commentary on Fritz Breuss', *Journal of Industry, Competition and Trade*, 4:4 (2004), 337–44; W. Kohler, 'The WTO Dispute Settlement Mechanism: Battlefield or Cooperation?'; B. P. Rosendorff, 'Stability and Rigidity: Politics and Design of the WTO's Dispute Settlement Procedures', *American Political Science Review*, 99:3 (2005), 389–400; S. A. B. Schropp, *Trade Policy Flexibility and Enforcement in the WTO: A Law and Economics Analysis*.

measure success and failure of the WTO enforcement system, SCOO amounting to expectation damages may very well yield higher welfare levels than those resulting from a reliance counterfactual.[105]

- The remedy of SCOO allows for unexplored ways of retaliation that do not have the self-mutilation (shot-in-the-foot) factor as tariff retaliation: cross-retaliation in the form of suspension of intellectual property rights (patents, copyrights, trademarks, etc.) is an already tested alternative to tariff retaliation. Alternative avenues, such as Canada's innovative and perceptive request to suspend the 'injury test' in anti-dumping investigations against the United States have to be tested in the future and may very well be free from self-inflicted harm for the retaliating country.[106]

To sum up, we believe that it is a bad idea to jettison the expectation damages measure of quantifying injury just because the remedy of SCOO is burdened with some systemic problems. Trade sanctions, albeit by no means a perfect remedy, have the advantage of allowing the victim to self-enact enforcement without the respondent's consent. It would be wrong for arbitrators to calculate suboptimal levels of NoI until a fairer and more equitable DSU remedy is found, because this may never be the case.

5.2 *Policy reforms*

In this chapter, we have uncovered some systemic shortcomings of the current practice of Article 22.4 arbitrations. These shortcomings are the result of an empty WTO rule book and questionable interpretations on the part of WTO arbitrators. We have argued against the contention that it is the *text of the WTO* which is flawed and that arbitrators are forced to abide by erroneous language. Instead, we have found that the WTO Agreement – regrettably enough – is *silent* on a number of important systemic and procedural issues, and that arbitrators' interpretation of the treaty language and application thereof has been unfortunate in a number of instances.

We have brought forth a long list of criticisms of WTO arbitrators' practice in cases under the purview of Article 22.4 of the DSU. What is the constructive reform agenda we have to offer? As argued in detail in

105 See S. A. B. Schropp, 'The Case for Tariff Compensation in WTO Dispute Settlement', *Aussenwirtschaft*, 60:IV (2005), 485–528.

106 Available at: http://canadagazette.gc.ca/part II/2005/20050504/html/sor106-e.html#a.

the last subsection, WTO drafters have left a remarkably clean slate to the membership when it comes to the implementation of trade sanctions. The good news for our agenda of reform is that it does not require any changes in the language of the DSU whatsoever. Since the WTO founding fathers have provided virtually no guidance of how to handle arbitrations, all our previous criticisms can be addressed by a new, progressive interpretation of Article 22 of the DSU. Hence, the only policy reform that is needed is a rethinking of previous arbitration practice, an improvement of legal practice and a renunciation of legal precedent.[107]

Future arbitrators would be doing a better job if they heeded the advice laid out in the following steps:

(1) Be transparent about your choices: arbitrators have become much better at explaining their reasoning.[108] More transparency, however, would be highly welcome.
(2) Avoid falling prey to 'tariffic' blinders: arbitrators should make efforts to be explicit about what is the *nature* of the offending measure. This may provide initial clarity on whether a direct trade-effects test is applicable at all, and which alternative quantification methods could be called upon.
(3) Actively address the trade-off between accuracy and speculation: given the nature of the offending measure, how can arbitrators calculate the *intensity* of the trade damage suffered by the complaining party – without having to be unduly speculative, and without considering claims that are too remote? What is the proper counterfactual against which to measure the current situation? What is the most adequate metric in which to measure NoI – and later on SCOO? When choosing the metric to measure NoI, how can arbitrators handle the trade-off between avoiding unfounded speculation (an

[107] Although dispute panels and the Appellate Body do not tire of pointing out that the WTO does not know *stare decisis* (*cf.* the arbitrator, *US–Byrd*, footnote 57: 'As a matter of fact, we do not consider previous arbitrations to be constitutive of "subsequent practice" within the meaning of that concept under public international law (see Vienna Convention, Article 31.3(b)'), dispute panels do cherish the concept of legal precedence.

[108] Whereas in the first arbitration (*EU–Bananas (US)* (Article 22.6)), the arbitrator justified his calculation of the retaliation award with a single sentence ('Using the various data provided on US market shares, and our knowledge of the current quota allocation and what we estimate it would be under the WTO-consistent counterfactual chosen by us, we determine that the level of nullification and impairment is US$191.4 million per year'; para. 7.8), recent arbitrations have laid out their methodologies and economic models in a fairly detailed manner. The recent Arbitrator's Report in *US–Cotton* (DS 267) underscores this trend.

argument in favour of straightforward measurement units based on hard evidence), and the need to choose proxies that are not *under-* or *over*compensatory?[109]

(4) Enter the virgin territory of 'quantification of retaliation': arbitrators must start tackling the task of calculating the level of SCOO that was assigned to them by the drafters of the WTO Agreement. This is the only way to properly determine equivalence with the level of NoI. The arbitrator may well leave it up to the complaining party to determine *nature* and *form* of retaliation (keeping in mind provisions like Articles 22.3 and 22.5 of the DSU). However, once the policy mix of retaliatory action is chosen by the complainant, the competence of fixing the maximal level of *intensity* of the retaliation must reside with the arbitrator. Quantifying the intensity of SCOO is the mirror-image calculation of that of NoI. The arbitrator must thereby use the identical methodology, that is, the same counterfactual, metric and scope, so as to be consistent and to actually make the two numbers comparable. Only with a coherent methodology can the two levels be called 'of equal value'. Having monetized both the level of damage suffered and of remedy granted suffices to make these actions equivalent. Thus, retaliatory action that uses a policy mix of *nature*, *form* and *intensity* other than the original offending measure is open for consideration.

(5) Establish clear procedural rules: in current arbitration practice, there is no specific procedure in place to structure the SCOO authorization process. The current practice is to let the *complainant* set the dollar figure of retaliation and to let it construe the retaliation package, which is then challenged by the responding member if it considers the list non-equivalent. The arbitrator so far essentially decides on the level of NoI and leaves it to the complainant to define and execute the nature and extent of trade sanctions. The respondent, in case it feels maltreated by the complainant's implementation of trade sanctions has no choice but to initiate a novel trade dispute (as happened in the recent *US–Hormones (Suspension)* case). This post-authorization process is counterproductive.

It would be better to have the respondent challenge the requested *level* of SCOO right at the beginning. The arbitrator, after having calculated the correct level of NoI, would request the complainant

[109] In earlier sections, we have revealed our preference for choosing *direct economic gains and losses* as proxy for trade damage, but this may change from case to case.

to come up with a retaliation list.[110] After having presented this list, containing *nature* and *form* of SCOO, the arbitrator should then be charged with engaging in the DSU, Article 22.3 test (testing practicability and effectiveness of retaliation in the same sector/agreement), and then with setting the *level* of this proposed retaliation mix. Thereafter, the complainant should start enacting its trade sanctions according to the arbitrator's finding.

Our proposal would mark a radical shift in the way in which arbitrations have been conducted in the past decade or so. We acknowledge that drafting a methodology for calculating the level of SCOO will be a challenging task for arbitrators. The same goes for the calculation of expectation damages and quantification of broader economic gains and losses. Tackling these issues will require a change in the skill-set of arbitration panels. Calculation of NoI and SCOO will become more 'technical' and empirical: work to be conducted by economic specialists. Yet it would be imprudent to condemn this endeavour just because it seems challenging. The membership should not lower its ambitions or jettison a reform agenda of Article 22.4 arbitrations simply for reasons of practicality. Rather, additional economic competence inside the WTO Secretariat or by outside experts may support arbitration panels in their work.[111]

[110] During this time, the retaliation process should be suspended. The complainant could take all the time necessary to compile its retaliation package. Once composed, the retaliation process would be resumed.

[111] As P. C. Mavroidis, 'Remedies in the WTO Legal System: Between a Rock and a Hard Place', 769 states: 'The fact, though, that full recovery [that is, expectation damages] is, in practice, sometimes hard to calculate, does not render the reparation exercise meaningless ... Although assessment of damages is the task of the judge, calculation of the damage is essentially a quantification exercise, that is, essentially the task of the economist' (see Chad Bown, chapter 19, above; see also A. Sapir and J. P. Trachtman, 'Subsidization, Price Suppression, and Expertise: Causation and Precision in Upland Cotton', *World Trade Review*, 7:1 (Special Issue) (2008), 183–209; H. Vandenbussche, 'Comment: Upland Cotton Case', *World Trade Review*, 7:1 (Special Issue) (2008), 211–17).

Comment on chapter 20

A general equilibrium interpretation of some WTO dispute settlement cases: four EU–US trade conflicts

FRITZ BREUSS*

Simon Schropp, in a structured law and economics approach, gives an excellent and critical survey of the major deficiencies of WTO arbitration. He discusses the different concepts of calculating the appropriate counterfactual in order to quantify the level of nullification and impairment. This leads him to conclude that it is nearly impossible to 'determine whether the level of suspension of concessions or other obligations (SCOO) is equivalent to the level of nullification or impairment (NoI)'. He shows in a nice little matrix that different scales (blocked trade or lost turnover; efficiency losses or lost profits; overall economic losses) and scopes (direct or sectoral impact and/or indirect or economy-wide effects) lead to different outcomes when measuring the NoI. In my analysis I assume that the goal of the WTO treaty is not only to increase trade flows (reciprocal exchanges of market access) but to enhance – at least in the long run – overall welfare. In addition, I am concerned about the spillovers or side effects of NoIs and also of any retaliation.

In order to underline my 'welfare cum general equilibrium effects' position I will refer to the results of calculations of the overall implications of some selected US–EU trade disputes. For this purpose I deal with a number of issues. First, is 'rebalancing' retaliation in WTO dispute settlement more a myth than reality? Second, I provide examples of unintended side effects in some transatlantic trade disputes – demonstrated in the case of the most prominent 'mini-trade wars' between the EU and the United States. Third, I offer suggestions for improvements of the dispute settlement system from an economic perspective.

* Europa Institut at the Vienna University of Economics and Business (WU Wien).

1 Is 'rebalancing' retaliation in WTO dispute settlement more a myth than reality?

The ability of the WTO to authorize trade retaliation as a response to persistent violations is perhaps the most salient, but also the most controversial feature of its dispute settlement system. Although the main purpose of retaliation is to achieve compliance, most authors seem to take it for granted that, by allowing the complaining member to suspend concessions and obligations under the WTO agreements vis-à-vis the responding member at a level equivalent to the level of nullification and impairment caused by the latter's WTO-inconsistent measure (Dispute Settlement Understanding (DSU), Article 22.4), the current system of trade retaliation performs some kind of 'rebalancing'. My main thesis is that rebalancing is more a myth than reality.

Due to several side effects, 'rebalancing' never means and never can be a restoration of the *status quo ante*. One reason is that even an identically specified measure will have different effects depending on the size and composition of the trade flow (sectoral implications). The other reason is that suspension must be targeted against the responding member, while the underlying violation will usually have covered trade with all members (third-country effects). But also the retaliation of one complainant against one violating member (for example, in many EU–US trade disputes) has external effects on other WTO members.

In practice, it is very difficult to 'calculate' the 'exact' damage or level of nullification or impairment. One simple approach, often applied by the WTO arbitrators is to approximate it by trade effects in the sense of lost trade (that is, lost turnover) as the relevant comparator. In *EC–Hormones* the calculation of the lost trade was by far the most transparent calculation. In *EC–Bananas* and in the other cases of EU–US trade disputes where sanctions were allowed, these calculations – according to Breuss (2004) – were neither transparent nor plausible. Whereas 'WTO retaliation authorizations are, in reality, arbitrary' (Spamann, 2006, 34), it seems that the outcome of the level of nullification is sometimes more the result of a political bazaar deal (Breuss, 2004, 2007).

Anderson (2002) shows theoretically that equal trade effects will only coincidentally, if ever, proxy for equal welfare effects. I have demonstrated elsewhere (Breuss, 2004, 2007) that the simply calculated forgone trade effects must, not however, coincide with the more proper welfare effects. Welfare effects are the standard comparator in economic policy analysis, and welfare improvements – and not only a simple increase in trade – are, or should be, also the ultimate goal of the WTO agreements. Although welfare effects are the only truly general comparator for the level of nullification, they are admittedly difficult to calculate. A shortcoming of all the WTO arbitrators' calculations of the level of damage (or level of nullification) is that primarily partial analytical calculations are applied. However, without a general equilibrium analysis it cannot be done properly. Kohler (2004) in commenting on my general equilibrium calculations of the economic impact of the four transatlantic trade disputes interprets the concept of 'rebalancing' by weighing 'economic values' against 'political values'. For him, this makes it more understandable that although, as I have shown, both the plaintiff and the defendant may lose in welfare terms, both governments – due to political economy motives – still prefer the outcome to the initial situation (the original agreement). In Kohler's interpretation 'the DSM is a useful vehicle to "re-balance" the agreement, towards a new political equilibrium'.

2 Examples of unintended side effects in some transatlantic trade disputes

Here I demonstrate examples of side effects from the most prominent 'mini-trade wars' between the EU and the United States.[1] In order to overcome the usual shortcomings of the partial analytical calculations of the WTO arbitrators in the analysis of the economic impact of the four most prominent EU–US trade conflicts I applied a computable general equilibrium (CGE) model (GTAP5) using twelve countries/regions and seven commodities/sectors (Breuss, 2004, 2007). Here I refer to the major findings of this exercise only.

With this CGE setting the four most prominent EU–US trade conflicts – that is, *EC–Hormones*, *EC–Bananas*, *US–FSC*, and *US–Steel Safeguards* – were analysed. When either the US or the EU is retaliating against one another because of having violated WTO agreements we have the situation of a (retaliatory) 'trade war': both parties reduce trade by imposing trade-contracting measures simultaneously. As these trade disputes have a fairly low dimension – they amount only to between 0.01 per cent and around 2 per cent of bilateral EU–US trade in each case – I call them

[1] Unfortunately, I cannot offer an equivalent quantitative analysis of the *US–Byrd Amendment* and the *US–Internet Gambling* cases.

'mini-trade wars'.[2] In the so-defined 'mini-trade wars' in three out of four cases both parties have or would have suffered a (slight) welfare deterioration. Only in *US–FSC* could the EU improve its welfare slightly.

2.1 Major findings

2.1.1 The level of damage

The four analysed cases showed that the estimation of the correct level of suspension of concessions 'equal to the nullification or impairment' is practically impossible. The calculation always involves the comparison between the actual situations with one hypothetical in which the trade measures would be WTO-legal. As such calculations always have to be made under uncertainty one should at least do this exercise under two conditions: (1) the arbitrators should make sensitivity analyses when fixing the level of impairment; and (2) they should allow for much more transparency. The concept of equivalence draws more on notions of fairness than on economic accuracy.

Hence, a complete 'rebalancing' is an illusion. If allowed to introduce retaliatory import tariffs in the amount of the 'damage', this will enhance reactions by importers and will reduce imports of the targeted products either completely (100 per cent extra tariffs act prohibitively) or not fully. In short, the damage calculated by WTO arbitrators may be quite different from the overall economic impact of the introduction of retaliatory measures in the economies of the complainant, respondent and also in third countries.

There are other flaws in the WTO dispute settlement system. It looks at future actions only. Past wrongs go uncompensated. Trade retaliation under the WTO targets non-compliance only after a 'reasonable period of time' has elapsed following a panel or Appellate Body finding against a respondent's illegal policy regime. The damage caused to the complainant's export industry in preceding years is simply ignored by DSU procedures. Furthermore, by retaliating it is the complainant's import-competing industries that enjoy temporary assistance because of the prohibitive retaliatory tariffs imposed. This does not help the export industry that has been denied market access by the respondent's wrong policy in the first place.

[2] A more detailed description of the history of these cases can be found in Breuss (2004, 2007).

2.1.2 Questionable system of retaliation

The WTO dispute settlement system's objective is twofold: (1) to obtain a satisfactory solution to the dispute in the interest of the disputing parties; and (2) more broadly to guarantee compliance in the interest of all WTO members. The present tariff sanction system is questionable for several reasons:

- it is counterproductive because it leads to trade contraction and hence goes against the very trade liberalizing principles of the GATT/WTO;
- retaliation does not bring relief to the exporters injured by the WTO-illegal measures;
- trade retaliation also damages innocent bystanders (external side effects);
- existing remedies are unwieldy: the more trade of a country is affected by WTO-illegal measures, the more difficult it is to find imports that can be restricted without hurting consumers.

Additionally, theory and the empirical evidence (via simulations with CGE trade models) suggest that import tariffs may lead to a trade war. Trade wars can only be won by large (and hence, powerful) countries. This is the result of optimum tariff theory. That means that small (and more so, poor) less developed countries (LDCs) are discriminated against in two respects. On the one hand, due to a lack of legal resources they make less use of the WTO dispute settlement system, and on the other hand, if they are authorized to retaliate against a large country or trading bloc (like the EU), they do not implement such sanctions (for example, Ecuador in its 'cross-retaliation' case against the EU) either because they fear losing the trade war or necessary aid from the donor country (for example, from the EU) or they hope for preferential treatment in debt negotiations in the Paris Club. Countermeasures in the form of retaliatory tariffs are bad policy and amount to 'shooting oneself in the foot'. Through countermeasures, a small and poor WTO member imposes an additional cost on its own society. Precisely because of the budgetary constraints, adoption of countermeasures is simply not an option for the poorer WTO members. The present system of compensation in the WTO illustrates the disadvantageous position of LDCs. Even 'cross-retaliation' in the area of TRIPS, which may have seemed promising from the perspective of compliance-seeking developing countries, does not offer them the relief they hoped for, as can be seen in Ecuador's experience in *EC–Bananas*.

2.1.3 Unpleasant implications of tariff retaliation

Retaliatory measures via import tariffs have a whole series of incalculable and unpleasant impacts. *EC–Hormones*, *EC–Bananas*, and *US–FSC* have demonstrated that retaliatory measures tend to injure a motley assembly of exporters and importers that are often smaller companies that rarely, if ever, have an interest in the original dispute (for example, bananas against luxury bags from 'Gucci').

In addition to these anecdotes, one can strictly prove from general equilibrium analysis of trade policy measures that the imposed tariffs on a randomly selected list of products (sometimes aggravated by a 'carousel' method) can have implications which were not foreseen by WTO arbitrators if they did not have access to a very detailed CGE world trade model. As long as such modelling devices are not at hand, the WTO Dispute Settlement Body's (DSB) decisions on retaliatory tariffs – although not carrying them out on their own but on behalf of the WTO member states – are irresponsible. The first promising attempts to correct such omissions can be found in the decisions of the arbitrators in *US–FSC* and *US–Byrd Amendment*.

2.1.4 Who controls the retaliators?

Furthermore, besides the problem of calculating the level of damage a country suffers as a result of another member not complying with WTO rules, the dispute settlement architects also overlooked the question of who controls the retaliators? Once the amount of impairment is set by the arbitrators in the WTO dispute settlement procedure, who controls whether the country which has been permitted to retaliate really only reduces imports by the amount authorized by the WTO? Additionally, who controls the distribution of the retaliatory tariff revenues? Are any of the collected revenues redistributed to the companies suffering the damage? In practice companies suffering the damage by WTO-illegal measures are not compensated out of the tariff revenues collected by the complainant government.

3 Suggestions for improvements of the dispute settlement system from an economic perspective

There are numerous proposals for improving and clarifying the DSU which refer to institutional and/or procedural changes. Nevertheless, rarely do they touch intrinsic economic problems with the dispute settlement system.

3.1 *Transfers instead of tariffs for retaliation*

A wide range of proposals for improving the WTO's system of remedies has already been put forward: my findings confirm that tariffs are very poor instruments for countermeasures. According to international law, in cases of compliance a basic principle is the right to request financial reparation for a wrongful act, including damage incurred in the past. The crucial remaining question is, with which instruments should one execute the sanctions?

A much more efficient and easier retaliation instrument than tariffs would be direct transfers from the government of the non-complying country to the government of the country having got the authorization for compensation by the WTO. The latter government could then easily redistribute the received transfers to the companies which suffered the concrete loss. Such form of retaliation is often called 'financial compensation'. This is not a novel idea: reparation by governments of injury for which they can be held responsible is part of the tradition of public international law. It had already been proposed in the GATT in 1966 (see Bronckers and van den Broek, 2005, 110) and was also proposed more recently in the WTO. Such a transfer or financial compensation scheme has several advantages over the present tariff-ridden retaliation system. It solves more or less all the problems inherent in the retaliation system by tariffs. This method of retaliation would come closer to the ideal of 'rebalancing' because there would be no negative external and distorting effects as with a tariff. Whether transfers as retaliatory measures would also be covered by the present DSU legislation is an open question. Article 22.1 of the DSU does not refer to tariffs explicitly, only to 'compensation and the suspension of concessions or other obligations'.

Suspension of concessions as a rule implies the reintroduction of tariffs since the major part of concessions in former GATT rounds consisted of tariff reductions. One could (newly!) interpret 'other obligations' as the duty of countries not complying with WTO rules to pay transfers to the countries hurt by the non-compliant action. This should be a recoverable claim, determined by the usual DSU procedure. The problem, however, is that the complainant would interfere in the respondent's national sovereignty – something excluded from the present WTO system. In any case, this would require amendment of the DSU (see also Bronckers and van den Broek, 2005, 123ff).

3.2 *Compensation instead of retaliation*

There are other suggestions put forward to improve the retaliatory procedure. Anderson (2002) pleads for compensation instead of retaliation. A complainant unhappy with the respondent's policy reform should be entitled to seek compensation until satisfactory reforms are implemented. Compensation could come in the form of temporarily lowering the respondent's import barriers on some other products on a most-favoured-nation (MFN) basis. Instead of the restrictive effect of retaliation to both countries involved in the trade dispute, compensation in this form would simply mean trade liberalization. According to Anderson (2002), the concept of compensation would not only favour the complainant but also third countries, and by granting compensation the respondent would gain greater control of procedures. With retaliation, by contrast, the complainant can keep pressure on the respondent until the latter complies. Anderson's suggestion, however, would confuse the ongoing general liberalization rounds under WTO. What Bronckers and van den Broek (2005, 107) have called a 'mandatory compensation' system also has its disadvantages.

The advantage of trade compensation, as opposed to retaliation, is that compensation does not restrict trade but actually opens it up, albeit temporarily, for as long as the non-complying measure remains in place. In practice, however, compensation is hardly ever offered because it is very difficult for countries to find and offer compensatory reductions of trade barriers.

3.3 *Tradable retaliation rights*

Mexico has proposed that retaliation rights be made tradable (Bagwell, Mavroidis and Staiger, 2006). Its proposal came out of recognition of the problem that small and developing countries have difficulty in finding the capacity to retaliate effectively against trading partners. Bagwell, Mavroidis and Staiger (2007) offer a first formal analysis of the possibility that retaliation rights within the WTO system be allocated through auctions and present results that are, however, highly sensitive to the auction format chosen.

References

Anderson, Kym 2002. 'Peculiarities of Retaliation in WTO Dispute Settlement', *World Trade Review,* 1(2):123–34.

Bagwell, Kyle, Petros C. Mavroidis and Robert W. Staiger 2006. 'The Case for Tradable Remedies in WTO Dispute Settlement' in Simon J. Evenett and Bernard M. Hoekman (eds.), *Economic Development and Multilateral Trade Cooperation* (Washington, DC: Palgrave Macmillan and the World Bank).

Bagwell, Kyle, Petros C. Mavroidis and Robert W. Staiger 2007. 'Auctioning Countermeasures in the WTO', *Journal of International Economics*, 73(2): 309–32.

Breuss, Fritz 2004. 'WTO Dispute Settlement: An Economic Analysis of Four EU–US Mini Trade Wars – A Survey', *Journal of Industry, Competition and Trade*, 4(4): 275–315.

2007. 'Economic Integration, EU–US Trade Conflicts and WTO Dispute Settlement', FIW Working Paper, No. 001, April.

Bronckers, Marco and Naboth van den Broek 2005. 'Financial Compensation in the WTO: Improving the Remedies of WTO Dispute Settlement', *Journal of International Economic Law*, 8(1): 101–26.

Kohler, Wilhelm 2004. 'The WTO Dispute Settlement Mechanism: Battlefield or Cooperation? A Commentary on Fritz Breuss', *Journal of Industry, Competition and Trade*, 4(4): 317–36.

Spamann, Holger 2006. 'The Myth of "Rebalancing" Retaliation in WTO Dispute Settlement Practice', *Journal of International Economic Law*, 9(1): 31–79.

PART VI

New frontiers and lessons from other fields

21

Cross-retaliation and suspension under the GATS and TRIPS agreements

WERNER ZDOUC*

1 Background and context

This chapter discusses the rules and procedures for cross-retaliation under the Dispute Settlement Understanding (DSU) and relevant dispute settlement practice and problems arising in the context of suspension of concessions or other obligations under the GATS and the TRIPS Agreement. Under the DSU, countermeasures in response to non-compliance with Dispute Settlement Body (DSB) recommendations and rulings are subject to certain disciplines. Most importantly, Articles 22 and 23 of the DSU require *prior authorization* of suspension of concessions or other obligations by the DSB. Article 22.4 provides that the level of suspension must be *equivalent* to the nullification or impairment resulting from non-compliance with DSB recommendations or rulings. According to Article 22.8, suspension shall be temporary and be applied only until such time as the measure found to be inconsistent with a covered agreement has been removed or another mutually satisfactory solution is achieved. In principle, countermeasures are to be taken in the same trade sector and under the same covered agreement in respect of which the DSB made recommendations and rulings. However, the DSB may authorize suspension of concessions or other obligations across trade sectors, or under another agreement, provided that the

* Director of the WTO Appellate Body Secretariat. The views expressed should not be attributed to the Appellate Body or its Secretariat. I would like to thank my colleagues at the Secretariat, Kaarlo Castren, Andreas Sennekamp, Liz Upton and Gisele Kapterian for their contributions to this chapter. These comments were prepared for the Interdisciplinary Workshop 'The Calculation and Design of Trade Sanctions in WTO Dispute Settlement' held at the Graduate Institute, Geneva on Saturday, 19 July 2008, for the session entitled 'How to Improve the Current System', Panel 5: 'Improvements and new approaches from a legal perspective'.

requirements and conditions set out in Article 22.3 for so-called *cross-retaliation* are met.

Some similarities, and some differences, exist with public international law standards on countermeasures, as reflected in the International Law Commission's Draft Articles on State Responsibility. For example, countermeasures must be 'commensurate with the injury suffered, taking into account the gravity of the internationally wrongful act and the rights in question.'[1] Moreover, countermeasures 'shall be terminated as soon as the responsible State ha[s] complied with its obligations … in relation to the internationally wrongful act'.[2] However, the Draft Articles on State Responsibility do not regulate and constrain countermeasures in the same way that Article 22.3 does with respect to cross-retaliation.[3]

Obviously, WTO members could request authorization to cross-retaliate under the Multilateral Agreements on Trade in Goods listed in Annex 1A to the WTO Agreement in response to breaches of the GATS or the TRIPS Agreement. However, to date, all requests and authorizations of cross-retaliation have concerned the GATS and the TRIPS Agreement and were made in response to non-compliance with DSB recommendations and rulings under the GATT 1994 or the GATS. Such requests for cross-retaliation have been made in three cases: (1) by Ecuador in *EC–Bananas III (Ecuador)*; (2) by Antigua and Barbuda (hereinafter 'Antigua') in *US–Gambling*; and (3) by Brazil in *US–Upland Cotton*. Ecuador requested and obtained authorization to suspend TRIPS obligations (copyrights and related rights, geographical indications and industrial designs) in reaction to breaches by the EC of its obligations under the GATT 1994 and the GATS.[4] In response to the failure by the United States to comply with its commitments under the GATS in the sector of 'recreational, cultural and sporting services', Antigua requested and obtained authorization to suspend GATS commitments in another sector (communication services) and 'horizontal' (that is, across the board) GATS commitments as well as TRIPS obligations (copyrights and related rights, trademarks, industrial designs, patents and protection of undisclosed

[1] Article 51 of the Draft Articles on State Responsibility.

[2] Article 53 of the Draft Articles on State Responsibility.

[3] Article 55 provides that the rules and standards of the Draft Articles on State Responsibility do not apply to the extent that content or implementation of the international responsibility of a state is governed by special rules of international law such as those set out in the DSU.

[4] WTO document, WT/DS27/52, 9 November 1999. Decision by the arbitrators, *EC–Bananas III (Ecuador)* (Article 22.6 – EC), WTO document, WT/DS27/ARB/ECU, 24 March 2000 (DSR 2000:V, 2237).

information).[5] Neither Ecuador nor Antigua have exercised their rights to impose sanctions under the TRIPS Agreement. In October 2005, Brazil sought authorization for retaliation against the United States including under the GATS (business, communication, construction and related engineering services) and the TRIPS Agreement (copyrights and related rights, trademarks, industrial designs, patents and protection of undisclosed information).[6] Brazil reactivated its request after the DSB adopted the panel and Appellate Body reports in Article 21.5 proceedings in June 2008.[7] The arbitration proceedings pursuant to Articles 22.2 and 22.3 on the level of suspension and the permissibility of cross-retaliation are pending at the time of writing.

Article 22.7 provides that 'if the matter referred to arbitration includes a claim that the principles and procedures set forth in paragraph 3 have not been followed, the arbitrator shall examine that claim' and that '[i]n the event the arbitrator determines that those principles and procedures have not been followed, the complaining party shall apply them consistent with paragraph 3'. A number of complexities arise for a WTO member seeking authorization for cross-retaliation. Specifically, Article 22.3 of the DSU provides, as a general principle, that the complaining member should first seek to suspend concessions or other obligations with respect to the same 'sector' as that in which the panel or Appellate Body has found nullification or impairment resulting from non-compliance with DSB recommendations and rulings. If the complaining member considers that it is not practicable or effective to suspend concessions or other obligations with respect to the same sector(s), the DSB may authorize suspension of concessions in other sectors under the same agreement if certain conditions are met. Retaliation in other sectors under another covered agreement is permitted only if the arbitrators acting pursuant to Article 22.3 find that suspending concessions with respect to other sectors under the same agreement 'is not practicable or effective' and the 'circumstances are serious enough' to warrant cross-retaliation. Furthermore, when requesting suspension of concessions, the complaining member shall take into account: (1) the trade in the sector or under the agreement where nullification or

[5] WTO document, WT/DS285/22, 22 June 2007. Decision by the arbitrators, *US–Gambling* (Article 22.6 – US), WTO document, WT/DS285/ARB, 21 December 2007. Subsequently, in response to questioning by the arbitrators, Antigua clarified that it was only seeking authorization to cross-retaliate under the TRIPS Agreement (Decision by the arbitrators, *US–Gambling*, para. 2.17).

[6] WTO document, WT/DS267/26, 7 October 2005.

[7] WTO document, WT/DS267/38, 15 October 2008.

impairment was found, and the 'importance' of such trade to the complaining party; and (2) the broader economic elements related to the nullification and impairment suffered by the member requesting suspension and the broader economic consequences of the suspension of concessions for the non-complying member. Article 22.3 of the DSU further requires the complaining member requesting authorization to suspend concessions in other sectors under the same, or another, agreement, to state the reasons for doing so in its request. Subparagraphs (f) and (g) set out definitions for the terms 'sector' and 'agreement' with respect to trade in goods and trade in services, and trade-related intellectual property rights.

It is not clear why, for purposes of Article 22.3, all agreements regulating trade in goods (contained in Annex 1A to the WTO Agreement) constitute one sector, while the GATS and the TRIPS Agreement are subdivided into service sectors and types of intellectual property rights, respectively. It appears that the trade-in-goods sector is no less heterogeneous than the services sector or the sector of trade-related intellectual property rights, especially given the variety of twelve agreements and six understandings regulating various aspects of trade in goods listed in Annex 1A to the WTO Agreement.[8] Nevertheless, if a member decides, for example, to request authorization to suspend obligations under the SPS Agreement when another member fails to comply with DSB recommendations or rulings

[8] In this respect, Canada made a creative request for authorization of appropriate countermeasures under Article 4.10 of the SCM Agreement and Article 22.2 of the DSU when Brazil was found to have failed to comply with DSB recommendations and rulings concerning Article 3 of the SCM Agreement on prohibited export subsidies in the Article 21.5 proceedings in *Brazil–Aircraft*. Canada requested suspension of the requirement to determine that subsidization caused (threat of) material injury before imposing countervailing measures; it also requested suspension of its obligations under the Agreement on Textiles and Clothing relative to quantitative restrictions on textile and clothing imports from Brazil and suspension of its obligations under the Agreement on Import Licensing Procedures relative to licensing for imports from Brazil. Finally, Canada requested authorization to remove Brazil from the list of developing countries eligible for preferential treatment under the Enabling Clause (see WTO document, WT/DS46/16).

Brazil, in its request for arbitration under Article 22.6 of the DSU and Article 4.11 of the SCM Agreement 'maintain[ed] that the principles and procedures set out in Articles 22.3 ha[d] not been followed' (see WTO document, WT/DS46/18).

In their award, the arbitrators acting pursuant to Article 22.6 of the DSU and Article 4.11 of the SCM Agreement found that it was within their jurisdiction to review the scope of their mandate also in relation to Article 22.3 of the DSU (Decision by the arbitrators, *Brazil–Aircraft* (Article 22.6 – Brazil) (DSR 2002:I, 19), paras. 3.14–17). They also stated that Brazil had acknowledged at the arbitration hearing that Canada's request fell under Article 22.3(a), that is, under the same sector as that in which nullification and impairment had occurred (para. 3.13).

concerning the Antidumping Agreement (or vice versa), the arbitrator is entitled to pronounce only on the level of the suspension sought, not on the nature of that suspension of concessions or other obligations provided it remains within the framework of the twelve agreements and six understandings listed in Annex 1A. However, in *EC–Bananas III (Ecuador/US)*, *Brazil–Aircraft* and *US–Gambling*, the arbitrators noted that they had the authority to review not only requests under Article 22.3(b) and (c), but also whether requests under Article 22.3(a) should have been made in full or in part under Article 22.3(b) or (c), that is, as requests for cross-retaliation.[9]

Arbitrators acting pursuant to Article 22 also concluded that the *burden of proof* for this question falls on the implementing member, although the member proposing the sanctions must come forward with reasons and explanations for its proposed sanctions.[10] This allocation of the evidentiary burden is unobjectionable, but it also highlights the dilemma faced by arbitrators in obtaining essential information. It makes sense to ask the member seeking authorization for suspension to explain the methodology underlying its request in a so-called reference paper. At the same time, the suspending member may consider that providing too much detail might enable the non-complying member to rebut its request more effectively; in these circumstances, the member seeking suspension may well decide to rely on the fact that the ultimate burden of proof lies with the member that has been found not to be in compliance with its WTO obligations in both the original and the Article 21.5 proceedings.

[9] Decisions by the arbitrators, *EC–Bananas III (Ecuador)* (Article 22.6 – EC), paras. 45 and 46; *Brazil–Aircraft*, paras. 3.14 and 3.15; *US–Gambling*, paras. 4.1–19. The arbitrators stated that they have the authority 'to broadly judge whether the complaining party in question has considered the necessary facts objectively and whether, on the basis of these facts, it could plausibly arrive at the conclusion that it was not practicable or effective to seek suspension within the same sector under the same agreements' (Decision by the arbitrators, *EC–Bananas III (Ecuador)* (Article 22.6 – EC), para. 52). The arbitrators in *EC–Bananas III (US)* (Article 22.6 – EC) concluded that, because Article 22 makes clear that the general rule is that suspension of concessions/obligations should be in the *same* sector and relate to the *same* agreement as the violations, the authority of arbitrators to determine whether the principles and procedures of subparagraphs (b) and (c) have been followed implies that they have the competence to examine whether a request under subparagraph (a) should have been made under subparagraphs (b) or (c); in that case, because violations had been found in both the services and the goods sectors, the US request to suspend concessions on trade in goods fell within the terms of subparagraph (a) (Decision by the arbitrators, *EC–Bananas III (US)* (Article 22.6 – EC) (DSR 1999:II, 725), paras. 3.1–10).

[10] Decision by the arbitrators, *EC–Bananas III (Ecuador)* (Article 22.6 – EC), paras. 59 and 60.

This disincentive to be forthcoming in providing evidence exists in any Article 22.6 arbitration, but it complicates matters further when arbitrators also have to determine whether the rules and procedures of Article 22.3 for cross-retaliation have been followed. It comes as no surprise that arbitrators have faced difficulties in gathering sufficient information on whether suspension in the same sector and under the same agreement was, indeed, 'not practicable or effective' and 'circumstances serious enough' to justify cross-retaliation.

The arbitrators in *EC–Bananas III (Ecuador)* relied on the fact that a great imbalance in terms of trade volume and economic power existed between the complaining member seeking suspension and the non-complying member, and that in situations where the complaining member 'is highly dependent on imports from the other party, it may happen that the suspension of certain concessions or certain other obligations entails more harmful effects for the party seeking suspension than for the other party'.[11] In the view of the arbitrators:

> in these circumstances, a consideration by the complaining party in which sector or under which agreement suspension may be expected to be least harmful to itself would seem sufficient for us to find a consideration by the complaining party of the effectiveness criterion to be consistent with the requirement to follow the principles and procedures set forth in Article 22.3.[12]

The arbitrators in *US–Gambling* were not entirely persuaded by this approach. They considered that:

> general statements relating to the size of the complaining party's economy or the relative size of the economies of both parties do not justify a departure from the requirements of Article 22.3 of the DSU ... an explanation of how such circumstances affect the practicability or effectiveness of the proposed suspension would in our view be required, in order for these considerations to validly support a determination that it is not practicable or effective to suspend concessions or other obligations in other sectors under the same agreement within the meaning of Article 22.3.[13]

Ultimately, however, the approach chosen by the arbitrators in *US–Gambling* is not very different from that of the arbitrators in *EC–Bananas III (Ecuador)*. They found that Antigua had not limited itself

[11] Decision by the arbitrators, *EC–Bananas III (Ecuador)* (Article 22.6 – EC), para. 73 (footnote omitted).

[12] Decision by the arbitrators, *EC–Bananas III (Ecuador)* (Article 22.6 – EC), para. 73.

[13] Decision by the arbitrators, *US–Gambling* (Article 22.6 – US), para. 4.91.

to general assertions as to the size of its economy, in itself or relative to the US economy. Antigua had also provided arguments to explain how the potential adverse impact of suspension of obligations would manifest itself in various specific sectors under the GATS in respect of which suspension might be considered. The arbitrators agreed with Antigua that if it were to suspend concessions with respect to its most important service sectors (travel, transportation and insurance services) – given the low level of these imports – such suspension would have virtually no impact upon the United States. The consequent need to replace these services from other service providers, if reasonably practicable at all, would most likely prove to be more expensive to Antiguan consumers.[14] Thus, suspension of obligations in respect of such services would have the potential to adversely affect Antigua's economy, while not necessarily having any perceptible impact on inducing compliance by the United States. Similarly, the arbitrators in *EC–Bananas III (Ecuador)* reasoned that it was not practicable or effective for Ecuador to retaliate in trade in goods or service sectors other than distribution because Ecuador could be adversely affected by the lack of access to capital goods and disinvestment of European commercial presence in its service sectors.

The arbitrators in *US–Gambling* further noted that, by their very nature, services transactions are closely woven into a country's domestic economic fabric, with many cross-sectoral linkages (for example, in infrastructural services, such as large segments of the transport, telecommunications and financial services sectors). They found that the risk of economic disruption in the case of forced divestiture of US firms established in Antigua in such sectors, or similar measures, was not negligible, in particular for such a small economy. For instance, it was not clear to what extent Antiguan services suppliers would be able or willing to step in for US services suppliers obliged to suspend their operations or even leave

[14] The arbitrators also noted that 'the IMF Balance of Payments statistics do not reflect any volumes of imports by Antigua in relation to "Personal, Cultural and Recreational Services" between 1998 and 2005. This would tend to suggest that no significant volumes of imports of such services takes place.' They also noted that the United States had not, in fact, suggested that any amount of imports takes place with respect to sector 10 from the United States, that could form the basis for suspension of obligations under the GATS. In addition, the arbitrators referred to Antigua's argument that '[t]he trade disparity is so great that United States service providers would suffer little harm at all, if any, while Antiguan consumers would be forced to scramble for replacement services at uncertain cost', and the fact that the United States had not given any specific indication that Antigua's assessment in respect of the practicability or effectiveness of suspension of other obligations under sector 10 was incorrect (Decision by the arbitrators, *US–Gambling* (Article 22.6 – US), para. 4.49).

the country. Finally, the arbitrators considered that 'legislative and other measures protecting foreign investors may make it difficult in practice to take and enforce action against them'.[15]

Overall, arbitrators and economists have found the criteria mentioned in Article 22.3, such as 'effectiveness', 'practicability' and 'seriousness of circumstances', difficult to apply in practice. Many developing country members view the strings attached by Article 22.3 to cross-retaliation as too cumbersome. They consider that 'impracticability' and 'ineffectiveness' of retaliation in the same sector or under the same agreement should be presumed when developing countries are successful in a complaint against a developed country. Similarly, they do not believe that requests for cross-retaliation should depend on the 'importance' of trade impaired by the inconsistent measure or the 'broader economic elements' or 'broader economic consequences' of nullification and suspension. Accordingly, in the negotiations on DSU review in July 2006, Cuba, India and Malaysia proposed the insertion of a new Article 22.3*bis* stating that:

> Notwithstanding the provisions contained in paragraph 3, in a dispute between a developing country Member and a developed country Member, the developing country Member shall have the right to seek authorization to suspend concessions or other obligations in any sectors under any covered agreements.

In other words, a developing country member would be free to seek DSB authorization to retaliate against a developed country member that had failed to comply with DSB recommendations or rulings in any trade sector and under any covered agreement. It would no longer have to state reasons why retaliation in the same sector or under the same agreement is not practicable or effective and why the circumstances are serious enough to warrant a DSB authorization of cross-retaliation. Whether that approach is to be preferred depends on what Sykes refers to as the purpose for imposing trade sanctions.[16] If the philosophy underlying countermeasures is to rebalance rights and obligations distorted by the breach of WTO law in a way that ensures that the price of such a breach is not too high and not too low, the *status quo* of cross-retaliation is to be preferred. If the objective is to induce compliance by using the most effective form of retaliation or to punish the perpetrator for its non-compliance, then the

[15] Decision by the arbitrators, *US–Gambling* (Article 22.6 – US), para. 4.98.

[16] Alan O. Sykes, 'Optimal Sanctions in the WTO: The Case of Decoupling (and the Uneasy Case for the *Status Quo*)', Chapter 16, section 1, above.

new Article 22.3*bis* proposed in the DSU review negotiations is the more promising alternative.

2 Cross-retaliation and suspension under the TRIPS Agreement

Suspension of obligations under the TRIPS Agreement poses problems and complexities that are different from those arising when sanctions are imposed on trade in goods. At the same time, suspension of TRIPS obligations may also be more practicable and effective in inducing compliance by a developed country, especially if implemented by a developing country. The arbitrators in *EC–Bananas III (Ecuador)* made some general remarks on suspension of TRIPS obligations. They first addressed the scope of such suspension. The authorization by the DSB would permit Ecuador to suspend the treatment provided for in the TRIPS Agreement with respect to *nationals* of the thirteen EC member states to which Ecuador's request for suspension referred.[17] Recalling that Ecuador's request for the suspension of TRIPS obligations referred to Article 14 of section 1 of the TRIPS Agreement on 'Copyright and related rights,' as well as section 3 on 'Geographical indications' and section 4 on 'Industrial designs', the arbitrators observed that in respect of the protection of performers, producers of phonograms (sound recordings) and broadcasting organizations, there could be different right holders of the different rights related to phonograms and these right holders might not necessarily all have the nationality, within the meaning of Article 1.3 of the TRIPS Agreement, of one of those thirteen member states in question, even if the phonogram concerned has been produced in one of those member states. For example, 'the performer having rights to a phonogram under Article 14 may be a non-national of these 13 member States, but the producer of the phonogram may be a national of those member States'. The arbitrators said that such 'complicated situations' would have to be 'carefully considered by Ecuador in implementing the suspension of TRIPS obligations, if authorized by the DSB, so as not to adversely affect right holders who cannot be regarded as nationals of those 13 EC member States'.[18] Similar problems could arise in respect of the criteria for eligibility for the protection

[17] Ecuador's request for suspension excluded Denmark and the Netherlands, that is, those member states of the EC that had voted against the common market organization on bananas in the European Council.

[18] Decision by the arbitrators, *EC–Bananas III (Ecuador)* (Article 22.6 – EC), para. 144.

of industrial designs as defined in the Paris Convention[19] if not all right holders of (parts of) the industrial designs are attributable to the member states targeted by the trade sanctions. In addition, goods manufactured using the protected industrial design need not be attributable to the targeted member states under the applicable rules of origin of goods.

The arbitrators in *EC–Bananas III (Ecuador)* considered how to minimize undesired effects on other WTO members of the suspension of TRIPS Agreement obligations by Ecuador vis-à-vis the EC. In their view, distortions on markets of other WTO members could be avoided if Ecuador suspended the intellectual property rights in question only for the purposes of supply destined for its *domestic market*.[20] For example, with respect to phonograms produced in Ecuador without the consent of the right holder, but consistent with a DSB-authorized suspension of copyright protection, the prohibition in Article 51 of the TRIPS Agreement of trade in counterfeit and pirated goods would continue apply.[21] This caveat limits the reach and effect of cross-retaliation and raises difficult enforcement problems. How can the suspending member ensure that goods incorporating suspended TRIPS rights are sold on the domestic market and not exported? Ecuador proposed in this respect a licensing and registration system so as to trace goods incorporating suspended TRIPS rights and ensure that such production does not exceed the authorized level of suspension.

The problem of distinguishing between 'overlapping' intellectual property rights held by right holders from different countries (and rules of origin of goods incorporating protected intellectual property rights) is less virulent in the case of geographical indications. The protection of geographical indications applies to 'interested parties' within the meaning of Articles 22.2 and 23.1 of the TRIPS Agreement. Given that the Agreement requires a clear link between a region, locality or territory and a protectable geographical indication, the suspension of protection of geographical indications would concern parties with an interest in geographical indications which identify a good as originating in the territory of one of the EC member states, or a region or locality in that territory.[22] The goods protected by geographic indications will have the origin of the WTO member in which the region, locality or territory is located, and the producers in that region that qualify as 'interested parties' are likely to have the nationality of the same WTO member.

[19] Decision by the arbitrators, *EC–Bananas III (Ecuador)* (Article 22.6 – EC), para. 145.
[20] Decision by the arbitrators, *EC–Bananas III (Ecuador)* (Article 22.6 – EC), para. 156.
[21] Decision by the arbitrators, *EC–Bananas III (Ecuador)* (Article 22.6 – EC), para. 155.
[22] Decision by the arbitrators, *EC–Bananas III (Ecuador)* (Article 22.6 – EC), para. 146.

At the same time, the potential multiplicity of right holders, 'overlapping' intellectual property rights, and their incorporation in patented, copyrighted, trademark-protected goods and services, may improve the position of the member authorized to suspend TRIPS obligations in forcing compliance by the recalcitrant member. Had Ecuador merely requested authorization to suspend concessions under the GATT 1994 vis-à-vis the EC, Ecuador would have obstructed its access to European capital goods that could be crucial for its development. Had Antigua merely requested suspension of its GATS commitments vis-à-vis the United States, Antigua would have impeded, for example, foreign direct investment through the commercial presence of US suppliers of tourism or other services. These effects would have been more detrimental for Ecuador and Antigua than for the EC and the United States, respectively.

As the arbitrators in *EC–Bananas III (Ecuador)* noted, 'the interference with private property rights of individuals or companies may be perceived as more far-reaching under the TRIPS Agreement [than under the GATT 1994 or the GATS], given the potentially unlimited possibility to copy phonograms or use other intellectual property rights'. By contrast, producers of goods and service suppliers that are affected by the suspension of concessions or other obligations under the GATT 1994 or the GATS may cease exporting to the member imposing such suspension.[23] In other words, retaliation under the GATT 1994 or the GATS simply impedes or interrupts trade flows in goods or services. By contrast, Ecuador and Antigua improved their bargaining position vis-à-vis the EC and the United States by requesting and obtaining authorization to suspend TRIPS obligations, because such suspension has an effect different to the suspension of GATT 1994 and GATS rights. In the area of intellectual property rights, patent holders, copyright collecting societies, owners of trademarks and industrial designs and associations of interested parties in geographical indications may be numerous and organized in powerful interest groups capable of lobbying governments effectively to comply with their WTO obligations so as to avert further damage to the intellectual property rights they hold. Such interest groups are motivated to lobby their governments because the sale of low-quality goods may damage the reputation of geographical indications, trademarks or trade names for the longer term, even after the suspension of TRIPS obligations is terminated. Likewise, the value of copyrights or patents is compromised in the long run if the market has been saturated by goods incorporating the patent

[23] Decision by the arbitrators, *EC–Bananas III (Ecuador)* (Article 22.6 – EC), para. 157.

or copyright during the suspension of its protection. The obstruction of trade in goods by imposing prohibitive tariffs does not have similar long-term effects once terminated (except where product substitution effects occur in a given market). Therefore, retaliation under the TRIPS Agreement may have a 'snowball effect' in mobilizing private intellectual property right holders against non-complying governments, and, in turn, may empower developing country members against more powerful WTO members. As Sykes puts it, cross-retaliation under the TRIPS Agreement may enable developing country members to more precisely 'calibrate sanctions' and target them at interest groups of foreign exporters who are likely to lobby their governments to cure breaches of WTO laws in order to end trade sanctions.[24]

Another complication resulting from the suspension of TRIPS obligations is the relationship between the TRIPS Agreement and certain international conventions on the protection of intellectual property rights administered by the WIPO. Article 2.2 of the TRIPS Agreement states that nothing in Parts I to IV of the Agreement 'shall derogate' from obligations under the Paris Convention, the Berne Convention, the Rome Convention and the Treaty on Intellectual Property in Respect of Integrated Circuits. Article 2.2 mentions only Parts I to IV of the TRIPS Agreement, while the relevant dispute settlement provisions are found in Part V. The dispute settlement provisions in Part V of the TRIPS Agreement do not exclude the application of Article 22 of the DSU, including the suspension of TRIPS obligations.[25] In these circumstances, the arbitrators in *EC–Bananas III (Ecuador)* stated that it was not within their jurisdiction under Articles 22.3 to 22.6 of the DSU to pass judgment on whether Ecuador, by suspending certain TRIPS obligations, following authorization by the DSB, would be acting inconsistently with its international obligations under treaties other than the WTO covered agreements (for example, the Paris, Berne and Rome conventions which Ecuador has ratified). As a result, it was left to Ecuador or other parties to international treaties on the protection of intellectual property rights to assess whether the particular manner in which Ecuador chose to implement the suspension of certain TRIPS obligations gave rise to difficulties in legal or practical terms under such treaties.[26] These considerations highlight the potential for legal conflict between DSB-authorized suspension of TRIPS obligations and other

[24] Alan O. Sykes, Chapter 16, section 2, above.

[25] Decision by the arbitrators, *EC–Bananas III (Ecuador)* (Article 22.6 – EC), para. 150.

[26] Decision by the arbitrators, *EC–Bananas III (Ecuador)* (Article 22.6 – EC), para. 152.

international regimes for the protection of intellectual property rights. Cross-retaliation under the TRIPS Agreement cannot induce compliance effectively unless structures are developed to avoid a situation where a WTO member exercising its DSB-authorized right to suspend TRIPS obligations faces conflict with its obligations other international or national regimes.

In addition, DSB-authorized suspension of TRIPS obligations may undermine the protection of rights acquired by private individuals. Intellectual property is a form of *property* which is widely protected in municipal law or non-WTO international law. This may implicate guarantees of fundamental rights and property rights protection under international and national law. In that vein, in relation to Brazil's request for cross-retaliation in *US–Upland Cotton*, a bill has been submitted to the Brazilian parliament to permit derogation from domestic intellectual property rights protection standards and guarantees (see Salles, Chapter 13, above).[27]

Ensuring that the level of suspension of TRIPS obligations is equivalent to the nullification and impairment resulting from non-compliance with DSB recommendations and rulings requires quantification of intellectual property rights. This is, indeed, a challenging task (as developed by Abbott, Chapter 22, below). What is a patent worth? What is the value of a copyright? In *US–Copyright Act*, the arbitrators acting pursuant to Article 25 of the DSU assessed compensation for nullification and impairment resulting from the breach of copyright protection in terms of royalty income forgone by EC right holders after the introduction by the United States of its TRIPS-inconsistent measure.[28] This may provide an estimate for compensation of actual losses incurred; however, the criterion of revenue forgone does not provide a precise benchmark for the potential value of intellectual property rights.

In *EC–Bananas III (Ecuador)*, the arbitrators noted 'with approval' that, with regard to implementing the suspension of certain TRIPS obligations

[27] Projeto de Lei nº 1893, submitted on 28 August 2007, which regulates temporary measures suspending intellectual property rights in case of non-compliance with WTO obligations. Available at: www2.camara.gov.br/internet/proposicoes/chamadaExterna.html?link= www.camara.gov.br/internet/sileg/Prop_Detalhe.asp?id=364818 (12 December 2008).

[28] Award of the arbitrators, *US–Section 110(5) Copyright Act* (Article 25), WT/DS160/ARB25/1, 9 November 2001, DSR 2001:II, 667, para. 3.19. That arbitration was conducted pursuant to Article 25 of the DSU, not Article 22. However, in that arbitration the question arose as to how to quantify the nullification or damage caused by the breach of copyrights.

of an amount not exceeding the level authorized by the DSB, Ecuador submitted that it did not intend to simply abolish all rules on 'related rights' and put all EC-produced phonograms in the public domain. Rather, it would establish a licensing system whereby companies or individuals in Ecuador could obtain authorization from the Ecuadorian government to apply the suspension of obligations derived from Article 14 of the TRIPS Agreement within the Ecuadorian territory. This authorization would be granted through a licensing system that would limit the suspension of obligations in terms of quantity, value and time. The Ecuadorian government would reserve its right to revoke these licences at any time. The suspension of obligations related to geographical indications and industrial designs could be licensed in similar terms as explained for phonograms above.[29] By contrast, in *US–Gambling*, Antigua refused to disclose to the arbitrators how it would go about putting the suspension of TRIPS obligations into effect once authorized.[30] The arbitrators found that this information was not indispensable to reach a conclusion on whether cross-retaliation was justified, but noted that it was 'incumbent upon Antigua' to ensure that, in applying such suspension, it would not exceed the authorized level of US$21 million.[31] The arbitrators noted, however, that:

> the suspension of obligations under the TRIPS Agreement may involve more complex means of implementation than, for example, the imposition of higher import duties on goods, and that the exact assessment of the value of the rights affected by the suspension is also likely to be more complex.[32]

Commentators have tried to tackle the question of quantification of intellectual property rights. For example, Keith Maskus highlights the difficulty of quantifying the effects of losses in intellectual property rights, since 'unlike tariffs and taxes, IPRs are not readily measurable'.[33] Maskus proposes output and input analysis as possible methods for the quantification of intellectual property rights, but expresses a preference

[29] Decision by the arbitrators, *EC–Bananas III (Ecuador)* (Article 22.6 – EC), paras. 159–62.

[30] Decision by the arbitrators, *US–Gambling* (Article 22.6 – US), paras. 5.1–5.

[31] Decision by the arbitrators, *US–Gambling* (Article 22.6 – US), paras. 5.7–9.

[32] This is illustrated well by the explanations provided by Ecuador in the *EC–Bananas III (Ecuador)* (Article 22.6 – EC) case as to how it proposed to implement the proposed suspension of TRIPS obligations, including through the setting up of specific government-run schemes (Decision by the arbitrators, *US–Gambling* (Article 22.6 – US), para. 5.10).

[33] Keith E. Maskus, *Intellectual Property Rights in the Global Economy* (Washington, DC: Institute for International Economics, 2000), 88ff.

for the latter. The *output* analysis method measures trade flows in goods and services incorporating intellectual property rights.[34] By contrast, the *input* analysis method focuses on measuring inputs, labour, overheads and transport costs in respect of products whose production involves intellectual property rights.[35] Total input prices are deducted from the sales price: the difference equals the value of the intellectual property right concerned. The method could work with compact disks, patented products, products incorporating industrial designs and products bearing trademarks or geographical indications. These two methods may provide a basis for measuring actual trade flows in goods or services incorporating intellectual property rights; but they do not offer precise benchmarks for assessing the potential value of intellectual property rights protection, the extent of their exploitation and enforcement and changing market conditions and demand for those intellectual property rights in the future.

One would also have to factor into the calculation of the value of intellectual property rights divergences in levels of intellectual property right protection and enforcement between various countries, especially between developed and developing countries. It should not be forgotten that the TRIPS Agreement sets international minimum standards for protection and enforcement, which should serve as a benchmark for quantifying intellectual property rights. The benchmark for quantifying intellectual property rights protection in the TRIPS Agreement should not be the more intensive intellectual property rights protection and enforcement found in domestic legal systems reflecting a higher standard. Differences in the level of intellectual property rights protection in various jurisdictions may have an impact on the price of patented products or products incorporating or produced with intellectual property rights. Problems also arise in terms of access to information on registered intellectual property rights, as registration affects the value of those rights and the goods and services incorporating them.

Quantification of intellectual property rights is, first and foremost, a problem when failure to comply with DSB recommendations or rulings concerns the TRIPS Agreement, regardless of whether authorization for suspension is sought under the same Agreement or in the form of cross-retaliation under the GATT 1994 or the GATS. In that case, it would be for the member seeking DSB authorization of suspension to explain its approach to quantification of nullified or impaired intellectual property

[34] Keith E. Maskus, *Intellectual Property Rights in the Global Economy*, 100.
[35] Keith E. Maskus, *Intellectual Property Rights in the Global Economy*, 88.

rights in a so-called reference paper to be submitted to the arbitrators, which may be commented on or rebutted by the member that has failed to comply with its TRIPS obligations in a timely manner. In cases where cross-retaliation under the TRIPS Agreement is sought to counter non-compliance with DSB recommendations and rulings concerning the GATT 1994 or the GATS, it is for the suspending member to ensure that the suspension of its TRIPS obligation does not exceed the level of nullification and impairment found under the GATT 1994 or the GATS.

As noted earlier, in *EC–Bananas III*, Ecuador explained how it intended to implement the suspension of certain TRIPS obligations vis-à-vis the EC, while Antigua declined to provide such information in *US–Gambling*. The arbitrators in the latter case did not believe that the lack of such information prevented them from reaching an affirmative conclusion with respect to Antigua's request. They simply noted that 'the United States may have recourse to the appropriate dispute settlement procedures in the event that it considers that the level of concessions or other obligations suspended by Antigua exceeds the level of nullification or impairment we have determined for purposes of the award'.[36] However, it would then be incumbent upon the United States as the non-complying member to show that the level of suspension actually imposed by Antigua was in excess of the level authorized by the DSB. One may wonder if a key reason for the attractiveness of suspension of TRIPS obligations is the apparent opportunity to escape or alleviate the 'equivalence' ceiling on the amount of sanctions imposed by Article 22.4 of the DSU.[37] Given the difficulties in quantifying the value of intellectual property rights and their protection, it may also be more difficult for the non-complying member to establish that it is subject to suspension of TRIPS obligations in excess of the level authorized.

3 Cross-retaliation and suspension under the GATS

Suspension of commitments and other obligations under the GATS also faces a number of difficulties (further developed by Appleton, Chapter 23, below). The arbitrators in *EC–Bananas III (Ecuador)* gave some guidance on this point when examining whether suspension of commitments under the GATS in a sector *other than distribution services* is 'not practicable or effective' within the meaning of Article 22.3(b) of the DSU. Accordingly,

[36] Decision by the arbitrators, *US–Gambling* (Article 22.6 – US), para. 5.12.

[37] Alan Sykes, Chapter 16, section 1, above.

the proper analysis of this question would involve the following steps: in which sector or subsector does the member seeking authorization to suspend have binding commitments? In which modes of supply? Do these commitments cover alternative modes of supply and/or multiple modes of supply? Are there horizontal commitments that apply across the board to entire service sectors that could be suspended?

First, suspension of commitments is possible only with respect to those service sectors and those modes of supply bound in the retaliating member's schedule of specific commitments.[38] Generally applicable requirements and commitments are rare under GATS, they concern essentially Articles II and III of the GATS (most-favoured-nation treatment, however, with exemptions as well as transparency). The arbitrators in *EC–Bananas III (Ecuador)* observed that, in most of the service sectors covered by its commitments, Ecuador had not bound all four modes of service and that many of Ecuador's specific commitments excluded the cross-border mode of supply. In other words, suspension of commitments with respect to that mode of supply would not have been possible in the first place. Many developing country members have similar commitment patterns in their GATS schedules. Moreover, even if cross-border supply of certain services were covered by a specific commitment that could be suspended, it may be technically feasible to provide such services through alternative channels of supply, that is, either through consumption abroad or commercial presence. If such alternative supply channels exist, it would be ineffective to suspend GATS commitments with respect to cross-border supply only.[39] In addition, there may be technical difficulties (such as telecommunication flows) with blocking service trade across borders in certain sectors.

Second, as regards the suspension of commitments in relation to commercial presence (the third mode of service supply), suspension of such commitments would distort the investment climate in the suspending member for actual and potential investors from the non-complying member in a way that could harm the suspending member more than the non-complying member. In this regard, the arbitrators in *EC–Bananas III (Ecuador)* observed that 'the effects of the suspension of commitments concerning commercial presence could be particularly detrimental to a developing country member such as Ecuador because it is highly dependent on foreign direct investment'.[40] For example, suspension

[38] Decision by the arbitrators, *EC–Bananas III (Ecuador)* (Article 22.6 – EC), para. 106.
[39] Decision by the arbitrators, *EC–Bananas III (Ecuador)* (Article 22.6 – EC), para. 117.
[40] Decision by the arbitrators, *EC–Bananas III (Ecuador)* (Article 22.6 – EC), para. 110.

could induce European service suppliers who have actually invested in Ecuador to transfer their commercial presence to other countries. Similarly, European service suppliers who are potential investors in Ecuador (in the pre-establishment phase) could turn to other host countries with a view to avoiding the impact of suspension of GATS commitments on commercial presence. The withdrawal of commitments would not necessarily require the immediate closure of a commercial presence owned or controlled by European nationals within the meaning of Article XXVIII(m–n) of the GATS, but it may mean that EC service suppliers lose the legal protection, and legal certainty and predictability, reflected in GATS disciplines.[41]

Practical difficulties with implementing suspension of commitments on commercial presence may arise from the legal protection enjoyed by natural or juridical persons under domestic or international law (for example, equal treatment obligations embodied in municipal law or international investment treaties) when the suspending member seeks to close or limit the output of a commercially present service supplier of a particular foreign origin.[42] Therefore, implementing DSB-authorized suspension of GATS rights and obligations will be less problematic in the pre-establishment phase than in the post-establishment phase of commercially present legal or natural persons supplying services. Non-WTO international or domestic law may require respecting the rights of locally established service suppliers of foreign origin, even if the DSB has exonerated the suspending member of its obligations under the GATS. The suspending member will be well advised to take into account differences between origin-related GATS obligations and rules of origin and rules on the attribution of private actors to states under domestic law or other international law. Similar considerations may apply *mutatis mutandis* to suspension of GATS obligations with respect to the movement of natural persons, that is, the fourth mode of service supply.

Moreover, multiple alternative channels of supply under different modes of supply could be used to circumvent suspension of GATS commitments in relation to particular modes of service supply. Such problems have not yet surfaced in arbitrations under Article 22 of the DSU. However, complexities discussed in the context of negotiations on emergency safeguard

[41] Decision by the arbitrators, *EC–Bananas III (Ecuador)* (Article 22.6 – EC), para. 111.
[42] Decision by the arbitrators, *EC–Bananas III (Ecuador)* (Article 22.6 – EC), paras. 113 and 114.

measures (ESM) under the GATS are instructive in this respect.[43] In particular, it has been argued that mode-specific safeguard action could create economic distortions, and that such action might not be effective since it could be circumvented by foreign suppliers switching to unrestricted modes of service supply. For example, a safeguard applied under supply mode three (commercial presence) may lead to alternative service delivery through the other modes of supply (such as cross-border supply, consumption abroad or movement of natural persons). Others have argued that the possibility for circumvention would be remote because switching between modes of supply would imply significant costs ('sunk costs' for establishing a commercial presence or transport channels in the case of cross-border movement etc.). In other words, 'it might be counterproductive to target all modes; for instance, if the purpose of safeguard action was to prevent unemployment, it would be unreasonable to restrict new investment or take action against locally established foreign firms'.[44] In addition – as is the case with the suspension of commitments under the GATS generally – it may be more difficult to enforce a safeguard mechanism in certain modes or sectors than in others. Under supply mode two (consumption abroad), a tax, a quantitative limitation or a regulation of some kind affecting consumption abroad could operate as a safeguard measure. In this scenario, it would be the consumer who 'would be taxed or restricted in some way, or a regulation might seek to ration or restrict consumption abroad of the service concerned'. Under supply mode three (commercial presence), it would seem possible to impose additional taxes or restrict service output. Under supply mode four (movement of natural persons), the physical movement of a natural person might be subject to a surtax or restricted in other ways.

Therefore, it has been proposed that safeguard actions under certain modes of supply should be given priority over others; for example, safeguard measures under modes three and four (commercial presence and movement

[43] See, for example, Working Party on GATS Rules, Emergency Safeguard Measures in the GATS: The Applicability of Concepts Applied in the WTO Agreement on Safeguards, Note by the Secretariat, WTO document S/WPGR/W/8, 6 March 1996; Working Party on GATS Rules, Issues for Future Discussions on Emergency Safeguards, Note by WTO Secretariat, WTO document, S/WPGR/W/27/Rev.2, 16 September 1999; and Working Party on GATS Rules, Communication for Brunei Darussalam, Cambodia, Indonesia, Malaysia, Myanmar, the Philippines, Thailand and Vietnam, Draft Annex on Article X Emergency Safeguard Measures, WTO document JOB(07)/155, 19 October 2007.

[44] See Note by WTO Secretariat, Issues for Future Discussions on Emergency Safeguards, S/WPGR/W/27/Rev.2 (1999).

of natural persons) could be taken only after safeguard measures under modes one and two (cross-border supply and consumption abroad) have proven ineffective.[45] These considerations may provide a basis for reflection by members authorized to suspend GATS commitments in developing strategies on how best to implement such suspension. In addition, it is difficult to predict and measure the value of potential future service supply through commercial presence or movement of natural persons before natural or legal persons are established and – to a lesser extent – after they have established themselves in the member suspending GATS commitments.

As with the quantification of the value of intellectual property rights protection, no precise estimate of potential service supply forgone due to suspension of GATS commitments is possible. Matters are further complicated by the potential for circumvention of such suspension through alternative channels of service supply. These difficulties in quantifying the impact of suspension of GATS commitments and TRIPS obligations on service supply and intellectual property rights provide support for Sykes' point that retaliation under the DSU should not be replaced with direct monetary compensation to exporters injured by non-compliance with DSB recommendations and rulings because similar problems with quantification would arise with respect to compensation.[46]

As a practical matter, it may be the case that the services market of developing countries is so small that suspension of GATS commitments has no real effect in bringing about compliance. For such countries, suspension of TRIPS commitments may serve as a more effective tool for bringing about compliance for the reasons explained above. Sykes suggests in Chapter 16, above, that 'the addition of TRIPS to the WTO system may empower weaker nations considerably with a prospect of cross-retaliation'.[47] Right holders and producers affected by cross-retaliation under the TRIPS Agreement would be likely to lobby non-complying governments to do what is necessary to avoid such suspension or, if already in place, to have suspension lifted as early as possible. In a way, suspension of TRIPS obligations may alleviate asymmetries in market size, economic power and technological capacity between suspending developing country members and non-complying developed country members.[48]

[45] Note by WTO Secretariat, Issues for Future Discussions on Emergency Safeguards, S/WPGR/W/27/Rev.2 (1999), para. 14.

[46] Alan Sykes, Chapter 16, section 3, above. [47] Alan Sykes, Chapter 16, section 1, above.

[48] For a discussion of the pros and cons of TRIPS suspension, see Henning Grosse Ruse-Khan, 'A Pirate in the Caribbean? The Attractions of Suspending TRIPS Obligations', *Journal of International Economic Law*, 11: 2 (2008), 313–64.

Finally, there may be effective alternatives to suspension of GATS commitments and TRIPS obligations. Would collective countermeasures imposed by the WTO membership more effectively induce compliance than cross-retaliation? Should the winning party obtain the right to request the losing party to lower or remove trade barriers as chosen by the winning party at its discretion? Should compensation in monetary form be introduced in order to make enforcement work for developing country members? Would developed members simply 'pay off' breaches of WTO law and perpetuate non-compliance?

22

Cross-retaliation in TRIPS: issues of law and practice

FREDERICK M. ABBOTT*

1 Introduction

This contribution addresses a WTO dispute settlement remedy commonly known as "cross-retaliation," and specifically the mechanism by which a WTO member suspends concessions in the field of trade-related intellectual property rights (TRIPS) to redress an injury suffered with respect to trade in goods or services.

A WTO member enforces compliance with a ruling by the Dispute Settlement Body (DSB) by suspending trade concessions enjoyed by the non-compliant member. This might involve raising tariffs on products imported from the non-compliant member. Economically powerful WTO members are not likely to be harmed by suspension of trade concessions in goods or services by substantially less powerful members. The trade impact will be too small to "induce compliance" and, equally important, the types of suspension that may be used in the fields of goods and services may cause economic harm to the less powerful members using them. The WTO dispute settlement process strongly favors economically powerful countries, leaving most developing and least developed members with few options for inducing compliance.

Attention is increasingly focusing on the possibility of developing members suspending concessions relating to intellectual property rights (IPRs) as a means to induce compliance by developed members. Cross-retaliation is expressly contemplated by the WTO Dispute Settlement Understanding (DSU). WTO arbitrators have so far approved TRIPS

* Edward Ball Eminent Scholar Professor of International Law, Florida State University College of Law. This chapter is excerpted from a paper prepared for the International Centre on Trade and Sustainable Development. The author gratefully acknowledges comments and suggestions on drafts of this chapter from William Davey, Carsten Fink, Ahmed Abdel Latif, Sisule Musungu, Pedro Roffe, and David Vivas-Eugui.

cross-retaliation on two occasions; in favor of Ecuador (against the EC) and Antigua (against the United States).

Constructing and implementing a cross-retaliation program involving IPRs raises a substantial number of complex legal questions. The DSU establishes principles and procedures that must be respected. The various forms of IPR – copyright, patent, trademark, etc. – serve different social and industrial policy functions and have their own unique characteristics. There are multilateral and bilateral agreements and rules outside the WTO context that may influence the shaping of a cross-retaliation program. National constitutions and rules relating to property rights need to be addressed.

This chapter anticipates many legal questions raised by cross-retaliation in TRIPS and seeks to provide answers. It analyzes the cross-cutting issues raised by external commitments and national IPRs-related rules, and looks at each major form of IPR to suggest practical approaches to suspending (or not suspending) those forms.

It is sometimes suggested that difficulty in valuing IPRs presents a significant obstacle to TRIPS cross-retaliation. It is true that predicting how general changes to IPRs legislation will affect a national economy is very difficult. But, establishing the value of TRIPS cross-retaliation is a different exercise involving valuation of "IP assets" (and the economic effect of withdrawing IP protection). In fact, businesses and investment analysts value IP assets routinely and in fairly precise ways. Valuing the suspension of concessions in IP is not an obstacle to building a successful cross-retaliation program.

The WIPO conventions referenced in the TRIPS Agreement will not provide an independent basis for IPRs holders to challenge cross-retaliation in the International Court of Justice (ICJ) (or elsewhere). Nor will the more recent WIPO Copyright Treaty (WCT) or WIPO Performances and Phonograms Treaty (WPPT) provide such an independent basis. Bilateral and regional trade agreements that include TRIPS-plus commitments in their IP and investment chapters may pose challenges, but these can be overcome by tailoring suspension regimes to be coextensive with TRIPS commitments.

National constitutions and legislation may discourage uncompensated 'takings' of property, including intellectual property. However, cross-retaliation programs can be designed to avoid potential characterization as takings of property. Suspension programs may be limited in time, may affect only a portion of the "basket of rights" characterizing IPRs, and may allow continued use of the subject matter by IPRs holders.

There are likely to be contexts in which existing national legislation can be used to implement a suspension regime. For example, with respect to patents, existing compulsory licensing and government use legislation can be used to suspend concessions. A determination of adequate remuneration will reflect the circumstances of the case, namely, that of inducing compliance with the decision of the WTO DSB. There may be no royalty, or a limited one.

The digital format of many copyrighted works provides both opportunities and challenges for the suspension of concessions. By using a metered download distribution system a WTO member can control the extent of distribution and adjust the level of suspension. By the same token, it will be important to consider digital rights management and technical means of protection to prevent unauthorized redistribution.

A suspension regime need not affect all of the rights in the basket of the IPRs holder. A copyright suspension regime might authorize the reproduction and sale of DVDs, but leave the copyright holder with television broadcast rights.

One of the difficult challenges less powerful WTO members face in seeking to implement cross-retaliation in TRIPS is political pressure from industry groups and governments of more powerful members. While exporters of goods have not persuaded international media outlets that suspension of tariff concessions is "piracy of trade rights," IP-dependent industry groups use sophisticated and expensive propaganda campaigns that result in media portrayal of IPRs suspension as "piracy" and "theft." WTO members must be prepared to deal with industry-induced media pressure. Of course, it will be wise to prepare press releases, but there may be no better answer than a "tough skin." WTO members contemplating cross-retaliation in TRIPS should not be under the illusion that this will be easy.

2 WTO jurisprudence

There are a substantial number of complex technical legal issues – such as how various WTO dispute settlement procedures are sequenced – that arise in the interpretation and application of Article 22 of the TRIPS Agreement that governs the suspension of concessions, including cross-retaliation. To briefly summarize, when the complained-against member in a WTO dispute has failed to properly implement a recommendation to conform its measures, the complaining member will be authorized by the DSB to suspend concessions equivalent to the level of nullification or impairment. As a matter of principle, the complaining member should seek to suspend concessions in the same sector as the area of non-compliance. However, should the complaining member determine that suspension in the same sector, or alternatively under the same covered agreement, will not be practicable or effective and the matter is serious enough, that complaining member may suspend concessions under another covered agreement. The complained-against member may demand arbitration regarding whether the complaining member has followed the prescribed principles and procedures for making its determination, including whether the level of concessions it intends to suspend are equivalent to the level of the nullification or impairment. Once the arbitrators render their determination, and assuming that some level of suspension is authorized, the complaining member may then secure formal authorization for the suspension from the DSB. This DSB authorization is essentially "automatic" if requested by the complaining member.

In sum, the main issues likely to be examined by arbitrators in the context of cross-retaliation are whether the complaining member has adequately followed the prescribed principles and procedures of Article 22, whether the difficulties facing the complaining member warrant cross-retaliation, and what level of suspension is appropriate. The arbitrators are not authorized to examine the "nature" of the obligations to be suspended by the complaining member.

Cross-retaliation under the TRIPS Agreement has twice been approved by WTO dispute settlement arbitrators. Ecuador followed up on arbitrator approval by requesting, and the DSB authorized, TRIPS cross-retaliation against the EC. Cross-retaliation under TRIPS has not yet been implemented by any authorized country. There has been an additional cross-retaliation request by Brazil against the United States, but arbitration of that request is presently suspended by agreement of the parties to the dispute.

(a) EC–Bananas III – *Article 22.6, DSU arbitration with Ecuador*

The first proceeding under the DSU in which a WTO member requested DSB authorization to suspend concessions under the TRIPS Agreement, also the first proceeding in which TRIPS suspension was requested as a matter of "cross-retaliation," involved Ecuador's claim against the EC in respect of the latter's banana trading regime.[1] Ecuador requested authorization pursuant to Article 22.2 of the DSU to suspend concessions or other obligations under the TRIPS Agreement, GATT, and GATS, in

[1] *EC–Regime for the Importation, Sale and Distribution of Bananas*, Recourse to Arbitration by the European Communities under Article 22.6 of the DSU, Decision by the arbitrators, WT/DS27/ARB/ECU, March 24, 2000 (DSR 2000:V, 2237).

respect of findings of inconsistencies regarding the EC's banana regime under the GATT and GATS. The EC thereupon requested arbitration pursuant to Article 22.6 of the DSU.

The panel determined that although Ecuador had a certain margin of appreciation in determining whether suspension of concessions in the same sector as that in which the injury occurred would be practicable or effective, its discretion was limited by the requirements of Article 22.3(b)–(d) with respect to the principles and procedures for making its determinations. The arbitrators are authorized to review compliance with the applicable principles and procedures.[2] The arbitrators concluded that:

> In our view, the margin of review by the Arbitrators implies the authority to broadly judge whether the complaining party in question has considered the necessary facts objectively and whether, on the basis of these facts, it could plausibly arrive at the conclusion that it was not practicable or effective to seek suspension within the same sector under the same agreements, or only under another agreement provided that the circumstances were serious enough.[3]

The arbitrators observed that the objective of suspension of concessions is to induce the complained-against party to fulfil its obligations, and that as a practical matter this may be extremely difficult in cases where there is a great imbalance in terms of trade volume and economic power between the country seeking to suspend concessions and the complained-against country.[4] Particularly in respect to "primary goods" and "investment goods" (referring to inputs and capital equipment), it may well be counterproductive to suspend concessions (that is, to increase tariffs) because this will increase costs for local manufacturers.[5] Effects on consumer goods may be less important from the standpoint of establishing the practicability or effectiveness of suspension.[6] Because Ecuador's banana sector formed a major part of its economic activity, and because the EC's failure to implement the decision adopted by the DSB plausibly contributed to a severe disruption of Ecuador's economy, Ecuador clearly demonstrated that circumstances were "serious enough" to seek suspension of concessions under a covered agreement (that is, under the TRIPS Agreement) other than where the violation was found.[7]

[2] *See EC–Bananas III*, for example, para. 57.
[3] *EC–Bananas III*, para. 52.
[4] *EC–Bananas III*, paras. 73, 125–6.
[5] *EC–Bananas III*, for example, paras. 94–6.
[6] *EC–Bananas III*, for example, paras. 100–1.
[7] *EC–Bananas III*, for example, paras. 129, 132 and 137.

The arbitrators said that although Article 22 of the DSU does not expressly direct the arbitrators to make suggestions regarding how to implement their decision, in light of this being the first decision to address suspension under the TRIPS Agreement and Ecuador's expressed interest in hearing the arbitrators' views, there is nothing to prevent the arbitrators from making suggestions regarding implementation of the suspension.[8]

The arbitrators noted that Ecuador should take care that suspension of intellectual property rights affects only nationals of members subject to the suspension. In some circumstances it may be difficult to determine the nationality of right holders.[9]

The arbitrators favorably noted Ecuador's stated intention to implement the suspension by a government-sanctioned licensing system for the reproduction of certain copyrighted works (that is, phonograms), as well as geographic indications and industrial design rights, suggesting this was perhaps a better approach than "simply abolish[ing]" IP rights and placing materials in the public domain. This licensing system would permit Ecuador to monitor the level of suspended concessions and terminate the suspension when appropriate.[10] The panel also noted that economic operators in Ecuador should be cautious about reliance on a transitory suspension regime for investments "which might not prove viable in the longer term."[11]

The arbitrators said that authorization of suspension of TRIPS obligations within Ecuador does not affect intellectual property rights in other WTO members.[12] The panel stated:

> Distortions in third-country markets could be avoided if Ecuador would suspend the intellectual property rights in question only for the purposes of supply destined for the domestic market. An authorization of a suspension requested by Ecuador does of course not entitle other WTO

[8] *EC–Bananas III*, for example, para. 139.

[9] *EC–Bananas III*, for example, paras. 141–7.

[10] *EC–Bananas III*, paras. 159–64. [11] *EC–Bananas III*, para. 165.

[12] In considering exports of phonograms produced under a suspension regime, the arbitrators said that Ecuador should consider footnotes 13 and 14 to Article 51 of the TRIPS Agreement. While footnote 13 provides that a member is not under obligation to block imports of goods put on the market in another member by, or with, the consent of the copyright holder, phonogram copies authorized under a suspension regime would not be put on the market with consent. Members would remain obligated to apply Article 51 border measures with respect to goods produced without consent. This is the view expressed by the arbitrators. Recall, however, that paragraph 5(d) of the Doha Declaration on the TRIPS Agreement and Public Health confirms that relevant provisions of the TRIPS Agreement "leave each Member free to establish its own regime for such exhaustion without challenge." It is not clear that the arbitrators sufficiently accounted for this confirmed interpretation of the TRIPS Agreement.

> Members to derogate from any of their obligations under the TRIPS Agreement. Consequently, such DSB authorization to Ecuador cannot be construed by other WTO Members to reduce their obligations under Part III of the TRIPS Agreement in regard to imports entering their customs territories.[13]

The arbitrators took note that implementation of suspension of TRIPS obligations "may give rise to legal difficulties or conflicts within the domestic legal system of the Member so authorized (and perhaps even of the Member(s) affected by such suspension)." They further noted that this is a matter entirely within the prerogative of the suspending members, and that their domestic legal situation may be influenced by the specific measures used to implement the suspension.[14]

In the *EC–Bananas III* arbitration, the arbitrators said it is not for WTO arbitrators to pass judgment on whether Ecuador, once authorized by the DSB to suspend TRIPS commitments, might act inconsistently with obligations under relevant WIPO conventions. This is for Ecuador and the other parties to such treaties to consider.[15]

The arbitrators authorized Ecuador to request suspension of concessions under the TRIPS Agreement from the DSB. The DSB authorized the suspension.[16] However, Ecuador did not implement the suspension following successful negotiation of a settlement with the EU.

(b) US–Gambling – *Article 22.6, DSU arbitration with Antigua and Barbuda*[17]

The second arbitration involving a request to suspend concessions under the TRIPS Agreement was initiated by the United States in response to a request for authorization by Antigua and Barbuda (hereinafter Antigua). Antigua had prevailed against the United States on its claim that US restrictions on cross-border gambling services were inconsistent with US commitments under the GATS, and the United States was determined by a panel pursuant to Article 21.5 of the DSU to have failed to implement the

[13] *EC–Bananas III*, para. 156.

[14] *EC–Bananas III*, paras. 157–8. [15] *EC–Bananas III*, para. 152.

[16] The WTO Secretariat Summary of Dispute DS27 notes: "On 18 May 2000, the DSB authorized Ecuador to suspend concessions to the European Communities as requested." Available at: www.wto.org/english/tratop_e/dispu_e/cases_e/ds27_e.htm.

[17] *US–Measures Affecting the Cross-Border Supply of Gambling and Betting Services*, Recourse to arbitration by the United States under Article 22.6 of the DSU, Decision by the arbitrator, WT/DS285/ARB, December 21, 2007.

decision adopted by the DSB. Antigua thereupon requested authorization to suspend concessions under the GATS and TRIPS Agreement.[18] Before the arbitration Antigua dropped its request to suspend concessions under the GATS, and pursued only suspension under the TRIPS Agreement.[19]

The United States challenged Antigua on grounds that it had failed to follow the principles and procedures established in Article 22.3 of the DSU. The arbitrators in this proceeding largely followed the line of analysis and assessment used by the arbitrators in the *EC–Bananas III* arbitration, discussed above.

The arbitrators accepted that Antigua's relative economic and trade position compared with the United States made it exceedingly difficult to suspend concessions in a way that would induce compliance because (a) the relative size of Antigua's services import market meant that suspending concessions in services would have a negligible impact on the United States, and (b) that suspension of concessions in the services sector would impose additional costs on Antigua's consumers, as well as adversely affecting its travel, tourism, and other services industries.[20] In this regard, the arbitrators in the *US–Gambling* arbitration were more receptive to argumentation concerning impact on consumers in the suspending country than were the arbitrators in the *EC –Bananas III* arbitration.[21]

Antigua had indicated its intention to suspend concessions under TRIPS Agreement "Section 1: Copyright and related rights, Section 2: Trademarks,

[18] In Antigua's proceeding against the United States, the parties agreed on sequencing in accordance with this generally accepted practice (see WTO Secretariat Dispute Settlement Summary for Dispute DS285, *US–Measures Affecting the Cross-Border Supply of Gambling and Betting Services*, available at: www.wto.org).

[19] *US–Gambling*, above, note 41, at para. 4.20.

[20] *US–Gambling*, for example, paras. 4.90–100.

[21] On the question of whether circumstances were sufficiently serious (that is, "serious enough") to justify cross-retaliation among covered agreements, the arbitrators had little difficulty accepting Antigua's position based upon (1) serious disparity in national economic circumstances, (2) dependency on services trade leading to vulnerability to external factors, and (3) the need for Antigua to diversify its economy. After stating its acceptance of Antigua's position, the arbitrators said:

> 4.114 We note in this respect that the extremely unbalanced nature of the trading relations between the parties makes it all the more difficult for Antigua to find a way of ensuring the effectiveness of a suspension of concessions or other obligations against the United States under the same agreement. We also note that the heavy reliance of Antigua's economy on the very sectors that would be candidates for retaliation under the GATS increases the likelihood that an adverse impact would arise for Antigua itself, including for low-wage workers. (*US–Gambling*, paras. 4.90–100)

Section 4: Industrial designs, Section 5: Patents and Section 7: Protection of undisclosed information."[22] In contrast to Ecuador in *EC–Bananas III*, Antigua did not provide further details regarding its plans to implement the TRIPS suspension. The United States argued that the arbitrators should require Antigua to provide that information because otherwise it would not be possible for the arbitrators to determine the level of suspension intended by Antigua. The United States sought to support its argument by arguing that Antigua had turned a blind eye toward (that is, failed to regulate) activities taking place in Antigua that violated US criminal law. In the US view, because Antigua had not indicated how it would supervise the suspension of TRIPS concessions its failure to regulate may "encourage rampant and uncontrolled IPR piracy."[23]

The arbitrators rejected the US demand for a specific plan of implementation. While regretting that Antigua had not provided explanations as to how it proposed to implement the TRIPS suspension, the arbitrators found that they did not have a mandate to consider the "nature" of the obligations to be suspended and could not question the complaining party's choice of specific obligations to be suspended.[24]

The arbitrators favorably invoked the decision in *EC–Bananas III* and indicated that the same considerations would apply with respect to Antigua's suspension regime.[25]

The arbitrators authorized Antigua to request suspension of concessions under the TRIPS Agreement. Antigua has not yet requested authorization from the DSB to proceed with this suspension.[26]

[22] *US–Gambling*, para. 5.6. [23] *US–Gambling*, para. 5.3.

[24] The panel said:

> 5.10 At the same time, it is important that the form that is chosen in order to enact the suspension is such as to ensure that equivalence can and will be respected in the application of the suspension, once authorized. The form should also be transparent, so as to allow an assessment of whether the level of suspension does not exceed the level of nullification. We also note that the suspension of obligations under the TRIPS Agreement may involve more complex means of implementation than, for example, the imposition of higher import duties on goods, and that the exact assessment of the value of the rights affected by the suspension is also likely to be more complex. (*US–Gambling*, para 5.3)

[25] *US–Gambling*, para. 5.11.

[26] See WTO Secretariat Dispute Settlement Summary for Dispute DS285, *US–Measures Affecting the Cross-Border Supply of Gambling and Betting Services*, available at: www.wto.org. Recall that Article 22.7 of the DSU provides "The DSB shall be informed promptly of the decision of the arbitrator and shall *upon request*, grant authorization to suspend

(c) *Brazil's suspension request*

On October 6, 2005, Brazil requested authorization to suspend concessions under the TRIPS Agreement in response to the failure by the United States to implement the decision of the DSB in the *US–Upland Cotton* case.[27] The request for suspension preceded a panel decision under Article 21.5 of the DSU that the United States had not fully implemented the underlying decision.[28] Pursuant to an Agreed Procedure between the parties, the United States submitted a request for arbitration pursuant to Article 22.6, but requested suspension of the proceeding. Brazil suspended its request for authorization pursuant to an understanding with the United States pending negotiations on a satisfactory resolution of this dispute.[29]

3 The economic rationale for cross-retaliation under the TRIPS Agreement

(a) *Imbalance in trade flows between developed and developing economies*

As a practical matter, developing countries are not often in a position to enforce compliance with DSB decisions effectively because the domestic markets of those countries are not sufficiently large that restricting access to a developed country will significantly affect the economy of the developed country.[30] This is not always the case. A number of the larger economy developing countries – such as Brazil, China, and India – do

concessions or other obligations where the request is consistent with the decision of the arbitrator, unless the DSB decides by consensus to reject the request" (emphasis added).

27 "Brazil Asks to Suspend TRIPS, GATS Rules in US Cotton Retaliation," *Inside US Trade*, October 7, 2005, arising out of *US–Subsidies on Upland Cotton*, AB-2004–5, Report of the Appellate Body, WT/DS267/AB/R, March 3, 2005 (DSR 2005:I, 3).

28 *US–Subsidies on Upland Cotton*, Recourse to Article 21.5 of the DSU by Brazil, Report of the Panel, WT/DS267/RW, December 18, 2007.

29 In Brazil's proceeding against the United States in the *Uplands Cotton* proceeding, the parties also accepted the generally agreed sequencing framework (see WTO Secretariat Dispute Settlement Summary for Dispute DS267, *US–Subsidies on Upland Cotton*, available at: www.wto.org). See generally, John H. Jackson, William J. Davey, and Alan O. Sykes, *Legal Problems of International Economic Relations: Cases, Materials, and Text*, 5th edn. (St. Paul, MN: West Publishing, 2008), 348–50.

30 There is a general problem that confronts many developing countries in initiating and prosecuting WTO dispute settlement actions because of limited financial and personnel resources. This problem is at least partially mitigated through operation of the WTO Advisory Centre that provides legal assistance for developing countries.

have domestic markets sufficiently large that market access restrictions may have a material impact on developed country exporters and investors.[31] But, for smaller economy developing countries, and least developed countries, it is very unlikely that market access restrictions will materially impact the developed country economy.

The imbalance in the compliance-enforcement capacity of developed and developing countries is a long-standing and well-known critique of the WTO legal system. Starting in the GATT 1947 era, proposals were made that would require some form of compensation from developed to developing countries as a means to induce compliance, or at least to penalize "bad behavior," because otherwise developing countries would be perpetually without effective recourse for developed country failure to abide by commitments. To date such proposals have not been seriously taken up, which has led to the current interest in cross-retaliation in TRIPS as a means of providing developing countries with some leverage in dispute settlement.

One strong indicator of the degree to which the threat of TRIPS retaliation stimulates political pressure from potentially affected constituencies is the hyperbolic language used by those constituencies and/or their proxies when the possibility of TRIPS suspension is raised. WTO members threatening suspension are referred to as "pirates,"[32] and threats are made that suspension will lead to reduction in foreign direct investment. By contrast, such language is not deployed when a WTO member threatens to suspend tariff concessions on imported goods. This reflects the successful deployment of propaganda by IPRs-dependent industries. Based upon the degree of caution with which government officials approach the possibility of cross-retaliation in TRIPS, this propaganda appears to have some influence. Lawfully adopted measures limiting monopoly positions are transformed into the equivalent of "criminal theft," while lawfully adopted measures aimed at raising prices on imported goods are treated as normal regulatory activities.

[31] This does not mean that larger economy developing countries may not determine that withdrawal of concessions in the same sector (for example, goods), or under the same agreement, will not be practical or effective. That determination involves a number of factors including, for example, the extent to which increased tariffs would raise primary or intermediate goods input costs for local manufacturers, thereby rendering those manufacturers less competitive. The above text is intended only to distinguish smaller economy developing countries with virtually no possibility of retaliation at a level which may have an impact on a non-compliant developed member from those that may be large enough to create a material impact, even though the latter may harm themselves through retaliation in the same sector or under the same agreement.

[32] See, for example, James Kanter and Gary Rivlin, "In Trade Ruling, Antigua Wins a Right to Piracy," *The New York Times*, December 22, 2007.

The inability of a developing country to induce compliance with a DSB ruling because of a lack of sufficient domestic market size should be sufficient to constitute grounds of ineffectiveness or impracticability in the suspension of concessions under the GATT or GATS. It seems reasonable also to suggest that very few developing countries choose to initiate dispute settlement proceedings against developed countries in circumstances that are "not serious," given the diplomatic discomfort that is virtually certain to be generated for those developing countries.

(b) *The self-destructive impact of raising tariffs and service barriers*

The theory behind authorizing suspension of concessions is that, at least in the short term, political constituencies (that is, private operators) in the country against which trade barriers are imposed will exercise their influence on the government to bring trade measures into conformity in order to avoid harm to themselves.

For many developing countries, the economic harm caused to manufacturers, service providers, and consumers from suspending concessions (that is, raising trade barriers) will outweigh the economic harm inflicted on a complained-against developed country. For manufacturers, raising tariffs may increase the cost of inputs that will raise the price of their end products destined for domestic and international markets. This will hurt the manufacturers. There may be some manufacturers that will benefit from operating behind a higher tariff wall because they will be able to raise domestic prices and/or increase local market share. But it may be difficult for manufacturers to raise domestic prices without raising export prices as well, potentially causing a loss of export sales.

Local service providers may benefit from regulatory barriers imposed upon service providers from the complained-against member. Local service providers may enjoy increased pricing power. This pricing power will affect consumers who will pay more for services. Major questions for most developing countries seeking to withdraw concessions in the field of services will be whether the domestic services market is sufficiently large that restricting it will significantly affect a developed country, and how consumers will react to higher prices.

(c) *The basic economic distinction of TRIPS concessions*

IPRs typically entitle the right holder to exclude third parties from the market. These rights are granted based on different considerations, including promotion of innovation and investment in innovation (by patent and trade secret), promotion of creative expression (by copyright and industrial design), and to provide a means of identifing the goods and services of enterprises and regions (by trademark and geographical indication). To different extents, and depending on the characteristics of the relevant market, IPRs enable producers to obtain a premium price for their products based on the right to exclude others. Economists refer to the economic return from IPRs as "rents" or "royalties" that may be imputed in the price of goods or services, or may be collected separately as licensing fees.

As a general proposition, the suspension of IPRs should not have the same negative impact on the country undertaking the suspension as would imposing increased tariffs on goods or restricting access to the services market. Rents or royalties paid to foreign holders of IPRs typically represent payment outflows from a host country to a home country.[33] Suspending rent or royalty outflows based on suspension of TRIPS concessions should not generate the same type of adverse impact as raising tariffs on goods or restricting services. Local producers should not face increased costs for inputs and consumers should not pay higher prices for consumer goods. The suspension should mainly affect foreign IPR holders whose rent income is reduced, curtailing outflows to the country against which the suspension is imposed.

The observation in the preceding paragraph is not without qualification. A country authorizing suspension of IPRs under the TRIPS Agreement needs to consider the potential for disrupting ongoing business relations between enterprises in the suspending and suspended-against country. Some such relationships may depend upon local recognition of IPRs as to which suspension could trigger contractual problems. Some suppliers of IPR-protected products from the suspended-against country may decide to curtail exports during the period of suspension, and alternative sources of supply may be limited. Some foreign investors could alter their view of the investment environment within the suspending country depending upon the characteristics of the suspension. It could also be argued that suspension of IPRs will adversely affect the local research and development environment (R&D), thereby having a "net negative" impact on global R&D, and limiting the emergence of new technologies worldwide.[34]

[33] This is not invariably the case as rents or royalties may be reinvested locally.

[34] Even if there is some net R&D inhibiting effect, this seems unlikely to be a key factor in the decision making of particular developing countries given the comparatively low proportion of global R&D conducted in developing countries, particularly in small economy developing countries.

Other things being equal, a WTO member suspending IPRs should be reducing its costs and payment outflows during the period of suspension, without raising prices on inputs for local producers or to consumers. This is preferable from an economic standpoint to raising tariffs on goods or restricting access to the services market. And, it may be the only viable mechanism for placing economic pressure on the suspended-against country.

(d) *Conceptual distinction between IPRs and traditional trade regulation subject matter*

Concessions under the TRIPS Agreement are of a different character or nature than concessions under the GATT or GATS. The differences raise novel legal issues when assessing the suspension of concessions under TRIPS.

The TRIPS Agreement evidences several basic features. It incorporates basic principles, such as national and most-favored-nation (MFN) treatment, which are largely common across international trade law. The principal feature of the TRIPS Agreement is minimum substantive standards applicable to different fields of intellectual property: copyright, trademark, geographical indication, design protection, integrated circuit layout protection, patent, and undisclosed information. A novel feature of the TRIPS Agreement from an international economic law standpoint is the introduction of minimum standards of enforcement. The Agreement also includes various transition arrangements and institutional mechanisms.

From a "suspension of concessions" standpoint, an important aspect of the TRIPS Agreement is reflected in the preamble that "*Recogniz[es]* that intellectual property rights are private rights" (original emphasis). This provision was introduced during the Uruguay Round negotiations to clarify that private right holders are expected to enforce intellectual property rights through civil litigation, and that the Agreement does not impose on governments an obligation to undertake general enforcement activity.[35] Yet the provision points to a key distinction with other WTO agreements. Generally speaking, trade instruments and measures address classes of economic operators. A tariff is adopted with respect to a class of goods and when implemented it applies to imports (or exports) by

[35] Recognizing that the TRIPS Agreement does impose certain limited obligations on governments with respect to criminal enforcement. See UNCTAD–ICTSD, *Resource Book on TRIPS and Development* (Cambridge University Press, 2005), 619–21.

all economic operators dealing with that class of goods. A service regulation (such as a banking or tourist industry regulation) is adopted to affect a class or category of service providers. As a general rule, no particular enterprise or operator has a "property interest" in, or a specific legal entitlement to, tariff, quota system, service regulation, or other form of trade regulation.

An IPR holder takes advantage of a generally applicable system of regulation (that is, the laws and regulations under which IPRs are granted), but is understood to have a specific legal entitlement to the intellectual property right that is granted to it. There is substantial theoretical debate about whether an IPR is genuinely a form of "property" in the sense of real property or movable personal property. Because an IPR is typically (though not exclusively) granted for a limited period, with effects closely determined by government industrial policy regulation, it is of a different character than perpetual ownership of land or entitlement to specific personal property. Some courts and government regulations have elected to treat IPRs much as other forms of "property," and we will revert to this discussion in section 7. But, whether or not an IPR is considered "property" as such, the right accorded to the owner or "right holder" is specific to that holder (though it may well be transferable).

When a government suspends concessions or intellectual property rights previously granted in favor of foreign IPR holders, it will be suspending or affecting specific legal entitlements held by private operators. This is different than suspending tariff concessions (that is, by imposing higher tariff rates) because importers and manufacturers generally are not understood to have specific legal entitlements to tariff rates.

Private operators have attempted to enforce claimed entitlements to tariff, quota, and service regulations. Perhaps the best-known example of such attempts involved the efforts by German importers and distributors of bananas to prevent the European Council and Commission from adopting and enforcing changes to tariffs, quotas, and service regulations on the basis of property rights or legitimate expectations. The European Court of Justice rejected these efforts.[36] While a complete canvassing of

[36] See judgment of the court, October 5, 1994 – *Federal Republic of Germany* v. *Council of the European Union* – Bananas – Common organization of the markets – Import regime – Case C-280/93. From the Summary:

> 7. The same considerations justify the restriction on the freedom of traders who previously operated on open markets to pursue their trade or business, the substance of that right not being impaired.

national court decisions regarding changes to tariff, quota, and services regulation is beyond the scope of this chapter, there is substantial evidence that most governments and courts do not consider private operators to have specific entitlements to particular trade measures. National (and regional) legislatures change such rules with regularity, and it would be problematic if such rule changes gave private operators grounds for legal challenge. An analogy would be allowing individual taxpayers to challenge changes to tax codes on the ground that taxpayers have a specific legal entitlement to particular tax rates and/or rules. Such challenges are not generally permitted before national courts.

Governments can, and do, change intellectual property rules, and with some degree of frequency. And, private IPR holders generally cannot assert claims against the government arguing that changes to those rules have adversely affected their "specific entitlement." But if a government interferes with a specific intellectual property interest of a private right holder there may, under certain circumstances, be a requirement to award compensation to that right holder, such as awarding a royalty when a compulsory license is granted in the ordinary course of commercial use.

Specific IPR holders might seek to challenge suspension of concessions under TRIPS claiming interference with existing rights in property. Because the concept of a general suspension of IP rights to enforce compliance with a trade agreement is new to the post-1995 WTO era, and has not previously been done, national (and regional) courts would face a new situation. As a matter of general principle, because governments have historically modified intellectual property rules in ways that affect pre-existing specific entitlements of private operators, for example, by modifying exhaustion doctrines, there is substantial precedent to support the conclusion that suspension of TRIPS-based IPRs would be treated as other forms of regulatory change, such as changes in tariff rates. Nonetheless, it is important to be aware of the possibility of

> With respect to those traders' right to property, the loss of market shares does not impact that right, since the market share held before the establishment of a common organization of a market constitutes only a momentary economic position exposed to the risks of changing circumstances and is not covered by the right to property. Similarly, a position on the market resulting from an existing situation cannot, especially if that situation is contrary to the rules of the common market, benefit from protection on the basis of acquired rights or legitimate expectation.

challenge based on claims of government taking of specific property interests.[37]

4 Multilateral, regional and bilateral commitments

(a) Multilateral commitments

The TRIPS Agreement incorporates by reference provisions of certain multilateral agreements, including most notably the Paris Convention on the Protection of Industrial Property and the Berne Convention on the Protection of Literary and Artistic Works.

While the TRIPS Agreement and DSU contemplate that obligations under the Paris and Berne conventions may be suspended, the question remains whether a suspension of concessions or obligations may, nonetheless, constitute an independent breach by the suspending WTO member of obligations under the associated conventions. In other words, assuming that a WTO member is not breaching WTO obligations by suspending TRIPS concessions that refer to the Paris or Berne Convention, might the complained-against member successfully pursue a separate dispute settlement claim under the Paris or Berne Convention?

It is important to examine the relevant rules of the Vienna Convention on the Law of Treaties (VCLT) with respect to the application of successive treaties between the same parties.[38] Article 30 of the VCLT does not clearly prescribe a rule that accounts for the relationship between the

[37] See further discussion below, section 7(b).

[38] The Vienna Convention provides:

> Article 30
> Application of successive treaties relating to the same subject-matter
>
> 1. Subject to Article 103 of the Charter of the United Nations, the rights and obligations of States parties to successive treaties relating to the same subject-matter shall be determined in accordance with the following paragraphs.
> 2. When a treaty specifies that it is subject to, or that it is not to be considered as incompatible with, an earlier or later treaty, the provisions of that other treaty prevail.
> 3. When all the parties to the earlier treaty are parties also to the later treaty but the earlier treaty is not terminated or suspended in operation under article 59, the earlier treaty applies only to the extent that its provisions are compatible with those of the latter treaty.
> 4. When the parties to the later treaty do not include all the parties to the earlier one:

TRIPS Agreement, the DSU and the Paris and Berne conventions in the suspension context.

The TRIPS Agreement was adopted subsequent to the Paris and Berne conventions. Article 2.1 of the TRIPS Agreement provides that WTO members should "comply" with certain provisions of the Paris Convention, but (a) not stating that TRIPS Agreement rules are "subject to" the Paris Convention rules, and (b) expressly leaving out TRIPS Agreement provisions relating to dispute settlement. Article 9.1 of the TRIPS Agreement provides that WTO members should "comply" with certain provisions of the Berne Convention. But, the provision on non-derogation with existing obligations applying both to the Paris and Berne conventions does not incorporate WTO dispute settlement.

The Paris Convention has 172 state parties as of 2008, and the Berne Convention has 163. In all, or virtually all, cases, a member of the WTO will also be a party to the Paris and Berne conventions. The conventions permit state parties to initiate dispute settlement before the ICJ. Such dispute settlement under the Paris or Berne Convention is unlikely to be successful based upon suspension of concessions under the WTO DSU and TRIPS Agreement. This is not because the ICJ would necessarily find that the WTO agreements take precedence over the WIPO conventions as a matter of applying Article 30 of the VCLT and the rules regarding successor agreements – though it might. Instead, in examining the two sets of obligations (WTO and WIPO), the ICJ would find that the complaining and responding states had each expressly accepted the suspension regime prescribed by WTO DSU rules. A state party to the Paris or Berne Convention would be objecting to application of a rule of enforcement that it had clearly accepted under WTO rules. By accepting the WTO suspension rule, a state party would appear to have waived the right to independently enforce a complementary substantive obligation under the cross-referenced Paris or Berne regimes that would effectively nullify the suspension. Put another way, a member of the WTO would be equitably

(a) as between States parties to both treaties the same rule applies as in paragraph 3;
(b) as between a State party to both treaties and a State party to only one of the treaties, the treaty to which both States are parties governs their mutual rights and obligations.

5. Paragraph 4 is without prejudice to article 41, or to any question of the termination or suspension of the operation of a treaty under article 60 or to any question of responsibility which may arise for a State from the conclusion or application of a treaty the provisions of which are incompatible with its obligations towards another State under another treaty.

estopped from attempting to independently enforce an obligation under a WIPO Convention as a means of preventing effective enforcement of its WTO obligation.[39]

A result that authorized a WTO member to challenge a suspension of concessions by seeking an independent judgment from the ICJ on the

[39] Under general principles of equity, an "estoppel" arises when a first party promises or engages in conduct indicating its intention to act in a certain way, thereby establishing a legitimate expectation for a second party. The first party may not thereafter engage in conduct intended to defeat the legitimate expectation of the second party.

The *Nuclear Tests* case (*Australia* v. *France*), ICJ judgment of December 20, 1974 (I.C.J. Rep. 1974, at 253) is a widely noted decision of the ICJ in which France established an estoppel (that is, a binding legal obligation) against further nuclear testing in the Pacific by its own formal unilateral pronouncements.

In the WTO panel decision in the *US–Section 301* case (United States – Sections 301–310 of the Trade Act of 1974, Report of the Panel, WT/DS152/R, December 22, 1999), the parties extensively briefed the significance of the *Nuclear Tests* case. The panel ultimately determined with regard to unilateral statements of the United States:

> Accordingly, we find that these statements by the US express the unambiguous and official position of the US representing, in a manner that can be relied upon by all Members, an undertaking that the discretion of the USTR has been limited so as to prevent a determination of inconsistency before exhaustion of DSU proceedings. (at para. 7.125) …
>
> It of course follows that should the US repudiate or remove in any way these undertakings, the US would incur State responsibility since its law would be rendered inconsistent with the obligations under Article 23. (at para. 7.126)

The principle determines that states may by their conduct and/or pronouncements establish legal obligations against conduct inconsistent with such conduct and/or pronouncements. By accepting the rules on cross-retaliation that apply to the TRIPS Agreement, WTO members have by their own conduct accepted an obligation not to defeat those rules by recourse to alternative forums.

See also, for example, *Hass* v. *Darigold Dairy Products* (9th Cir. 1985) 751 F.2d 1096 (US), stating:

> Equitable estoppel has been defined as
>
> the doctrine by which a person may be precluded by his act or conduct … from asserting a right which he otherwise would have had. [Citation.] The effect of voluntary conduct of a party whereby he is precluded from asserting rights against another who has justifiably relied upon such conduct and changed his position so that he will suffer injury if the former is allowed to repudiate the conduct.
>
> *Black's Law Dictionary* 483 (5th edn. 1979), cited in part in Jablon, 657 F.2d at 1068; the doctrine has also been described as standing for the principle that where one party has by his representations or his conduct induced the other party to a transaction to give him an advantage which it would be against equity and good conscience for him to assert, he would not in a court of justice be permitted to avail himself of that advantage. *Amalgamated Clothing,*

same subject matter would undermine the effectiveness of the WTO dispute settlement system. Such action would appear to be inconsistent with Article 23.1 of the DSU, which provides that:

> When Members seek the redress of a violation of obligations or other nullification or impairment of benefits under the covered agreements or an impediment to the attainment of any objective of the covered agreements, they shall have recourse to, and abide by, the rules and procedures of this Understanding.

The initiation of a dispute before the ICJ under the Paris or Berne Convention might also be viewed as a breach of obligation to perform the WTO agreements in good faith. A WTO member that initiated such a claim would essentially be attempting to nullify its obligations under the WTO agreements by recourse to an alternative forum. Particularly in light of the fact that WTO members accepted their TRIPS obligations in full knowledge of their corresponding equivalent Paris and Berne Convention obligations, it would be difficult for WTO members to argue that they reserved the right to block effective operation of the WTO dispute settlement system through parallel treaties. It seems doubtful that the ICJ would interpret the WTO agreements to have contemplated a result defeating the purpose of the DSU suspension system.

The WCT and WPPT were adopted subsequent to the WTO agreements, including the DSU and the TRIPS Agreement. The WCT and WPPT are not incorporated by reference or otherwise in the TRIPS Agreement. As of September 7, 2008, the WCT has sixty-seven member states and WPPT has sixty-six. Each treaty contains provisions that obligate the members to provide remedies against circumvention of effective measures of technological protection (TPMs) and interference with digital rights management (DRM) information.[40] However, in each case the obligation is qualified only to require remedies where the relevant act is not "permitted by law" or is undertaken "without authority." If a WTO member that is also a party to the WCT or WPPT acts to suspend copyright and to authorize the use of copyright subject matter, actions by the government

602 F.2d at 1370 (quoting *Union Mutual Insurance Co.* v. *Wilkinson*, 80 US (13 Wall.) 222, 233, 20 L.Ed. 617 (1872)).

[40] Article 11 of the WCT provides: "Contracting Parties shall provide adequate legal protection and effective legal remedies against the circumvention of effective technological measures that are used by authors in connection with the exercise of their rights under this Treaty or the Berne Convention and that restrict acts, in respect of their works, which are not authorized by the authors concerned or permitted by law." Article 12(1) of the WTO provides:

or third parties to circumvent TPMs or interfere with DRM information would be "permitted by law" and undertaken with "authority." Each of the WCT and WPPT permit member states to adopt limited exceptions to the protections otherwise afforded under the agreements, at Articles 10 and 16, respectively, and such provisions would permit the member states to fulfill their commitments under the WTO DSU.

Human rights instruments, such as the Universal Declaration of Human Rights (at Article 27(2)), and the International Convention on Economic, Social and Cultural Rights (at Article 15), reference the right of everyone to benefit from moral and material interests resulting from scientific, literary, or artistic productions of which they are author. These treaty references are not sufficiently specific to constitute an obstacle to the temporary suspension of IPRs under the TRIPS Agreement. In any case, the WTO agreements were adopted subsequent to the relevant human rights instruments. Unless the provisions of the human rights conventions referred to above were considered peremptory norms (or core human rights, at minimum), and that is not the case, WTO members accepted to suspend those rights by operation of the DSU. A suspended-against member should be precluded from asserting a claim based upon a suspension procedure it has accepted.

Just as governments may have implemented Paris and Berne Convention obligations into national law through provisions that are effectively independent of those treaties, so may governments have implemented human rights obligations into national law through provisions that are effectively independent of corresponding international obligations. Human rights are not infrequently protected under national constitutions. To the extent that the suspension of an intellectual property right may be argued to contravene a constitutional right that reflects an international human rights obligation, the relevant

> Contracting Parties shall provide adequate and effective legal remedies against any person knowingly performing any of the following acts knowing, or with respect to civil remedies having reasonable grounds to know, that it will induce, enable, facilitate or conceal an infringement of any right covered by this Treaty or the Berne Convention:
> (i) to remove or alter any electronic rights management information without authority;
> (ii) to distribute, import for distribution, broadcast or communicate to the public, without authority, works or copies of works knowing that electronic rights management information has been removed or altered without authority.

Articles 18 and 19 of the WPPT, respectively, provide the same.

issues are addressed below in the context of potential claims involving the taking of property.

(b) *Regional and bilateral commitments*

From both a conceptual and practical standpoint, bilateral and regional commitments of WTO members may be more likely to present difficulties in the context of suspension of concessions than the multilateral WIPO conventions. The TRIPS Agreement and the DSU were negotiated subsequent to the Paris and Berne conventions, and the latter are integrated into the text of the TRIPS Agreement. Each of the aforementioned agreements is broadly applicable to the same treaty parties. Coherence between the two systems of IP regulation was anticipated.

The negotiating environment and the object and purpose of many of the recently concluded bilateral and regional trade agreements are different insofar as intellectual property rights are concerned. Most, though not all, of these agreements were negotiated subsequent to the conclusion of the TRIPS Agreement. The set of bilateral and regional free trade agreements (FTAs) between the United States and various developed and developing countries are specifically intended to enhance the scope and enforceability of IPRs, and to reduce flexibilities available to party governments. While the FTAs address the relationship with the WTO agreements, they do so in a way that leaves many questions unanswered. Among those questions is how suspension of concessions pursuant to WTO DSB authorization would be treated under the FTAs. It is important to note at the outset that, unlike the WTO agreements, the FTAs include chapters on the protection of investment that provide third-party dispute settlement rights to private investors. Those chapters are largely untested so far as they may address intellectual property. And, there is a significant number of earlier bilateral investment treaties (BITS) negotiated by the United States, in addition to the FTAs, that do not include chapters detailing IPRs substantive commitments, but which include intellectual property subject matter within the scope of investment protection subject to dispute settlement, including third-party investor–state dispute resolution.[41]

[41] See Frederick M. Abbott, "Protecting First World Assets in the Third World: Intellectual Property Negotiations in the GATT Multilateral Framework," *Vanderbilt Journal of Transnational Law*, 22(1989), 689.

There are many regional and bilateral agreements that provide for the protection of investment beyond those concluded by or with the United States. The trend toward bilateral and regional arrangements is a worldwide phenomenon.[42] The US model agreements are used here to illustrate a phenomenon, recognizing that similar issues will arise in non-US contexts. The provisions of the Dominican Republic–Central America–United States Free Trade Agreement (CAFTA) will be used to illustrate the issues raised. There are variations among specific terms in the US-negotiated FTAs, but the CAFTA is broadly representative of those agreements.

Chapter 15 on intellectual property, as similar intellectual property chapters in other US-negotiated FTAs, incorporates a wide range of substantive and enforcement-related obligations. A substantial number of these obligations are duplicative of obligations established by the TRIPS Agreement. However, a number of such obligations are so-called "TRIPS-plus", meaning that they establish IP-protection obligations higher and/or more restrictive than those established by the TRIPS Agreement. A number of research papers have described the TRIPS-plus obligations established by the US-negotiated FTAs. That analysis is not repeated here.[43] As an illustration, the pharmaceutical regulatory data protection provisions of the FTAs are substantially more restrictive (that is, protective of right-holder interests) than Article 39.3 of the TRIPS Agreement. A state party to the CAFTA might breach its obligations under Article 15.10: Measures Related to Certain Regulated Products, without breaching the TRIPS Agreement.

Article 10.28: Definitions, in Chapter 10, Investment, defines "investment" to include: "(f) intellectual property rights; (g) licenses, authorizations, permits, and similar rights conferred pursuant to domestic law." The investment chapter incorporates national treatment,[44] MFN obligations,[45] and provides for fair and equitable treatment, and full

[42] See, for example, Frederick M. Abbott, "A New Dominant Trade Species Emerges: Is Bilateralism a Threat?" *Journal of International Economic Law.*

[43] See, for example, Frederick M. Abbott, "Intellectual Property Provisions of Bilateral and Regional Trade Agreements in Light of U.S. Federal Law," ICTSD–UNCTAD Issue Paper No. 12, 2006; Carsten Fink and Patrick Reichenmiller, "Tightening TRIPS: The Intellectual Property Provisions of Recent US Free Trade Agreements," World Bank Trade Note No. 20, 2005; Pedro Roffe, "Bilateral Agreements and a TRIPS-Plus World: The Chile–USA Free Trade Agreement," QIAP TRIPS Issues Papers No. 4, 2004; David Vivas-Eugui, "Regional and Bilateral Agreements and a TRIPS-Plus World: The Free Trade Area of the Americas (FTAA)," QIAP/QUNO TRIPS Issues Papers No. 1, 2003.

[44] CAFTA, Article 10.3. [45] CAFTA, Article 10.4.

security,[46] according to public international law standards, as well as protecting against expropriation without adequate compensation.[47]

Disputes between state parties are generally subject to the provisions of Chapter 20 on Dispute Settlement. In Chapter 10 on Investment, pursuant to Section B: Investor–State Dispute Settlement, private investors of state parties may initiate third-party arbitration of investment claims using the facilities of ICSID, or under UNCITRAL rules. Comparable third-party arbitration facilities provided for in the North American Free Trade Agreement (NAFTA) have been used fairly extensively, and there is no reason to expect that CAFTA investors in the field of intellectual property would be reluctant to use the relevant provisions.

The question presented is whether a CAFTA state party that prevailed in a WTO dispute settlement proceeding, and thereafter suspended commitments under the TRIPS Agreement, might independently breach its obligations under the CAFTA IP or Investment Chapter, and with what consequences.

To the extent that a CAFTA state party suspends TRIPS obligations that are coextensive with CAFTA IP obligations, there is probably no independent basis for claiming a violation of the CAFTA. As between the state parties, suspension of WTO obligations implies that the initial dispute settlement claim was brought under the WTO DSU, and the CAFTA provides that the initial choice of forum is determinative and exclusive. A second claim on the same subject matter could not be brought to CAFTA dispute settlement.

Similarly with respect to coextensive claims, it is difficult to conclude that a private investor could prevail in third-party arbitration on the ground that a CAFTA state party acting pursuant to authorization by the DSB had breached an investment protection obligation. This is principally because an unlawful taking of IP property presupposes contravention of customary international law standards regarding protection of the property of aliens (see CAFTA, Article 10.5(2)). And, it is doubtful that temporary suspension of rights pursuant to DSB authorization would be considered an expropriation or nationalization due to its transitory nature and the fact that it is authorized under international law.

A more difficult set of issues would arise both as to state parties and private investors if, pursuant to a suspension authorized by the DSB, the suspending country addressed IP subject matter that is not regulated by

[46] CAFTA, Article 10.5.
[47] CAFTA, Article 10.7.

the TRIPS Agreement, and thus not technically covered by the authorization. As to that subject matter, the DSB would not be providing the international legal authorization for suspension because TRIPS concessions would not be involved. In that context, claims under CAFTA and the WTO agreements would not be coextensive, and independent claims under CAFTA might be foreseen.

Because independent claims might arise under the terms of the CAFTA and other FTAs, a country that is party to an FTA with the United States and that is preparing to suspend obligations pursuant to WTO DSB authorization may avoid difficulties by selecting TRIPS commitments that are effectively coextensive under both agreements.

5 Broad level of suspension issues under the TRIPS Agreement

(a) *Valuing changes in IP legislation generally*

The absence of reliable data and economic models with respect to the economic impact of changes in intellectual property regulation is a matter of distinguished pedigree. Seminal studies of the US patent system from the 1940s and 1950s stressed the limitations faced by economists in assessing the economic impact of the patent system.[48] From the outset of the Uruguay Round, a lack of reliable data regarding the prevalence, distribution, and economic impact of intellectual property rights was in evidence. Studies relied upon by developed country governments to promote the TRIPS Agreement were deeply and transparently flawed.[49] The few economic analyses brought out to support demands for stronger IP protection were generated by industry trade associations[50] or were tentative abstract exercises.[51] This does not mean that developed country industry groups demanding

[48] See Walton Hamilton, Senate Temporary National Economic Committee, 76th Congress, 3rd Session, "Investigation of Concentration of Economic Power: Patents and Free Enterprise," 164 (Comm. Print 1941) (W. Hamilton Monograph No. 31); and Fritz Machlup, "An Economic Review of the Patent System," Subcommittee of Committee on Patents, Trademarks and Copyrights, of the Committee on the Judiciary, 85th Congress 2nd Session 21 (Comm. Print 1958), and others cited in Abbott, "Protecting First World Assets," above, note 41.

[49] See, for example, USITC study written by former Pfizer employee, R. Sherwood, directly transposing unverified data from industry questionnaire, discussed in Abbott, "Protecting First World Assets," above, note 41.

[50] See, for example, R. M. Gadbaw and T. Richards (eds.), *Intellectual Property: Global Consensus, Global Conflict?* (Boulder, Co: Westview Press, 1988).

[51] See, for example, Burstein, "Diffusion of Knowledge-Based Products: Applications to Developing Economies," *Economic Inquiry*, 22 (1984), 612.

stronger international IP protection were not confronting a problem in IP-rent collection. These groups are run by serious-minded people who perceived a business problem and sought to address it. But it does highlight that there was virtually no serious *ex ante* assessment of the value of concessions in the field of TRIPS. And, although there has been some improvement over the past two decades in the collection of data regarding IP rights and in the capacity for reliable economic modeling of the impact of changes in rules, the improvements should not be exaggerated.[52] The most sophisticated studies of the economic impact of changes in IP rules do as much to highlight incomplete understanding of this complex area as they do to enhance the reliability of assessment and prediction.[53]

The extent to which IP rights induce invention and/or creative activity is not well established. Because this correlation is not well understood, it is difficult to predict how changes in IP rules will promote or retard innovation and, by definition, what will be the impact. Furthermore, IP rights function within complex political and regulatory frameworks that help to determine the direction of economic activity.[54] In order to understand the impact of changes to IP laws it is necessary to determine the impact of the external regulatory regime. In other words, changes to IP regimes are difficult to study in isolation. Third, technologies are constantly changing and it is difficult to predict the impact of new technologies on economic activity. Fourth, changes in IP regimes may have different implications for stakeholder groups, including producer and consumer groups. In assessing changes in IP regimes, it is also necessary to ask, "changes for whom?"

(b) *Valuing IP assets distinguished*

An important distinction must be drawn between the problem of valuing or predicting changes in general IP regulation, such as changing the

[52] For example, see the Fifth Annual BSA and IDC Global Software Piracy Study to illustrate the type of assumptions made by industry groups to support assertions of financial losses, available at: http://global.bsa.org/idcglobalstudy2007//studies/2007_global_piracy_study.pdf. Compare that with the model and assumptions used by Chaudhuri *et al.* in note 53, below.

[53] See, for example, Shubham Chaudhuri, Pinelopi K. Goldberg, and Panle Jia, "Estimating the Effects of Global Patent Protection in Pharmaceuticals: A Case Study of Quinolones in India," *American Economic Review*, 1477, December 2006; Carsten Fink, "Patent Protection, Transnational Corporations, and Market Structure: A Simulation Study of the Indian Pharmaceutical Industry," *Journal of Industry, Competition & Trade*, 1 (2001), 101; Jayashree Watal, "Pharmaceutical Patents, Prices and Welfare Losses: Policy Options for India Under the WTO TRIPS Agreement," *World Economics*, 23 (2000), 733.

[54] See generally, Keith E. Maskus, *Intellectual Property Rights in the Global Economy* (Washington, DC: Institute for International Economics, 2000).

criteria of patentability, and the problem of valuing IP assets and suspending rights in those assets.

It is *not* unusually difficult to determine the value of a particular intellectual property asset in isolation and on a static basis.[55] For example, once the popularity of a particular film has been determined by the marketplace, it will have a future value to its owner based upon a reasonably predictable flow of royalties and/or sales. The value is largely based upon copyright protection since that is what prevents free copying, even if imperfectly. Removing copyright protection from the film will reduce its future value. By aggregating a group of films and removing copyright protection from them it would be possible to establish a value of nullification or impairment of rights in the particular case. Similarly, when patent protection on a pharmaceutical product expires and generic producers enter the market there is a reasonably predictable fall-off in earnings from the pharmaceutical product. Stock market analysts are familiar with valuing the transition from patented to generic products in particular cases. In selecting a group of patented pharmaceutical products for the suspension of patent protection, the value of the nullification or impairment in the specific case could be reasonably predicted.

A TRIPS suspension regime would be intended to affect existing "IP assets," not the future development of inventive or creative works. Existing IP assets are capable of fairly accurate valuation in a process that, as a practical matter, is routinely undertaken by business enterprises and government regulators. A number of market-making institutions are reported to be working on public listing of IP-related financial products, and standardization projects for the valuation of the IP assets are underway.[56] The acquisition by one technology-dependent business of another depends upon the valuation of a "patent portfolio." The purchase, sale or merger of an originator pharmaceutical company involves the valuation of the medicines patent portfolio. Mergers and acquisitions among entertainment industry enterprises involve evaluation of future revenue streams from existing copyrighted works. Portfolios of copyrighted music have recently been subject to securitization for purposes of establishing loan

55 See, for example, "Intellectual Property Financing – An Introduction," *WIPO Magazine* (acknowledging Lucinda Longcroft, Senior Legal Officer), September 2008, including references to various securitized transactions, such as bonds backed by copyright royalties, and the treatment of patents and other IP rights as commercial assets subject to securitization.

56 See, for example, "Intellectual Property Financing," *WIPO Magazine*, September 2008, discussing activities of the American Stock Exchange and the German Institute for Standardization, as well as the International Organization for Standardization (ISO).

collateral. Competition and antitrust authorities examine present and future value markets based upon IPR holdings in technology-dependent industries. Investment banking firms following the pharmaceutical sector generate fairly comprehensive predictive reports concerning the economic impact of patent expirations in various markets. The types of analysis used in those reports could be applied to a pharmaceutical patent suspension regime, where suspension is a proxy for patent expiration. Valuation of IP assets is not especially mysterious. Valuing suspension of rights in IP assets should not be especially mysterious.

This is not to suggest that data will be readily or equally available in all IPR-dependent industry sectors. The Article 25 DSU arbitration in the *US–Copyright* case regarding the level of nullification or impairment of TRIPS obligations illustrates some of the potential difficulties in obtaining robust information even within certain industry segments in highly developed economies.[57] These difficulties include issues of confidentiality in respect to royalty data. Nonetheless, operating in conditions of imperfect information, arbitrators in the *US–Copyright* case were able to establish a value of the nullification or impairment of rights in a discrete copyright subject-matter setting.

(c) *Nationality*

For all categories of intellectual property it will be necessary for the suspending country to develop a methodology for determining the nationality of IPR holders. Following the panel decision in the *US–Copyright Act* case, the EU and the United States agreed to arbitrate under Article 25 of the DSU the question of the level of nullification and impairment suffered by the EU as a consequence of the US failure to implement its TRIPS obligations. This required the arbitrators to determine the value of the US failure to enforce copyright in favor of EU right holders. The question of nationality of right holders in this arbitration was simplified by the existence of collective management organizations that paid over royalties to artists' rights societies that distributed the royalties to identified right holders.[58]

In the *EC–Geographical Indications* case, the panel observed that there are no explicit rules governing this issue in the TRIPS Agreement.[59] The

[57] *US–Section 110(5) of the US Copyright Act*, Recourse to arbitration under Article 25 of the DSU, Award of the arbitrators, WT/DS160/ARB25/1, November 9, 2001 (DSR 2001:II, 667).

[58] See *US–Section 110(5) of the US Copyright Act.*

[59] *EC–Protection of Trademarks and Geographical Indications for Agricultural Products and Foodstuffs*, Report of the Panel, WT/DS174/R, March 15, 2005 (DSR 2005:VIII–IX, 3499), paras. 7.141–171.

panel looked to the practice for determining nationality within the EU, which the United States accepted. According to the panel, "The criteria used by the EC member States to determine the nationality of a legal person may vary and include criteria such as the place of incorporation and the place of the seat of the company or a combination of such criteria."[60]

As a practical matter, for IPRs that are registered, such as patents, trademarks, and geographical indications, and for some cases of industrial designs and copyrights, determining the nationality of the right holder by the address provided in the registration will greatly facilitate determining the right holders against whom a suspension will be effective. This will not provide a clear result in all cases as registrations may be held by locally addressed affiliate enterprises that are controlled from the suspended-against member. A suspension should be directed against the beneficial owner of the IPR on the basis of the nationality of that beneficial owner.

6 Subject-matter specific level of suspension issues

(a) Categories

Each of the "categories" of intellectual property rights specified in Sections 1 through 7 of Part II of the TRIPS Agreement are defined as a separate sector. The seven category headings are, in respective order: (1) Copyright and Related Rights; (2) Trademarks; (3) Geographical Indications; (4) Industrial Designs; (5) Patents; (6) Layout-Designs (Topographies) of Integrated Circuits; and (7) Protection of Undisclosed Information. Section 8 of Part II, Control of Anti-Competitive Practices in Contractual Licences is not referenced as a sector.

It is apparent from the text of the TRIPS Agreement, as now confirmed by the Appellate Body in the *US–Havana Club* decision,[61] that the topic headings of Part II do not limit each category to a single form of intellectual property. Section 5 on Patents, for example, also addresses *sui generis* forms of plant variety protection, implicitly including the forms of protection regulated by UPOV. Section 4 on Industrial Designs allows members to use various forms of IP protection, including (but not limited to), copyright, trade dress and *sui generis* industrial design protection. By incorporation of Article 8 of the Paris Convention (in Article 2.1 of the TRIPS Agreement), Section 2 on Trademarks implicitly regulates trade names.

[60] *EC–Protection of Trademarks*, at para. 7.149.

[61] *US–Section 211 Omnibus Appropriations Act of 1998*, AB-2001–7, WT/DS176/AB/R, January 2, 2002 (DSR 2002:II, 589).

Protection of Undisclosed Information can be undertaken through a variety of legal mechanisms or forms of intellectual property.

Part III, Enforcement of Intellectual Property Rights, and Part IV, Acquisition and Maintenance of Intellectual Property Rights and Related *Inter-Partes* Procedures, are also established as separate sectors under the TRIPS Agreement. An obligation to enforce intellectual property rights is not a classical trade "concession" in the sense of reducing a tariff barrier or eliminating a quota and raises valuation issues.

The list of sectors in Article 22.3(f)(iii) of the DSU does not cover all of the concessions or other obligations in the TRIPS Agreement, such as the national treatment and MFN treatment obligations which are elaborated in Part I. This presumably means that such other obligations are not considered separate sectors for purposes of assessing suspension of concessions, but does not appear to mean that those concessions or other obligations cannot be suspended because, *inter alia*, subparagraph (c) refers to suspension of concessions under another "covered agreement," and subparagraph (d)(i) refers to trade "under the agreement" in which a violation has been found. Although the matter is not free from doubt, the definition of "sector" does not appear to limit suspension of concessions or other obligations to enumerated sectors only, but may extend to other obligations under a "covered agreement." Virtually by definition, suspension of intellectual property rights as to the nationals of one WTO member will require limited waiver of the national and MFN treatment principles, which must be contemplated by the suspension system.

(b) Copyright

The suspension of copyright could take the form of a limitation on the distribution of royalties that would otherwise be received from licensees of copyrighted works, without affecting the basic right of the copyright holders to exclude others from the use of their works. Such a mechanism of suspension is suggested by the arbitration under Article 25 of the DSU to determine the level of nullification or impairment suffered by the EC as a consequence of US failure to protect EU copyright holders.[62] In that arbitration the level of nullification or impairment was determined by examining the level of royalty payments that would (and should) have been paid to EU copyright holders based upon collection of fees from

[62] *US–Section 110(5) of the US Copyright Act*, Recourse to Arbitration under Article 25 of the DSU, Award of the arbitrators, WT/DS160/ARB25/1, November 9, 2001 (DSR 2001:II, 667).

relevant business establishments in the United States by collective management organizations.[63]

Assume that royalties were, in fact, being collected by collective management organizations in the suspending country and paid to relevant artists' rights societies for the suspended-against country. In such circumstances, a WTO member could give effect to suspension of copyright by diverting such royalties into a fund reflecting the level of the suspension. The fund could be used for a purpose deemed appropriate by the suspending member. The use of this particular type of suspension system depends upon the existence of a collection organization and appropriate identification of the nationality of recipients/copyright holders.[64] Such facts may not be present in many cases. Nevertheless, the basic outlines of the model could be used to fashion various royalty "diversion" methodologies.

Given the duration of the copyright term, suspension of copyright protection would not ordinarily be expected to last for the full remaining term. In this regard, "suspension" of copyright protection would not seem to anticipate that the underlying copyrighted work would fall into the "public domain" upon suspension. The restoration of complete protection would presumably be envisioned at some point. Rules regarding restoration would need to exempt acts undertaken during the period of suspension from liability.

Because copyrighted works are uniquely susceptible to digitization, electronic reproduction, and transmission, suspension of copyright raises some difficult questions with respect to control over the underlying work in the digital environment. The TRIPS Agreement did not specifically address digital media with respect to copyright, but there is no reason to conclude that the rules of the Berne Convention incorporated by reference do not apply in the electronic environment. Negotiation of the WIPO Copyright Treaty and WIPO Performances and Phonograms Treaty was undertaken immediately following entry into force of the TRIPS Agreement, and these new agreements clarify and extend copyright rules with respect to the digital environment, including by addition of obligations regarding technological measures of protection. However, they are not part of the TRIPS Agreement.[65]

[63] *US–Section 110(5) of the US Copyright Act*, paras. 3.36–58.

[64] An additional useful feature of the collective management system reference in the US Copyright Act arbitration was that it identified copyright holders by their nationality, which is another factor that needs to be addressed by a suspension system. See *US–Section 110(5)*, paras. 3.54–56.

[65] The panel in the *US–Copyright* case used the WIPO Copyright Treaty as a source of interpretative guidance. This practice was questionable in light of the limited number of parties to the WCT.

Suspension of copyright in a digital or digitally reproduced expressive work may expose that work to extensive retransmission and reproduction on a worldwide basis. Such Internet-based copying may be difficult to control even when copyright protection is present. TPMs or DRM may be used to control reproduction and retransmission. For example, the Apple iTunes system used to license movies for personal viewing incorporates a technical termination of access system that appears to make it difficult to circumvent copyright protection.[66]

A second important aspect of DRM and TPMs is that such measures employed by copyright holders may make it technologically infeasible for members undertaking cross-retaliation to access and make available the relevant digital media content.[67] From a technical standpoint, it may be necessary for members undertaking cross-retaliation to obtain the technology or access codes necessary to use the underlying media content as authorized by the DSB. This would require the cooperation of the members against which cross-retaliation is undertaken in securing the relevant technology or access codes, or would require the members undertaking cross-retaliation to legally enforce demands within their own territories to obtain the access-enabling technologies from their holders. A requirement to initiate legal proceedings might entail considerable delay. Alternatively, members undertaking cross-retaliation may need to engage the services of "hackers" with the technical know-how to "break" access restrictions. If the option to break relevant TPMs and to bypass DRM is used, such government action must not be considered inconsistent with any obligations under the WCT or WPPT. This legal issue was discussed in section 4(a) above.

The issue of digital reproduction and transmission is connected to the issue of the territorial scope of an authorization to suspend concessions. Copyright is granted on a country-to-country basis and is subject to the principle of independence.[68] The TRIPS Agreement and the DSU do not expressly address the question of whether the suspension of copyright or other intellectual property right would permit exportation of the subject matter generated by third parties under the terms of the suspension.

Suspension of copyright protection in country A, pursuant to the principle of independence, will not suspend parallel copyright protection

[66] Virtually any system of digital rights management can be "broken." The process of digital rights management from the standpoint of copyright holders is to stay sufficiently ahead of the deconstruction technology to earn a return on content.

[67] This aspect of the problem was identified by Sisule Musungu's email of July 27, 2008.

[68] Berne Convention, Article 5(2).

in country B. Under ordinary circumstances, an importer in country B could not lawfully sell the local copyright holder's reproduced work from country A because the copyright in country B would remain valid and enforceable.

A complexity arises when the doctrine of exhaustion of rights is introduced, and this complexity must consider a certain debated issue in WTO law. That is, whether exhaustion takes place only with respect to goods placed on the market with the "consent" of the IPR holder, or whether lawful government action (such as the issuance of a compulsory license) may also establish the basis for international exhaustion.[69] A number of developed country courts have interpreted exhaustion as a function of "consent,"[70] and under the consent theory a copyrighted work placed on the market under a suspension regime would not be free of the copyright holder's parallel IP right in an importing country that has adopted international exhaustion.[71] If an importing country follows the "lawfully placed on the market" theory of exhaustion that does not require consent of the IP holder, then a parallel IP right in an importing country would be exhausted under a suspension regime. A copyrighted work, for example, put on the market in the suspending country could be imported in a country under international exhaustion without the consent of the parallel copyright holder.

To be sure, the foregoing discussion of exhaustion doctrine adds a layer of complexity to the suspension of concessions question that may be difficult for national legislatures and courts to navigate. The question might be resolved by an explicit provision in the authorization of suspension addressing whether it is intended to allow export of the products placed on the market under the suspension regime.

Perhaps more important from the suspending country standpoint, the extent of an open parallel export market would likely be taken into

[69] See, for example, Carlos M. Correa, "Bilateral Investment Agreements: Agents of New Global Standards for the Protection of Intellectual Property Rights?" GRAIN 2004.

[70] See, for example, case law from various jurisdictions cited in Frederick M. Abbott, "Second Report (Final) to the Committee on International Trade Law of the International Law Association on the Subject of the Exhaustion of Intellectual Property Rights and Parallel Importation," London, July 2000, 69th Conference International Law Association, rev. 1.1, available at: http://frederickabbott.com; and see Frederick M. Abbott, "The Doha Declaration on the TRIPS Agreement and Public Health: Lighting a Dark Corner at the WTO," *Journal of International Economic Law*, 5 (2002), discussing different perspectives on "consent" issue.

[71] The arbitration panel in *EC–Bananas III*, discussed above, refers to footnotes 13 and 14 of Article 51 of the TRIPS Agreement to suggest that, at least in the field of copyright "piracy," WTO members have recognized a doctrine of "consent."

account in determining the "level" of suspension of concessions. This is because the value of the IPR in the suspending country is based upon volume of sales that can be made by the right holder in consequence of its exclusive position. Whether sales are of products that are consumed/used locally or are of products ultimately consumed/used in foreign markets does not appear material to valuing the loss of right holder's exclusive interests. Parallel exports would reduce the market share in importing countries of the affected copyright holder from the complained-against country. Presumably this would be taken into account by an arbitrator when assessing the level of suspension.

(c) Patent

The level of suspension of patent rights should also be subject to reasonable calculation. The national identity of patent holders is among the information typically gathered by patent offices, and the extent to which patents are relied upon in respect to the sale of goods (or licensing) is something that should also be capable of approximation. Some countries, such as the United States, report data on the collection of technology licensing royalties as part of their trade statistics, implying that such data can be broken down on a country-by-country basis. Such data may be useful in approximating the value of IP rights that may be suspended. As discussed earlier, valuation of suspension of patent rights in pharmaceutical products for a national market should be a relatively straightforward matter. The price of a medicine under patent in the local market and the level of sales should be available from existing data sources. If generic products are available from a foreign source, prices should be available for these products. Some preliminary assumptions will need to be made about the extent to which demand for generic products can be substituted for patented products. If the government public health system is a purchaser, some fair degree of certainty could be introduced into that process. The estimated lost value of sales of the patented originator product would constitute the level of suspension.

Suspension of patent rights might conceptually take a wide variety of forms. Such a suspension could apply across the entire range of patents that have been granted by the suspending country, or alternatively could apply to specific patents or categories of patents. One advantage of patent right suspension is that the patent holder has presumably already disclosed the invention in a way that will allow third parties to practice the invention. There may nevertheless be additional technical information important to the effective use of the patented technology that has not been disclosed.

In addition, a suspending country may elect to suspend certain rights of the patent holder and not others. For example, rights to prevent importation, local sale (and offering), and use could be suspended without granting third parties the right to make a product in the domestic market.

Because suspension is intended to be temporary, the suspending country will presumably envisage reintroduction of patent protection when the suspension is terminated. Such reintroduction would need to address issues such as the right to sell off remaining inventories, continued use of patented products sold during suspension, and exemption from infringement claims for activities during the term of suspension.

Suspension of patent rights also raises the question of exportation. Patents are granted on a country-to-country basis and are subject to the principle of independence. Suspension of patent rights in country A does not suspend patent rights in countries B, C or D. Therefore, a product manufactured in country A under a suspension regime could not be imported in country B if there is a parallel patent in country B, unless country B adopts an international exhaustion regime that is not dependent upon the consent of the patent holder in country A to placement of the goods on the market in country A. As with respect to copyright, there is debate in the scholarly literature as to whether parallel importation may be based on "lawful placement of goods on the market" or only upon "consent."

While copyright protection attaches automatically across a wide range of countries pursuant to the Berne Convention, patents are often applied for and granted for particular inventions in a relative handful of countries only. This is somewhat industry-dependent as, for example, pharmaceutical enterprises are more likely to patent across a wider geographic scope than most other enterprises. Nevertheless, it is quite likely that for any invention placed on the market in a suspending country there will be a significant number of potential export destinations where parallel patents will not be in force. In such circumstances, there should not be a legal obstacle to exporting otherwise patented products produced or acquired under a suspension regime. Yet, the availability of export markets might well be taken into account in determining the "level" of suspension of concessions. If exported products reduce the market share in third countries of patent holders from the complained-against country, this would have an economic impact on the complained-against country.

A complained-against WTO member may object to the export of products on political grounds that suspension is only intended to be in favor of the country adopting the suspension, and not to provide the basis for a wider marketing of affected products. There is no express legal basis within the TRIPS Agreement or DSU for this position. As noted above, potential exports might be considered in determining the level of the suspension.

There is nothing that would prevent a complaining member from treating suspension of patent rights under Article 22 in a manner equivalent to issuing a compulsory license, but without providing for the payment of compensation, or reducing compensation, during the period of suspension. When the suspension ended, a local manufacturer might continue production under the terms of the compulsory license but with a royalty added. This might assist with a potential problem faced by local manufacturers under a patent suspension regime that the period of suspension is indeterminate and/or subject to rapid termination.

Plant variety protection falls under the category of patents in Section 5 of Part II of the TRIPS Agreement, specifically referenced in Article 27.3(b). A suspension may, therefore, involve rights established by plant breeder certificates or other *sui generis* forms of plant variety protection. If seeds or other reproductive materials with respect to a protective variety are available generically from outside the suspending country, those seeds or other reproductive materials could be imported, distributed, planted, harvested, and sold during the period of suspension. Similarly, if plant breeder rights or plant patent rights ordinarily prevent the replanting of seeds (that is, the exercise of a farmer's rights) within the suspending country, replanting and related activities could be authorized during the period of suspension.

(d) Trademark

Trademarks are signs or symbols that distinguish the goods or services of one enterprise from another in commerce. Trademarks are of a potentially indefinite duration, though in many jurisdictions validity is dependent upon continued use in commerce. Trademarks are subject to limited exception, and are also subject to fair use by third parties, such as in comparative advertising. In some countries, the grant of trademark rights is based exclusively on registration. In other countries, trademark rights may arise in "common law" from use in commerce, and also be subject to registration. A trademark permits its holder to prevent others from affixing it to goods or services in commerce and from using it in the course of trade.

The suspension of trademark rights might permit the manufacture and sale of goods bearing an unauthorized trademark. By licensing or allocating such rights a country suspending them could determine the extent to which local production (or importation) would be substituting for authorized supply by the affected trademark holders.

Because trademarks serve a consumer protection function by identifying the source, and implicitly the quality or characteristics, of goods and services, it is not obvious that suspension of trademark protection will provide a net benefit to consumers. Consumers that purchase goods or services with an unauthorized trademark may find that these are of inferior quality. This may also lead to long-term damage to the reputation of the trademark holder in the local market.

Conceptually, it may be possible to distinguish between unauthorized use of trademarks on goods that are essentially identical to those bearing trademarks, and those that are inferior and may deceive and/or harm the consumer. This would require assessment of the local producer market by the government, and presumably some form of active regulatory control.

To explain this further, allowing persons other than the trademark owner to provide goods identified by the trademark risks the situation where local consumers would be purchasing inferior products. In some cases, such products may be dangerous. Because products would not, in fact, be supplied by the trademark owner consumers would not have recourse against the trademark owner for damages that they may suffer. A WTO member considering authorization of third-party use of trademarks should consider carefully the types of goods or services for which those marks may be used, as well as whether its consumers would, in fact, benefit from the arrangement. The government authorizing third-party use of trademarks may provoke consumer dissatisfaction. In principle, the government might adopt a quality control and inspection program that would avoid the potential problems raised above, but this may entail significant government regulatory action.

Nevertheless, a decision as to whether to suspend trademark protection may be influenced by whether the suspending country already maintains a significant "counterfeit" market. If it does, and if consumers do not expect to purchase genuine trademarked goods under ordinary circumstances, the risk or harm from suspending trademark protection may be reduced. Moreover, a suspending country could view the suspension of trademarks owned by particular enterprises based in the complained-against country as a particularly strong form of retaliation and consider that the potential injury suffered by those enterprises would create heightened pressure within the complained-against member to bring its measures into conformity. Many large multinational corporations invest heavily in advertising of their trademarks, and suspension of rights in those trademarks might place considerable pressure on those companies and their home government.

Like copyrights and patents, trademarks are granted on a country-to-country basis and are subject to the rule of independence. Therefore, the suspension of trademark protection within one national (or regional) territory will not suspend such protection in other national territories. Exports of goods or services using unauthorized trademarks would potentially face legal action for infringement in third countries. As with copyright and trademarks, there would be an issue as to whether the importing country had adopted a rule of international exhaustion and whether that country recognized exhaustion based only on the "consent" of the trademark holder or on the wider basis of "lawfully placed on the market" (for example, under a suspension regime). If products produced under the trademark suspension regime were exported, this would affect the calculation of the level of suspension.

Although suspension of trademark protection is certainly permitted by Article 22.5, there may be reasonable policy grounds for a suspending country to choose a different sector in which to suspend TRIPS concessions.

(e) Geographical indication

A "geographical indication" (GI) is a name or symbol that associates a product with a place based upon attributes of products or upon the goodwill of producers of that place. Geographical indications are typically associated with food products, including wines and spirits. There is no limitation on the term of protection by geographical indication, provided that the producing region continues to maintain the requisite association. Only producers of the region associated with the geographical indication are entitled to use it on products. Because geographical indications are tied to specific producing regions they are not assignable or transferable for use on goods produced outside the identified producing region.

The suspension of protection by geographical indication would presumably permit local producers of the suspending country to label their products with a geographical indication notwithstanding that the product was produced locally. As with trademarks, because geographical indications are used to convey information to consumers about the quality or characteristics of goods, there are policy reasons why allowing unauthorized use of geographical indications may not be beneficial from a consumer welfare standpoint. That is, consumers purchasing goods with the expectation of a certain quality or characteristic may find that the locally produced version is not what they expected. Consumers may benefit from a lower price, but may ultimately be dissatisfied. This would not benefit governments authorizing third-party use of GIs. As with respect to trademarks, the government could impose some form of quality control mechanism with respect to third-party GI users to attempt to protect consumers, but this may entail significant regulatory costs.

As with trademarks, if enforcement of GIs in the suspending country has traditionally been weak, consumers may not have built up a strong expectation of association so suspension may not result in unanticipated quality deficiencies. Furthermore, not all goods identified by GIs are of a quality that is objectively distinct from comparable goods not protected by GIs. GIs not only protect objective differences, they may also be used to protect the "goodwill" of producers in the region. In some cases, authorizing third-party use of GIs may have limited effect on consumers.

As with respect to trademarks, if enterprises of the complained-against country are substantially reliant on protection by GI, the suspension of such protection may be a more powerful tool in the hands of the suspending country to encourage compliance with the ruling of the DSB.

(f) Industrial design protection

Suspension of protection for industrial design may be a useful mechanism for inducing compliance with DSB decisions. For example, with respect to textiles and clothing, manufacturers in the suspending country might be authorized to produce copies of designs from the complained-against member. This could be done without (or with) also authorizing use of the foreign trademark. In that way, consumers could be offered similar or identical textile products without (or with) encountering potentially misleading information concerning the producer of that product.

Of course, in developing a program of suspension the suspending country must take into account its own particular legislative mechanisms for protecting industrial design. As noted above, those mechanisms vary substantially among countries.

(g) Integrated circuit layout protection

The utility of suspension of integrated circuit (IC) layout-design may largely be limited to countries with a capacity to produce integrated circuits. IC production is highly capital and technology intensive. It would be very difficult to rapidly take advantage of a suspension regime absent an existing production base. It may also be difficult to sell ICs produced under a suspension regime for export – which is typically necessary to justify investment in IC production facilities – because holders of rights in import markets would likely seek to block imports of products incorporating ICs infringing rights in the import market. While the potential for suspension of rights in ICs exists, this is a subject matter area that is likely to be of interest to a limited number of potential suspending countries in a limited number of situations.

(h) Protection of undisclosed information

The TRIPS Agreement protects different types of so-called "undisclosed information." The first is information that would traditionally be understood as "trade secret" information. Trade secret information is commercially valuable information that an enterprise has taken reasonable steps to protect from public disclosure. The second is certain types of regulatory data with respect to pharmaceutical and agricultural chemical products.

Trade secret protection may be provided by various legal means. It may be covered by unfair competition law or by specific statute. Traditional trade secret protection is of indefinite duration. It remains available so long as its holder continues to take reasonable steps to keep protected information secret. Third parties who acquire trade secret information by dishonest means are subject to liability under trade secret protection law. Trade secret information that is publicly disclosed by its holder loses protection.

Based upon the definition of traditional trade secret protection, it is not an obvious candidate for the suspension of TRIPS concessions because the information subject to protection is, by definition, not publicly available. There would be little immediate gain to third parties from the suspension of trade secret protection because additional information would become available only in cases where the trade secret holder elected to disclose it, or if third parties were encouraged to engage in dishonest commercial practices (which seems an unlikely avenue for governments to encourage). Compare the situation of patent rights for which the relevant technology is disclosed in the patent application thereby allowing it to be used by third parties. An additional problem with suspending trade secret protection is that secret information that became public during a suspension regime could not be effectively "put back" upon termination of the suspension regime. Thus, calculation of the level of suspension would need to take into account the continuing nature of the effect upon the trade secret holder.

Of substantially greater potential utility under a suspension regime is undisclosed pharmaceutical and agricultural chemical regulatory data with respect to new chemical entities submitted to regulatory authorities in the course of seeking approval for marketing. In a number of countries, such regulatory data is protected by "exclusive marketing rights" granted to the originators of the data. Such exclusive marketing rights prevent third parties from registering and marketing "generic" versions of the same chemical entities during the term of protection. That term of protection tends to range from five to ten years depending on the country. It is important to note that the TRIPS Agreement, at Article 39.3, does *not* require a government to adopt marketing exclusivity to protect pharmaceutical and agricultural regulatory data. The obligation is to prevent against "unfair commercial use" of the data.

If regulatory data is not protected by exclusive marketing rights, but is more generally protected against unfair commercial use, it may nevertheless be difficult for generic producers to register pharmaceutical or agricultural chemical products without reference to the information submitted by the originator to the regulatory authority depending upon the protection scheme used in the subject country.

Suspension of regulatory data protection would allow generic producers to register and market pharmaceutical and/or agricultural chemical products without challenge from the originator based on such data. It is important to note that a product protected by regulatory data protection may also be protected by patent. Therefore, in deciding upon a suspension regime, governments must consider both the patent situation and the regulatory data protection situation when pharmaceuticals and agricultural chemicals are at issue.

Protection of regulatory data takes place on a country-to-country basis. If a pharmaceutical or agricultural product is registered in the suspending country, there is no assurance that such product may be registered in third countries where protection may remain in force. This will affect assessments of export potential.

A significant issue concerning suspension of data protection with respect to pharmaceuticals and agricultural chemicals is how newly registered products (that is, taking advantage of the suspension) would be treated when the suspension is terminated. Under a marketing exclusivity regime, originators may argue that restoration of protection should foreclose further marketing and sale of the newly registered products. If there is no marketing exclusivity rule as such, but rather only protection against use of data for registration purposes, that issue presumably should not arise since a third-party pharmaceutical or agricultural chemical product would already be registered. The suspending government will need to address the question of rights upon termination of the suspension, particularly in respect of marketing exclusivity. In this regard, it is essential to recognize that marketing exclusivity is not required by the TRIPS Agreement, so that restoration of marketing exclusivity likewise is not required upon termination of a suspension regime. A suspending government might well adopt a new rule exempting previously approved products from marketing exclusivity without contravening TRIPS obligations. This is because third parties that had registered generic versions of pharmaceuticals or agricultural chemicals would not again be seeking to rely on undisclosed regulatory data.

(i) Enforcement

One potentially effective route for the suspension of concessions under the TRIPS Agreement is to suspend the right of IP holders to initiate enforcement proceedings during the pendency of the suspension, and to suspend rights to initiate proceedings subsequent to the suspension with respect to activities that had taken place during the suspension. By suspending enforcement without technically suspending the underlying IP rights, the government might simplify the suspension rules. Termination of the suspension would reinstate rights to enforce, but exclude activities taking place during the term of the suspension. The suspension of enforcement rights could be prescribed for a limited set of IP rights, or for a limited set of remedies.

With respect to limiting IP rights, suspension of enforcement could, for example, be prescribed with respect to patents and regulatory data protection. The suspending member could provide that no injunctions would be available during the term of the suspension, and that no compensation could be claimed either during or after the suspension of activities during the suspension. In the United States, as an illustration, owners of patents are precluded from obtaining injunctions against the government for unauthorized use of their patents.[72] This is essentially a government use licensing mechanism, with a specialized court determining a royalty. In the suspension context there may be no royalty requirement.[73]

Suspension of enforcement rights may raise some interesting questions regarding exhaustion. An IP right holder might argue that because the IP right itself has not been suspended, a first sale by a third party is not a "lawful" placing on the market and, therefore, does not constitute the basis for exhaustion. This is a difficult conceptual argument to address. If an action is technically prohibited, but liability is excused, is that action lawful (because liability does not attach) or unlawful (because it is technically prohibited)? Plausible arguments can be made for both questions. The government might resolve the matter by specifying an outcome in the suspension legislation.

Suspension of enforcement would also require valuation. Presumably this would follow the same lines as suspension of the underlying IP rights.

(j) Acquisition and maintenance of IP

Part IV of the TRIPS Agreement is established by Article 22.3(f)(iii) as a sector from the standpoint of suspension. Part IV addresses "Acquisition and Maintenance of Intellectual Property Rights and Related *Inter-Partes* Procedures."

The principal obligation of members under Part IV is to provide for the grant and/or registration of IP rights within a reasonable period of time,

[72] Instead, the patent holder is allowed to seek compensation before a specialized court for the government's use of the patents.

[73] If the government suspends IP rights in copyright or trademarks, it may be useful to simultaneously suspend criminal enforcement penalties for copyright piracy and/or trademark infringement on a commercial scale because the type of activity that the government is allowing might, under ordinary circumstances, constitute criminal activity. Although a private operator under a suspension regime presumably would not evidence the requisite "intent" to violate criminal law, it would nonetheless avoid confusion to suspend penalties along with related IP rights.

in a fair and equitable way, and without unnecessary cost or complexity, consistent with relevant IP rules.

Suspension of Part IV obligations might entail preventing or delaying applications for the grant and/or registration of IP rights during the suspension period. If, for example, inventors were prevented from filing patent applications, or having those applications processed, during a period of suspension, this would delay whatever exclusive rights might be obtained under the patent. By allowing the filing, but suspending processing, the suspending member might avoid problems such as loss of priority for the patent applicant. This is an intriguing route for a potential suspending member to induce compliance, particularly since it would affect only "future interests" in IP rights, and not previously granted rights.[74] It may be difficult to calculate precisely the value of this form of suspension, but presumably it could be based upon historic trends in patenting and a general valuation of patent rights.

A similar alternative approach might involve imposing additional fees or taxes in respect of registrations and/or renewals of IP registrations for nationals of the WTO member against which suspension is undertaken. This would essentially involve a suspension of the national treatment obligation with respect to IP application and maintenance. It might, however, be difficult to engage in "effective" cross-retaliation through this mechanism because it may not yield significant amounts of revenue (at least undertaken in isolation).

7 Practical considerations for developing countries regarding suspension of concessions under the TRIPS Agreement

The foregoing legal and policy analysis indicates that there is a range of legal options available to governments considering the suspension of concessions under the TRIPS Agreement in the context of cross-retaliation. It also suggests that some options may be preferable to others in terms of identifying the level of suspension and in avoiding legal conflicts.

[74] Third parties might find disclosure of the information otherwise included in a patent application from other countries so that use could be made of the inventions during the suspension period. Or, the suspending government might publish patent applications according to its ordinary schedule, but delay further processing of applications.

(a) *National legislation and constitutional concerns*

Assuming that a government has implemented TRIPS obligations in domestic/national intellectual property law, it will be necessary in some cases for the national legislature to adopt enabling legislation to authorize or implement a suspension of TRIPS concessions. National law will ordinarily prescribe the terms and conditions of the grant and termination of IPRs, as well as the conditions for the exercise of rights. Most governments have not included in general IP legislation a grant of authority to the executive to suspend rights or alter the conditions of exercise on the basis of retaliation authorized by the WTO DSB. Conceptually such authorization might be found in trade implementation authority granted to the executive, but because IPRs include a domestic law aspect,[75] this is somewhat less likely to have been expressly built in to trade authority than in other implementation areas.

IPRs holders from the country against which retaliation is proposed may object to "discriminatory" changes to domestic intellectual property rules on constitutional grounds. However, most national constitutions do not accord equivalent rights to foreign nationals as to local nationals.[76] An obligation to treat foreign IPRs holders on the same basis as local IPRs holders most likely arises from international treaty commitments, and not from the national constitution. Since the WTO DSB authorization effectively waives national and MFN obligations under the WTO agreements, the national legislature would not be contravening international obligations by differential treatment of nationals of the suspending country. This applies to obligations under the WIPO conventions based upon the analysis provided earlier in this chapter. That is, because the country against which the suspension is proposed will have expressly consented to the suspension of concessions pursuant to the WTO agreements, it will effectively have waived any claim under corresponding commitments at the multilateral level.

There are mechanisms based upon the use of pre-existing IPRs legislation for eliminating or minimizing the requirements for new legislative

[75] See the decision of the European Court of Justice in *Re The Uruguay Round Treaties* (Opinion 1/94), [1995] 1 C.M.L.R. 205, November 15, 1994.

[76] There is no uniform rule regarding whether local incorporation of a legal entity will entitle a foreign national owner to treatment as a domestic person from a constitutional protection standpoint. Courts may grant domestic constitutional protection to a locally incorporated enterprise, or they may treat the foreign beneficial owner of the local enterprise as the real party in interest and apply the constitutional treatment accorded to aliens. This may depend upon the extent of control exercised from abroad.

action. Virtually all governments have enacted legislation that authorizes the grant of compulsory and/or government use licenses in respect of patents. The TRIPS Agreement regulates such licensing in its Article 31 that, as confirmed by the Doha Declaration on the TRIPS Agreement and Public Health, does not restrict the grounds upon which compulsory patent licenses may be granted. A government seeking to suspend TRIPS obligations could do so by granting government use or compulsory licenses under the terms of its patent legislation, using as grounds the "public interest" in establishing compliance with trade agreements, or a related ground conforming to national legislation. Because the requirement to pay "adequate remuneration" under the TRIPS Agreement Article 31(h) is assessed with reference to "the circumstances of each case, taking into account the economic value of the authorization,"[77] and because the circumstances of suspension of concessions cases would entail the absence of a remuneration payment (that is, hypothetical royalties would offset the nullification or impairment), licenses could be granted on a royalty-free basis. For that matter, governments might decide to pay a reduced royalty as a matter of discretion.

Article 30 of the TRIPS Agreement permits the grant of "limited exceptions" to the rights of patent holders. A WTO member might also make use of limited exceptions existing under national patent law in suspending concessions, though this route may not provide as clear a path as the Article 31 route from the standpoint of pre-existing legislation.

The IPRs legislation of each WTO member is likely to contain other express exceptions or compulsory licensing provisions with respect to different fields of activity. Many countries provide for compulsory licensing with respect to broadcasts of copyrighted media content contingent upon the payment of equitable remuneration. Compulsory licensing of broadcasts and musical composition is expressly authorized by the Berne Convention, Articles 11*bis*(2) and 13(1). As with respect to compulsory licensing of patents under the TRIPS Agreement, the Berne Convention obligation with respect to equitable remuneration would take into account the suspension of concessions context. Equitable remuneration in the context of authorized suspension of rights may be quite limited.

Trademark rights are typically subject to "fair use" and other "limited exceptions" as also authorized under the TRIPS Agreement. It seems somewhat less likely that a government will have pre-existing trademark exception legislation that would expressly encompass the type of

[77] TRIPS Agreement, Article 31(h).

suspension that might be contemplated under a DSB authorization. This is partly because Article 21 of the TRIPS Agreement expressly precludes compulsory licensing of trademarks. The national legislature might declare that for the duration of the suspension third-party use of a trademark will be deemed "fair use," but this would presumably require new legislation.

It would be a matter for each government to examine national IPRs legislation with respect to industrial design, geographical indication, IC layout-design and trade secret rights to determine whether there is pre-existing legislative authority for suspension of rights in the nature, for example, of compulsory licensing provisions.

A practical area of promise also lies in legislation regarding protection of regulatory data submitted with respect to pharmaceutical and/or agricultural chemical products. Such legislation may include authority of the government to make use of, or authorize use of, regulatory data for purposes that do not constitute "unfair commercial use" (which is the standard adopted in Article 39.3 of the TRIPS Agreement). For example, such authority may be included within the scope of authority to grant compulsory patent licenses as a matter of assuring that regulatory approval may also be granted. National legislation varies considerably regarding the nature of regulatory data protection, making it difficult to generalize as to the authority that may be included in pre-existing legislation. Nonetheless, governments considering the suspension of rights with respect to regulatory data may well examine pre-existing legislation for avenues of authority prior to proposing new legislation.

The executive is ordinarily responsible for the enforcement of criminal law, including IP law. The executive may be able to issue a directive under pre-existing legislation that suspends criminal prosecution of IP violators during the term of the suspension of TRIPS concessions. However, this is likely to raise difficult constitutional issues in terms of executive versus legislative authority. Similarly, the executive could undertake under existing authority (that is, without new legislation) to suspend processing of patent applications during the term of a suspension of concessions. This may be somewhat less likely to raise constitutional separation of powers issues, but could nevertheless be problematic.[78]

[78] For example, the *India–Mailbox* case decided by the WTO Appellate Body substantially involved in a question of allocation of authority to regulate patents within the Indian constitutional framework (*India–Patent Protection for Pharmaceutical and Agricultural Products*, AB-1997–5, WT/DS50/AB/R, December 15, 1997, DSR 1998:I, 9).

(b) *Ordinary regulation and takings*

As previously discussed, neither national constitutions nor international law are likely to pose a genuine legal impediment to the suspension of TRIPS concessions in light of the fact that such suspensions will have been authorized by the WTO DSB under an agreed-upon set of international legal rules. Nonetheless, this does not mean that governments contemplating suspension of TRIPS concessions should not attempt, as a matter of operational efficiency, to formulate such suspensions in ways that are less likely to provoke constitutional challenges.

Most constitutional systems differentiate between government "takings" of property and government "regulation" of property. A taking is generally understood involve a permanent transfer to the government or other third-party owner. However, many constitutional systems also recognize the concept of a "regulatory taking." A regulatory taking may occur when restrictions on the use of property imposed by the government are sufficiently severe that effective use of the property is precluded, thereby constituting a taking in all but name and form. Much ordinary government regulation, on the other hand, restricts the uses that may be made of property, whether real, movable or intangible. Real property is typically "zoned" for specific types of uses, such as "commercial" or "residential," and within those categories a myriad of government regulations apply to the uses.

It is beyond the practical scope of this chapter to assess as a matter of comparative national/constitutional law where the border will be between government "taking" and ordinary government "regulation." However, the suggestion made here is that in implementing a "suspension" regime that is inherently intended to be transitory, the government should avoid steps that would be construed as "permanent takings."

First, this may be accomplished by expressly limiting the duration of the suspension, though it might be subject to renewal based on external events. Regulatory restrictions that are transitory are less likely to be considered "takings" as beneficial use of the property is intended to revert to its holder.

Second, suspension of a limited number of the "panoply" of IP rights is less likely to constitute regulatory taking. Effective use of the property would not be eliminated. Thus, for example, suspension of rights in films might be limited to the reproduction of DVDs, while copyright holders maintain the right of broadcast and public showing of the films (or vice versa).

Third, a suspension may be structured as an assessment against royalties or licensing fees with a limited duration. In principle, this assessment could be set at less than 100 per cent of the subject royalties, further limiting the potential for characterization as a regulatory taking.

Fourth, compulsory and government use licensing authorizes third-party use, while allowing the right holder to continue making use of its protected subject matter. The government could, though it need not, limit the number of licensees or the extent of licensed use with respect to relevant subject matter. This would further limit the characteristics of "taking." If the government elected to pay a minimal royalty or use fee, this would further erode any argument concerning "taking."

Fifth, temporary limitations on the enforcement of IPRs may be difficult to characterize as "regulatory taking" because the use of the IPR content by its owner is not restricted. A temporary interference with a right to enforce property rights is a limited measure.

(c) Exports and the Internet

A suspension of concessions regime is intended to be temporary. Revenues from exports would increase the level of economic benefit from the suspension, thereby promoting compliance and offsetting economic injury to the suspending country. There are, however, legal and practical obstacles to using a suspension regime as an export platform. While those obstacles might be addressed in a satisfactory way over a period of time, a government contemplating suspension might be better served by focusing on domestic market opportunities.

The principal legal obstacle to exports, as elaborated earlier, is that IPRs as a general proposition are granted and enforced on a country-to-country basis. Suspension of rights in the exporting country will not suspend rights in the importing country. There may not be corresponding or parallel IPRs in the importing country, or the importing country may have adopted a regime of international exhaustion of rights which *may* recognize exhaustion based on "lawful" placement on the market as opposed to "consent." In such cases exports and imports would be legal under a suspension regime, though the country against which the suspension is imposed may object politically on grounds that it is not the intention of a suspension regime to interfere with market opportunities outside the country imposing the suspension. While these concerns could be addressed by the suspending country it is not so clear that the complexities introduced by exports under the suspension regime will justify the inefficiency costs associated with addressing them.

Revenues from exports would need to be counted as part of the value of the suspension. It might be preferable on policy grounds to obtain the economic and social welfare gains from suspension from domestic activity.

As a practical matter, except in limited cases, it will be difficult for industry to establish itself in the export sector in the limited and uncertain period of time provided under a suspension regime. Capital investment based upon a regime that is subject to termination on short notice may not be advisable.

This is not to suggest that in specific cases suspension of TRIPS concessions that may involve exports will not be warranted and/or necessary to accomplish the objective of inducing compliance. It is, however, to suggest that a government contemplating routes for suspension should consider the legal and practical issues associated with exports carefully.

The Internet has had a profound effect on almost all areas of business activity. The Internet would certainly be relevant to most or all suspension regimes involving copyright subject matter that typically is subject to reproduction and digital transmission. In order to establish the level of suspension in many areas regulated by copyright, a government will probably need to adopt some form of digital rights management (DRM) control that can "meter" the use of copyrighted material. Here, of course, suspending governments will face the same problems faced by the copyright-dependent industries, namely that DRM controls are subject to circumvention. It is an interesting question whether a government metering otherwise copyright-protected materials under a suspension regime would be liable for unauthorized use of those materials. There is no obvious WTO precedent for addressing that question.

In this regard, a suspending country might attempt to avoid difficulties by limiting the suspension to activities that are less prone to circumvention. This could include television broadcast of copyrighted works, theater showings of copyrighted works, reproduction of books, physical reproduction of DVDs and/or compact discs (possibly) incorporating DRM protection, and radio broadcasts of copyrighted works. Another way to avoid difficulties with regard to circumvention would be to use a suspension mechanism involving assessment against licensing fees or royalties that would leave the initial matter of collection in the hands of the copyright holder. The suspending country would not play a role in production and distribution of the expressive work, and so would not be responsible with respect to circumvention. By assessing at less than 100 per cent of royalties or licensing fees otherwise payable, the suspending country would leave copyright holders with an incentive to collect payment.

(d) *Social welfare and inducing compliance*

The suspending country government should well consider the social welfare consequences of its actions. A government might choose to address public health issues through the mechanism of a suspension, such as by suspending patent protection for pharmaceutical products that are used to address significant public health concerns. Often times, a pharmaceutical product will be patented within a prospective importing country, but not in some countries from which exports may be available. A suspending country might fairly readily issue compulsory licenses for the importation of generic pharmaceutical products that could be substituted for patented products already on its market. This is a context in which there would be reasonable certainty in valuing the suspension of concessions because the price and volume of patented products on the market is information which is generally available from public or private data sources, and governments should be able to calculate the savings that can, and do, accrue from substituting imported generic products. The government could direct customs authorities to specifically track imports of generic pharmaceutical products during the period of suspension should they not already do so.

The suspension of plant patent or *sui generis* plant variety protection rights may also have an important positive social welfare impact. As noted earlier, a suspending country that did not otherwise permit the exercise of farmers' replanting rights could allow this during the suspension. If seed or plant varieties are ordinarily protected by patent or breeders' rights, but are available for import from a country that does not provide equivalent protection, importation and related uses during the suspension term may be beneficial (recognizing that the suspension would cover harvesting and sale of crops).

A government may also improve social welfare by making available entertainment-related products at lower cost through copyright suspension. It is not unreasonable to suppose that such "making available" would be well received by people within the country, thus increasing support for government policy. The same might be said for making available copies of popular clothing products.

It is also important to recall that a main purpose of suspension of concessions is to induce compliance by the country against which the suspension is imposed. It is important, therefore, to adopt a suspension regime that will affect the political constituencies (that is, private operators) that will exert pressure to bring the complained-against country into compliance. The principal proponents of the TRIPS Agreement were the originator pharmaceutical industry and the copyright/entertainment industry. These two sectors remain the most powerful political constituencies demanding strong intellectual property protection. It is fair to assume that retaliatory measures addressing either of those industry sectors will generate political pressure within the affected country.

At the same time, it is as well to recognize that those industries may not limit political counterpressure to seeking compliance by their governments with WTO obligations. They may urge their home government to make strong diplomatic representations, and to exert economic pressure. It is very important for WTO members contemplating suspension to be able to address this pressure.

(e) *Politics, asymmetry, and the DSU*

From a legal standpoint, suspension of TRIPS concessions in the context of cross-retaliation is certainly manageable. While suspending concessions on trade in goods by imposing increased tariffs on imported goods may be less complicated, suspending concessions on trade in services would present its own potentially complex picture. In essence, the incorporation of the "new area" agreements of GATS and TRIPS as a consequence of the Uruguay Round negotiations introduced a more complex era in dispute settlement and retaliation. That is a fact of "modern" trade life.

For many developing countries, as a consequence of asymmetry in economic power, suspension of concessions in TRIPS may represent the only practical mechanism for inducing compliance by developed countries with WTO obligations. For many developing countries, other routes of suspension are likely to cause more harm than good from an economic standpoint.

Yet experience in the field of public health and the TRIPS Agreement teaches that legal rights are only part of the suspension equation. The main obstacle developing countries will face with regard to cross-retaliation in TRIPS is political. Industries reliant on intellectual property rights are willing to invest heavily in government lobbying and media propaganda campaigns. Although intellectual property is a creature of industrial policy, just as are tariffs and services regulation, the IP-dependent industries have historically been able to persuade governments and media outlets that any interference with IP rights is equivalent to "theft," implying criminal intent. Raising tariffs may equally interfere with the business interests of private operators by restricting market access, but private operators have not been able to equate increased tariffs with "theft of trading rights."

A government proposing a suspension regime in TRIPS must prepare itself for counterpressure. The government might well prepare press releases and diplomatic replies in advance. The government proposing the suspension should not be under the illusion that it will have the power to control external portrayal of its actions. It must be prepared to move forward in the face of external criticism and, perhaps, internal pressure from multinational corporations. This is the realistic way forward in the present international environment.

23

Preliminary thoughts on WTO retaliation in the services sector

ARTHUR E. APPLETON*

1 Introduction

As of November 2008 there have been seventeen Article 22.6 arbitrations involving ten distinct WTO disputes. The great majority of these arbitrations were in the goods sector. The Dispute Settlement Body (DSB) has authorised suspension of concessions related to services in one case[1] and intellectual property rights in two cases.[2] *EC–Bananas III (Ecuador)* involved trade in both goods and services, and the complaining party won the right to suspend GATT, GATS and TRIPs commitments.[3] *US–Gambling* dealt also with trade in services, and the complaining party

* Arthur E. Appleton, J.D., Ph.D., Partner, Appleton Luff – International Lawyers. This chapter is an abridged version of a work commissioned by the International Centre for Trade and Sustainable Development (ICTSD) with support from the Hewlett Foundation, SIDA and DGIS. The full paper is available in A. Appleton, 'Suspension of Concessions in the Services Sector: Legal, Technical and Economic Problems', ICTSD Dispute Settlement and Legal Aspects of International Trade, Issue Paper No. 7, March 2009, International Centre for Trade and Sustainable Development, Geneva, Switzerland. The author appreciates ICTSD's agreement to allow publication of an abridged version. The author gratefully acknowledges the contribution of Marcia Aribela de Lima Gomes Pereira for her valuable research and editing assistance. The author also appreciates comments provided by Joost Pauwelyn, Niall Meagher, Johannes Bernabe, Sheila Sabune and Umberto Celli Jr, on an earlier draft. Any errors that remain are the author's alone.

[1] *EC–Regime for the Importation, Sale and Distribution of Bananas*, Recourse to Arbitration by the European Communities under Article 22.6 of the DSU, WT/DS27/ARB/ECU, 24 March 2000, DSR 2000:V, 2237 (*EC–Bananas III (Ecuador)*).

[2] *EC–Bananas III (Ecuador)* and *US–Measures Affecting the Cross-Border Supply of Gambling and Betting Services*, Recourse to Arbitration by the United States under Article 22.6 of the DSU, Decision by the arbitrator, WT/DS285/ARB, 21 December 2007 (*US–Gambling*).

[3] *EC–Bananas III (Ecuador)*, para. 173.

won the right to suspend TRIPs commitments.[4] At the time of writing (end of 2008) Brazil is again threatening cross-retaliation in *US–Cotton* under the GATS and TRIPs agreements.[5]

There is little experience with GATS retaliation and cross-retaliation and few articles have discussed this subject. This explains the cautious title of this chapter. Why have there not been more Article 22.6 arbitrations involving suspension of GATS concessions and other obligations? In part, this reflects the small number of GATS disputes, and in part this is because many developing countries made few commitments in the services sector. There may also be other reasons why there have not been more disputes involving GATS suspensions. This chapter examines the viability of retaliation and cross-retaliation in the services sector, and the extent to which they might provide a means to induce compliance with DSB decisions.

2 Summary of the legal framework

Article 22.3 of the DSU sets forth the general rules applicable to suspension of concessions, including the rules applicable to suspension of concessions in the services sector.[6] It provides 'a sequence of steps towards WTO-consistent suspension of concessions or other obligations'.[7] Article 22.4 sets forth an additional rule (equivalence) that must be followed for all suspensions of concessions or other obligations. The following rules apply:

(1) The 'complaining party should first seek to suspend concessions or other obligations with respect to the same sector(s) as that in which the panel or Appellate Body has found a violation or other nullification or impairment' (retaliation).[8]
(2) If suspension of concessions or other obligations in the same sector is not 'practicable or effective', the complaining party may seek 'to suspend concessions or other obligations in other sectors under the same agreement'.[9]

[4] *US–Gambling*, para. 6.1.

[5] *US–Subsidies on Upland Cotton*, WT/DS267, DSR 2005:I, 3 (*US–Cotton*); see 'Brazil to Seek US$4 Billion in Sanctions against US', vol. 12 *Bridges*, No. 23, 25 June 2008, available at: http://ictsd.net/i/news/bridgesweekly/12271/.

[6] Article 22.3 of the DSU should be read together with Article XXIII:2 of the GATS which applies the 'serious enough' standard to retaliation.

[7] *US–Gambling*, para. 4.19, quoting *EC–Bananas III (Ecuador)*, para 55.

[8] Article 22.3(a) of the DSU.

[9] Article 22.3(b) of the DSU.

(3) If suspension in other sectors under the same agreement is not 'practicable or effective', and the circumstances are 'serious enough', the complaining party 'may seek to suspend concessions or other obligations under another covered agreement' (cross-retaliation).[10]
(4) In applying the above principles, a complaining party must consider:
  (i) the trade in the sector or under the agreement under which the panel or Appellate Body has found a violation or other nullification or impairment, and the importance of such trade to that party;[11] and
  (ii) the broader economic elements related to the nullification or impairment and the broader economic consequences of the suspension of concessions or other obligations.[12]
(5) The level of suspension of concessions or other obligations must be 'equivalent to the level of the nullification or impairment'.[13]

Article 22.6 provides for arbitration if the member concerned: (1) objects to the level of suspension proposed, or (2) claims the principles and procedures in Article 22.3 have not been followed. In addition to judging claims that the principles and procedures of Article 22.3 have not been followed, the arbitrators are permitted to establish 'if the proposed suspension of concessions or other obligations is allowed under the covered agreement'.[14] Although the arbitrators are required to examine if the level of suspension (the 'trade effect') is 'equivalent' to the level of nullification or impairment, the arbitrators are not permitted to examine 'the nature of the concessions or other obligations to be suspended'.[15]

3 Relevant GATS terminology

3.1 *'Sectors' and 'agreements'*

Article 22.3(a) expresses the preference for suspension of concessions or other obligations in the same sector under the same agreement. Article 22.3(b) provides that if suspension in the same sector is not 'practicable or effective', a complaining party may seek to suspend concessions in another sector under the same agreement. Article 22.3(c) provides for suspension of concessions or other obligations under another

[10] Article 22.3(c) of the DSU. [11] Article 22.3(d)(i) of the DSU.
[12] Article 22.3(d)(ii) of the DSU. [13] Article 22.4 of the DSU.
[14] Article 22.7 of the DSU. [15] Article 22.7 of the DSU.

agreement (cross-retaliation) if suspension under the same agreement is not practicable or effective and the circumstances are 'serious enough'. The definitions of the terms 'sector' and 'agreement' appear in Article 22.3(f) and (g) of the DSU. With respect to services, 'sector' means 'a principal sector as identified in the current "Services Sectoral Classification List"' which sets forth twelve distinct sectors.[16] With respect to services, the term 'agreement' means the GATS.[17]

In a dispute involving trade in services, a complaining party must first seek to suspend GATS concessions or other obligations in the same service sector in which a panel or the Appellate Body has found a WTO violation or other nullification or impairment (retaliation).[18] Only if suspension in the same service sector would not be 'practicable or effective', and if the circumstances are 'serious enough',[19] may a complaining party seek to suspend concessions in another GATS sector pursuant to Article 22.3(b). If suspension under the GATS would not be practicable or effective, and the circumstances are serious enough, a complaining party may seek suspension under another 'agreement' pursuant to Article 22.3(c).

When a dispute arises under another 'agreement',[20] Article 22 of the DSU permits a suspension in the services sector (cross-retaliation) only when a suspension under the agreement where the violation or other nullification or impairment occurred is (1) not practicable or effective, (2) the circumstances are serious enough, and (3) the equivalence requirement is met.

[16] The 'Services Sectoral Classification List' identifies twelve service sectors: (1) business services; (2) communication services; (3) construction and related engineering services; (4) distribution services; (5) educational services; (6) environmental services; (7) financial services; (8) health-related and social services; (9) tourism and travel-related services; (10) recreational, cultural and sporting services; (11) transport services; and (12) other services not included elsewhere.

The first eleven sectors are the principal sectors. They are divided into subsectors. The Services Sectoral Classification List also provides the corresponding Central Product Classification (CPC) code used by the United Nations Statistics Division to classify goods and services. See the Services Sectoral Classification List, WTO Document (MTN.GNS/W/120). See also http://unstats.un.org/unsd/cr/registry/regcst.asp?Cl=16 for the CPC Codes.

[17] Article 22.3(f)(ii).

[18] A complaining party should refer initially to the Services Sectoral Classification List to determine whether a suspension is in the same sector. Not all members have based their schedules on the Services Sectoral Classification List. A complaining party must exercise care when identifying concessions or other obligations for suspension.

[19] Article XXIII.2 of the GATS imposes an additional requirement that the circumstances be 'serious enough' before the suspension of GATS 'obligations and specific commitments' in accordance with Article 22 of the DSU.

[20] An agreement other than the GATS as defined in Article 22.3(g) of the DSU.

3.2 'Concessions' and 'other obligations'

Article 22.2 of the DSU permits a complaining party to ask the DSB for authorisation to suspend 'concessions or other obligations' when a member fails to bring a WTO-inconsistent measure into conformity with a covered agreement.[21] The GATS distinguishes between 'General Obligations and Disciplines' (Part II of GATS) and 'Specific Commitments' (Part III of GATS). General obligations and disciplines include the most-favoured-nation (MFN) obligation. General obligations are applicable regardless of whether a member has scheduled commitments in specific service sectors. Specific commitments are comprised of market access limitations, national treatment limitations and additional commitments. Specific commitments apply only when a member makes a commitment in a service sector or subsector.

Members may schedule specific commitments in each of the twelve service sectors and in a large number of subsectors. 'Specific commitments' are scheduled based on how a service is delivered. The term 'modes of supply' refers to the distinct manner in which a particular service is delivered.

3.3 Modes of supply

The GATS distinguishes between four modes of supply:

- Mode 1 – cross-border supply
- Mode 2 – consumption abroad
- Mode 3 – commercial presence
- Mode 4 – presence of natural persons.

The four modes of supply are described in greater detail in section 4 where the suspension of specific commitments is considered in each mode.

The following table reflects that commitments in Modes 1 and 2 directly affect the service consumer and that commitments in Modes 3 and 4 directly affect the service supplier.[22]

[21] Article XXIII:2 of the GATS allows the DSB to authorise a member to suspend 'obligations and specific commitments in accordance with Article 22 of the DSU'. Both provisions use similar but not identical terminology.

[22] This table is adapted from a similar table that appears in Guidelines for the Scheduling of Specific Commitments under the General Agreement on Trade in Services (GATS), adopted by the Council for Trade in Services on 23 March 2001, S/L/92 (28 March 2001), 9.

Table 23.1. *Modes of supply*

Mode of supply	Supplier presence	Other criteria
Cross-border supply (Mode 1)	Service supplier *not present* within the territory of the member making commitments	Service delivered *within* the territory of the member making commitments, from the territory of another member
Consumption abroad (Mode 2)		Service delivered *outside* the territory of the member making commitments, in the territory of another member, to a service consumer or the goods of the member
Commercial presence (Mode 3)	Service supplier *present* within the territory of the member making commitments	Service delivered within the territory of the member making commitments, through the commercial presence of the supplier
Presence of natural person (Mode 4)		Service delivered within the territory of the member making commitments, with supplier present as a *natural* person

In Modes 1 and 2, the service supplier is not present in the territory of the member making commitments, while in Modes 3 and 4 the service supplier is present. Many services are capable of being delivered in more than one mode of supply. For example, an accounting firm in member A can provide accountancy services to a client in member B by email (Mode 1), by receiving the client in its office in member A (Mode 2), by constructing an office in member B (Mode 3) or by travelling to member B (Mode 4). Predicting how retaliation and cross-retaliation might work requires an understanding of the specific commitments.

3.4 *Scheduling specific commitments*

The GATS provides for three forms of 'specific commitments':

- *Market access limitations*: market access is provided for in Article XVI of the GATS and is scheduled in column 2 of the service schedules. Article XVI:1 contains an MFN obligation based on the conditions specified in a member's schedule. Article XVI:2 provides an *exhaustive* list of market access measures (quantitative restrictions, foreign capital restrictions and restrictions on the type of legal entity) which must be scheduled if they are to be maintained by a member. Importantly, although Article XVI provides an exhaustive list, it does not include all market access measures that could restrict market access. In particular, fiscal measures are not covered.[23]
- *National treatment limitations*: national treatment is provided for in Article XVII of the GATS and is scheduled in column 3 of the service schedules. Measures that are inconsistent with both the market access rules in Article XVI and the national treatment rules in Article XVII are inscribed in column 2.[24] National treatment limitations result in less favourable treatment for foreign services or service suppliers over domestic services and domestic service suppliers. Article XVII does not provide an 'exhaustive list' of national treatment limitations. Examples of national treatment measures drawn from member schedules are set forth in the 'Scheduling Guidelines' and include certain tax and financial measures, nationality and residency requirements, technology transfer and training requirements and property ownership requirements.[25]
- *Additional commitments*: the possibility of a member assuming additional commitments is provided for in Article XVIII of the GATS. Additional commitments are scheduled in column 4 of the service schedules. They relate to qualifications, technical standards, licensing requirements or procedures and domestic regulations consistent with Article VI. They are expressed in the member schedule as 'undertakings' and *not* 'limitations',[26] with the result that they are less relevant for

[23] See A. Mattoo, 'National Treatment in the GATS: Corner-stone or Pandora's Box' (22 January 1997), available at: www.wto.org/english/res_E/reser_E/tisd-96-02.doc.

[24] Article XX of the GATS.

[25] Guidelines for the Scheduling of Specific Commitments under the General Agreement on Trade in Services (GATS), adopted by the Council for Trade in Services on 23 March 2001, S/L/92 (28 March 2001), 5–6, 16–18.

[26] Guidelines for the Scheduling of Specific Commitments under the General Agreement on Trade in Services (GATS), adopted by the Council for Trade in Services on 23 March

this chapter. An example would be when a member assumes additional commitments pursuant to the telecommunications 'Reference Paper'.

The suspension of specific commitments means the suspension of market access and national treatment commitments that a member has scheduled in specific service sectors or subsectors. If 'NONE' appears in the market access or national treatment columns of a member's service schedule, the member has undertaken not to impose limitations with respect to the applicable service sector (or subsector) and mode of supply. This is a 'full commitment' in which there are no limitations. A suspension of specific commitments (market access and national treatment limitations) is possible in such sectors.

Members may also choose to schedule 'limited commitments' (commitments with specific limitations that favour domestic services and service suppliers). In such cases a member must provide a detailed description of the applicable limitation, that is, the measures inconsistent with market access and/or national treatment provisions. To the extent that a member has assumed market access and national treatment obligations, there may be room for suspension of specific commitments.

Suspension of specific commitments is not possible when a member schedules a sector as 'UNBOUND' or 'UNBOUND*'. In both cases there is no specific commitment to suspend – in the first case because the member has made no commitment and is free to introduce limitations on market access or national treatment; in the second case because no commitment is technically feasible.

To what extent is a suspension of the specific commitments practicable? The answer depends on the specific commitments scheduled by a member and how these commitments function.

4 Practical limitations on the suspension of specific commitments

4.1 *Specific commitments*

4.1.1 Article XVI

Assume that a complaining party has made specific commitments in a sector or subsector and is considering the suspension of these commitments as a form of retaliation or cross-retaliation. Within the category

2001, S/L/92 (28 March 2001), 7; and Note by the Secretariat, Additional Commitments under Article XVIII of the GATS, S/CSC/W/34 (16 July 2002), 1.

of specific commitments, the withdrawal of market access commitments offers the easiest form of retaliation or cross-retaliation. The complaining party's choice of suspensions is, however, circumscribed by the fact that Article XVI provides only a narrow range of permissible market access limitations. They are set forth in an exhaustive list from which the outline of possible suspensions can be drawn.[27] Market access limitations consist of quantitative restrictions affecting the number of service suppliers, the total value of service operations, the total quantity of service output, limitations on the number of natural persons employed in a particular service sector and limitations on permitted legal entities and foreign capital limitations. The suspensions of market access commitments means the imposition or re-imposition of some or all of these quantitative limitations. Other market access limitations, including the imposition of discriminatory taxation regimes, are not authorised by Article XVI.

4.1.2 Article XVII

There is some overlap between Articles XVI and XVII.[28] However, unlike market access commitments, the national treatment provision of Article XVII does not provide an exhaustive list of permissible limitations. Members have scheduled a wide range of conditions and qualifications that favour domestic services and service providers and function to some extent like market access limitations. This causes some of the confusion between Articles XVI and XVII.[29] As noted above, among the national treatment measures that members have scheduled are discriminatory tax and financial measures, nationality and residency requirements, technology transfer and training requirements and property ownership requirements. Members apply measures scheduled under Article XVII on an MFN basis, but as these measures derogate from the national treatment principle, they favour domestic over foreign services and service suppliers. The suspensions of national treatment commitments means the imposition or re-imposition of measures that discriminate in favour of domestic services and service suppliers.

[27] See Article XVI:2 of the GATS. These limitations must be scheduled and are due for an eventual phase-out.

[28] See Mattoo, 'National Treatment in the GATS: Corner-stone or Pandora's Box', 1.

[29] Mattoo notes that Article XVI covers 'quantitative measures' and Article XVII covers 'discriminatory measures', but that there is an overlap between the two provisions which is reflected in the scheduling instruction provided in Article XX:2. Mattoo, 'National Treatment in the GATS: Corner-stone or Pandora's Box', 8.

The practicality of suspending national treatment commitments under Article XVII has been the subject of a lively debate among the trade cognoscenti in Geneva. This author takes the view that a suspension of national treatment commitments will seldom be desirable in the light of the Article 22.6 decision in *US–Gambling*, which suggests a far superior remedy for the complaining party – the suspension of other obligations (general obligations), in particular MFN treatment.

First, the MFN obligation is a better source for an Article 22.6 suspension. The suspension of the national treatment obligation is only viable if a member has made a full commitment or a limited commitment in a relevant service sector or subsector (and mode) and has not already protected domestic services and service suppliers in the form of a scheduled limitation. Otherwise, the complaining party has no relevant national treatment obligations. Unlike the national treatment obligation, MFN is a general obligation and is applicable *regardless* of whether the offending party has made a specific commitment in a particular sector or subsector.[30] The potential scope of an MFN suspension is, therefore, much greater.

Second, when GATS retaliation and cross-retaliation are discussed, there is sometimes a failure to differentiate between MFN and national treatment and which way the obligations run in practice. In trade in goods, both MFN and national treatment function as general obligations which together make up the non-discrimination obligation that protects against tax and regulatory discrimination between like foreign products and between like domestic and foreign products. (In fact, when retaliation occurs in the goods sector, the complaining party simply raises tariffs and the debate between MFN and national treatment is usually avoided.)

In trade in services, the MFN obligation is analogous to its GATT relative – it is aimed (in the absence of listed Article II exemptions) at discrimination between all foreign services and service suppliers. However, under GATS, the national treatment obligation is significantly different. Four points warrant attention. First, the national treatment obligation is most effective at preventing discrimination between domestic and foreign services and service suppliers when a full commitment is scheduled in all subsectors and all modes of supply. Second, when either full or limited specific commitments are scheduled, foreign services and service suppliers are likely to be subject to domestic regulations (Article VI of the GATS)

[30] In this case, it does not matter if the complaining party has scheduled exemptions in its Annex on Article II Exemptions.

which may be discriminatory in nature. Third, when limited commitments are scheduled, they frequently serve to legalise discrimination in favour of domestic services and service suppliers. Fourth, a complaining party that has made national treatment commitments has obligations under this principle to other WTO members. A *suspension* of national treatment commitments will, therefore, not take the form of a tax credit or a regulatory advantage operating directly in favour of domestic services and service suppliers. Instead, it can only take the form of a discriminatory tax or regulation imposed on services and service suppliers from the offending party (in derogation of the MFN obligation). Pursuant to the GATS MFN principle, all other WTO members are going to be able to fill the void left by the reduction in the supply of services once provided by the offending party.

These considerations regarding national treatment lead to an interesting strategic question. When a developing country seeks to suspend concessions against an offending party's services or service suppliers in the form of higher taxes or an increased regulatory burden, should it suspend the national treatment or the MFN obligation? Although the answer might depend on the developing country's service schedule, for most developing countries the better choice is almost always going to be an MFN suspension. Developing countries made significantly fewer national treatment commitments than developed countries and in fewer sectors – so they have fewer commitments available for suspension.

4.1.3 Article XVIII

Article XVIII permits a member to schedule additional commitments. It provides 'a legal framework for Members to negotiate and schedule specific commitments ... in relation to any measures which do not fall within the scope of Article XVI or XVII'.[31] By doing so a member assumes additional obligations. Article XVIII allows a member to recognise in its schedule, consistent with Article VI (domestic regulation), foreign or international standards, procedures, licences and qualifications in sectors or subsectors where it has made full or partial commitments.

There are two reasons why the suspension of additional commitments is unlikely. First, the assumption of additional commitments is relatively rare, although it is found in the telecommunications subsector,

[31] Note by the Secretariat, Additional Commitments under Article XVIII of the GATS, S/CSC/W/34 (16 July 2002), para. 2.

and sometimes in the professional services subsectors.[32] Second, the suspension of additional commitments related to the application of international standards may risk reducing the quality of services provided to and in the complaining party.

4.2 *Suspension of specific commitments in each mode of supply*

Assume now that a complaining party has scheduled specific commitments and is considering suspension of these commitments in various modes of supply. The following section discusses problems associated with retaliation and cross-retaliation in each mode of supply. Arguments raised in the Article 22.6 arbitral decisions in *US–Gambling* and the *EC–Bananas III (Ecuador)* are incorporated into the analysis. The discussion of taxation schemes is deferred until section 5, below, where the suspension of general obligations, in particular MFN suspensions, is addressed.

There are a wide range of legal, technical and economic obstacles that may hinder the viability of a suspension of specific commitments. Overarching issues include:

(1) Will the suspension of concessions or other obligations be *equivalent* (as required by Article 22.4 of the DSU) to the level of nullification or impairment? More specifically, will the suspension's effect on trade from the party found to be in violation of the WTO Agreement be equivalent to the nullification or impairment of the complaining party's trade caused by the illegal trade measure? Can equivalence be quantified for certain forms of suspension?
(2) Would a proposed suspension have trade effects that endure beyond the date that the WTO-inconsistent measure is withdrawn? By excluding a member from a market on a short-term basis, would the excluded member be permanently disadvantaged? To what extent might this violate Article 22.4 of the DSU?
(3) Will the suspension of concessions be *impracticable or ineffective*? Is the complaining party a developing country that lacks substantial trade volumes or economic power vis-à-vis the offending member?

[32] Professional licensing and qualifications are frequently treated under Article VI (domestic regulations).

Will the suspension be devoid of a significant economic impact on the offending country?

(4) Will the suspension bring economic harm to the complaining party? Is the complaining party highly dependent on service imports from the offending country? Will the suspension result in unemployment in the complaining party?

(5) What effect will the suspension have on the investment climate in the complaining party and on the complaining party's economic development?

(6) Will the suspension of concessions or other obligations violate rights under national laws (including the complaining party's constitution), or under bilateral, regional or other international agreements ratified by the complaining party?

(7) Will the complaining party need to enact or change its domestic law to allow retaliation or cross-retaliation in specific sectors and to suspend concessions or other obligations?

(8) How should a proposed suspension be distributed or apportioned among service providers or recipients from an offending country (in particular in Modes 3 and 4)?

(9) Can the suspension be avoided or circumvented? Do alternative modes of supply exist to supply the service in question?

(10) Will consumers and businesses in the complaining party's territory be forced to contract more expensive domestic or foreign service suppliers or providers? (Will the member shoot itself in the foot by applying the measure?)

(11) Will the suspension disrupt the supply chain of various businesses? Will businesses in a complaining party be less inclined to purchase goods and services from a member targeted for retaliation or cross-retaliation in the service sector. For example, retaliation imposed on distribution services may affect trade in goods. Businesses in the complaining country may stop purchasing goods from countries whose transport companies are unable to deliver goods on time.

(12) Will the suspension disrupt regional efforts toward economic integration? If the complaining party and offending party are members of a regional trade agreement, retaliation or cross-retaliation may affect regional integration efforts.

These reoccurring questions are frequently present in the discussion of the suspension of specific commitments in the four modes of supply. The following subsections briefly describe each mode of supply and examine the possibility of suspending specific commitments in each mode.[33]

4.2.1 Cross-border supply (Mode 1)

Cross-border supply (Mode 1) refers to 'the possibility for non-resident service suppliers to supply services cross-border into the Member's territory'.[34] Cross-border supply occurs, for example, when an attorney, medical practitioner, accountant, engineer, architect or consultant in the territory of one member delivers an opinion, plans or a report by video link, telephone, fax, email or post to a recipient in the territory of another member. Mode 1 also includes services supplied through a physical medium, such as drawings, a USB key, a computer diskette, etc. The member in which the service is *received* schedules the specific commitments and limitations. Mode 1 is the only mode of service supply that is 'directly comparable' with the 'notion of importation' in trade in goods.[35]

The market access rules of Article XVI of the GATS provide substantial insight into potential retaliatory measures. Article XVI(a)–(c) suggests several market access limitations that are viable in Mode 1 – limitations on the number of service suppliers from the offending member, limitations on the total value of services supplied by the offending party and limitations on the total number of service operations. A complaining party could apply these limitations to restrict or prohibit the cross-border supply of services in Mode 1 from an offending party. For example, a complaining party could establish a 'zero quota' on the cross-border purchase of services from an offending party, such as legal or accountancy services or fire, automobile, life or property insurance from insurers located in the offending member. A complaining party applying a limitation on the number or value of services provided by an offending party in Mode 1

[33] For an introduction to the four modes of supply see the Guidelines for the Scheduling of Specific Commitments under the General Agreement on Trade in Services (GATS), adopted by the Council for Trade in Services on 23 March 2001, S/L/92 (28 March 2001), 9–10; see also the WTO Secretariat, Guide to Reading the GATS Schedules of Specific Commitments and the List of Article II (MFN) Exemptions, available at: www.wto.org/english/tratop_E/serv_E/guide1_E.htm.

[34] WTO Secretariat, Guide to Reading the GATS Schedules of Specific Commitments and the List of Article II (MFN) Exemptions. This Guide, although helpful, is not an authoritative legal interpretation of the GATS. See the definition provided in Article 1.2(a) of the GATS for the supply of a service in Mode 1: 'from the territory of one Member into the territory of any other Member'.

[35] A similar point is made in a Note by the Secretariat, 'Emergency Safeguard Measures in GATS: The Applicability of Concepts Applied in the WTO Agreement on Safeguards', S/WPGR/W/8 (6 March 1996), para. 4.

would need to ensure that the trade effect of the retaliatory measure does not exceed the level of nullification or impairment – in other words, that the equivalence requirement is met.

In addition to problems associated with equivalence, there are other problems of a practical nature associated with market access restrictions in Mode 1. The cross-border supply of services, such as legal services by phone, email, fax or post, is often difficult for members to regulate or control. In many instances services are supplied across borders without the government being aware that a service has been provided. Often WTO members learn that a service has been provided in Mode 1 only when a foreign service supplier makes a tax declaration related to income tax or VAT, when a bank transfer to a foreign service provider is notified to the authorities or when the service recipient seeks to deduct payment for the service provided for tax purposes. The success of a suspension of concessions or other obligations in Mode 1 may depend largely on the honesty of service suppliers and service recipients.

The 'camouflaged' nature of services delivered in Mode 1 can make an effective suspension in Mode 1 difficult if not impossible. Monitoring the means of delivery in Mode 1 (phone, email, fax, etc.) to prevent the delivery or receipt of services subject to suspension will often pose technical challenges and may threaten the privacy and contract rights in both the complaining member and in the offending member. Suspensions in Mode 1 may also threaten economic interests dependent on delivery of the service sought, and eliminate competition faced by domestic service suppliers – resulting in price increases and reductions in quality of competing domestic services.

The arbitrators in *EC–Bananas III (Ecuador)* recognised that a suspension of commitments concerning cross-border supply could create 'practical difficulties and remain ineffective in certain service sectors. For example, it would be technically difficult to cut certain service trade across borders such as telecommunications flows.'[36]

The arbitrators in *EC–Bananas III (Ecuador)* also recognised that obstacles associated with the availability of alternative modes of supply may make a particular form of retaliation or cross-retaliation ineffective and may pose practical difficulties.[37] When it is technically feasible to provide services through alternative modes of supply, it becomes difficult to implement a suspension of commitments applicable in only one mode of supply. A suspension of concessions in Mode 1 risks being

[36] *EC–Bananas III (Ecuador)*, para. 115. [37] *EC–Bananas III (Ecuador)*, para. 117.

impracticable or ineffective if the suspension does not encompass other modes of supply since services delivered in Mode 1 are often capable of being delivered in other modes. For example, if a complaining party only suspends commitments governing the cross-border supply of legal services in Mode 1, the same service might be provided in Mode 2 if the client travels to the foreign service supplier's office; in Mode 3 if the law firm establishes a commercial presence in the service recipient's territory; and in Mode 4 if the foreign attorney travels to the service recipient's office. In such cases, a suspension in Mode 1 would need to be reinforced by a suspension in other modes of supply if it is to be practicable and effective.

4.2.2 Consumption abroad (Mode 2)

Consumption abroad refers to 'the freedom for the Member's residents to purchase services in the territory of another Member'.[38] For example, when a resident in the territory of one member is allowed by that member to consume a service in the territory of another member – perhaps as a tourist, a patient in a foreign hospital, as a student abroad or an individual seeking accounting, consulting or legal services. Mode 2 includes servicing one's property in the territory of another member – for example, when a national or a company from one member has a ship, automobile, computer or airplane repaired in the territory of another member. In Mode 2, commitments and limitations are scheduled by the member whose nationals or residents are seeking a particular service abroad, and *not* by the member offering the service.

Retaliation or cross-retaliation in Mode 2 assumes that the complaining party has made full or partial commitments in at least one service sector or subsector. Retaliation or cross-retaliation in Mode 2 will take different forms depending on whether the physical movement of consumers or the movement of objects is involved. If the movement of consumers is involved, retaliatory measures might consist of market access restrictions, such as quantitative limitations on the total value or number of service transactions received by service recipients abroad. Quantitative limitations could take the form of limitations or prohibitions (a zero quota) on the consumption of services by consumers from the complaining country

[38] WTO Secretariat, Guide to Reading the GATS Schedules of Specific Commitments and the List of Article II (MFN) Exemptions. See the definition provided in Article 1.2(b) of the GATS for the supply of a service in Mode 3: 'in the territory of one Member to the service consumer of any other Member'.

in the offending country.[39] For example, the complaining party could (1) prohibit its residents from travelling as tourists to the offending party, (2) prohibit its residents from purchasing medical, dental, legal, educational, consulting or other services in the territory of the offending party, or perhaps (3) prohibit its insurance providers from reimbursing its residents for medical services received abroad.

When the movement of objects for servicing is involved (for example, the service or repair abroad of an automobile, ship, airplane or computer) the transaction itself may be targeted.[40] Measures could include (1) numerical limitations on the total value of repairs consigned by the complaining party to foreign repair facilities in the offending country, (2) numerical limitations on the number of service operations permitted in the offending country on goods from the complaining party, and perhaps (3) prohibitions on insurance coverage for goods serviced abroad in the offending country.[41]

Many of the problems associated with retaliation or cross-retaliation in Mode 1 also exist in Mode 2. Establishing equivalence remains an obstacle. In some cases the complaining party may find it difficult to establish that its proposed suspension does not exceed the level of nullification or impairment of the offending party's illegal trade measure. For example, it may be difficult to ascertain the value of medical, dental, tourist or repair services that the complaining party's residents and businesses are receiving in the offending party. Without this statistical information, it will be difficult to establish that the trade effects of the suspension do not exceed the level of nullification or impairment.

On a more practical level, it may prove difficult to prevent residents from travelling abroad to receive services in the offending party. While restrictions are conceivable, for example, US law imposes restrictions on the travel of its citizens to Cuba, limiting the travel of US citizens to Cuba through third countries has proven difficult. Furthermore, in some countries, limitations on the free movement of citizens may raise constitutional issues.[42] The same problem may arise with respect to the repair

[39] For an analogous position within the context of services safeguards, see 'Emergency Safeguard Measures in GATS: The Applicability of Concepts Applied in the WTO Agreement on Safeguards', S/WPGR/W/8 (6 March 1996), para. 11.

[40] *Cf.* 'Emergency Safeguard Measures in GATS: The Applicability of Concepts Applied in the WTO Agreement on Safeguards', S/WPGR/W/8 (6 March 1996), para. 11.

[41] See Rudolf Adlung and Aaditya Mattoo, Module 1: The GATS, Draft 11.04.04, 3, available at: http://siteresources.worldbank.org/INTRANETTRADE/Resources/WBI-Training/288464-1121285527226/AdlungMattooGATS1219f-Paper.pdf.

[42] See, for example, Article 5 of the Brazilian Constitution.

or maintenance of objects in the offending party. Often it will be hard to detect when a ship or plane is serviced abroad.

Mode 2 limitations suffer from other potential shortcomings. Service providers and consumers in the complaining party may object to restrictions on Mode 2 travel. For example, in the United States, health insurers have begun to establish partnerships with foreign hospitals where high quality medical procedures are sometimes offered at a substantially lower cost. Health insurers, and consumers paying health insurance premiums, may benefit from the possibility of travelling abroad for such medical procedures.[43]

Although tourism services and certain medical services may depend upon travel abroad, other professional services (including architectural, engineering and legal services) can often be offered in a different mode of supply. Circumvention is again an issue. The decision of the arbitrators in *EC–Bananas III (Ecuador)* discussed this point and made specific mention of Mode 2.[44]

Restrictions on the receipt of services abroad may also cause inconvenience, increase prices and risk harming service recipients. For example, restricting the ability of consumers to obtain services within the territory of the offending party could reduce competition and result in an increase in prices (and a reduction in quality) of services offered in the complaining party. Restrictions on the maintenance of ships and aircraft in the offending party could also result in safety risks for consumers in the complaining party, and elsewhere, who use these ships and aircraft.

4.2.3 Commercial presence (Mode 3)

Commercial presence, known also as Mode 3, refers to 'opportunities for foreign service suppliers to establish, operate or expand a commercial presence in the Member's territory, such as a branch, agency, or wholly owned subsidiary'.[45] Commercial presence is a form of foreign direct investment (FDI) in the service sector. The member in which the service is offered (where the commercial presence is or will be established, that is, where the investment will occur) schedules the commitments and limitations.

[43] See, for example, *The Economist*, 16–22 August 2008, 66–8.

[44] *EC–Bananas III (Ecuador)*, paras. 115–18.

[45] WTO Secretariat, Guide to Reading the GATS Schedules of Specific Commitments and the List of Article II (MFN) Exemptions. See the definition provided in Article 1.2(c) of the GATS which defines Mode 3 as the supply of a service: 'by a service supplier of one Member, through commercial presence in the territory of any other Member'.

WTO members divide activity in Mode 3 into two categories: the pre-establishment stage (when the investment flow occurs); and the post-establishment stage (when the actual service or 'output' is provided).[46] An example of Mode 3 in the pre-establishment stage is when a foreign law firm, bank or insurance company opens an office to provide services in the territory of another member. The post-establishment stage consists of the actual provision of services.

As with the other modes of supply, the market access limitations present in Article XVI suggest restrictions that a complaining party may impose as either retaliation or cross-retaliation in sectors and subsectors where it has scheduled full or partial commitments. In the pre-establishment stage retaliation or cross-retaliation against an offending party could take the form of: (1) limitations on the number of service suppliers from the offending party permitted to supply services in the complaining party, (2) limitations on the total number of natural persons that a service supplier from the offending party may employ in the complaining party, (3) measures that restrict or require service suppliers from the offending party to establish a specific type of legal entity or joint venture through which it will supply services in the complaining party (for example, limitations on foreign ownership or a requirement that the service supplier from the offending party enter into a joint venture with a local partner) and (4) limitations on the participation of foreign capital (for example, maximum percentage limits on investment or ownership by service suppliers from the offending party).

In the post-establishment phase, retaliation or cross-retaliation against an offending party could take the form of (1) limitations on the value of service transactions supplied by service providers from the offending party within the complaining party's territory, and (2) limitations on the total number of service operations or on the total quantity of service output supplied by the offending party's service suppliers within the complaining party.

In both the pre-establishment and post-establishment stages, the complaining party must ensure that the effect of its suspension of specific commitments on the offending party's service sector does not exceed the level of nullification or impairment resulting from the offending party's illegal trade measure. Establishing equivalence in the post-establishment stage

[46] See, for example, 'Emergency Safeguard Measures in GATS: The Applicability of Concepts Applied in the WTO Agreement on Safeguards', S/WPGR/W/8 (6 March 1996), para. 11, and *EC–Bananas III (Ecuador)*, paras. 6 and 11.

is somewhat easier than establishing equivalence in the pre-establishment stage. In the post-establishment stage the trade effects from the suspension are more readily quantifiable – it is easier for the complaining party to project the service trade that the offending party would lose as a result of a suspension. In the pre-establishment stage the trade effects can be more difficult to quantify. While such a calculation may be possible with respect to limitations on the number of service suppliers and limitations on the number of natural persons that a service supplier may hire, it may be more difficult with respect to suspensions that require the offending party's service suppliers to establish a specific type of legal entity or that impose limitations on investment or ownership.

A suspension of specific commitments in Mode 3 may raise questions pursuant to the national law of the complaining party. For example, would a complaining party be permitted by its national law to retaliate or cross-retaliate in Mode 3 against a foreign-owned service supplier that enjoys legal personality under the complaining party's national laws? Do national laws need to be changed to differentiate between foreign service providers that have acquired rights under domestic law and local service providers? Why should foreign service providers 'legally established' in the complaining party's territory be treated differently from domestic service providers? These questions are difficult because the GATS deals not only with 'importation' of services (Mode 1), but also with the 'establishment' of foreign service providers (Modes 3 and 4). Furthermore, the GATS definition of a 'service supplier' within the context of commercial presence recognises a distinction between foreign and domestic service suppliers established within the same member's territory.[47]

The suspension of specific commitments in Mode 3 will raise important questions for developing country members. The practicality and effectiveness of such suspensions was examined from a developing-country perspective in *EC–Bananas III (Ecuador)*. The arbitrators recognised that the effects of a suspension of commitments related to commercial presence could be particularly detrimental to developing country

[47] See Note by the Secretariat, 'Issues for Future Discussions on Emergency Safeguards', S/WPGR/W/27/Rev.1 (7 May 1999), paras. 9–11; Communication from Switzerland, 'Safeguards and Trade in Services', S/WPGR/W/14 (10 October 1996), 2; and Note by the Secretariat, 'Emergency Safeguard Measures in GATS: The Applicability of Concepts Applied in the WTO Agreement on Safeguards', S/WPGR/W/8 (6 March 1996), paras. 4–6. See also the definition of 'commercial presence' in Article XXVIII(d) and the definition of the 'service of another Member' in Article XXVIII(f)(ii) and (g) of the GATS. See also note 12 to Article XXVIII.

members if they are 'highly dependent on foreign direct investment'.[48] In their analysis of developing-country implications, the arbitrators distinguished between: (1) suspensions against foreign service suppliers who were potential investors in the complaining party (the 'pre-establishment' stage) and (2) suspensions made against foreign service suppliers who were already commercially present in the complaining party (the 'post-establishment' stage). They reasoned that suspensions at both the pre- and post-establishment stages could harm a developing country's economy.[49] Although cross-retaliation at the pre-establishment stage would not be difficult, it would discourage foreign service suppliers from investing in the complaining party and would provide an incentive for foreign service suppliers to take their FDI to another host country where there was no suspension of concessions on commercial presence.[50] Significant harm could be inflicted on the developing country that lost the FDI.

At the post-establishment (or post-investment) stage the complaining party (Ecuador) noted that it could, if authorised by the DSB, order a 'commercially present service supplier to stop its activities or impose a supplementary tax on each unit of its service output'. Ecuador argued, however, that this would not be practicable, since such actions 'against service suppliers of a particular foreign origin' could lead to conflicts with rights such as 'equal treatment embodied in national legislation or international treaties and would entail substantial administrative difficulties'.[51] The arbitrators reasoned that a suspension of concessions at the post-establishment stage could also be detrimental to a developing country. Foreign service suppliers at the post-establishment stage would lose the 'legal protection, predictability and certainty which the GATS standards provide', and the suspension could provide an incentive for commercially present service suppliers to transfer their investment to another country thus causing 'significant harm' to Ecuador's economy.[52]

The arbitrators also recognised that at the post-establishment stage it may be difficult to prevent 'legally established' foreign service providers from supplying services within a complaining party's territory. They cited the possible legal and administrative difficulties arising under national and international law 'to close or limit the service output' of foreign enterprises with legal personality, or branch or representative offices. They

[48] *EC–Bananas III (Ecuador)*, para. 110. [49] *EC–Bananas III (Ecuador)*, paras. 111–12.
[50] *EC–Bananas III (Ecuador)*, paras. 112 and 114.
[51] *EC–Bananas III (Ecuador)*, para. 113. [52] *EC–Bananas III (Ecuador)*, para. 111.

noted that such service providers may enjoy legal personality and legal protection under national or international law.[53]

In conclusion, *EC–Bananas III (Ecuador)* suggests several reasons why the suspension of specific commitments in Mode 3 might be impracticable or ineffective for purposes of GATS retaliation:

(1) *There is a violation or conflict with national or international law*: a foreign service provider who has already established a commercial presence in a complaining party's territory may have property rights under national law, rights to equal treatment under national law, constitutional protections or rights as an investor under a bilateral investment treaty or other international agreement, any of which may make the imposition of legal restrictions or taxes on commercial presence legally difficult or impracticable.
(2) *There are adverse effects on the economy of the member undertaking cross-retaliation*: suspending or placing limitations on existing or future foreign direct investment may pose administrative difficulties, and may distort the investment climate, discourage foreign direct investment and have other adverse effects for the economy of the complaining country. A suspension may also cause uncertainty for existing investors and discourage prospective investors. Foreign investors contemplating investment in a country considering cross-retaliation in Mode 3, or with a history of having implemented cross-retaliation in Mode 3, may view the investment climate as unpredictable.
(3) *There is no significant effect on the offending country*: a suspension may be impracticable or ineffective if it is harmful to the complaining party or does not have a significant economic effect on the offending country. For example, a suspension affecting the provision of services by foreign engineers could affect domestic production. It could harm the complaining party more than the offending party if no alternative service providers are available at a reasonable price. If the foreign engineers quickly find work in another country, the suspension might also have no effect on the offending party.[54]
(4) *There are difficulties establishing equivalence*: suspensions in Mode 3 raise the same questions with regard to equivalence as were

[53] *EC–Bananas III (Ecuador)*, para. 114.

[54] A suspension of concessions may not be practicable and effective for a developing country when 'transitional costs' of changing and adjusting to new service suppliers are high. For an analogous argument related to trade in goods, see *EC–Bananas III (Ecuador)*, para. 94.

discussed with respect to Modes 1 and 2. Arbitrators must estimate the complaining party's 'losses in actual or potential trade and trade opportunities in the relevant goods and service sectors'.[55]

4.2.4 Presence of natural persons (Mode 4)

Mode 4 refers to 'the possibilities offered for the entry and temporary stay in the Member's territory of foreign individuals in order to supply a service'.[56] Pursuant to the GATS, the member in which the service is offered (in the territory where the natural person offers the service) schedules the commitments and limitations. For example, supply in Mode 4 occurs when a natural person, such as a civil engineer, attorney, architect, lawyer, accountant or medical professional travels abroad on a temporary basis to render services in the territory of another member. Like Mode 3, Mode 4 has both a pre-establishment phase and a post-establishment phase.[57]

The suspension of specific commitments in Mode 4 is again likely to be based on the market access provisions of Article XVI. Assuming equivalence, at the pre-establishment stage, suspension of specific commitments may include the following limitations imposed by the complaining party on service suppliers (natural persons) from the offending party: (1) numerical limitations on the number of foreign service suppliers (natural persons) permitted to provide temporary services within the complaining party's territory; (2) limitations on the number of natural persons that may be employed in a particular service sector or that a service supplier may employ within the complaining party's territory; and (3) measures that restrict or require the creation of specific legal entities or joint ventures through which natural persons from the offending party are permitted to provide services within the complaining party's territory.

Assuming equivalence, at the post-establishment stage, suspension of specific commitments might include the following limitations imposed by the complaining party on service suppliers (natural persons) from the offending party: (1) limitations on the value of services provided by foreign

[55] *See EC–Bananas III (Ecuador)*, para. 159.

[56] WTO Secretariat, Guide to Reading the GATS Schedules of Specific Commitments and the List of Article II (MFN) Exemptions. See Article 1.2(d) which defines Mode 4 as the supply of a service 'by a service supplier of one Member, through presence of natural persons of a Member in the territory of any other Member'.

[57] Note by the Secretariat, 'Emergency Safeguard Measures in GATS: The Applicability of Concepts Applied in the WTO Agreement on Safeguards', S/WPGR/W/8 (6 March 1996), paras. 8 and 11.

service suppliers within the complaining party's territory or within a particular region in its territory; and (2) limitations on the number of service operations or on the total quantity of service output.

In addition to problems related to equivalence, suspensions in Mode 4 face obstacles that may limit their effectiveness and practicality. Many of these obstacles are similar to those encountered in Mode 3. Suspension in Mode 4 may violate the private contractual rights of service providers lawfully working in the complaining party's territory. For example, if an engineer signs a contract and receives a visa to work on a construction project, a suspension of concessions relative to the provision of construction services (coupled with the deportation of the engineer) may place the engineer in breach of his or her contract. Faced with such insecure work conditions, a WTO member, in particular a developing country member, may find it difficult to attract foreign service suppliers.

Limiting the value of services that a foreign national provides may also have adverse effects, particularly for developing countries. For example, a suspension of specific commitments may lead to uncertainty and insecurity if, due to the suspension, foreign doctors are barred from temporary work in the territory of the complaining party. Such restrictions may also make it more difficult to attract skilled foreign service suppliers to fill temporary contracts.

Suspensions in Mode 4 may also have adverse effects for enterprises offering services in Mode 3. If a foreign hospital builds a clinic in a developing country and occasionally sends foreign experts to provide medical consultations, a suspension of concessions in Mode 4 applicable to temporary visits by foreign doctors from an offending party may lessen the quality of services offered in Mode 3.

In many instances limiting the temporary access of foreign service suppliers may cause more harm than good to a complaining party. In some specialised fields, WTO members from developing countries are dependent on the knowledge and skills of foreign service suppliers. While in many cases the services offered may be acquired from other foreign suppliers, linguistic, economic, cultural and geographic factors may limit the availability of alternate service suppliers.

5 Suspension of 'other obligations': the MFN obligation

In addition to the suspensions of specific commitments under the GATS, Article 22.3 of the DSU permits a complaining party to suspend 'other obligations'. In the GATS context, 'other obligations' are different from specific commitments in one important respect – they apply even when a member has not made commitments in the service sector where the violation occurred, or in another sector under the GATS Agreement. The phrase 'other obligations' refers to the list of obligations in Part II of the GATS ('General Obligations and Disciplines'):

> Article II – Most Favoured-Nation Treatment; Article III – Transparency; Article III*bis* – Disclosure of Confidential Information; Article IV–Increasing Participation of Developing Countries; Article V – Economic Integration; Article V*bis* – Labour Markets Integration Agreements; Article VI – Domestic Regulation; Article VII – Recognition; Article VIII – Monopolies and Exclusive Service Suppliers; Article IX – Business Practices; Article X Emergency Safeguard Measures, Article XI – Payments and Transfers; Article XII – Restrictions to Safeguard the Balance of Payments; Article XIII – Government Procurement; Article XIV – General Exceptions; Article XIV *bis* – Security Exceptions; and Article XV – Subsidies.

The MFN obligation, set forth in Article II of the GATS is among these obligations. Despite the large number of obligations in Part II of the GATS, arbitral decisions on the suspension of 'other obligations' have only examined suspension of the MFN obligation.[58] This reflects MFN's importance among the 'other obligations'. It may also reflect the difficulty of establishing the trade effect of a suspension of most of the 'other obligations'. For example, it would be very difficult for purposes of establishing equivalence to quantify the effect on trade in services resulting from the complaining party's suspension of the Article III Transparency obligation.

Both *EC–Bananas III (Ecuador)* and *US–Gambling* examined suspension of other obligations (primarily the MFN obligation) but reached different conclusions. In *EC–Bananas III (Ecuador)*, the arbitrators concluded that the complaining party cannot suspend other obligations in subsectors where it has not entered into specific commitments.[59] Pursuant to the arbitrators' reasoning, if a member does not enter into specific commitments in a subsector, a complaining party would not be entitled

[58] *See EC–Bananas III (Ecuador)*, para. 103 and *US–Gambling*, paras. 4.45–60.

[59] *See EC–Bananas III (Ecuador)*, para. 103 and note 36. See also Eric Vranes, 'Fundamental WTO Issues' in F. Breuss, S. Griller and E. Vranes (eds.), *The Banana Dispute: An Economic and Legal Analysis*, vol. 19 (Schriftenreihe des Forschungsinstituts für Europafragen der Wirtschaftsuniversität Wien 93) (New York: Springer, 2003).

to suspend its application of the MFN obligation in that subsector.[60] The arbitrators also found that the same conclusion would apply if the complaining party 'had scheduled exemptions from MFN treatment' under Article II:2 of the GATS.[61]

In *US–Gambling* the arbitrators reached the opposite conclusion. They observed that the text of Article 22.3 of the DSU refers to 'concessions *or other obligations*' (emphasis added) with respect to the relevant sector and reasoned that the 'entire range' of obligations is relevant when considering whether a suspension is practicable or effective in a sector. This led the arbitrators to conclude that the review of other obligations should include an assessment of whether a suspension of the MFN obligation would be practicable or effective.[62] In reaching their decision, the arbitrators explicitly rejected the finding of *EC–Bananas*, ruling instead that 'the scope of the relevant obligations is not limited, in our view, to specific commitments bound in Antigua's GATS schedule'.[63]

[60] The arbitrators found in para. 103 that:

> Ecuador has not entered into specific commitments on market access or national treatment in any of those sub-sectors with the exception of 'wholesale trade services'. It is, therefore, evident for us that Ecuador cannot suspend commitments or other obligations in sub-sectors of the distribution service sector in respect of which it has not entered into specific commitments in the first place. (footnotes omitted)

[61] Pursuant to Article II:2 of the GATS, members can schedule MFN exemptions at the time of entry into force of the GATS (or the date of their accession). Contrary to the GATS, which uses a positive list approach, the MFN exemptions take the form of a negative list approach (an opt-out). Unlike national treatment and market access exceptions, which are made in sectors where members have made commitments, MFN exemptions can be listed in sectors where members have not made commitments. Paragraph 6 of the Annex provides that 'in principal the exemption should not exceed a period of ten years. In any event, they shall be subject to negotiation in subsequent trade-liberalizing rounds.' In practice most MFN exceptions remain in place and more than eighty members currently maintain such exemptions. They relate primarily to regional trade preferences. The sectors most frequently covered are road transport and audiovisual services, 'followed by maritime transport and banking services'. See www.wto.org/english/tratop_e/serv_e/cbt_course_e/c2s2p1_e.htm.

[62] *US–Gambling*, paras. 4.45, 4.54, 4.58 where the arbitrators found that:

> In considering this matter, we first note that there is only a limited number of such 'other obligations' under the GATS, that Antigua would be able to suspend under the whole of Sector 10 … In our view, the main relevant obligation in this respect is the MFN obligation, contained [sic] GATS Article II, which obliges Antigua to accord immediately and unconditionally to US services and service suppliers treatment no less favourable than that it accords to like services and service suppliers of any other country.

[63] *US–Gambling*, para. 4.52, note 305.

The view of the arbitrators in *US–Gambling* is compelling. Not only is *US–Gambling* a more recent decision (seven years after the *EC–Bananas III (Ecuador)* arbitration), it also provides a well reasoned and more detailed analysis that gives full meaning to the language of Article 22.3 of the DSU. The arbitrators' interpretation of Article 22.3 of the DSU is also consistent with similar language in Article XXIII:2 of the GATS.[64]

The argument on the applicability of 'general obligations' in instances when members have not made specific commitments has its roots in an old debate. When GATT Article III (national treatment) was negotiated a similar issue arose. Some countries argued that the national treatment principle should apply only when a country has made tariff concessions pursuant to GATT Article II. The view that prevailed was that a trade agreement should have 'certain basic general provisions'.[65] The MFN obligation within the GATS can be viewed as one of these 'basic general principles'.

Pursuant to *US–Gambling*, a suspension of 'other obligations' in accord with Article 22.3 of the DSU would permit a complaining party to suspend its Article II MFN obligation regardless of whether it has scheduled specific commitments in a particular sector. Provided that the complaining party has not already listed MFN exceptions in the Annex on Article II Exceptions,[66] a complaining party would be relieved of its Article II:1 obligation to accord 'immediately and unconditionally to services and service suppliers of any other Member treatment no less favourable than that it accords to like services and service suppliers of any other country'. As with trade in goods, such retaliatory measures are likely to take the form of (1) discriminatory regulations or (2) discriminatory duties and charges of any kind (taxes).

[64] Article 22.3 of the DSU allows a complaining party to suspend 'other obligations'. Article XXIII:2 of the GATS allows a member to suspend 'obligations and specific commitments in accordance with Article 22 of the DSU'. Article XXIII:2 of the GATS and Article 22 of the DSU can be read together with little difficulty.

[65] Mattoo, 'National Treatment in the GATS: Corner-stone or Pandora's Box', 7 (citing John Jackson and A. Ahnlid).

[66] As noted by the WTO Secretariat in its non-authoritative 'Guide to Reading the GATS Schedules of Specific Commitments and the List of Article II (MFN) Exemptions':

> It is a basic principle of the Agreement that specific commitments are applied on an MFN basis. Where commitments are entered, therefore, the effect of an MFN exemption can only be to permit more favourable treatment to be given to the country to which the exemption applies than is given to all other Members. Where there are no commitments, however, an MFN exemption may also permit less favourable treatment to be given.

In *US–Gambling* the arbitrators reviewed Antigua's determination of the practicality and effectiveness of suspending 'concessions or other obligations', first in the sector[67] where the nullification or impairment occurred (Sector 10 – recreational, cultural and sporting services),[68] and once that was confirmed not to be practicable and effective, then in other GATS sectors.[69] In each case, the arbitrators considered subsectors where the complaining party had not made specific commitments on the grounds that the MFN obligation nevertheless applied.[70]

The arbitrators merged their consideration of the suspension of specific commitments and other obligations with their analysis of the practicality and effectiveness of a suspension in other sectors under the GATS.[71] The arbitrators noted that the complaining party, in its explanation of how a suspension would work in the services sector, raised the possibility of 'higher duties, tariff, [sic] fees or other restrictions'.[72] Such measures are examples of potential retaliatory action involving a suspension of the MFN obligation. If authorised to suspend the MFN obligation, a complaining party would be able to apply discriminatory taxes and regulations against services from the offending party until the effect on the offending party's service trade equalled the level of nullification or impairment.

It is useful to consider how an MFN suspension might work in each of the four modes of supply. In each mode, the complaining party could apply taxation and regulatory schemes to discriminate against the offending

[67] Antigua accepted that the entirety of Sector 10 (recreational, cultural and sporting services) was relevant for determining retaliation in the same sector: *US–Gambling*, para. 4.43. Neither Antigua nor the United States was able to produce statistics demonstrating Antiguan imports of entertainment services from the United States. The arbitrators accepted that such trade was negligible and that it was it was plausible for Antigua to conclude that suspending concessions in Sector 10.a (entertainment services), the only subsector in which Antigua had made a specific commitment, would not be practicable or effective: *US–Gambling*, paras. 4.52–6.

[68] *US–Gambling*, paras. 4.39–65. [69] *US–Gambling*, paras. 4.66–105.

[70] See *US–Gambling*, para. 4.76. Antigua and Barbuda made specific commitments in (1) business services: (a) professional services, (b) computer and related services and (c) research and development services; (2) communications services: (c) telecommunications services; (7) financial services: (a) insurance, (c) re-insurance only; (9) tourism and travel-related services: (a) hotel and resort development – construction and management; (10) recreational, cultural and sporting services: (a) entertainment services; and (11) transport services: (a) maritime transport services, (b) freight transport services and (d) maintenance and repair of vessels. See Antigua and Barbuda, Schedule of Specific Commitments, GATS/SC/2 (15 April 1994) and Schedule of Specific Commitments, Supplement 1, GATS/SC/2/Suppl.1 (11 April 1997).

[71] *US–Gambling*, para. 4.76. Antigua's position was less precise – discussing the effect of a suspension on both goods and services: *US–Gambling*, para. 4.87.

[72] *US–Gambling*, para. 4.87.

party. The equivalence rule would apply to all measures to ensure that the trade effect of a tax or regulatory measure does not exceed the level of nullification or impairment.

In Mode 1, a tax could be imposed by the complaining party on the sale or receipt of services from the offending party. Since trade in services in Mode 1 resembles importation of goods under the multilateral agreements on trade in goods, the tax that a complaining party would impose is somewhat analogous to a retaliatory tariff increase (retaliation or cross-retaliation) in the goods sector. A similar result would be achieved if instead of discriminatory tax measures, services exports from the offending party were subject to a discriminatory regulatory requirement. However, taxation schemes do not require conformity assessment measures and would appear to be easier to apply.

In Mode 2 taxation and regulatory schemes are also both viable. When the movement of consumers is at issue, discrimination against the offending party could take the form of (1) taxes on consumers travelling abroad to receive services and (2) regulations limiting or restricting consumption abroad by consumers.[73] More specifically, discriminatory measures could include: (1) restricting or prohibiting a member's nationals from purchasing medical, dental, legal, consulting or other professional services in the territory of another member; (2) exit taxes on nationals travelling abroad to targeted countries as tourists; (3) limitations on the number of residents allowed to travel to a specific country for tourism; (4) taxes on nationals travelling abroad to targeted countries for dental work and to receive other professional services; (5) prohibitions on coverage under a member's public health insurance scheme for medical treatment received abroad; and (6) a tax on insurance purchased abroad.

When the movement of objects as opposed to consumers is at issue in Mode 2 (for example, the service or repair of an automobile, ship, airplane or computer abroad), the complaining party must target the transaction itself.[74] Discriminatory measures that would affect the offending country might include: (1) a prohibition by the complaining party on the use

[73] For an analogous position within the context of services safeguards, see 'Emergency Safeguard Measures in GATS: The Applicability of Concepts Applied in the WTO Agreement on Safeguards', S/WPGR/W/8 (6 March 1996), para. 11.

[74] *Cf.* 'Emergency Safeguard Measures in GATS: The Applicability of Concepts Applied in the WTO Agreement on Safeguards', S/WPGR/W/8 (6 March 1996), para. 11.

of foreign repair facilities in the offending party; (2) taxes imposed on the value of maintenance and repairs performed on goods from the complaining party in the offending party; and (3) limitations on insurance coverage in the complaining party for goods serviced or repaired in the offending party.[75]

In Mode 3 the complaining party could apply discriminatory taxes and regulations at both the pre-establishment and post-establishment stages against the offending party's service suppliers. At the pre-establishment stage, special fees could be assessed before a foreign commercial presence is authorised in the complaining party's territory. At the post-establishment stage, the complaining party could impose taxes on the offending party's service suppliers operating in its territory based on service output, commercial presence, the number of foreign employees, the amount of capital invested, as well as on many other criteria. Discriminatory regulations, such as with a requirement that a foreign firm from the offending party must hire a minimum number of local workers at a set wage, are also feasible, but more difficult to quantify for purposes of assessing equivalence.

Both discriminatory taxation and regulatory measures are also conceivable in Mode 4. A complaining party could impose taxes as a condition of entry (pre-establishment taxes) and on the service output (post-establishment taxes). A complaining party could also impose regulations limiting the recognition of foreign degrees or qualifications. Likewise the complaining party could require skilled foreign service providers from the offending party to train its nationals,[76] but this may raise questions regarding the establishment of an equivalent trade effect.

In addition to possible difficulties regarding the establishment of equivalent trade effects, there are two other caveats to consider. First, when a developing country complaining party suspends its MFN obligation vis-à-vis an offending party, many of the same economic and political difficulties will arise as when it seeks to suspend its specific commitments. Second, in instances when a complaining party has made specific commitments under Article XVI (Market Access) and Article XVII (National Treatment), the complaining party may need to consider whether it is necessary to suspend these commitments in conjunction with an MFN suspension.

[75] See Rudolf Adlung and Aaditya Mattoo, Module 1: The GATS, Draft 11.04.04, 3.

[76] See Rudolf Adlung and Aaditya Mattoo, Module 1: The GATS, Draft 11.04.04, 3.

6 Conclusion: some developing country considerations

The WTO DSU may be the 'jewel in the crown' of the Uruguay Round, but sometimes jewels need polishing. Implementation and enforcement are the DSU's weakest links. Suspension of concessions or other obligations to induce compliance (also known as retaliation and cross-retaliation) favour the largest trading members – in particular the EC and the United States. Many developing country members lack the volume of trade and political strength required for retaliation and cross-retaliation to be effective. Other factors also constrain the ability of developing countries to retaliate or cross-retaliate, such as the risk of losing economic assistance or preferential market access granted by developed countries. Most violating parties bring their WTO-inconsistent measures in line with the covered agreements in order to be 'good WTO citizens' and not because they fear the effects of retaliation or cross-retaliation.

As with suspensions of concessions or other obligations in the goods sector, suspensions in the services sector may not exert sufficient leverage to induce compliance with the covered agreements – unless politically powerful (and vulnerable) sectors are targeted. This is because most developing country members have made relatively few GATS commitments, and few developing countries engage in enough service trade to exert significant leverage over a particular developed country.

Furthermore, suspension of service commitments may disproportionately hurt developing countries, more specifically the employment prospects of their citizens, as well as their consumers and businesses. In particular, suspension in the services sector risks inflicting economic damage on domestic businesses that rely on skilled foreign service providers, on individuals employed by foreign service providers and on consumers seeking services from foreign service providers. Suspensions also risk chilling the climate for foreign direct investment. Developing countries are particularly susceptible to these risks.

GATS suspensions may also pose difficult questions under national laws (including various constitutions) with respect to the treatment of private rights and commitments assumed under various bilateral and regional trade and investment agreements. In certain service sectors and modes of supply questions may also arise as to whether a suspension of GATS concessions or other obligations can be administered in conformity with Article 22.4's equivalence requirement. When implementing any form of suspension, including an MFN suspension, the complaining party must ensure that the trade effects do not exceed the level of nullification or impairment that result from the illegal trade measure. The equivalence requirement of Article 22.4 of the DSU provides an avenue by which an offending party may limit retaliation and cross-retaliation.

Despite this overall negative assessment, avenues exist for members intent upon pursuing the suspension of GATS concessions or other obligations, even if such suspensions are likely to remain the exception and not the rule. The 'suspension of concessions' or 'specific commitments' under Part III of the GATS is the most obvious form of suspension available to complaining parties. The suspension of specific commitments, such as market access commitments, is available to complaining parties that have scheduled specific commitments under the GATS. Such suspensions are probably more practicable and more effective in Modes 3 and 4 where enforcement appears easier. Developed countries are likely to place more value on foreign direct investment (establishing the foreign commercial presence of their service suppliers, such as banks and insurance companies) and on the temporary presence abroad of their skilled professionals (medical professionals, accountants, lawyers, etc.). Offending parties may be more willing to respond to numerical limitations and other restrictions in Modes 3 and 4, in particular in the financial service sector. In part this is because foreign financial service providers frequently have the political power to influence their government's trade policies.

The suspension of 'other obligations' is another viable form of suspension in the services sector. The arbitrators in *US–Gambling* found that Article 22 of the DSU permits a complaining party to suspend application of the GATS MFN obligation in sectors where it has not made specific commitments. Such a suspension would relieve a complaining party of its obligation to accord 'immediately and unconditionally to services and service suppliers of any other Member treatment no less favourable than that it accords to like services and service suppliers of any other country'. A suspension of the MFN obligation could permit a complaining party to impose duties and charges (higher taxes and fees), as well as domestic regulations, on services and service providers from the member violating the covered agreements. Services and service providers from the offending party would be subject to financial and/or regulatory discrimination. Cross-retaliating in the form of a suspension of MFN commitments depends upon future Article 22.6 arbitrators following the approach set forth in *US–Gambling*.

How then can WTO members, in particular developing country members, benefit from cross-retaliation in services? There is one lesson to be learned from cross-retaliation in TRIPs. By selecting high profile and politically influential service sectors for suspension, it may be possible for a member to pressure another member to meet its obligations under the covered agreements, or at least negotiate a mutually satisfactory solution. The financial service sector is often capable of mustering the political pressure required to convince its government to change trade policies. The financial service sector, in particular the banking and insurance industries, is also among the most vulnerable and most easily targeted by members for retaliatory measures. Assuming financial firms from the violating party have a substantial commercial presence in the complaining party, the suspension of specific commitments in Mode 3, or the imposition of taxation measures (through a suspension of MFN) are likely to provide the easiest means of influencing already established financial service providers. The success of measures taken against the financial service sector will, of course, depend on the ability of the targeted sector (or targeted companies) to lobby their governments for a change in trade policy, and the permissibility of such measures pursuant to local, regional and international law. Disruption to domestic business interests must also be factored into the complaining party's decision to retaliate or cross-retaliate against this sector.

Retaliatory measures in Modes 1 and 2 are less likely to be successful than retaliatory measures in Modes 3 and 4. Retaliatory measures in Modes 1 and 2 are too easily circumvented to be effective. Frequently, services provided in Modes 1 and 2 escape the attention of national governments entirely. Although retaliation may help domestic service suppliers (or foreign service suppliers from third countries), it is more likely that consumer interests and other domestic interests will be harmed.

Retaliation in Modes 3 and 4 offers greater possibilities for exerting political pressure on an offending party. However, to the extent that the complaining party's nationals work for an entity established under Mode 3, retaliation is likely to cause domestic unemployment. Likewise, while retaliation in Mode 4 may protect domestic jobs, it is also likely to prevent needed professionals from working in the retaliating country. Furthermore, Mode 4 is often difficult to discipline. For example, a large number of consultants, lawyers and accountants enter foreign countries to provide short-term professional services on tourist visas.

In most cases retaliation and cross-retaliation in services is unlikely to be successful and will be detrimental to the complaining party – particularly to complaining parties from developing countries. In certain modes of supply fundamental questions exist as to whether a suspension of GATS concessions or other obligations can be administered in conformity with

Article 22.4 of the DSU (equivalence). In other instances, basic economic considerations mean that retaliation and cross-retaliation in services is an unpalatable alternative – either ineffective or impracticable – or both.

In conclusion, neither suspension of GATS concessions nor the suspension of other obligations provides an adequate cure for the relative impotence of developing countries seeking to enforce the covered agreements. The problem remains that, as Debra Steger, the former Director of the WTO's Appellate Body Secretariat, noted in 2005:

> It is in the area of compliance/implementation that most of the Members' attention should be focused. Suspension of concessions or retaliation is a blunt instrument that realistically only the two most powerful Members, the United States and the European Communities, can use effectively; most Members recognize that other means need to be found to encourage Members to implement when encouragement is needed.[77]

The paradigm of suspending trade concessions and other obligations does little to further trade liberalisation, and is not realistically in reach of most developing country members. Even in instances when it is in reach, the suspension of TRIPs commitments may be a more viable and less painful way of fulfilling developing-country objectives. When developing countries suspend GATS concessions and other obligations, they will suffer. When developing countries suspend TRIPs concessions, the developed world is more likely to suffer.

[77] Debra P. Steger, 'WTO Dispute Settlement: Systemic Issues', Roundtable, University of Ottawa Faculty of Law (16 February 2005), 68, available at: www.international.gc.ca/eet/research/TPR-2005/TPR-2005_Chapter_03_-_Steger.pdf.

24

Compensation assessments: perspectives from investment arbitration

GABRIELLE KAUFMANN-KOHLER*

1 Introduction: similarities and differences between investment and trade law

The organizers of the workshop and editors of this volume have asked me to draw lessons from the compensation assessments made in international investment law for use in international trade law. Therefore, one must first inquire about the similarities and differences between these two fields of law in order to determine to what extent lessons learned in one field can be applied to the other.

There are obvious differences between international trade transactions and the classical notion of foreign investment. It has even been asserted that the broad concept of investment enshrined in Article 25 of the ICSID Convention can be characterized by drawing a contrast with international trade transactions.[1] Yet, international trade and foreign investment law are two subfields of international economic law and the differences between the two result more from the function of the different regulatory angles which they adopt, rather than from the underlying economic realities.[2]

* Professor of International Law at Geneva University Law School and Partner with Lévy Kaufmann-Kohler.

[1] On the notion of investment see: C. Schreuer, *The ICSID Convention: A Commentary* (2001), ad art. 25, 149ff; N. Rubins, 'The Notion of "Investment" in International Investment Arbitration' in N. Horn (ed.), *Arbitrating Foreign Investment Disputes* (The Hague: Kluwer Law, 2004), 283ff; R. Dolzer, 'The Notion of Investment in Recent Practice' in S. Charnovitz, D. P. Steger and P. Van Den Bosche (eds.), *Essays in Honour of Florentino Feliciano* (Cambridge University Press, 2005), 261ff; R. Dolzer and C. Schreuer, *Principles of International Investment Law* (Oxford University Press, 2008), 60ff; E. Schlemmer, 'Investment, Investor, Nationality, and Shareholders' in P. Muchlinski, F. Ortino and C. Schreuer (eds.), *The Oxford Handbook of International Investment Law* (Oxford University Press, 2008), 49ff.

[2] See also Nicholas DiMascio and Joost Pauwelyn, 'Nondiscrimination in Trade and Investment Treaties: Worlds Apart or Two Sides of the Same Coin?', *American Journal of International Law*, 102 (2008), 48, 52ff.

With the present complexity of international business transactions, it is increasingly difficult to draw a clear line between the economic realities of foreign investment and trade, as a transborder transaction (such as a sale of goods or the provision of services) may well constitute a component of a larger investment scheme.[3]

In spite of the commonalities in terms of underlying realities, the present contribution focuses on the specific regulatory angles used by international trade law, on the one hand, and international investment law, on the other hand. Indeed, this approach appears better suited to explore the potential contribution of investment law to trade law with respect to monetary remedies for breach of a given norm or standard of conduct.

In this respect, a first difference relates to the purpose of the remedies available in each field. One may argue whether remedies in international trade seek to achieve compliance or compensation or both.[4] By contrast, there is no doubt that the primary purpose of the remedies provided by investment law is to compensate an investor for the losses caused by an act of a state.[5] The purpose of investment treaties is to protect foreign direct investment by granting investors guarantees against expropriation, unfair and inequitable treatment and discrimination (by way of standards of national treatment and most-favoured-nation treatment). Consequently, the approach in investment arbitration is clearly compensatory.

A second important difference between the two regulatory approaches is that international trade law focuses on the harm suffered by one (or more) state(s), while investment law deals with the damage incurred by a particular investor or group of investors. Thus, compensation in the WTO system does not necessarily entail that the industry segment of a state which has been affected by a measure taken by a foreign state will reap the benefits of compensatory measures adopted by that state. This

[3] As noted by the tribunal in *CSOB* v. *Slovak Republic*, 'an international transaction which contributes to cooperation designed to promote the economic development of a Contracting State may be deemed to be an investment as that term is understood in the [ICSID] Convention', *Ceskoslovenska Obchodni Banka AS (CSOB)* v. *The Slovak Republic*, ICSID Case No. ARB/97/4, Decision of 24 May 1999, para. 64.

[4] See the contribution of Joost Pauwelyn, 'The Calculation and Design of Trade Retaliation in Context: What is the Goal of Suspending WTO Obligations?', Chapter 2, above.

[5] The role played by non-pecuniary remedies in investment arbitration remains very limited. On this issue see C. McLachlan, L. Shore and M. Weiniger, *International Investment Arbitration: Substantive Principles* (2007), 341ff; C. Schreuer, 'Non-Pecuniary Remedies in ICSID Arbitration', *Arbitration International*, 20:4 (2004), 325ff.

may be one of the reasons why compensation is relatively rare in the WTO context.[6]

One should keep in mind these differences when seeking to draw parallels or analogies between international investment and international trade with respect to the issue of compensation. Therefore, rather than drawing lessons from investment law for trade law, which may be of limited use, the following developments more modestly seek to provide a few perspectives from the standpoint of an investment arbitrator. For this purpose, section 2 explains how investment arbitrators determine compensation and section 3 highlights two main characteristics of this determination. These two sections will provide the basis for a brief discussion (section 4) of comments made by international trade law specialists on the possibility of reforming the WTO sanction system to enhance the role of compensatory remedies.

2 Compensation in international investment law and practice

2.1 Terminology

The terminology used by investment arbitral tribunals with respect to compensation is not uniform. Often, terms such as 'reparation', 'compensation', 'damages', 'indemnity' and others are used interchangeably.[7] It has been suggested that the term 'compensation' should be reserved for monetary remedies in the event of a lawful expropriation, while the words 'damages' or 'indemnity' should apply to unlawful expropriation or non-expropriatory breaches of investment law protections.[8]

[6] As noted by D. Palmeter and P. Mavroidis (*Dispute Settlement in the WTO: Practice and Procedure* (Cambridge University Press, 2004), 266), compensation entails important drawbacks both for the complainant and the defendant states:

> From the complainant's point of view, compensation by way of lower barriers in other areas does nothing to eliminate non-compliance in the area that was the subject to the dispute. Particularly from the perspective of the concerned industry in the territory of the complaining Member, compensation does nothing. By the same token, Members whose measures are found not to be in compliance have difficulty 'volunteering' a sector of the economy for increased foreign competition for the explicit reason of protecting another sector that benefits from that violation.

[7] See T. Wälde and B. Sabahi, 'Compensation, Damages, and Valuation' in P. Muchlinski, F. Ortino and C. Schreuer (eds.), *The Oxford Handbook of International Investment Law* (Oxford University Press, 2008), 1050ff, 1052–3.

[8] See *LG&E* v. *Argentina*, ICSID Case No. ARB/02/1 (United States/Argentina BIT), Damages Award of 25 July 2007 (hereafter LG&E Damages), para. 38.

In reality, pursuant to Articles 31(1) and 34 of the International Law Commission's Articles on State Responsibility (ILC Articles), reparation is the term that encompasses all forms of relief and includes compensation, restitution and satisfaction,[9] the latter two being irrelevant for present purposes.

This contribution follows the terminology of the ILC Articles. It uses 'compensation' in connection with the monetary reparation for lawful expropriation, and 'compensation' or 'damages' in connection with monetary relief for unlawful expropriation and other breaches of investment guarantees.

2.2 *Compensation for lawful expropriation*

Most modern BITs and multilateral investment treaties, such as Chapter 11 of the North American Free Trade Agreement (NAFTA)[10] or the Energy Charter Treaty,[11] expressly require payment of 'prompt, adequate, and effective compensation'. Many also provide the standards of compensation and state that the compensation must represent the fair market value of the expropriated assets.[12] Others merely refer to the 'genuine'[13] or '"real"

[9] Responsibility of States for Internationally Wrongful Acts, G.A. Res. 56/83, para. 25, U.N. Doc. A/RES/56/83 (28 January 2002).

[10] North American Free Trade Agreement (NAFTA), adopted on 17 December 1992, entered into force on 1 January 1994.

[11] Energy Charter Treaty (ECT), signed on 17 December 1994, entered into force on 16 April 1998.

[12] See, for example Article 6(1) of the US Model BIT, which states in relevant part:

> 'The compensation referred to in paragraph 1(c) shall:
>
> (a) be paid without delay;
> (b) be equivalent to the fair market value of the expropriated investment immediately before the expropriation took place ('the date of expropriation');
> (c) not reflect any change in value occurring because the intended expropriation had become known earlier; and be fully realizable and freely transferable.

[13] See, for example, Article 5(1) of the UK Model BIT (2005), which states in relevant part:

> Such compensation shall amount to the genuine value of the investment expropriated immediately before the expropriation or before the impending expropriation became public knowledge, whichever is the earlier, shall include interest at a normal commercial rate until the date of payment, shall be made without delay, be effectively realizable and be freely transferable.

value',[14] or even sometimes only to 'the value'.[15] In addition, some treaties refer to certain valuation criteria. Article 1110(2) of NAFTA, for instance, provides that the compensation shall be equivalent to the fair market value of the investment to be assessed using valuation criteria, such as going concern or asset value:

> Compensation shall be equivalent to the fair market value of the expropriated investment immediately before the expropriation took place ('date of expropriation'), and shall not reflect any change in value occurring because the intended expropriation had become known earlier. Valuation criteria shall include going concern value, asset value including declared tax value of tangible property, and other criteria, as appropriate, to determine fair market value.

The overriding principle which is brought to bear in these provisions is that the investor must be made whole for the deprivation of his assets. In

[14] See, for example, Article 6(2) of the French Model BIT (2006), which states in relevant part:

> Toutes les mesures de dépossession qui pourraient être prises doivent donner lieu au paiement d'une indemnité prompte et adéquate dont le montant, égal à la valeur réelle des investissements concernés, doit être évalué par rapport à une situation économique normale et antérieure à toute menace de dépossession.
>
> Cette indemnité, son montant et ses modalités de versement sont fixés au plus tard à la date de la dépossession. Cette indemnité est effectivement réalisable, versée sans retard et librement transférable. Elle produit, jusqu'à la date de versement, des intérêts calculés au taux d'intérêt de marché approprié.

[15] See, for example, Article 4(2) of the Chinese Model BIT, which reads as follows:

> The compensation mentioned in Paragraph 1 of this Article shall be equivalent to the value of the expropriated investments immediately before the expropriation is taken or the impending expropriation becomes public knowledge, whichever is earlier. The value shall be determined in accordance with generally recognized principles of valuation. The compensation shall include interest at a normal commercial rate from the date of expropriation until the date of payment. The compensation shall also be made without delay, be effectively realizable and freely transferable.

Similarly, Article 4(2) of the German Model BIT (2005) reads in relevant part:

> Such compensation shall be equivalent to the value of the expropriated investment immediately before the date on which the actual or threatened expropriation, nationalization or comparable measure has become publicly known. The compensation shall be paid without delay and shall carry the usual bank interest until the time of payment; it shall be effectively realizable and freely transferable. Provision shall have been made in an appropriate manner at or prior to the time of expropriation, nationalization or comparable measure for the determination and payment of such compensation.

other words, the level of compensation must be sufficient to eliminate the effects of the expropriation. This principle is well established in customary international law, for which reference is made to the PCIJ's *Factory at Chorzów* case.[16]

Even where the treaty specifies compensation standards and valuation criteria, such as the NAFTA provision just quoted, the practical implementation of the full compensation principle lies within the tribunal's discretion. How do tribunals exercise this discretion?

The method most commonly used, at least with respect to the valuation of a commercial or industrial enterprise, is the discounted cash flow (DCF) analysis. The DCF method measures the value of an enterprise by discounting projected future cash flows over a given period of time to net present value. It has the advantage of recognizing that the real economic value of a business lies in its potential to generate profits.[17] In applying the DCF methodology, arbitrators proceed in three steps: first, they determine the net cash flows expected to be generated by the assets from the time of expropriation until a certain point in time in the future; second, they choose the appropriate discount rate; third, they discount the cash flows to reach the net present value of the future income streams, which then represents the compensation awarded.

This method calls for three main comments. First, it covers future lost profits or so-called expectation damages as opposed to reliance damages. In other words, the method places the investor in the situation in which he would have been had the host State complied with all of its obligations over the entire duration of the investment.

Second, the methodology implies several partially subjective assessments. One such assessment deals with the determination of future cash flows. How certain must future cash flows be to be taken into account? By nature, future events are uncertain. It is, therefore, necessary to draw a line beyond which cash flows are too uncertain or speculative to be compensable. Another partially subjective assessment lies in the determination of the discount rate. What risks must be reflected in the discount rate? To what extent does it have to account for business risk and project risk, inflation and currency risk, country risk and sovereign risk? The

[16] *Factory at Chorzów, Germany* v. *Poland*, Judgment on the Merits (1928) P.C.I.J. Series A, No. 17, 47.

[17] H. Weisburg and C. Ryan, 'Means to Be Made Whole – Damages in the Context of International Investment Arbitration' in Y. Derains and R. Kreindler (eds.), *Evaluation of Damages in International Arbitration* (Paris: Dossiers ICC, 2006), 173–4 with references.

answer to these questions is often made more difficult because the parties present widely divergent views regarding the level of an appropriate rate.

The third comment is linked to the uncertainty of future profits addressed above. Indeed, tribunals have found it difficult to apply the DCF method when there is no proven record of profitability, for instance, because the expropriated assets make losses or because the project has not started, or has failed at the preparatory negotiation or financing stage. Apposite illustrations of such situations are provided by *Tecmed* v. *Mexico*,[18] *Aucoven* v. *Venezuela*[19] or *PSEG* v. *Turkey*.[20] In cases such as these, the DCF methodology is often abandoned to avoid a speculative result.

In such cases, as well as in others where the DCF method appears inadequate because of the nature of the investment, arbitral tribunals resort to a number of other valuation methods. Often they will resort to the cost of the investment, that is, the costs and expenses incurred by the investor in connection with the investment.[21] In other words, the sum awarded is equivalent to reliance as opposed to expectation damages. They may also resort to the so-called replacement value, that is, the price one would have paid to buy the assets composing the expropriated investment on the day preceding the taking.[22] Although theoretically available, the valuations relying on book value or liquidation value of the assets are not generally considered to provide full compensation and are thus not, or seldom, used.

2.3 Compensation for unlawful expropriation and non-expropriatory breaches

Most investment treaties only contain provisions on compensation for lawful expropriation. They have no rules for unlawful expropriation and other illegal acts, such as breaches of fair and equitable treatment, national treatment or full protection and security standards.

[18] *Tecnicas Medioambientales Tecmed SA* v. *United Mexican States*, ICSID Case No. ARB(AF)/00/2, Award of 29 May 2003, paras. 185–6.

[19] *Autopistas Concesionadas de Venezuela CA* v. *Bolivarian Republic of Venezuela*, ICSID Case No. ARB/00/5, Award of 23 September 2003, paras. 353–65.

[20] *PSEG Global Inc. and Konya Iegin Elektrik Uretim ve Ticaret Limited Sirketi* v. *Turkey*, ICSID Case No. ARB/02/5, Award of 19 January 2007, paras. 305–9.

[21] See *Autopistas Concesionadas* Award, above, note 19, paras. 236–306; PSEG Award, paras. 316–40.

[22] See, for instance, *Government of the State of Kuwait* v. *American Independent Oil Co. (AMINOIL)*, Award of 24 March 1982, 21 I.L.M. (1982), paras. 164–7, 976ff.

Faced with such a gap, tribunals generally consider that damage awards should represent full reparation in accordance with the *Factory at Chorzów* case and that it is their task to establish standards of compensation in the light of the circumstances of the case.[23] Thus, for instance, the tribunal in the NAFTA dispute *Feldman* v. *Mexico* stated that the measure of compensation was the loss or damage actually incurred.[24]

If there is total loss or substantial deprivation of the assets, then the arbitrators often tend to resort to the fair market value standard and the DCF methodology by analogy to lawful expropriation. For example, the tribunal in *CMS* v. *Argentina*[25] held that fair market value was an appropriate measure for breaches resulting in long-term losses:

> Unlike the circumstances in the Feldman case, however, the Tribunal is persuaded that the cumulative nature of the breaches discussed here is best dealt with by resorting to the standard of fair market value. While this standard figures prominently in respect of expropriation, it is not

[23] See *Feldman (Marvin)* v. *Mexico*, ICSID Case No. ARB (AF)/99/1 (NAFTA), Award of 16 December 2002 (hereafter *Feldman* Award), paras. 195–7, referring to *S.D. Myers* v. *Government of Canada*, Partial Award, 13 November 2000, paras. 303–19 and *Pope & Talbot* v. *Government of Canada*, Award in Respect of Damages, 31 May 2002, paras. 81–90.

[24] See, for example *Feldman* Award, para. 194:

> NAFTA provides no further guidance as to the proper measure of damages or compensation for situations that do not fall under Article 1110 (expropriation); the only detailed measure of damages specifically provided in Chapter 11 is in Article 1110(2–3), 'fair market value', which necessarily applies only to situations that fall within that Article 1110. It follows that, in case of discrimination that constitutes a breach of Article 1110, what is owed by the responding Party is the amount of loss or damage that is adequately connected to the breach. In the absence of discrimination that also constitutes indirect expropriation or is tantamount to expropriation, a claimant would not be entitled to the full market value of the investment which is granted by NAFTA Article 1110. Thus, if loss or damage is the requirement for the submission of a claim, it arguably follows that the Tribunal may direct compensation in the amount of the loss or damage actually incurred.

A comparable approach was followed by the Tribunal in *MTD* v. *Chile*. See also *MTD Equity Sdn Bhd & MTD Chile S.A.* v. *Chile*, ICSID Case No. ARB/01/7 (Malaysia/Chile BIT), Award of 25 March 2004, para. 238.

[25] *CMS Gas Transmission Co.* v. *Argentina*, ICSID Case No. ARB/01/08 (United States/Argentina BIT), Award of 12 May 2005 (hereafter *CMS* Award), Annulment Decision of 25 September 2007 (hereafter *CMS* Annulment); see also *Metalclad Corp.* v. *United Mexican States*, ICSID Case No. ARB(AF)/97/1 (NAFTA), Award of 30 August 2000, reprinted in YO I.L.M. 36, 2001.

> excluded that it might also be appropriate for breaches different from expropriation if their effect results in important long-term losses.[26]

However, there are other situations in which the extent of the injury or the nature of the investment call for different solutions. The computation will thus often focus on actual losses, sometimes including lost profits. In this respect, arbitrators tend to place a strong emphasis on causation.[27]

In *LG&E* v. *Argentina*, for instance, the tribunal retained the 'actual loss' standard of compensation on the basis of a causation analysis:

> For the Tribunal, compensation in this case cannot be determined by the impact on the asset value; it does not reflect the actual damage incurred by Claimants. The measure of compensation has to be different.

Adding a few paragraphs later:

> The issue that the Tribunal has to address is that of the identification of the 'actual loss' suffered by the investor 'as a result' of Argentina's conduct. The question is one of 'causation': what did the investor lose by reason of the unlawful acts?[28]

In essence, the preceding discussion suggests that for most breaches of investment guarantees, arbitral tribunals enjoy considerable discretionary power when setting compensation.

2.4 *Compensation-reducing factors*

Several factors may conceivably reduce compensation.[29] First, it can occur that the injury was caused by concurrent causes, only one of which is attributable to the respondent state. Such concurrent causes can either be ascribed to the victim of the breach, which has then committed contributory negligence or fault, or to a third party. Second, the victim of the breach may have failed to mitigate the damage once it has materialized.

In respect of concurrent causes, the *CME* v. *Czech Republic* tribunal noted, by reference to the ILC Articles, that these would not justify a reduction unless the cause rested with the victim:

[26] *CMS* Award, para. 410. See also *Sempra Energy* v. *Argentina*, ICSID Case No. ARB/02/16 (United States/Argentina BIT), Award of 28 September 2007 (hereafter *Sempra* Award), paras. 402–4.

[27] See T. Wälde and B. Sabahi, 'Compensation, Damages, and Valuation', 1093ff.

[28] *LG&E* Damages, above, note 8, paras. 36 and 45.

[29] See on this issue: T. Wälde and B. Sabahi, 'Compensation, Damages, and Valuation', 1093ff; C. McLachlan, L. Shore and M. Weiniger, *International Investment Arbitration Substantive Principles*, 335ff.

> International practice and the decisions of international tribunals do not support the reduction or attenuation of reparation of concurrent causes, except in cases of contributory fault.[30]

In support of this statement, the *CME* tribunal referred in particular to the Commentary of the Articles of the ILC, which reads as follows:

> It is true that cases can occur where an identifiable element of injury can properly be allocated to one of several concurrently operating causes alone. But unless some part of the injury can be shown to be severable in causal terms from that attributed to the responsible State, the latter is held responsible for all the consequences, not being too remote, of its wrongful conduct.[31]

In other words, it appears that compensation may generally be reduced if it is established that a certain proportion of the damage is due to a cause other than the respondent state's act, be it to an act of a third party or of the victim itself. This being so, the allocation of the burden of proof becomes critical. The burden of proving compensation-reducing facts rests *a priori* on the respondent, once the claimant has established the damage and a causal link between the illegal act and the damage.[32]

On this basis, tribunals have reduced the measure of compensation because part of the damage resulted from a misjudgement of the investor,[33] for instance, when the victim of the injury had overinvested. As an illustration, one can cite a situation which arose in an unreported case where the investor had increased the value of its investment at a time when it was likely that the government was about to take measures affecting the investment.[34]

Similarly, tribunals reduce the amount of damages if the investor has failed to take action to mitigate the harm caused by the state's act. The tribunal in *Middle East Cement* v. *Egypt* recognized the duty to mitigate in the following terms:

[30] *CME Czech Republic BV* v. *Czech Republic*, UNCITRAL Arbitration Rules, I.I.C. 61 (2001), Partial Award and Separate Opinion of 13 September 2001, para. 583.

[31] *CME Czech Republic BV* v. *Czech Republic* quoting Commentary 13 to Article 31 of the ILC Articles.

[32] See T. Wälde and B. Sabahi, 'Compensation, Damages, and Valuation', 1111.

[33] X. W. M. Reisman and R. D. Sloane, 'Indirect Expropriation and its Valuation in the BIT Generation', in *British Yearbook of International Law*, 74 (2003), 118, 130; see also Article 39, ILC Articles on contribution to the injury by the injured state.

[34] See also *MTD Equity Sdn Bhd and MTD Chile S.A.* v *Republic of Chile*, ICSID Case No. ARB/01/7, Award of 25 May 2004, paras. 242–3; *Azurix Corp.* v *Republic of Argentine*, ICSID Case No. ARB/01/12, Award of 14 July 2006, para. 426.

> The duty to mitigate damages is not expressly mentioned in the BIT. However, this duty can be considered to be part of the General Principles of Law which, in turn, are part of the rules of international law which are applicable in this dispute according to Art. 42 of the ICSID Convention.[35]

A reduction on this ground would, for example, be justified if the state's illegal act prevented the investor from producing certain goods and he failed to undertake the production of similar unrestricted goods when the change was reasonably feasible, a situation present in the unreported case mentioned earlier. By contrast, in *Middle East Cement* v. *Egypt*, the arbitral tribunal found that the supply of similar unrestricted goods was not an 'economically feasible alternative'[36] to the supply of the restricted goods.[37]

Another question that arises in the context of compensation-reducing factors is whether the capacity to pay of the respondent state should be taken into consideration. Among scholars the opinions are divided.[38] Arbitral tribunals have avoided addressing the issue directly, though they may have impliedly integrated paying capacity in their thinking when assessing compensation. Moreover, in reliance on the practice of the European Court of Human Rights which applies proportionality when reviewing the level of indemnities for expropriations,[39] tribunals may conceivably reduce compensation on this ground. There is an indication to this effect in *CMS* v. *Argentina*, where the tribunal held that it was unrealistic to believe that no adjustments would have been made to a pay-or-ship contract as a result of the crisis, in other words as a result of Argentina's financial difficulties.[40]

[35] See *Middle East Cement Shipping and Handling Co. SA* v. *Egypt*, ICSID Case No. ARB/99/6, Award of 12 April 2002, para. 167.

[36] *Middle East Cement* v. *Egypt*, para. 168.

[37] Similarly, in *Amco* the failure by an investor to sell its contractual interests to a third party following the revocation of an investment licence was not considered a breach of the duty to mitigate, as 'there was no realistic prospect of it being able to mitigate its loss'. See *Amco Asia Corporation, Pan American Development Ltd and PT Amco Indonesia* v. *Republic of Indonesia*, ICSID Case No. ARB/81/8, Award of 5 June 1990, paras. 78–9.

[38] T. Wälde and B. Sabahi, 'Compensation, Damages, and Valuation', 1098 and citations in footnote 209.

[39] See extensive discussion in U. Kriebaum, 'Eigentumsschutz im Völkerrecht. Eine vergleichende Untersuchung zum internationalen Investitionsrecht sowie zum Menschenrechtsschutz', Duncker und Humblot, 2008, 506ff.

[40] *CMS* Award, para. 444.

3 Characteristics of damage assessment in investment arbitration

3.1 Discretion

The preceding section shows that the standards and methodologies used for the determination of compensation leave wide discretion to investment arbitral tribunals. Such discretion can be seen at different levels of the process.

First, absent a specific treaty provision, arbitral tribunals have wide discretion to select the proper standard of compensation. Such standards include the fair market value of an investment or the actual loss incurred by an investor to name just a few. Second, arbitral tribunals also have considerable discretion with respect to the selection of a valuation methodology, such as DCF or replacement costs. Moreover, even when one standard has been selected, tribunals may wish to add some adjustments, for instance, by the introduction of a proportionality analysis in the computation of compensation for a regulatory taking. Third, even when a methodology has been selected, arbitral tribunals retain control over the particular manner in which such methodology is applied to the facts.

This state of the law and practice has led the tribunal in *Himpurna* to inquire whether:

> the result [of the application of one methodology] – in that case and often elsewhere – is not to create an illusion of scientific analysis to mask the reality of subjective approximation.[41]

Be this as it may, it is certain that damage assessments as they are presently conducted by investment tribunals involve a substantial degree of discretion.

3.2 Complexity

The surge in investment disputes in the last several years has carried with it a wide variety of issues upon which tribunals are called to decide, including in the area of compensation. As investors explore the limits of the protections granted by investment treaties with increasingly sophisticated complex arguments in disputes with growing stakes, it becomes

[41] See *Himpurna California Energy Ltd* v. *P.T. (Persero) Perusahaan Listruik Negara*, Award of 4 May 1999, *Yearbook Commercial Arbitration*, vol. XXV (2000), 11–432, para. 373.

more and more difficult in practice for arbitrators with a legal background to reach meaningful results.

A first difficulty relates to the availability of the data necessary to conduct a reasonably accurate assessment of damages. Although from a legal standpoint this difficulty could be mastered by resorting to the rules on burden of proof,[42] such an approach may be unsatisfactory from both the practical and economic points of view.

A second difficulty arises in connection with the assessment of the accuracy of conflicting expert valuations produced by the parties. Given the often sophisticated techniques used by party-appointed experts, the predominantly legal backgrounds of arbitrators and the not infrequent ambiguity of the source data, it is often difficult for the tribunal to assess the relative merits of the divergent reports presented by the parties' experts.

A possible solution to this second difficulty, which has been adopted in recent cases, is the appointment by the tribunal of its own damage expert to assist it in evaluating the evidence of the party-appointed experts. Because of the complexity of the economic issues, there is certainly a need for more involvement of economists in investment arbitration. To this extent, the appointment of tribunal experts is a welcome development. This course of action may, however, give rise to breaches of due process if the expert is allowed to give input to the tribunal without the parties having access to and being able to comment on such input. The mission of the tribunal expert must thus be defined in a manner that complies with due process guarantees.

4 Discretion and direct compensation in the WTO system as viewed from investment law

4.1 *Preliminary remarks*

Building on the preceding discussion, this section examines two criticisms voiced by trade specialists against the assessment of compensation in the WTO context. These criticisms are of particular interest here because they relate to important similarities between the WTO and the investment regimes.

[42] On the allocation of the burden of proof see: A. Reiner, 'The Standards and Burden of Proof in International Arbitration', *Arbitration International*, 10 (1994), 328ff; M. Kazazi, *Burden of Proof and Related Issues: A Study of Evidence before International Tribunals* (The Hague: Kluwer Law, 1996); T. Wälde and B. Sabahi, 'Compensation, Damages, and Valuation', 1110ff.

The first criticism is put forward by Simon Schropp in Chapter 20, above.[43] It deals with the manner in which arbitrators acting under Article 22 of the Dispute Settlement Understanding (DSU)[44] and tasked with the equivalence assessment between the level of 'nullification or impairment' (NoI) suffered by the injured state and the level of the 'suspension of concessions or other obligations under the covered agreements' (SCOO) have so far exercised their mandate.[45]

The second criticism is developed by Alan Sykes in Chapter 16, above.[46] It is targeted at recent proposals to replace or supplement trade sanctions with direct monetary compensation to injured exporters.[47]

4.2 *Discretion in the assessment of compensation in the WTO system?*

The main argument of Schropp's contribution is that arbitrators acting pursuant to Article 22 of the DSU have largely misunderstood their

[43] Simon Schropp, 'The Equivalence Standard under Article 22.4 DSU: A "Tariffic" Misunderstanding?', Chapter 20, above.

[44] Understanding on Rules and Procedures Governing the Settlement of Disputes, Annex 2 to the Agreement Establishing the World Trade Organization, opened for signature on 15 April 1994 and entered into force on 1 January 1995.

[45] Article 22(7) of the DSU states:

> The arbitrator acting pursuant to paragraph 6 shall not examine the nature of the concessions or other obligations to be suspended but shall determine whether the level of such suspension is equivalent to the level of nullification or impairment. The arbitrator may also determine if the proposed suspension of concessions or other obligations is allowed under the covered agreement. However, if the matter referred to arbitration includes a claim that the principles and procedures set forth in paragraph 3 have not been followed, the arbitrator shall examine that claim. In the event the arbitrator determines that those principles and procedures have not been followed, the complaining party shall apply them consistent with paragraph.

[46] Alan Sykes, 'Optimal Sanctions in the WTO: The Case for Decoupling (and the Uneasy Case for the *Status Quo*)', Chapter 16, above.

[47] Sykes refers in this regard to: K. Bagwell, P. Mavroidis and R. Staiger, 'Auctioning Countermeasures in the WTO', *Journal of International Economics*, 73 (2007), 309ff; M. Bronckers and N. van den Broek, 'Financial Compensation in the WTO: Improving the Remedies of WTO Dispute Settlement', *Journal of International Economic Law*, 8 (2005), 101ff; S. Charnovitz, 'Rethinking WTO Trade Sanctions', *American Journal of International Law*, 95 (2001), 792ff; W. Davey, 'The Sutherland Report on Dispute Settlement: A Comment', *Journal of International Economic Law*, 8 (2005), 321ff; R. Lawrence, *Crimes and Punishments: Retaliation under the WTO* (Washington, DC: Institute for International Economics, 2003); J. Pauwelyn, 'Enforcement and Countermeasures in the WTO: Rules are Rules – Toward a More Collective Approach', *American Journal of International Law*, 94 (2000), 335ff.

mandate or at least misapplied the relevant provisions when seeking to assess whether the level of the SCOO contemplated by the complaining member state, as a response to a breach of the WTO obligations by another member state, was equivalent to the level of the NoI caused by such breach.

This is because arbitrators have: (1) used the wrong measure of damages to assess NoI by focusing on the actual loss suffered by the complaining member state instead of more fully taking into account the economic expectations in the absence of a breach or 'expectation damages'; and (2) used the wrong metrics or valuation techniques to assess such 'expectation damages', namely, instead of taking into account the overall 'economic gains and losses' resulting from the breach they have focused on the trade directly blocked by such breach. In essence, to put this argument in terms closer to investment law, what is lacking in the assessment of NoI by WTO arbitrators is the lost profits dimension of damages. Schropp further argues that WTO arbitrators have adopted a hands-off approach to the calculation of SCOO. To address these difficulties, Schropp suggests a change in the manner in which WTO arbitrators interpret Article 22 of the DSU and more room for economic expert analysis. He advocates 'a rethinking of previous arbitration practice, an improvement of legal practice and a renunciation of legal precedent'[48] and a move away from flexibility and discretion.

This radical proposition calls for three comments from the perspective of international investment arbitration, it being understood that the other aspects of Schropp's comments are specific to the regulatory angle adopted by trade law.

First, abandoning consistent previous practice is not a step that can be taken easily. Even in the absence of a formal rule of *stare decisis*, the inclination of international tribunals is to take account of earlier cases, especially when they can rely on a series of consistent decisions.[49] In

[48] Simon Schropp, Chapter 20, above, section 5.2. Schropp refers in this regard to the constant reminder by arbitrators, dispute panels and the WTO Appellate Body that the WTO does not know the rule of *stare decisis* and quotes footnote 57 of *US–Byrd* which reads: 'As a matter of fact, we do not consider previous arbitrations to be constitutive of "subsequent practice" within the meaning of that concept under public international law.'

[49] On the use of precedents in international arbitration, see G. Kaufmann-Kohler, 'Arbitral Precedent: Dream, Necessity or Excuse?', *Arbitration International*, 23 (2007), 357ff and Y. Banifatemi (ed.), *Precedent in International Arbitration*, IAI Series in International Arbitration, No. 5, (Paris: IAI, 2008).

investment arbitration, there is precisely a debate on how to foster consistency.[50] A recent report of the WTO Appellate Body also emphasizes the need for consistency.[51]

Second, the practice in investment arbitration shows that arbitral tribunals enjoy broad discretion when fixing compensation. This allows them to take into consideration the nature of the investment and all the surrounding circumstances, which can vary significantly. It possibly further allows them to factor into their end result some considerations of fairness. As always, flexibility certainly implies an element of unpredictability. It is, nevertheless, valuable because it allows one to reach an outcome that appears generally adequate under the circumstances.

Third, as noted in the preceding section, the increasing complexity involved in the assessment of compensation is a real challenge for arbitrators. In this regard, there is no doubt that more room for economic experts is welcome under both the WTO and the investment regimes, provided due process is safeguarded. Moreover, better elaboration of the reasons explaining the damage assessment would also be welcome as it would buttress the legitimacy of the system.

4.3 Direct compensation to injured exporters in the WTO system?

Another criticism of the WTO system, which presents a direct connection with the regulatory angle adopted by investment law, is that advanced by Alan Sykes against the reform proposals seeking to directly compensate injured exporters.[52]

Sykes' argument takes as a starting point the characterization of the WTO sanctions system as a 'decoupled' one, namely, one in which 'recalcitrant violator nations may pay a price in the form of trade sanctions, but the exporters injured by violations do not receive compensation for the harm caused by violations'.[53] Sykes then sets out to examine 'the wisdom of moving away from a decoupled system in the direction of a system that provides direct compensation to exporters' and concludes that the current decoupled system seems preferable to a reformed system.

[50] See, for example, G. Kaufmann-Kohler, 'In Search of Transparency or Consistency: ICSID Reform Proposals, International Dispute management', *Transnational Dispute Management*, 2: 5 (2005), 8.

[51] World Trade Organization, Report of the Appellate Body, United States – Final AntiDumping Measures on Stainless Steel from Mexico, 30 April 2008, para. 160.

[52] See above, note 47. [53] Alan Sykes, Chapter 16, above, Introduction.

Five reasons support this conclusion. They will be reviewed here from the perspective of international investment law. First, Sykes argues that compensating injured exporters, even when a breach is 'efficient', may incite firms relying on market access or full compensation (in case of access restriction) to overinvest in anticipation of serving that particular market.[54] Investment arbitration shows that the risk of overinvestment can be dealt with by reducing compensation to take into account that the investor has contributed to create a portion of the damage.

Sykes' second reason against designing a direct compensation regime relates to the difficulty and cost of taking the damage analysis from the level of aggregate trade volume to that of a particular exporting firm, and further to the other firms that indirectly benefit from the business of exporters. That second objection appears mainly empirical in nature and is thus difficult to assess in a context different from trade law, but suffice it to say that the challenges appear real and could certainly be mastered only with the increased involvement of damage experts.

The same comment applies *mutatis mutandis* to Sykes' third reason, which refers to the deadweight cost of protection which could allegedly be avoided through monetary compensation of exporters. Sykes argues that whether or not such deadweight cost saving could be attained would depend upon the deadweight costs of the taxes imposed to raise the funds for compensation,[55] the relationship between the two being an empirical one.

The fourth reason points to likely higher cost and volume of litigation if exporters were entitled to direct compensation, whether they are given a private right of action or not. The risk of additional litigation and extra costs, which among others would burden the budgets of developing countries, is real if one is to judge from the experience of investment law. The incorporation into a growing number of investment treaties of a private right of the investor to bring claims against the host state of the investment has brought about an increasing number of cases. Current estimates speak of approximately 300 pending investment arbitrations in 2007, as opposed to about ten to twenty, 10 years earlier.[56] Yet, despite the surge in investor claims and the fact that developing countries are frequently involved in investment disputes,[57] the current system appears to work adequately.

[54] Alan Sykes, Chapter 16, above, section 3. [55] Alan Sykes, Chapter 16, above, section 3.

[56] UNCTAD, 'Latest Developments in Investor–State Dispute Settlement', *IIA Monitor*, No. 1 (2008), 1.

[57] Forty-four out of seventy-three governments involved in investment arbitrations in 2007 were from the developing world (UNCTAD, 'Latest Developments in Investor–State Dispute Settlement', *IIA Monitor*, No. 1 (2008), 2).

It is true that investment arbitration faces criticism which is in part legitimate. The criticism focuses primarily on the lack of transparency of the process. To a lesser extent, it also addresses the lack of consistency in outcome on certain legal issues, as well as a perceived deficiency in democratic legitimacy of the decision makers. Interestingly, the number of cases and the resulting costs are not the subject of any meaningful criticism.

The fifth and final objection asserts that compensation may represent a heavy burden for developing countries, especially when the breaches are a result of limited compliance capacity rather than deliberate non-compliance. Here again, the experience gathered in investment arbitration does not appear to support this concern. Moreover, as the discussion in the context of investment arbitration has shown, there are arguments in favour of adjusting the level of compensation to the paying capacity of the respondent state. This can be done by integrating a proportionality analysis into the determination of the quantum or by relying on considerations of fairness, whether expressed or implied in some of the subjective factors of compensation assessment.

5 Concluding remarks

In summary, the different regulatory angles adopted by trade and investment law should guard against any hasty transposition. This said, some insight can certainly be gained from the practice of investment arbitration. Overall, that practice shows that with a fair level of discretion in the choice of the methodology and valuation techniques and an increasing measure of expert assistance, investment arbitrators are in a position to assess direct compensation. It is hoped that the experience so gathered in investment arbitration may provide some avenues for further exploration by trade specialists. More generally, the interactions and possible areas of cross-fertilization between these two fields of international economic law are certainly worth monitoring closely in the years to come.

25

Reforming WTO retaliation: any lessons from competition law?

SIMON J. EVENETT*

Introduction and preliminary observations

Perhaps it is because both competition law (or antitrust law as it is known in North America) and international trade law ultimately influence commercial outcomes that the question arises as to whether the regime of sanctions applied in one branch of law may have lessons for the other. The purpose of this brief chapter is to describe, where the author feels it is legitimate and appropriate, the possible implications of the sanctions regimes employed in competition law for the enforcement of international trade law and the WTO agreements in particular.

One challenge in drawing any implications for trade law is that, while competition laws have been on the statute books in some jurisdictions for over a hundred years, in fact, competition laws are for much of the world a relatively new phenomenon. Experience has revealed that the political machinations necessary to get many competition laws enacted in the first place often requires substantial compromise and, quite frankly, weakening of both the law's substantive provisions and sanctions regime.

Moreover, once a competition law regime is in place and the deficiencies associated with its initial implementation become well appreciated, then second generation reforms tend to be implemented. The latter typically involve the strengthening the sanctions regime of competition laws: that is, raising maximum fines, including the possibility of triple or multiple damages for injured parties, as well as including the possibility of incarcerating persons who have engaged in certain anticompetitive acts. In short, competition laws and their sanction regimes have been evolving over time

* Professor of International Trade and Economic Development, Department of Economics, University of St. Gallen, Switzerland. Co-Director, International Trade and Regional Economics Programme, Centre for Economic Policy Research, London.

and while this evolution may inform thinking about the preferred sanctions regime for the WTO, certain caveats necessarily arise as well.

Another factor that needs to be taken into account is that the provisions of competition law can relate to the behaviour of private commercial enterprises as well as to state bodies. Some of the sanctions contained in competition law for private parties may not be feasible or allowable for state parties, such as the incarceration of an individual involved in a so-called hard core cartel. This limits the set of possible implications of competition law's sanctions regime for the design of WTO dispute settlement. Moreover, as will be argued below, some of the sanctions which relate to state violations of competition law may be of greatest relevance to the potential reform of WTO procedures.

It is also important to remember that there is typically a body of law and process that stands behind any particular sanction used in an economic law, and that the former are important in determining the credibility of the latter. A private party can be credibly fined for violating some aspect of national competition law precisely because it is understood that if the fine is not paid some other, perhaps more severe, sanction will be imposed on the party involved. Similar considerations apply in the context of international trade law where the parties are states or government bodies. In the latter case, even if fines could be imposed for violating a WTO agreement, ultimately the credibility of fining a state will depend on the fact that more traditional trade sanctions (typically taking the form of the withdrawal of prior tariff concessions) can be imposed if the fine is not paid. These considerations also imply that any two possible sanctions may not be such stark alternatives as initially thought, limiting perhaps the extent to which sanctions used under competition law in fact add to the set of sanctions that can be employed in international trade disputes.

One factor that may be partly responsible for any differences in the sanctioning regimes of competition and international trade law is that the very purpose of the sanctions differs across these laws. In the case of competition law, it may be the case that the allowed sanctions are designed with the goal of deterring and punishing anticompetitive acts (it being recognised that deterrence and punishment are distinct matters). Whereas, if the purpose of a dispute settlement procedure in a trade agreement is to encourage any party to come back into compliance at the earliest possible moment, as appears to be the case in WTO dispute settlement, then the very notion of 'sanctions' and of 'punishing' a party may be unnecessary and possibly even counterproductive. Indeed, the sanctions regime to discourage a party from deviating from an international trade accord may be different from the measures necessary to encourage a party to come back into compliance. Ultimately policymakers and analysts may have to choose between these two objectives, with potential implications for the degree to which competition law and its sanctions regime have to offer discussions on the reform of WTO dispute settlement procedures.

With these preliminary remarks in mind, the discussion now turns to some (hopefully first-order) implications of the sanctions regimes of competition law for the potential reform of the measures taken during WTO dispute settlement.

The use of fines

As is well known, a long-standing concern with using tariff increases as a form of trade sanction is that they reduce the welfare of the party imposing the sanction. Fines, that in this context are essentially what economists refer to as a transfer between nations, do not distort the allocation of resources and so are efficient. While it is certainly not novel to advocate the replacement of tariff increases with fines in the sanctions regimes of international trade accords, what is of particular interest here is the experience with employing fines in competition law, bearing in mind that in many jurisdictions fines are a permitted sanction under national competition laws for numerous infringements.

From time to time the Organisation for Economic Co-operation and Development (OECD) collects data on the total magnitude of fines imposed against parties involved in anticompetitive acts and the estimates of the private gains from undertaking these acts. The associated findings are consistently depressing in that the total fines are always a fraction of the total private gains. Competition agencies appear, therefore, to be reluctant to set fines at levels necessary to deter anticompetitive conduct or even to remove the benefits from illicit acts! The question arises as to whether an international agency or board would be similarly cowed into setting too low fines against national governments found to be violating international trade agreements. At a minimum one might ask what procedures need to be put in place to ensure the correct levels of fines are put in place.

One reason why the fines of private actors under competition law have tended to be too low is that in cases where the anticompetitive act is expected to last several years the fine necessary to deter illicit behaviour, reflecting the probability of the private actors being caught and, therefore, being a multiple of the private gain, is large enough so as to bankrupt the firms involved. This 'bankruptcy' constraint may not have a direct analogue in the case of national governments, not least because states have access to streams of tax revenues over time, even so there could be effectively a political constraint in that fines paid to an international body are seen as coming at the expense of sensitive government expenditures, such as those on health, education, and the like.

The use of cease and desist orders

In many first generation competition laws official agencies were given the right to order parties involved in anticompetitive acts to cease and desist. Cartels, in particular, were often ordered to cease and desist. Does this experience have anything to offer for resolving international trade disputes? In principle, the attractiveness of this option is that the adverse practice ceases without any punitive measures being taken, measures that in the trade context could be provocative, politically unacceptable or distortive of economic resources.

If anything, however, experience seems to discount this option, not least because the competition agency has to check whether any order is being complied with and frequently this was not so. In the case of cartels there has been a progressive replacement of cease and desist orders with stronger sanctions (fines and in some cases incarceration) as competition laws have been revised. Another weakness of cease and desist orders is that they provided no deterrence to anticompetitive conduct in the first place.

The use of behavioural and structural remedies

Fines are by no means the only measure that competition authorities can impose. Two other, and often very controversial, measures that can be taken are so-called behavioural remedies and structural remedies. Behavioural remedies are steps ordered by a competition authority that parties have to undertake or refrain from undertaking that do not involve a change in the ownership of the firms involved or subsidiaries of the firms involved. Behavioural remedies include restrictions on prices charged, investment and employment decisions and contractual terms with suppliers. Structural remedies involve a party being ordered to sell off or liquidate commercial assets associated with a subsidiary. The latter are, therefore, often associated with 'breaking up' of a company.

It should be acknowledged that there are sharp disagreements among competition law experts as to the merits of such remedies in specific cases;

even so, these remedies do point to measures that a competition authority can take that are more intrusive than fines. The question here is whether there is any applicability to international trade disputes? To the extent that such remedies can act as a substitute for fines then they may well correct aberrant behaviour and, it should be recognised, discouraging the latter in the first place. The first-order matter, however, may be whether it is an acceptable intrusion on national sovereignty for a WTO body to specify precisely how a member state should come back into compliance with an international trade accord. In particular, the imposition of structural remedies, that in this context could amount to the creation of new government agencies or reallocation of functions from one agency to another, may be regarded as too great a constraint on national autonomy. Still, any consideration of the experience from competition law ought to point to this logical possibility.

The matter of state subsidies or state aids

Perhaps the element of competition law that is most directly related to international trade law concerns provisions relating to the state subsidisation of commercial parties, be they private or public. Laws constraining and even banning state subsidies to parties engaged in commercial activity, especially those parties that compete with other parties, are known as state aids legislation in the EU. Given that EU competition law has either provided the template for many other jurisdictions' competition laws or has influenced the latter, state aids legislation is by no means confined to Europe.

The motivation for state aid legislation is related to the international integration of markets, typically through trade reform and ultimately the creation of free trade agreements, customs unions and so-called single markets. The concern is expressed that after formal trade barriers have fallen governments would seek to 'tilt' the playing field in favour of firms located in their jurisdiction by offering them financial payments or by exempting such firms from payments they would have otherwise made to the state. Such subsidies distort competition between firms and the purpose of state aid legislation is to constrain, and, ultimately, ban the use of such financial measures. Unlike much of competition law that seeks to influence the behaviour of private firms, the object of state aid legislation is public bodies that can grant such financial favours. Therefore, in this respect state aid legislation comes close to international trade accords whose signatories are also public authorities.

Within the EU there appears to have been a shift over time in the manner through which sanctions and remedies associated with state aids have been implemented. Initially state aid investigations typically resulted in fines, thereby punishing violators. Over time, however, repayment of any sums advanced to private parties has been stressed, with the goal apparently to establish a structure of sanctions that ultimately discourages firms from seeking financial support in the first place. Again, as noted above, the lessons to be drawn depend crucially on the objective of the sanctions regime.

For completeness' sake it must also be noted how controversial the implementation of state aids legislation has been within the EU. Investigations associated with these matters frequently put the European Commission at loggerheads with national governments and were it not for the established importance of the former then the latter would surely prevail. Should the WTO or any associated body take on strong powers in the area of state aids, or sanctions modelled on state aids, then the question arises as to whether a backlash from member states could be contained after an adverse judgment. In the light of the recent (fourth quarter, 2008) relaxation of European state aid rules during the current sharp global economic downturn, questions must surely be raised as to the long-term viability of any particularly strict set of state aids rules and sanctions. A set of sanctions may be viable when one party contemplates breaking the rules, but when circumstances lead many parties to (almost simultaneously) consider breaking a set of rules then those rules and associated sanctions may not survive a pronounced collective deviation.

Concluding remarks

According to the United Nations approximately a hundred jurisdictions have some form of competition law on their statute books, and one might think that the associated experience could offer lessons for the potential reform of the sanctions regime of WTO dispute settlement. In this short chapter it has been argued that there may be fewer implications for the latter than one might have thought. This is because the object and purpose of sanctions under competition law is often different from that under international trade law. As far as the purpose is concerned, a major reform choice would be between a sanctions regime that encourages WTO members to come back into compliance as quickly as possible (as appears to be the current regime) or a sanctions regime that discourages WTO members from deviating from international accords in the first place.

Another theme developed here was that the experience with competition law shows that there may be limitations in the application of certain sanctions or remedies in the international trade arena. Some of those limitations may be technical and others may be related to their political viability, as the discussion on behavioural and structural remedies made clear. Moreover, even if non-distortive sanctions can be applied (such as fines) one may need the credible threat of distortive trade sanctions to ensure the former are complied with. It may, therefore, not be appropriate to think of distinct options for sanctions but rather of sets of mutually reinforcing instruments that seek to encourage desired state behaviour.

INDEX

additional commitments
  GATS provision for 595–6
  suspension of 599–600
adjudication *see* arbitration
'agreements', definition of 591–2
agricultural chemical regulatory data, suspension of protection of 575–7, 582
alternatives to retaliation
  behavioural remedies 644–5
  cease and desist orders 644
  compatibility with dispute settlement 90–1
  compensation 364
  fines 643–4
  structural remedies 644–5
  use of 83, 90
'amount of monetary cost imposed' metric for NoI 107
'amount-of-subsidy' approach *see* appropriateness standard of level of retaliation
antidumping penalties, US use of 236
Antigua and Barbuda
  ability to retaliate against United States 321
  concern over self-damage from imposing sanctions 322–3
  consideration of relevant factors in cross-retaliation request 123
  cross-retaliation in *US–Internet Gambling* 81–2, 310–13
    arbitrators' decision on cross-retaliation request 520–2
    GATS, implications of 314–16
    overview of jurisprudence 542–4
    quantifying IP rights 528
    reasons for not imposing sanctions 334–5
    request for cross-retaliation 516–17
    scope of chapter 310
    use to improve negotiating position 525–6
  retaliation under TRIPS, application of 313–14
  statement on applying sanctions 15
  use of sanctions 76–8, 81
appellate review of decisions, need for 260–1
appropriateness standard of level of retaliation
  'amount-of-subsidy' approach
    description 114–16
    reasons for 116–18
  'appropriate'
    arbitrators' approaches to defining 118
    interpretation of 137–40
    meaning of 117
  'appropriate countermeasures', full amount of subsidy as basis for calculating 139–40
  'equality-of-harm' approach, use of 118
  rules for 114–18
arbitration *see also* decisions
  appellate review of decisions, need for 260–1
  authorization request for retaliation following 97–8
  causation issues in 369–71
  de Vattel on 27
  deciding level of 31–3

distinction between legal and non-legal disputes 26–31
'final offer' 443–4
improved interpretation as reform agenda 449
precedential effect of prior awards 97
process 95–7, 344
provision for 25
reasons for introducing 344–5
role of 25–6
third-party adjudication 107–8
use of 25–6

arbitration reports
identifying goal of retaliation, as basis for 49
list 2
page length of (table) 421

arbitrators 20
ability to calculate authorized level of retaliation
Byrd Amendment dispute, in 20
investment disputes, in 20
statement in *US–Gambling* 15–16
approach to export subsidies, need for consistent 5
'appropriate', approaches to defining 118
assessment of harm caused by trade rule violation 1
assessment of practicability and effectiveness of cross-retaliation 120–2
assessment of sanctions, scope for 136
authority to review cross-retaliation requests 518
burden of proof in cross-retaliation, decision on 519–20
calculation of NoI 100–11
assessment of 479
Canada–Aircraft dispute, collection of evidence in 20
chilling effect of violations, consideration of 369–70
choice of benchmarks and counterfactuals 1
choice of own calculation of level of sanctions 136–7
compensation, critique of approach to 635–6
compliance claim following retaliation in *EC–Hormones*, decision on 371–2
conformity of measure, decision on 29–30
conformity with Bagwell and Staiger theory 17
cross-retaliation under TRIPS
general remarks on 523–4
jurisprudence 538–9
data and evidence used by
collection of 19–20
improving quality of 133–4
decision-making process, economic modelling of 152
decision on cross-retaliation 1
decision on initial request for authorization 96–7
decision on level of retaliation 31–2
decision on purpose of retaliation 123–6
direct-trade-blocked metric, use of 447
discretion
consider non-legal issues, to 18
degree of 31
disputes, in (table) 406
economic analysis and modelling from WTO Secretariat, use of *see* World Trade Organization (WTO)
economists as 404–5
'effectiveness' of retaliation, interpretation of 40
entitlement to use different metrics for NoI 106–7
'equality-of-harm' approach, use of 99–113
equivalence standard, interpretation of 478–9
arguments against flawed interpretation thesis 494
improved practice, suggestions for 500–2

arbitrators (*cont.*)
estimating future damages, role in 32
'final offer arbitration', role in 18
final word in decisions 29
influence on members' economic policies, examples of 391–2
instructions on level of SCOO 16
interpretation of equivalence standard 138
interpretation of preconditions for authorizing cross-retaliation 15
justification for recalculation of level of sanctions 137
legal and technical support from Secretariat 392
limitation on power to examine proposed retaliation 95–6
mandate 95–7
NoI calculation baseline used by 481
reasonable period of time for compliance, decision on 30–1
reciprocity model, use of 4
review of cross-retaliation request 119
SCOO
consideration of 447, 448, 486–9
restriction on 495
opinion on calculation of level of 489–92
statements by, as basis for identifying goal of retaliation 42, 48–9 *see also specific disputes*
tasks of 446
terms of reference 96
US–Internet Gambling, award in 310–13
Argentina, disputes involving valuing of compensation 630–1
Asociación Latinoamericana de Integración (ALADI), *Peru–Computers* dispute 288–9
authorization procedure for retaliation 1
arbitrators' decision on initial request 96–7
burden of proof 97
grants of authorization 329
initial request 94–5
post-award request 97–8
precedential effect of prior awards 97
role of economics in 1
rules on 94–9
ultra vires, ensuring that measures are not 98
authorized level of retaliation
identifying goal of retaliation, as basis for 41–2
law of
conclusions of chapter 126–7
scope of chapter 89–90
limits on 282–4
'efficient breach' argument for 346
reasons for 345–7
auxiliary entitlements 455–6

Bagwell and Staiger reciprocity model *see* reciprocity model of retaliation
'banana waiver' 26
benchmark
arbitrators' choice of 1
export subsidy amount as 5
impact of reciprocity versus welfare debate on choice of 6–7
importance of goal of retaliation in choosing 39
trade loss as, for NoI 142–3
undercompensatory 17
Berne Convention, interaction with TRIPS 553
bilateral investment treaties (BITS)
compensation provisions 626–7
relation to TRIPS 557–60
bilateral trade agreements, relation to TRIPS 557–60
Brazil
Canadian retaliation against, effectiveness of 279–80
cross-retaliation request 516–17, 545
MERCOSUR obligations 301

procedures for retaliation
conclusions of chapter 308–9
design of sanctions 299–300
implementing 301–3
scope of chapter 297–9
reasons for not imposing sanctions in *Canada–Aircraft* 333–4
suspension of IP rights, threat of 82
TRIPS Agreement, retaliation under 302
legislation for 303–8
US–Cotton Subsidies
legislation in response to 297, 300, 302
US–Cotton Subsidies dispute
retaliation request in 118
use of sanctions 76–8, 81, 82

Brazil–Aircraft dispute
'amount-of-subsidy' approach, use of 114–15
'appropriate', meaning of 117
arbitrators' authority to review 519
Canadian retaliation in 279–80
economic modelling 180–2
effective compliance aim of retaliation, statement on 138
full amount of subsidy, effect of 139
statement on goal of retaliation in 52–3
use of economic models 141

'broad list' approach to sanctions *see* sanctions

broadcasts, compulsory licensing of 581

burden of proof
authorization of retaliation, for 97
compliance claim following retaliation 371–2
cross-retaliation 519–20
level of retaliation exceeding authorized 530
reducing compensation, for 632

CAFTA (as, e.g., of FTA)
definition of 'investment' 558
relation to TRIPS 558

calculation of authorized level of retaliation
'about right' aim 18
'accuracy impossible' argument, summary of 15–20
appropriateness standard
historical development of 43
rules on 92
arbitration relating to, features of 31–3
arbitrators' discretion to consider non-legal issues 18
arbitrators' role in 31–2
arbitrators' statement in *US–Gambling* dispute 15–16
art rather than science, as 17–18
causation as factor in 370
commensurateness standard 92
counterfactual as basis for 5–6
data and evidence, use of 19–20
EC–Hormones dispute 16
economics, role of 19
equivalence standard
see equivalence standard for level of retaliation
'exactly right', need to be 17
expectation damages as basis for 5–6
importance of goal of retaliation for 38–9
investment disputes, in 20
present stage of development, scope of chapter 135–6
process of 16
rules on 92–3
scientificness of 15

Canada
disputes involving 277
effectiveness of retaliation
Brazil, against 279–80
conclusions of chapter 280
EC, against 279
US, against 278
preparation of target list 277–8
retaliation by 277–80
retaliation in *Byrd Amendment* dispute 10, 81
retaliation request in *Brazil–Aircraft* 114–15
trade with US 278

Canada (*cont.*)
US–CDSOA dispute, retaliation in 278
use of sanctions 76–8
Canada–Aircraft dispute
adjustment of level of sanctions 139
'amount-of-subsidy' approach, use of 115–16
arbitrators' collection of evidence 20
Brazil's reasons for not imposing sanctions 333–4
Brazil's retaliation 82
causal link between violation and loss, whether 108–9
decision on purpose of retaliation 124, 126
economic modelling 180–2
'equality-of-harm' approach, use of 116
full amount of subsidy, effect of 139
Canada–Export Credits and Guarantees dispute, statement on goal of retaliation in 53
carousel approach to 'smart sanctions' *see* United States
causation
establishing effect of retaliation 370–1
harm by trade rule violation, of 6, 108–10
assessment of 1
Canada–Aircraft 108–9
EC–Bananas 109–10
EC–Hormones 109
NoI, as 6
US–Internet Gambling 109
welfare model focus on 7
indirect or intangible effects, treatment of 369–70
issues in arbitration 369–71
NoI by 'marketing effort driven' additional exports, of 110
retaliation by optimal tariffs 5
setting retaliation level, as factor in 370
central banks, use of economic analysis 418–22
Centre for Trade and Economic Integration, Workshop on WTO trade sanctions 2
'chocolate cake' scenario *see* Mexico
CME v. *Czech Republic*, reduced compensation in 631–2
CMS v. *Argentina* dispute, valuing of compensation 630–1
collective retaliation
collective retaliation, rather than cross-retaliation 535
UN Charter, under 91–2
use of 91–2
'commensurate', retaliation to be 118
commercial presence commitments, suspension of 531–2, 606–11
compensation
alternative to sanctions, as 350–4, 364
arbitrators' approach, critique of 635–6
BITS provisions 626–7
burden of proof for reducing 632
cooperation from defaulting state, need for 358
cost of, compared with cost of retaliation 339–40
DCF analysis for quantifying level of 628
EC firms' right to claim 270–4
enforceability of 364
enforcement objective, as 496–7
failure to mitigate damages, reduction for 632–3
Fedon claim for 356–8
focus of 37
goal of retaliation, as 37, 74–5
historical development 43–9
government procurement, in 358
importance of goal of retaliation in awarding 40
increasing NoI levels 364–5
insights on compensation *see* compensation
instead of retaliation 510
investment law and practice, in *see* investment
investment law insights on

conclusions of chapter 640
scope of chapter 623–5
investor misjudgement reducing 632
issues for operation of system
cost of measuring losses from violations 351–2
cost of taxation to fund compensation 352
developing countries, effect on *see* developing countries
'liquidated' damages, use of 351–2
litigation cost and volume 352–3
over-reliance on expectation damages 350–1
lawful expropriation, for 626–9
losses from imposing sanctions, for 12
methods of 355
non-expropriatory breaches of agreements, for 629–31
principle of 627–8
private parties' right to claim 355–6, 364
proposal for 364–5
quantifying, DCF analysis for 628
reduction factors 631–3
reform proposals, critique of 638–40
reparation, as 365
respondent's ability to pay reducing 633
retaliation as 497–9
system in dispute resolution, case for
conclusions of chapter 354
contract law insights 345–6
Fedon judgment 356–8
issues for operation of system 340
need for reform 339
scope of chapter 339–41
terminology in investment law and practice 625–6
tribunals' practice 628
unlawful expropriation, for 629–31
US–Byrd Amendment negotiation on 283
US–Copyright, agreement in 355
valuation methods 628
competition authorities, use of economic analysis 424–5
competition law insights
behavioural remedies, use of 644–5
cease and desist orders instead of retaliation 644
conclusions of chapter 646–7
fines instead of retaliation 643–4
scope of chapter 641–3
state subsidies and state aids, measures against 645–6
structural remedies, use of 644–5
complainants
assessment of effectiveness of retaliation 284
responsibility to set correct level of suspension 529–30
compliance with trade rules
see also violations of trade rules
aim of dispute settlement, as 24
Brazil's TRIPS retaliation bill as inducing 303–8
capacity for retaliation, importance for inducing 325–7
choice to face retaliation instead of 5
counterfactual, as 7
developing countries' aim of inducing 84–5
effective compliance aim of retaliation, statement on 138
effectiveness of retaliation in inducing 58–60, 255
exporters' support for measures inducing 76
following retaliation 371–2
burden of proof 371–2
GATT success rate 328
disputes involving developing countries, in 328
goal of retaliation, as 49, 74–5
EC, by *see* European Communities (EC)
'inducing compliance' concept 137–40
informal remedies as drivers for 9
partial retaliation to achieve 83–4
'plausible or reasonable compliance scenario' as counterfactual 103

compliance with trade rules (*cont.*)
primary purpose of retaliation, as 82
'quality' of 360–1
rate of 326–7, 360
disputes involving developing countries, in 327
reasonable period of time for, arbitrators' decision on 30–1
retaliation as key factor in 320
factors other than 328–9
retaliation as sole remedy for non-compliance 90–1
shift of goal of retaliation to sanctions from 44
threat of sanctions achieving 81, 83
time until
US–Brooms Safeguard 291
US–Byrd Amendment 284, 291
timeliness of 361–2
countries failing in timely compliance 362
compulsory licensing in IP legislation 580–2
'concessions', definition of 593
consensus statement, use in dispute settlement 442–3
consultations prior to imposing sanctions 11
consumer goods, Ecuador required to suspend concessions on 122
contract law insights for operation of compensation 345–6
copyright, suspension of 565–9
copyrighted works in digital format, opportunities and challenges for cross-retaliation 538
cost of retaliation
compared with cost of compensation 339–40
cost of, success factor, as 375
Costa Rica, ability to impose sanctions 202–3
counterfactual
accuracy of, dependence on trade data 140–2
bases for calculation of retaliation, as 5–6
choice of
approaches to 7–8
arbitrators' 1, 101–6
definition of 7
EC–Bananas dispute as example 102
EC–Hormones as example 8, 101–2
US–Gambling as example 7–8, 102–4
WTO-consistency requirement 131–3
consistency with WTO rules 103–6
constructing appropriate 457–67
defendant's compliance with rules as 7
impact of reciprocity versus welfare debate on choice of 6–7
inappropriate, use of 447
non-existence of violation as 7–8
'plausible or reasonable compliance scenario' as 103
reliance damages as 17, 480–3
scenarios 457
comparison 461–7
expectation measure 461
reliance measure 458–9
restitution measure 459–61
use of 367–8
countermeasures *see* sanctions
cross-retaliation 510
arbitrators' authority to review 518
arbitrators' decision on 1
arbitrators' interpretation of preconditions for authorizing 15
arbitrators' review of request for 119
assessment of practicability and effectiveness of 120–2
authorization to developing countries 15
burden of proof 519–20
level of retaliation exceeding authorized 530
circumstances serious enough for, whether 122–3
collective retaliation rather than 535
comparison with international law standards on countermeasures 516

developing countries' use of
see developing countries
factors for practical and effective 121
factors to take into account 123
GATS, under *see* General Agreement on Trade in Services (GATS)
GATT, under 119
goods by sectors in WTO, TRIPS and GATS 518–19
importance of goal of retaliation for 40
potential effectiveness of 335–6
preconditions for 40–1
proposals to improve developing countries' access to 522–3
reasons for, requirement to state 95
requests for 335, 516–17
provisions for 517–18
right to object to request for 95
rules 118–23
services sector, in *see* services sector
suspension of IP rights 1, 14
TRIPS Agreement, under *see* TRIPS Agreement
welfare enhancing, as 14, 336
withholding of royalties 14
Czech Republic, *CME* v. *Czech Republic*, reduced compensation in 631–2

damages
arbitrators' role in estimating future 32
assessment in investment arbitration *see* investment
comparison as baselines for NoI calculation (figure) 462
direct-trade damages as NoI measurement 483–6
expectation
analogy with sanctions 341–2, 347
baseline for calculation of NoI, as (figure) 462
bases for calculation of retaliation, as 5–6
DCF analysis, in 628
over-reliance on 350–1
private contract theory, in 17
reciprocity model of retaliation applied to 349–50
sanctions equivalent to 347–50
failure to mitigate, reduced compensation for 632–3
'liquidated' 351–2
reliance
baseline for calculation of NoI, as (figure) 458
counterfactual, as 17, 480–3
DCF analysis, in 628
restitution, baseline for calculation of NoI, as (figure) 460
data and evidence
dependency of accurate counterfactuals on availability of 140–2
improving quality of 133–4
quality of 205
importance for selecting target products 295–6
quantifying deterrent effect of retaliation, analysis for 205–29
use of 19–20
decision-making process
arbitrators' *see* arbitrators
economic modelling of *see* economic modelling
WTO members' domestic
approach to regulation of 378–86
conclusions of chapter 386–7
consensus for regulation, need for 378–9
current DSU regulation of 377–8
importance of 373–8
need for regulation of 378
'notice-and-comment' procedure, use of 379
priority for regulation of 378
proposed DSU amendments 387–90
scope of chapter 373
SPS and TBT agreements as models for regulation of 379
decision on retaliation 289–94
Mexico's in *Peru–Computers* 288–9
type of retaliation, responsibility for 35

decisions
  'banana waiver' 26
  elements of system for implementing 23–4
defendant's compliance with rules as counterfactual 7
design of retaliation
  importance of 377
  regulation of domestic processes for *see* decision-making process
deterrent effect of retaliation, quantifying
  'actionable' exports
    computing amount of 206–16
    computing growth of 210–16
  conclusions of chapter 229–30
  data analysis 205–29
  developing countries' contribution to value of deterrence 201, 227–8
    degree of incentive 202
    factors 202–3
  differences in countries' potential for enforcement role 201
  enforcers
    criteria for potential 216
    exports from potential, computing percentage of 220–3
    identifying potential 216–23
      specific countries, for 216–19
    ranking of 219–20
  exports from potential enforcers 201
  factors for value of deterrence 199
  findings of study 200–1
  'homogeneous' goods, identifying 207–10
  imports from potential enforcers, computing percentage of 224–9
  literature survey 202–5
  methodology 200, 203
  'non-actionable' exports, identifying 207–10
  outsourcing, effect of 204
  parts and components, identifying 207–10
  potential enforcers, number of 201
  relative pressure to conform on industrialized and developing economies 228
  scope of chapter 198–201
  symmetry between WTO protection and enforcement potential 224
developing countries
    see also 'retaliation does not work when developing countries win a case' argument
  ability to retaliate 202–3, 353–4
    effectiveness of sanctions 321–2
    problem of imbalance with developed countries 319, 321–2
  authorization for cross-retaliation 15
  authorization requests by 330–1
  commercial presence (Mode 3) suspension, utility of 608–11
  compensation, economic effects
    defendant, as 353
    plaintiff, as 353
  compliance rate in disputes involving 327
    GATT disputes 328
  contribution to value of deterrence 201
    computing 227–8
    degree of incentive 202
    factors 202–3
  cross-retaliation
    services sector 619–22
      benefits from 620–2
      financial services 621
      MFN status suspension 620
      'specific commitments' suspension 620
    utility of dispute settlement for 620
  cross-retaliation by 14–15
    authorizations granted 336–7
    constitutional and legislative issues 580–2, 619–20
    intellectual property rights, suspension of 335–7

challenge of political pressure against 538
use to improve negotiating position 525–6
legal issues 579
potential effectiveness of 335–6, 587–8
proposals to improve access to 522–3
requests for 335
size of services market as factor in suspending GATS or TRIPS commitments 534–5, 619
welfare enhancing, as 336
disadvantage under dispute settlement 536
exports from potential enforcers 201
implementation of retaliation 10
contrast to developed countries 331
reasons for not imposing 331, 335
US–Byrd Amendment, in 334
inducing compliance, aim of 84–5
inequalities with developed countries, problem of 9
membership of 'WTO enforcement club' 11
potential effectiveness of sanctions by 15
ranking of 205–6
relative pressure to conform on industrialized and 228
variation in 228–9
retaliation by 10, 81–2, 330–5
self-damage from suspending concessions 547, 619
services sector retaliation, opportunities for 620
'shooting yourself in the foot' argument applied to 322
utility of dispute settlement for 9–10, 329–30
arguments that retaliation rules undermine 320
conclusions of chapter 337–8
effect of retaliation as sole remedy 363
retaliation rules do not undermine 325
retaliation rules skewed against developing countries 323–4
retaliation rules undermine 324–5
sanctions lead to self-damage 322–3
scope of chapter 319–20
strength of arguments 325
welfare reduction, fear of 203
digital formats, copyrighted works in, opportunities and challenges for cross-retaliation 538
direct-trade-blocked metric, arbitrators' use of 447
discounted cash flow (DCF) analysis 628
dispute settlement *see also* arbitration; *see also specific disputes*
advantage for developed countries 536
categories of disputes 149–50
clarification of WTO provisions as by-product of 441
compatibility of non-retaliatory measures with 90–1
compensation, case for system of *see* compensation
consensus statement, use of 442–3
decisions *see* decisions
disadvantage for developing countries 536
economic effect of, evidence for 396–8
economists' role in *see* economists' role in dispute settlement
effectiveness of
developing countries, for *see* developing countries
importance of goal of retaliation for 41
GATT and WTO compared 327–8
guidelines
calculation of NoI 443
usefulness of 443
improvements, proposals for 508–10
law, role of 29

dispute settlement (*cont.*)
legal and non-legal disputes
criteria for distinguishing 27
importance of distinction 28
overlap 28
legal profession, role of 29
penalties under 343–4
present stage of development 129–30
proposed amendments for regulation of domestic decision making 387–90
reasons for not using 362
reform of, case for system of compensation *see* compensation
role of economic analysis in 396–404
sanctions, role of *see* sanctions
services sector retaliation, opportunities for 619
symmetry between WTO protection and enforcement potential 224
system
compliance aim of 24
expansion of 28–9
features 23–4
historical development of goal of retaliation in 43–9
importance of 23
UN Charter provisions 27
utility for developing countries *see* developing countries
Dispute Settlement Understanding (DSU) *see* dispute settlement
disputes *see also specific countries and specific disputes*
categories of 149–50, 589–90
compliance rate 326–7
developing countries 327
distinction between legal and non-legal 26–31
criteria for distinguishing 27
importance of distinction 28
overlap 28
economic modelling of *see* reciprocity model of retaliation
effects of 505–8
GATT compliance success rate for developing countries 328
general equilibrium interpretation of, scope of chapter 503
investment disputes, calculation of authorized level of retaliation in 20
'mini-trade wars', as 505–6
parties' responsibility for economic input 440
retaliation against import restrictions
non-tariff measures 172
quotas 160, 163–4
retaliation against subsidies 158–60
retaliation not imposed, where 331
SCOO calculation in 486
three-country model 179–80
two-country model 185–6

EC–Agricultural Biotech dispute, US threat of sanctions 83
EC–Bananas dispute
arbitrators' authority to review 519
arbitrators' general remarks on cross-retaliation under TRIPS 523–4
assessment of practicability and effectiveness of cross-retaliation 120–1
'carousel' sanctions by US 79, 237
causal link between violation and loss, whether 109–10
choice of counterfactual 102
commercial presence commitments, suspension of 531–2
commercial presence (Mode 3), suspension in 608–11
complainants 2
consumption abroad (Mode 2), suspension in 606
cross-border supply (Mode 1), suspension in 603
decision on Ecuador's cross-retaliation request 120–1, 520
economic modelling 164–5

Ecuador's consideration of relevant factors in cross-retaliation request 123
Ecuador's reasons for not imposing sanctions 332–3
Ecuador's retaliation 10, 527–8
'equality-of-harm' approach, use of 99–100
exporters' support for retaliation 78
GE model of 505–6
indirect or intangible effects of violation, treatment of 369
input by US interest groups 79
issue of case 142
metric for NoI, choice of 106
Mexico's negotiation approach 287–8, 293
MFN status, suspension of 613–14
NoI arising from retaliation, calculation of 112–14
overview of jurisprudence 539–42
reliance damages as counterfactual, use of 480–3
SCOO, calculation of 489–90
US claim of indirect effect of violation 469
US retaliation in 238–9, 356–7
use of 'smart sanctions' 80
EC–Bananas (Ecuador) report, statement on goal of retaliation in 51
EC–Bananas (US) report, statement on goal of retaliation in 50–1
EC–Beef Hormones dispute
arbitrators' influence on economic policies, as example of 392
arbitrators' justification for recalculation of level of sanctions 137
calculation of authorized level of retaliation 16
Canadian retaliation in 279
carousel sanctions by US 13–14, 79, 237
causal link between violation and loss, whether 109
choice of counterfactual 8, 101–2
complainants 2
compliance following retaliation, issue of 371–2
economic modelling 165–8
example of choosing goal of retaliation 36–8, 58
exporters' support for retaliation 78
GE model of 505–6
input by US interest groups 79
issue of case 142
lost trade claim in 369–70
'marketing-effort driven' additional exports cause of NoI, whether 110
requirement to identify products to be subject to suspension 94–5
SCOO, consideration of 486–9
statement on responsibility for deciding type of retaliation 35
US retaliation in 239–41
use of 'smart sanctions' 80–1
EC–Biotech dispute, proposed US retaliation in 241
EC–Commercial Vessels dispute, non-retaliatory measures consistent with dispute settlement, whether 90–1
EC–Geographical Indications dispute, identifying rights holders' nationality 563
economic analysis and modelling
appropriate use of 441–2
arbitrators' decision-making process, of 152
central banks' use of 418–22
competition authorities' use of 424–5
conclusions of chapter 190–1
DCF analysis for quantifying level of compensation 628
general equilibrium model *see* general equilibrium (GE) model of disputes
investigating agencies' use of 422–4
limitations of 141–2, 441
NoI level, of 156–7

economic analysis and modelling (*cont.*)
  parties' responsibility for input in disputes 440
  provision by WTO Secretariat *see* World Trade Organization (WTO)
  reciprocity model *see* reciprocity model of retaliation
  role of 444–5
  scope of chapter 149–53
  use of 140–2
economic effects of dispute settlement *see* dispute settlement
economic policies, arbitrators' influence on 391–2
economics
  role in calculation of level of retaliation 19
  role in retaliation authorization process 1
economists' role in dispute settlement
  arbitrations, in
    arbitrators and panellists, as 404–5, 435–6
    'called in' experts, as 417–18
    parties' behalf, on 440
    possible involvements 404–18
    Secretariat support staff, as 410–17
  'economic clarity', providing 441
  equal partners in arbitration process 400–3
  expert witness and interpretative 398–400
  limitations to 403–4
Ecuador
  ability to retaliate against EC 321
  arbitrators' decision on cross-retaliation request 120–1, 520, 523–4
  consideration of relevant factors in cross-retaliation request 123
  cross-retaliation in *EC–Bananas* 10, 81–2, 527–8
    overview of jurisprudence 539–42
    use to improve negotiating position 525–6
  reasons for not imposing sanctions in *EC–Bananas* 332–3
  request for cross-retaliation 516–17
  requirement to suspend concessions on consumer goods 122
  use of sanctions 76–8, 81
effect of retaliation 145–6
  causation as factor in establishing 370–1
  effect of 508
  trade volumes balanced with violation, on 4
effectiveness of retaliation 40, 58–60, 255
  complainants' assessment of, *US–Byrd Amendment* 284
  critique of 507
  factors for 374–5
'efficient breach'
  argument for limited retaliation 346
  cost of 363
  private contract theory, in 17
  theory of 17
Egypt, *Middle East Cement* v. *Egypt* dispute, reduced compensation for failure to mitigate damages 632–3
enforcement of trade rules
  compensation as objective of 496–7
  cross-retaliation under TRIPS 577–8
  enforcers
    criteria for potential 216
    exports from potential, computing percentage of 220–3
    identifying potential 216–23
      specific countries, for 216–19
    ranking of 219–20
  equivalence standard, role of 449
  factors determining capacity for 10–11
  features of system 90–3
  imports from potential enforcers, computing percentage of 224–9
  relative pressure to conform on industrialized and developing economies 228

variation in 228–9
symmetry between WTO protection and enforcement potential 224
US success in 241–2
'WTO enforcement club'
developing countries' membership 11
existence of 11
'equality-of-harm' approach
appropriateness standard, to 118
equivalence standard, to 99–113
alternative approaches 113–14
equivalence standard 16, 35
annual level of NoI approach to 114
arbitrators' interpretation of 138, 478–9
flawed interpretation thesis, arguments against 494
improved practice, suggestions for 500–2
attainment of 447
components of 450
conclusions of chapter 492–4
enforcement role of 449
'equality-of-harm' approach 99–113
alternatives to 113–14
establishing 448
general standard 99–114
historical development of 43
interpretation of, origin of problems with 494
law and economic aspects
introduction 449–51
NoI calculation *see* nullification or impairment (NoI)
MFN status suspension, applied to 617
policy improvements 499–502
rules on 92
safeguarding equivalence 477–8, 492
scope of chapter 446–9
European Communities (EC)
Canadian retaliation against, effectiveness of 279
claim of chilling effect of violation in *US–Antidumping Act 1916* 369–70
compensation for losses from imposing sanctions 270–4
compliance aim of retaliation 244–5, 246, 267–8
sole purpose, as 245
Ecuador's ability to retaliate against 321
Florida orange juice retaliation 13
'long list' approach 274–6
partial retaliation, use of 83–4
procedures for designing sanctions 246–7
punitive sanctions, avoidance of 245–6
sanctions applied by 255–6
sanctions used against 256–8
selecting sanctions, political and legal issues in
avoidance of substituting products in *US–Foreign Sales Corporations* dispute 269
member states' share of burden of imposing sanctions 268
member states' support for sanctions 267–70
scope of chapter 267
substitution of products on proposed target list 268–70
Swedish objections to sanctions 268
threat of sanctions by
effectiveness of 81
inducing compliance, as means of 83
US–1916 Act, retaliation in 252–3
US–Byrd Amendment
claim of indirect effect of violation 469
retaliation in 250–2
US–Foreign Sales Corporations (FSC), retaliation in 248–50
US–Section 110(5) US Copyright Act, retaliation in 253–4
US–Section 211 Omnibus Appropriations Act, retaliation in 254
US–Steel Safeguards, retaliation in 247–8

European Communities (*cont.*)
US–Wheat Gluten Safeguards, retaliation in 247–8
USA's success in enforcement against 242
use of sanctions 76–8
recent commencement of 244
scope of chapter 244–6
evidence
Canada-Aircraft dispute, collection in 20
collection of 19–20
'excess antidumping duties collected' metric, use of 107
expectation damages *see* damages
expectation measure as counterfactual 461
exporters' support for retaliation 76, 78
exports
'actionable'
computing amount of 206–16
computing growth of 210–16
effect of sanctions on 204
'homogeneous' goods
identifying 207–10
reasons for not targeting 206
'marketing-effort driven' additional exports as cause of NoI 110
'non-actionable' exports, identifying 207–10
parts and components, identifying 207–10
percentage from potential enforcers, computing 220–3
promotion measures, retaliation against
economic modelling of 177–86
Singapore, exports actionable by potential enforcers 222–3
subsidies *see* subsidies
expropriation, compensation for
lawful 626–9
non-expropriatory breaches of agreements 629–31
unlawful 629–31

Fedon compensation claim 356–8
'final offer arbitration' 18, 443–4
Florida orange juice, EC retaliation 13
France, Roquefort cheese retaliation by US 14
free trade agreements (FTAs), relation to TRIPS 557–60
'full commitments', scheduling under GATS 596

General Agreement on Tariffs and Trade (GATT)
compliance success rate 328
disputes involving developing countries, in 328
concessions compared with IPRs 549–52
consensus for retaliation, need for 46
cross-retaliation under 119
dispute settlement compared with WTO 327–8
historical development of goal of retaliation in 43–9
incidence of authorized retaliation compared with WTO 2, 373–4
Netherlands/US case 45
provisions for authorized retaliation 43
sanctions under 342–3
compared with WTO 343–7
General Agreement on Trade in Services (GATS)
additional commitments, provision for 595–6
concessions compared with IPRs 549–52
cross-retaliation under 530–5
commercial presence commitments 531–2
estimate of service supply forgone 534
safeguard actions 532–4
scope of chapter 515–23
sectors with binding commitments 531
size of developing countries' services market 534–5
steps for analysing 530–5

use of multiple channels of supply to circumvent 532–4
division of goods by sectors in 518–19
'full commitments', scheduling of 596
'limited commitments', scheduling of 596
market access limitations, provision for 595
modes of supply 593–4
national treatment limitations, provision for 595
obligations list 613
'specific commitments'
difference to 'other obligations' 612
forms of 595–6
suspension of 596
terminology compared with WTO 591–6
'UNBOUND' or 'UNBOUND*' commitments, scheduling of 596
US defence in *US–Internet Gambling* under 311–12, 314–16
general equilibrium (GE) model of disputes *see* disputes
effect of retaliation 508
SCOO, calculation of 506
geographical indications, suspension of protection by 524, 573–4, 582
goal of retaliation
choices of 36–8
compensation as 37
compliance as 49
conclusion of chapter 36, 64
differing views on 60–4
historical development in GATT and WTO provisions 43–9
identifying
historical development, as basis for identifying goal of retaliation 42–3
methods of 41
reasons for retaliation, from 42–3
use of retaliation, from compliance or compensation, for 74–5
exporters' support for compliance-inducing measures 76
full or partial retaliation 75
scope of chapter 73–4
'smart sanctions', use of 75–6
importance of 38–41
multiple purposes 70–2
optimal protection as 60–4
reasons for lack of formal statement of 43
'rebalancing' 504–5
sanctions as 37
scope of chapter 34–5
shift from compliance to sanction 44
statements on *see specific disputes*
variation 56–8
goods subject to retaliation
factors in selection of 294–5
goods subject to, data quality, importance of 295–6
government procurement, compensation applied to 358
guidelines for dispute settlement
calculation of NoI 443
usefulness of 443

Havana Charter, provisions on retaliation 44–5
'Havana Club' case *see US–Section 211 Omnibus Appropriations Act* dispute
'hostage taking' analogy for imposing sanctions *see* sanctions
human rights agreements, relation to TRIPS 556–7

impairment *see* nullification or impairment
imperfectly competitive markets, economic modelling of 186–7
imports
measures restricting, economic modelling of retaliation against 157–77

imports (*cont.*)
non-tariff measures, retaliation against
disputes 172
economic modelling of 170–2
potential enforcers, from, computing percentage of 224–9
quotas, retaliation against 160–3
disputes 163–4
economic modelling of 160–3
tariffs
retaliation against
disputes 160
economic modelling of 158–60
theoretical compliance effect 321
imposition of retaliation 329
developing and developed countries contrasted 331
imposition of, disputes where not imposed 331
reasons for not imposing 331
indirect or intangible effects of violation, treatment of 369–70
industrial designs, suspension of protection of 574–5, 582
informal remedies, drivers for compliance with trade rules, as 9
integrated circuits layout protection, suspension of 575, 582
intellectual property rights (IPRs)
acquisition and maintenance of, TRIPS provisions for 578–9
categories of 564–5
differences to GATT/GATS concessions 549–52
economic impact of IP legislation changes 560–1
identifying rights holders' nationality 563–4
operation of 547
suspension of 527
agricultural chemical regulatory data, protection of 575–7, 582
Brazil's legislation 302
broadcasts 581
compulsory licensing, use of 580–2
constitutional and legislative issues 580–2
copyright 565–9
cross-retaliation, as 1
developing countries, by 81–2
use to improve negotiating position 525–6
difference between 'takings' and 'regulation' of IP 583–4
differing levels of protection and enforcement between countries, allowance for 529
effect of 548
effectiveness as cross-retaliation 14
enforcement of 577–8
export of IP by Internet, issues of 584–6
geographical indications, protection by 524, 573–4, 582
industrial designs 574–5, 582
integrated circuits layout protection 575, 582
patent rights 569–71
pharmaceutical regulatory data, protection of 575–7, 582
quantifying, approaches to 528–9
'royalty income forgone' metric, use of 107
social welfare issues 586–7
taking of property, as 537, 583–4
trade secret protection 575–7, 582
trademark rights 571–3, 581
TRIPS, under *see* TRIPS Agreement
United States, by 236
WIPO, under *see* WIPO conventions
valuing IP assets 561–3
International Law Commission, drivers for compliance with trade rules, as 48–9
countermeasures provisions compared with cross-retaliation 516

international tribunals, goals of 66–9
Internet export of IP, issues for rights suspension 584–6
investigating agencies, use of economic analysis 422–4
investment
  BITS *see* bilateral investment treaties (BITS)
  CAFTA definition 558
  damages assessment in arbitration
    complexity 634–5
    tribunals' discretion 634
  disputes, arbitrators' ability to calculate authorized level of retaliation in 20
  law, comparison with trade law 623–5
  terminology applied to compensation 625–6
  treaty provisions for compensation 626–7
investors' reduced compensation
  failure to mitigate damages, because of 632–3
  misjudgement, because of 632
Irish music case *US–Section 110(5) US Copyright Act* dispute

Japan, use of sanctions 76–8
'juridical institutions', goals of 66–9

legal profession's role in dispute settlement 29
level of retaliation *see* authorized level of retaliation
LG&E v. *Argentina* dispute, valuing of compensation 631
liberalization of trade
  retaliation's role in 4
  WTO aim, as 4
'limited commitments', scheduling under GATS 596
lists
  arbitration reports 2
  authorized retaliations 2
  main arguments of title 3
  products to be targeted *see* target list of products
litigation over compensation, cost and volume of 352–3
'long list' approach to sanctions *see* sanctions
losses from rule violations *see* violations of trade rules
'lost profits' method for measuring NoI 468

main arguments of title
  list 3
  'shooting yourself in the foot', retaliation as *see* 'shooting yourself in the foot' argument, retaliation as market access limitations
  GATS provision for 595
  suspension of 596–7
'marketing-effort driven' additional exports as cause of NoI 110
measurement and metrics *see* nullification or impairment (NoI)
members of WTO *see* World Trade Organization (WTO)
MERCOSUR, Brazil's obligations 301
Mexico
  'chocolate cake' scenario 283, 289–90
  decision to retaliate 289–90
    Peru–Computers 288–9
  disputes involving 281
  goods subject to retaliation
    data quality, importance of 295–6
    factors in selection of 294–5
  negotiation, preference for 293–4
    EC–Bananas dispute 287–8, 293
    US–Trucking dispute 288, 293–4
  retaliation by
    conclusions of chapter 296
    duration of 291
    scope of chapter 281–2
    'smart sanctions' in *Byrd Amendment* dispute 13
  selection of targeted goods in *US–Byrd* and *US–Brooms* 285–7
  'smart sanctions' in *US–Brooms* 13

Mexico (*cont.*)
US–Brooms Safeguard, retaliation in 284–7, 286
US–Byrd Amendment dispute, retaliation in 10, 282–4
US–Byrd Amendment, retaliation in 286
use of sanctions 76–8
Middle East Cement v. *Egypt* dispute, reduced compensation for failure to mitigate damages 632–3
minimum standard entitlements 453–5
modes of supply (GATS) 593–4, 616–18
commercial presence (Mode 3), suspension in 606–11
taxation and regulatory measures applied to 618
consumption abroad (Mode 2), suspension in 604–6
taxation and regulatory measures applied to 617–18
cross-border supply (Mode 1), suspension in 602–4
taxation and regulatory measures applied to 617
effectiveness of retaliation in 621
MFN status suspension in 616–18
presence of natural persons (Mode 4), suspension in 611–12
taxation and regulatory measures applied to 618
table 594
most-favoured-nation (MFN) status, services sector suspension 598–9, 612–18
equivalence standard applied to 617
modes of supply, in 616–18
taxation and regulatory measures applied to 616–18
utility for developing countries 620
mutual rights and obligations of members
auxiliary entitlements 455–6
minimum standard entitlements 453–5
reciprocal market access entitlement 452–3
national treatment limitations
GATS provision for 595
suspension of 597–9
types of 597
Netherlands, GATT dispute with United States 45
non-compliance *see* compliance with trade rules
non-tariff measures on imports
economic modelling 170–2
US use of 236
North American Free Trade Area (NAFTA)
US–Brooms Safeguard dispute *see US–Brooms Safeguard* dispute
US–Trucking dispute *see US–Trucking* dispute
'notice-and-comment' procedure, use for domestic decision making 379
nullification or impairment (NoI)
'amount of monetary cost imposed' metric 107
annual level of, approach to equivalence based on 114
arbitrators' calculation baseline (figure) 481
arbitrators' entitlement to use different metrics for 106–7
calculation of 100–11, 369–70
assessment of arbitrators 479
direct trade effects, in terms of 447–8
gains and losses resulting from violation as measure 469
guidelines for 443
law and economic aspects 451
intensity of injury 457
nature and form of injury 452–6
'lost profits' method 468
measurement standards 471
choice of metric 471
comparison of 469–74
consideration of direct or indirect effects of violation 469
matrix of (figure) 469

restitution measure, using (figure) 460
retroactive 495–6
standards for, issues of 467–74
unit of measurement of loss 468–9
'trade-effects test' 468, 471
causal link between violation and loss, whether 108–10
changes in effect over time, assessment of 111
comparison of damages as baselines for calculation (figure) 462
compensation increasing levels of 364–5
definition under reciprocity and welfare models 6
economic modelling of level of 156–7
empirical issues in determining 110–11
'equality-of-harm' approach to deciding level of 100
equivalence to SCOO *see* equivalence standard
expectation damages as baseline for calculation of (figure) 462
experienced by third countries 107–8
intensity of, standards for measuring (figure) 470
loss quantifiable, whether 110
'marketing-effort driven' additional exports as cause of 110
measurement of, choice of metric 106–7, 130–1
measurement standards
direct trade damages, use of 483–6
net economic loss caused by violation as 6
reliance damages as baseline for calculation of (figure) 458
restitution damages as baseline for calculation of (figure) 460
retaliation, arising from, calculation of 112–13
time period for calculation of 366–7
trade effects of violation as 6
trade loss as benchmark for 142–3
US–Antidumping Act 1916 calculation 448, 484–5
US–Section 110(5) US Copyright Act calculation 448, 485–6
'value-of-trade-blocked' metric 106–7

optimal tariffs *see* tariffs
'other obligations'
definition of 593
difference to specific commitments 612
GATS, list of 613
outsourcing, effect on deterrent value of retaliation 204
over-retaliation risk 144

Paris Convention, interaction with TRIPS 553
patent rights, suspension of 569–71
Peru–Computers dispute, Mexico's decision to retaliate 288–9
pharmaceutical regulatory data, suspension of protection of 575–7, 582
'plausible or reasonable compliance scenario' as counterfactual 103
political influences on retaliation 187–90
examples 1–2
punitive sanctions, avoidance of 138–9
purpose of retaliation 82
arbitrators' decision on 123–6
compliance as, statement on 135
compliance as primary purpose 82

quotas, import, retaliation against, economic modelling of 160–3

Rauch, James, classification of SITC categories 207
reasonable period of time *see* compliance with trade rules
rebalancing *see* compensation

reciprocal market access entitlement 452–3
reciprocity model of retaliation 4–5, 194–7
arbitrators' use of 4
Bagwell–Staiger theory 153–7
conclusions of chapter 190–1
contrast with welfare model 5–6
definition of nullification and impairment 6
domestic production subsidies 173–5
expectation damages applied to 349–50
export-promoting measures 177–86
three-country model
disputes 179–80
economic modelling 177–9
two-country model
disputes 185–6
economic modelling 183–5
focus on trade volume effects 7
imperfectly competitive markets 186–7
import quotas 160–3
import restricting measures 157–77
import tariffs 158–60
non-political impacts of retaliation 187–90
non-tariff measures on imports 170–2
reciprocity versus welfare debate
economic perspectives 5–6
impact on choice of benchmarks and counterfactuals 6–7
legal perspectives 6
scope of chapter 149–53
theory 4, 17
use of 150–2
regional trade agreements, relation to TRIPS 557–60
reliance damages *see* damages
reliance measure as counterfactual 458–9
reparations, compensation as 365
restitution measure as counterfactual 459–61
retaliation 78, 363, 373–8, 497–8, *see also* cross-retaliation; sanctions; suspension of concessions or other obligations (SCOO)
alternatives to *see* alternatives to retaliation
appropriateness standard *see* appropriateness standard of level of retaliation
arbitrators' power to examine proposed, limitation on 95–6
authorization procedure *see* authorization procedure for retaliation
authorization requests 329, 330–1
authorized level of *see* authorized level of retaliation
behavioural remedies instead of 644–5
calculation of level of *see* calculation of authorized level of retaliation
capacity for, importance for inducing compliance 325–6, 327
cease and desist orders instead of 644
collective retaliation *see* collective retaliation
'commensurate', requirement to be 118
comparison of GATT and WTO provisions 43
compensation, as 497–9
compensation instead of 510
compliance following *see* compliance following retaliation
consensus for, need for 46
control of, responsibility for 508
cost of *see* cost of retaliation
decision on *see* decision on retaliation
design of *see* design of retaliation
deterrent effect of, quantifying *see* deterrent effect of retaliation, quantifying
developing countries, by *see* developing countries

duration of 291
early, use of 284–7
economic modelling *see* economic modelling
effect of *see* effect of retaliation
effect of rules on developing countries' use of dispute settlement *see* developing countries
effective compliance aim of, statement on 138
effectiveness of *see* effectiveness of retaliation
export subsidies, against 5
exporters' support for 76, 78
fairness of, as success factor 375–7
'final offer arbitration' 18
fines instead of 643–4
form of, rules on 92
goal of *see* goal of retaliation
goods subject to *see* goods subject to retaliation
Havana Charter provisions 44–5
imposition of *see* imposition of retaliation
increasing welfare 4–5
incremental, use of 75
interest groups commenting on proposed 79
key factor in compliance, as 320
other factors 328–9
liberalization of trade, role in 4
likelihood of optimal tariffs causing 5
list of authorizations 2
multiple purposes of 70–2
NoI arising from, calculation of 112–13
over-retaliation risk 144
partial, use of 75, 83–4
political impact of 10
political influences 1–2
purpose of *see* purpose of retaliation
'rebalancing', capacity for 504–5
reciprocity model *see* reciprocity model of retaliation
reform of, competition law insights *see* competition law insights
reluctance generally to use 242–3
request for *see* authorization procedure *above*
same 'agreement' requirement 92
same 'sector' requirement 92
sensitivity level of products to 291
services sector, in *see* General Agreement on Trade in Services (GATS); services sector
'shooting yourself in the foot' argument, as *see* 'shooting yourself in the foot' argument, retaliation as
sole remedy for non-compliance, as 90–1
effect on developing countries' use of dispute resolution 363
specific countries, by *see specific countries*
structural remedies instead of 644–5
success factors 374–7
symmetrical, requirement to be 92
system as undercompensatory 17–18
target list, requirement to provide 94–5
temporary, requirement to be 93
termination of 98–9
terminology describing 258–9
timing of *see* timing of retaliation
Tokyo Code provisions 46
tradable rights to 510
transfers instead of tariffs as 509
TRIPS, under *see* TRIPS Agreement
unilateral, need to control 344–5
US rules on lists 13
use of *see* use of retaliation
value of authorized 145
violator's choice to face 5
WIPO, under *see* WIPO conventions
'retaliation does not work when developing countries win a case' argument, summary of 9–15
Roquefort cheese retaliation by United States 14

royalties, withholding of, effectiveness as cross-retaliation 14
'royalty income forgone' metric, use of 107

safeguard actions under GATS cross-retaliation 532–4
sanctions *see also* retaliation; suspension of concessions or other obligations (SCOO)
adjustment of level of 139
arbitrators' choice of own calculation of level of 136–7
arbitrators' justification for recalculation of level of 137
arbitrators' scope for assessing 136
'broad list' approach *see* 'long list' approach *below*
calculation of, specific issues relating to 365
counterfactuals, use of 367–8
time period for calculation of NoI 366–7
Centre for Trade and Economic Integration Workshop 2
compensation as alternative to 350–4
consistency with WTO's trade liberalization aim 4
'decoupled' nature of 340–1
difference between legal status and imposition of 259–60
differing impact of 203–4
EC, use by *see* European Communities (EC)
effectiveness for developing countries 321–2
effectiveness of threat or authorization of 10
equivalent to expectation damages 347–50
estimation of impact of 10–11
expectation damages analogy 341–2, 347
export industries, effect on 204
focus of 37–8
form of 143–6
GATT and WTO compared 343–7
GATT, under 342–3
goal of retaliation, as 37
historical development 43–9
goods that are likely targets for, 206
implementing, specific issues relating to
'carousel' provisions 368–9
causation issues in arbitration 369–71
importance of goal of retaliation in choosing 39–40
imposition of 1
difference to suspension of obligations 259–60
'hostage taking' analogy 13, 14, 59
last resort, as 1
'long list' approach
EC, by 274–6
functions of 79–80
replacement of 'short list' 12
use of 83
potential effectiveness for developing countries 15
process for selecting and implementing 78–9
punitive, avoidance of 138–9
reputational impact 12
role in dispute settlement
conclusions of chapter 372
scope of chapter 360
self-damage to developing countries imposing 322–3
Antigua's concern over 322–3
shift of goal of retaliation from compliance to 44
'short list' approach
operation of 80–1
replacement by 'long list' 12
'smart sanctions'
Byrd Amendment dispute, use in 13
'carousel' approach by United States 13–14, 78, 79, 83–4, 236–7, 368–9
guidelines 11
low duties' effectiveness 13
maximizing impact on target 13–14, 255

minimizing harm to self
government compensation for victims 12
'long list' approach 12
prior consultations with stakeholders 11–12, 255
political impact of 13–14
Roquefort cheese retaliation by United States 14
US–Brooms dispute, use in 13
US–FSC dispute, use in 11, 12–13
use of 11–15, 75–6, 80–1, 82–3, 84, 255–6
targeted *see* 'smart sanctions' *above*
threat of, as means of inducing compliance 83
threat of, effectiveness of 81
WTO and GATT compared 343–7
scope of title 2–3
main arguments listed 3
'sectors', definition of 591–2
services sector
additional commitments, suspension of 599–600
commercial presence (Mode 3), suspension in 606–11
conclusions of chapter 619–22
consumption abroad (Mode 2), suspension in 604–6
cross-border supply (Mode 1), suspension in 602–4
current experience of retaliation 590
developing countries' retaliation in *see* developing countries
disputes 589–90
financial services, effectiveness of retaliation in 621
GATS retaliation *see* General Agreement on Trade in Services (GATS)
legal framework for retaliation 590–1
limitations on suspending specific commitments 596–612
market access limitations, suspension of 596–7
MFN status, suspension of 598–9, 612–18
modes of supply, in 616–18
national treatment limitations, suspension of 597–9
presence of natural persons (Mode 4), suspension in 611–12
scope of chapter 589–90
'specific commitments', suspension in modes of supply 600–2
terminology compared with GATS
'agreements' 591–2
'concessions' 593
'other obligations' 593
'sectors' 591–2
'shooting yourself in the foot', retaliation as 197–8
developing countries, applied to 322
summary 4–9, 8
'short list' approach to sanctions *see* sanctions
Singapore, exports actionable by potential enforcers 222–3
SITC product categories, Rauch classification of 207
'smart sanctions' *see* sanctions
'specific commitments'
GATS provisions *see* General Agreement on Trade in Services (GATS)
suspension in modes of supply *see* services sector
SPS agreements as models for regulation of domestic decision making on retaliation 379
state subsidies and state aids, measures against 645–6
subsidies
domestic production, retaliation against
disputes 175–7
economic modelling of 173–5
export
amount as benchmark 5
arbitrators' need for consistent approach to 5
retaliation against 5
full amount

subsidies (*cont.*)
calculation of 'appropriate countermeasures', as basis for 139–40
effect of 139,
state subsidies and state aids, measures against 645–6
suspension of concessions or other obligations (SCOO)
arbitrators' consideration of 447
restriction on 495
arbitrators' instructions on level of 16
calculation of 474–7, 486
arbitrators' approach to 486–9, 489–92
GE model of 506
definition of 'concessions' and 'other obligations' 593
difference to imposition of sanctions 259–60
equivalence to NoI *see* equivalence standard
provisions for prior authorization 515–16
quantifying 448
use of term 258–9
suspension of trade *see* retaliation
suspension of treaties
ILC Articles provisions 48–9
Vienna Convention provisions 48
Sweden, opposition to proposed EC sanctions 268

taking of property, cross-retaliation seen as 537
target list of products
'broad list' *see* sanctions
'long list' approach *see* sanctions
preliminary list, US consultation on 235
preparation of
Canadian procedure 277–8
Mexico's in *US–Byrd* and *US–Brooms* 285–7
substitution of products on proposed EC target list 268–70
US rules 13
requirement to provide 94–5
'short list' *see* sanctions
targeted sanctions *see* sanctions
tariffs
import
economic modelling of 158–60
theoretical compliance effect 321
optimal tariffs
level of 4
likelihood of causing retaliation 5
transfers instead of, as retaliation 509
US use of 236
taxation
fund compensation, to 352
MFN status suspension, applied to 616–18
TBT agreements as models for regulation of domestic decision making on retaliation 379
termination of retaliation 98–9
terminology 258–9
compensation in investment law, of 625–6
GATS and WTO compared 591–6
third-party adjudication 107–8
economic modelling of disputes
disputes 179–83
model 177–9
timeliness of compliance *see* compliance with trade rules
timing of retaliation
importance of goal of retaliation for 40–1
reasonable period of time (RPT) for compliance
arbitrators' decision on 30–1
rules on 93
Tokyo Code on Technical Barriers to Trade (Tokyo Code), provisions on retaliation 46
tradable retaliation rights 510
trade
agreements, relation to TRIPS 557–60
direct trade damages as NoI measurement 447, 483–6

imbalance between developed and developing countries 319, 321–2
law, comparison with investment law 623–5
liberalization *see* liberalization of trade
loss
benchmark for NoI, as 142–3
claim in *EC–Hormones* 369–70
rules *see* compliance with trade rules; enforcement of trade rules; violations of trade rules
sectors with binding commitments, suspension under GATS 531
suspension of *see* retaliation
volumes
balanced effect of violation and retaliation on 4
reciprocity model focus on 7
wars, disputes as 505–6
'trade-effects test' for measuring NoI 468, 471
trade secret protection, suspension of 575–7, 582
trademark rights, suspension of 571–3, 581
transfers instead of tariffs as retaliation 509
tribunals
compensation practice 628
damages assessment in investment arbitration 634
goals of 66–9
TRIPS Agreement
acquisition and maintenance of IPRs, provisions for 578–9
cross-retaliation under 15, 118–19, 264–6, 335–7, 523–30
Antigua, by 313–14
authorizations granted 336–7, 536–7
Brazil, by 302
Brazil's legislation 303–8
burden of proof 530
challenges from other conventions 537
complainants' responsibility to set correct level of suspension 529–30
developing countries, by *see* developing countries
digital formats, opportunities and challenges of 538
EC–Bananas, arbitrators' general remarks in 523–4
economic rationale for
differences between concessions under TRIPS and GATT/GATS 549–52
economic distinction of TRIPS concessions 547–9
imbalance in trade flows between developed and developing countries 545–7
self-damage to developing countries from suspending concessions 547
effect on rights of private individuals 527
interaction with
BITS 557–60
CAFTA (as, e.g., of FTA) 558
FTAs 557–60
human rights agreements 556–7
Paris and Berne conventions 553
regional and bilateral agreements 557–60
'TRIPS-plus' agreements 558
WIPO conventions 555
jurisprudence 538–9
legal issues for implementing 537
need to quantify IP rights 527
political pressure against 538
scope of chapter 515–23, 536–8
selective application of 538
size of services market as factor in suspending GATS or TRIPS commitments 534–5
suspension of obligations under other agreements 552–7
taking of property, as 537, 583–4
use of national legislation to implement 537–8

TRIPS Agreement (*cont.*)
valuing IP rights as barrier to 537
division of goods by sectors in 518–19
relation to WIPO conventions 526–7
standards for protection and enforcement 529
'TRIPS-plus' agreements, relation to TRIPS 558

ultra vires, ensuring that retaliatory measures are not 98
'UNBOUND' or 'UNBOUND*' commitments, scheduling under GATS 596
United Nations (UN) Charter
collective retaliation under 91–2
dispute settlement provisions 27
United States
antidumping penalties, use of 236
Antigua's ability to retaliate against 321
Canada, trade with 278
Canadian retaliation against, effectiveness of 278
'carousel' provision 13–14, 78, 79, 83–4, 236–7, 368–9
consultation on preliminary list of targeted products 235
EC–Bananas
claim of indirect effect of violation 469
retaliation in 238–9, 356–7
EC–Biotech, proposed retaliation in 241
EC–Hormones dispute, retaliation in 239–41
EC–Hormones, retaliation in 237
enforcement success 241–2
EC, against 242
Florida orange juice, EC retaliation 13
GATS defence in *US–Internet Gambling* 311–12, 314–16
GATT dispute with Netherlands 45
intellectual property rights, suspension of 236
interest groups' input into disputes 79
'long list' approach to sanctions 79
non-tariff measures, use of 236
objection to third-party adjudication 107–8
procedures for use of retaliation 235–7
Roquefort cheese retaliation 14
rules on target lists 13
'smart sanctions' by 80–1
tariffs, use of
100 per cent 236
graduated 236
threat of sanctions by 83
US–Internet Gambling
GATS defence 311–12, 314–16
withdrawal of cross-border gambling and betting commitment 314–16
US–Upland Cotton, failure to implement decision 545
use of sanctions 76–8, 235
reasons for limited 242–3
scope of chapter 241–3
US–Antidumping Act 1916 dispute
'amount of monetary cost imposed' metric 107
changes in effect of NoI over time, assessment of 111
choice of counterfactual 102
direct trade damages as NoI measurement 484–5
EC retaliation in 252–3
economic modelling 172
EC's claim of chilling effect of violation 369–70
issue of case 170
loss quantifiable, whether 110
NoI calculation 448
'qualitative' approach to equivalence, use of 113
statement on goal of retaliation in 54
trade loss, effect of 142
US–Brooms Safeguard dispute
compliance, time until 291
Mexico's retaliation 284–7
Mexico's selection of targeted goods 286

Mexico's use of 'smart sanctions' 13
US–Byrd Amendment dispute *see* *US–(Offset Act) Byrd Amendment* dispute
US–CDSOA dispute, Canadian retaliation in 278
US–Cotton Subsidies dispute
Brazilian legislation in response to 297, 300
Brazil's threat to suspend IP rights 82, 302
'commensurate' requirement for retaliation 118
US–Foreign Sales Corporations (FSC) dispute
'amount-of-subsidy' approach, use of 115–16
'appropriate', meaning of 117
avoidance of substituting products by EC 269
consultations prior to imposing sanctions, example of 11
EC retaliation in 248–50
economic modelling 179–80, 182–3
EC's threat of sanctions in 83
EC's use of incremental tariffs 76–8
EC's use of partial retaliation 83–4
effect of retaliation 145–6
full amount of subsidy, effect of 139–40
GE model of 505–6
trade loss, effect of 142, 143
use of economic models 140–1
use of 'smart sanctions' 12–13
US–Internet Gambling dispute
Antigua's reasons for not imposing sanctions 334–5
Antigua's retaliation in *see* Antigua and Barbuda
Antigua's statement on applying sanctions 15
appellate review, need for 260
arbitrators' authority to review 519
arbitrators' power to examine proposed retaliation 95–6
arbitrators' statement on ability to calculate authorized level of retaliation 15–16
assessment of practicability and effectiveness of cross-retaliation 121
burden of proof 530
causal link between violation and loss, whether 109
choice of counterfactual 7–8, 102–4
circumstances serious enough for cross-retaliation, whether 122
consideration of relevant factors in cross-retaliation request 123
critique of 261–4
decision on Antigua's cross-retaliation request 520–2
economic modelling 168–9
'effectiveness' of retaliation, arbitrators' interpretation of 40
loss quantifiable, whether 110
MFN status, suspension of 614–16
NoI assessment method 111
overview of jurisprudence 542–4
political approach to award 18
SCOO, consideration of 487–8
statement on goal of retaliation in 55–6, 63–4
third-party adjudication 108
US's GATS defence 311–12
US–(Offset Act) Byrd Amendment dispute 469
arbitrators' ability to calculate authorized level of retaliation in 20
authorization request for retaliation following arbitration 97–8
Canada's retaliation 10
Canadian 'smart sanctions' 81
changes in effect of NoI over time, assessment of 111
choice of counterfactual 102
complainants 2
compliance as aim of retaliation, statement on 135
compliance, time until 284, 291
decision on purpose of retaliation 124

US–(Offset Act) Byrd Amendment dispute (*cont.*)
EC claim of indirect effect of violation 469
EC retaliation in 250–2
economic modelling 175–7
effectiveness of retaliation, complainants' assessment of 284
form of sanctions 144
imposition of sanctions 334
limits on authorized retaliation 282–4
Mexico's retaliation 10, 76–8, 282–4
use of 'smart sanctions' 13
Mexico's selection of targeted goods 286
negotiation on compensation 283
NoI assessment method 111
'qualitative' approach to equivalence, use of 113–14
statement on goal of retaliation in 54–5
statement on need for clear goal of retaliation 34
third-party adjudication 107–8
trade loss, effect of 143
use of economic models 141
'value-of-trade-blocked' metric, use of 106–7
US–Section 110(5) US Copyright Act dispute
annual level of NoI approach to equivalence standard, use of 114
compensation agreement 355
EC retaliation in 253–4
identifying rights holders' nationality 563
NoI calculation 448, 485–6
quantifying IP rights 527
'royalty income forgone' metric, use of 107
valuing IP assets 563
US–Section 211 Omnibus Appropriations Act dispute, EC retaliation in 254
US–Softwood Lumber dispute, 'excess antidumping duties collected' metric, use of 107
US–Steel Safeguards dispute
arbitrators' influence on economic policies, as example of 391–2
EC retaliation in 247–8
EC's threat of sanctions in 76–8
effectiveness of EC's sanctions threat 81
GE model of 505–6
US–Tax Treatment for Foreign Sales Corporations dispute, EC's retaliation in 78–9
US–Trucking dispute, Mexico's negotiation approach 288, 293–4
US–Upland Cotton dispute, Brazil's cross-retaliation request 545
US–Wheat Gluten Safeguards dispute
EC retaliation in 247–8
EC's use of sanctions in 76–8
use of retaliation *see also specific countries*
identifying goal from 73
incidence of authorized 76–8, 82–3, 129
incidence of GATT and WTO authorized retaliation compared 2, 373–4

'value-of-trade-blocked' metric for NoI 106–7
Vattel, Emerich de, arbitration, on 27
Vienna Convention on the Law of Treaties (Vienna Convention), provisions on treaty suspension 48, 552
violation of trade rules
see also compliance with trade rules; 'efficient breach'
arbitrators' assessment 1
chilling effect of
arbitrators' consideration of 369–70
intangible effect, as 369–70
choice to face retaliation rather than comply 5
consideration of direct or indirect effects of 469
cost of measuring losses from 351–2
cost to violator 17

effect on trade volumes balanced with retaliation 4
gains and losses resulting from violation as measure of NoI 469
indirect or intangible effects of, treatment of 369–70
net economic loss caused by nullification or impairment, as 6
welfare model focus on 7
non-existence as counterfactual 7–8
trade effects as nullification or impairment 6

welfare
cross-retaliation enhancing 14, 336
IP rights suspension impacts on 586–7
model
contrast with reciprocity model
economic perspectives 5–6
impact on choice of benchmarks and counterfactuals 6–7
legal perspectives 6
focus of 7
reduction, developing countries' fear of 203
retaliation increasing 4–5
WIPO conventions
relation to TRIPS 526–7, 555
retaliation under 264–6
Workshop on WTO trade sanctions 2
World Trade Organization (WTO)
Dispute Settlement Understanding (DSU) *see* dispute settlement
division of goods by sectors in 518–19
economic analysis provided by Secretariat, use of 19
'called in' experts, use of 417–18, 436–40
comparisons with similar institutions 418
central banks 418–22
competition authorities 424–5
investigating agencies 422–4
conclusions of chapter 430–1
divisions providing support, data on 412–17
economists' role *see* economists' role in dispute settlement
importance of analysis 391, 393
improving communications between economic and legal divisions 427–30
need for 434
policy improvements 430–1
process of providing support 410–12
provision of more economic support 425–30, 436
role in dispute settlement 396–404
scope of chapter 391–6
selection of economic staff 426–7
members' decision-making processes *see* decision-making process
members' economic policies, arbitrators' influence on 391–2
members' mutual commitments *see* mutual rights and obligations of members
mercantilist institution, as 4
rules *see* compliance with trade rules; enforcement of trade rules; violations of trade rules
Secretariat staff numbers by division (table) 414
Secretariat's mandate to provide legal and technical support to arbitrators 392
trade liberalization aim, consistency of sanctions with 4
treaty as multi-objective and multi-entitlement 456
'WTO enforcement club' *see* enforcement of trade rules

Lightning Source UK Ltd.
Milton Keynes UK
UKOW01n2319300316

271206UK00002B/3/P